Best Editorial Cartoons of the Year

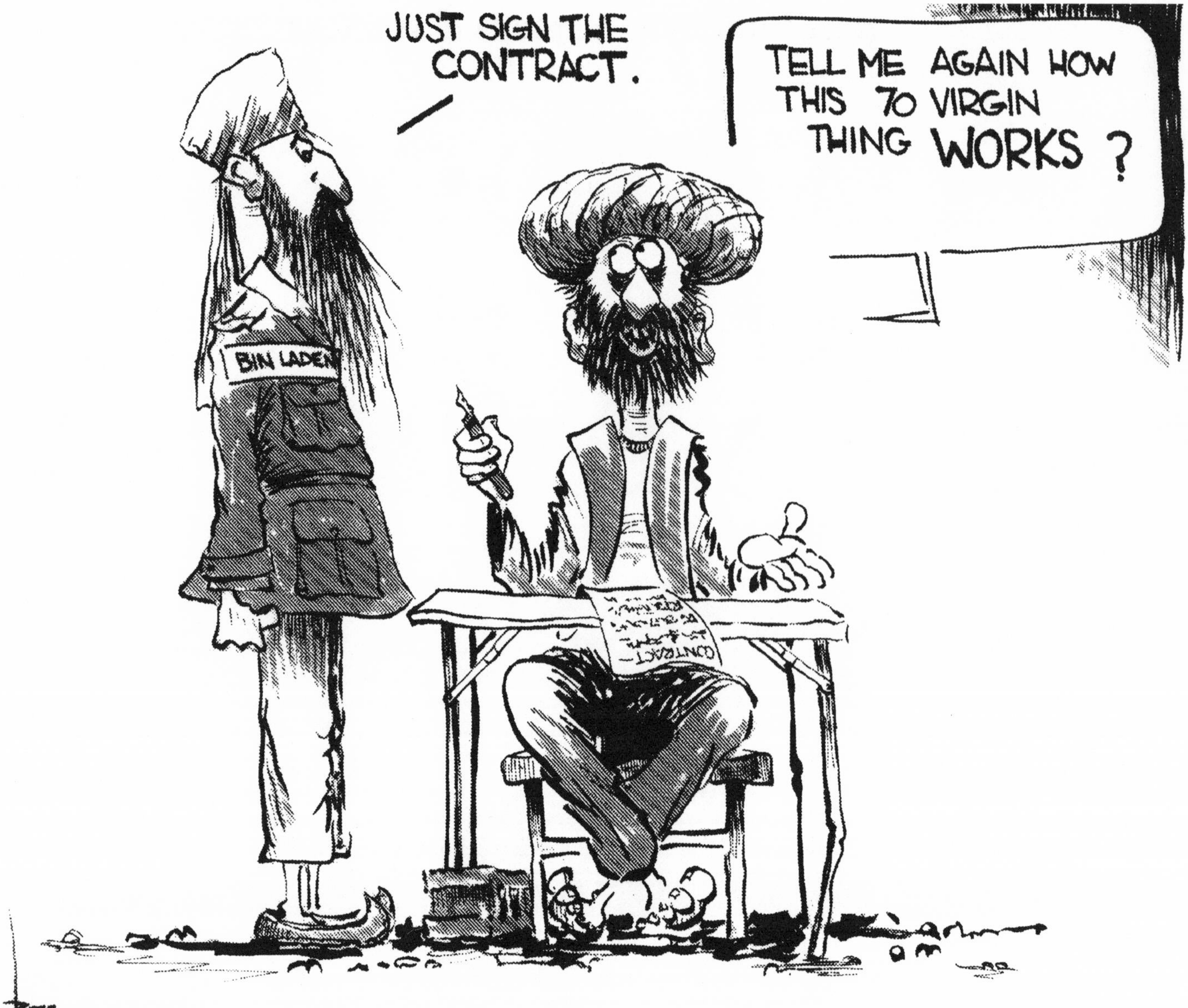
JUST SIGN THE CONTRACT.
TELL ME AGAIN HOW THIS 70 VIRGIN THING WORKS ?
BIN LADEN
CONTRACT
BILL MANGOLD
HERITAGE NEWSPAPERS 4-25-02

BILL MANGOLD
Courtesy Heritage Newspapers

BEST EDITORIAL CARTOONS OF THE YEAR

2003 EDITION

Edited by
CHARLES BROOKS

PELICAN PUBLISHING COMPANY
Gretna 2003

Library of Congress Serial Catalog Data

Best Editorial Cartoons, 1972-
Gretna [La.] Pelican Pub. Co.
v. 30 cm annual-
"A pictorial history of the year."

1. United States—Politics and government—
1969—Caricatures and Cartoons—Periodicals.
E839.5.B45 320.9'7309240207   73-643645
ISSN 0091-2220   MARC-S

Manufactured in the United States of America

Published by Pelican Publishing Company, Inc.
1000 Burmaster Street, Gretna, Louisiana 70053

Contents

Award-Winning Cartoons

2002 PULITZER PRIZE

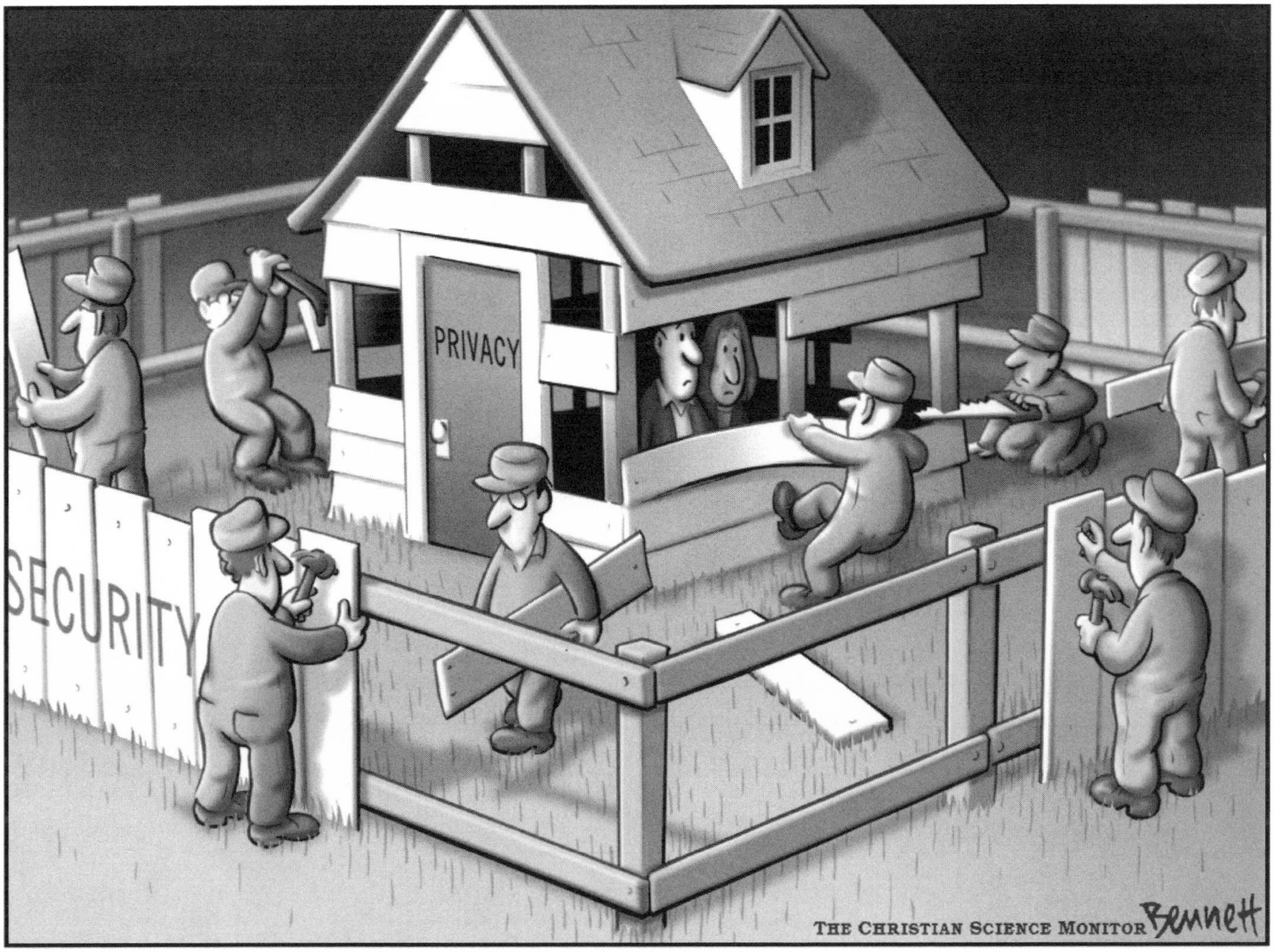
PRIVACY
SECURITY
THE CHRISTIAN SCIENCE MONITOR
Bennett

CLAY BENNETT

Editorial Cartoonist
Christian Science Monitor

Born in Clinton, South Carolina, in 1958; graduate of the University of North Alabama, 1980; editorial cartoonist for the *St. Petersburg Times,* 1981-94, and the *Christian Science Monitor,* 1998 to the present; also winner of the National Headliner Award for Cartooning, 1999 and 2000, the Fischetti Award, 2001, and the National Society of Professional Journalists Award, 2001.

2001 NATIONAL SOCIETY OF PROFESSIONAL JOURNALISTS AWARD

(Selected in 2002)

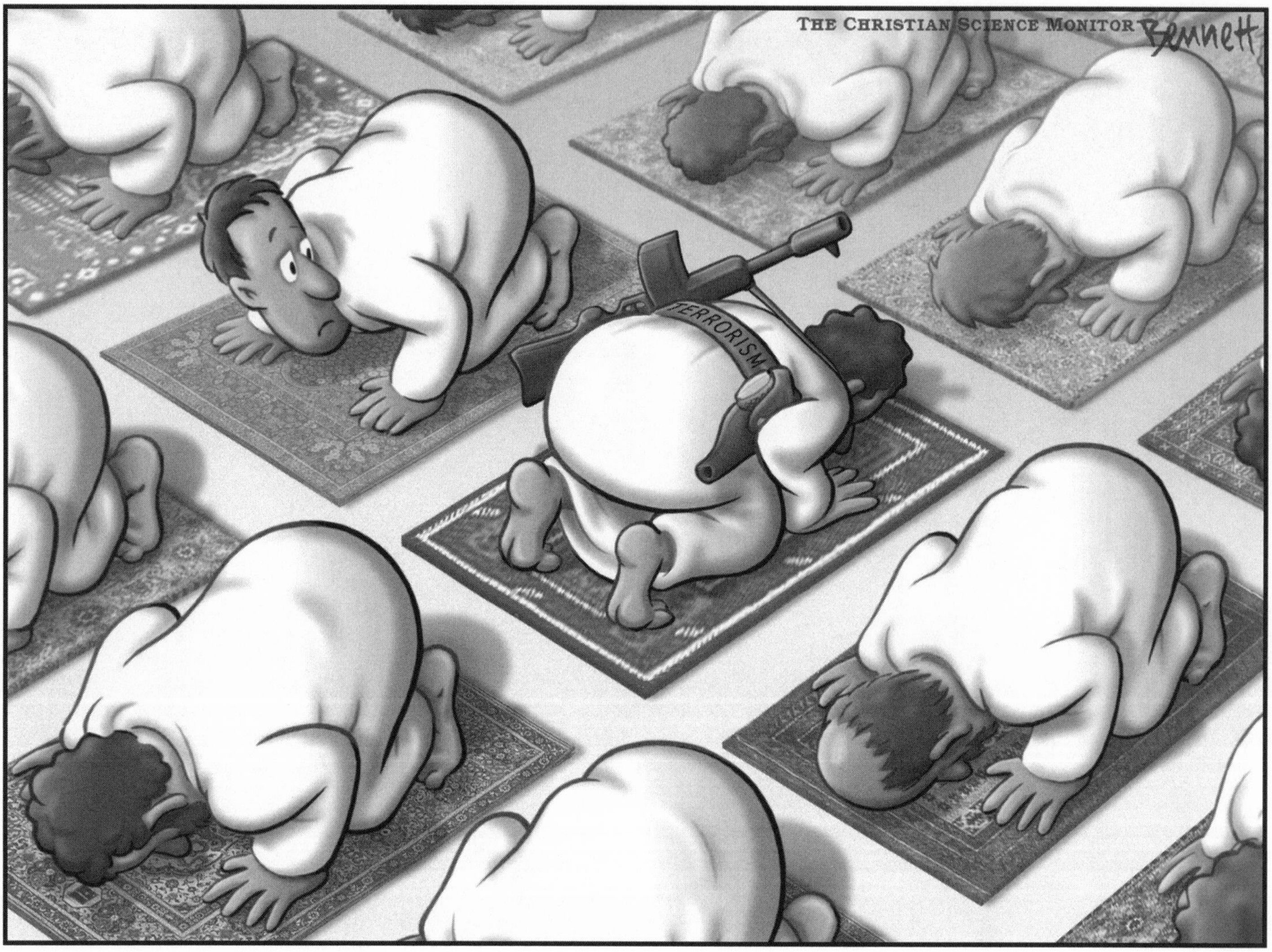
THE CHRISTIAN SCIENCE MONITOR
BENNETT
TERRORISM

CLAY BENNETT

Editorial Cartoonist
Christian Science Monitor

2001 FISCHETTI AWARD

(Selected in 2002)

SCIENCE
BENNETT THE CHRISTIAN SCIENCE MONITOR

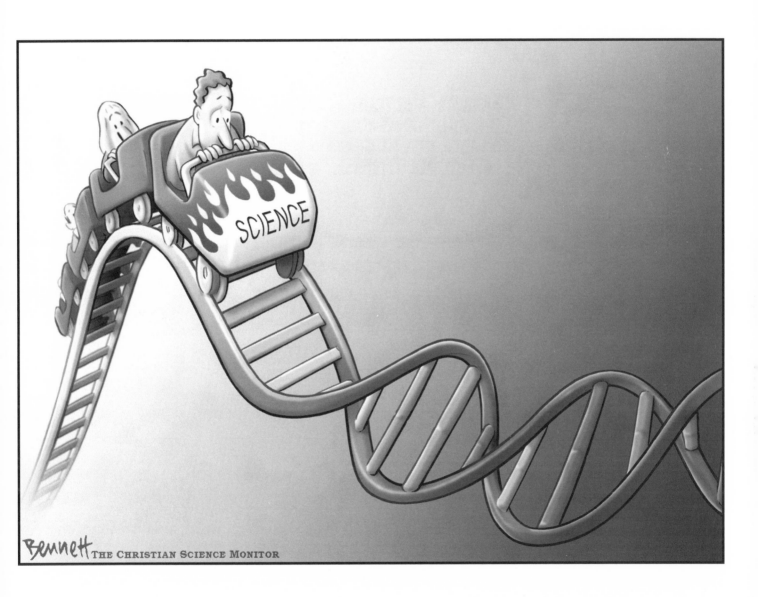

CLAY BENNETT

Editorial Cartoonist

Christian Science Monitor

2002 NATIONAL HEADLINER AWARD

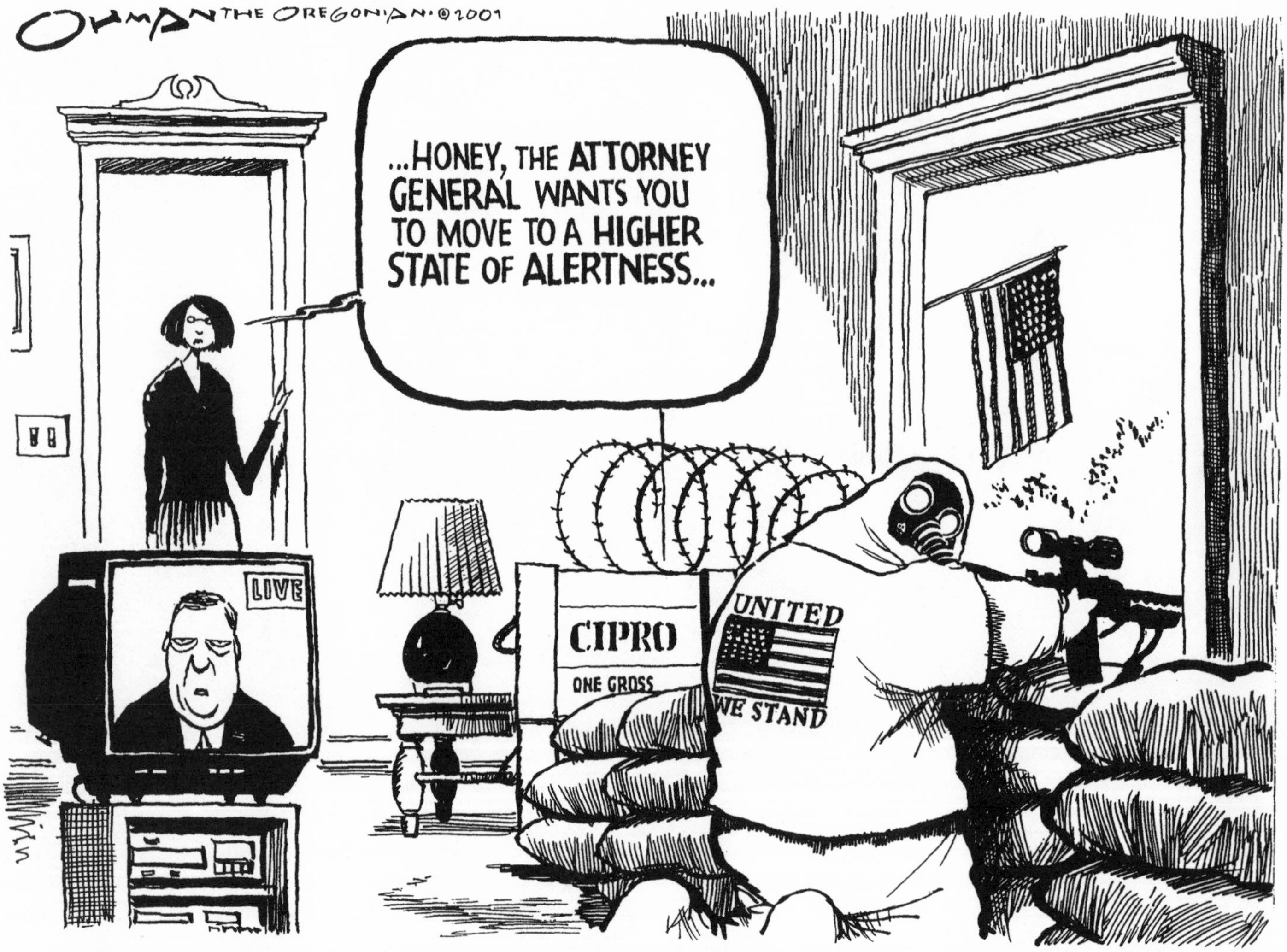
OHMAN THE OREGONIAN ©2001
...HONEY, THE ATTORNEY GENERAL WANTS YOU TO MOVE TO A HIGHER STATE OF ALERTNESS...
LIVE
CIPRO
ONE GROSS
UNITED WE STAND

JACK OHMAN

Editorial Cartoonist
The Oregonian

Born September 1, 1960, in St. Paul, Minnesota; earned bachelor's degree in history from Portland State University; editorial cartoonist for the *Columbus Dispatch,* 1981-82, the *Detroit Free Press,* 1982-83, and *The Oregonian,* 1983 to the present; drew comic strip "Mixed Media," 1994-98; also winner of the Overseas Press Club Award, 1995, syndicated in 300 newspapers by Tribune Media Services.

2002 OVERSEAS PRESS CLUB AWARD

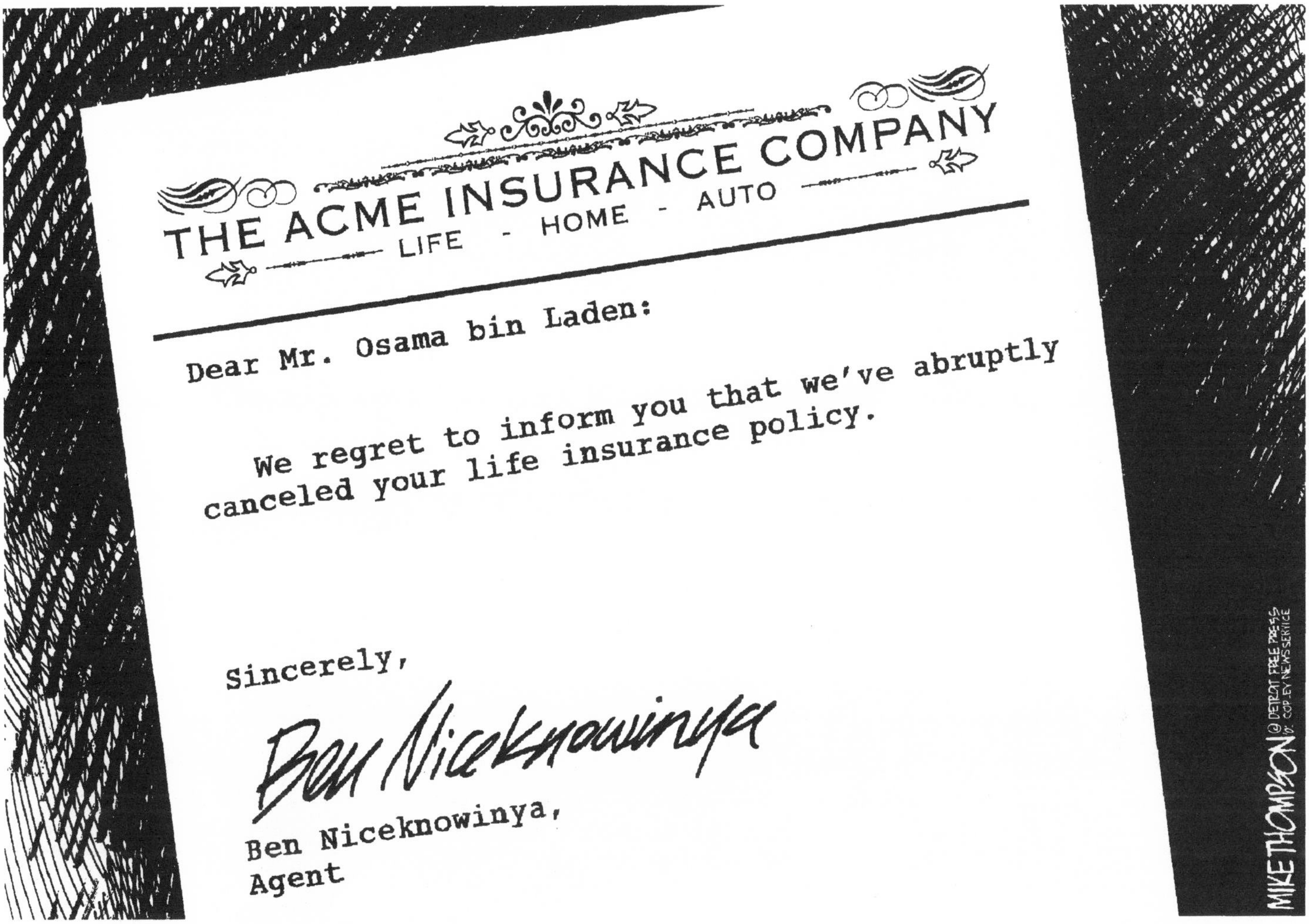
THE ACME INSURANCE COMPANY
LIFE - HOME - AUTO
Dear Mr. Osama bin Laden:
We regret to inform you that we've abruptly canceled your life insurance policy.
Sincerely,
Ben Niceknowinya
Ben Niceknowinya,
Agent
MIKE THOMPSON

MIKE THOMPSON

Editorial Cartoonist
Detroit Free Press

Born in 1964; graduate of the University of Wisconsin at Milwaukee; editorial cartoonist for the *Detroit Free Press,* 1998 to the present; also winner of the Scripps-Howard Award, 1988, the H. L. Mencken Award, 1994, the Berryman Award, 1999, and the National Society of Professional Journalists Award, 2000.

2002 BERRYMAN AWARD

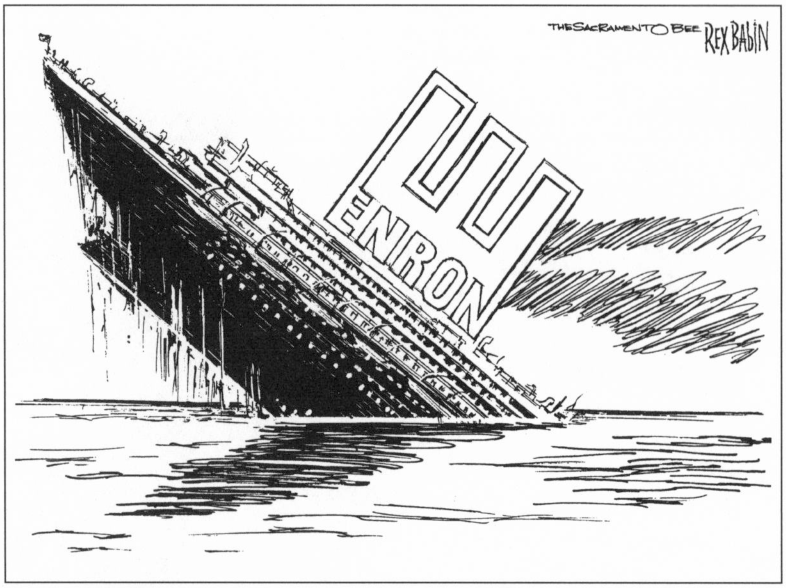
THE SACRAMENTO BEE REX BABIN
ENRON

REX BABIN

Editorial Cartoonist
Sacramento Bee

Born in Walnut Creek, California; graduate of San Diego State University, 1985; editorial cartoonist for the *Denver Post,* 1988-89, the *Albany (N. Y.) Times Union,* 1989-99, and the *Sacramento Bee*, 1999 to the present; cartoons syndicated by North American Syndicate.

2001 NATIONAL NEWSPAPER AWARD / CANADA

(Selected in 2002)

BRIAN GABLE

Editorial Cartoonist
Toronto Globe and Mail

Born in Saskatoon, Canada, in 1949; graduated from the University of Toronto in 1971; former editorial cartoonist for the *Brockville Recorder* and *Times* and the *Regina Leader-Post;* presently editorial cartoonist for the *Toronto Globe and Mail;* previous winner of the National Newspaper Award of Canada, 1986 and 1995.

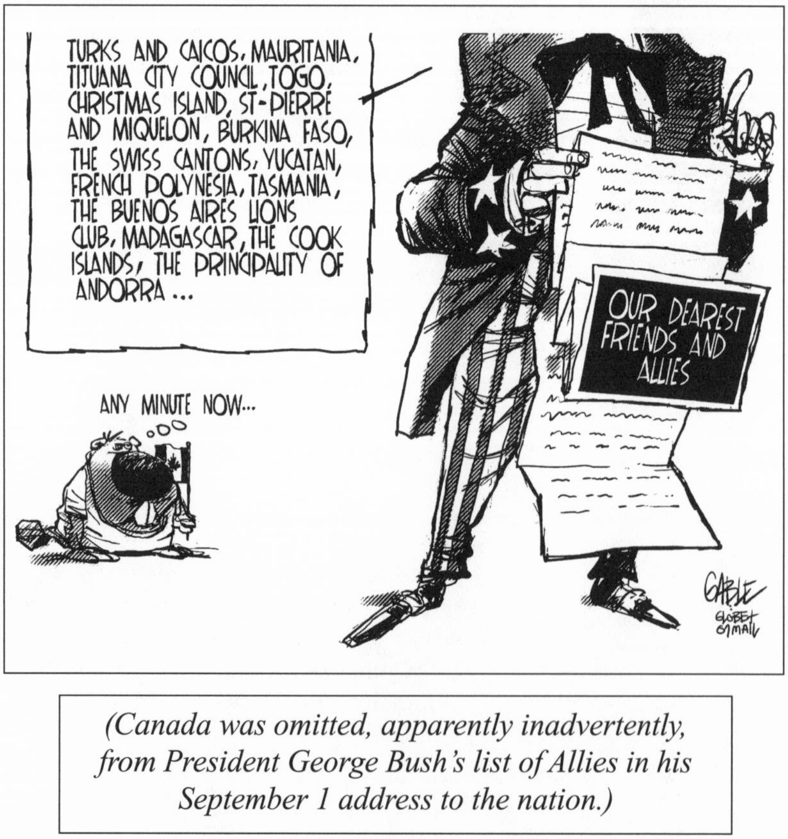
TURKS AND CAICOS, MAURITANIA, TIJUANA CITY COUNCIL, TOGO, CHRISTMAS ISLAND, ST-PIERRE AND MIQUELON, BURKINA FASO, THE SWISS CANTONS, YUCATAN, FRENCH POLYNESIA, TASMANIA, THE BUENOS AIRES LIONS CLUB, MADAGASCAR, THE COOK ISLANDS, THE PRINCIPALITY OF ANDORRA ...
OUR DEAREST FRIENDS AND ALLIES
ANY MINUTE NOW...
GABLE
GLOBE & MAIL

(Canada was omitted, apparently inadvertently, from President George Bush's list of Allies in his September 1 address to the nation.)

Best Editorial Cartoons of the Year

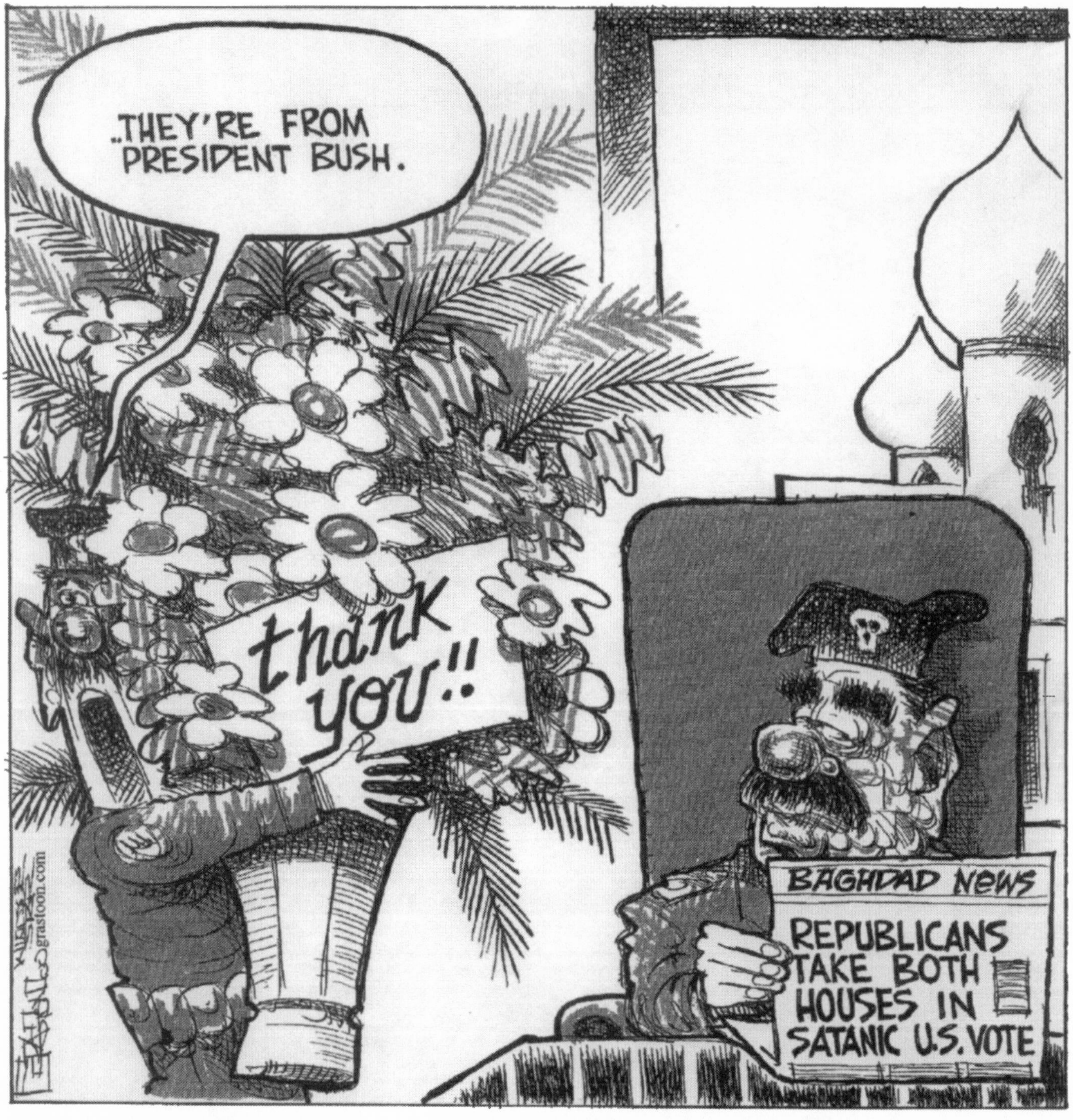
..THEY'RE FROM PRESIDENT BUSH.
thank you!!
BAGHDAD NEWS
REPUBLICANS TAKE BOTH HOUSES IN SATANIC U.S. VOTE
grastoon.com

MIKE GRASTON
Courtesy Windsor Star

The Bush Administration

President George W. Bush addressed terrorism in a September speech before the United Nations, telling members that the world was "challenged" by an "outlaw regime, exactly the kind of aggressive threat the United Nations was born to confront." He then described in detail how Iraq's Saddam Hussein had violated commitments for eleven years. With British Prime Minister Tony Blair firmly in his corner, Bush declared that if the U.N. would not hold Hussein accountable, then the U.S. would. Finally, after weeks of hemming and hawing, the U.N. voted to support Bush's position, as did the U.S. Congress.

Secretary of State Colin Powell made an extensive trip through the Middle East trying to line up support for Bush's plan. Investigations into the Enron collapse reached into the White House, but no evidence of wrongdoing was found. Democrats continued to demand that the president deal forcefully with corporate corruption and global warming.

The president urged Congress to pass legislation requiring insurance companies to offer affordable mental health coverage. Bush passed out at the White House when he choked on a pretzel but recovered unharmed and later joked about the incident.

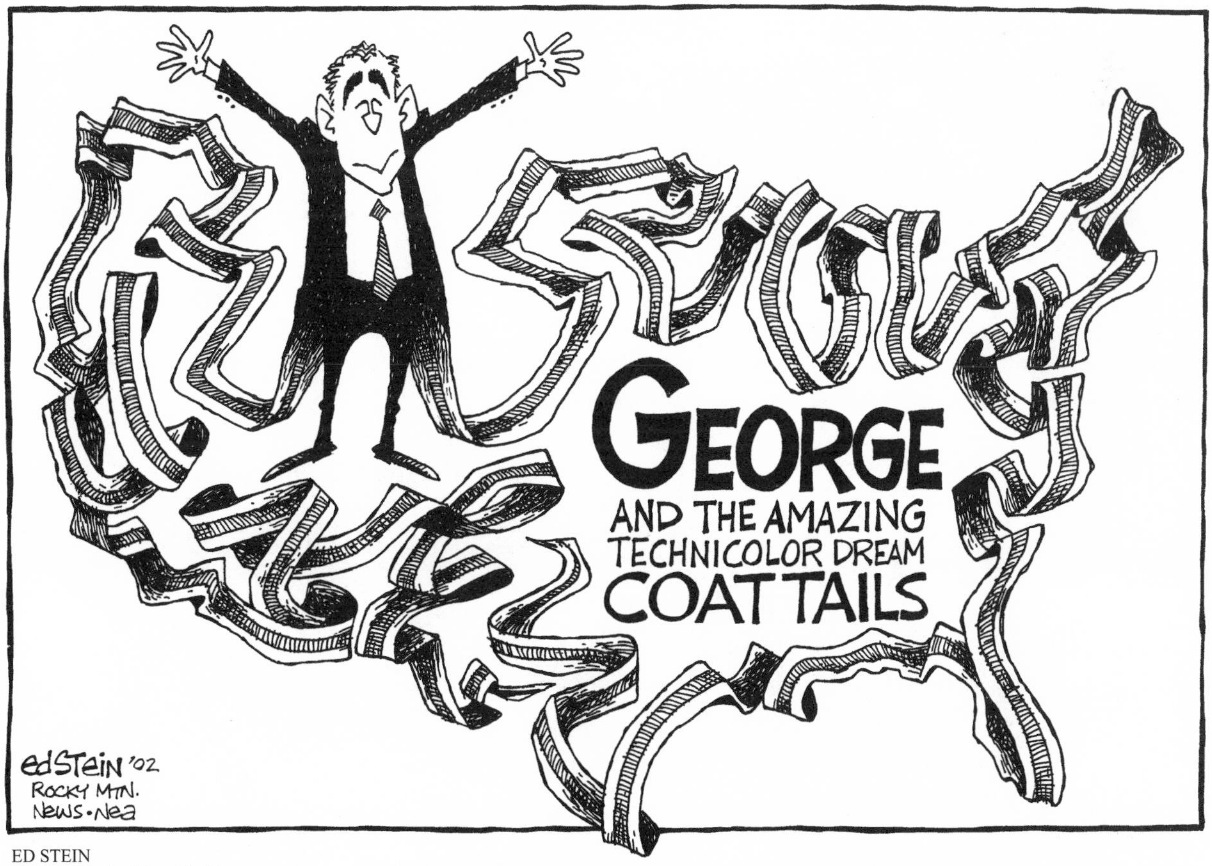
GEORGE
AND THE AMAZING
TECHNICOLOR DREAM
COATTAILS
edSTeiN '02
ROCKY MTN.
NEWS•NEA

ED STEIN
Courtesy Rocky Mountain News

JACK OHMAN
Courtesy The Oregonian

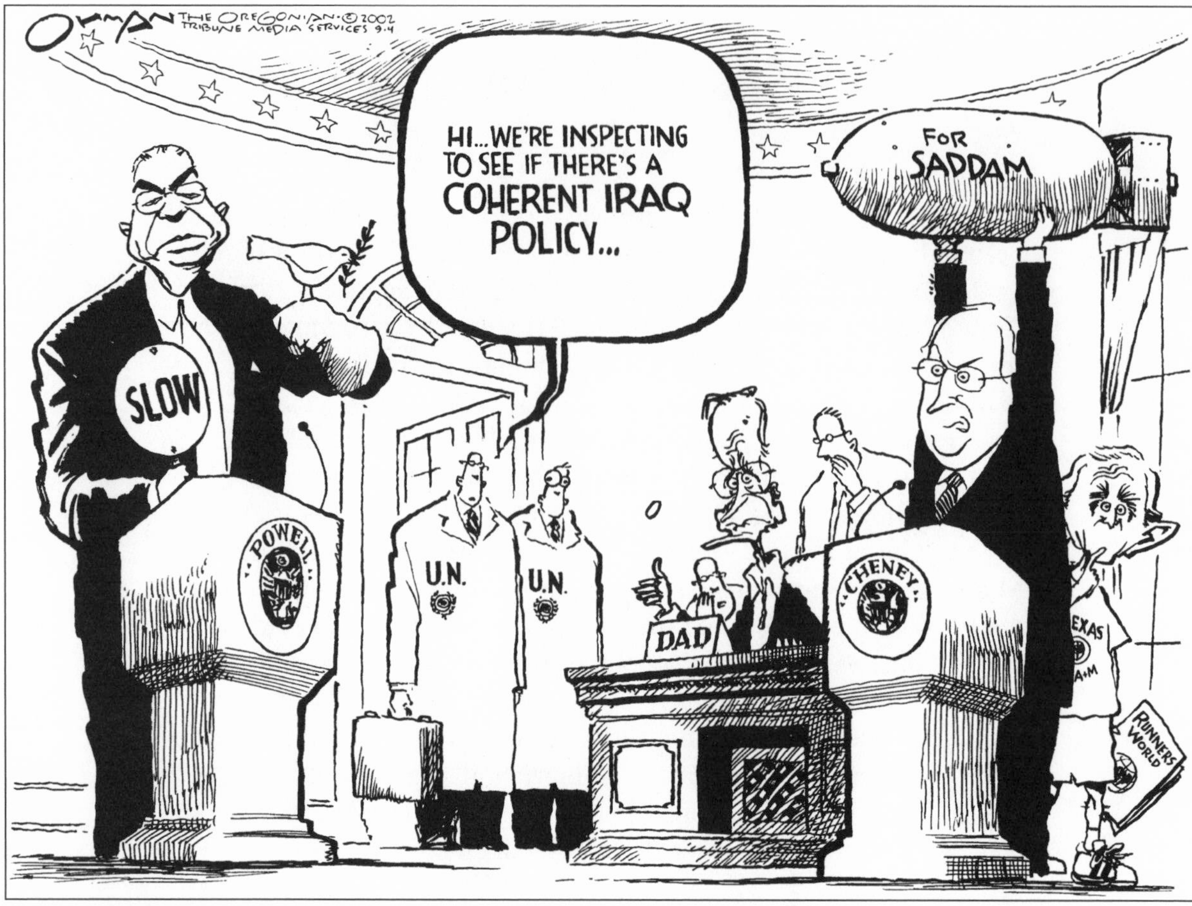
OHMAN THE OREGONIAN © 2002 TRIBUNE MEDIA SERVICES 9-4
HI...WE'RE INSPECTING TO SEE IF THERE'S A COHERENT IRAQ POLICY...
FOR SADDAM
SLOW
POWELL
U.N.
U.N.
DAD
CHENEY
TEXAS A&M
RUNNERS WORLD

BRIAN FAIRRINGTON
Courtesy Arizona Republic

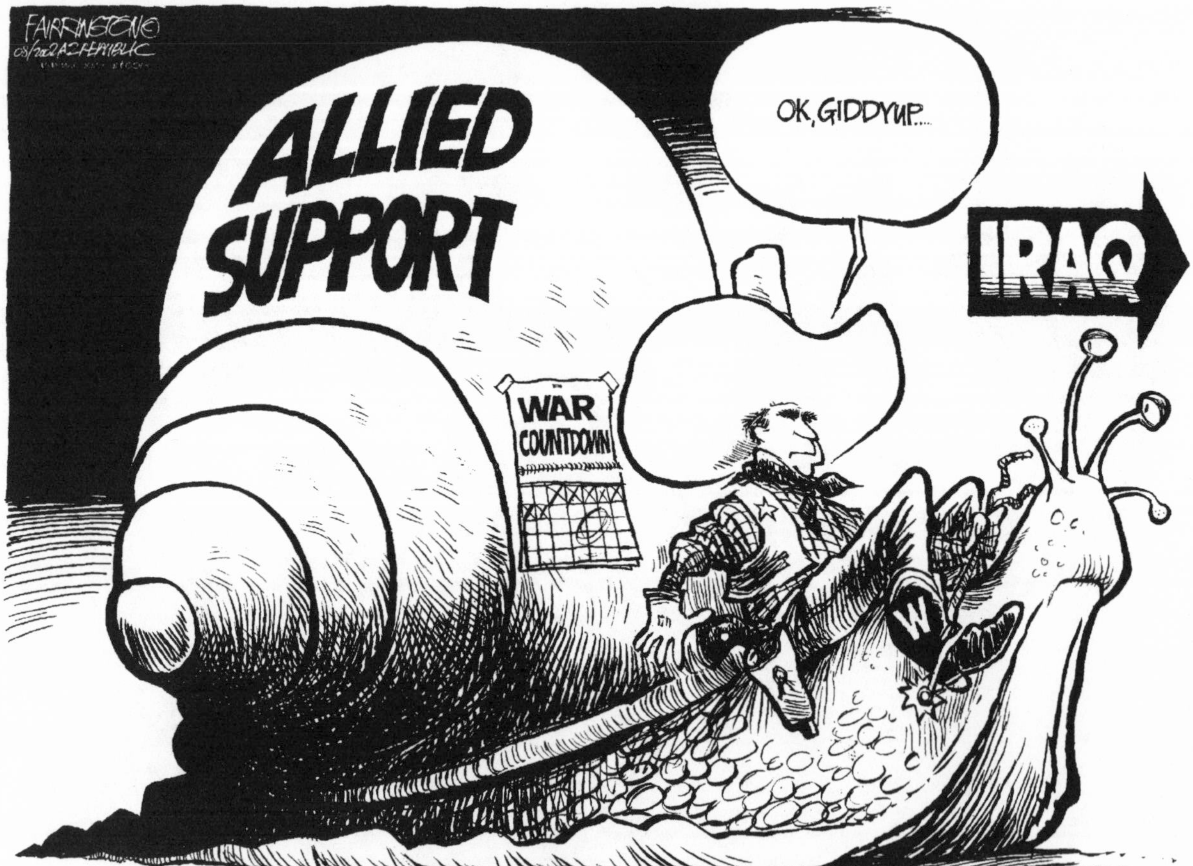
FAIRRINGTON©
ALLIED SUPPORT
OK, GIDDYUP....
IRAQ
WAR COUNTDOWN
W

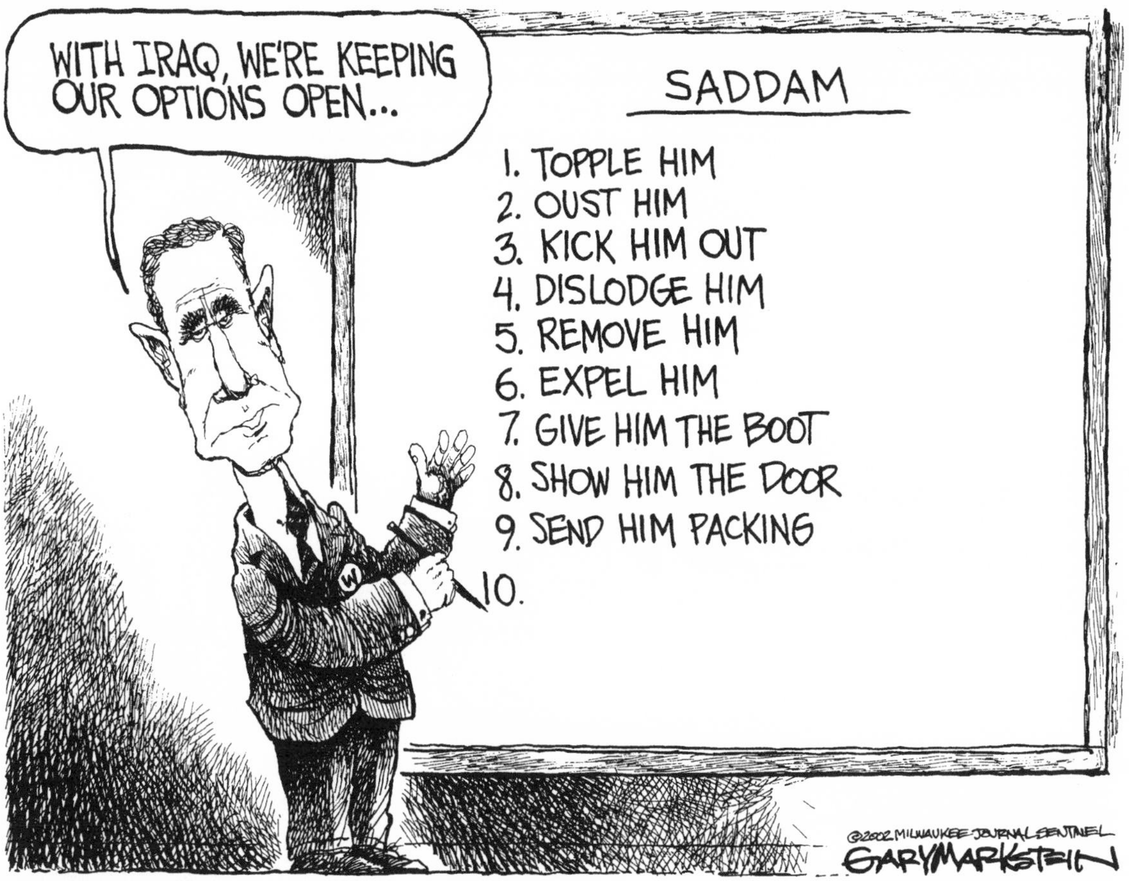
WITH IRAQ, WE'RE KEEPING OUR OPTIONS OPEN...
SADDAM
1. TOPPLE HIM
2. OUST HIM
3. KICK HIM OUT
4. DISLODGE HIM
5. REMOVE HIM
6. EXPEL HIM
7. GIVE HIM THE BOOT
8. SHOW HIM THE DOOR
9. SEND HIM PACKING
10.
©2002 MILWAUKEE JOURNAL SENTINEL
GARY MARKSTEIN

GARY MARKSTEIN
Courtesy Milwaukee Journal Sentinel

SVEN VAN ASSCHE
Courtesy Darien Times (Conn.)

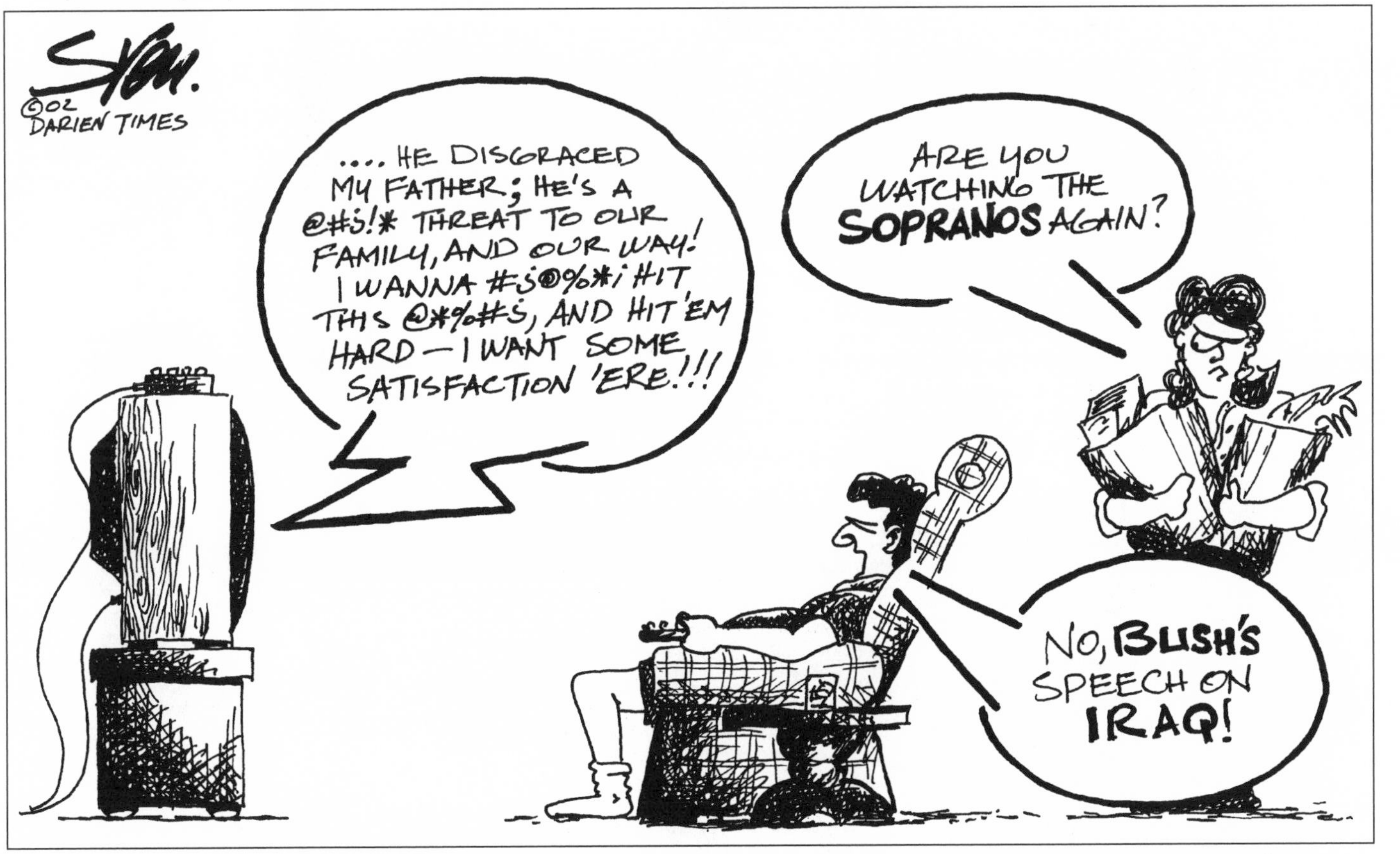
SVEN.
©02 DARIEN TIMES
....HE DISGRACED MY FATHER; HE'S A @#$!* THREAT TO OUR FAMILY, AND OUR WAY! I WANNA #$@%*i HIT THIS @*%#$, AND HIT 'EM HARD— I WANT SOME SATISFACTION 'ERE!!!
ARE YOU WATCHING THE SOPRANOS AGAIN?
NO, BUSH'S SPEECH ON IRAQ!

TOM BECK
Courtesy Freeport Journal-Standard (Ill.)

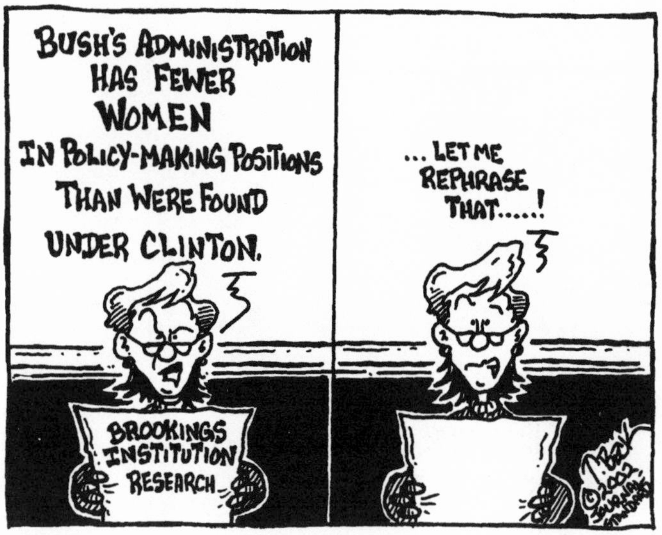
BUSH'S ADMINISTRATION HAS FEWER WOMEN IN POLICY-MAKING POSITIONS THAN WERE FOUND UNDER CLINTON.
BROOKINGS INSTITUTION RESEARCH
... LET ME REPHRASE THAT.....!

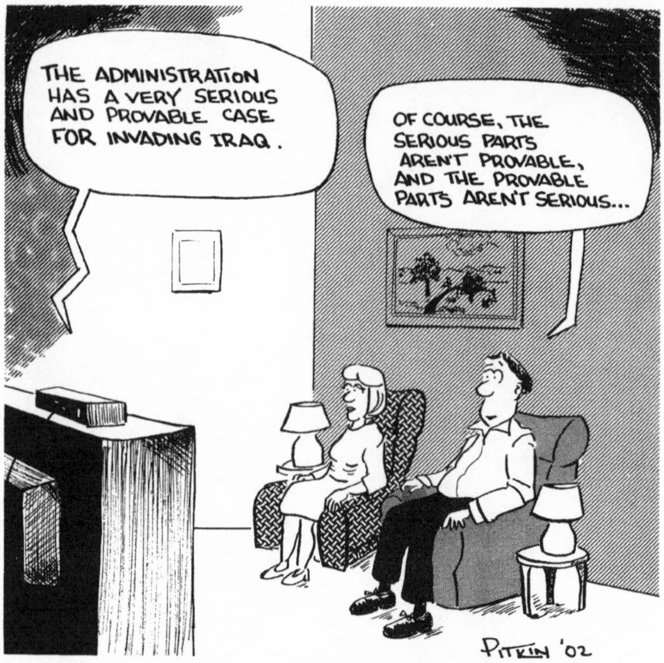
THE ADMINISTRATION HAS A VERY SERIOUS AND PROVABLE CASE FOR INVADING IRAQ.
OF COURSE, THE SERIOUS PARTS AREN'T PROVABLE, AND THE PROVABLE PARTS AREN'T SERIOUS...
PITKIN '02

HAP PITKIN
Courtesy Boulder Daily Camera

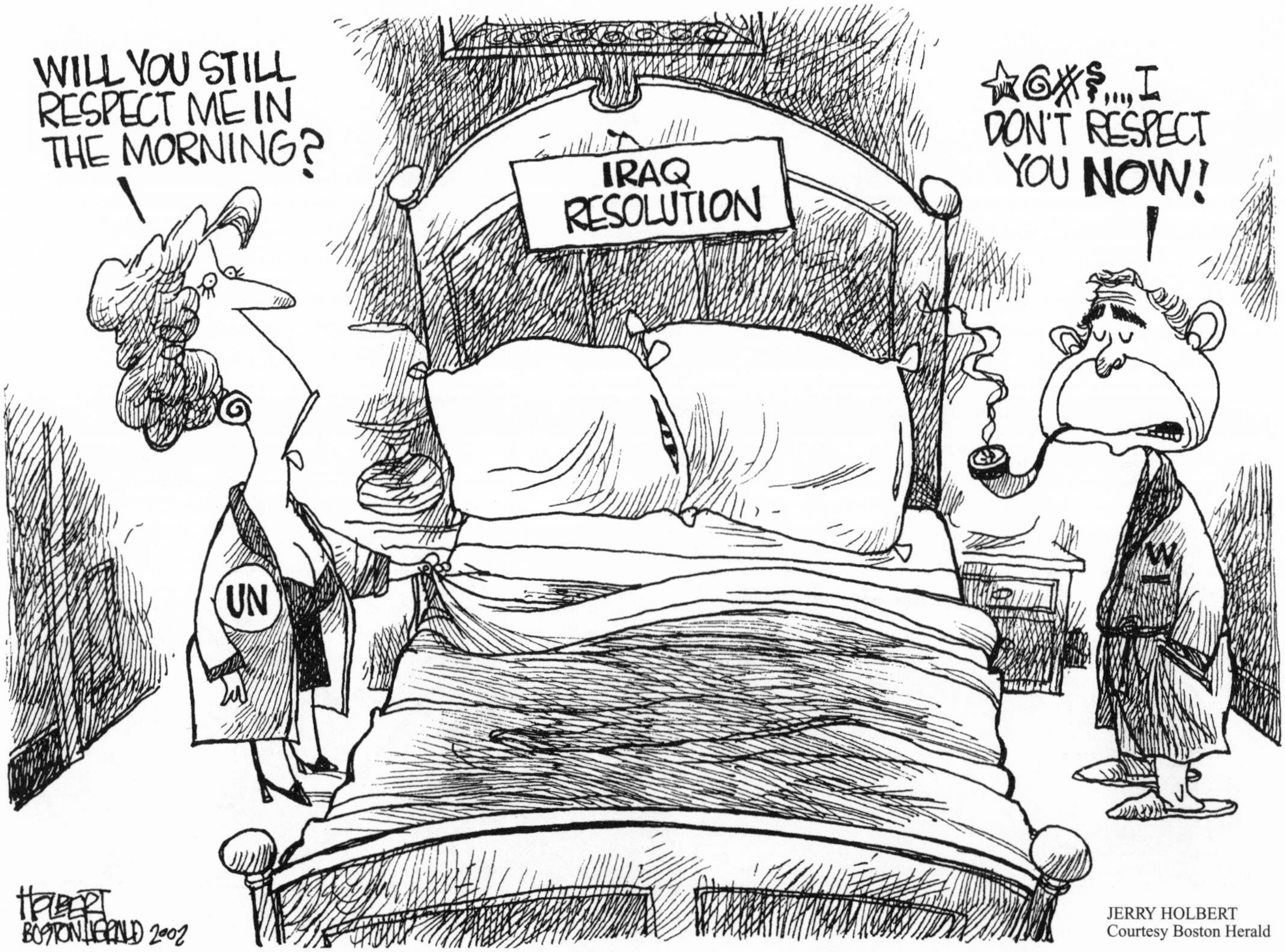
WILL YOU STILL RESPECT ME IN THE MORNING?
IRAQ RESOLUTION
☆@#$,..., I DON'T RESPECT YOU NOW!
UN
W
HOLBERT BOSTON HERALD 2002

JERRY HOLBERT
Courtesy Boston Herald

DICK LOCHER
Courtesy Chicago Tribune

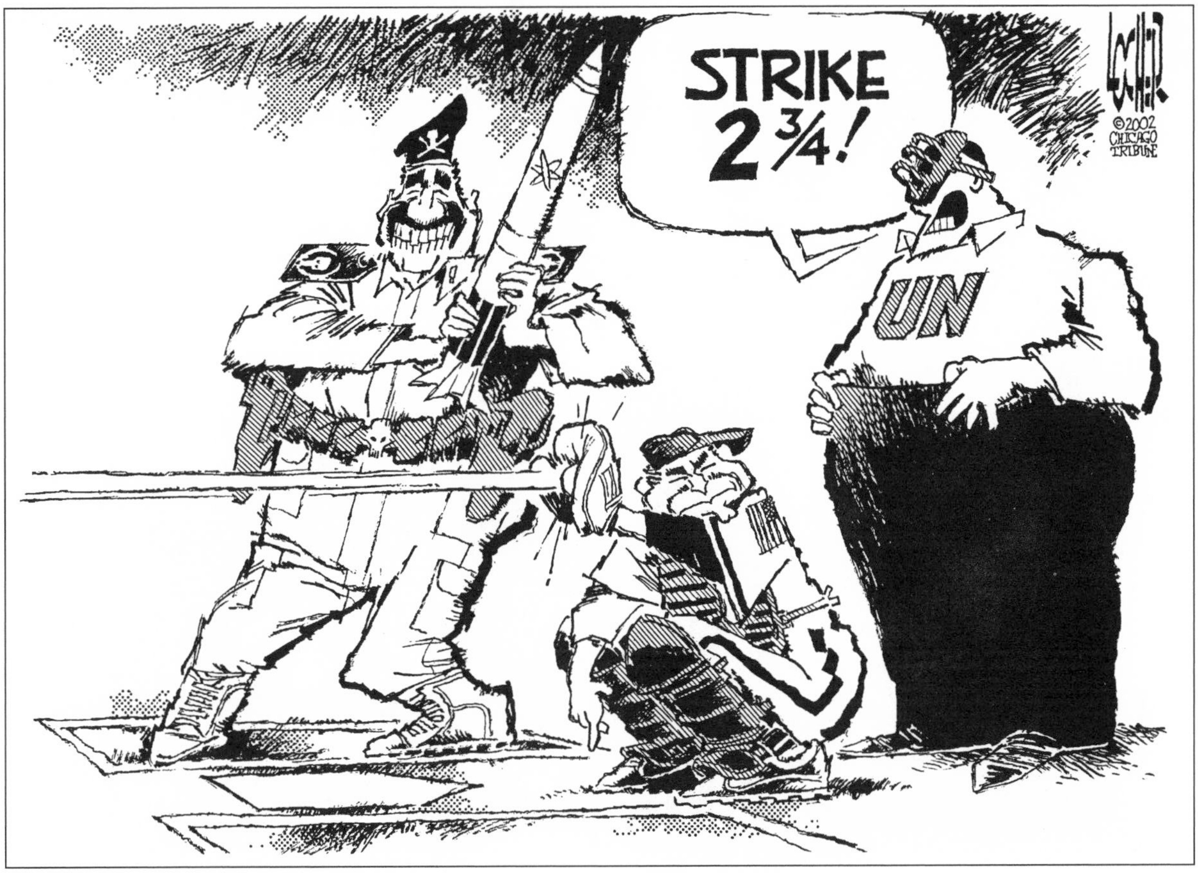
STRIKE 2 3/4!
UN
©2002 CHICAGO TRIBUNE

SCOTT STANTIS
Courtesy Birmingham News

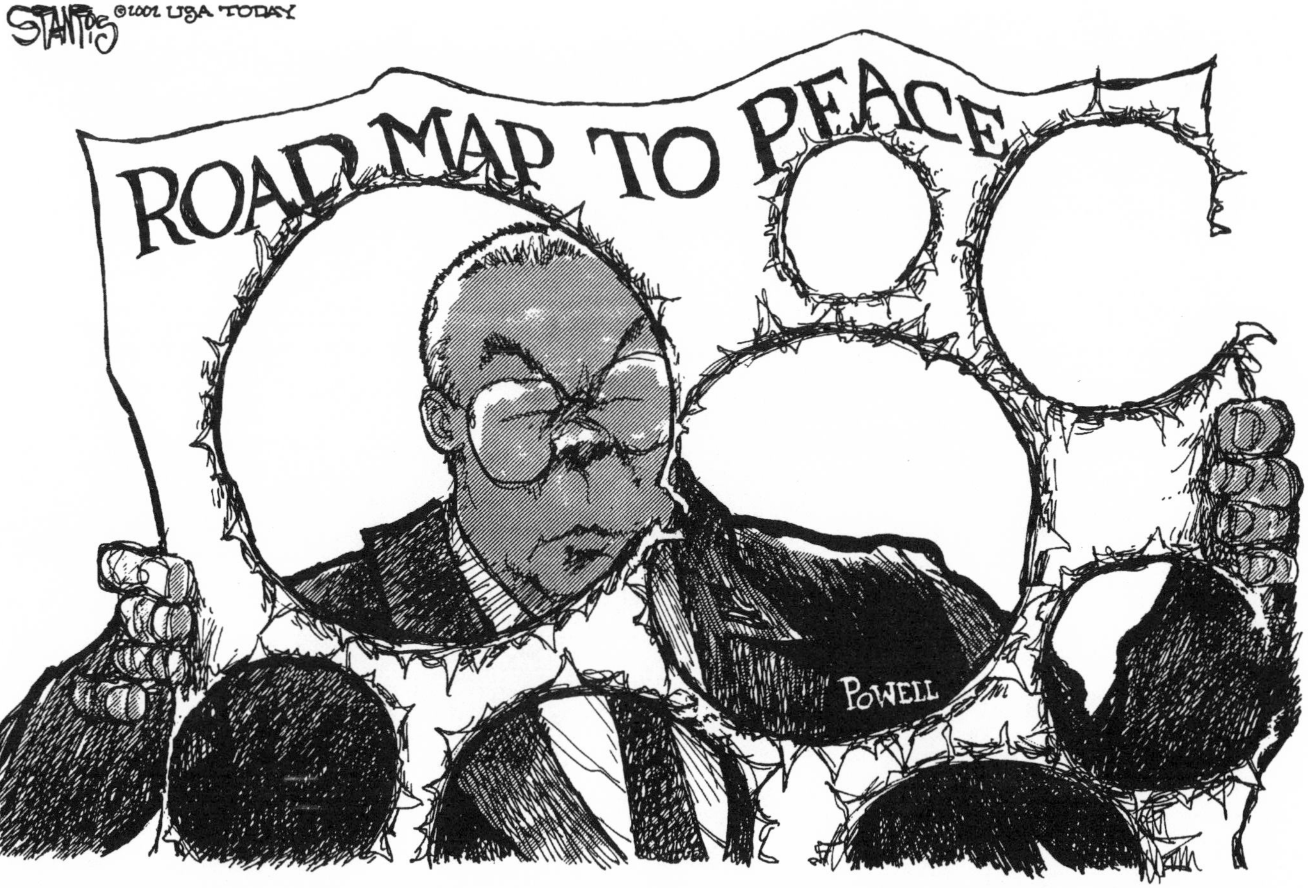
©2002 USA TODAY
ROAD MAP TO PEACE
POWELL

HENRY McCLURE
Courtesy Lawton Constitution (Okla.)

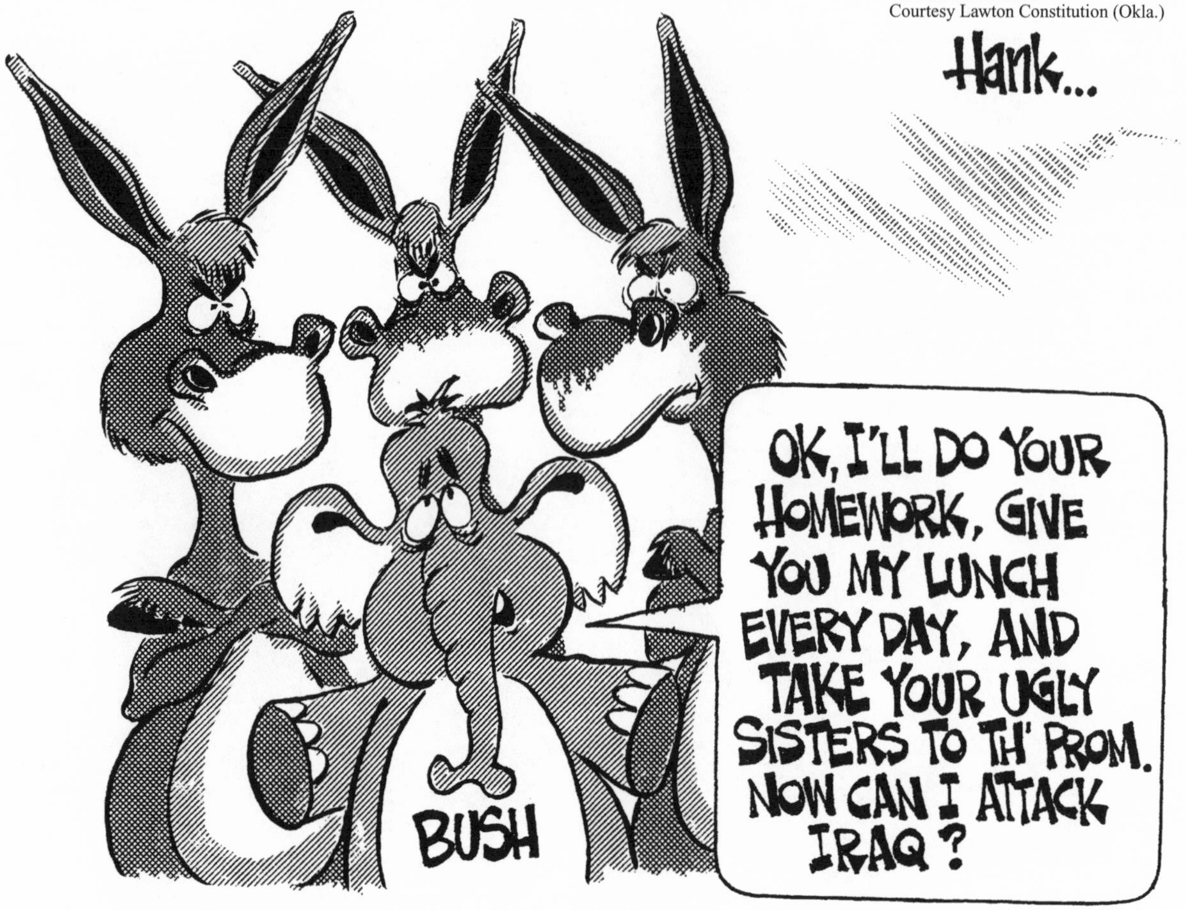
Hank...
OK, I'LL DO YOUR HOMEWORK, GIVE YOU MY LUNCH EVERY DAY, AND TAKE YOUR UGLY SISTERS TO TH' PROM. NOW CAN I ATTACK IRAQ?
BUSH

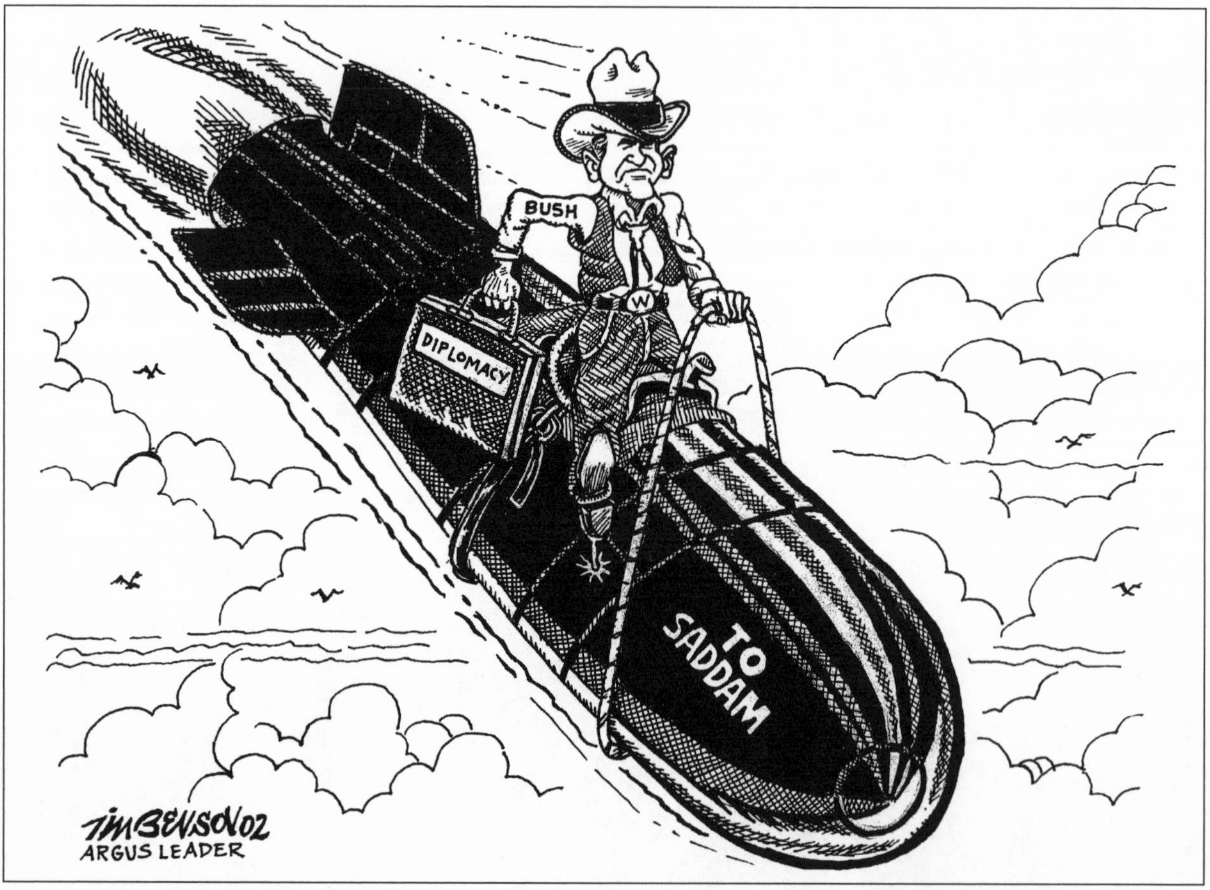
BUSH
DIPLOMACY
W
TO SADDAM
TIM BENSON 02
ARGUS LEADER

TIM BENSON
Courtesy The Argus-Leader (S.D.)

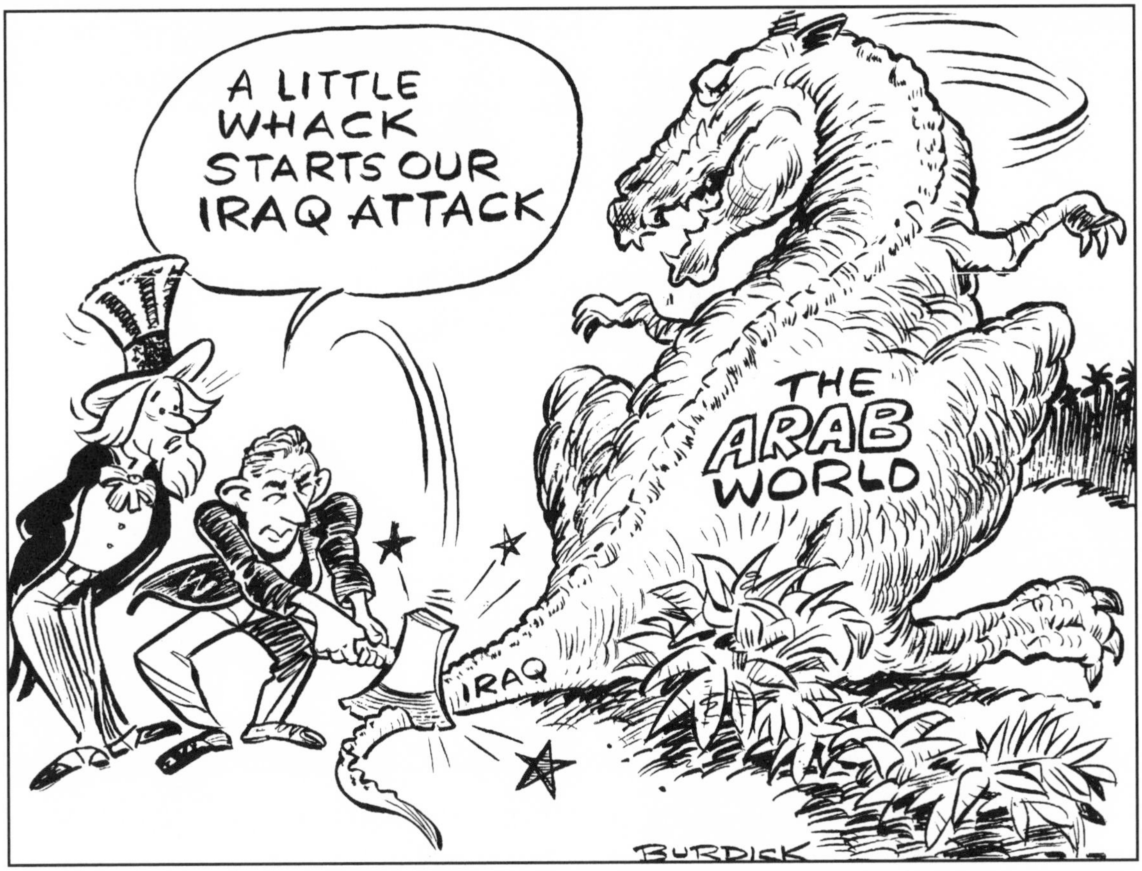
A LITTLE WHACK STARTS OUR IRAQ ATTACK
THE ARAB WORLD
IRAQ
BURDICK

STAN BURDICK
Courtesy Pennysaver News (N.Y.)

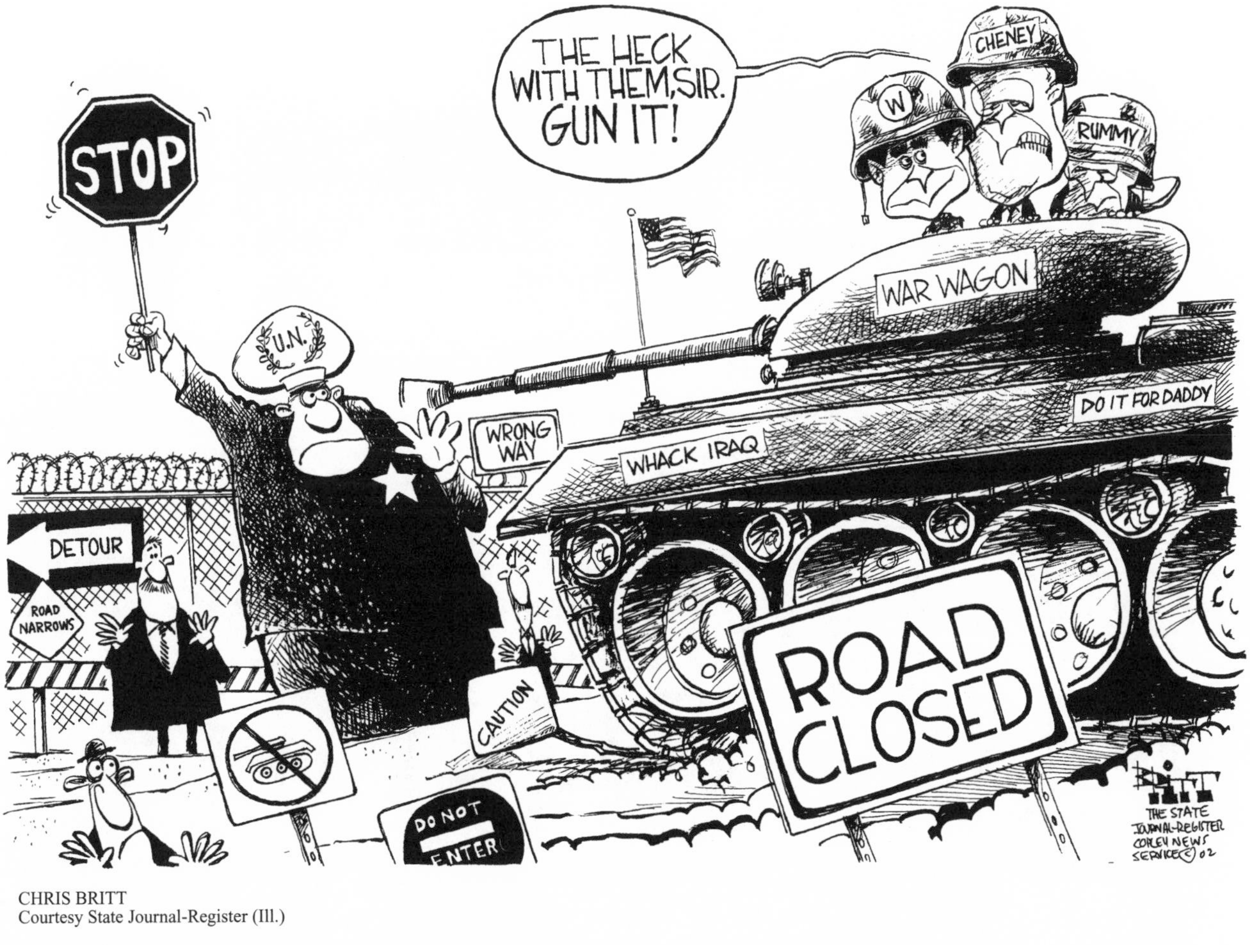
THE HECK WITH THEM, SIR. GUN IT!
W
CHENEY
RUMMY
STOP
U.N.
WAR WAGON
DO IT FOR DADDY
WRONG WAY
WHACK IRAQ
DETOUR
ROAD NARROWS
CAUTION
ROAD CLOSED
DO NOT ENTER
BRITT
THE STATE JOURNAL-REGISTER COPLEY NEWS SERVICE © 02

CHRIS BRITT
Courtesy State Journal-Register (Ill.)

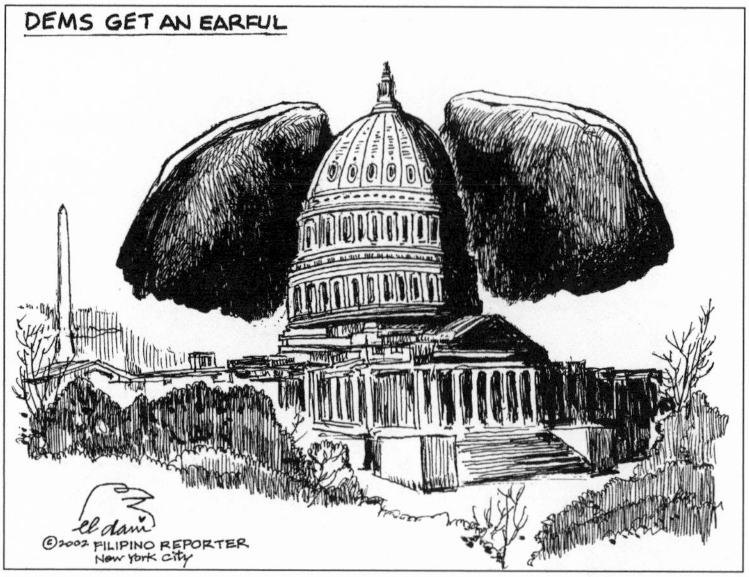
DEMS GET AN EARFUL
©2002 FILIPINO REPORTER
New York City

DANI AGUILA
Courtesy Filipino Reporter

KIRK ANDERSON
Courtesy St. Paul Pioneer Press

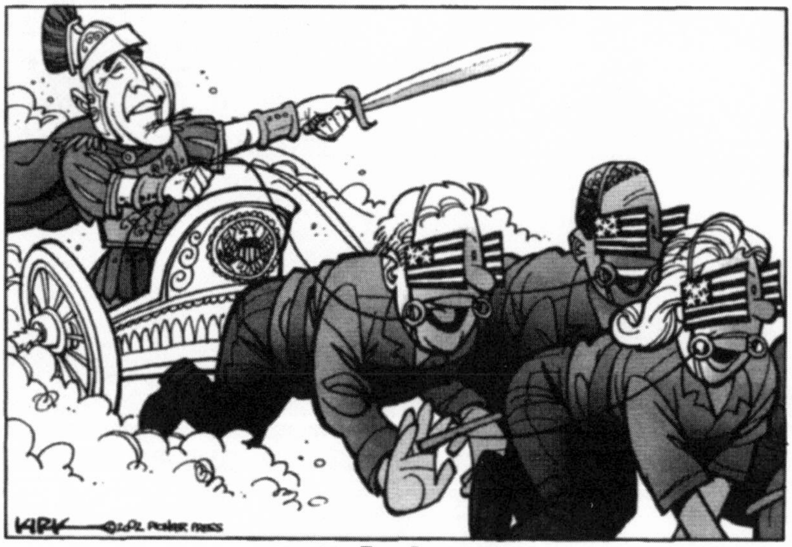
KIRK

BLIND PATRIOTISM

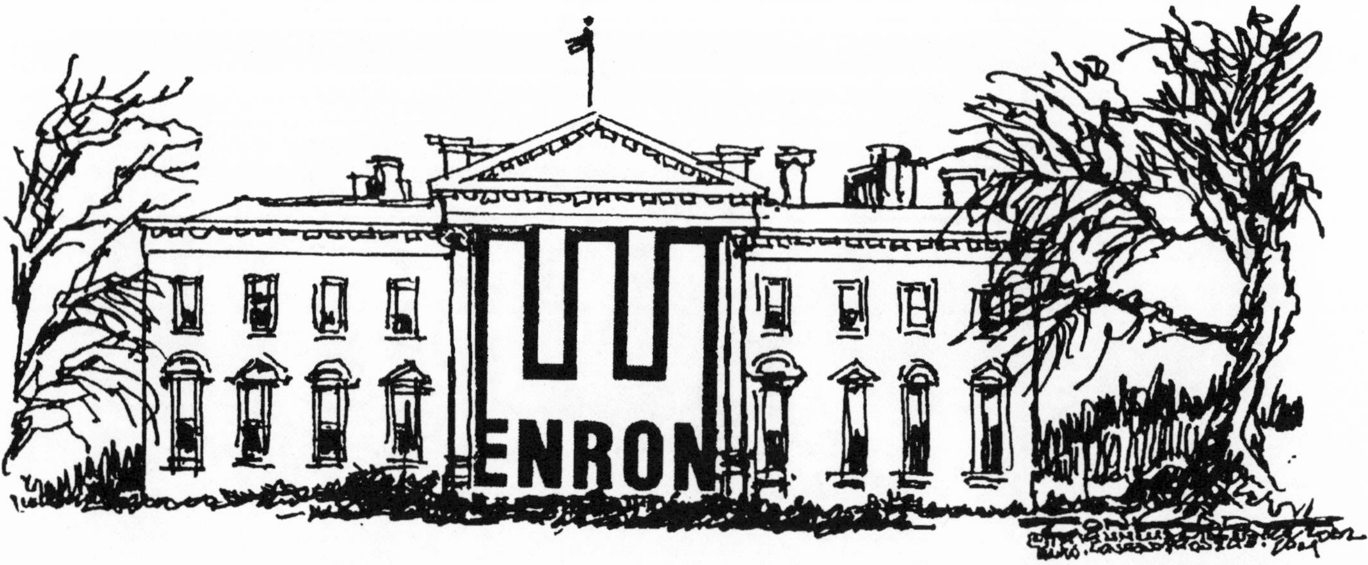
ENRON

PAUL CONRAD
Courtesy Los Angeles Times

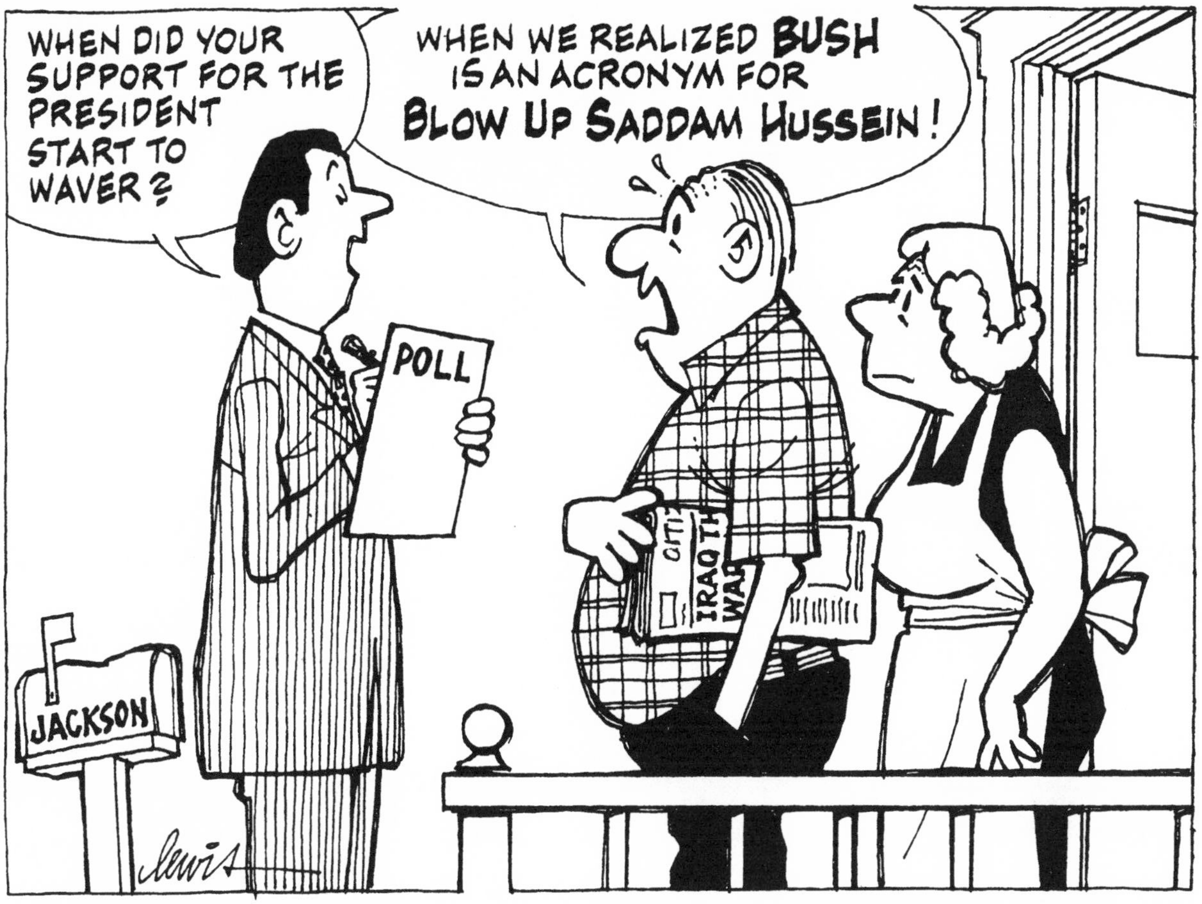
WHEN DID YOUR SUPPORT FOR THE PRESIDENT START TO WAVER?
WHEN WE REALIZED BUSH IS AN ACRONYM FOR BLOW UP SADDAM HUSSEIN!
POLL
IRAQ TH WAR
JACKSON
Lewis

LARRY LEWIS
Courtesy Jackson Citizen Patriot (Mich.)

BEN SARGENT
Courtesy Austin American-Statesman

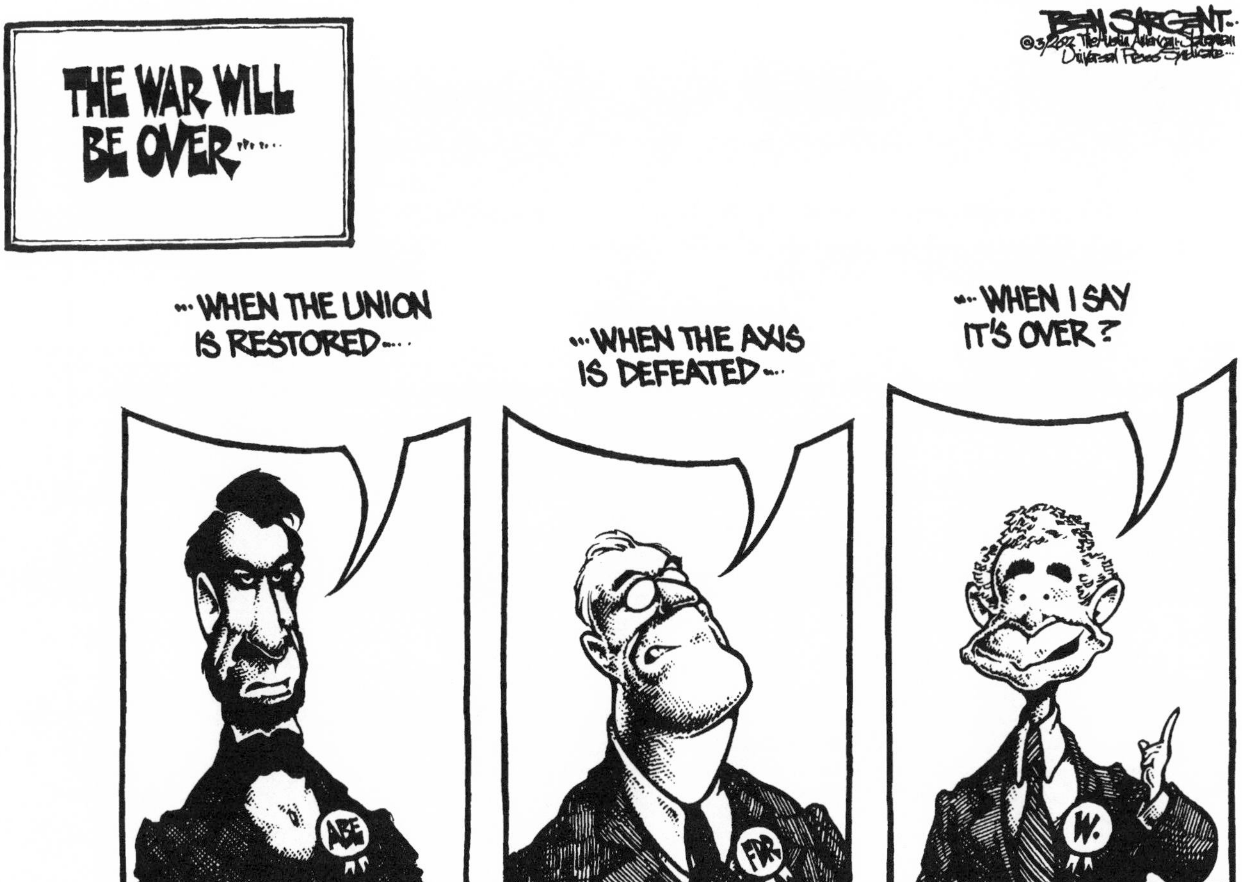
BEN SARGENT
THE WAR WILL BE OVER.....
...WHEN THE UNION IS RESTORED....
...WHEN THE AXIS IS DEFEATED...
...WHEN I SAY IT'S OVER?
ABE
FDR
W.

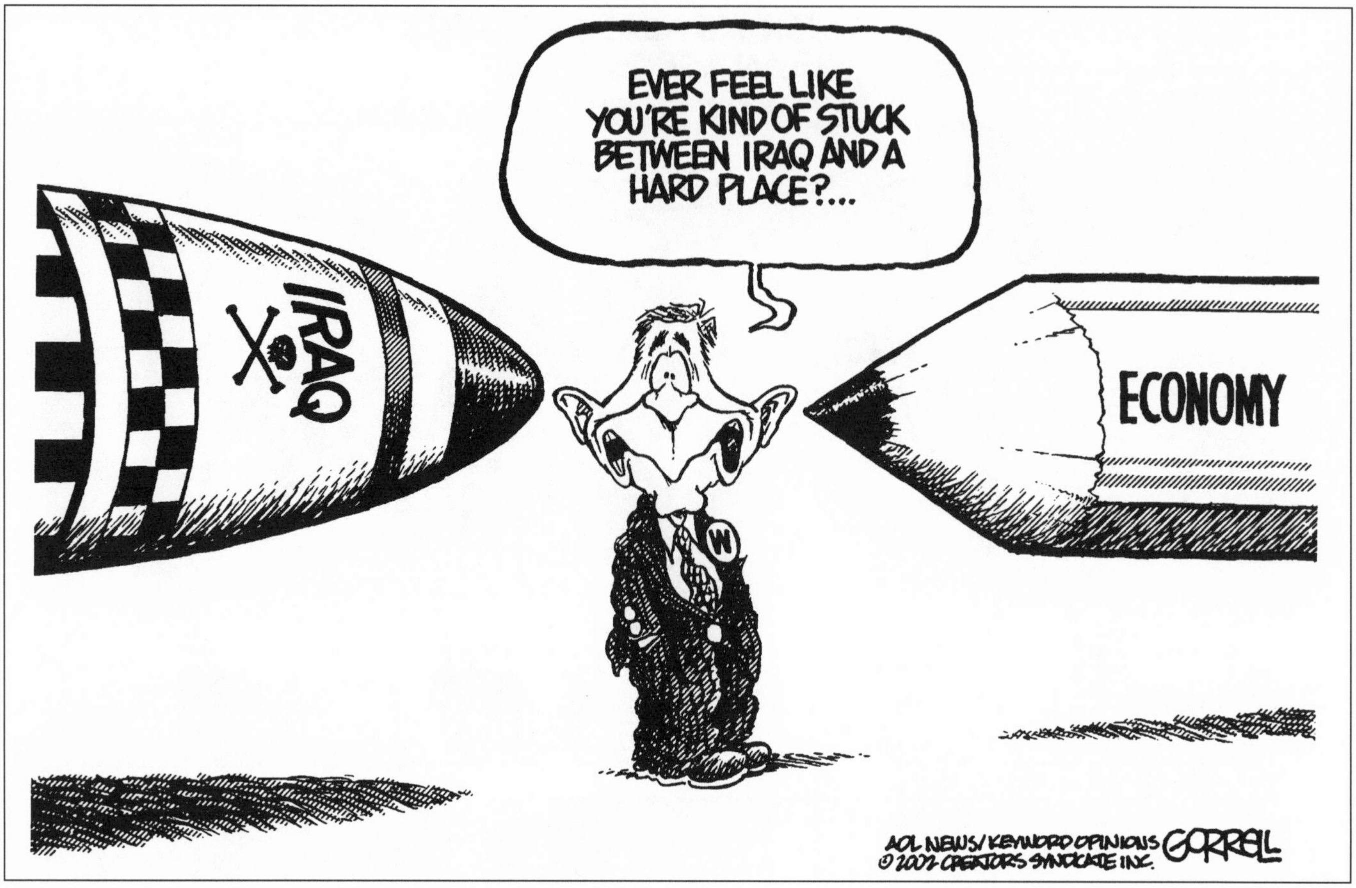
EVER FEEL LIKE YOU'RE KIND OF STUCK BETWEEN IRAQ AND A HARD PLACE?...
IRAQ
ECONOMY
W
AOL NEWS/KEYWORD OPINIONS GORRELL
© 2002 CREATORS SYNDICATE INC.

BOB GORRELL
Courtesy America Online News

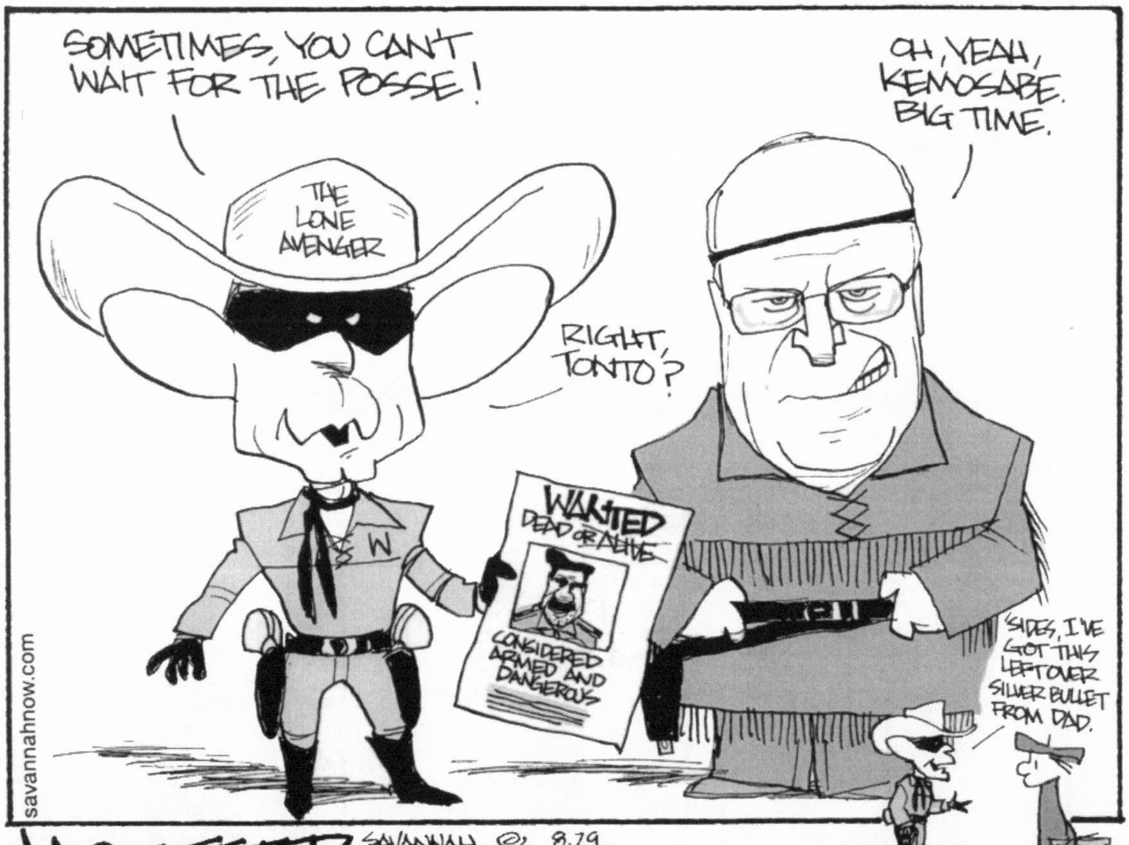
SOMETIMES, YOU CAN'T WAIT FOR THE POSSE!
OH, YEAH, KEMOSABE. BIG TIME.
THE LONE AVENGER
RIGHT, TONTO?
WANTED
DEAD OR ALIVE
CONSIDERED ARMED AND DANGEROUS
W
'SIDES, I'VE GOT THIS LEFTOVER SILVER BULLET FROM DAD.
savannahnow.com
MSTREETER SAVANNAH MORNING NEWS © 8.29 '02

MARK STREETER
Courtesy Savannah Morning News

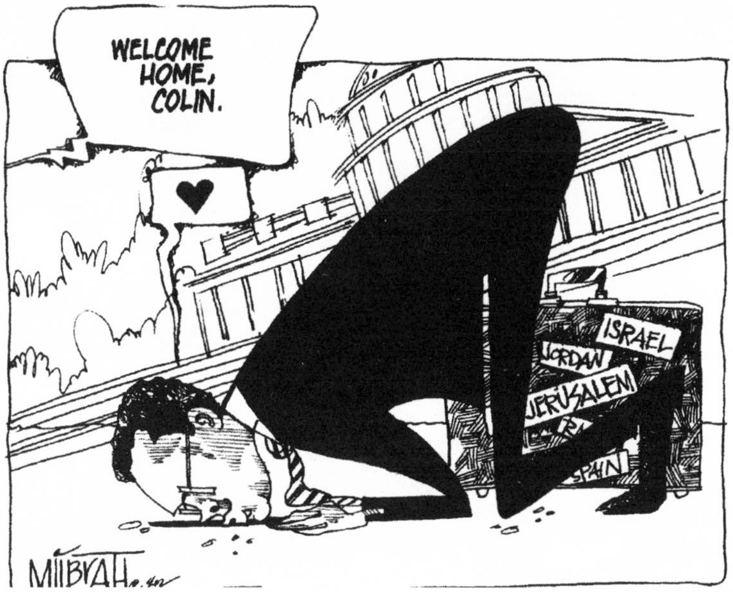
WELCOME HOME, COLIN.
ISRAEL
JORDAN
JERUSALEM
SPAIN
MILBRAH

DEB MILBRAH
Courtesy New York Daily News

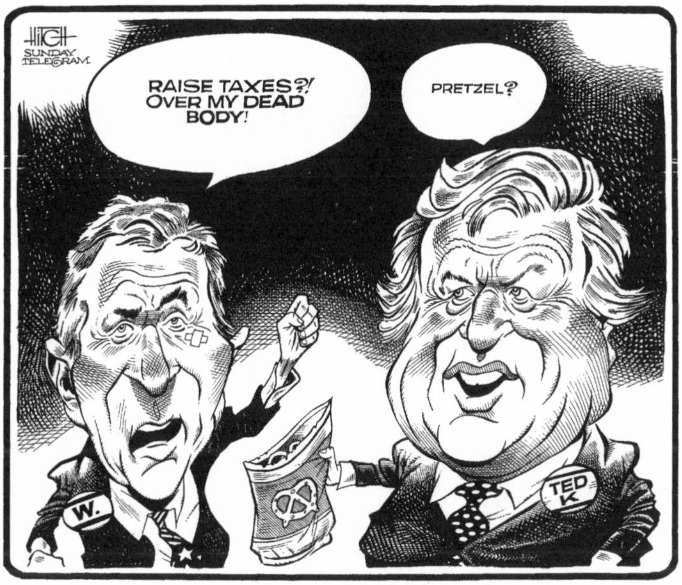
HITCH SUNDAY TELEGRAM
RAISE TAXES?! OVER MY DEAD BODY!
PRETZEL?
W.
TED K

DAVID HITCH
Courtesy Worcester Telegram and Gazette (Mass.)

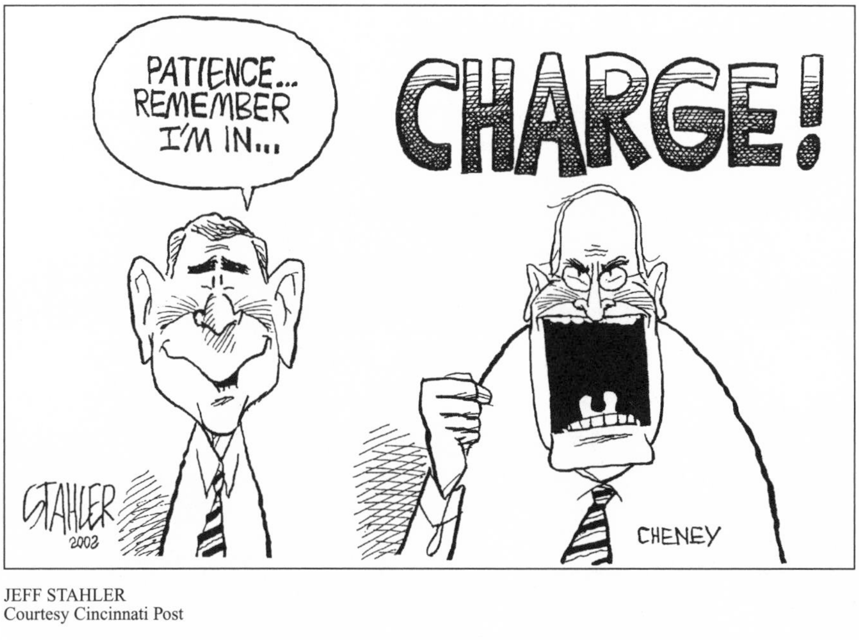
PATIENCE... REMEMBER I'M IN...
CHARGE!
STAHLER 2003
CHENEY

JEFF STAHLER
Courtesy Cincinnati Post

PAUL CONRAD
Courtesy Los Angeles Times

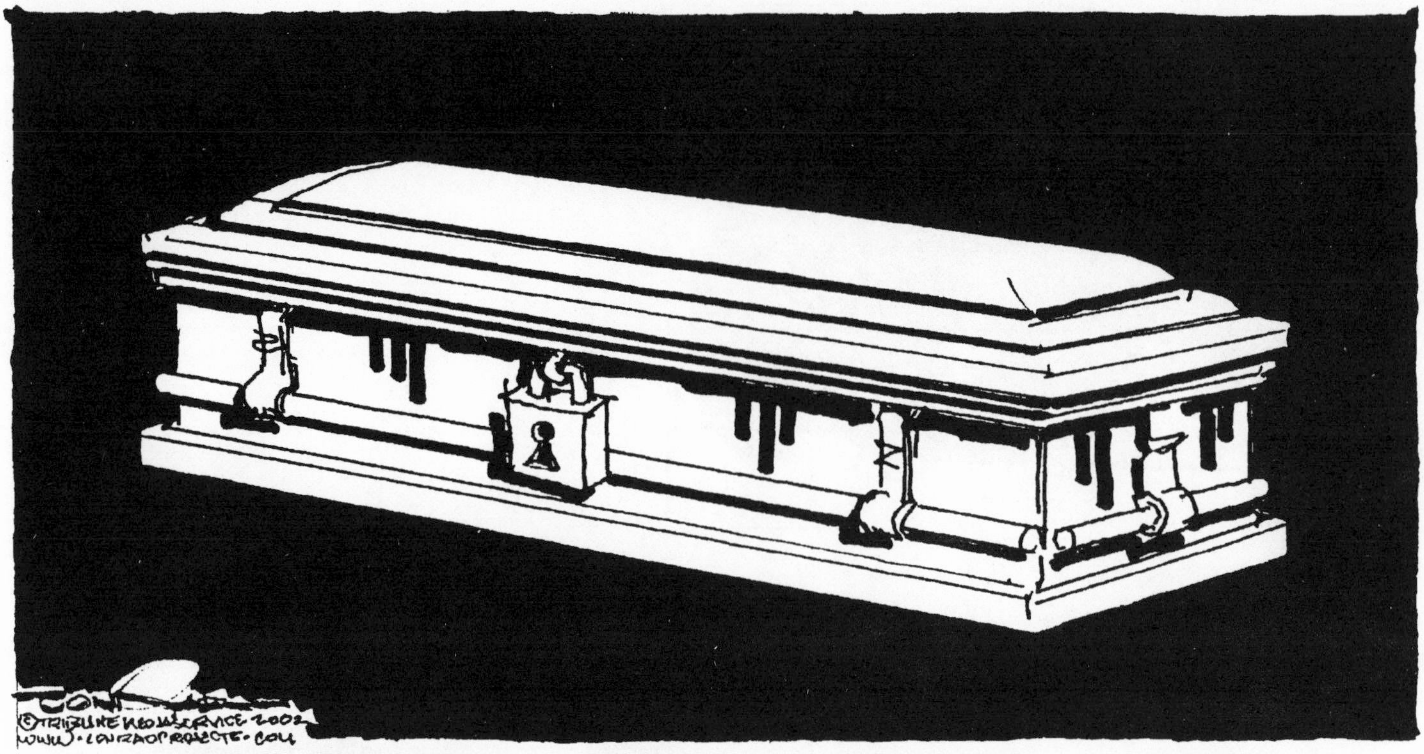

REPUBLICAN SOCIAL SECURITY AND MEDICARE LOCKBOX

ROB ROGERS
Courtesy Pittsburgh Post-Gazette

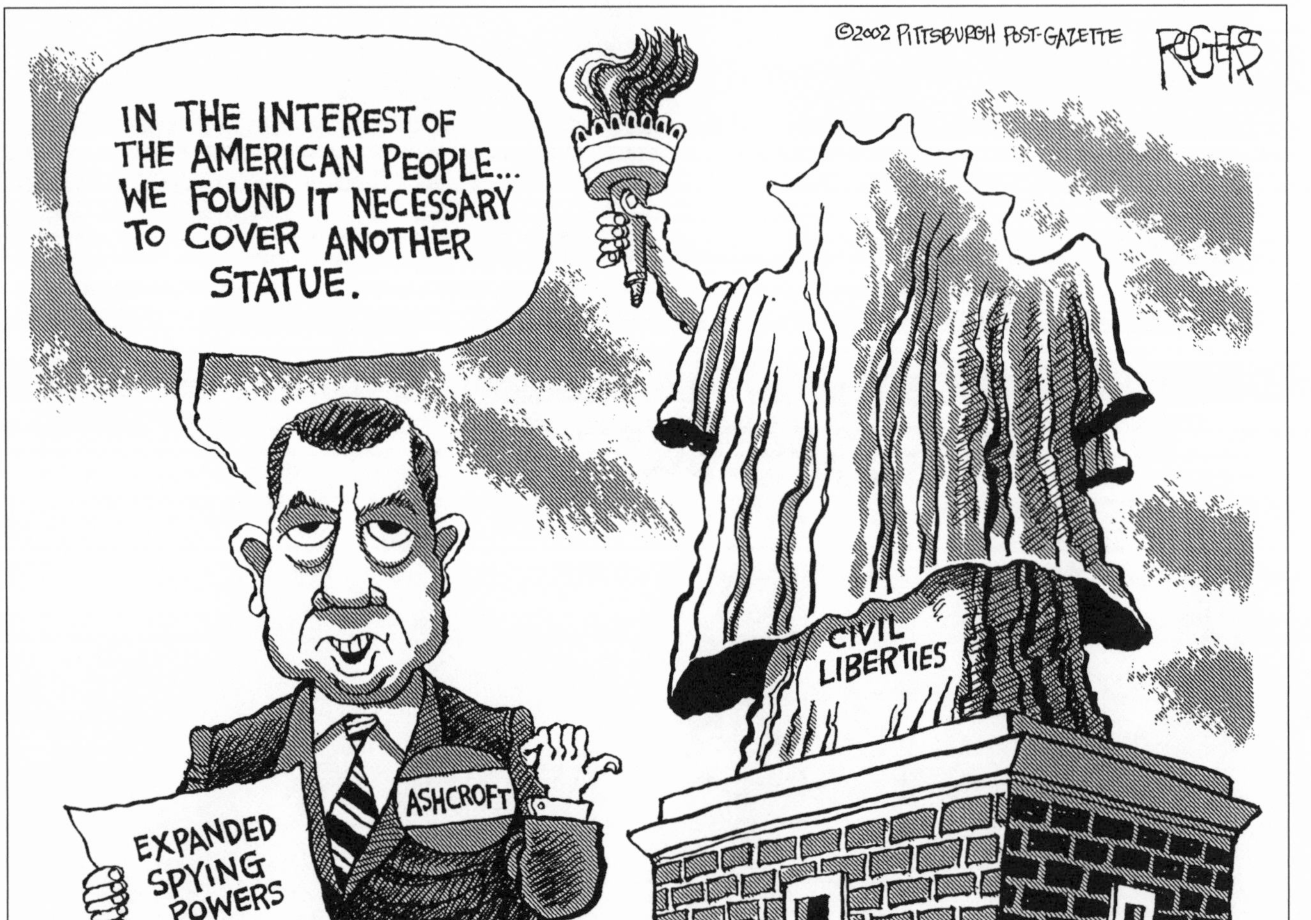
©2002 PITTSBURGH POST-GAZETTE
ROGERS
IN THE INTEREST OF THE AMERICAN PEOPLE... WE FOUND IT NECESSARY TO COVER ANOTHER STATUE.
CIVIL LIBERTIES
ASHCROFT
EXPANDED SPYING POWERS

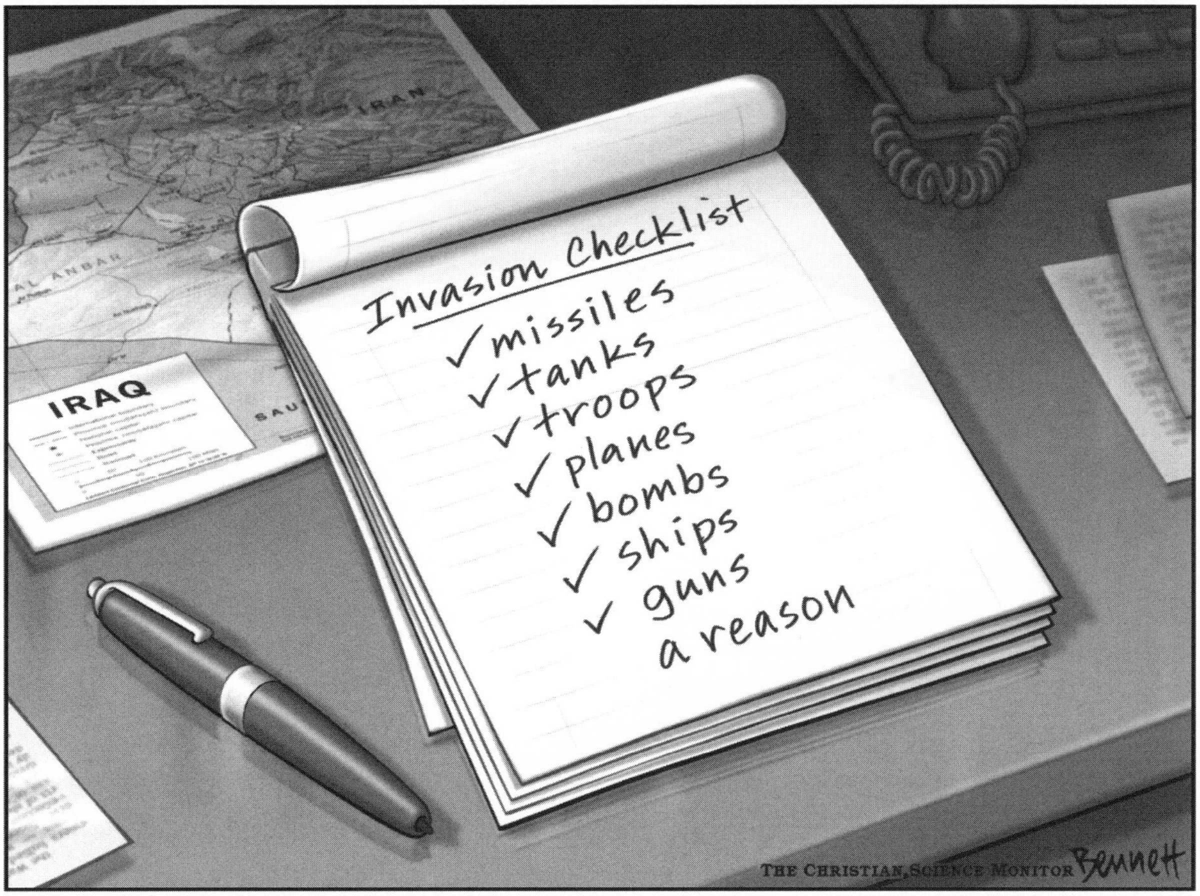

IRAN
AL ANBAR
IRAQ
Invasion Checklist
✓ missiles
✓ tanks
✓ troops
✓ planes
✓ bombs
✓ ships
✓ guns
a reason
THE CHRISTIAN SCIENCE MONITOR Bennett

CLAY BENNETT
Courtesy Christian Science Monitor

ROBERT ARIAIL
Courtesy The State (S.C.)

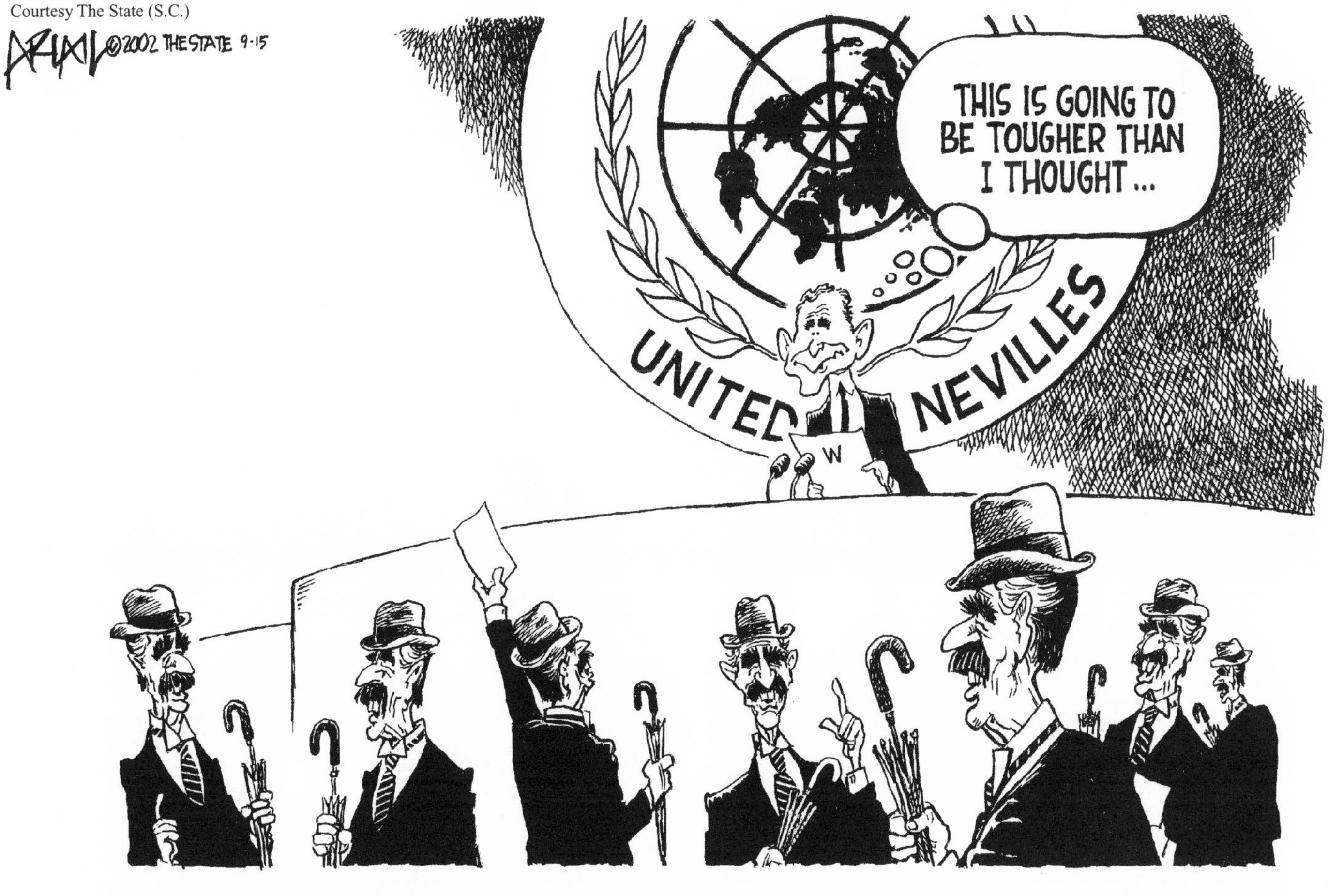

ARIAIL ©2002 THE STATE 9·15
THIS IS GOING TO BE TOUGHER THAN I THOUGHT ...
UNITED NEVILLES
W

YOU'RE ON BUSH'S ECONOMIC TEAM, RIGHT?
STAHLER '02
©THE CINCINNATI POST

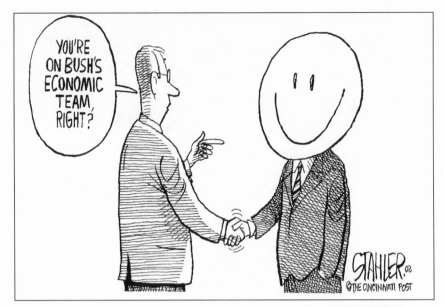

JEFF STAHLER
Courtesy Cincinnati Post

GEORGE W. BUSH's BRAIN
Everything Else
sgreenberg@insidevc.com www.greenberg-art.com
GREENBERG — VENTURA COUNTY STAR, 2002

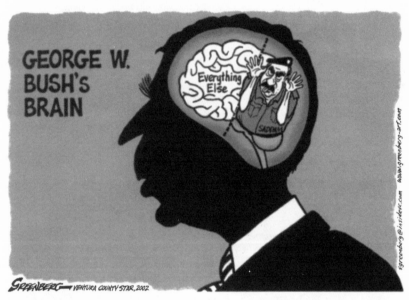

STEVE GREENBERG
Courtesy Ventura County Star (Calif.)

THAT'S IT — COME ON, COME ON...
NATIONS THAT START WARS
©LINDSTROM
DULUTH NEWS TRIBUNE 8-02

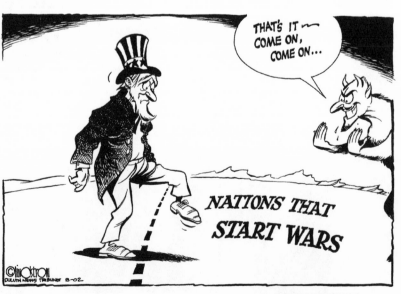

STEVE LINDSTROM
Courtesy Duluth News-Tribune

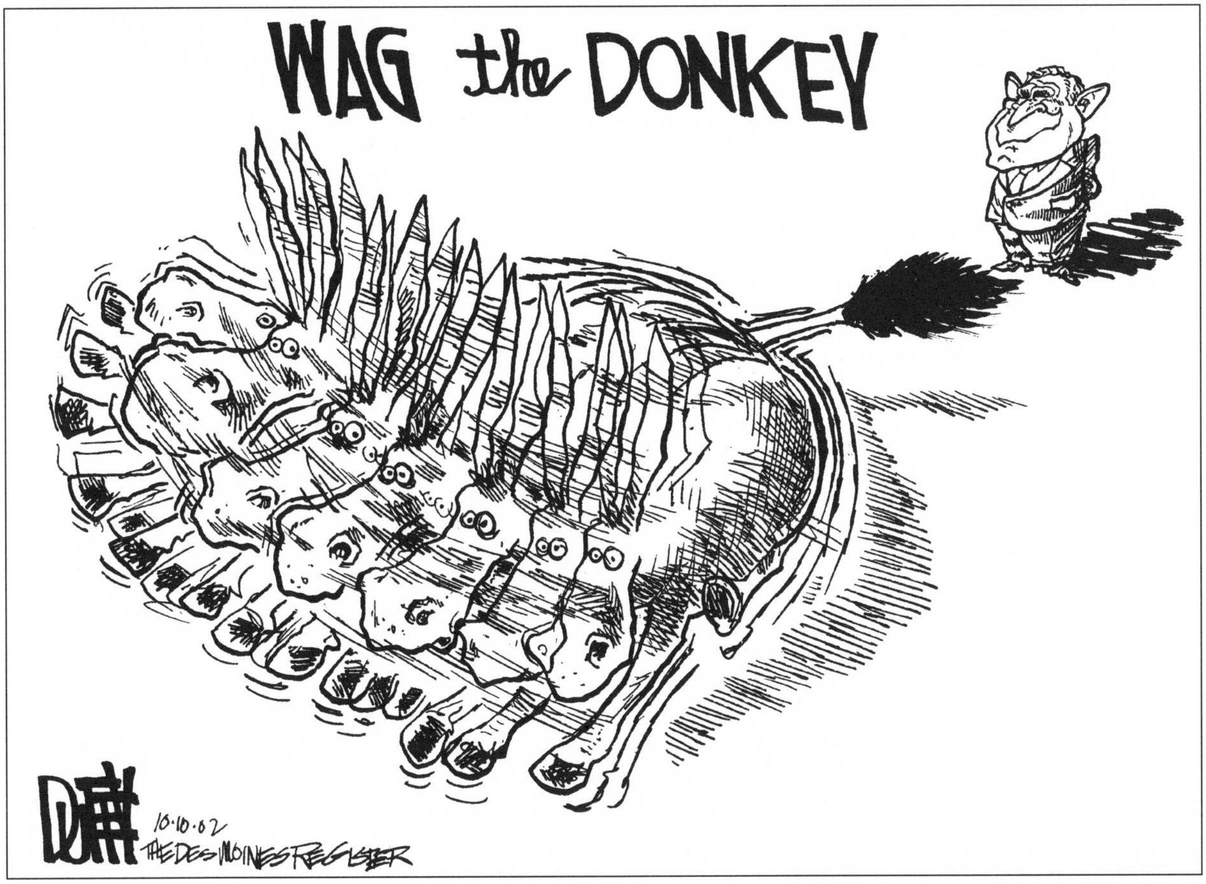
WAG the DONKEY
10·10·02
THE DES MOINES REGISTER

BRIAN DUFFY
Courtesy Des Moines Register

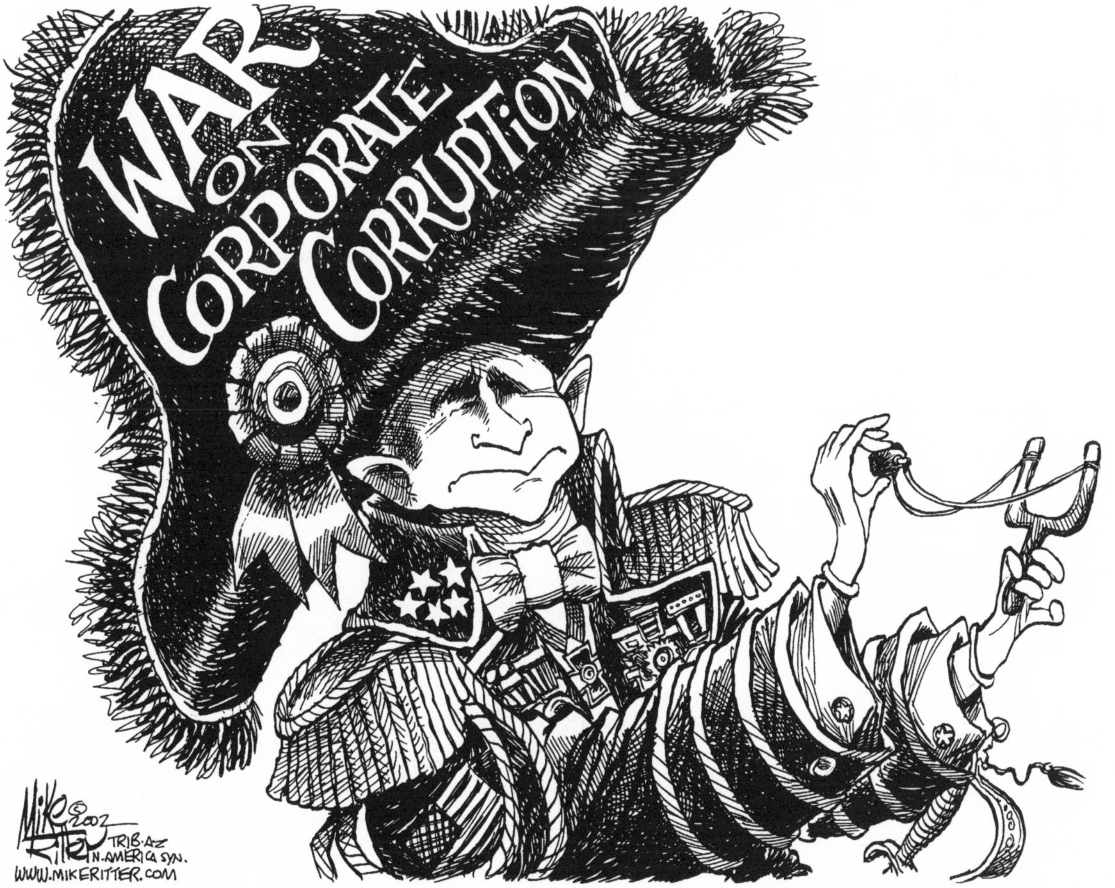
WAR ON CORPORATE CORRUPTION
MIKE RITTER ©2002
TRIB·AZ
N. AMERICA SYN.
WWW.MIKERITTER.COM

MIKE RITTER
Courtesy Tribune Newspapers

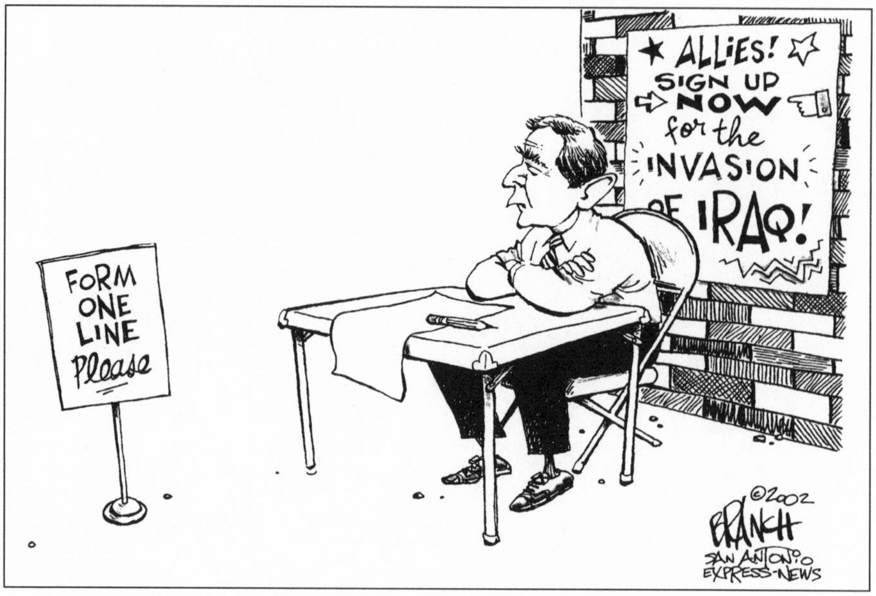
ALLIES! SIGN UP NOW for the INVASION OF IRAQ!
FORM ONE LINE Please
©2002
BRANCH
SAN ANTONIO EXPRESS-NEWS

JOHN BRANCH
Courtesy San Antonio Express-News

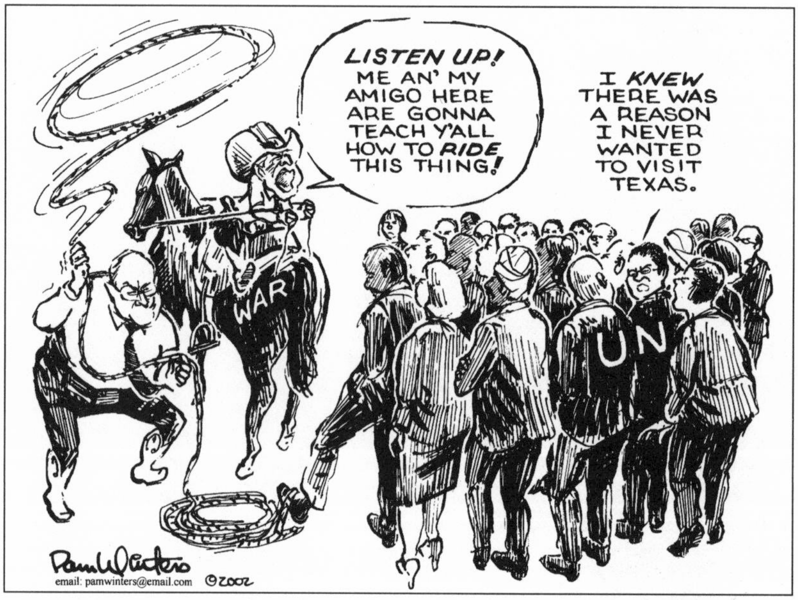
LISTEN UP! ME AN' MY AMIGO HERE ARE GONNA TEACH Y'ALL HOW TO RIDE THIS THING!
I KNEW THERE WAS A REASON I NEVER WANTED TO VISIT TEXAS.
WAR
UN
email: pamwinters@email.com
©2002

PAM WINTERS
Courtesy San Diego Union-Tribune

REX BABIN
Courtesy Sacramento Bee

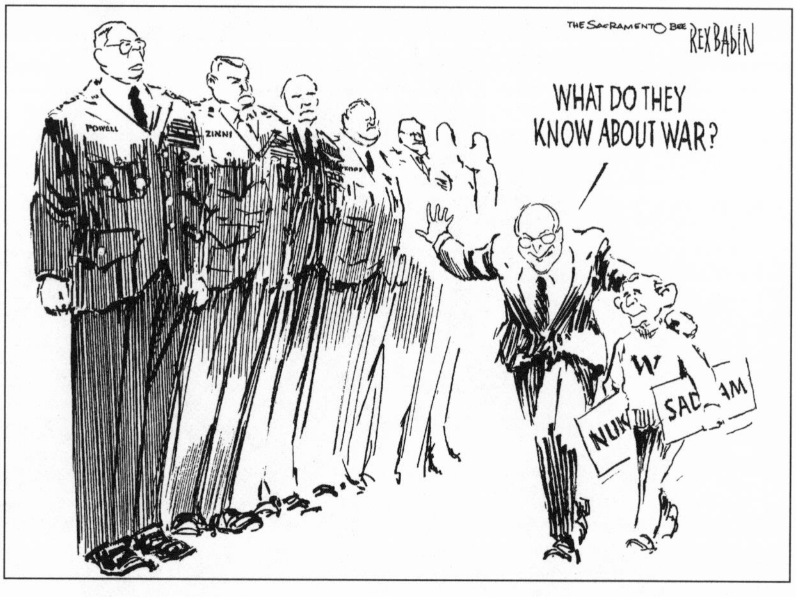
THE SACRAMENTO BEE
REX BABIN
WHAT DO THEY KNOW ABOUT WAR?
POWELL
ZINNI

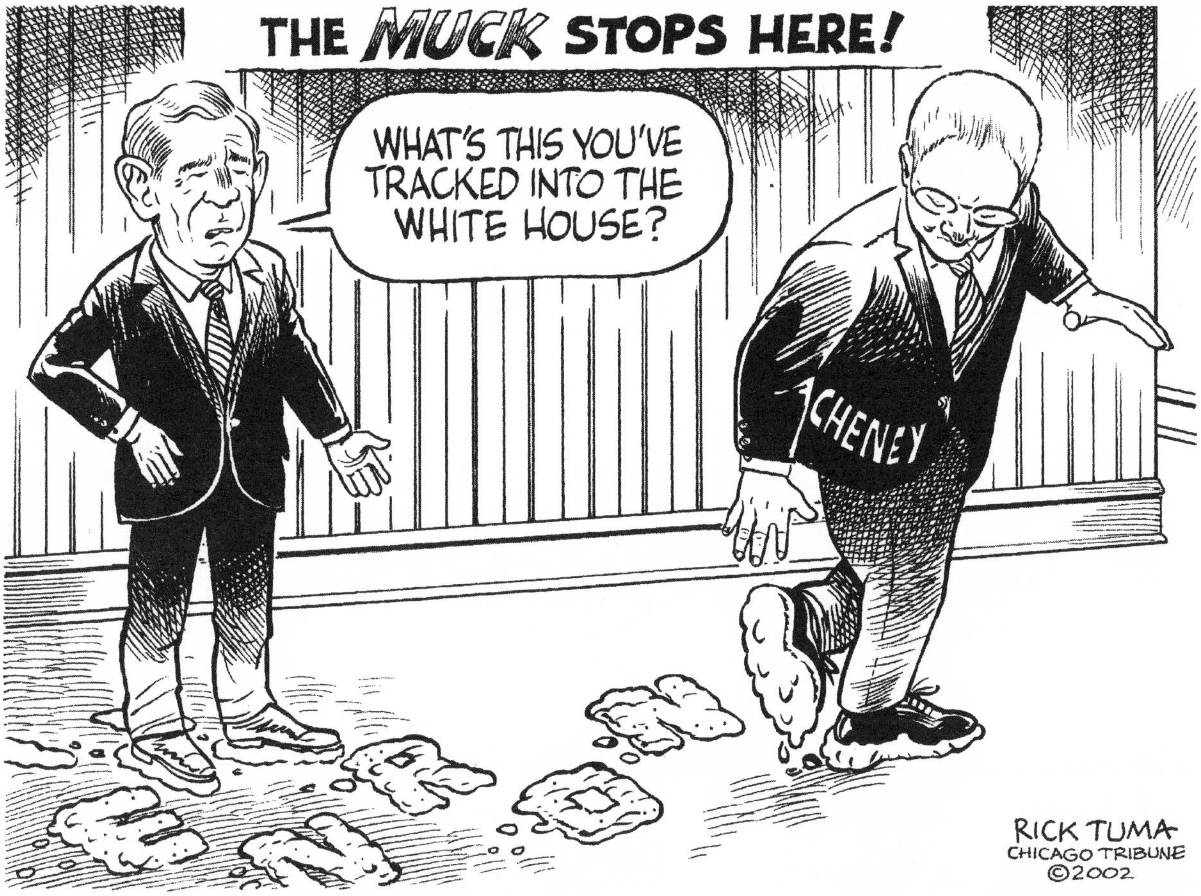
THE MUCK STOPS HERE!
WHAT'S THIS YOU'VE TRACKED INTO THE WHITE HOUSE?
CHENEY
RICK TUMA
CHICAGO TRIBUNE
©2002

RICK TUMA
Courtesy Chicago Tribune

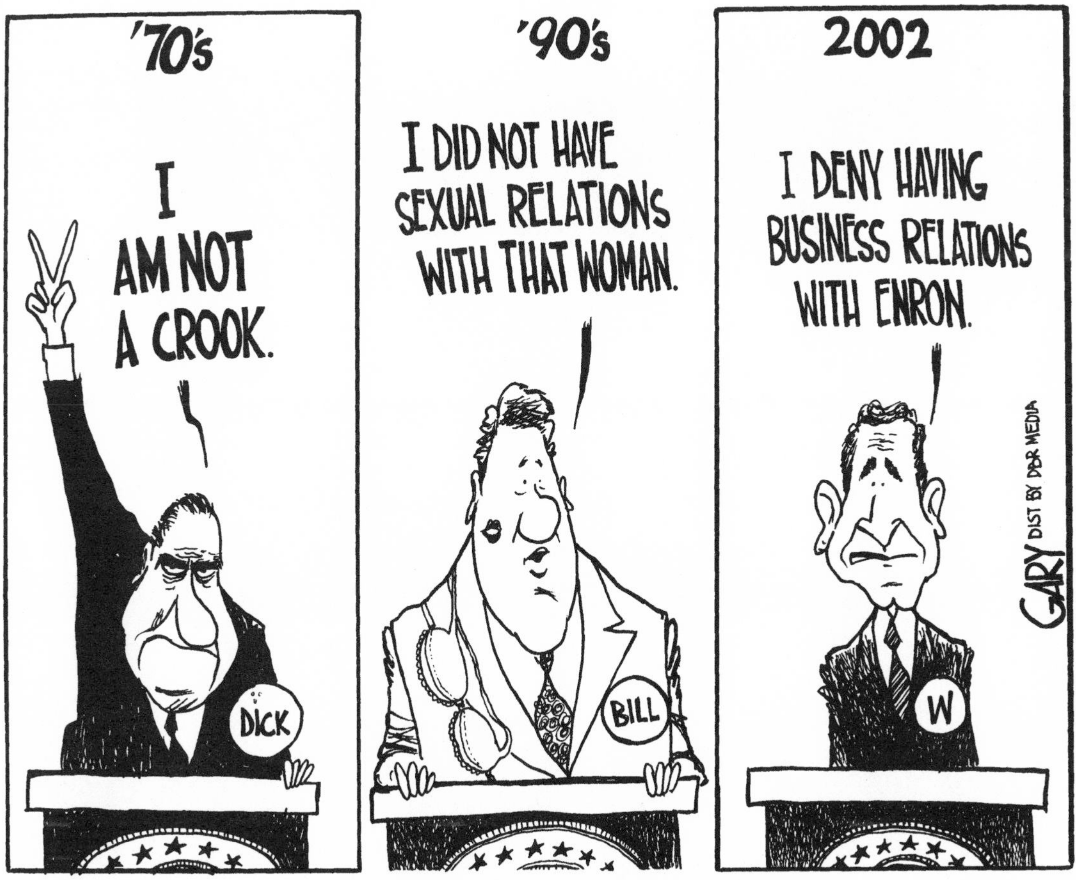
'70's
I AM NOT A CROOK.
DICK
'90's
I DID NOT HAVE SEXUAL RELATIONS WITH THAT WOMAN.
BILL
2002
I DENY HAVING BUSINESS RELATIONS WITH ENRON.
W
GARY DIST BY DBR MEDIA

CHARLOS GARY
Courtesy Chicago Tribune

BRUCE BEATTIE
Courtesy Daytona Beach News-Journal

©02 Daytona Beach News-Journal
Copley News Service
News-Journalonline.com
BEATTIE
MORE GORE
FOR 2004

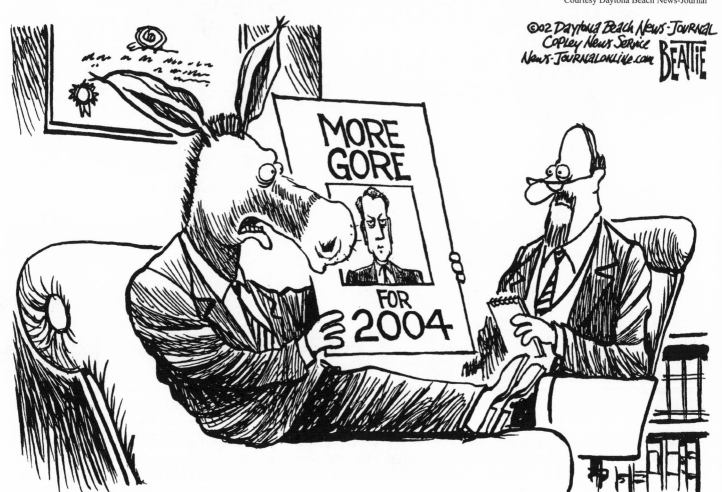

"I need help, Doc! Is this a great idea or a death wish?!"

The Democrats

The Democratic Party definitely did not enjoy its best year in 2002. Longtime Democratic Sen. Robert Torricelli withdrew suddenly from his reelection campaign in New Jersey because of ethics problems. He had been a heavy favorite but had plummeted in the polls. He was replaced on the ballot by former Sen. Frank Lautenberg in an apparent violation of state law, but the Supreme Court approved the unusual switch.

Sen. Paul Wellstone, locked in a tight race for reelection in Minnesota, died in a plane crash a few days before the balloting. The Democrats were doubly distressed because the popular senator's death further imperiled the party's one-seat majority. Former Vice President Walter Mondale was hastily recruited as a replacement on the ticket. Many voters felt that the resulting campaign overshadowed the Wellstone funeral.

In any event, Mondale lost in a stunning blow to the Democrats. When the results of all the congressional races were in, the Republicans had reclaimed control of the Senate with 51 seats and had increased slightly their margin in the House of Representatives. The Demos ended 2002 with seemingly no agenda and no compelling issues. Ultra-liberal Nancy Pelosi of California was named House party leader, signaling a further move left by Democrats, and Al Gore let it be known he would not be a candidate in 2004.

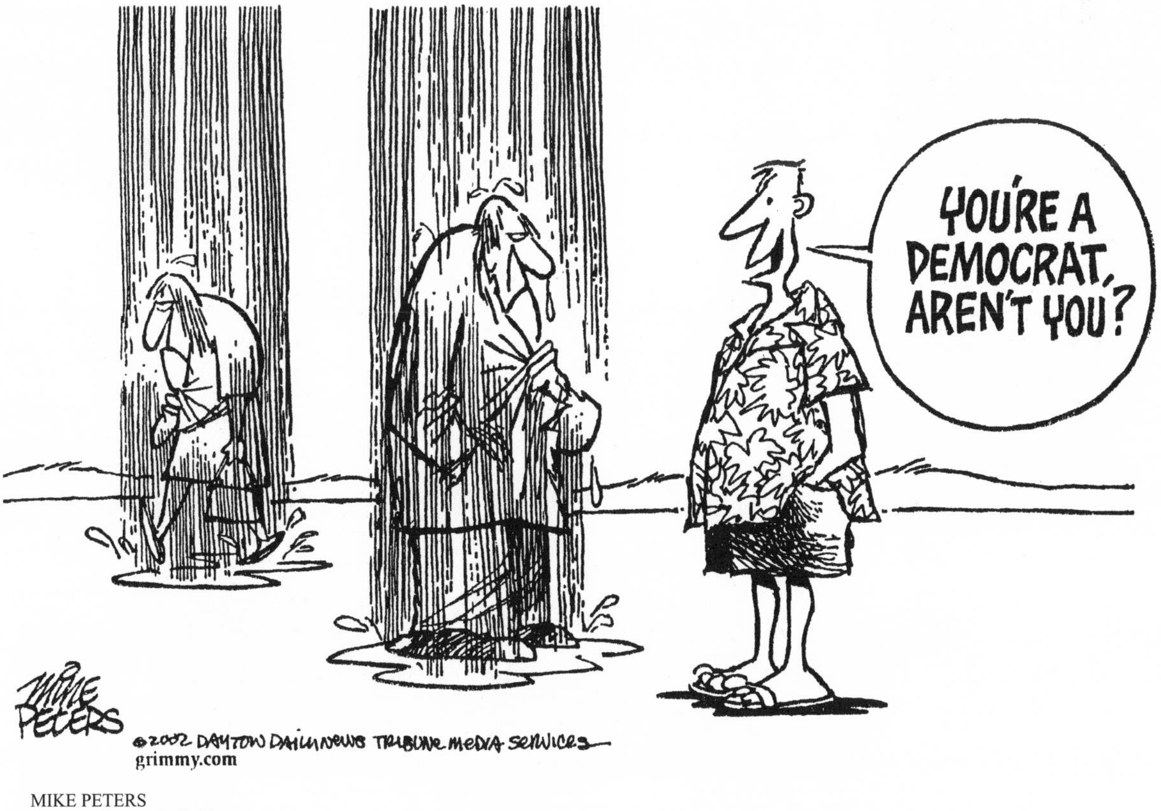
YOU'RE A DEMOCRAT, AREN'T YOU?
MIKE PETERS
©2002 DAYTON DAILY NEWS TRIBUNE MEDIA SERVICES
grimmy.com

MIKE PETERS
Courtesy Dayton Daily News

ED FISCHER
Courtesy Rochester Post-Bulletin (Minn.)

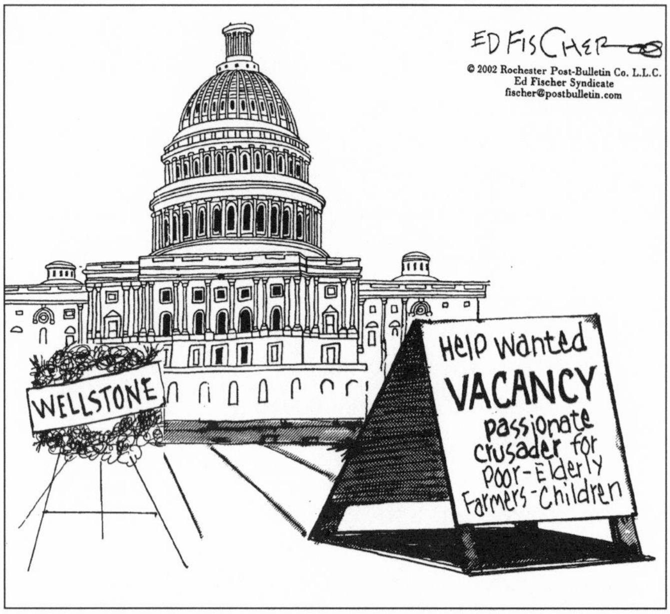
ED FISCHER
© 2002 Rochester Post-Bulletin Co. L.L.C.
Ed Fischer Syndicate
fischer@postbulletin.com
WELLSTONE
Help Wanted
VACANCY
passionate
crusader for
Poor-Elderly
Farmers-Children

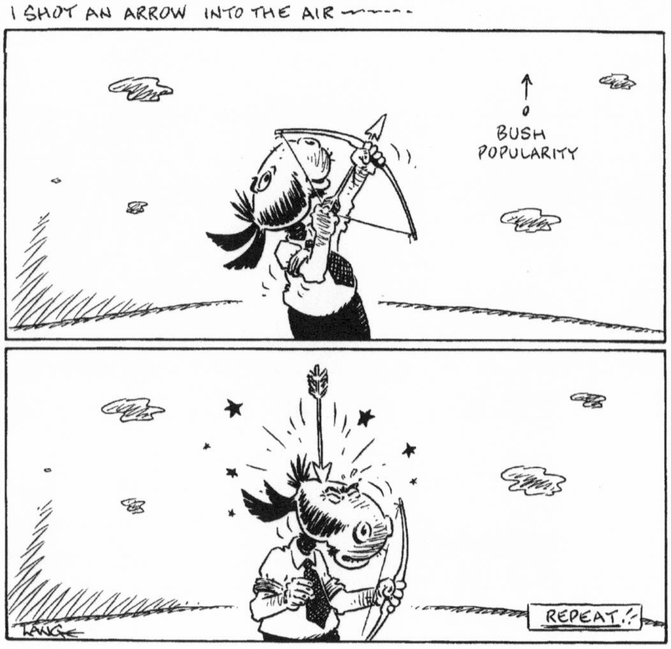
I SHOT AN ARROW INTO THE AIR
BUSH
POPULARITY
REPEAT
LANGE

JIM LANGE
Courtesy The Daily Oklahoman

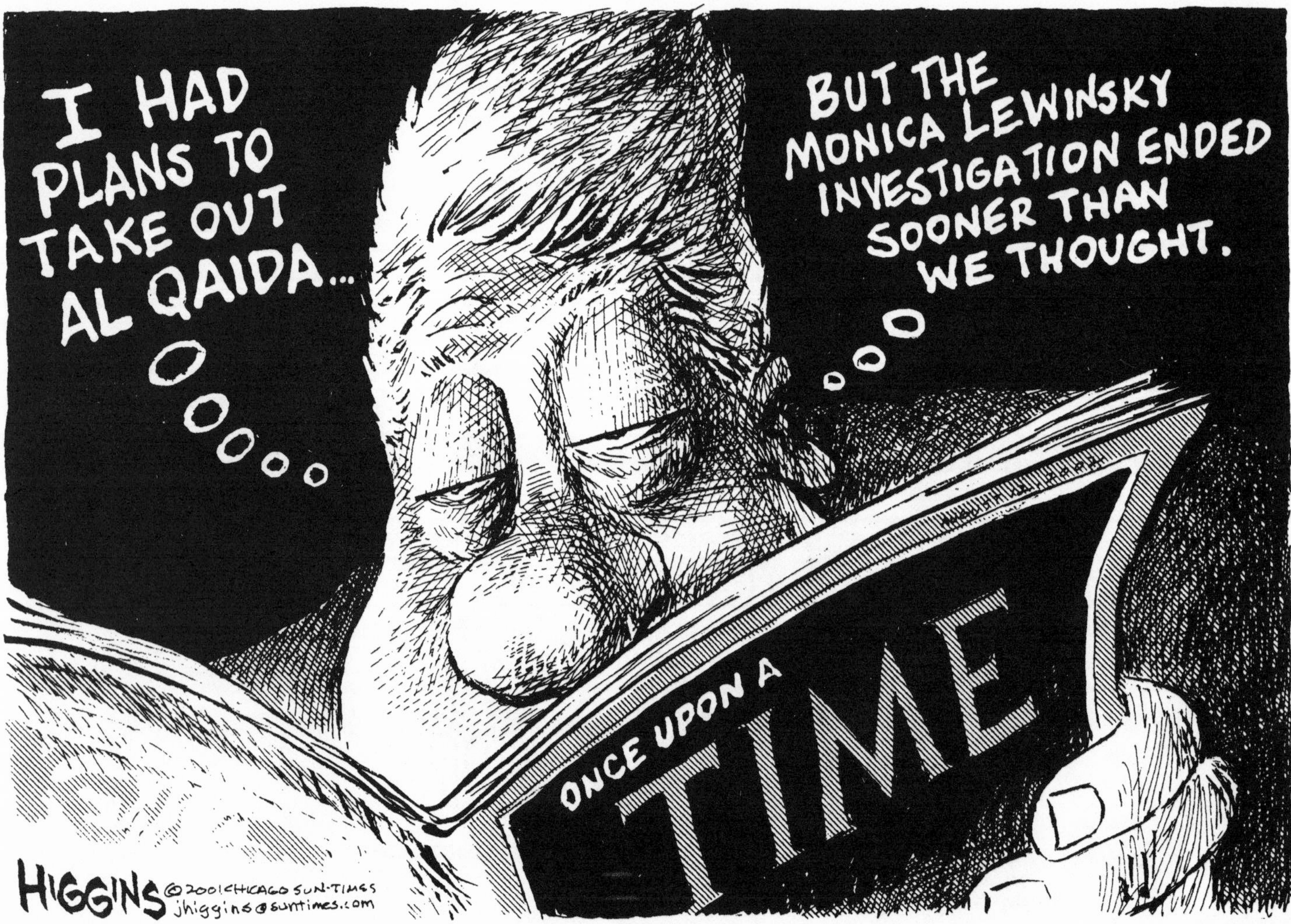
I HAD PLANS TO TAKE OUT AL QAIDA...
BUT THE MONICA LEWINSKY INVESTIGATION ENDED SOONER THAN WE THOUGHT.
ONCE UPON A
TIME
HIGGINS ©2001 CHICAGO SUN-TIMES
jhiggins@suntimes.com

JACK HIGGINS
Courtesy Chicago Sun-Times

TOM GIBB
Courtesy Johnstown Tribune-Democrat (Pa.)

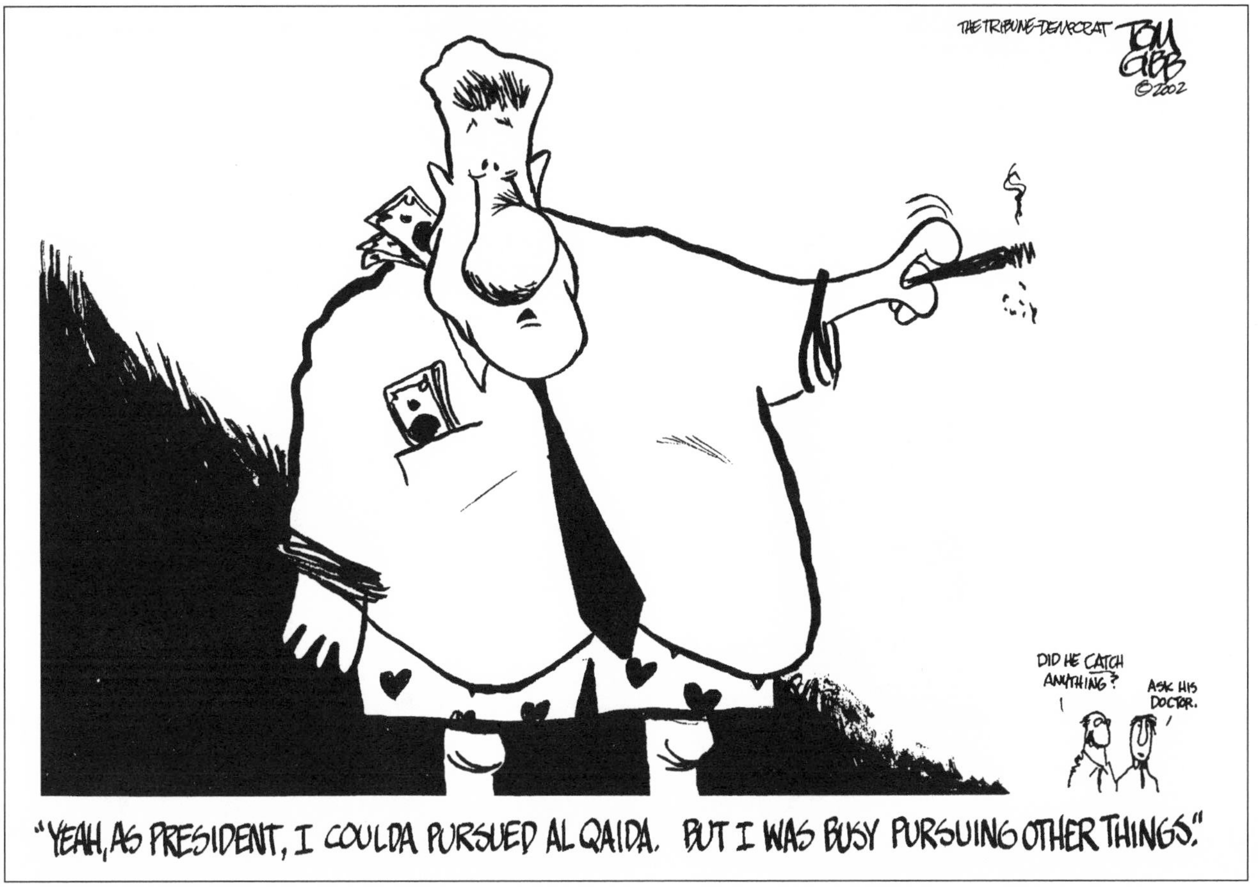
THE TRIBUNE-DEMOCRAT
TOM GIBB ©2002
DID HE CATCH ANYTHING?
ASK HIS DOCTOR.
"YEAH, AS PRESIDENT, I COULDA PURSUED AL QAIDA. BUT I WAS BUSY PURSUING OTHER THINGS."

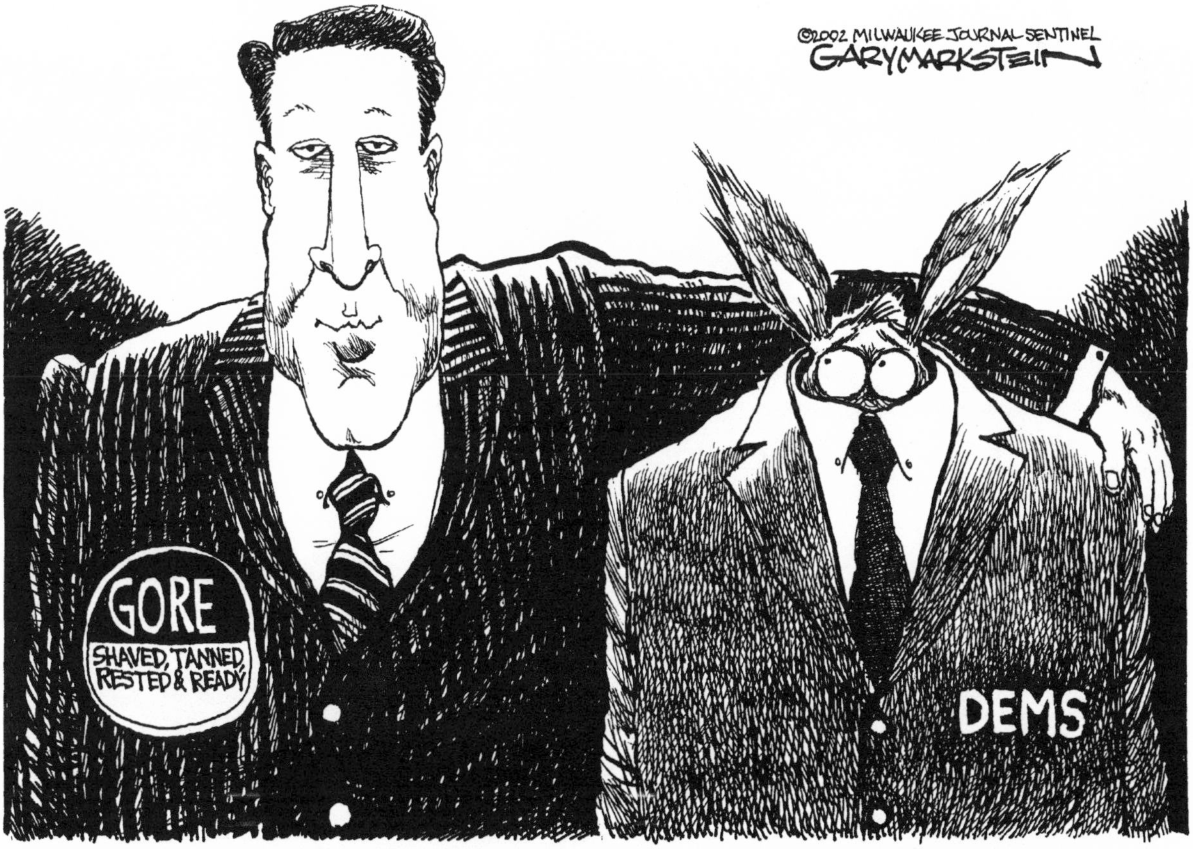
©2002 MILWAUKEE JOURNAL-SENTINEL
GARY MARKSTEIN
GORE
SHAVED, TANNED, RESTED & READY
DEMS

GARY MARKSTEIN
Courtesy Milwaukee Journal Sentinel

JACK OHMAN
Courtesy The Oregonian

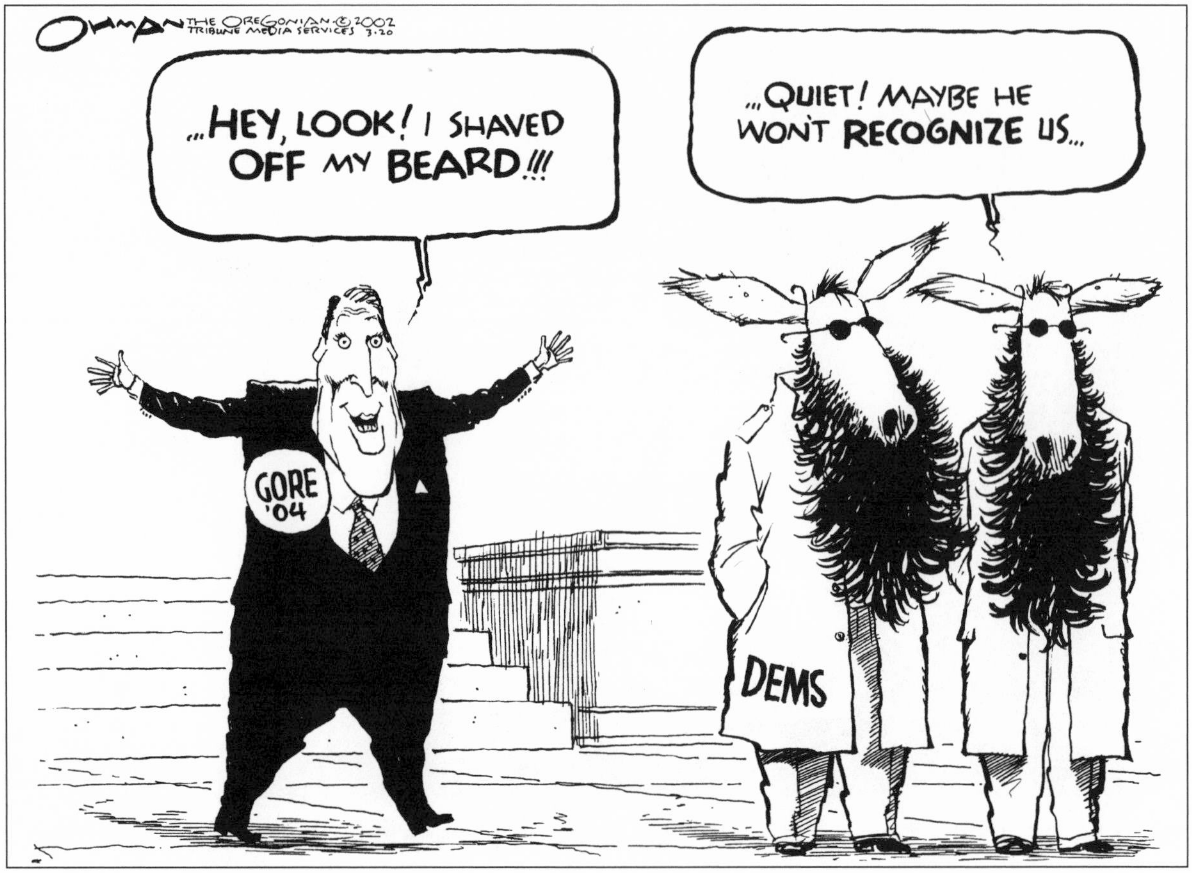
OHMAN THE OREGONIAN ©2002 TRIBUNE MEDIA SERVICES 3-20
...HEY, LOOK! I SHAVED OFF MY BEARD!!!
...QUIET! MAYBE HE WON'T RECOGNIZE US...
GORE '04
DEMS

MIKE LUCKOVICH
Courtesy Atlanta Constitution

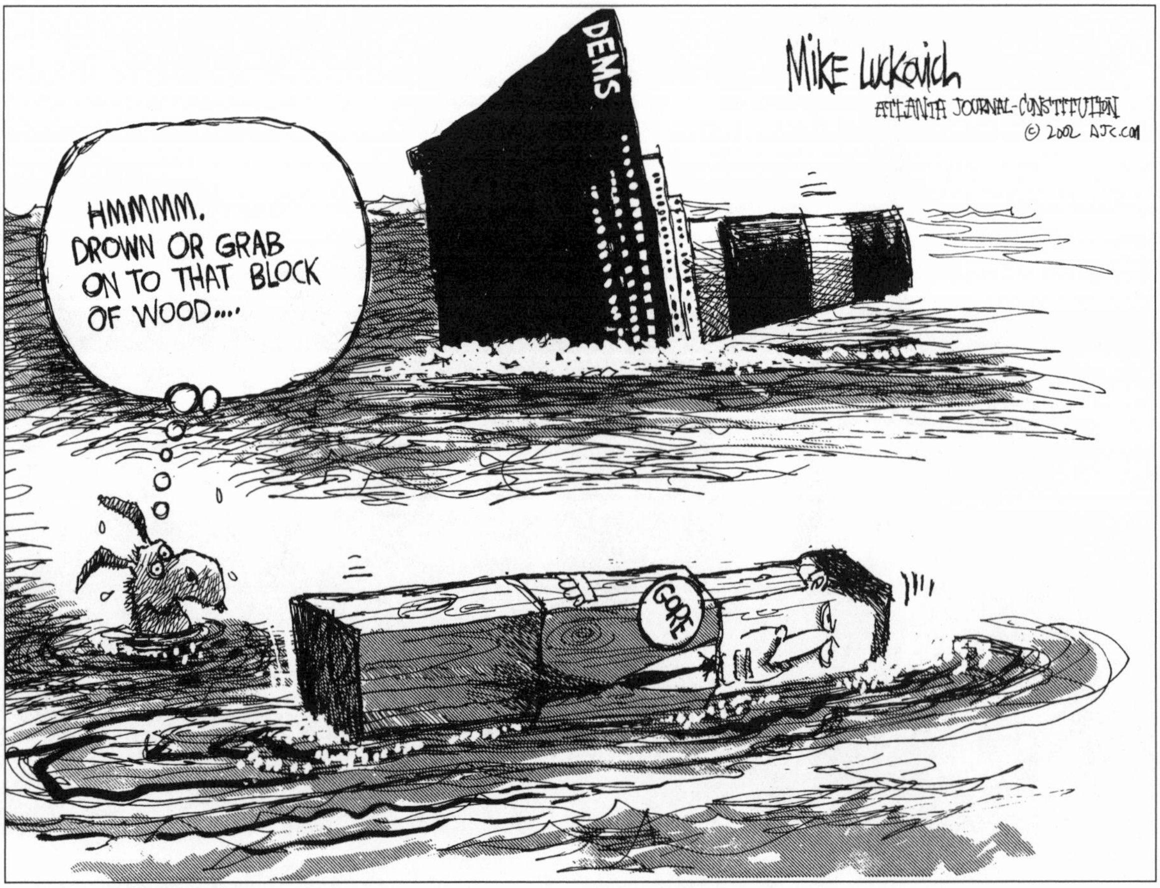
Mike Luckovich
ATLANTA JOURNAL-CONSTITUTION
© 2002 AJC.COM
DEMS
HMMMM. DROWN OR GRAB ON TO THAT BLOCK OF WOOD....
GORE

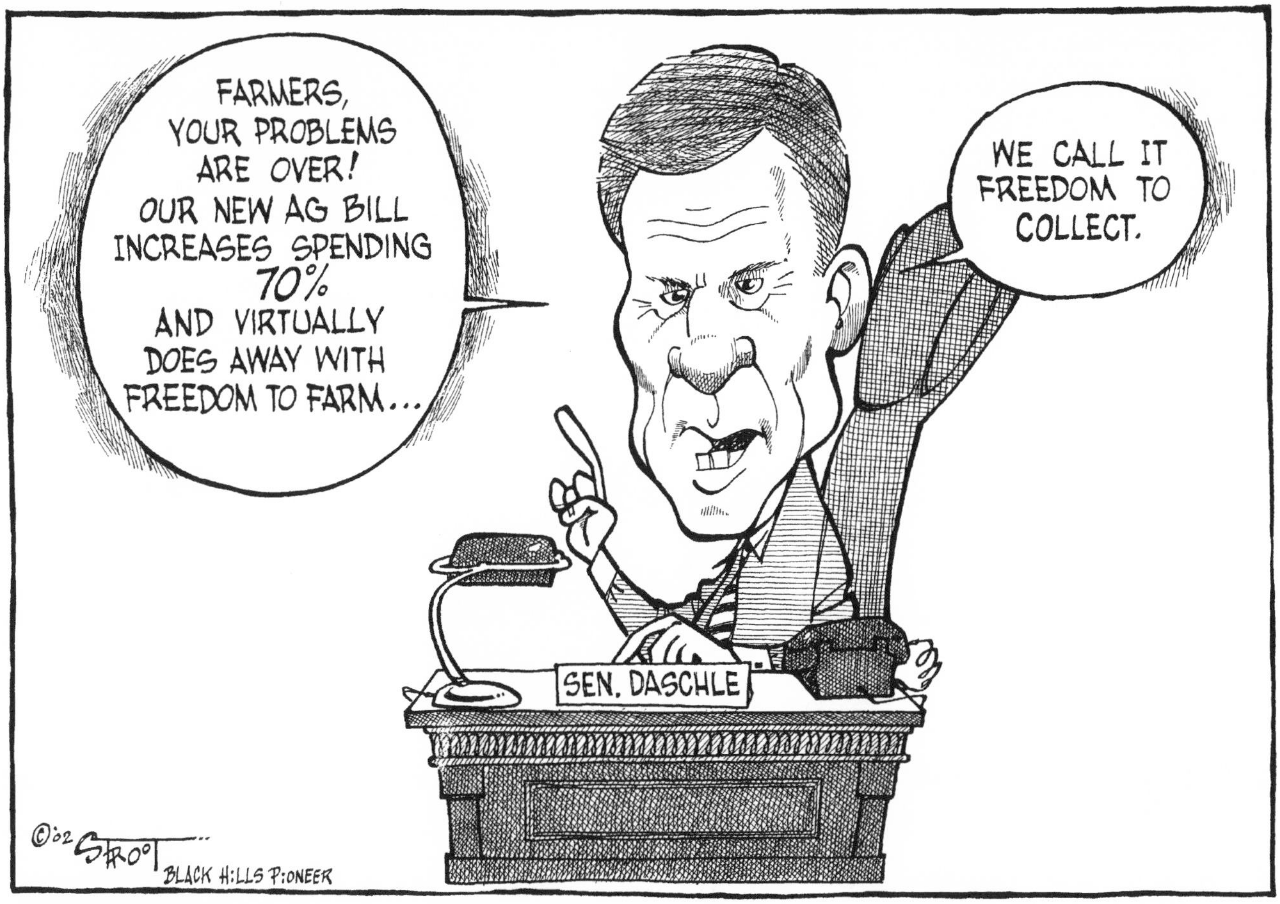
FARMERS, YOUR PROBLEMS ARE OVER! OUR NEW AG BILL INCREASES SPENDING 70% AND VIRTUALLY DOES AWAY WITH FREEDOM TO FARM...
WE CALL IT FREEDOM TO COLLECT.
SEN. DASCHLE
©'02 STROOT
BLACK HILLS PIONEER

WAYNE STROOT
Courtesy Hastings Tribune

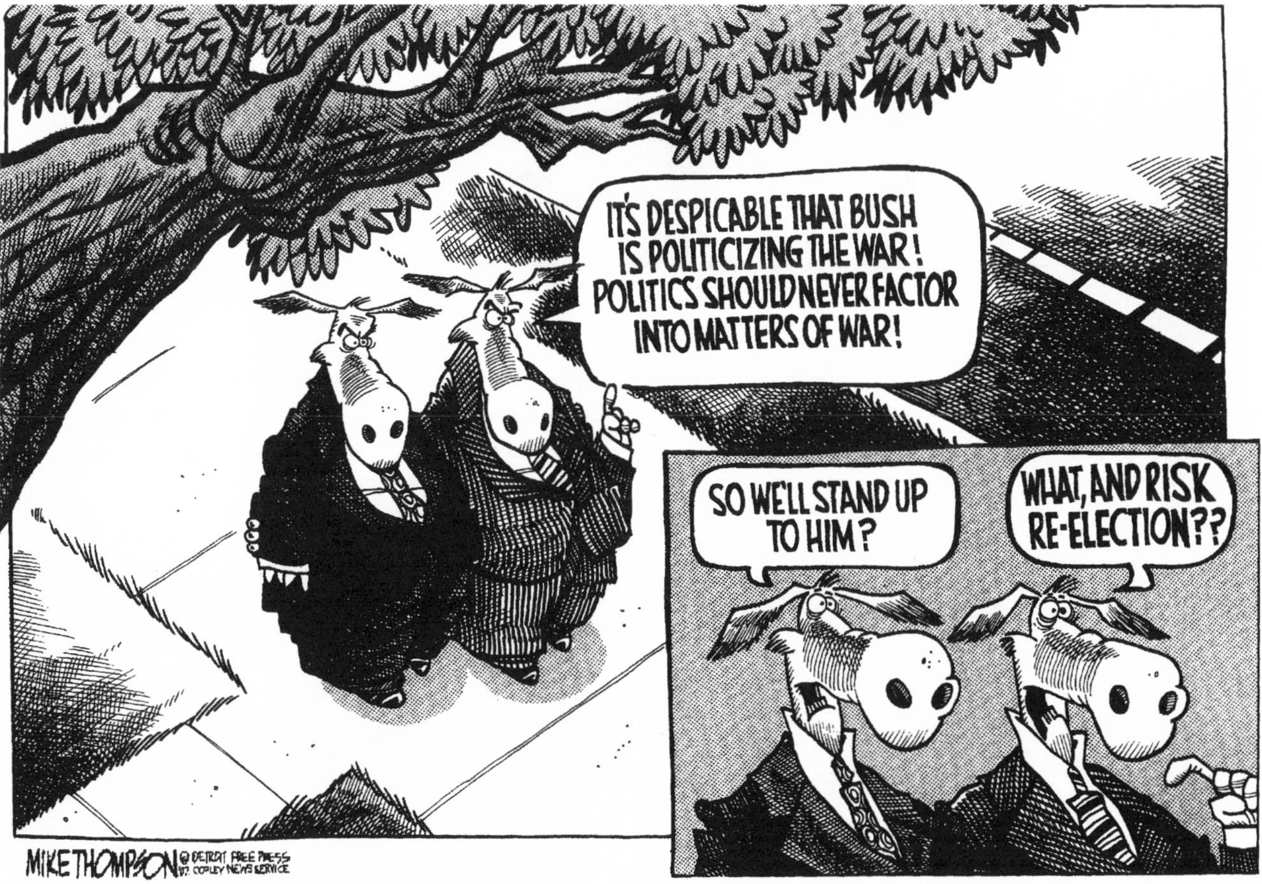
IT'S DESPICABLE THAT BUSH IS POLITICIZING THE WAR! POLITICS SHOULD NEVER FACTOR INTO MATTERS OF WAR!
SO WE'LL STAND UP TO HIM?
WHAT, AND RISK RE-ELECTION??
MIKE THOMPSON

MICHAEL THOMPSON
Courtesy Detroit Free Press

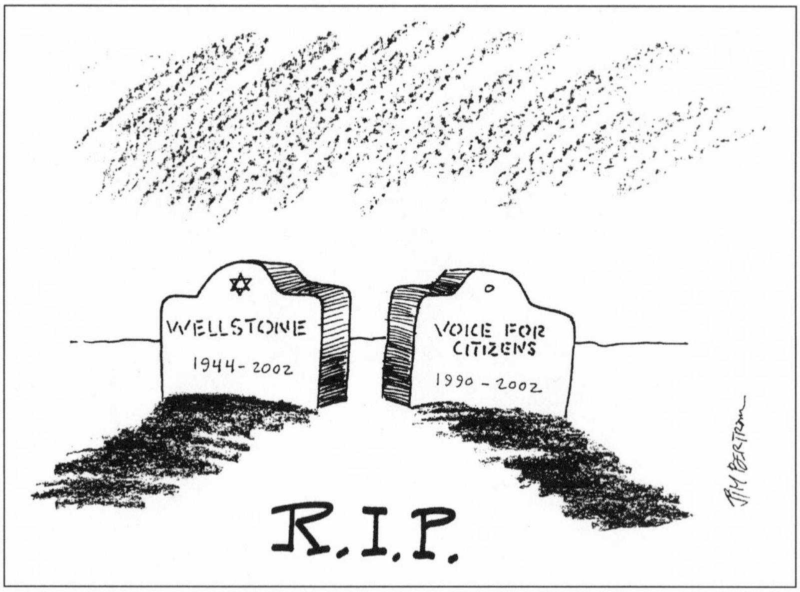
WELLSTONE
1944-2002
VOICE FOR CITIZENS
1990-2002
R.I.P.

JIM BERTRAM
Courtesy St. Cloud Times (Minn.)

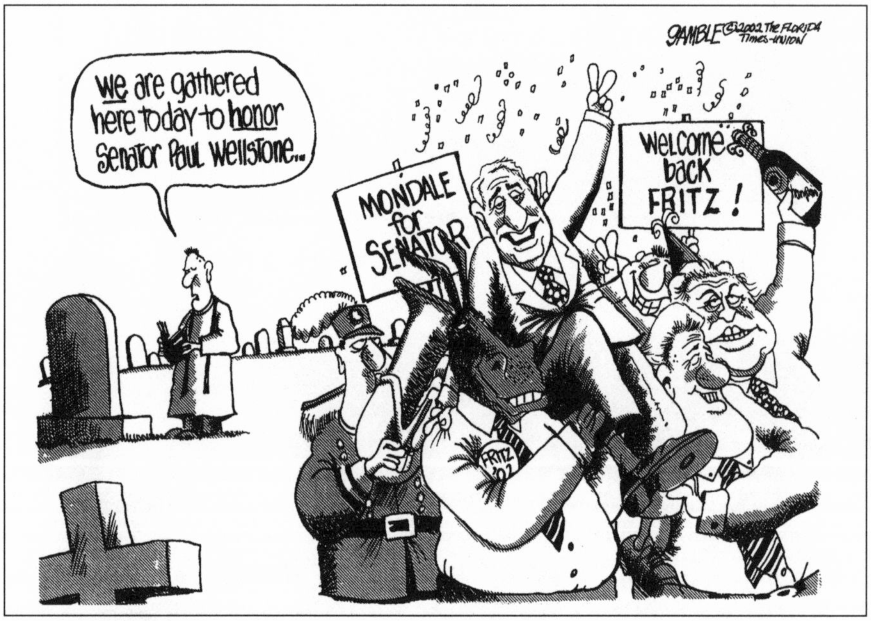
WE are gathered here today to honor Senator Paul Wellstone...
MONDALE for SENATOR
Welcome back FRITZ!
FRITZ '02

ED GAMBLE
Courtesy Florida Times-Union

RICK BALDWIN
Courtesy Metro Pulse (Tenn.)

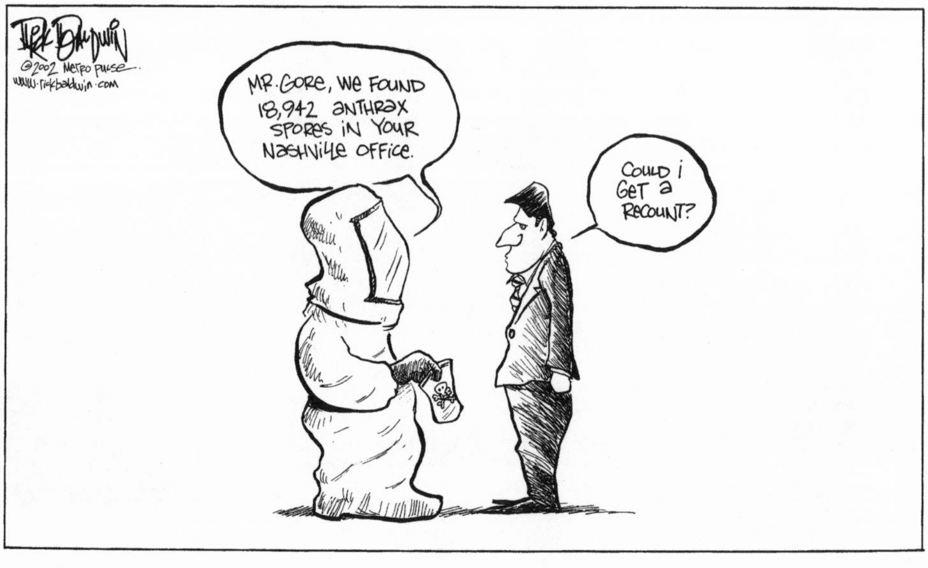
MR. GORE, WE FOUND 18,942 ANTHRAX SPORES IN YOUR NASHVILLE OFFICE.
COULD I GET A RECOUNT?

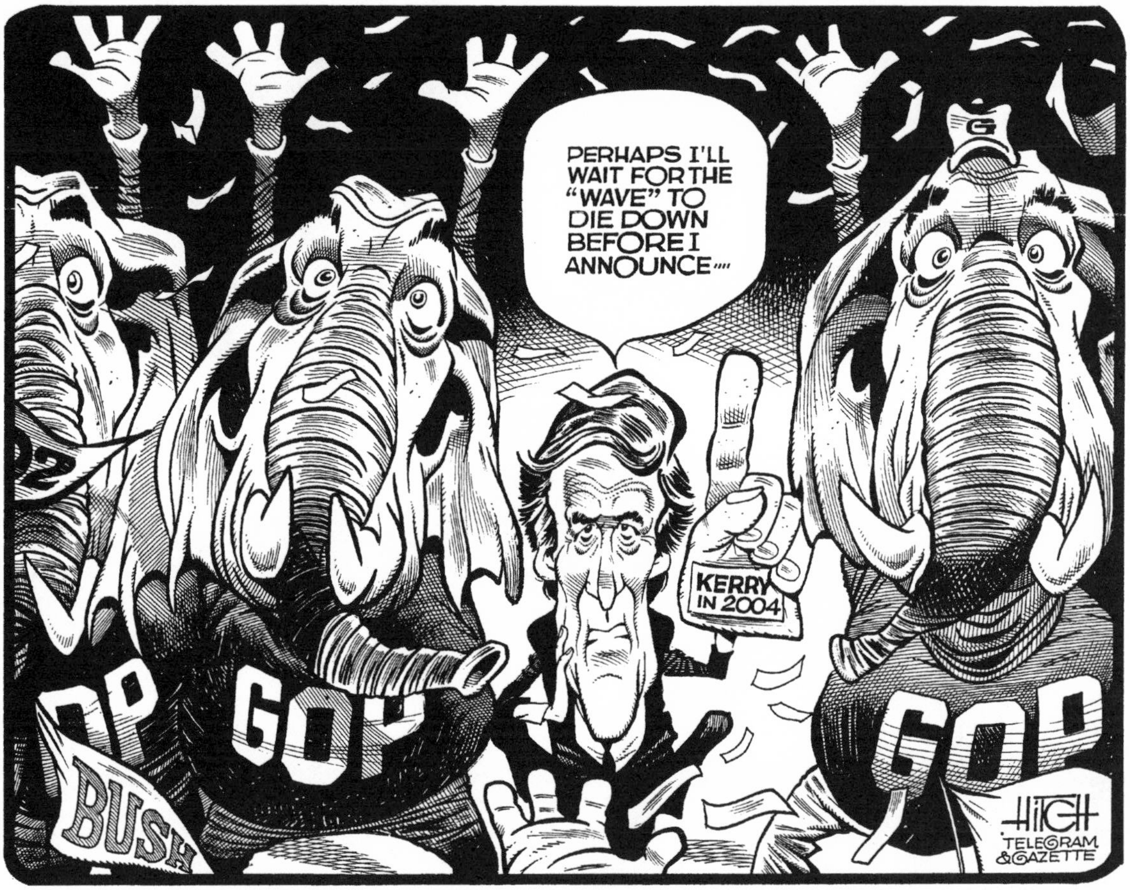
PERHAPS I'LL WAIT FOR THE "WAVE" TO DIE DOWN BEFORE I ANNOUNCE....
KERRY IN 2004
GOP
GOP
BUSH
HITCH TELEGRAM &GAZETTE

DAVID HITCH
Courtesy Worcester Telegram and Gazette (Mass.)

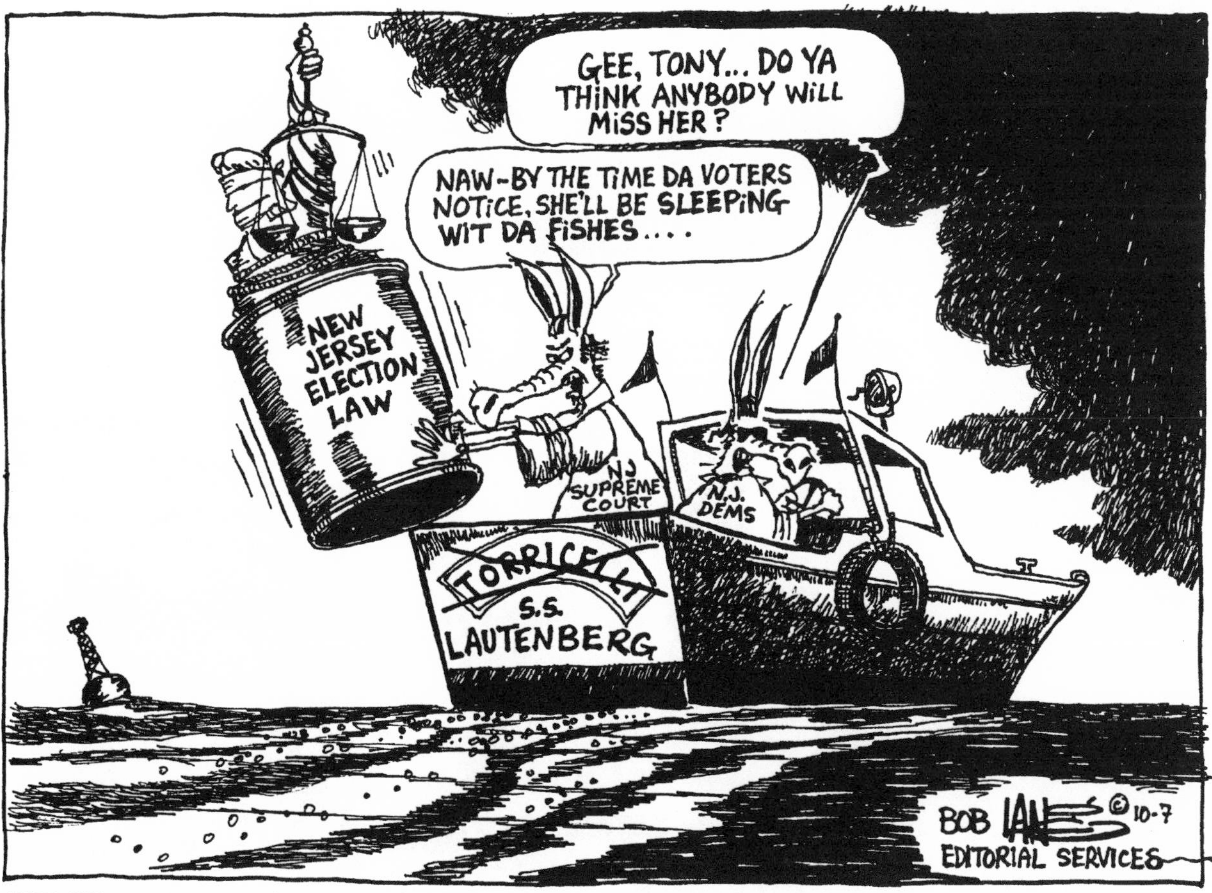
GEE, TONY... DO YA THINK ANYBODY WILL MISS HER?
NAW-BY THE TIME DA VOTERS NOTICE, SHE'LL BE SLEEPING WIT DA FISHES....
NEW JERSEY ELECTION LAW
NJ SUPREME COURT
N.J. DEMS
TORRICELLI
S.S. LAUTENBERG
BOB LANG © 10-7 EDITORIAL SERVICES

BOB LANG
Courtesy Editorial Services

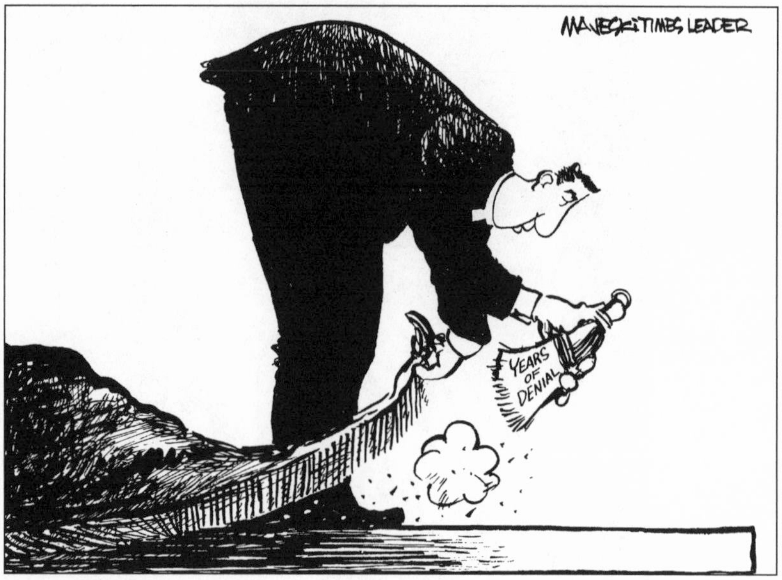

MAJESKI TIMES LEADER
YEARS OF DENIAL

JOE MAJESKI
Courtesy The Times-Leader (Pa.)

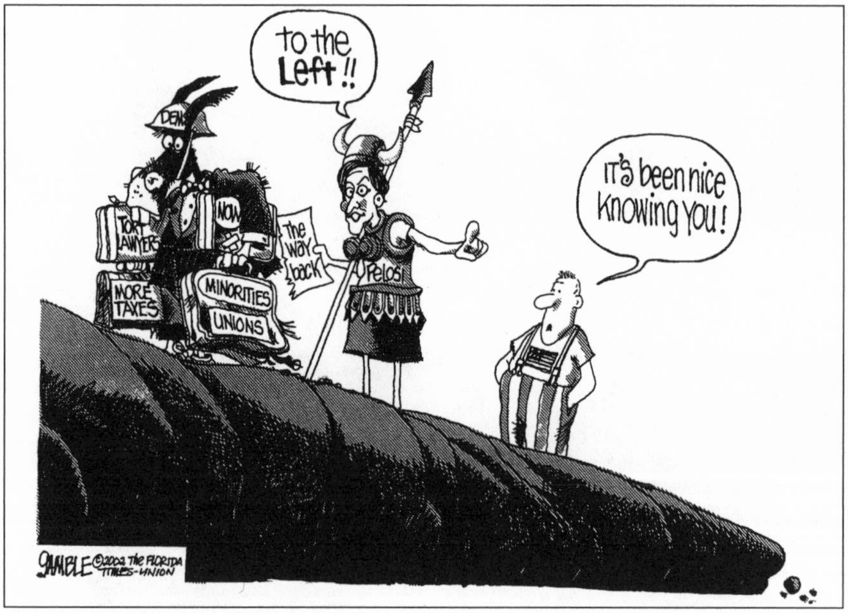

to the Left!!
It's been nice knowing you!
DEMS
TORT LAWYERS
NOW
MORE TAXES
MINORITIES
UNIONS
The way back
Pelosi
GAMBLE ©2002 The FLORIDA TIMES-UNION

ED GAMBLE
Courtesy Florida Times-Union

PAUL CONRAD
Courtesy Los Angeles Times

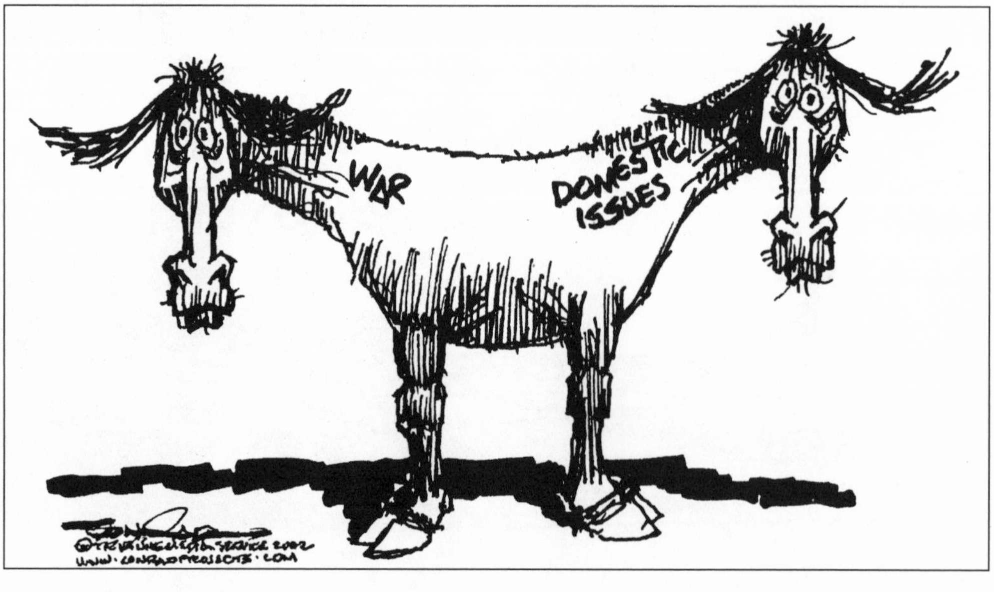

WAR
DOMESTIC ISSUES

RICK McKEE
Courtesy Augusta Chronicle

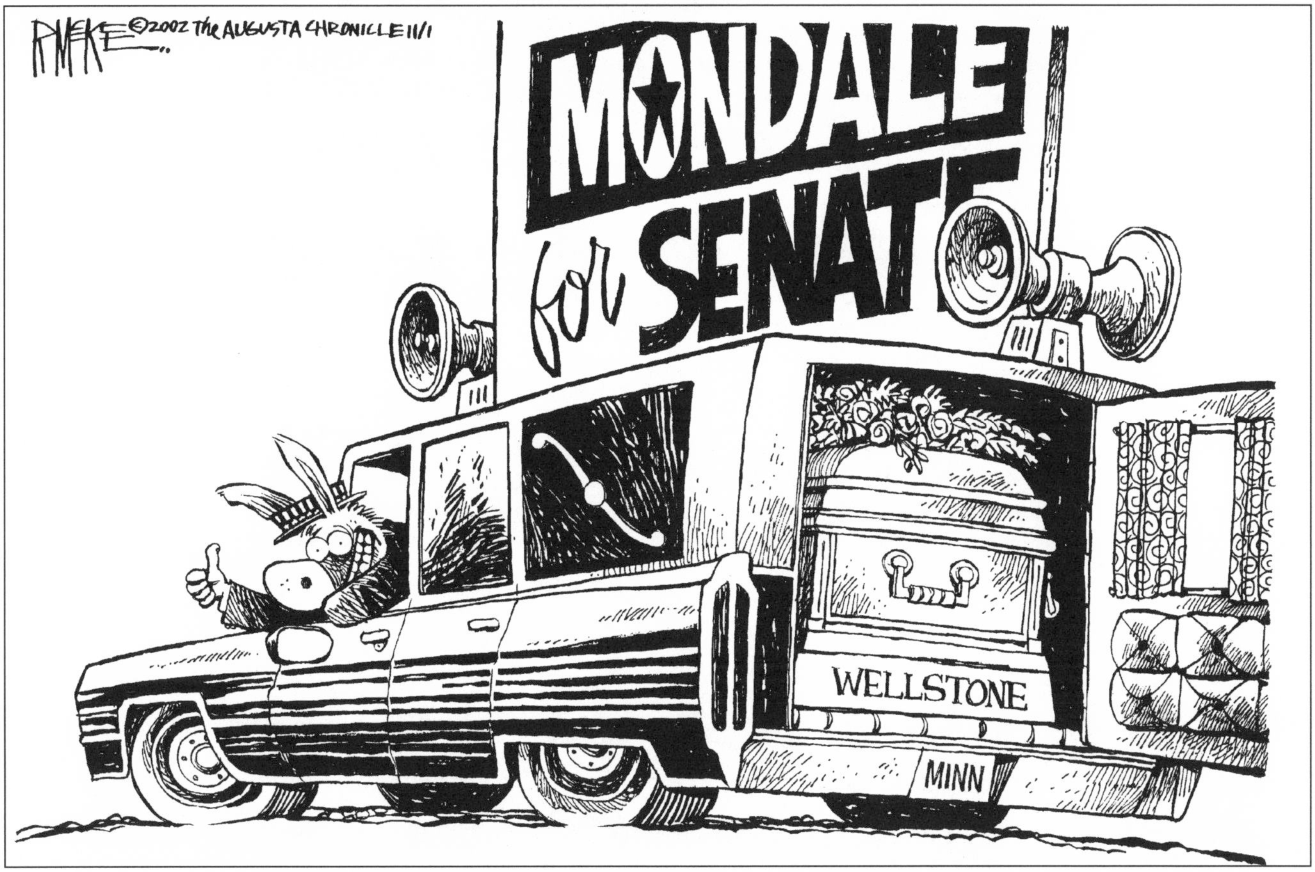
RMcKEE ©2002 The AUGUSTA CHRONICLE 11/1
MONDALE for SENATE
WELLSTONE
MINN

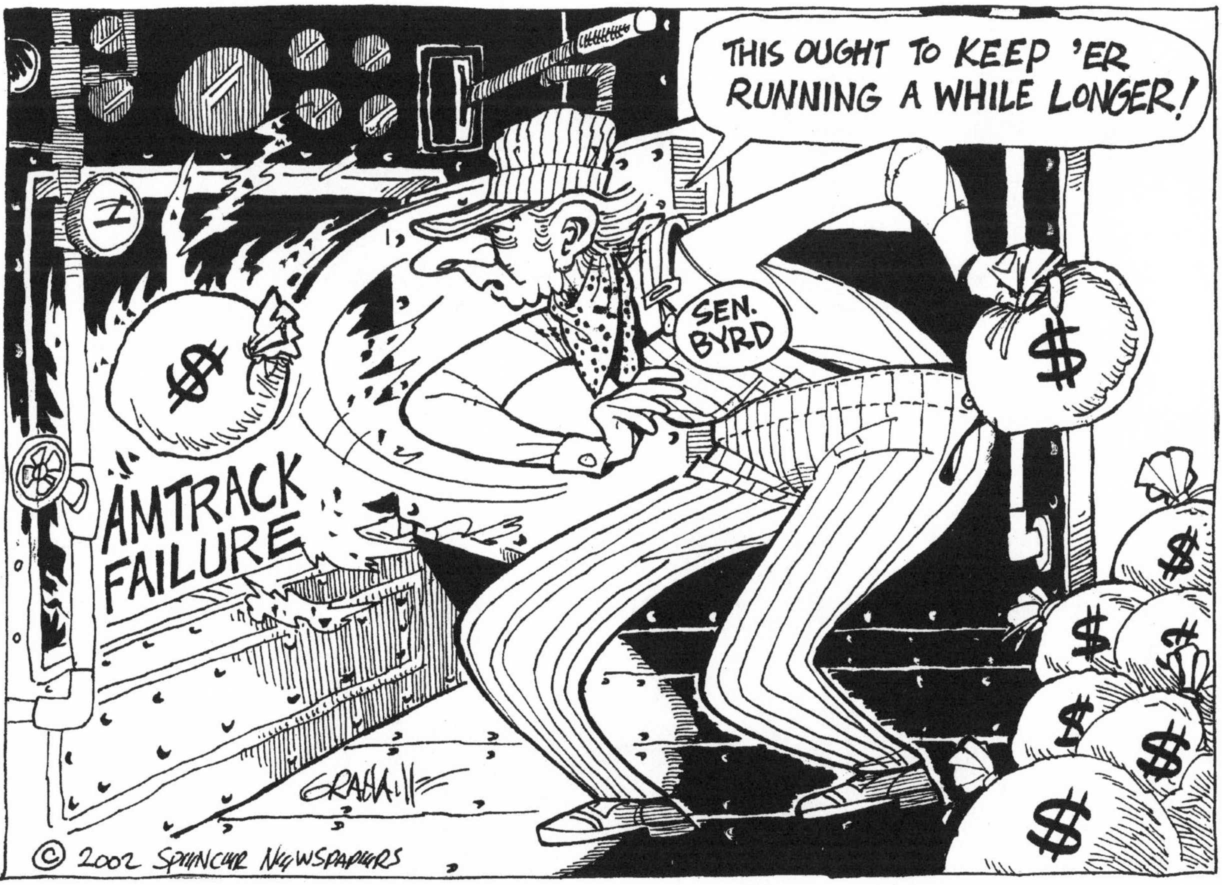
THIS OUGHT TO KEEP 'ER RUNNING A WHILE LONGER!
SEN. BYRD
AMTRACK FAILURE
GRAHAME
© 2002 SPENCER NEWSPAPERS

NEIL GRAHAME
Courtesy Spencer Newspapers

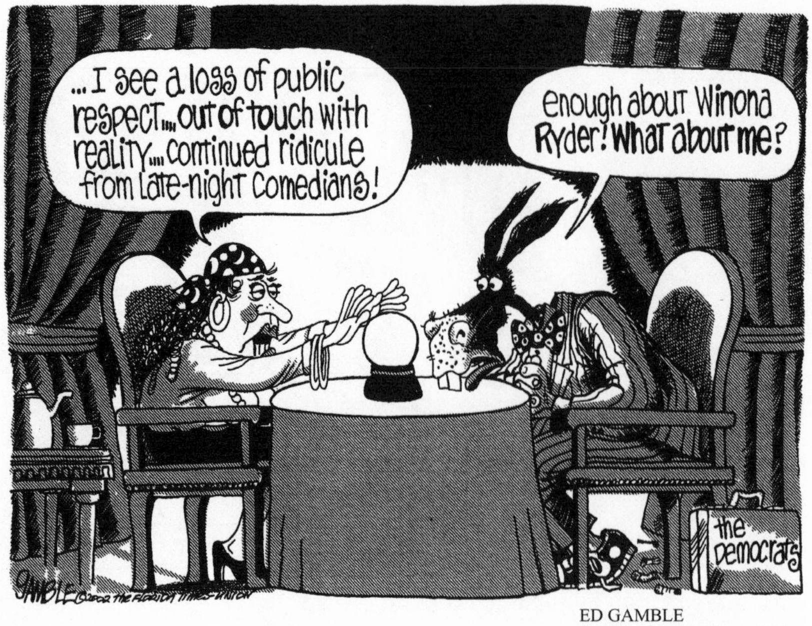

...I see a loss of public respect....out of touch with reality....continued ridicule from late-night comedians!
enough about Winona Ryder! What about me?
the Democrats

ED GAMBLE
Courtesy Florida Times-Union

REX BABIN
Courtesy Sacramento Bee

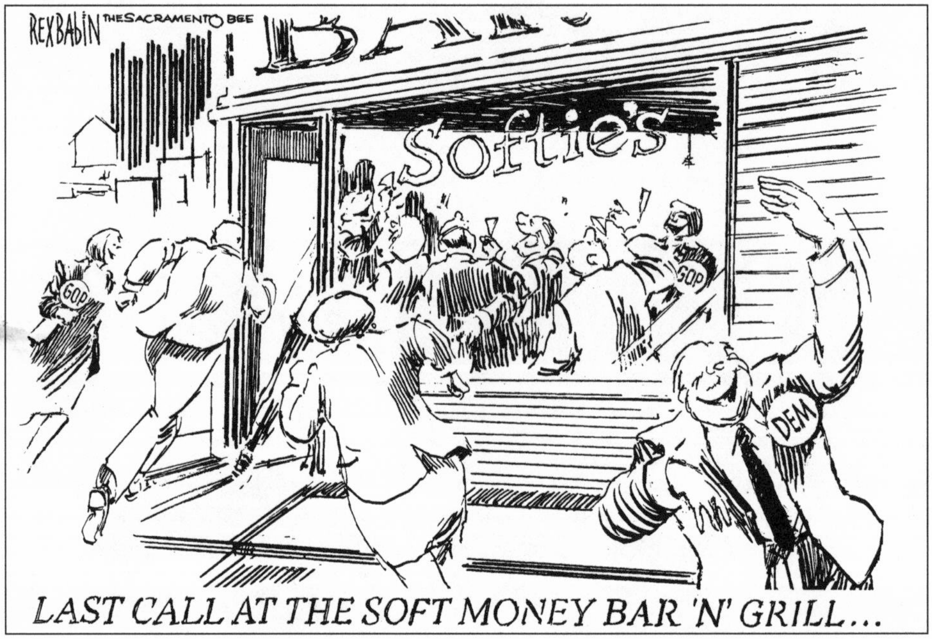

REX BABIN THE SACRAMENTO BEE
Softie's
GOP
GOP
DEM
LAST CALL AT THE SOFT MONEY BAR 'N' GRILL...

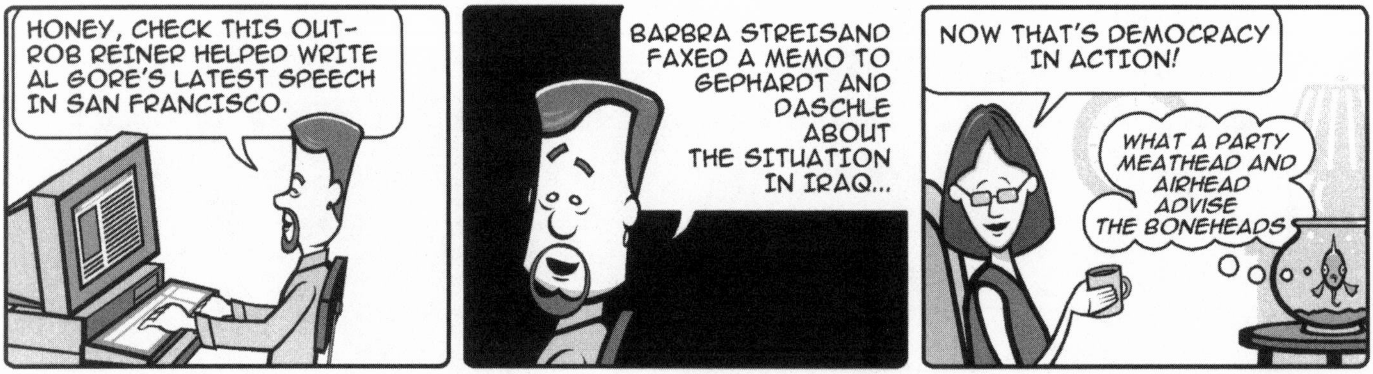

HONEY, CHECK THIS OUT-ROB REINER HELPED WRITE AL GORE'S LATEST SPEECH IN SAN FRANCISCO.
BARBRA STREISAND FAXED A MEMO TO GEPHARDT AND DASCHLE ABOUT THE SITUATION IN IRAQ...
NOW THAT'S DEMOCRACY IN ACTION!
WHAT A PARTY MEATHEAD AND AIRHEAD ADVISE THE BONEHEADS

COLIN T. HAYES
Courtesy Rightoons.com

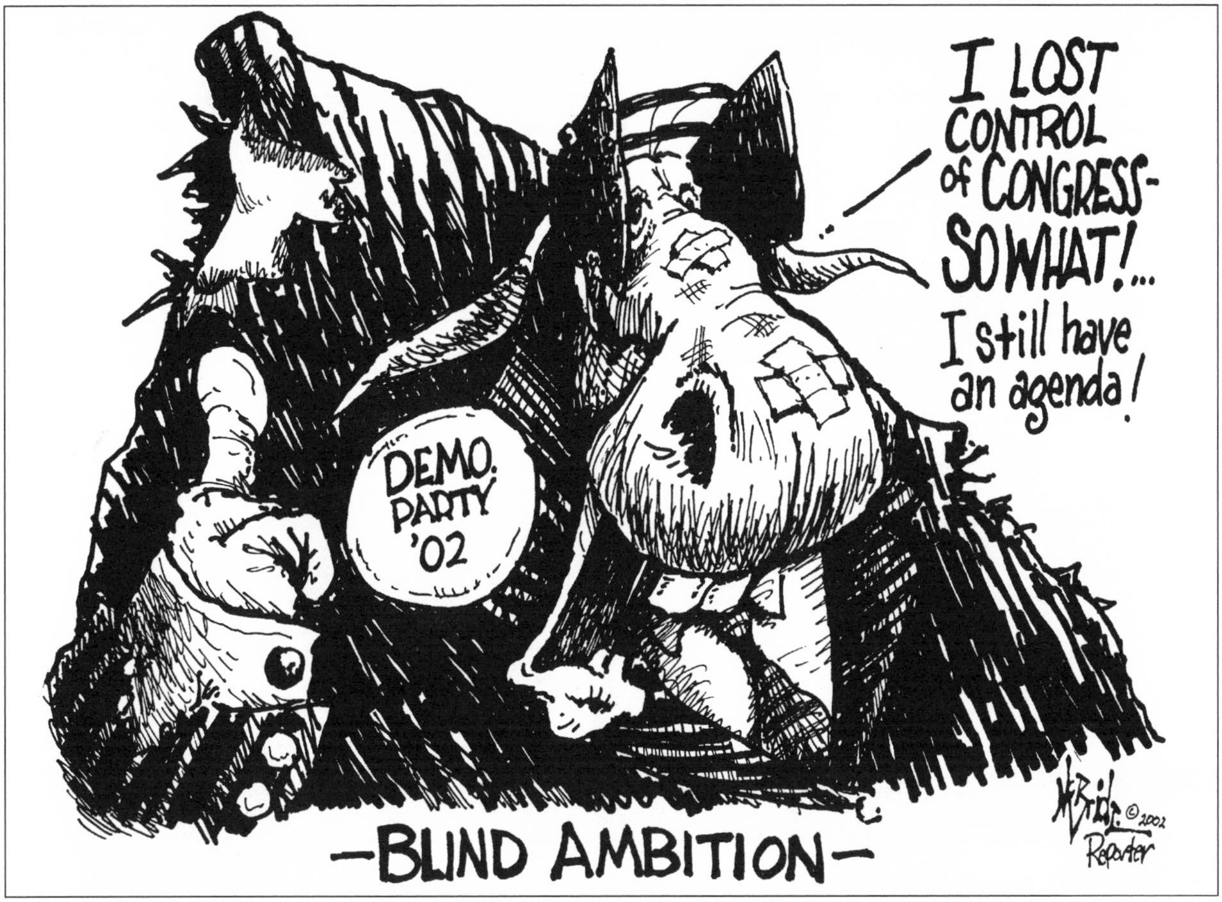
I LOST CONTROL of CONGRESS-SO WHAT!... I still have an agenda!
DEMO. PARTY '02
McBride © 2002 Reporter
-BLIND AMBITION-

STEVE McBRIDE
Courtesy Independence Daily Reporter (Kan.)

SCOTT STANTIS
Courtesy Birmingham News

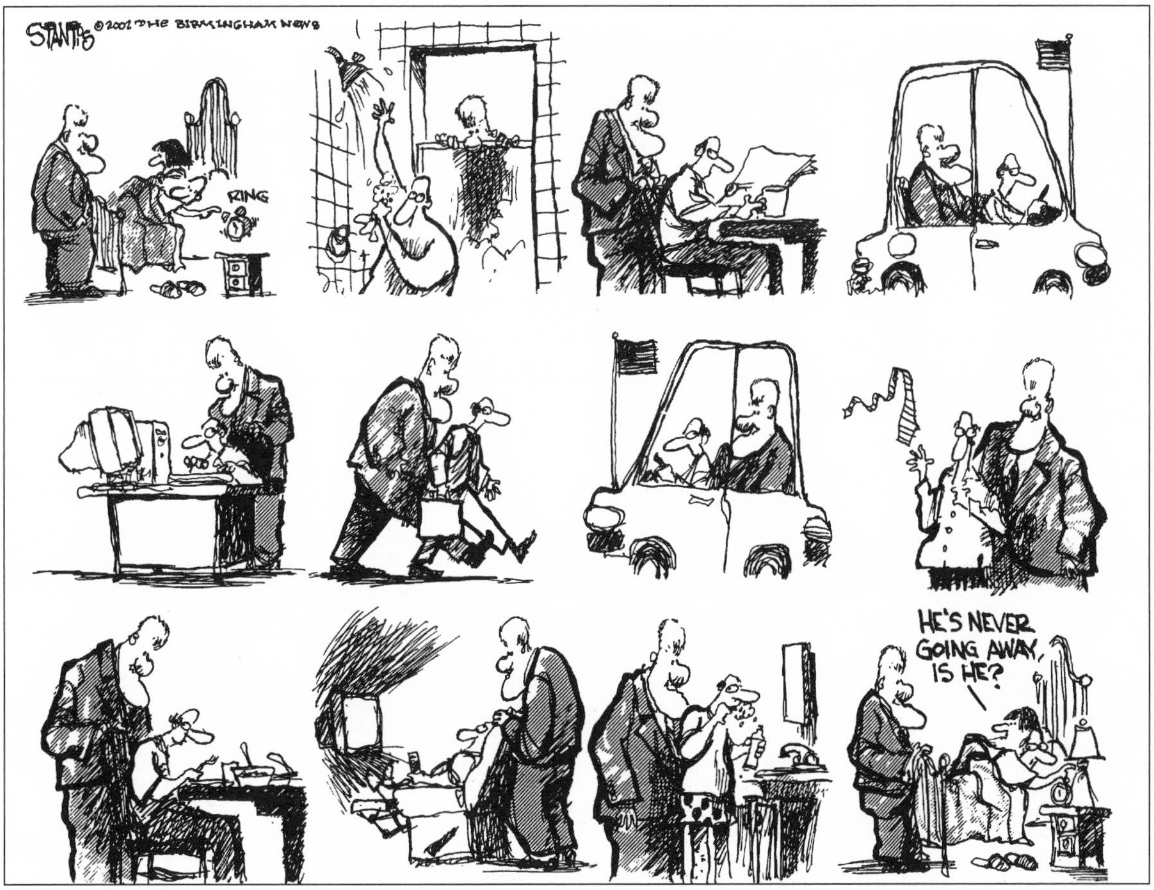
STANTIS ©2002 THE BIRMINGHAM NEWS
RING
HE'S NEVER GOING AWAY, IS HE?

GARY VARVEL
Courtesy Indianapolis Star

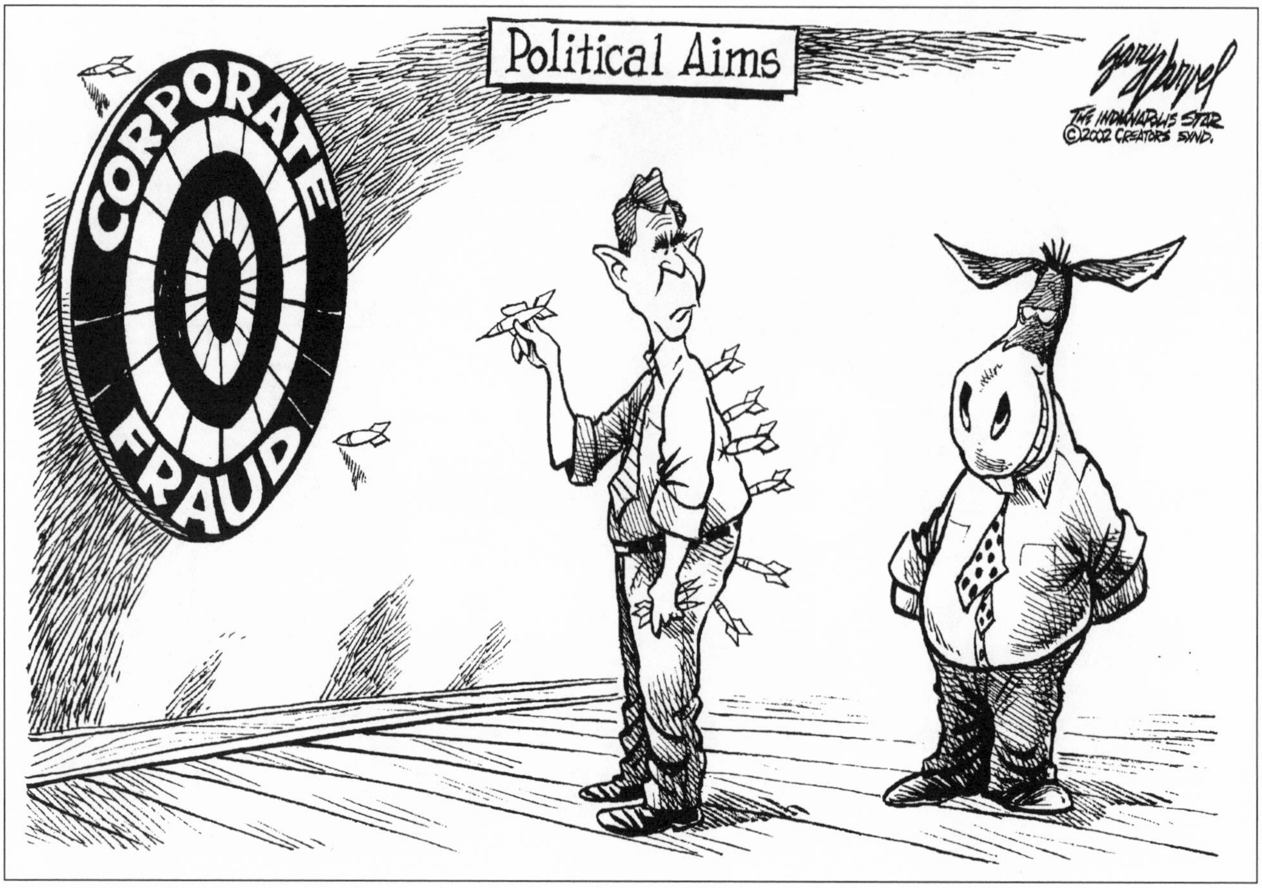
Political Aims
CORPORATE FRAUD
Gary Varvel
THE INDIANAPOLIS STAR ©2002 CREATORS SYND.

MARSHALL RAMSEY
Courtesy The Clarion Ledger

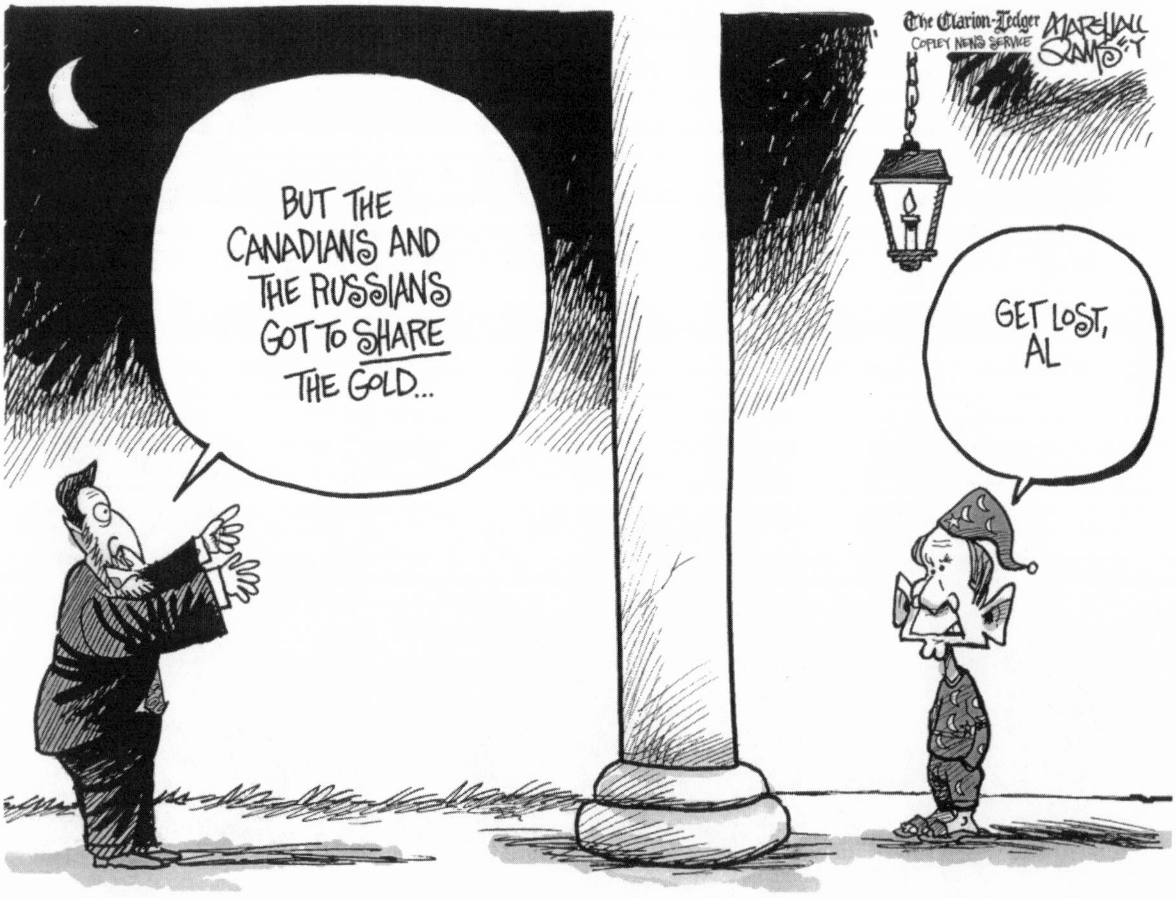
The Clarion-Ledger
COPLEY NEWS SERVICE
MARSHALL RAMSEY
BUT THE CANADIANS AND THE RUSSIANS GOT TO SHARE THE GOLD...
GET LOST, AL

JOHN TREVER
Courtesy Albuquerque Journal

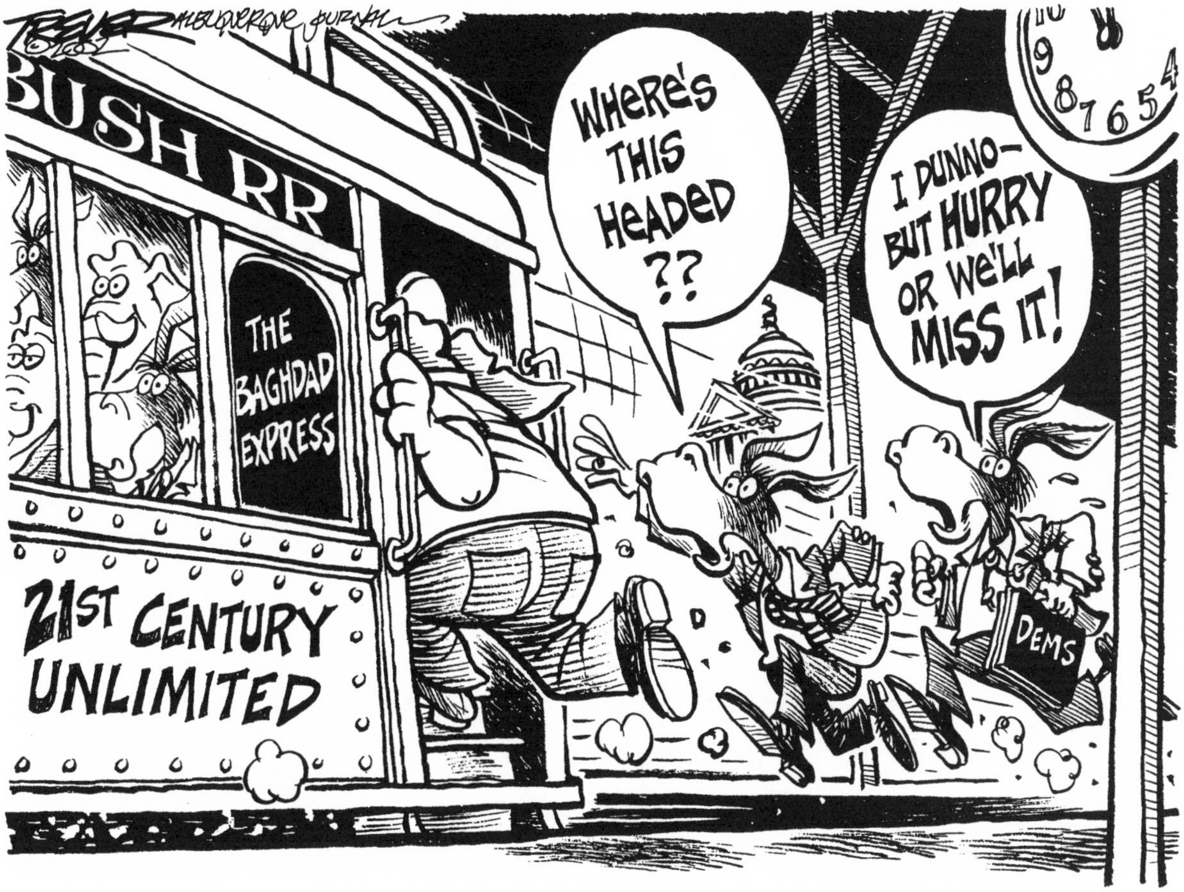

TREVER ALBUQUERQUE JOURNAL
BUSH RR
THE BAGHDAD EXPRESS
21ST CENTURY UNLIMITED
WHERE'S THIS HEADED ??
I DUNNO— BUT HURRY OR WE'LL MISS IT!
DEMS

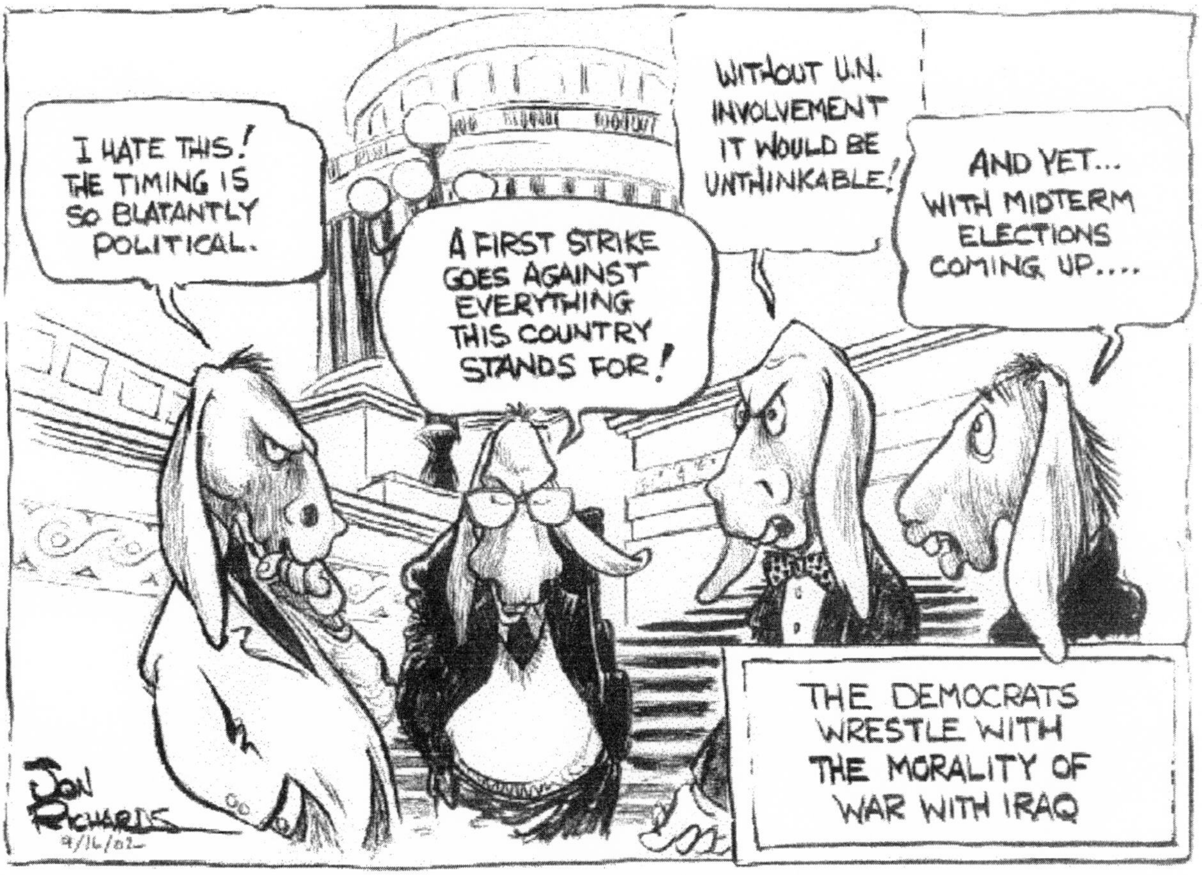

I HATE THIS! THE TIMING IS SO BLATANTLY POLITICAL.
A FIRST STRIKE GOES AGAINST EVERYTHING THIS COUNTRY STANDS FOR!
WITHOUT U.N. INVOLVEMENT IT WOULD BE UNTHINKABLE!
AND YET... WITH MIDTERM ELECTIONS COMING UP....
THE DEMOCRATS WRESTLE WITH THE MORALITY OF WAR WITH IRAQ
JON RICHARDS 9/16/02

JON RICHARDS
Courtesy Albuquerque Journal North

DREW CHAPMAN
Courtesy CommentaryPage.com

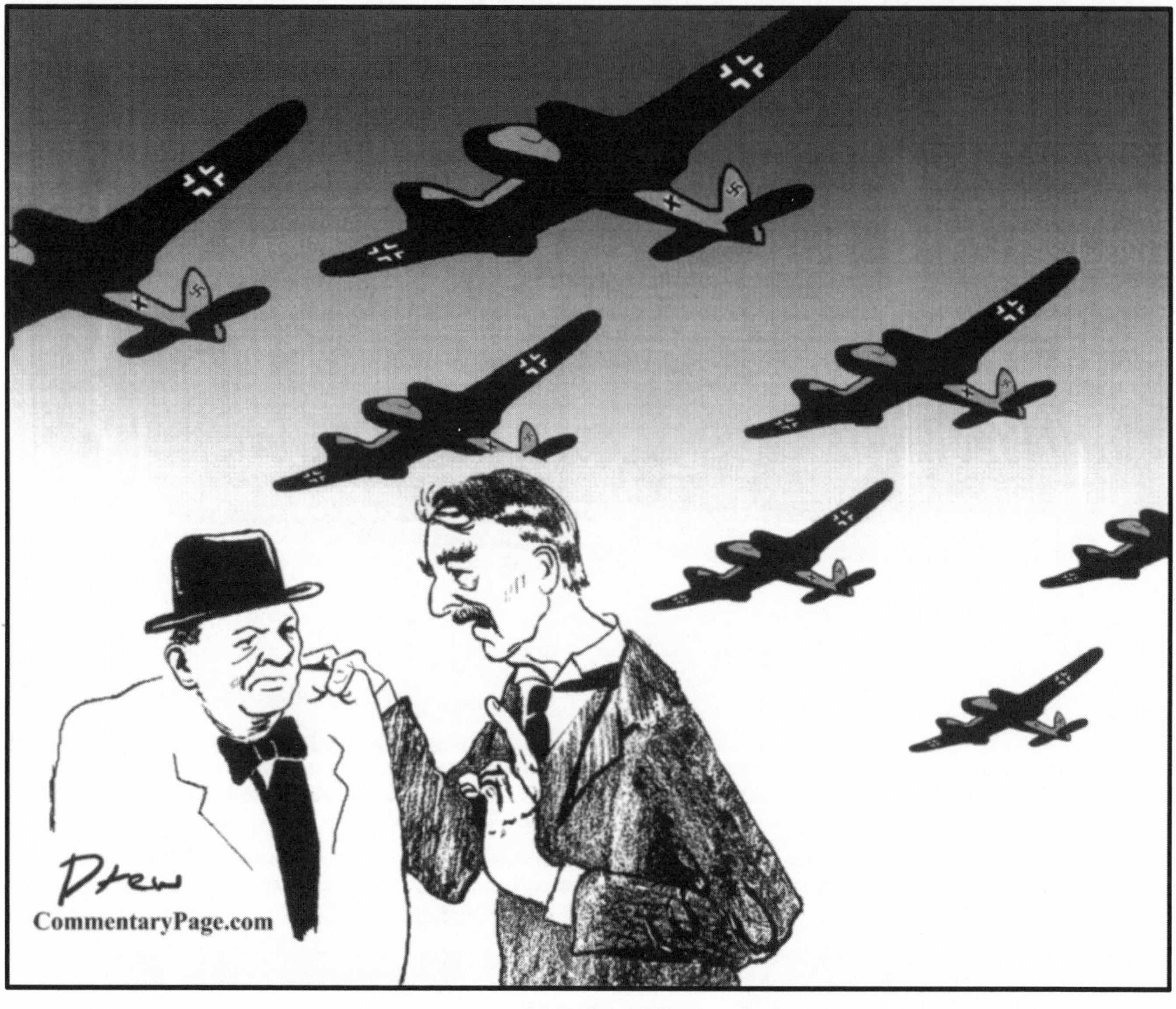
Drew
CommentaryPage.com

"My dear Mr. Churchill, have you considered the consequences of a preemptive strike?"

Foreign Affairs

Violence continued unabated in the Middle East during 2002. Yasser Arafat talked peace but constantly escalated the violence—which was always answered with further violence by Israel. Palestinian suicide bombers continued to strike buses, shopping malls, virtually any target they chose. Over a period of eighteen months, the people of Israel have suffered—when figured in proportion to the U.S. population—the equivalent of 16,000 deaths and 150,000 injured.

The threat of nuclear war hung over the India-Pakistan border for several months as the two countries argued angrily over the disputed territory of Kashmir. More than a million troops stood at the ready in the face off. Secretary of Defense Donald Rumsfeld and Secretary of State Colin Powell traveled to the region, seeking to calm nerves and recruit allies in the war on terror.

Saddam Hussein staged a make-believe referendum in October. He was declared the winner by a vote of 11 million to 0 as Iraqis demonstrated their solidarity against the United States. North Korea announced to the world that it has nuclear weapons—possibly a bomb—and that it has been continuing its nuclear weapons program. President Bush met with Chinese President Jiang Zemin in an effort to find a way to resolve peacefully this growing Asian crisis.

TOM GIBB
Courtesy Johnstown Tribune-Democrat (Pa.)

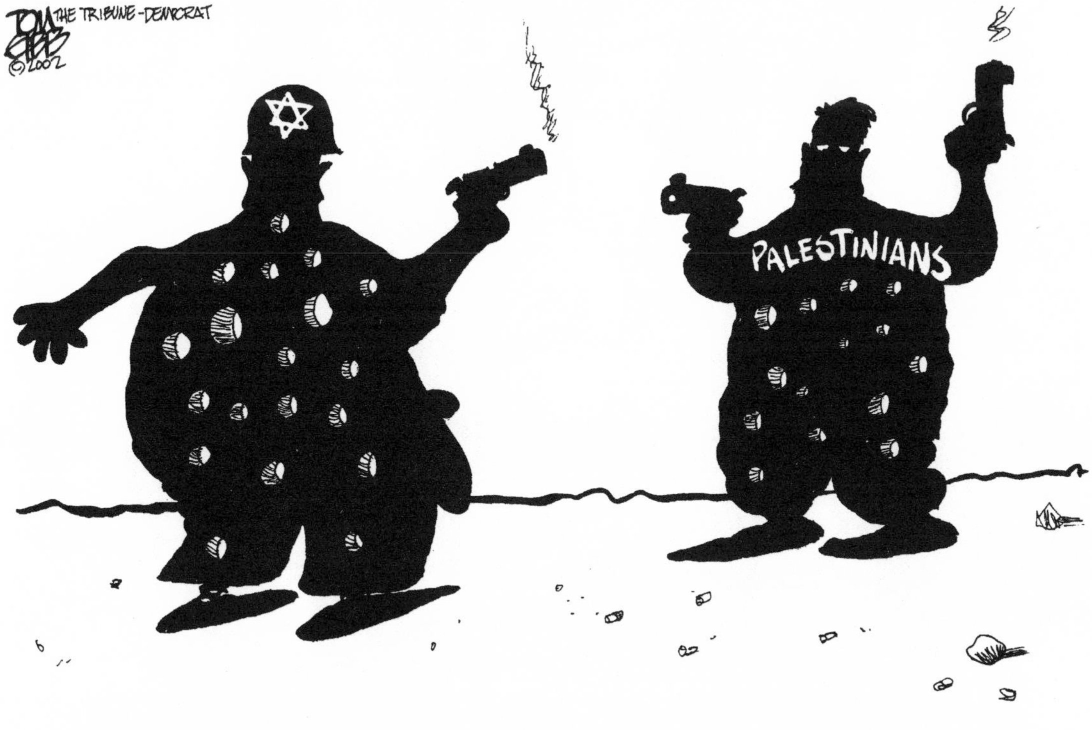
THE TRIBUNE-DEMOCRAT
©2002
PALESTINIANS

AWAITING THE GLIMMER OF RECOGNITION THAT VIOLENCE GETS THEM NOWHERE.

ED FISCHER
Courtesy Rochester Post-Bulletin (Minn.)

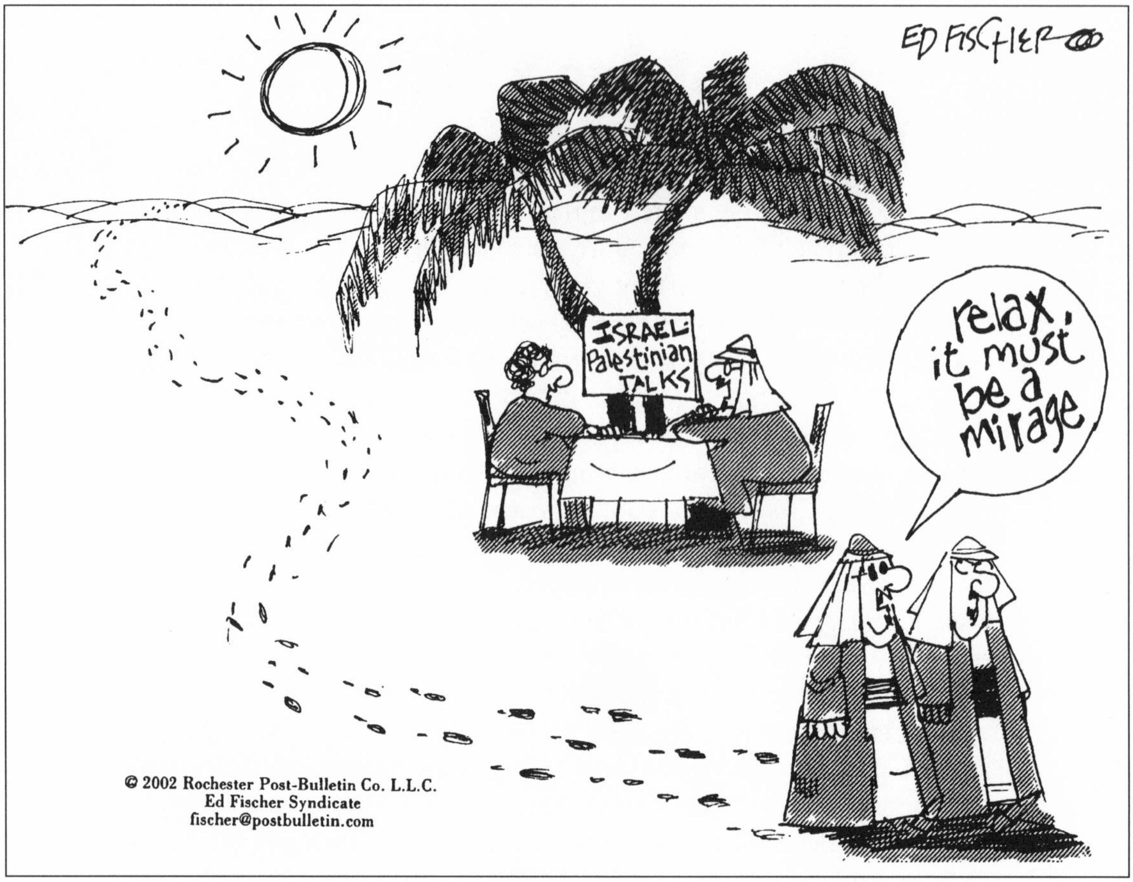
ED FISCHER ©00
ISRAEL-Palestinian TALKS
relax, it must be a mirage
© 2002 Rochester Post-Bulletin Co. L.L.C.
Ed Fischer Syndicate
fischer@postbulletin.com

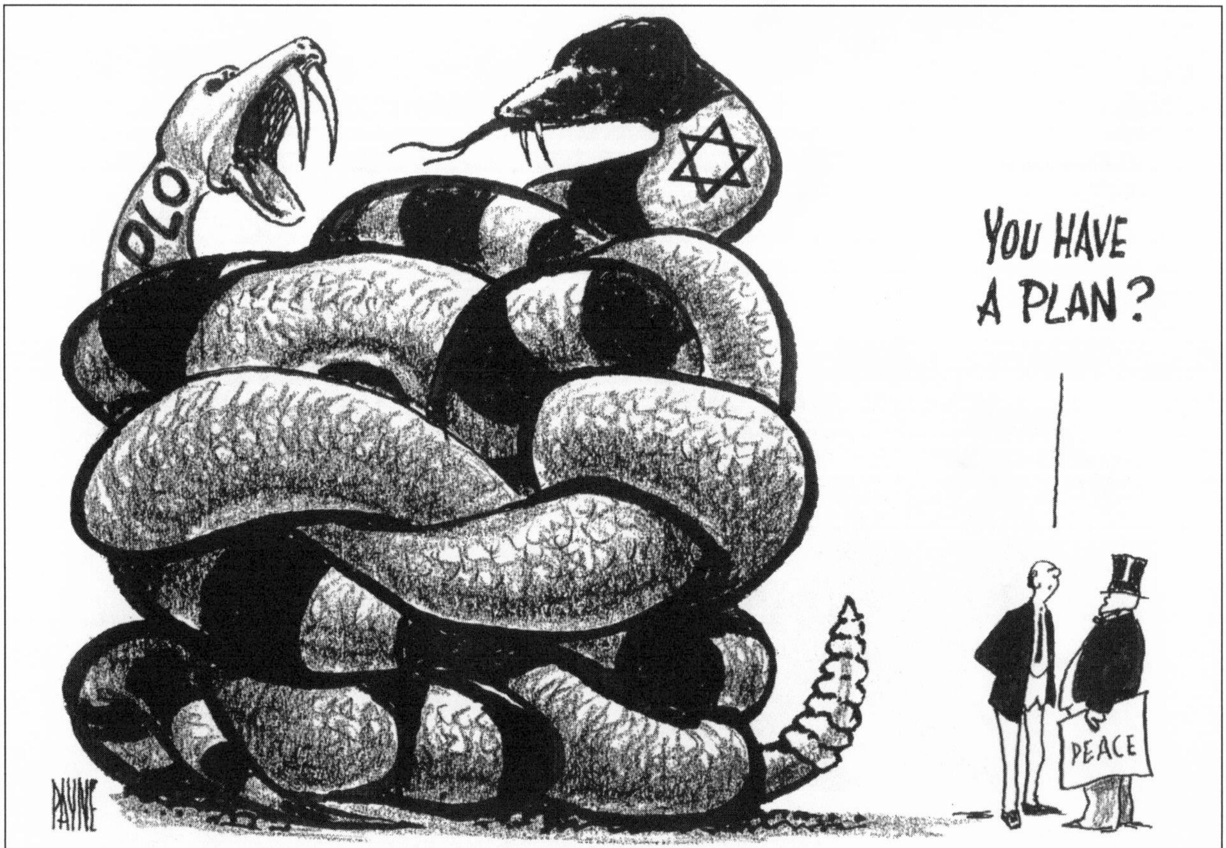
PLO
YOU HAVE A PLAN?
PEACE
PAYNE

EUGENE PAYNE
Courtesy Charlotte Observer

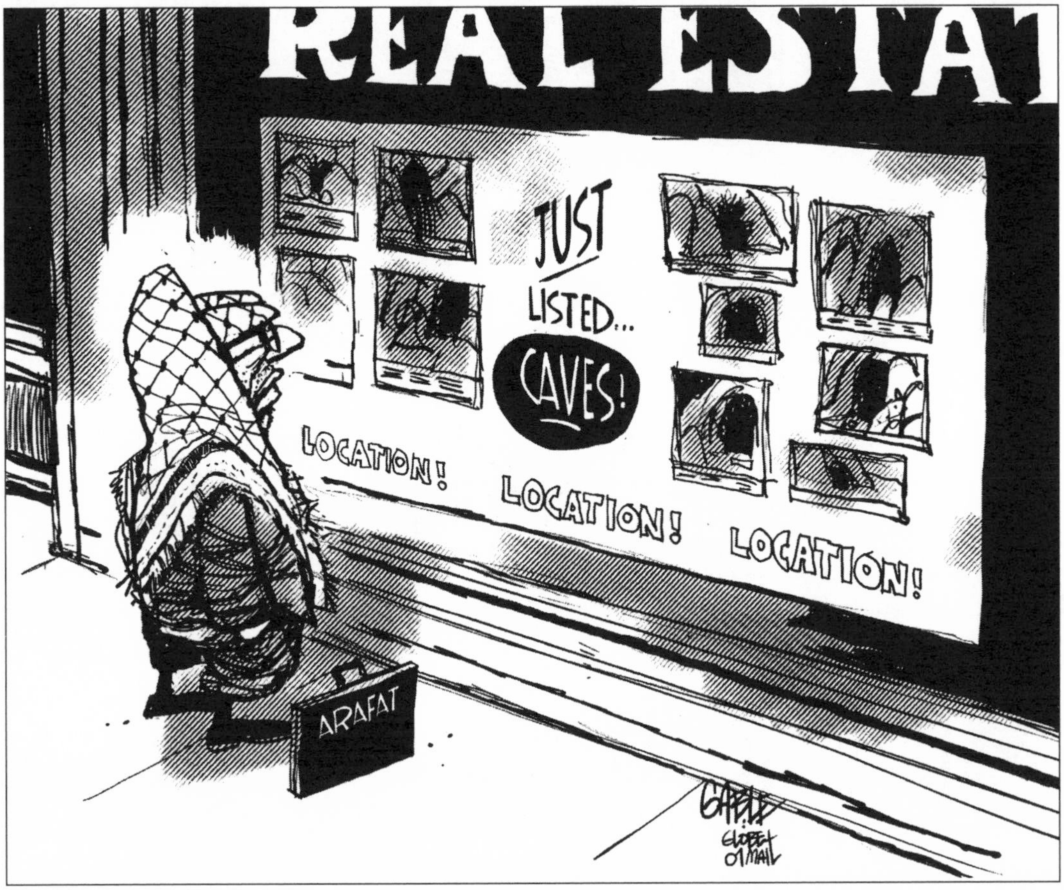
REAL ESTAT
JUST LISTED... CAVES!
LOCATION! LOCATION! LOCATION!
ARAFAT
GABLE
GLOBE & MAIL

BRIAN GABLE
Courtesy Globe and Mail (Canada)

MIKE KEEFE
Courtesy Denver Post

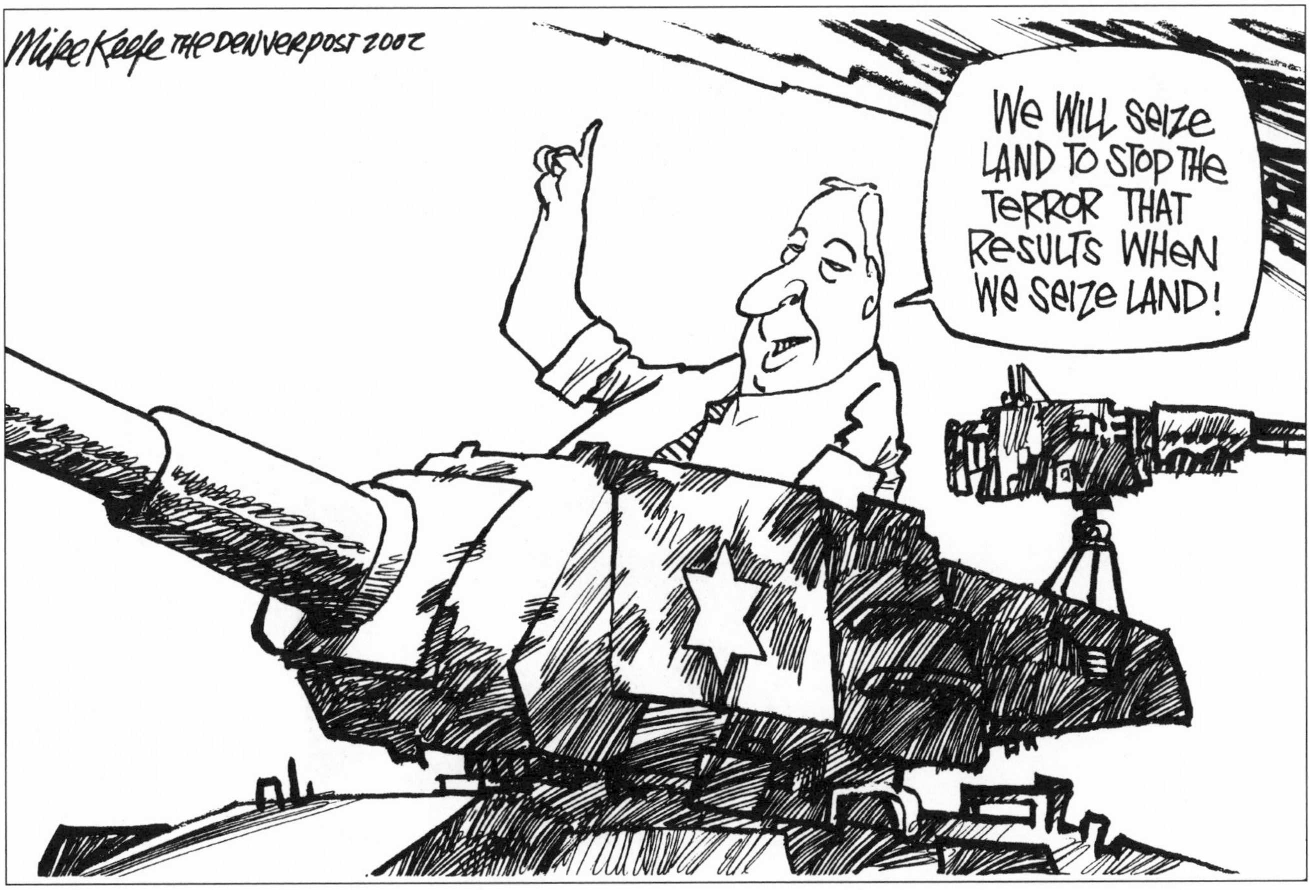
Mike Keefe THE DENVER POST 2002
WE WILL SEIZE LAND TO STOP THE TERROR THAT RESULTS WHEN WE SEIZE LAND!

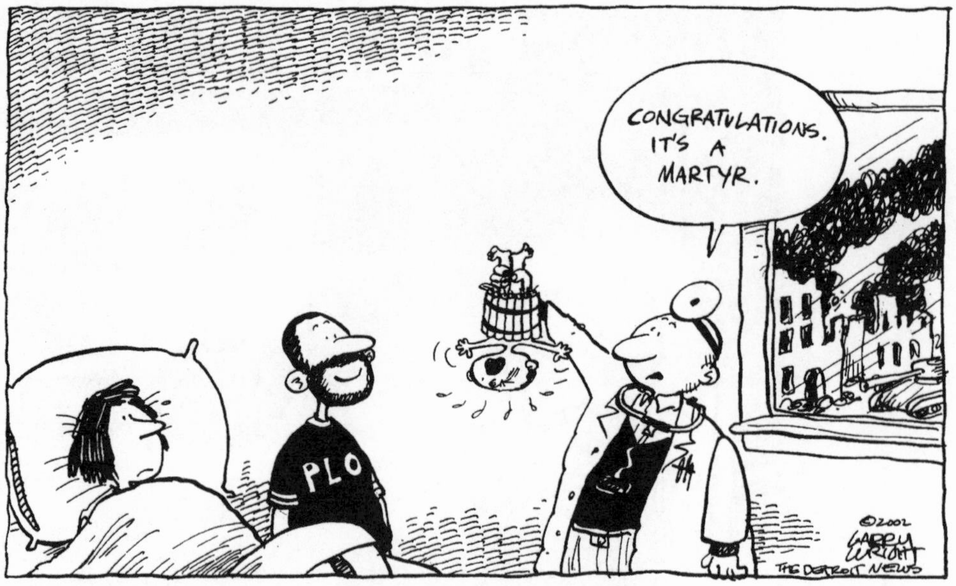
CONGRATULATIONS. IT'S A MARTYR.
PLO
©2002 LARRY WRIGHT THE DETROIT NEWS

LARRY WRIGHT
Courtesy Detroit News

ROBERT ARIAIL
Courtesy The State (S.C.)

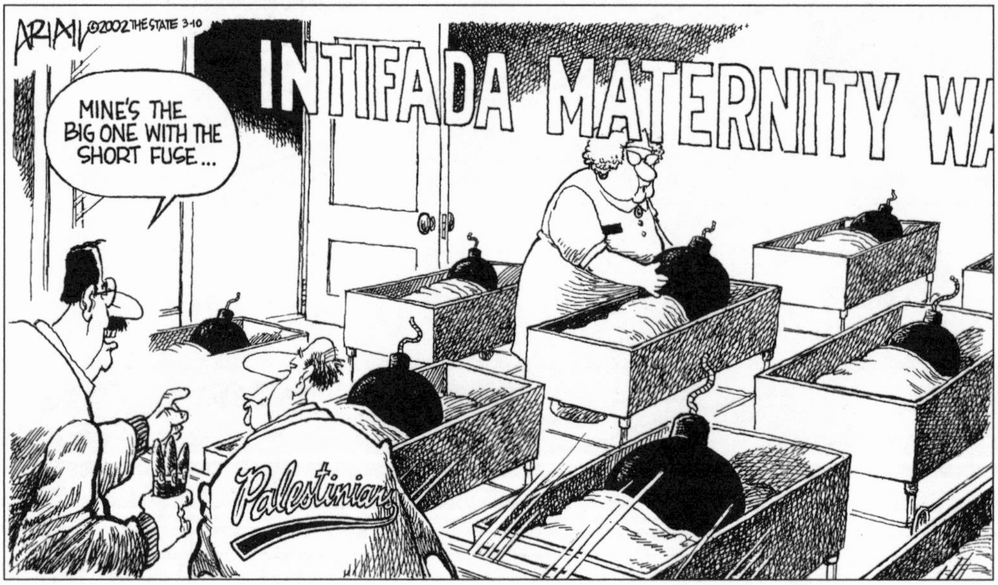
ARIAIL ©2002 THE STATE 3-10
INTIFADA MATERNITY WA
MINE'S THE BIG ONE WITH THE SHORT FUSE...
Palestinian

MILT PRIGGEE
Courtesy miltpriggee.com

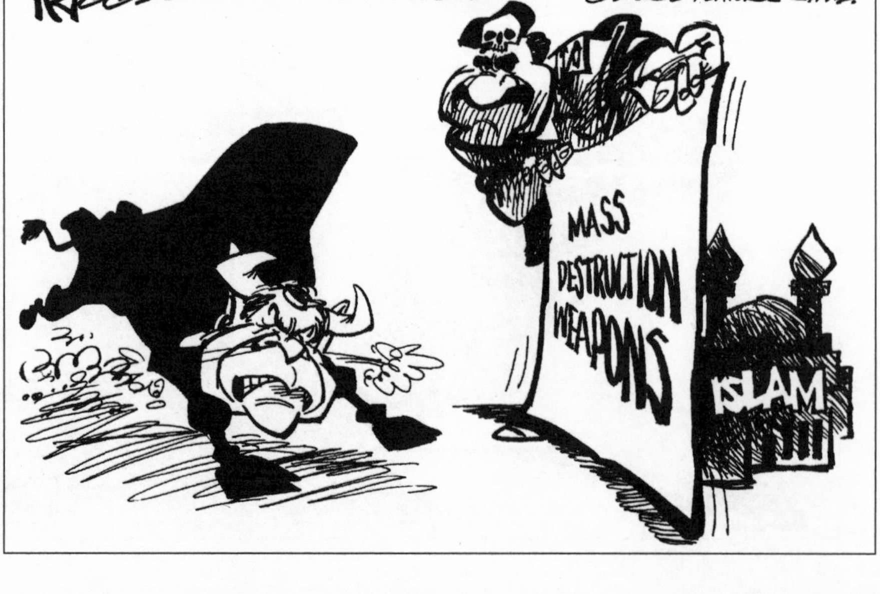
PRIGGEE ©02.10 WWW.MILTPRIGGEE.COM
@LARGE FEATURES SYND.
MASS DESTRUCTION WEAPONS
ISLAM

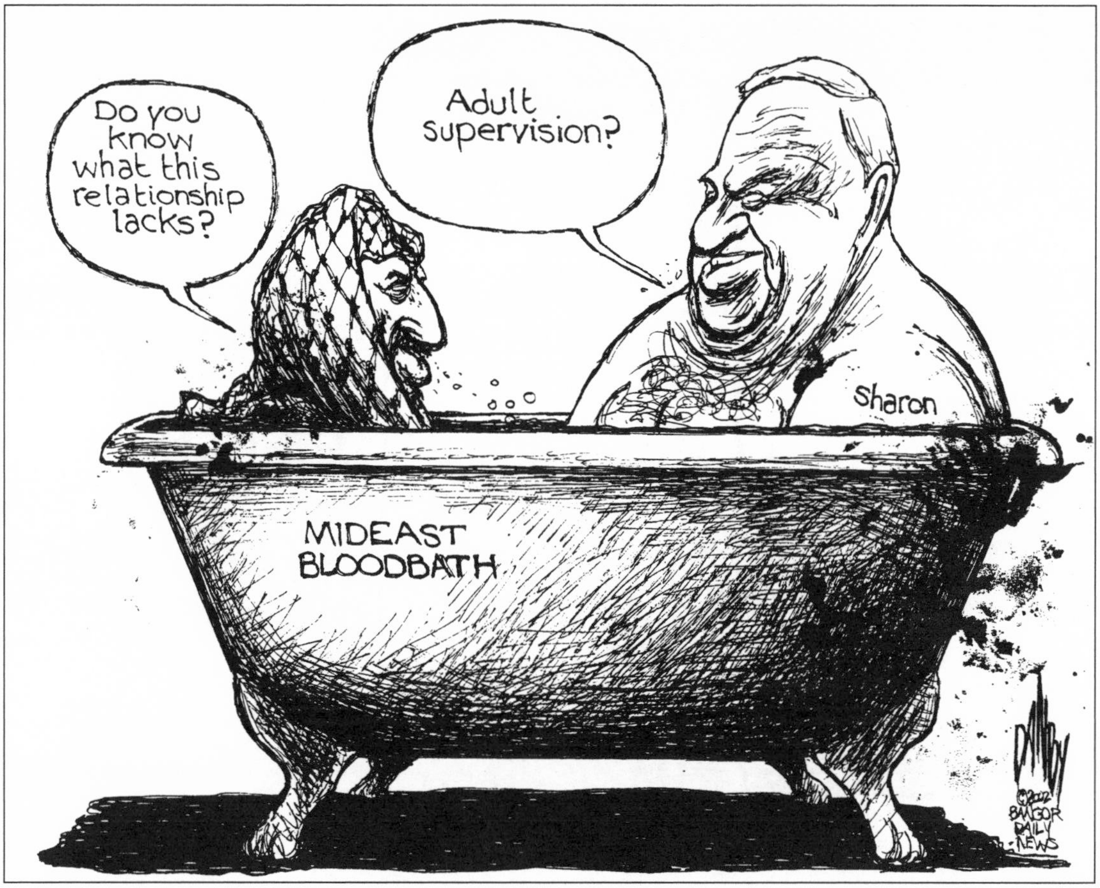
Do you know what this relationship lacks?
Adult supervision?
Sharon
MIDEAST BLOODBATH
DANBY
©2002 BANGOR DAILY NEWS

GEORGE DANBY
Courtesy Bangor Daily News

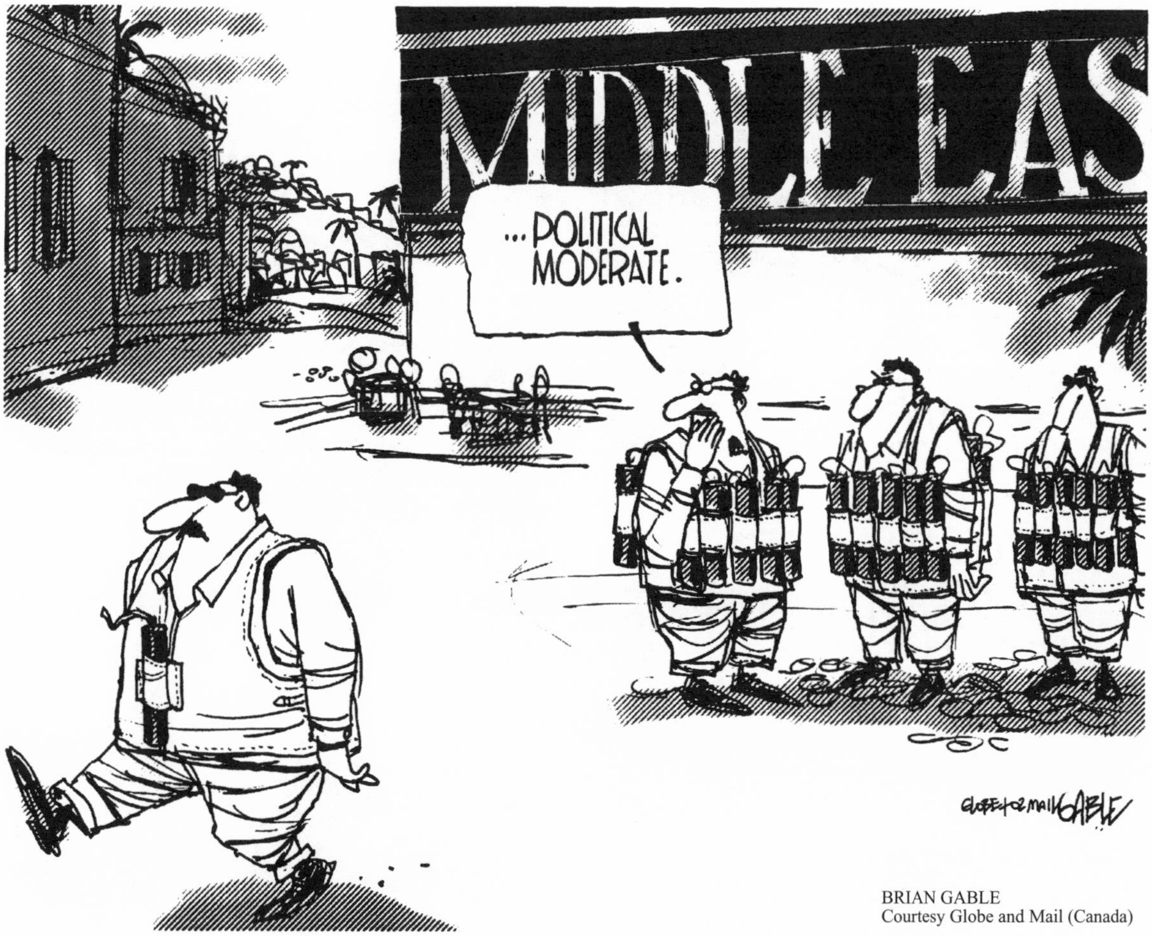
MIDDLE EAS
...POLITICAL MODERATE.
GLOBE+MAIL GABLE

BRIAN GABLE
Courtesy Globe and Mail (Canada)

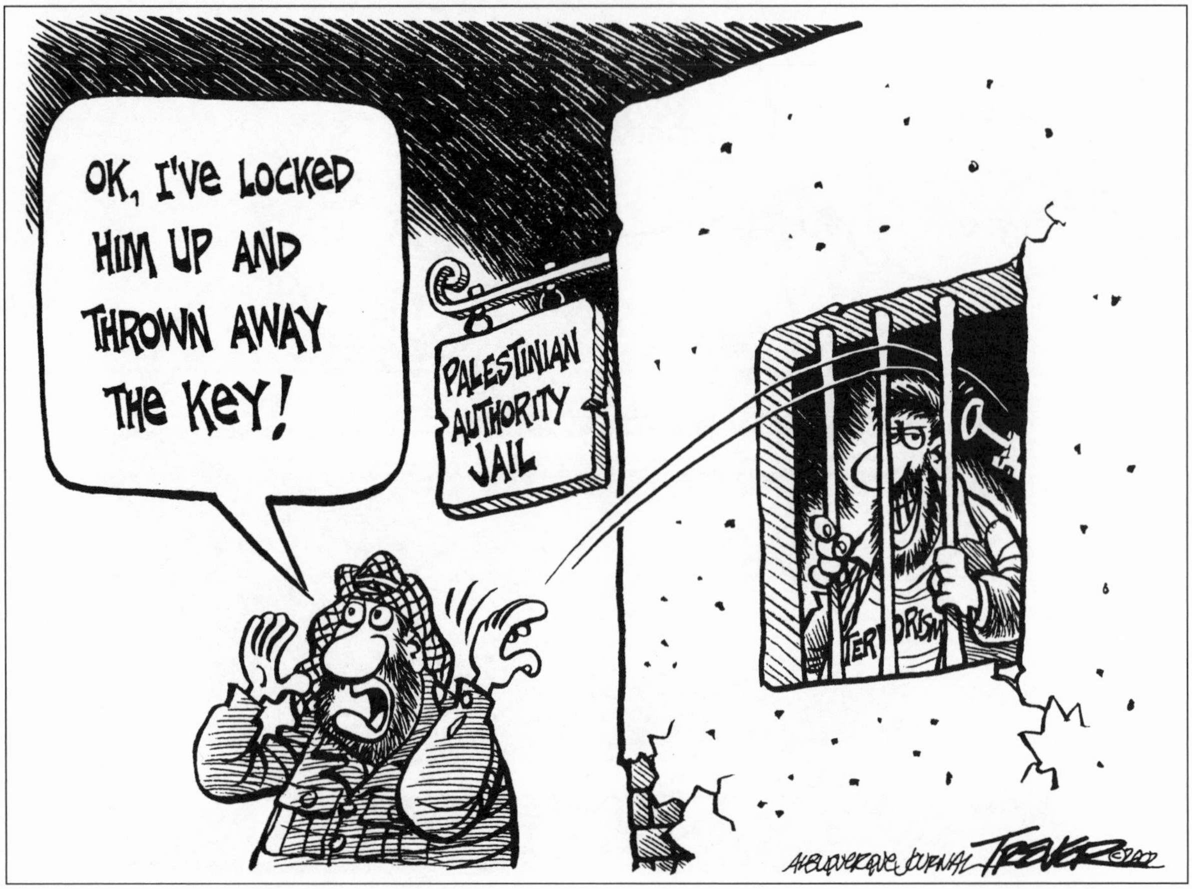
OK, I'VE LOCKED HIM UP AND THROWN AWAY THE KEY!
PALESTINIAN AUTHORITY JAIL
TERRORISM
ALBUQUERQUE JOURNAL TREVER

JOHN TREVER
Courtesy Albuquerque Journal

GARY BROOKINS
Courtesy Richmond Times-Dispatch

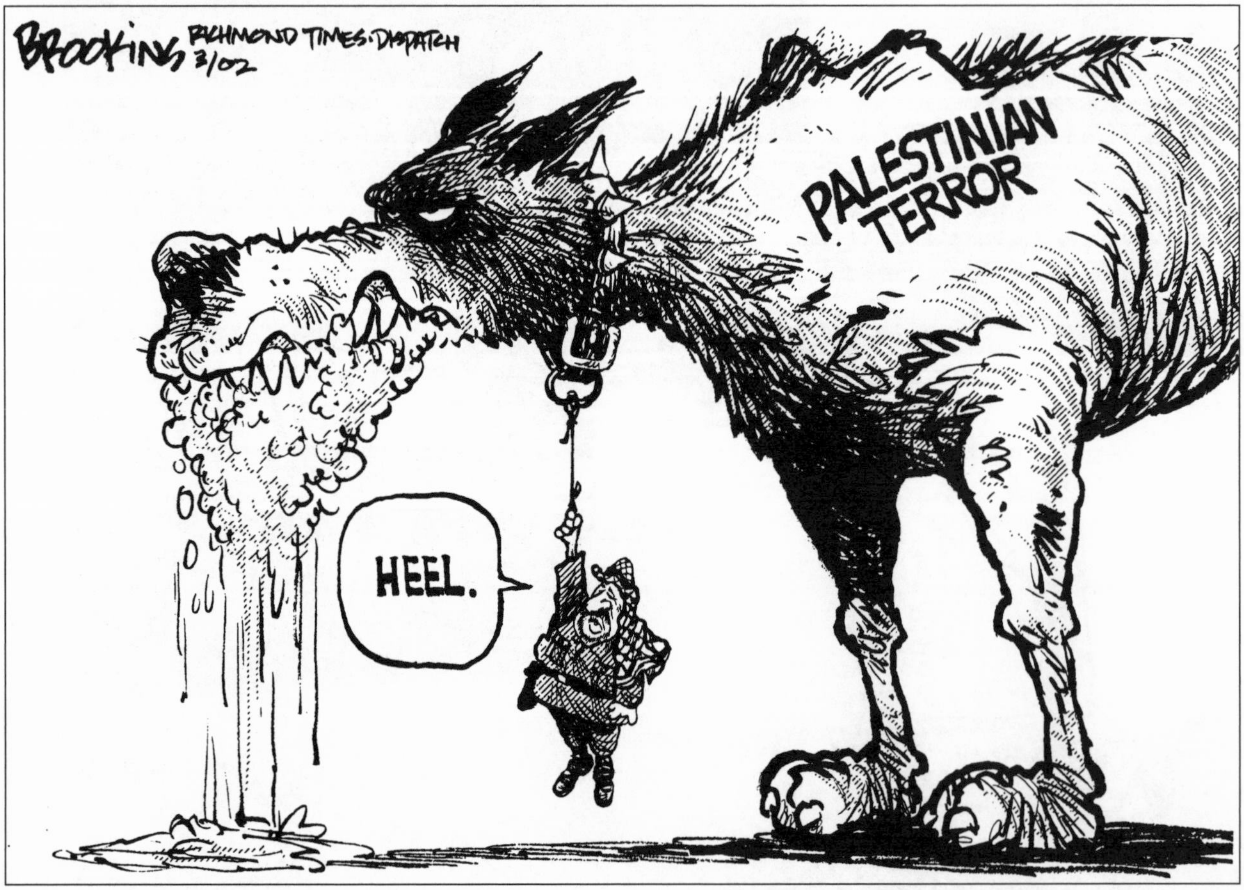
BROOKINS RICHMOND TIMES-DISPATCH 3/02
PALESTINIAN TERROR
HEEL.

BILL GARNER
Courtesy Washington Times

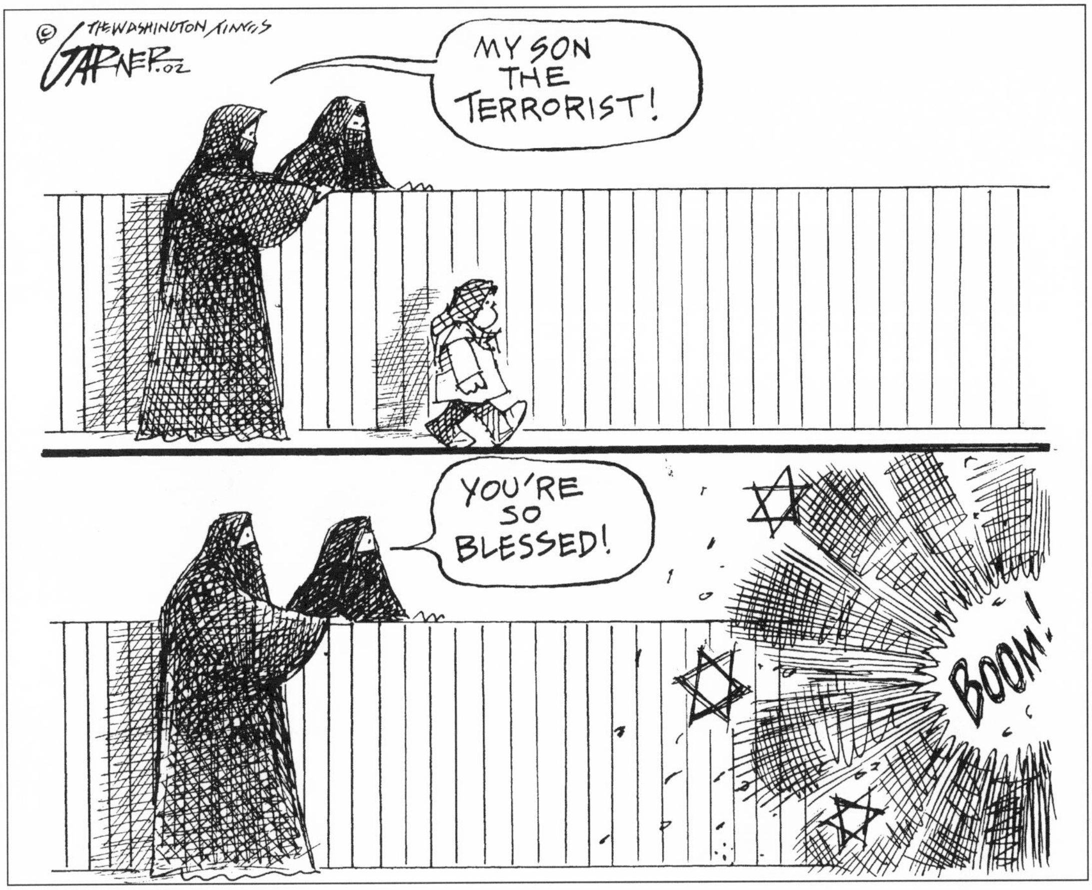
© THE WASHINGTON TIMES
GARNER '02
MY SON THE TERRORIST!
YOU'RE SO BLESSED!
BOOM!

JIMMY MARGULIES
Courtesy The Record (N.J.)

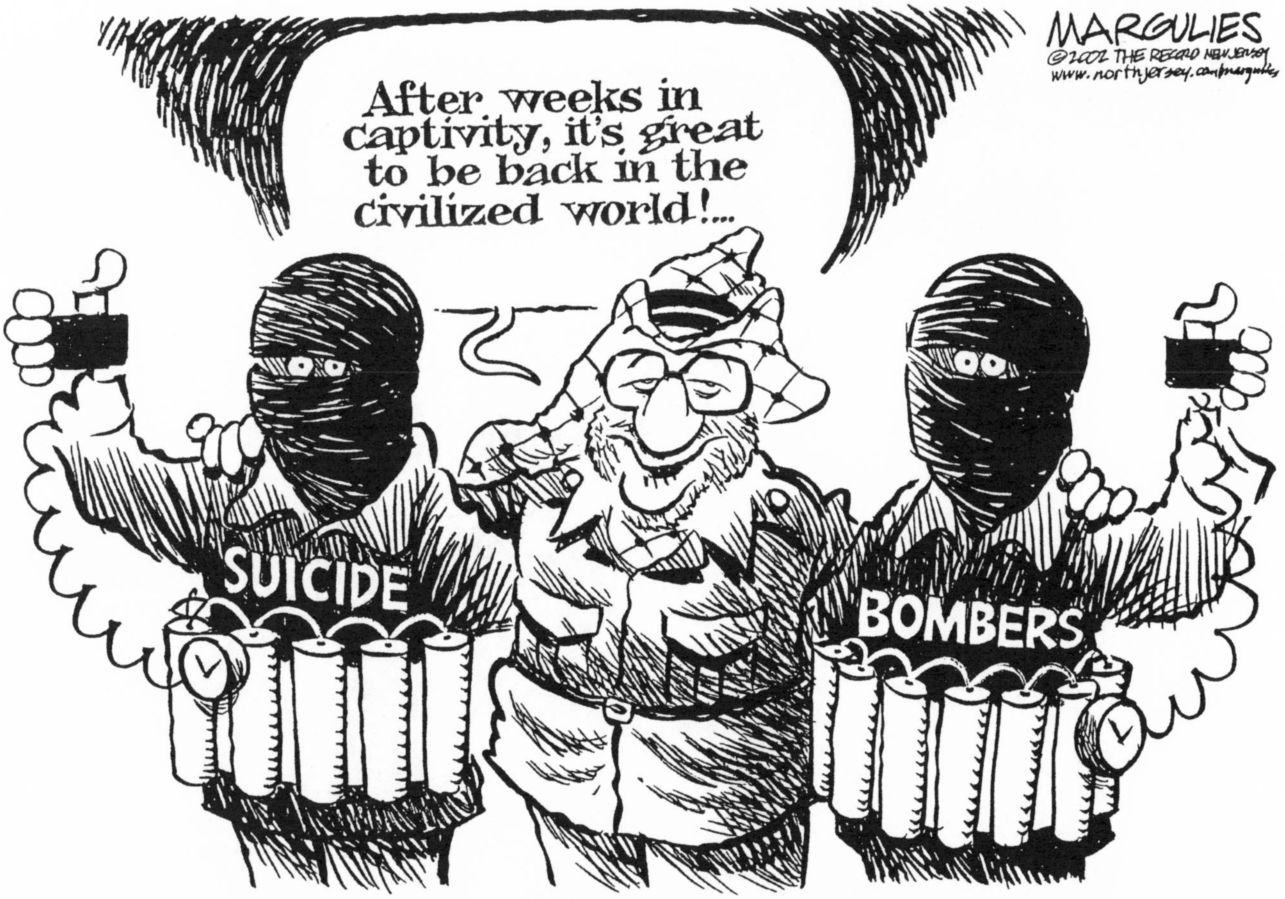
MARGULIES
©2002 THE RECORD NEW JERSEY
www.northjersey.com/margulies
After weeks in captivity, it's great to be back in the civilized world!...
SUICIDE
BOMBERS

BRUCE BEATTIE
Courtesy Daytona Beach News-Journal

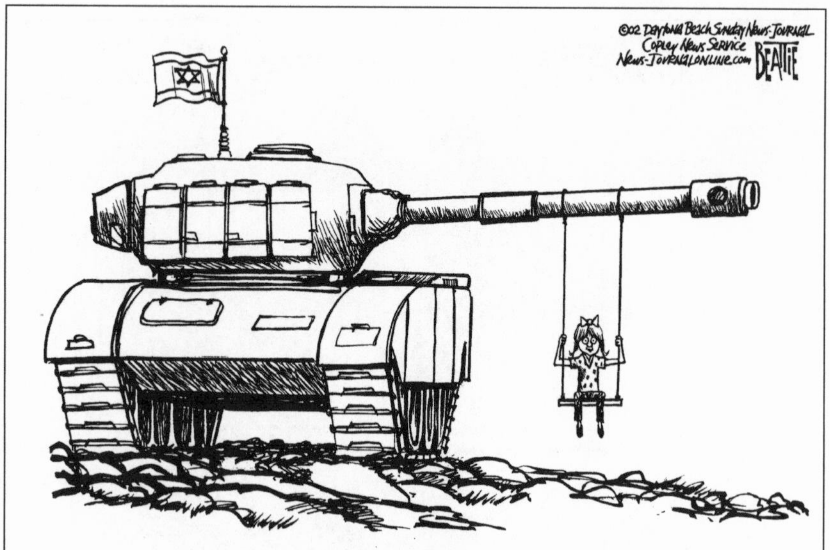

"It's nice having someplace safe to put up this swing set."

JIM BORGMAN
Courtesy Cincinnati Enquirer

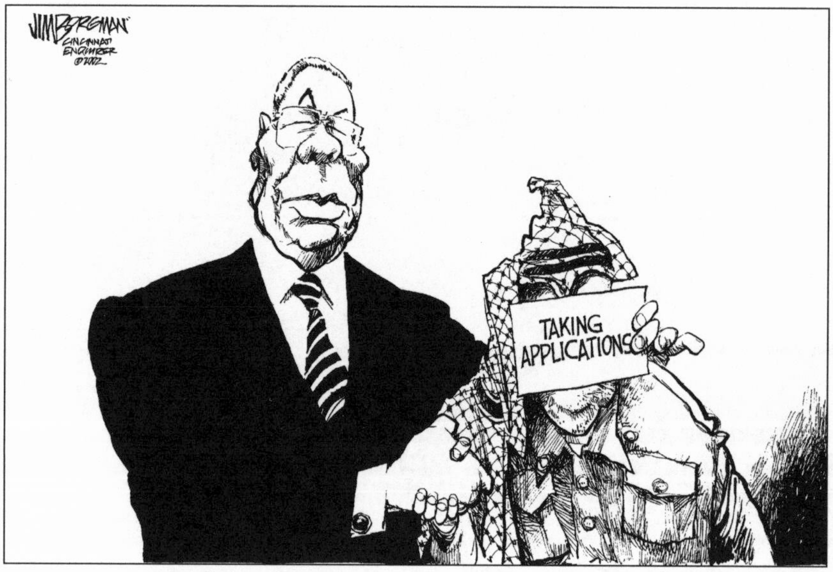
TAKING APPLICATIONS

GARY BROOKINS
Courtesy Richmond Times-Dispatch

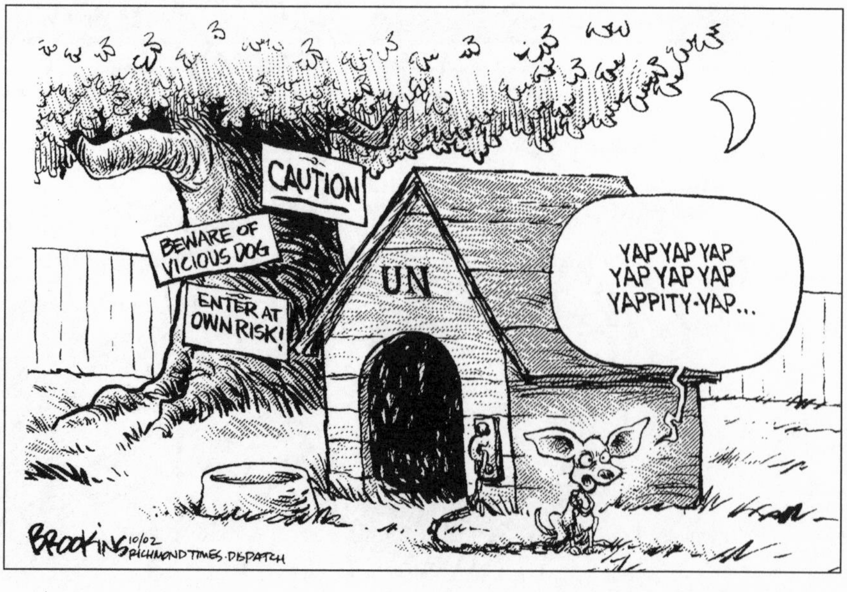
CAUTION
BEWARE OF VICIOUS DOG
ENTER AT OWN RISK!
UN
YAP YAP YAP
YAP YAP YAP YAP
YAPPITY-YAP...

VIC HARVILLE
Courtesy Donrey News (Ark.)

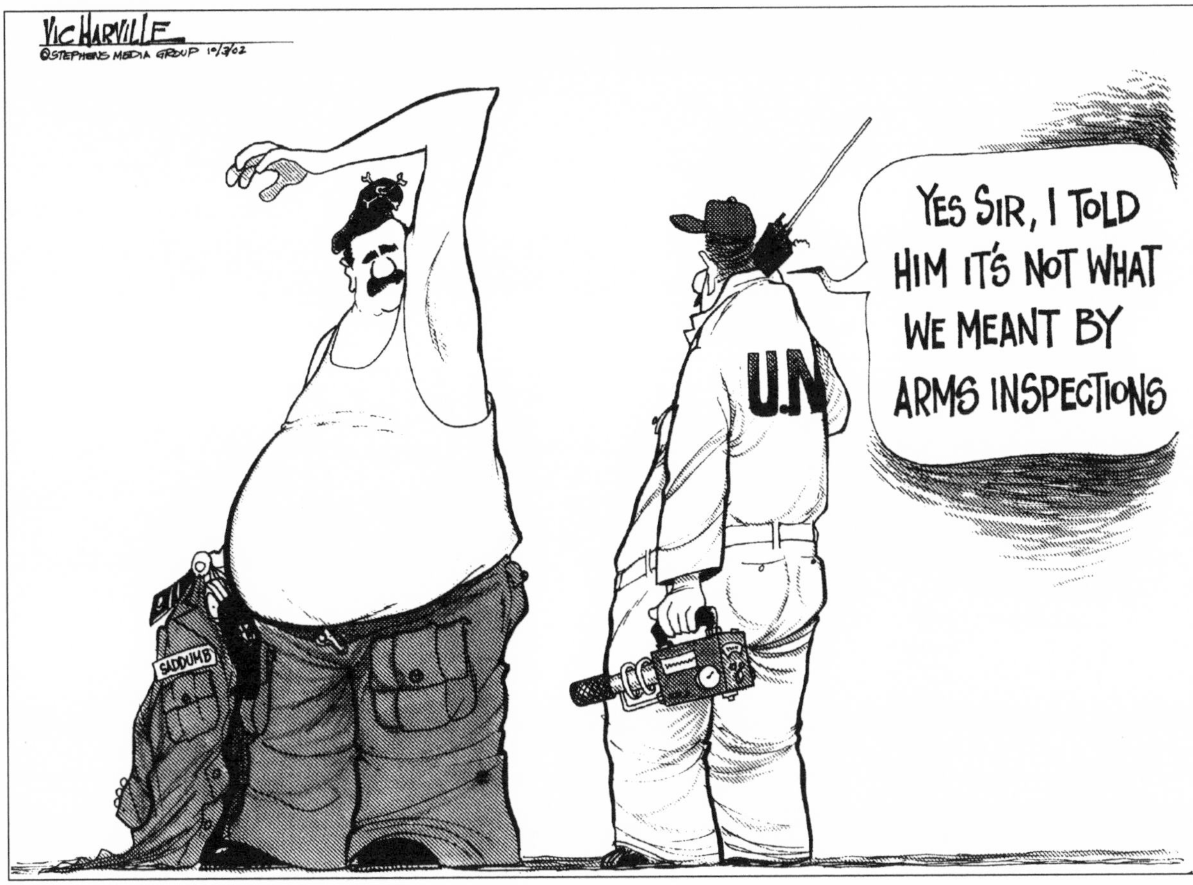
VIC HARVILLE
©STEPHENS MEDIA GROUP 10/3/02
SADDUMB
U.N
YES SIR, I TOLD HIM IT'S NOT WHAT WE MEANT BY ARMS INSPECTIONS

KIRK ANDERSON
Courtesy St. Paul Pioneer Press

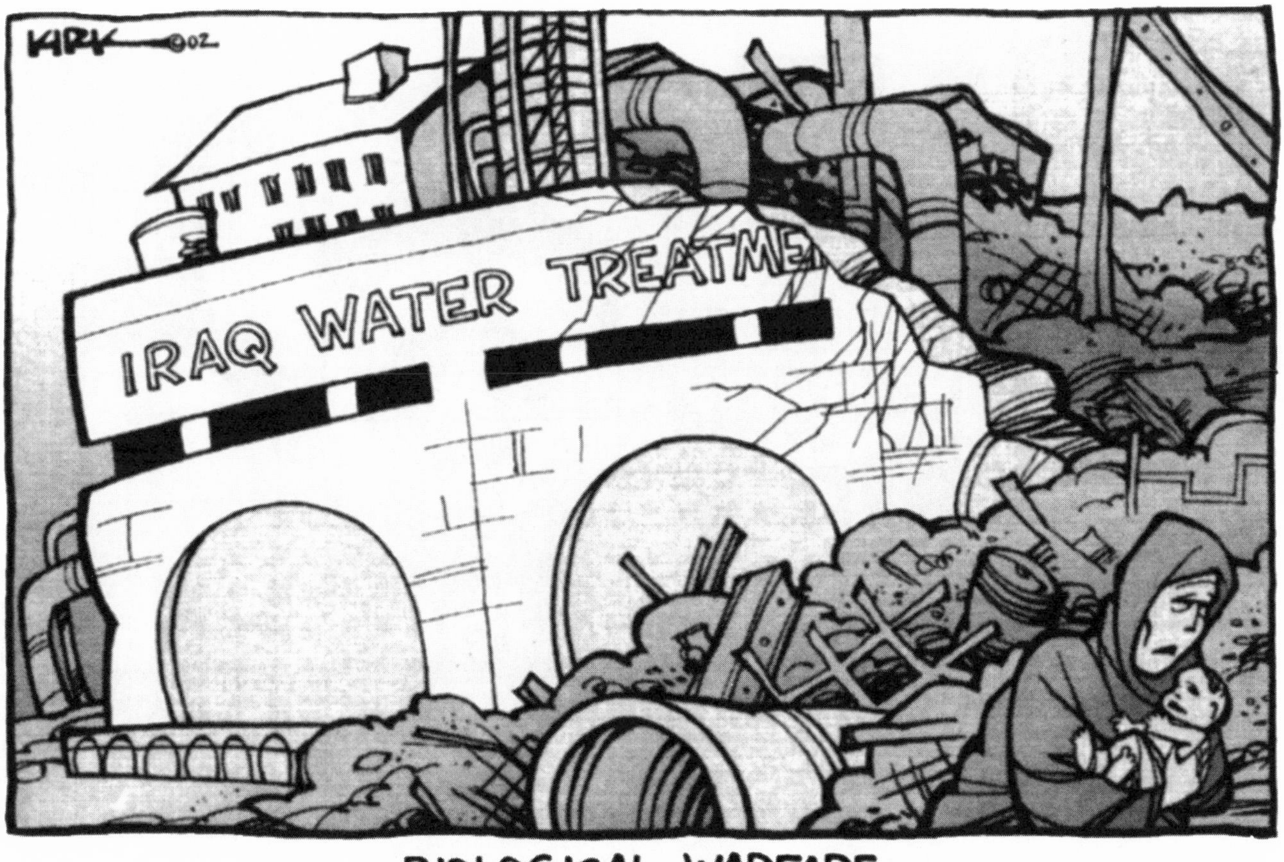
KIRK ©02
IRAQ WATER TREATME
BIOLOGICAL WARFARE

STEVE KELLEY
Courtesy The Times-Picayune (La.)

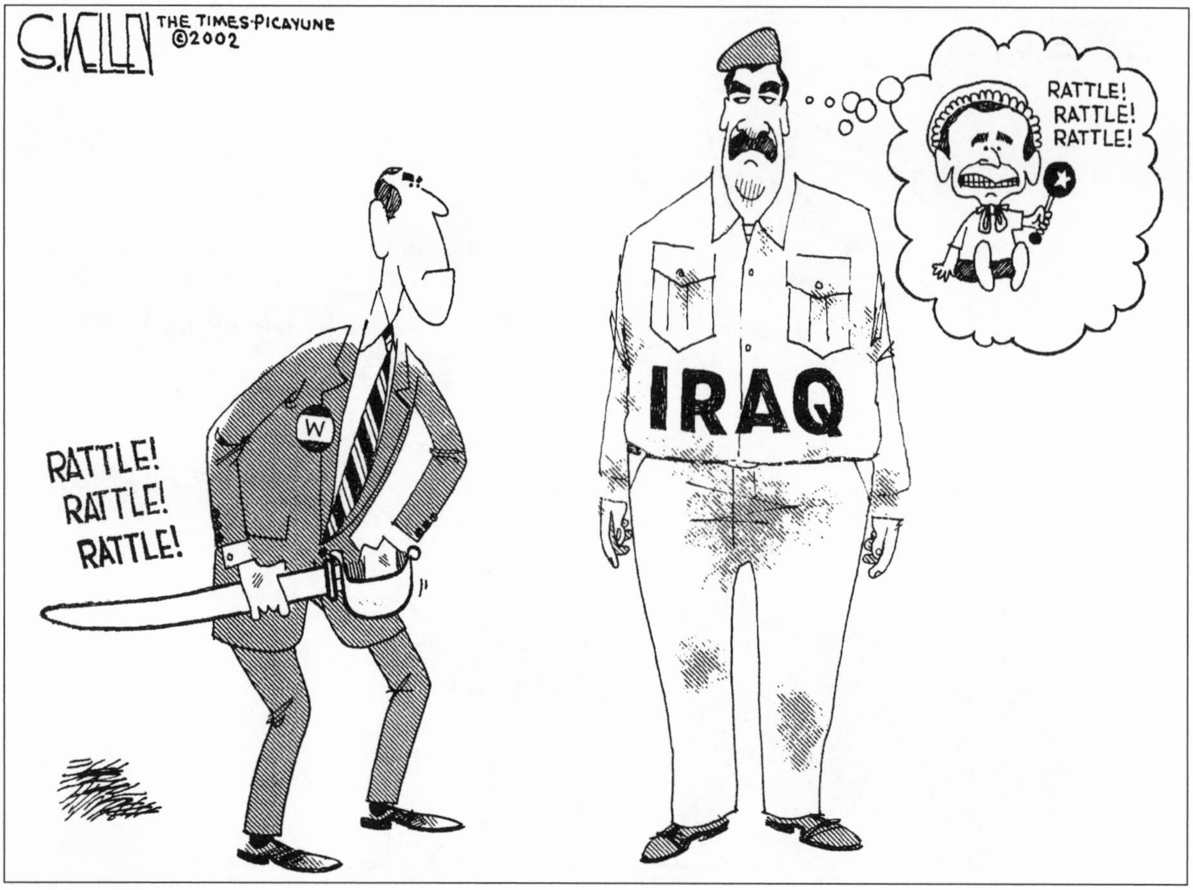
S.KELLEY THE TIMES-PICAYUNE ©2002
RATTLE! RATTLE! RATTLE!
W
IRAQ
RATTLE! RATTLE! RATTLE!

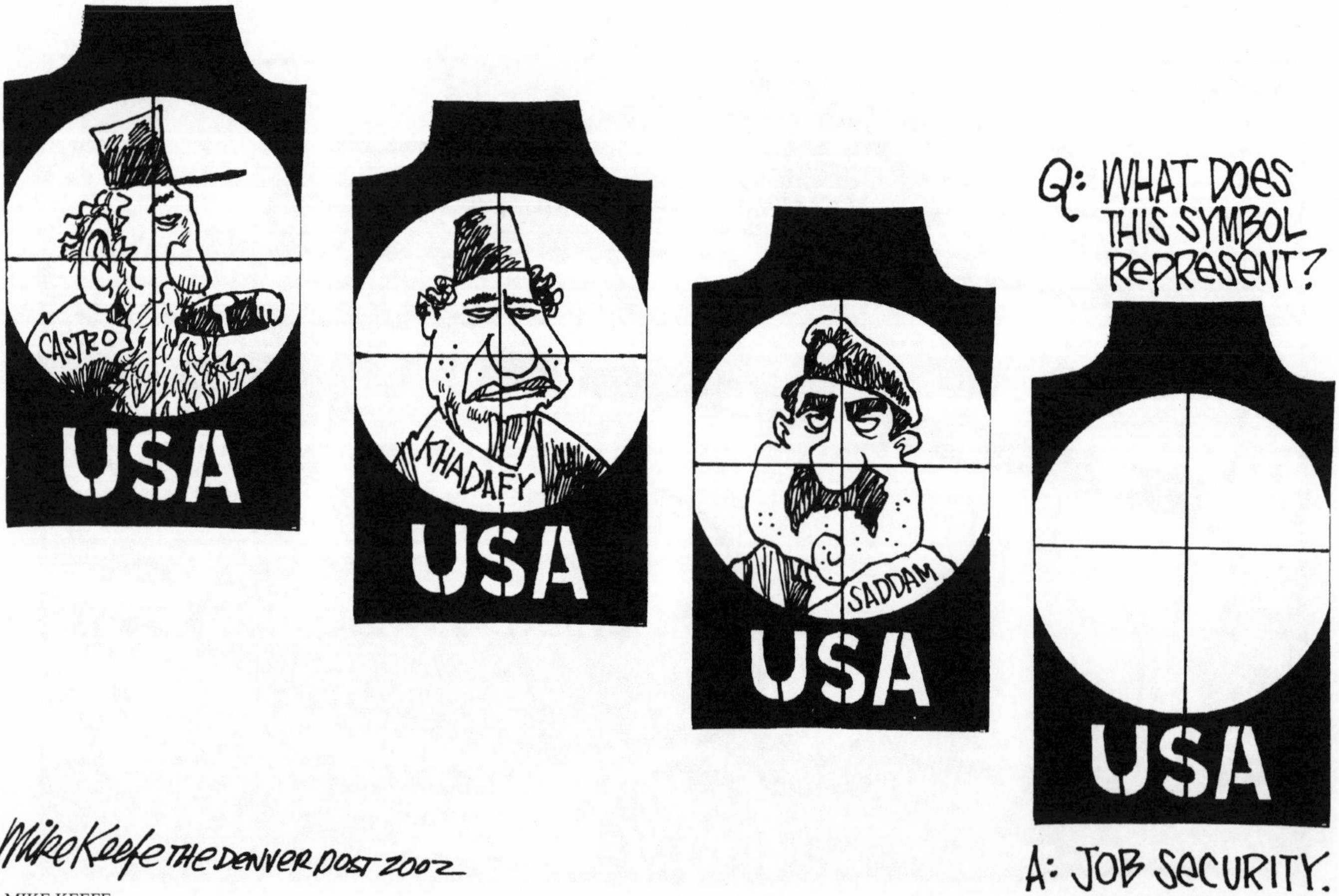
CASTRO
USA
KHADAFY
USA
SADDAM
USA
Q: WHAT DOES THIS SYMBOL REPRESENT?
USA
A: JOB SECURITY.
Mike Keefe THE DENVER POST 2002

MIKE KEEFE
Courtesy Denver Post

PETER DUNLOP-SHOHL
Courtesy Anchorage Daily News

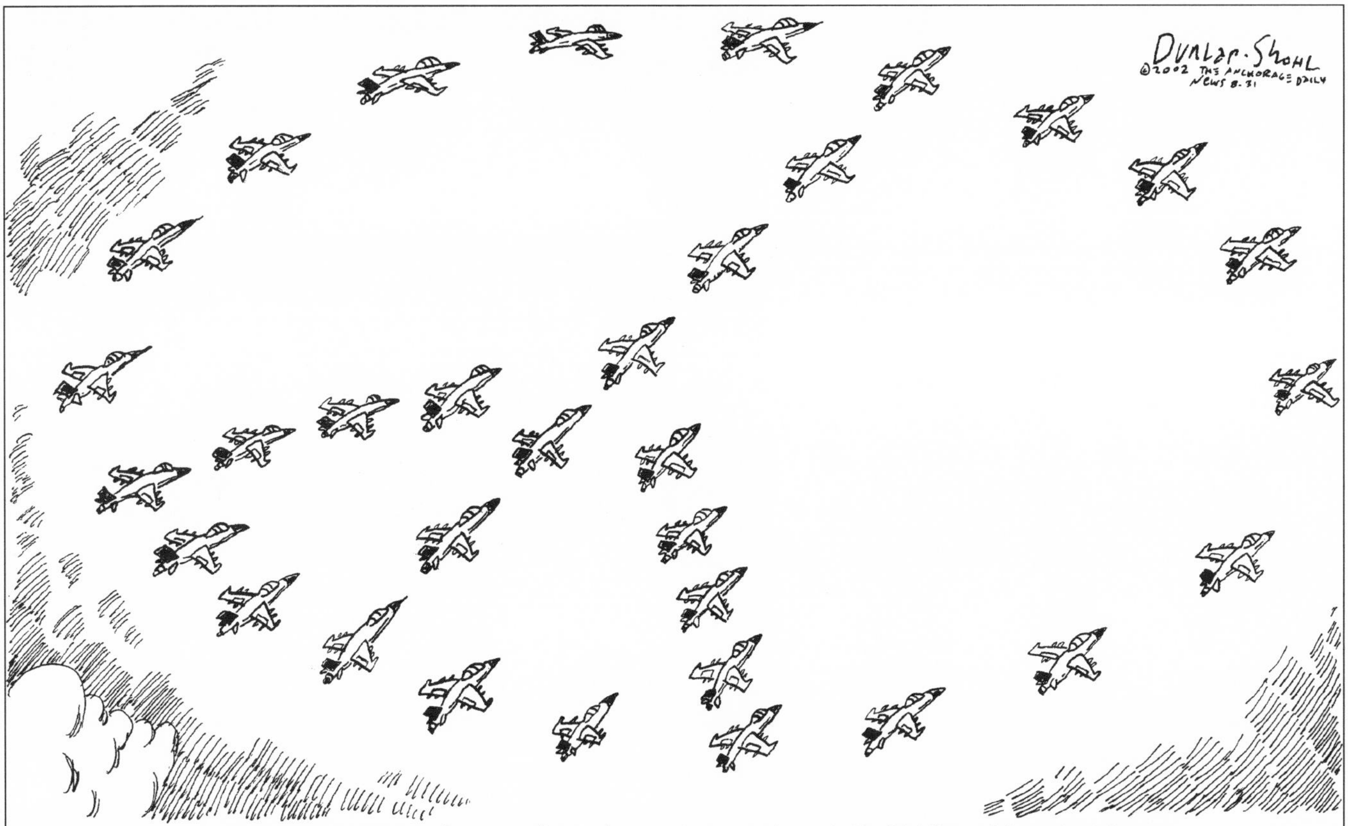
Dunlap-Shohl
©2002 The Anchorage Daily News 8.31

OUR EUROPEAN AND ARAB ALLIES FLYING IN FORMATION ON IRAQ.

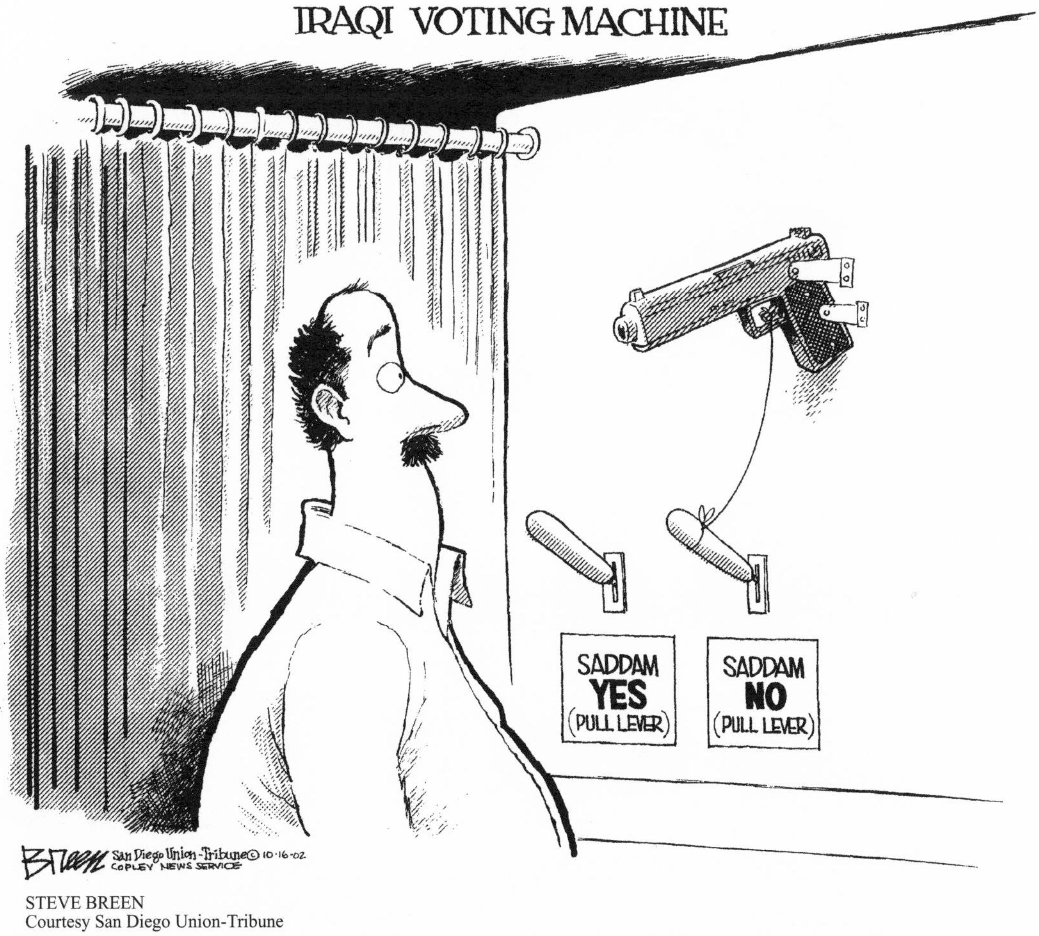
IRAQI VOTING MACHINE
SADDAM YES (PULL LEVER)
SADDAM NO (PULL LEVER)
Breen San Diego Union-Tribune © 10-16-02 COPLEY NEWS SERVICE

STEVE BREEN
Courtesy San Diego Union-Tribune

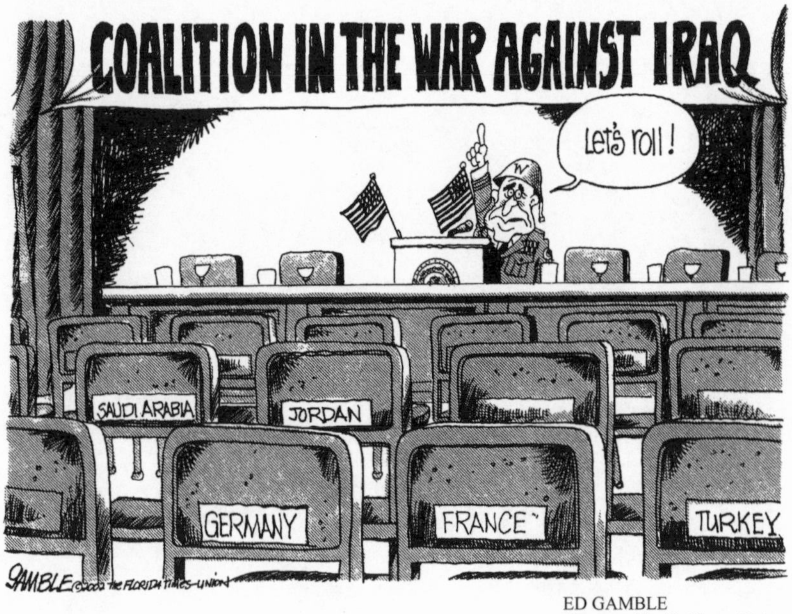
COALITION IN THE WAR AGAINST IRAQ
Let's roll!
SAUDI ARABIA
JORDAN
GERMANY
FRANCE
TURKEY
GAMBLE

ED GAMBLE
Courtesy Florida Times-Union

JAMES McCLOSKEY
Courtesy Daily News Leader (Va.)

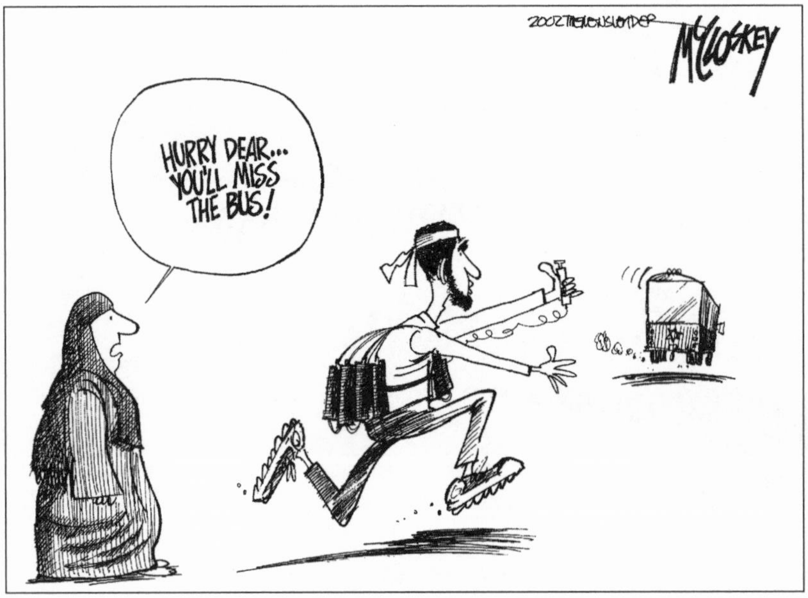
McCLOSKEY
HURRY DEAR... YOU'LL MISS THE BUS!

JIM BORGMAN
Courtesy Cincinnati Enquirer

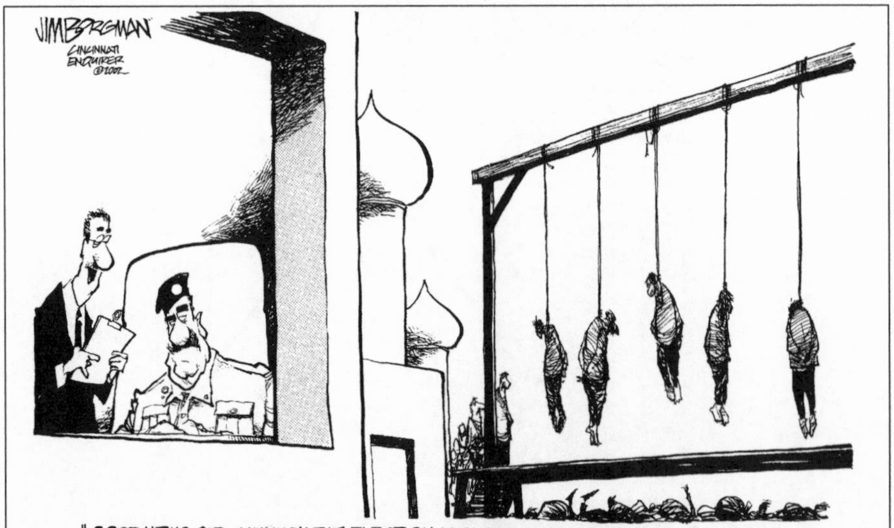
JIM BORGMAN
"GOOD NEWS, SIR... YOU WON THE ELECTION WITH 100 PERCENT OF THE VOTE.... AFTER YOU ELIMINATE THE HANGING CHADS, OF COURSE."

NICK ANDERSON
Courtesy Louisville Courier-Journal

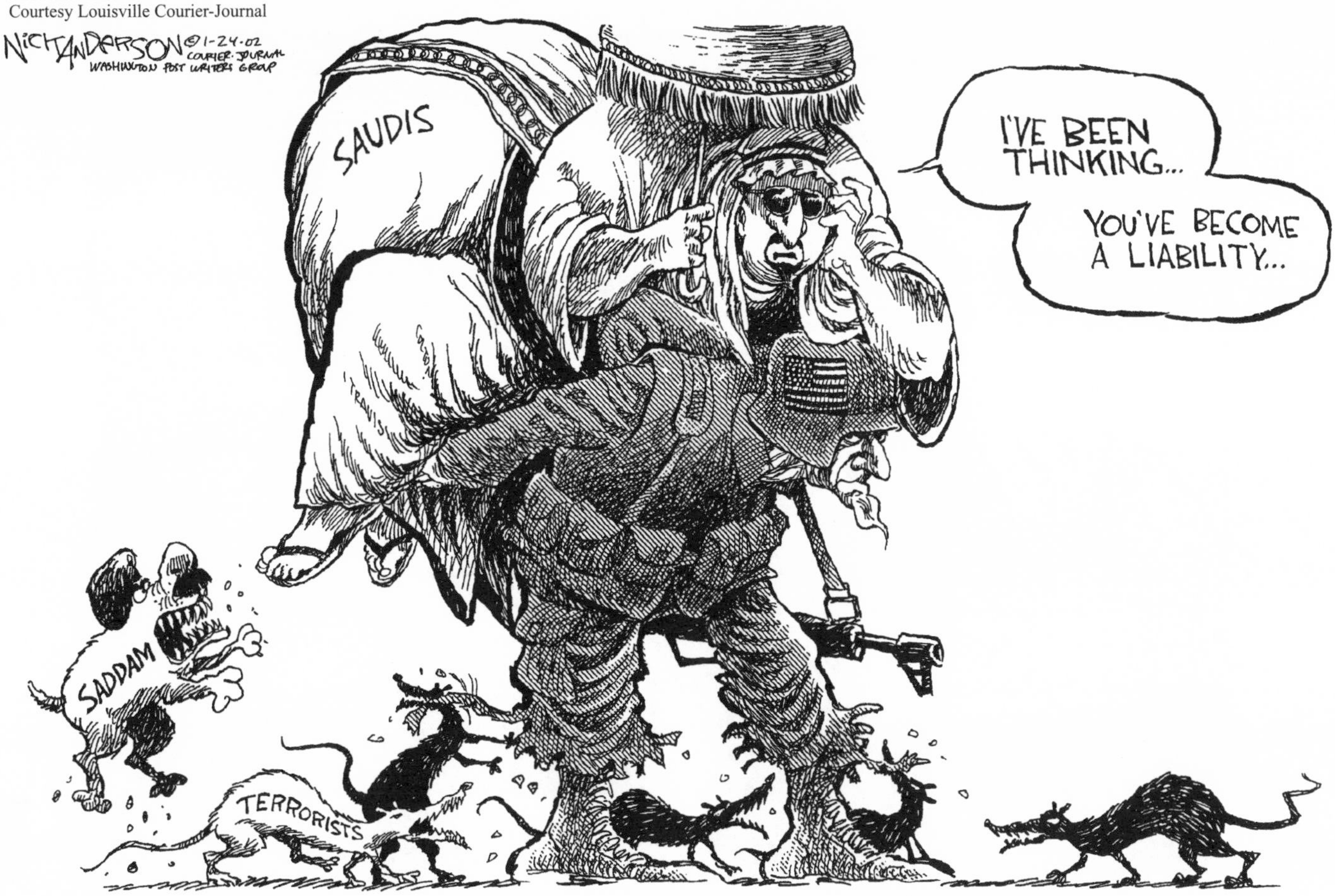

I'VE BEEN THINKING...
YOU'VE BECOME A LIABILITY...
SAUDIS
SADDAM
TERRORISTS

MIKE LUCKOVICH
Courtesy Atlanta Constitution

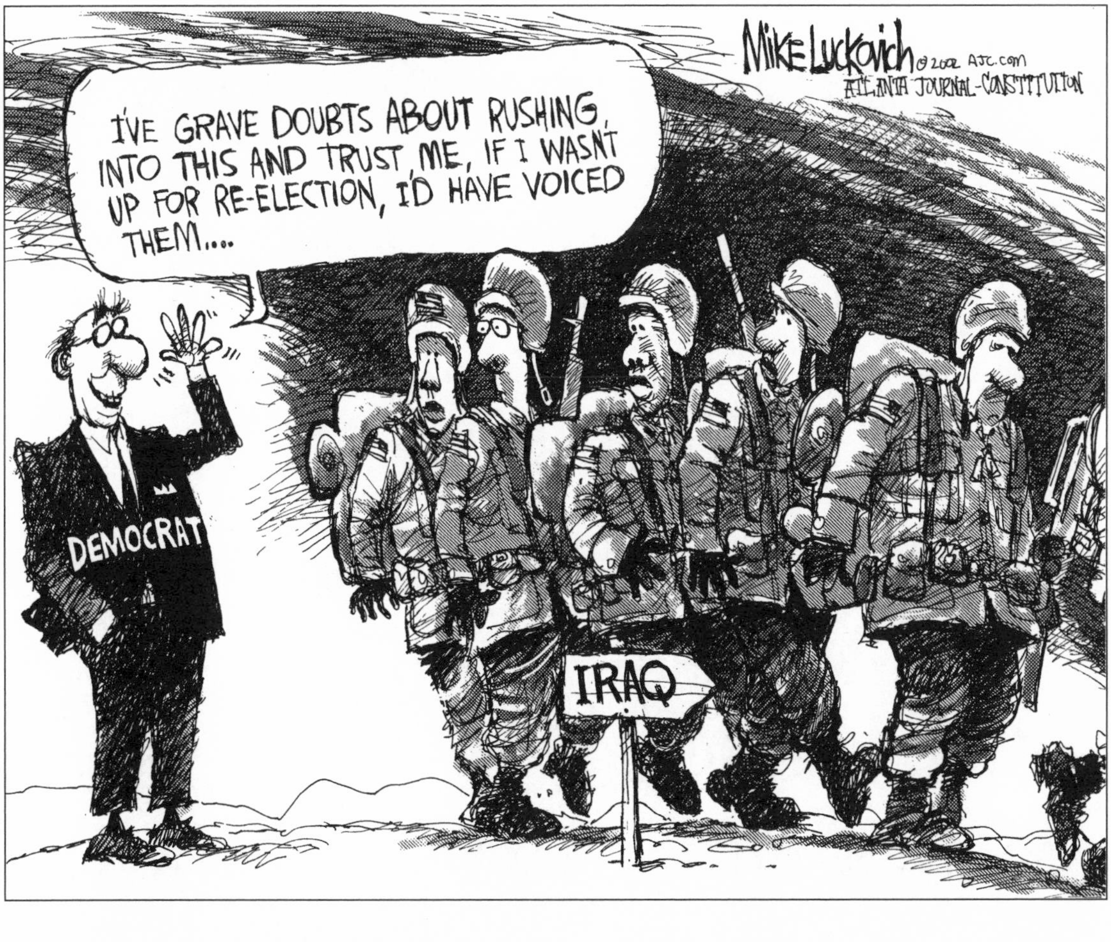

I'VE GRAVE DOUBTS ABOUT RUSHING INTO THIS AND TRUST ME, IF I WASN'T UP FOR RE-ELECTION, I'D HAVE VOICED THEM....
DEMOCRAT
IRAQ

BRIAN FAIRRINGTON
Courtesy Arizona Republic

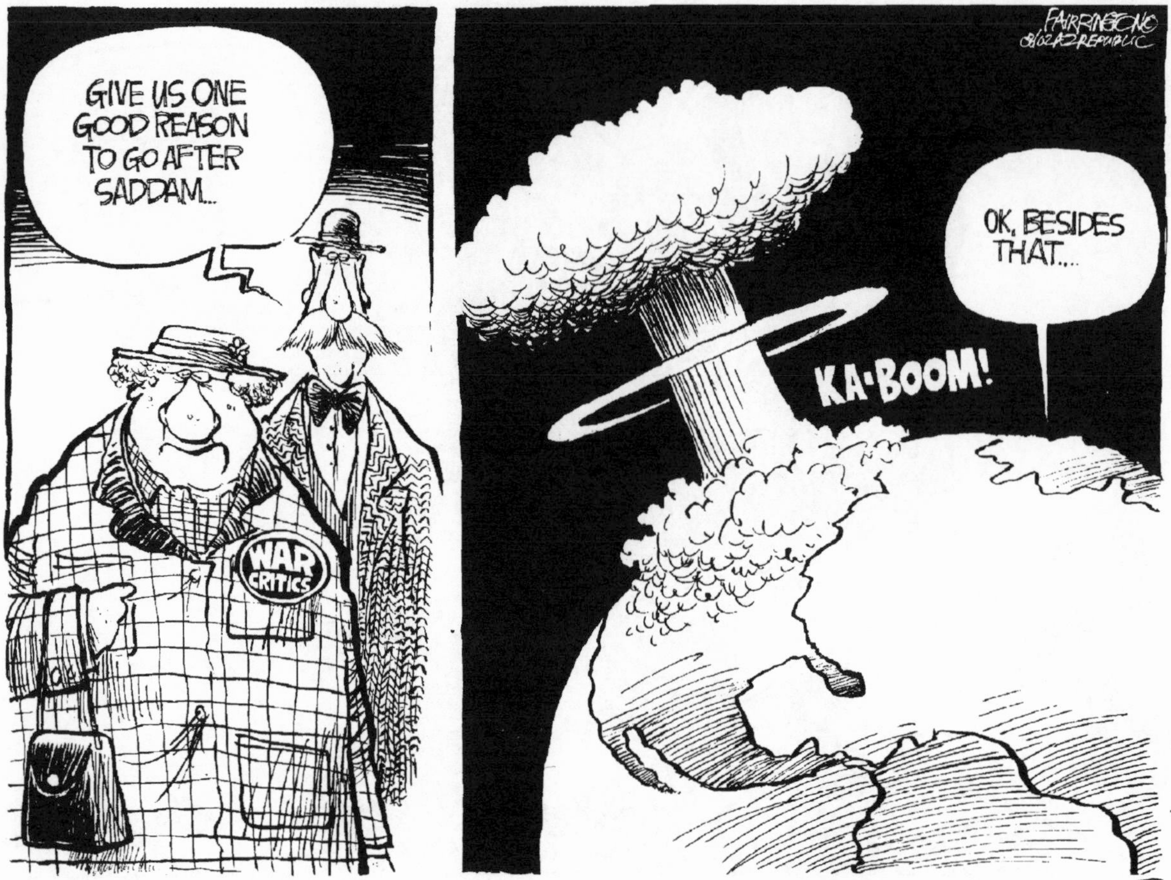
GIVE US ONE GOOD REASON TO GO AFTER SADDAM...
WAR CRITICS
FAIRRINGTON©
KA-BOOM!
OK, BESIDES THAT...

CHIP BECK
Courtesy Associated Features

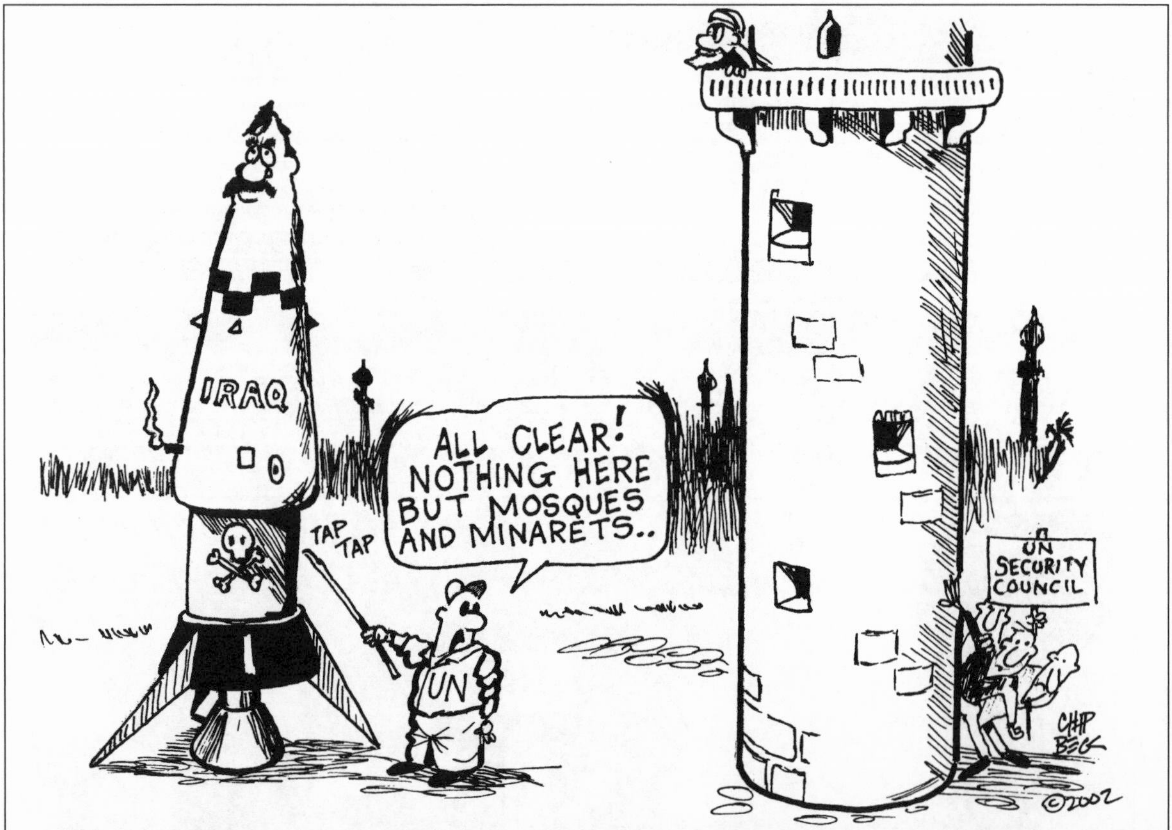
IRAQ
ALL CLEAR! NOTHING HERE BUT MOSQUES AND MINARETS..
TAP TAP
UN
UN SECURITY COUNCIL
CHIP BECK
©2002
IRAQI S.C.U.M. MISSILE WITH SADDAM WARHEAD & UN INSPECTOR

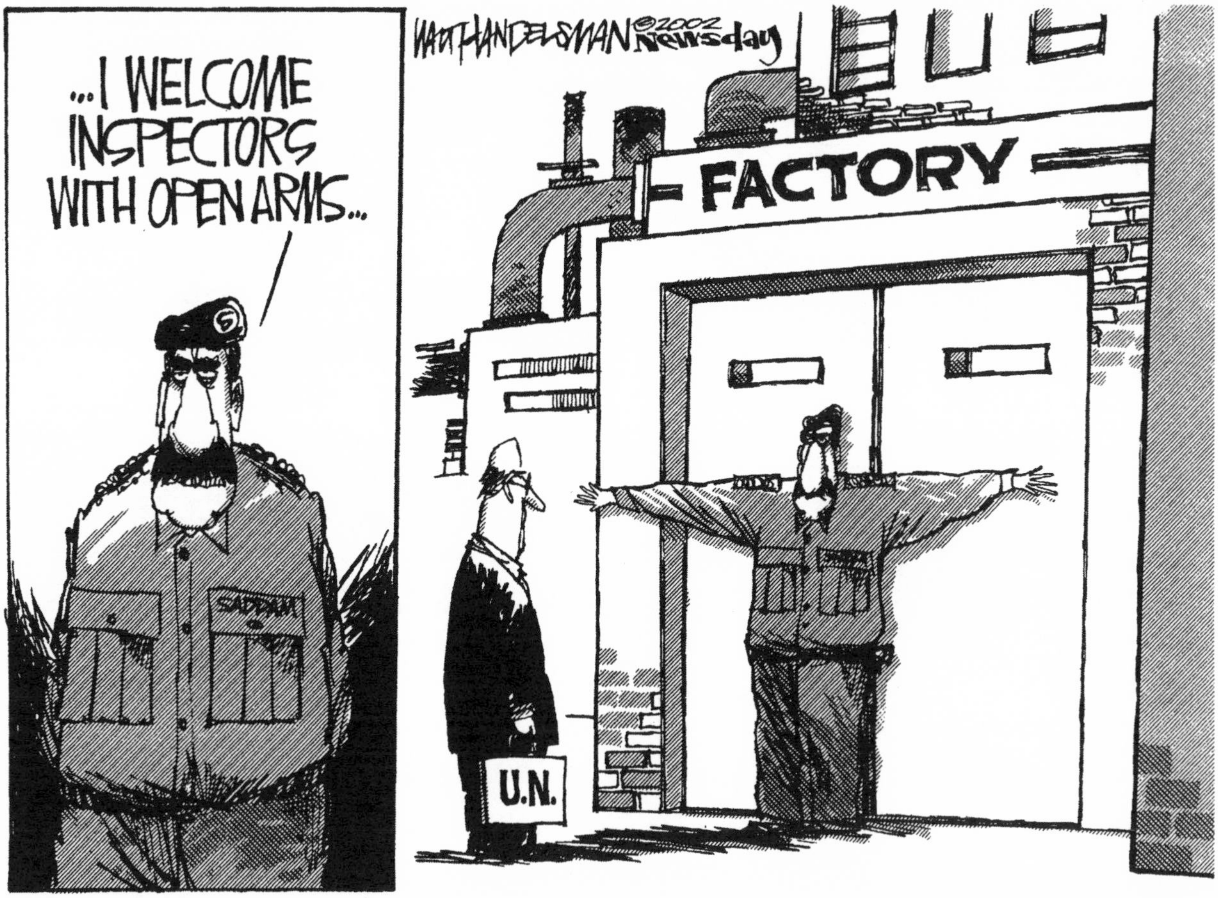
...I WELCOME INSPECTORS WITH OPEN ARMS...
WALT HANDELSMAN ©2002 Newsday
FACTORY
SADDAM
U.N.

WALT HANDELSMAN
Courtesy Newsday

BOB GORRELL
Courtesy America Online News

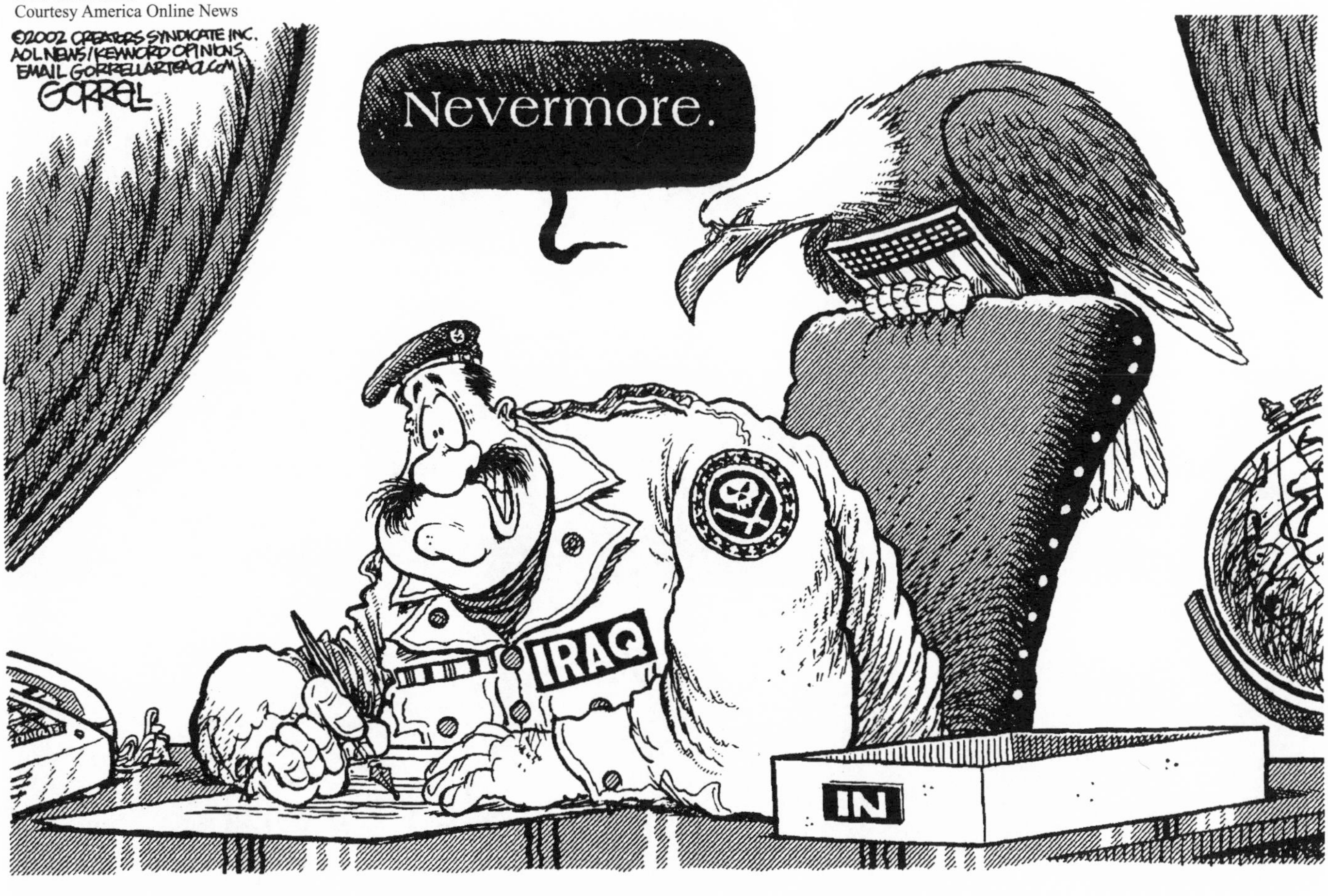
©2002 CREATORS SYNDICATE INC.
GORRELL
Nevermore.
IRAQ
IN

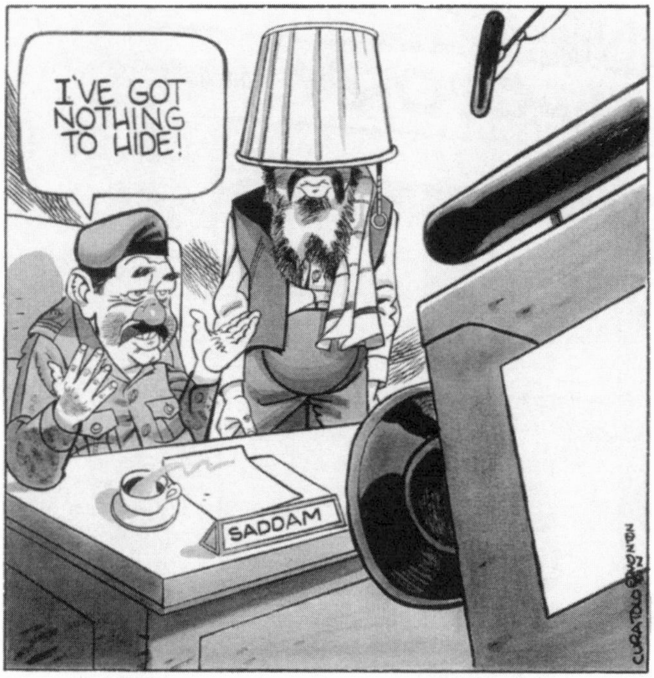
I'VE GOT NOTHING TO HIDE!
SADDAM

FRED CURATOLO
Courtesy Edmonton Sun

BRIAN GABLE
Courtesy Globe and Mail (Canada)

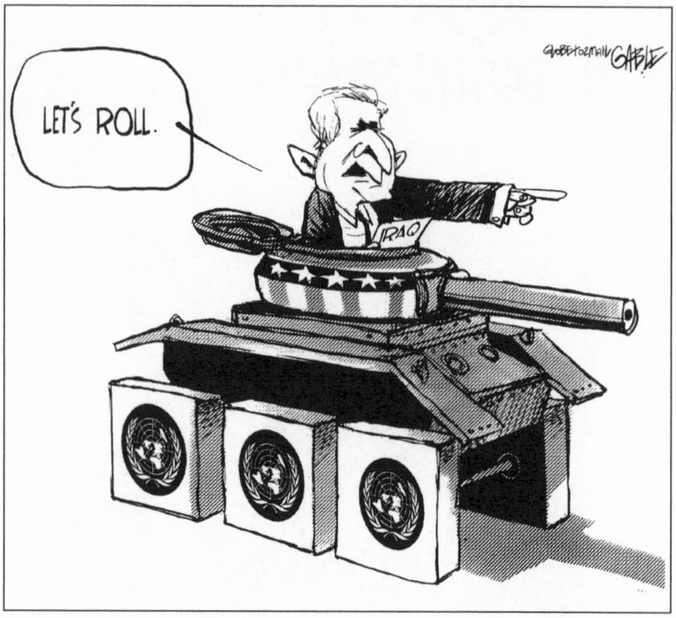
LET'S ROLL.
IRAQ
GABLE

MICHAEL RAMIREZ
Courtesy Los Angeles Times

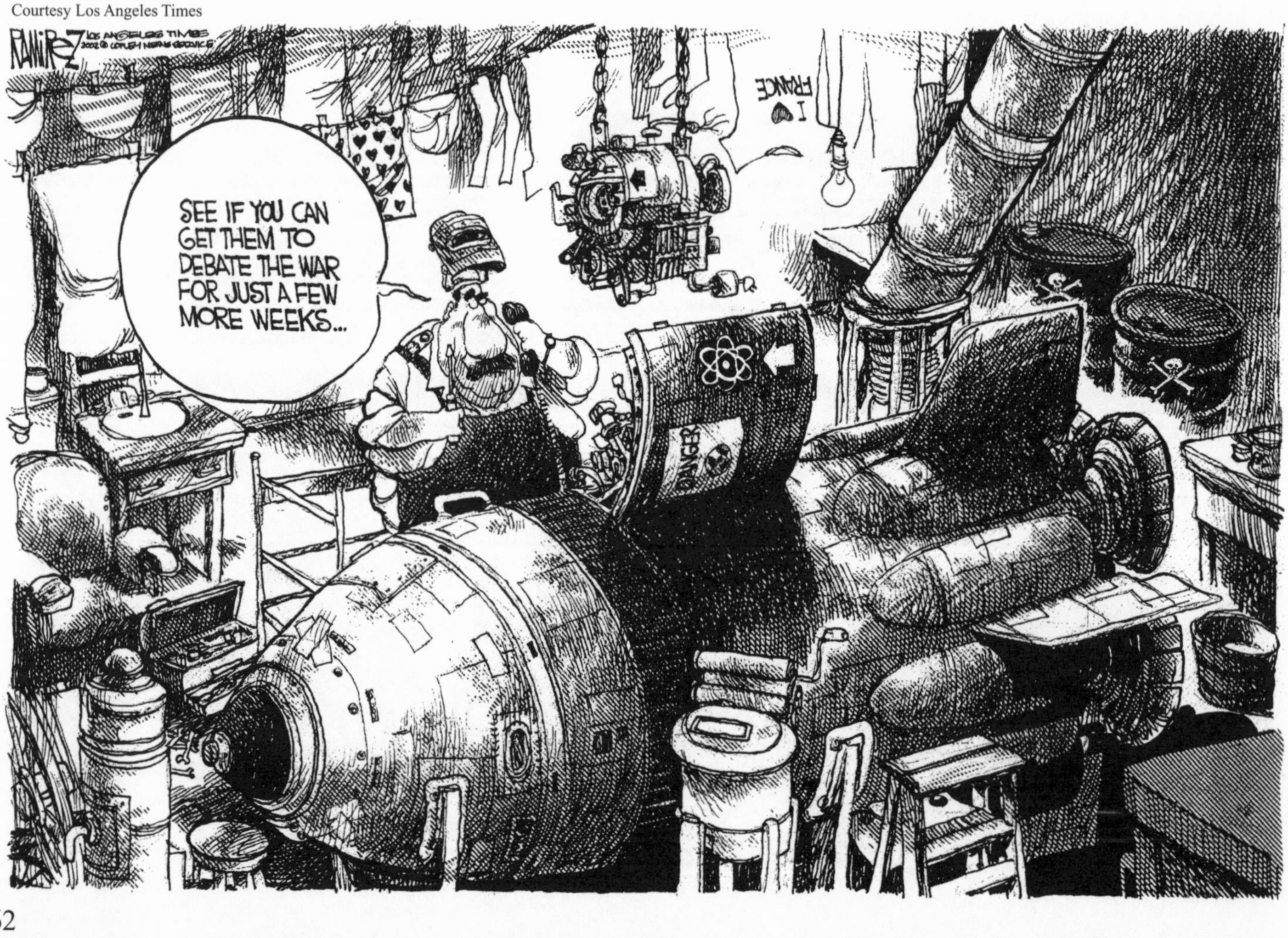
RAMIREZ
SEE IF YOU CAN GET THEM TO DEBATE THE WAR FOR JUST A FEW MORE WEEKS...
DANGER

JOE HELLER
Courtesy Green Bay Press-Gazette

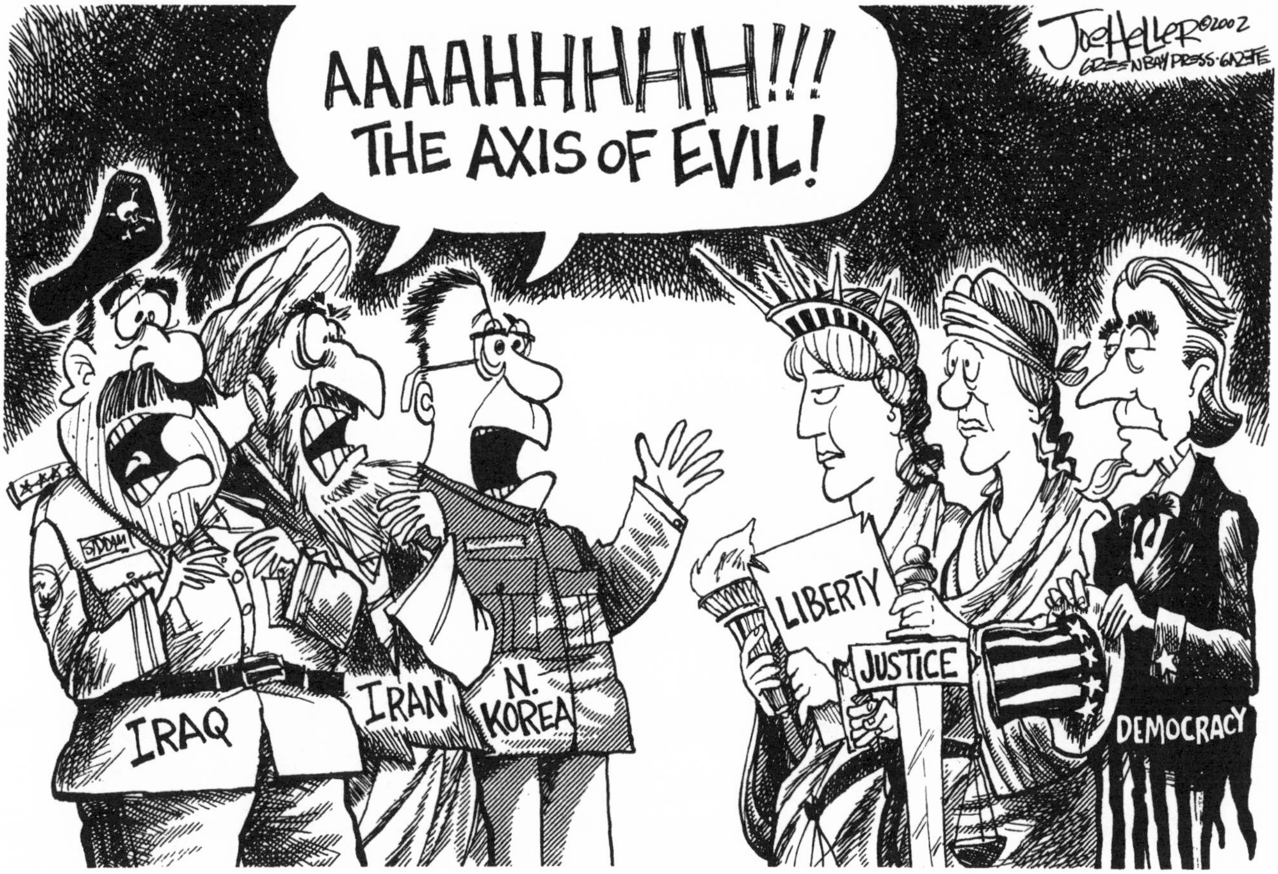

JoeHeller ©2002 GREEN BAY PRESS-GAZETTE
AAAAHHHHH!!!
THE AXIS OF EVIL!
SADDAM
IRAQ
IRAN
N. KOREA
LIBERTY
JUSTICE
DEMOCRACY

MIKE LUCKOVICH
Courtesy Atlanta Constitution

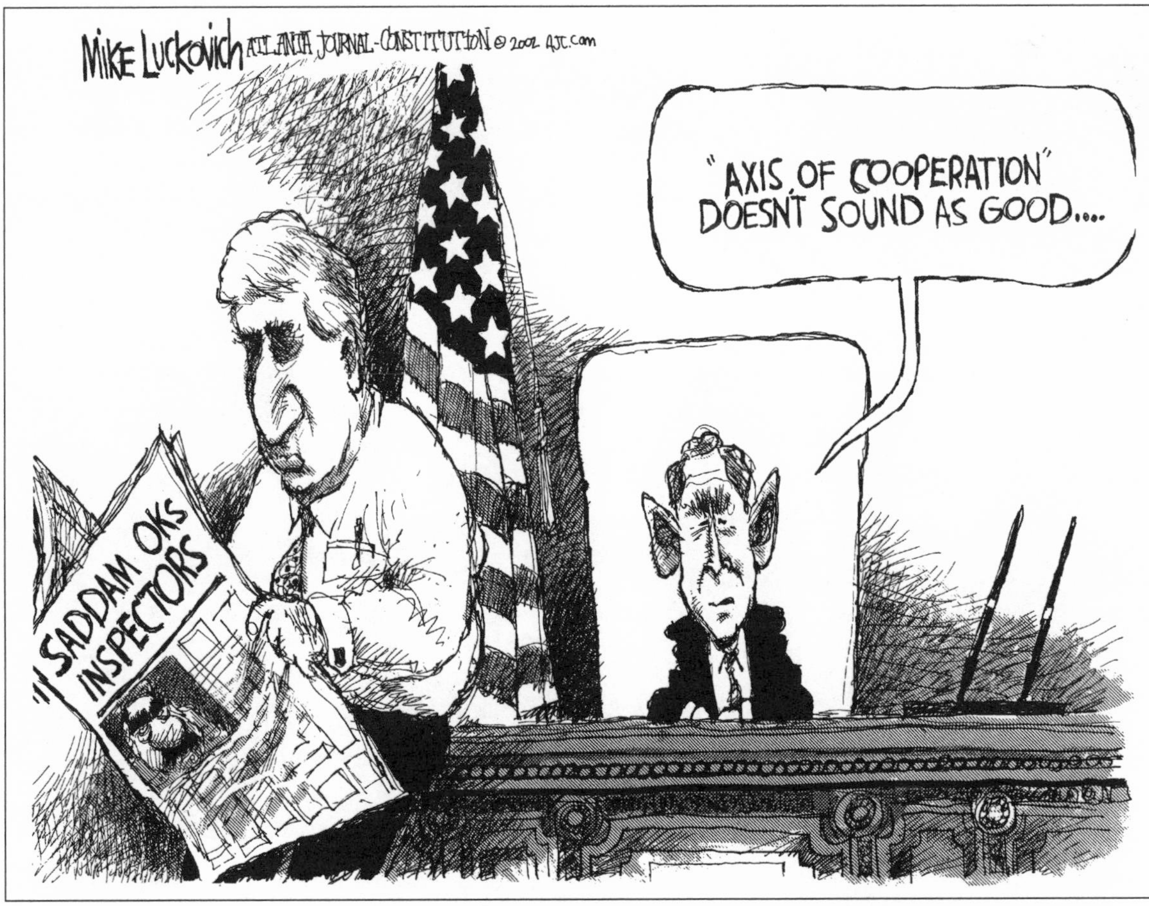

MIKE LUCKOVICH ATLANTA JOURNAL-CONSTITUTION © 2002 AJC.com
"AXIS OF COOPERATION" DOESN'T SOUND AS GOOD....
SADDAM OKS INSPECTORS

JOHN WEISS
Courtesy Santa Cruz Sentinel

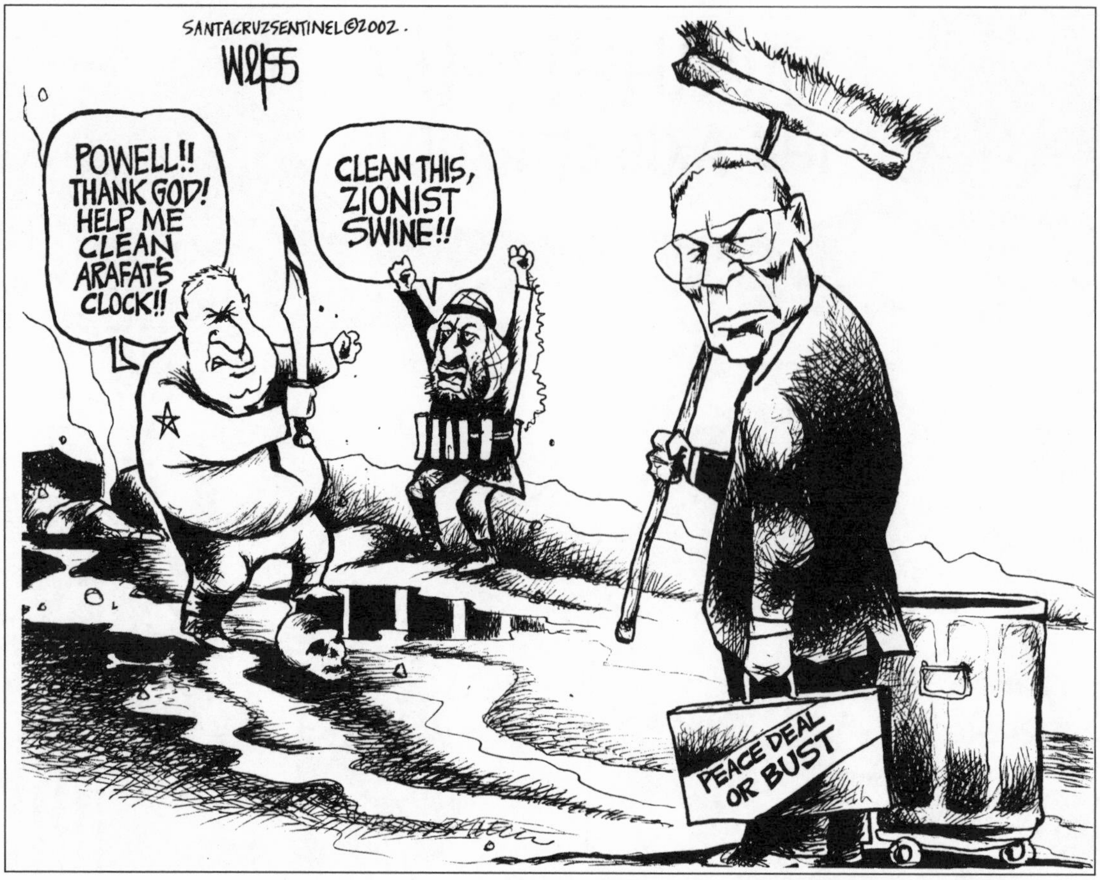
SANTACRUZSENTINEL©2002.
WEISS
POWELL!! THANK GOD! HELP ME CLEAN ARAFAT'S CLOCK!!
CLEAN THIS, ZIONIST SWINE!!
PEACE DEAL OR BUST

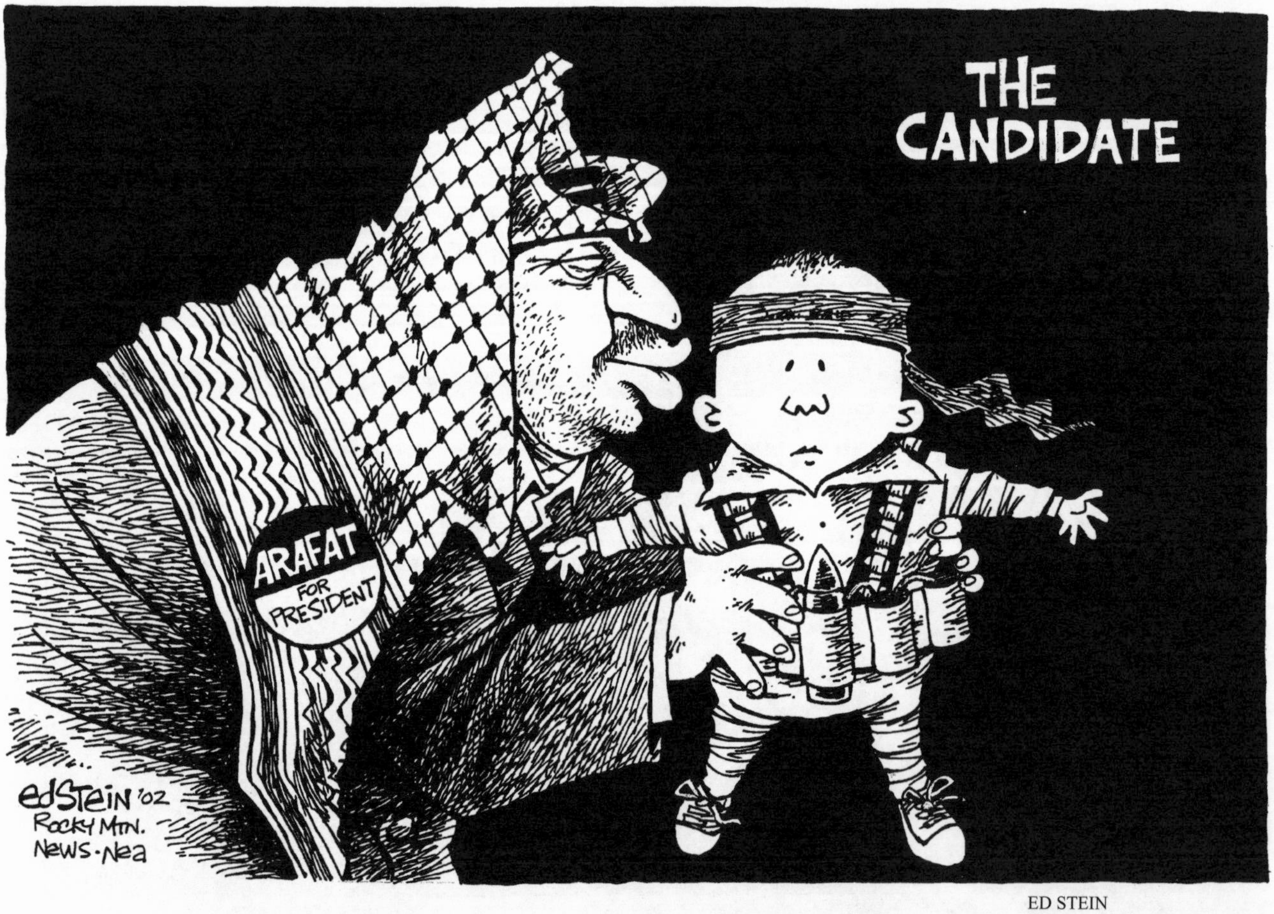
THE CANDIDATE
ARAFAT FOR PRESIDENT
edSTEIN '02 Rocky Mtn. News-Nea

ED STEIN
Courtesy Rocky Mountain News

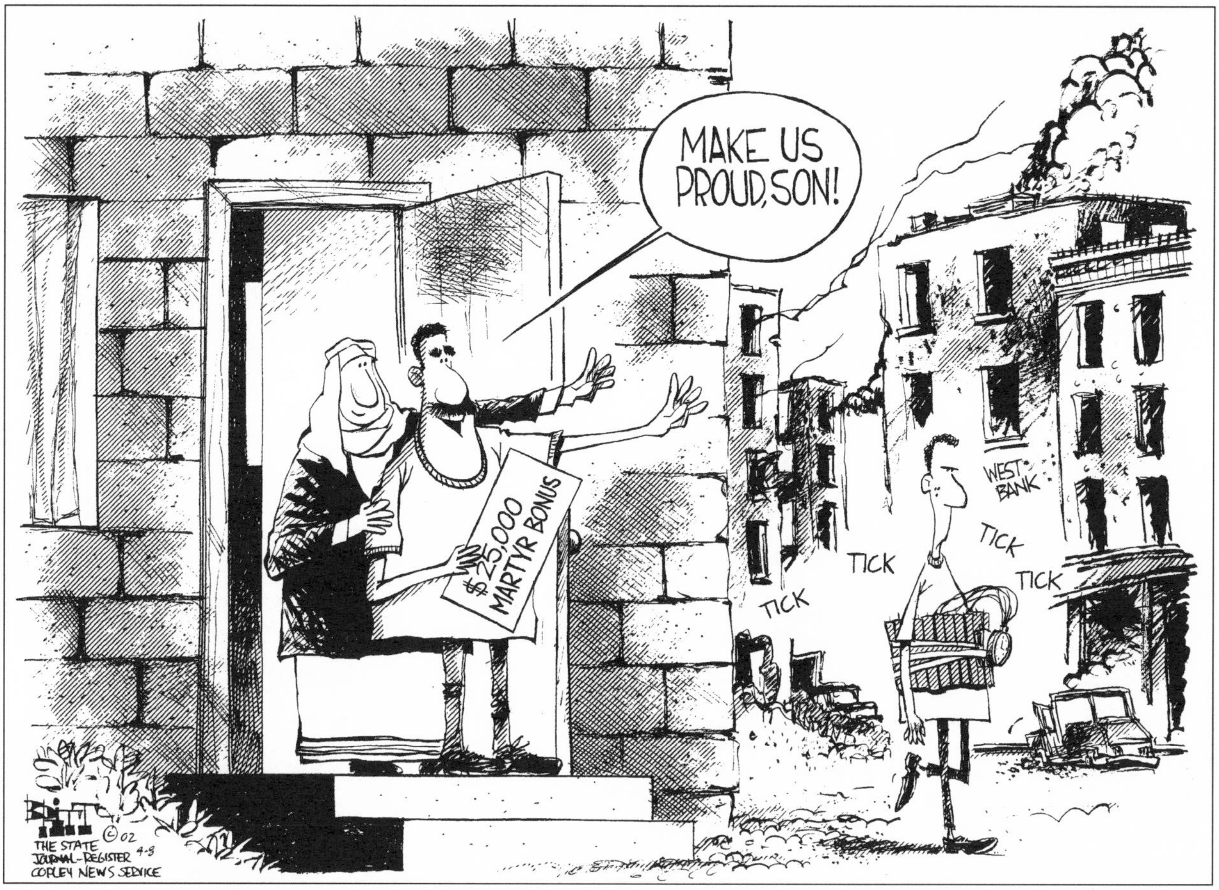
MAKE US PROUD, SON!
$25,000 MARTYR BONUS
TICK
TICK
TICK
TICK
WEST BANK
BRITT
©02
4-8
THE STATE JOURNAL-REGISTER
COPLEY NEWS SERVICE

CHRIS BRITT
Courtesy State Journal-Register (Ill.)

MICHAEL RAMIREZ
Courtesy Los Angeles Times

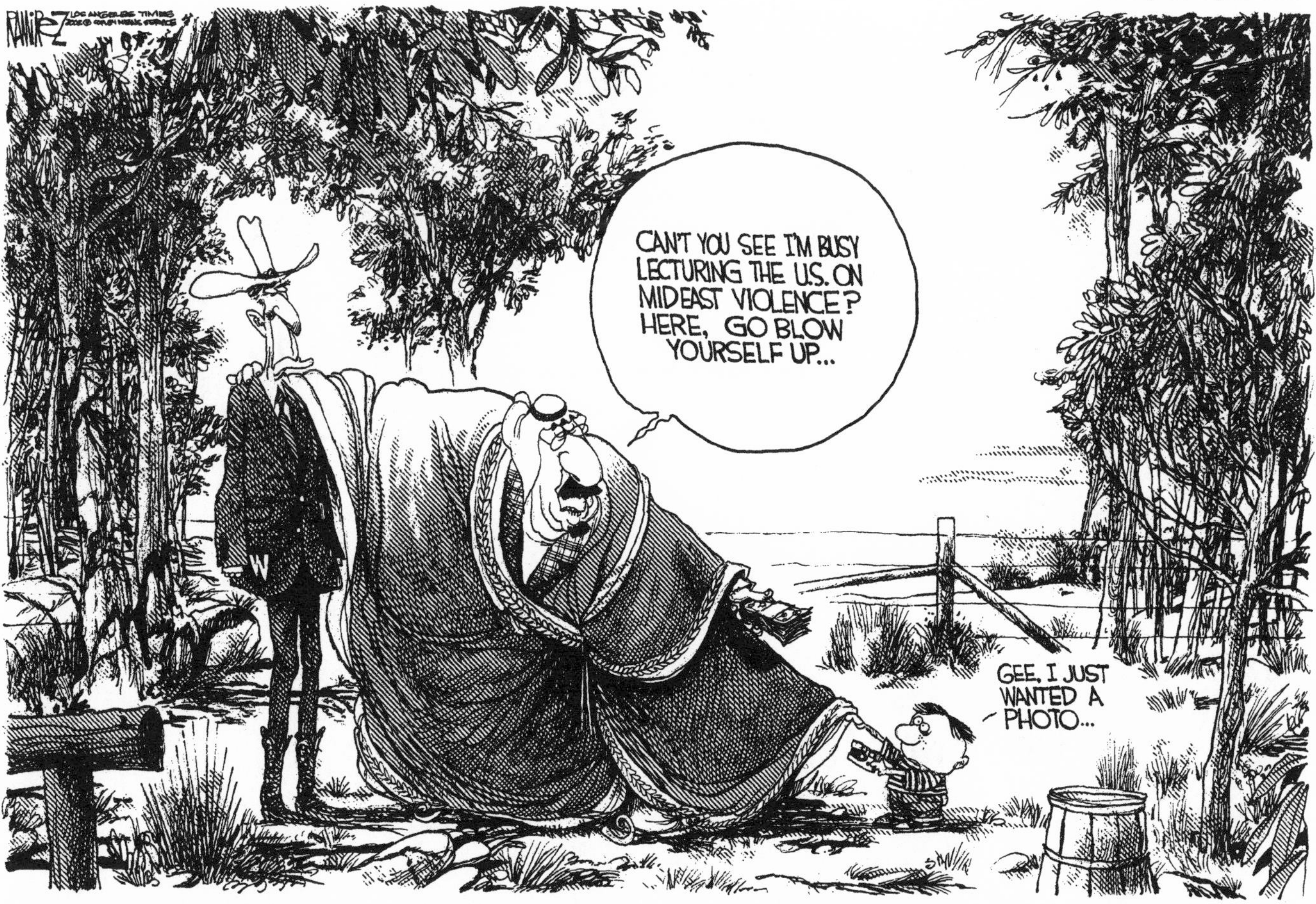
RAMIREZ
CAN'T YOU SEE I'M BUSY LECTURING THE U.S. ON MIDEAST VIOLENCE? HERE, GO BLOW YOURSELF UP...
GEE, I JUST WANTED A PHOTO...

MIKE GRASTON
Courtesy Windsor Star

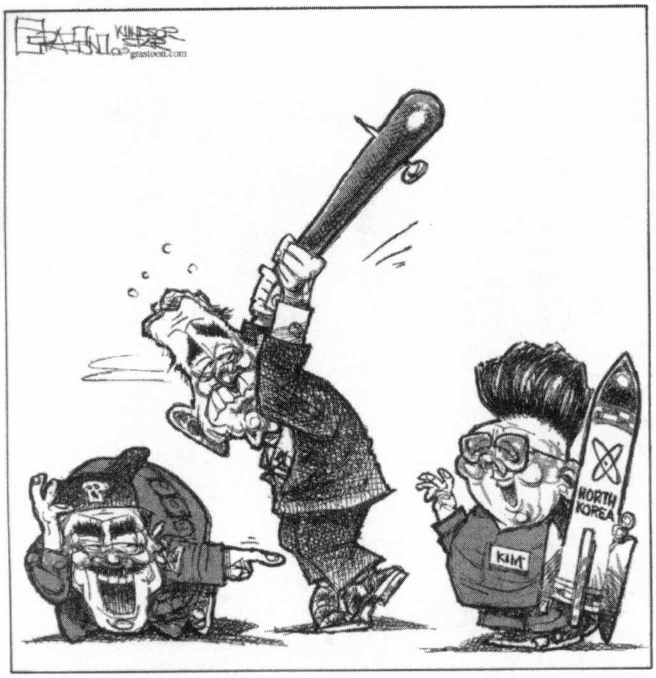
NORTH KOREA
KIM

BILL GARNER
Courtesy Washington Times

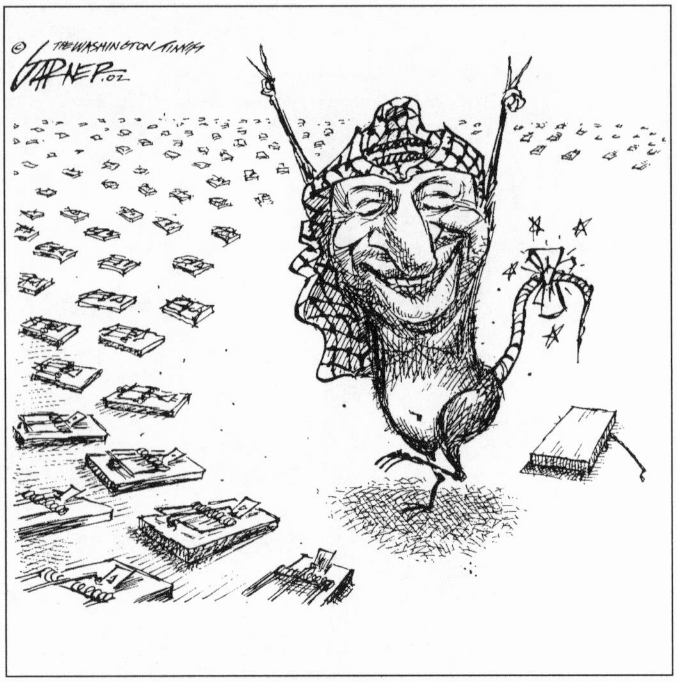

JIM BUSH
Courtesy Providence Journal (R.I.)

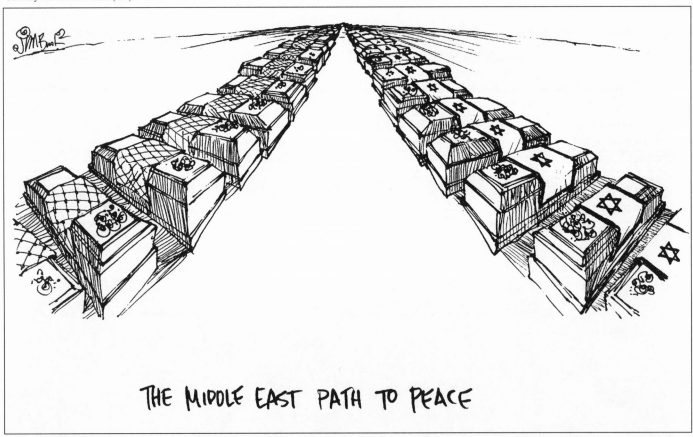

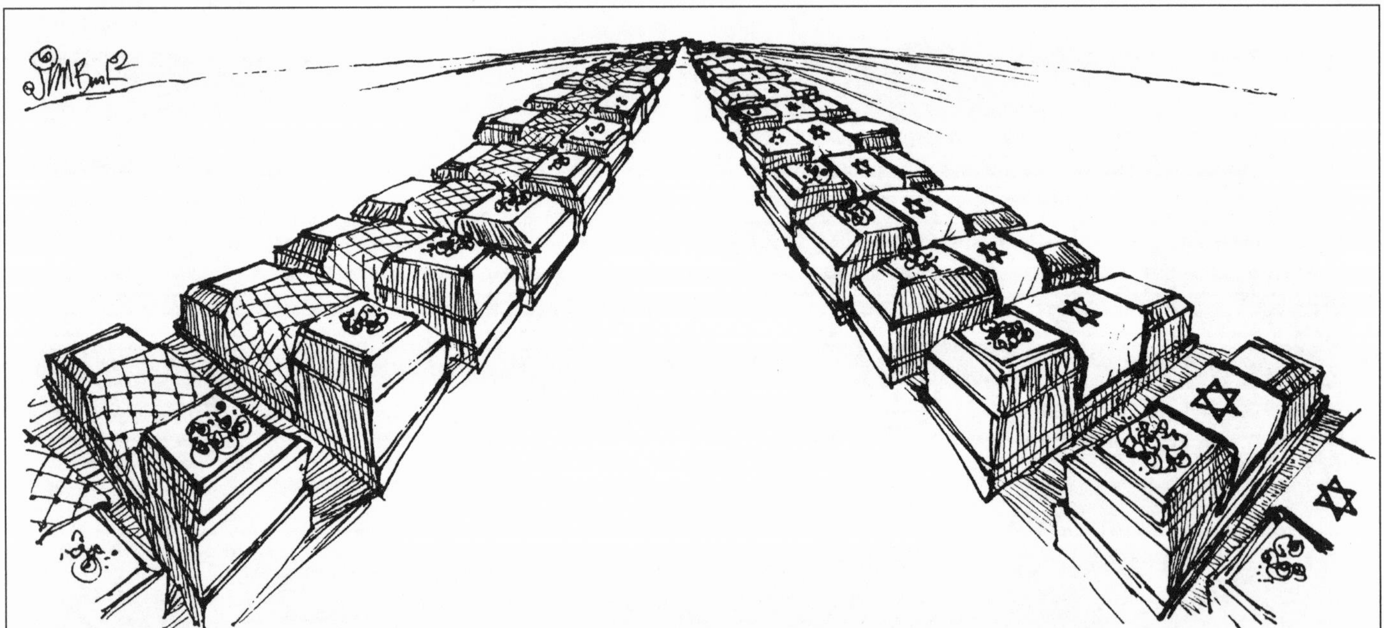
THE MIDDLE EAST PATH TO PEACE

STEVE BREEN
Courtesy San Diego Union-Tribune

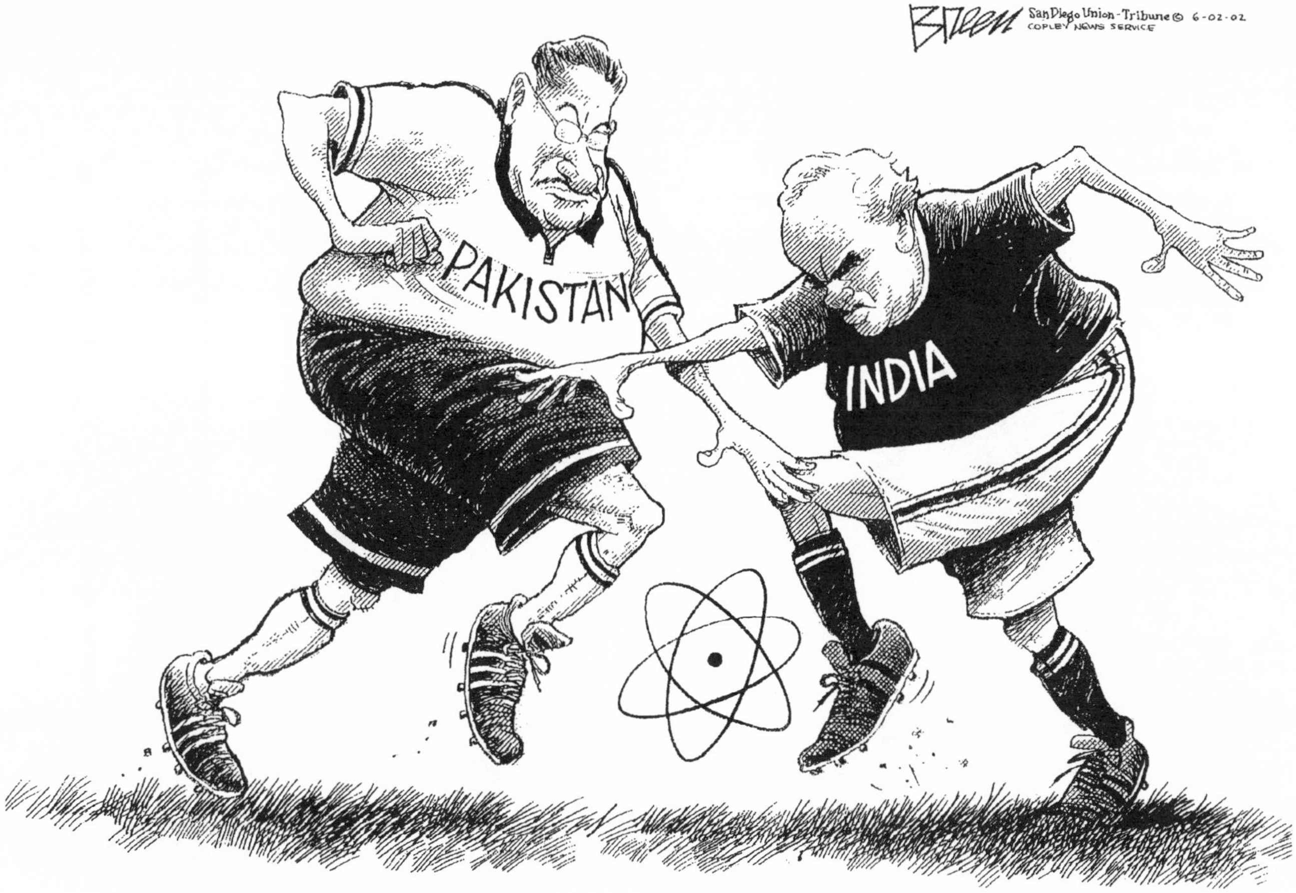
BREEN
San Diego Union-Tribune © 6-02-02
COPLEY NEWS SERVICE
PAKISTAN
INDIA

ANN CLEAVES
Courtesy Palisadian Post

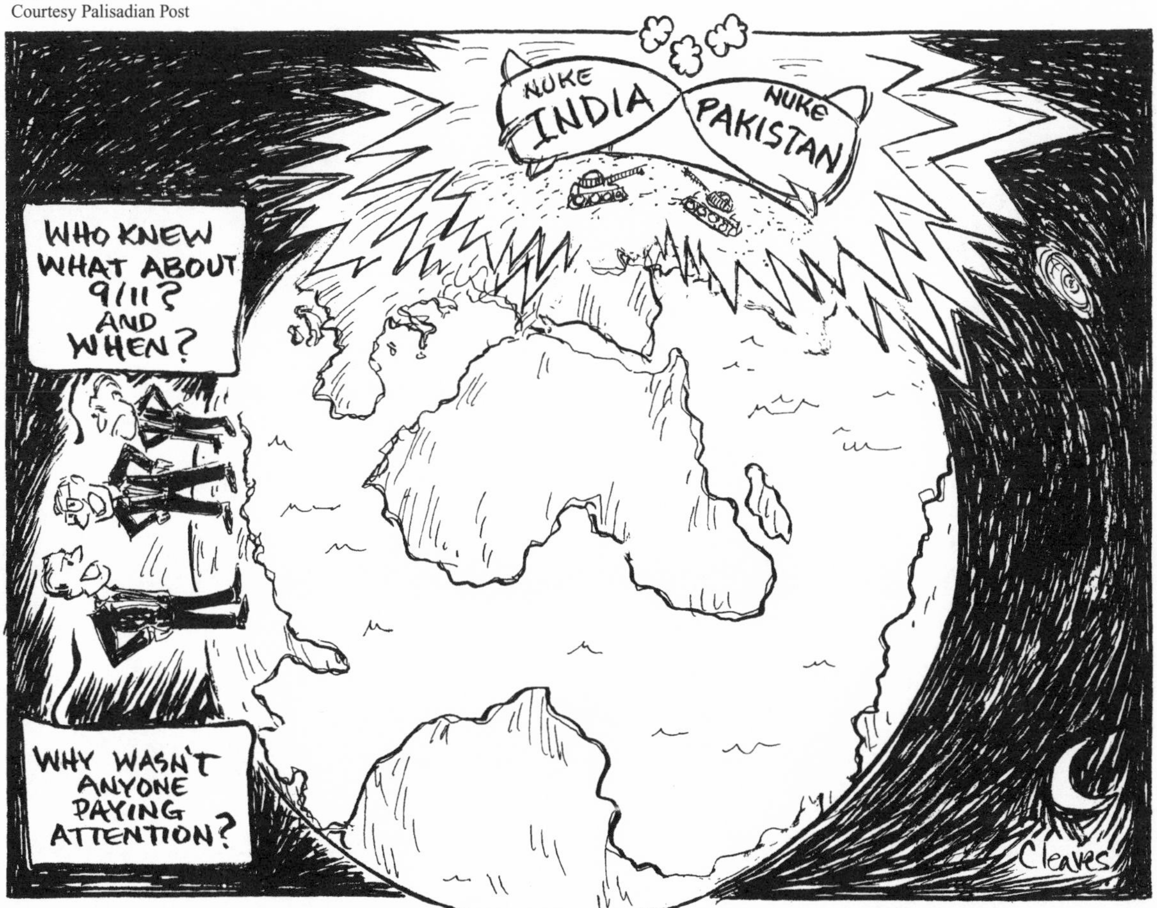
NUKE INDIA
NUKE PAKISTAN
WHO KNEW WHAT ABOUT 9/11? AND WHEN?
WHY WASN'T ANYONE PAYING ATTENTION?
Cleaves

ED GAMBLE
Courtesy Florida Times-Union

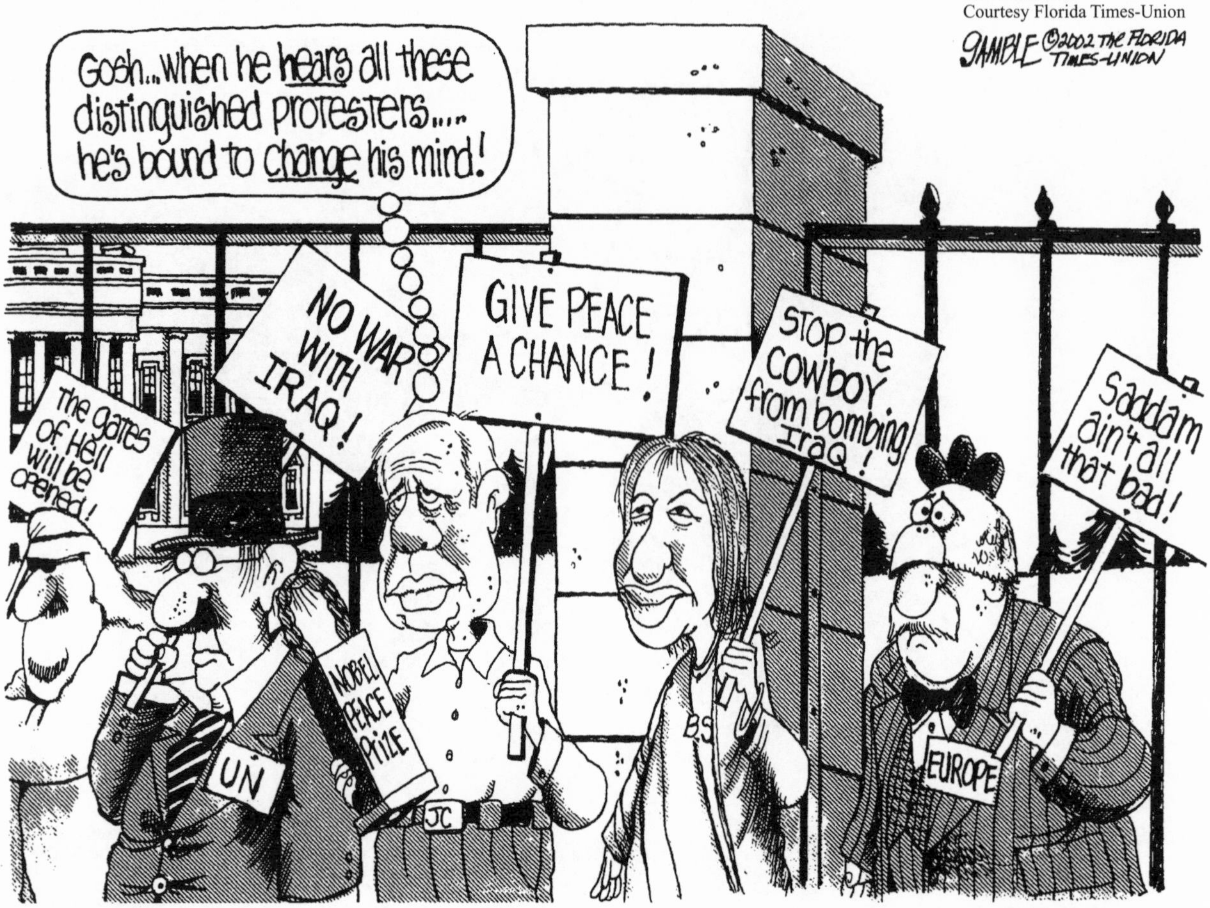
GAMBLE ©2002 THE FLORIDA TIMES-UNION
Gosh... when he hears all these distinguished protesters.... he's bound to change his mind!
The gates of Hell will be opened!
NO WAR WITH IRAQ!
GIVE PEACE A CHANCE!
Stop the COWBOY from bombing IRAQ!
Saddam ain't all that bad!
NOBEL PEACE PRIZE
UN
JC
BS
EUROPE

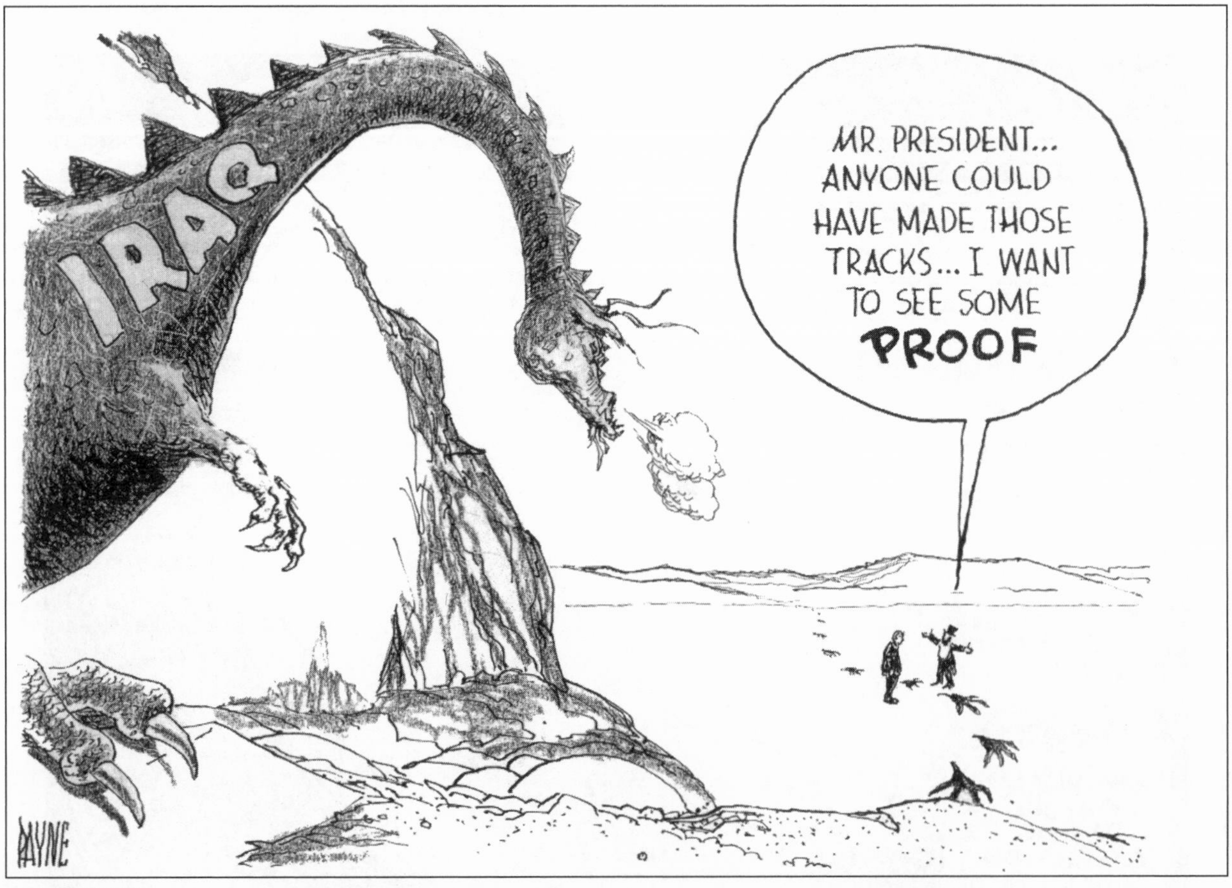
IRAQ
MR. PRESIDENT... ANYONE COULD HAVE MADE THOSE TRACKS... I WANT TO SEE SOME PROOF
PAYNE

EUGENE PAYNE
Courtesy Charlotte Observer

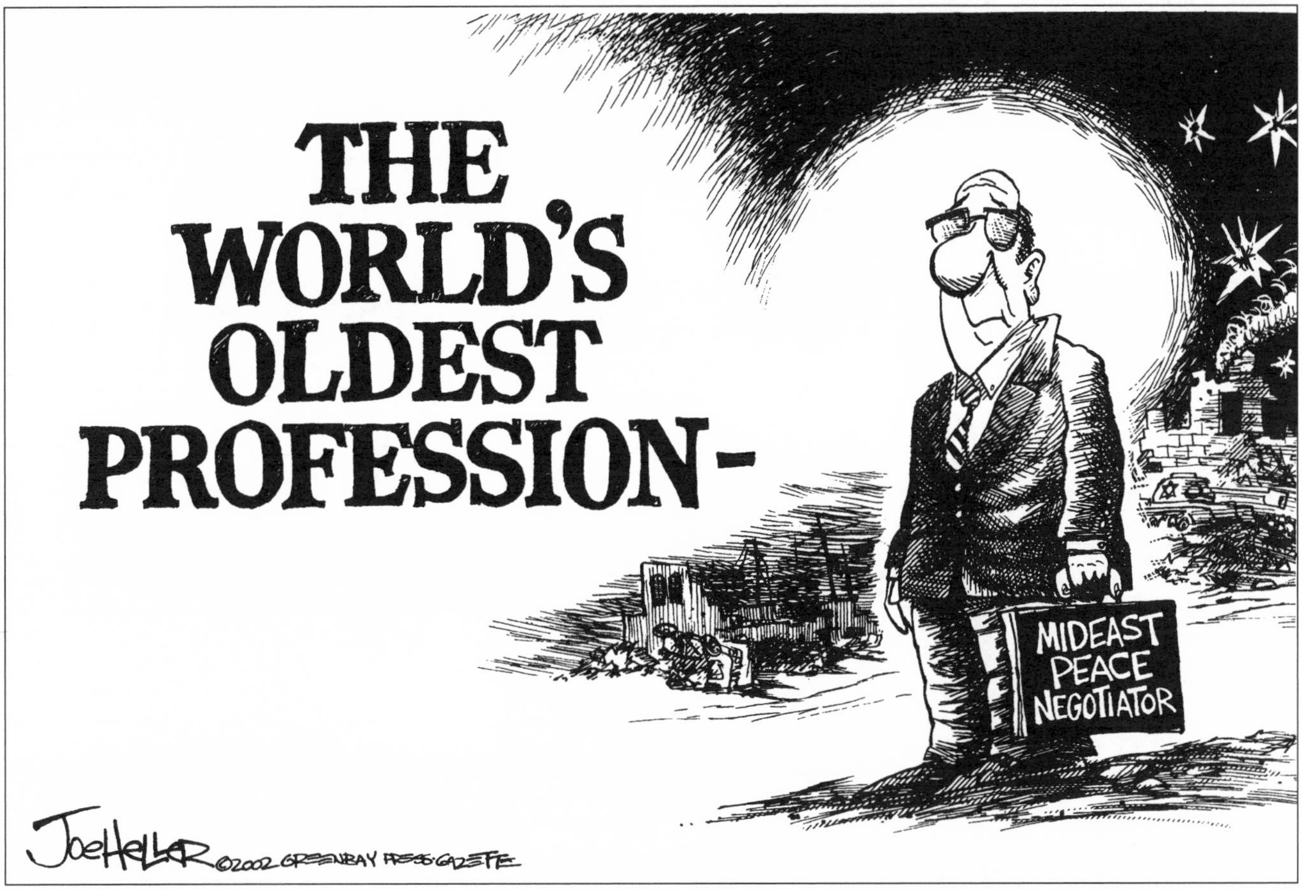
THE WORLD'S OLDEST PROFESSION-
MIDEAST PEACE NEGOTIATOR
JoeHeller ©2002 GREENBAY PRESS-GAZETTE

JOE HELLER
Courtesy Green Bay Press-Gazette

KIRK ANDERSON
Courtesy St. Paul Pioneer Press

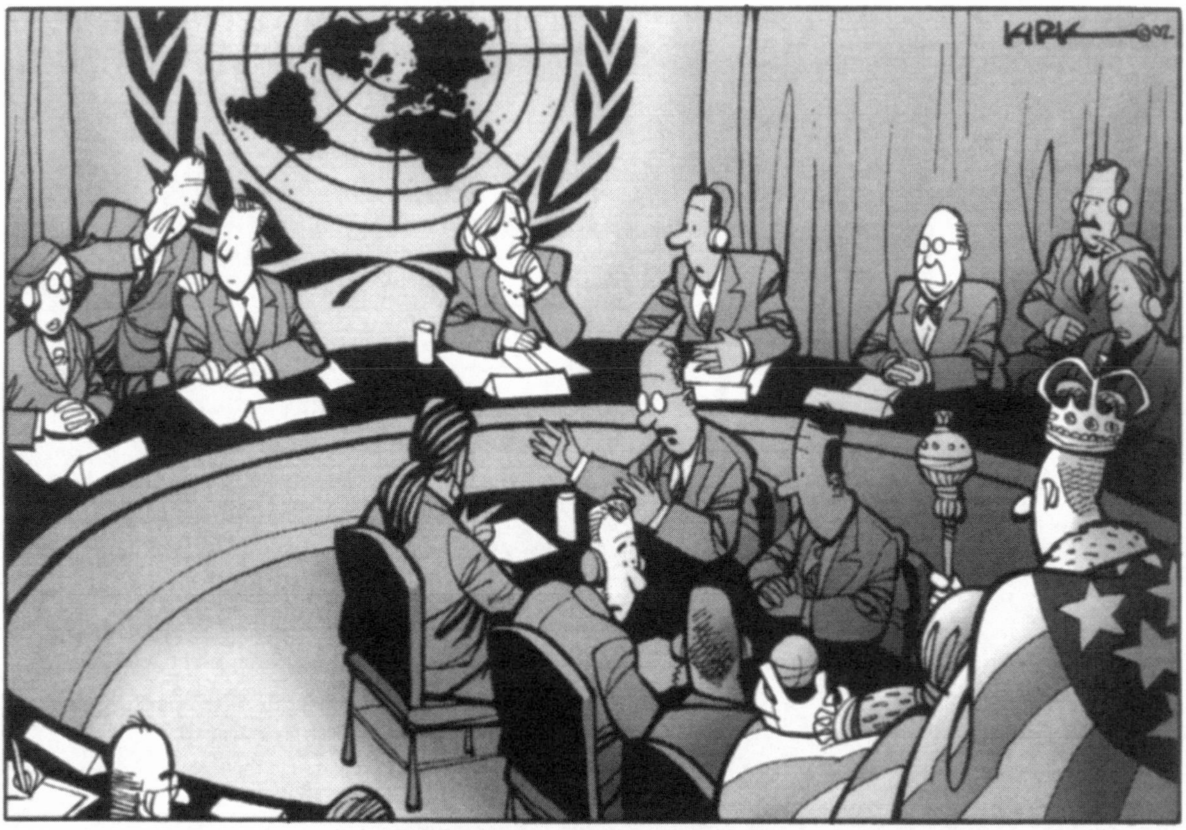
KIRK ©02

GLOBAL DEMOCRACY

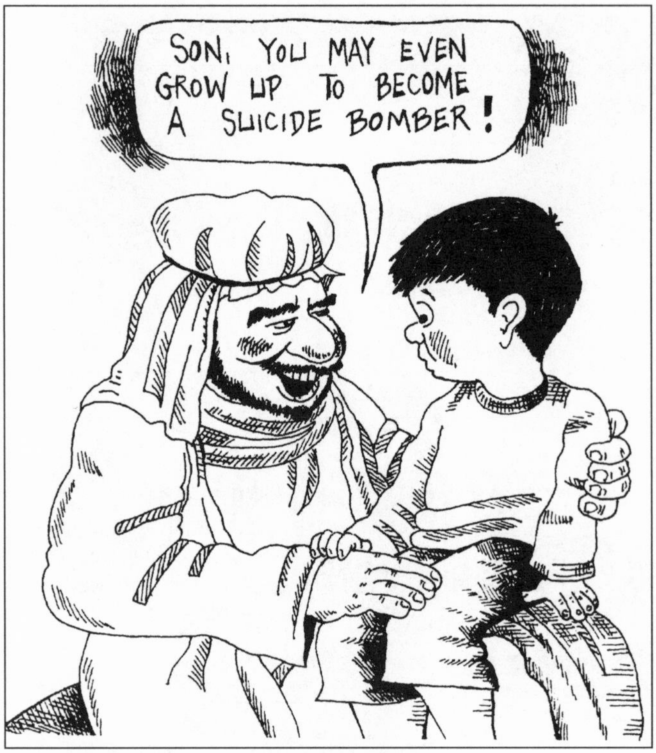
SON, YOU MAY EVEN GROW UP TO BECOME A SUICIDE BOMBER!

LINDA BOILEAU
Courtesy Frankfort State Journal (Ky.)

J. P. TROSTE
Courtesy Chapel Hill Herald

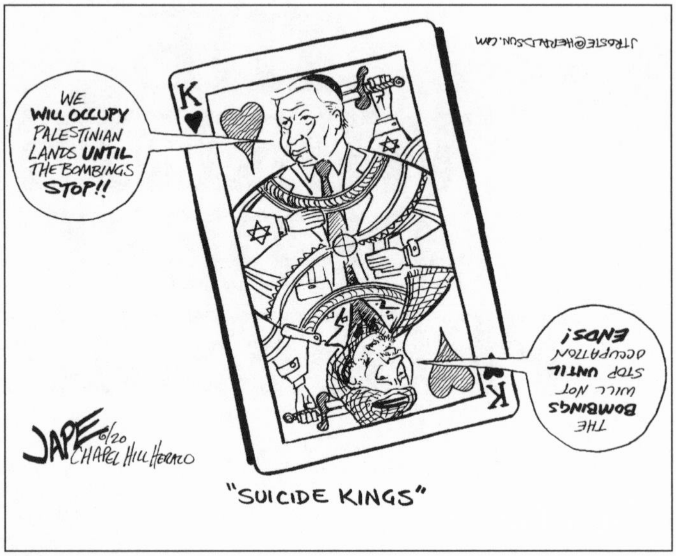
WE WILL OCCUPY PALESTINIAN LANDS UNTIL THE BOMBINGS STOP!!
THE BOMBINGS WILL NOT STOP UNTIL OCCUPATION ENDS!
JAPE 6/20 CHAPEL HILL HERALD
"SUICIDE KINGS"

JAMES CASCIARI
Courtesy Vero Beach Press-Journal

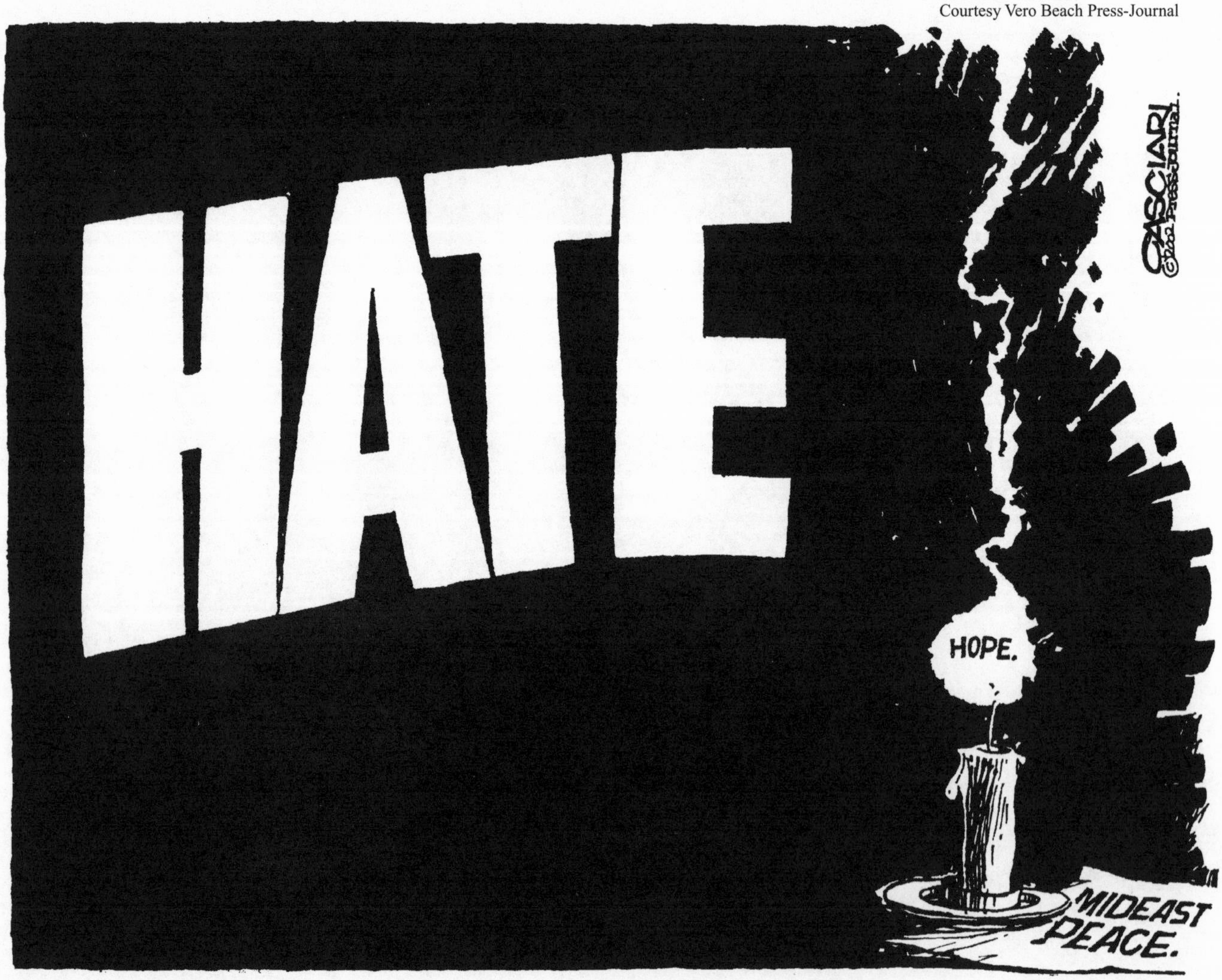
HATE
HOPE.
MIDEAST PEACE.
CASCIARI

STEVE KELLEY
Courtesy The Times-Picayune (La.)

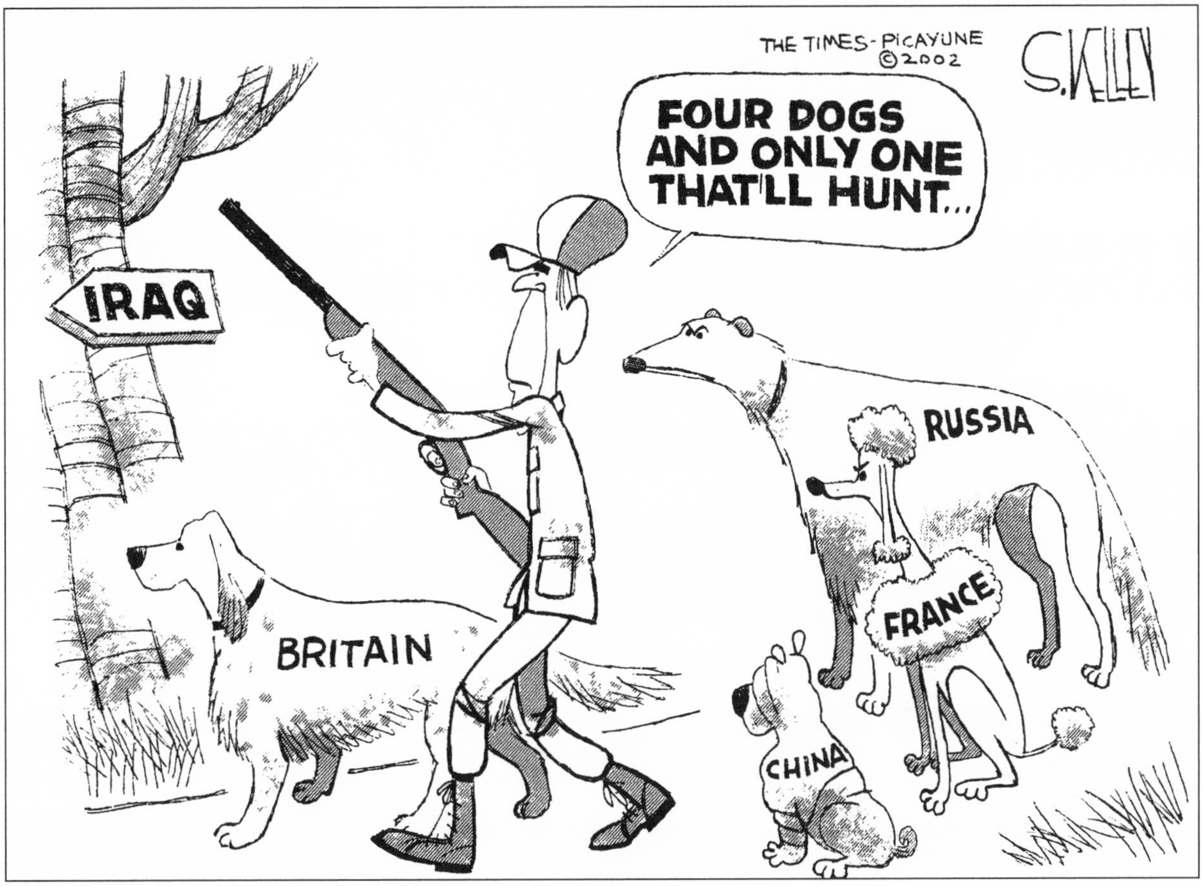
THE TIMES-PICAYUNE ©2002
S. KELLEY
FOUR DOGS AND ONLY ONE THAT'LL HUNT...
IRAQ
RUSSIA
FRANCE
BRITAIN
CHINA

STEVE McBRIDE
Courtesy Independence Daily Reporter (Kan.)

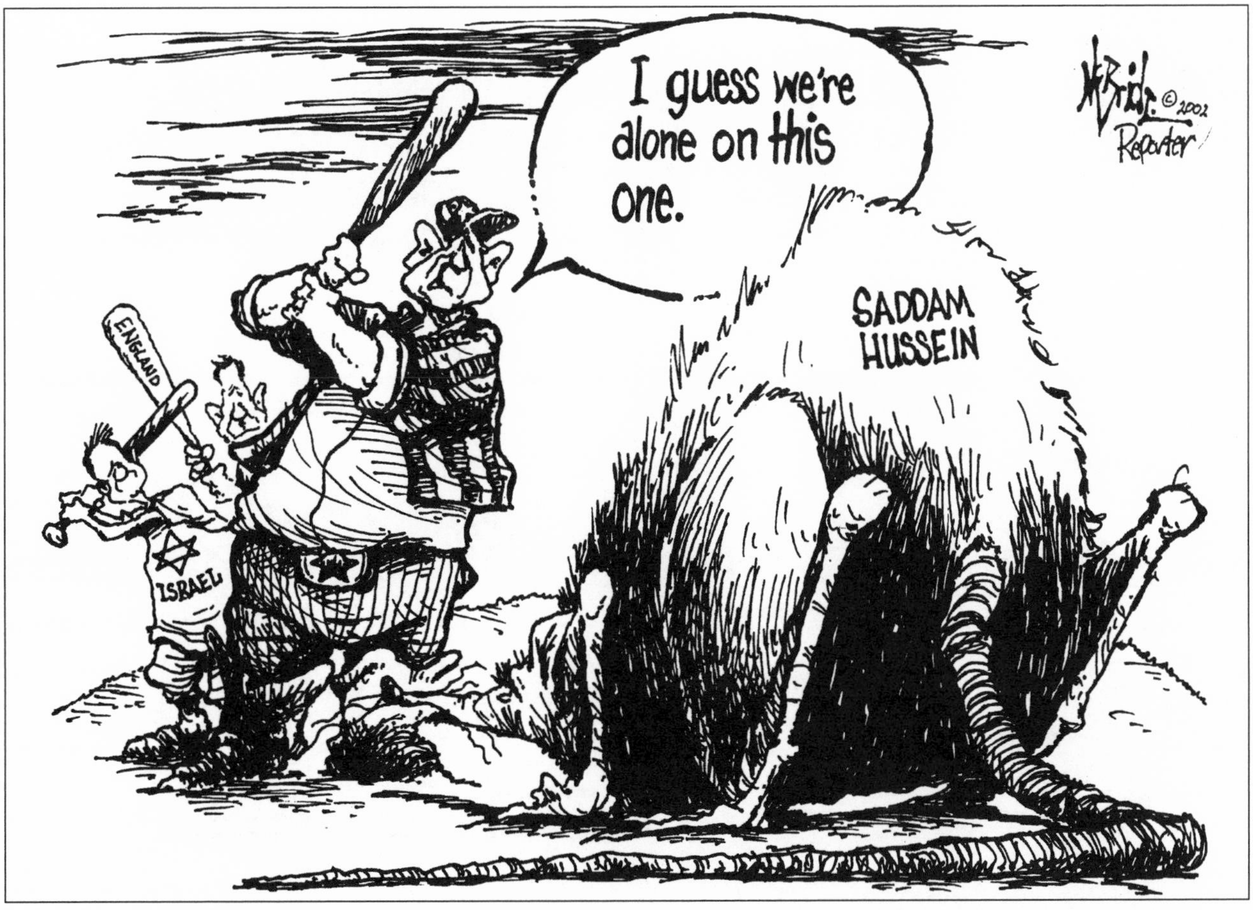
McBride ©2002 Reporter
I guess we're alone on this one.
SADDAM HUSSEIN
ENGLAND
ISRAEL

JAMES CASCIARI
Courtesy Vero Beach Press-Journal

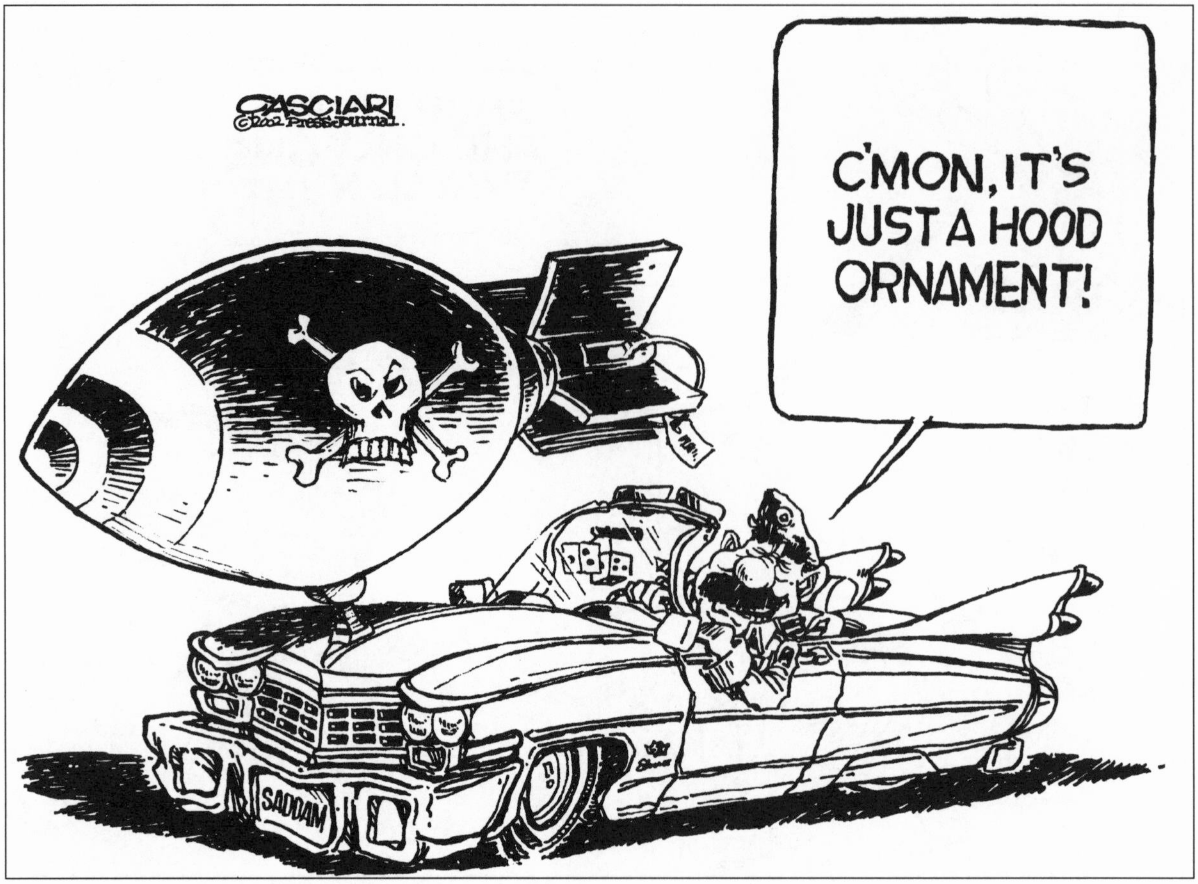
CASCIARI ©2002 Press-Journal
C'MON, IT'S JUST A HOOD ORNAMENT!
SADDAM

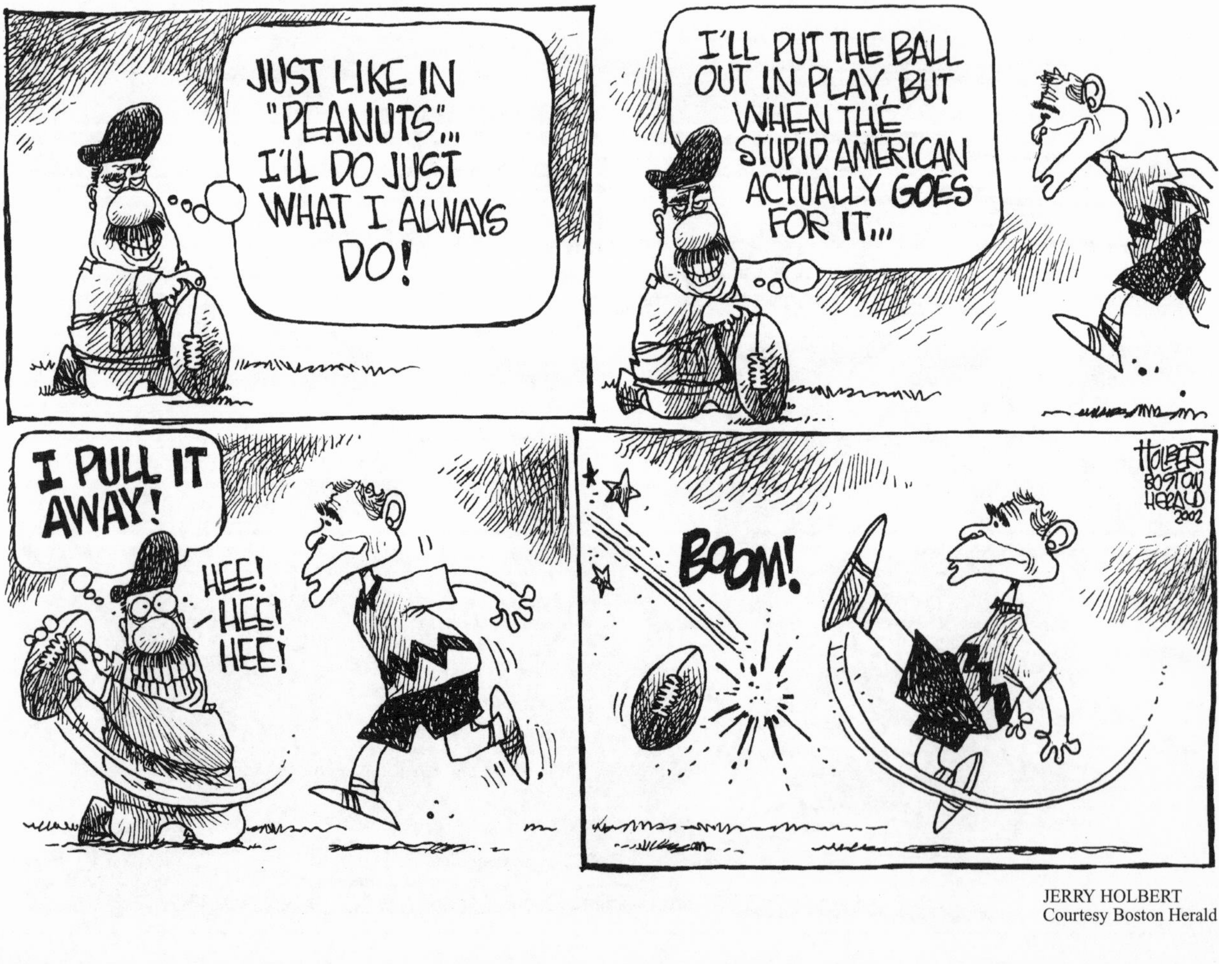
JUST LIKE IN "PEANUTS"... I'LL DO JUST WHAT I ALWAYS DO!
I'LL PUT THE BALL OUT IN PLAY, BUT WHEN THE STUPID AMERICAN ACTUALLY GOES FOR IT...
I PULL IT AWAY!
HEE! HEE! HEE!
BOOM!
HOLBERT BOSTON HERALD 2002

JERRY HOLBERT
Courtesy Boston Herald

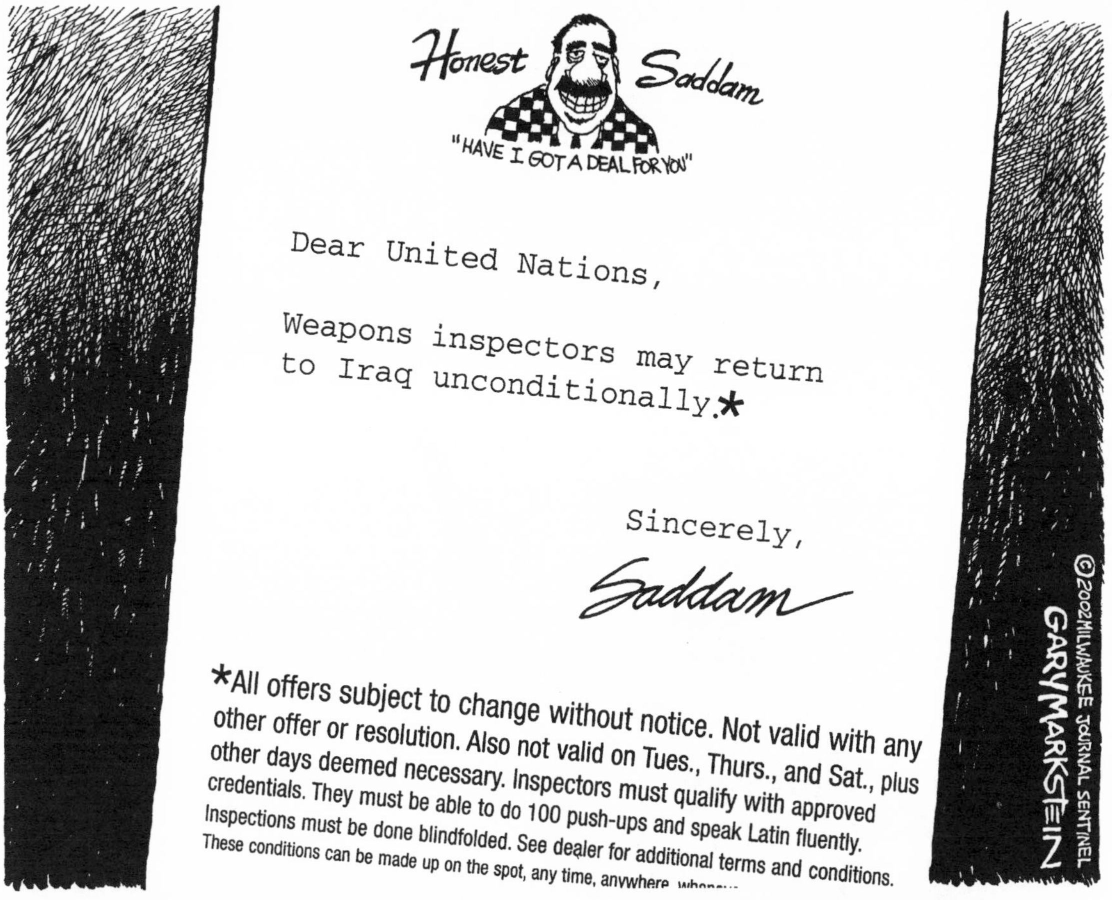
Honest Saddam
"HAVE I GOT A DEAL FOR YOU"
Dear United Nations,
Weapons inspectors may return to Iraq unconditionally.*
Sincerely,
Saddam
*All offers subject to change without notice. Not valid with any other offer or resolution. Also not valid on Tues., Thurs., and Sat., plus other days deemed necessary. Inspectors must qualify with approved credentials. They must be able to do 100 push-ups and speak Latin fluently. Inspections must be done blindfolded. See dealer for additional terms and conditions. These conditions can be made up on the spot, any time, anywhere
©2002 MILWAUKEE JOURNAL SENTINEL
GARYMARKSTEIN

GARY MARKSTEIN
Courtesy Milwaukee Journal Sentinel

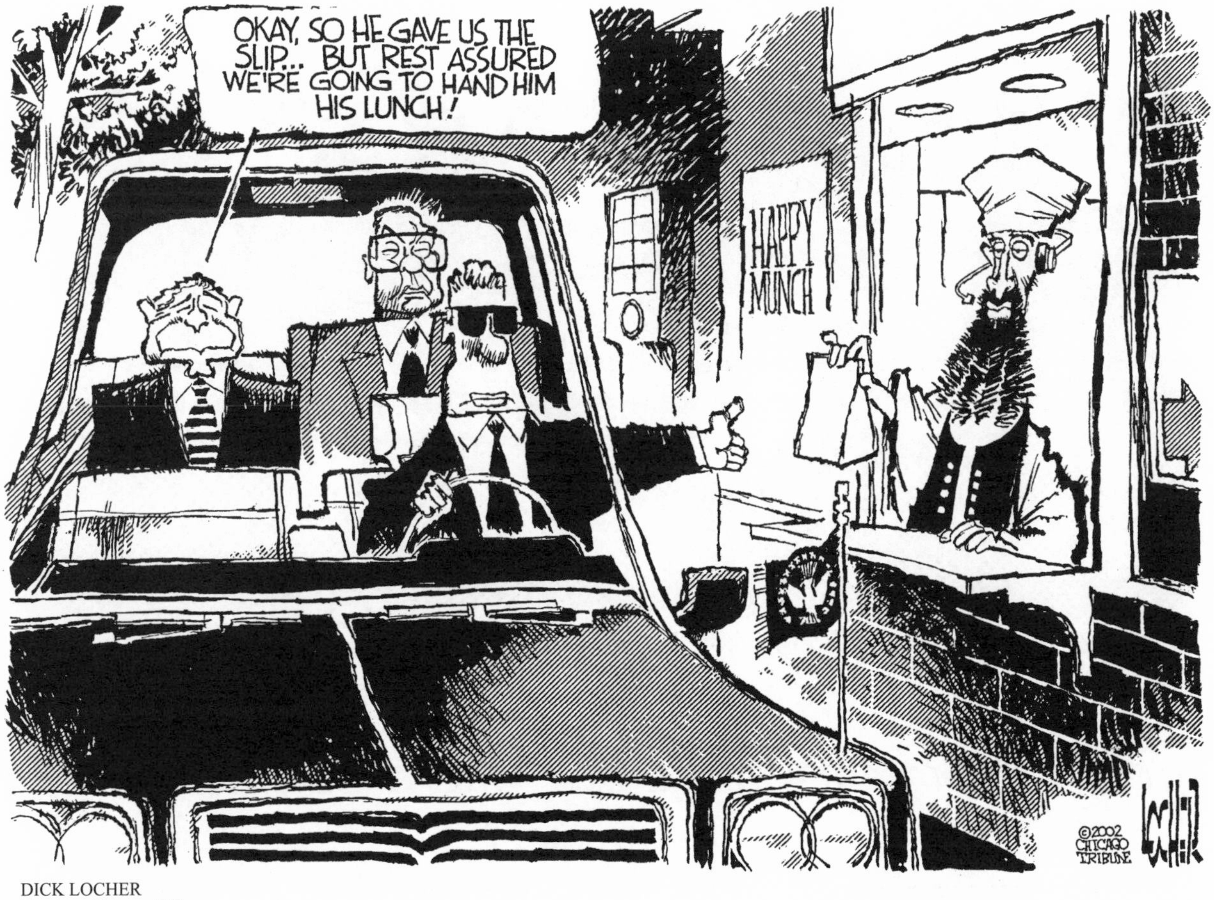
OKAY, SO HE GAVE US THE SLIP... BUT REST ASSURED WE'RE GOING TO HAND HIM HIS LUNCH!
HAPPY MUNCH
©2002 CHICAGO TRIBUNE
LOCHER

DICK LOCHER
Courtesy Chicago Tribune

JIM BERRY
Courtesy NEA

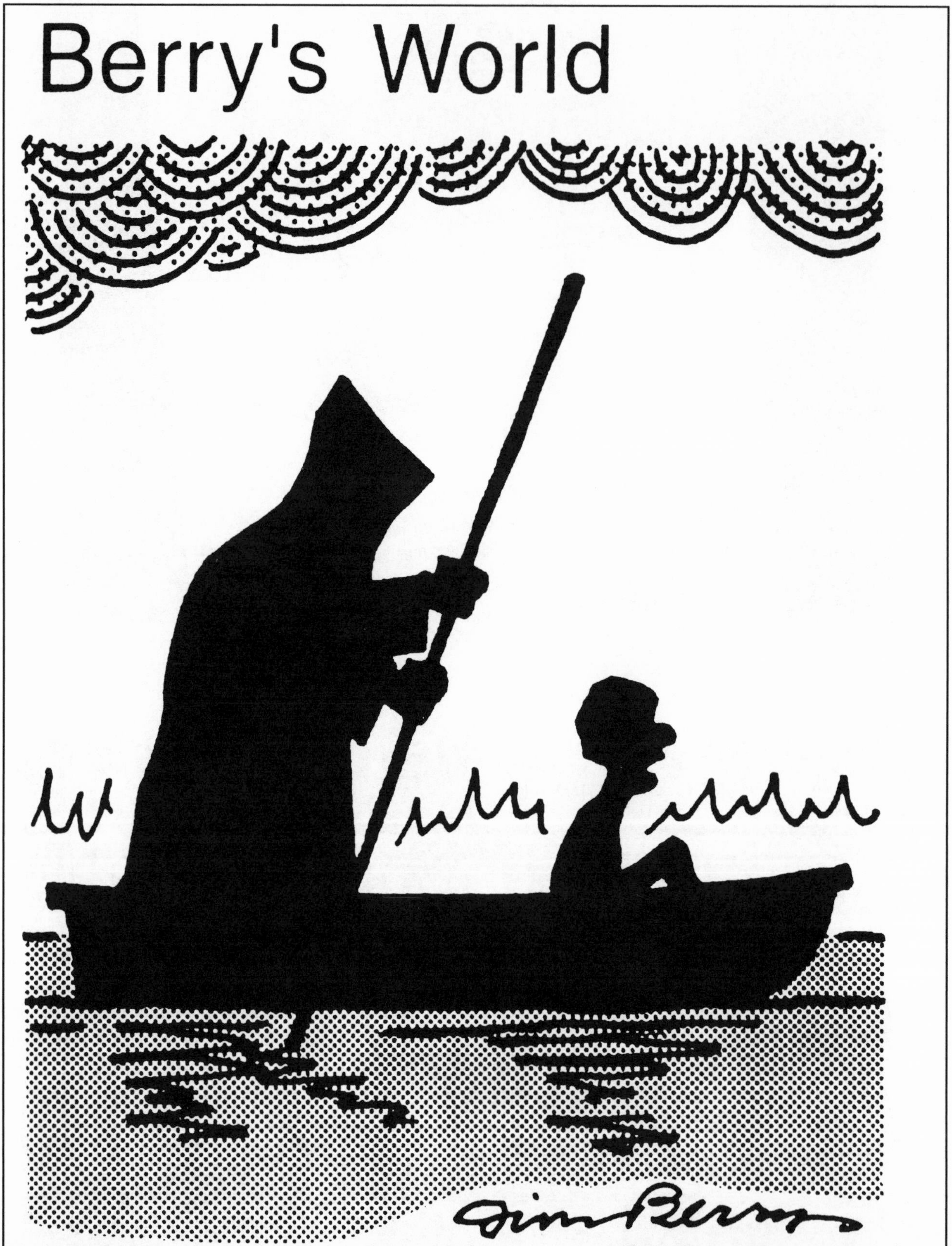
Berry's World
www.comics.com
© 2002 by NEA, Inc.

"Are you sure this is right? I was a suicide bomber. A martyr."

Terrorism

The war against international terrorism continued, with one-third of the top-ranking al-Qaida confirmed dead or captured. Intelligence from allies overseas was contributing mightily to rooting out terrorists around the globe. In late November, following President Bush's call for the creation of a special Department of Homeland Security, Congress approved legislation establishing this giant agency designed to better protect the U.S.

The FBI and the CIA clearly need to be restructured—along with other agencies—in the fight against terrorism. President Bush has repeatedly warned that it will be a long battle but that America will see it through. The enemies are Bin Laden, al-Qaida, Saddam Hussein, and every other person or nation that supports terrorists.

Most agree that America's armed forces are doing an excellent job in this unusual war where the enemy does not show itself. The troops made short work of the Taliban in Afghanistan, and continue to hunt down pockets of al-Qaida. Since September 11, 130,000 members of the National Guard and the Reserves have been called to duty to reinforce the regular Army. Commanders are preparing troops for war with Iraq in the event Saddam is found to possess weapons of mass destruction.

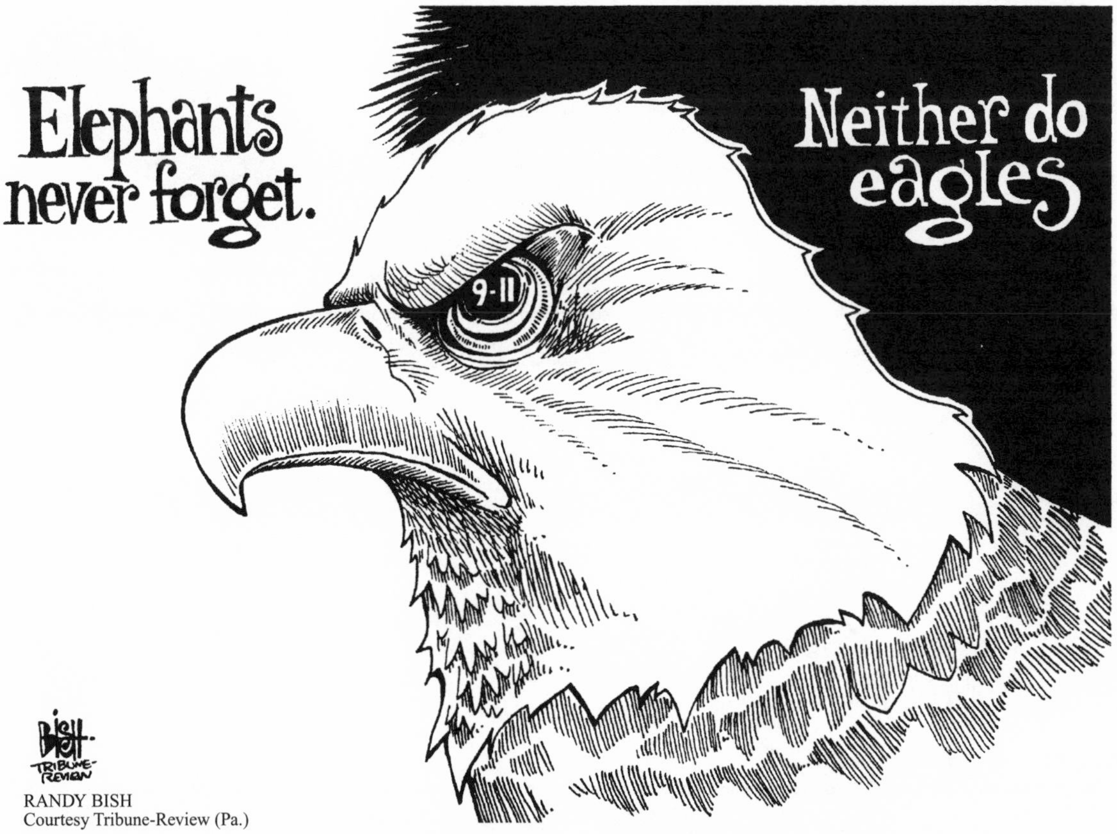

Elephants never forget.
Neither do eagles
9-11
BISH TRIBUNE-REVIEW

RANDY BISH
Courtesy Tribune-Review (Pa.)

FRESQUET®

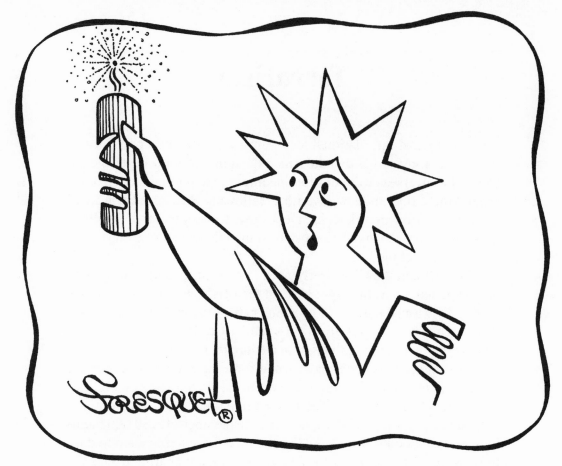

LAZARO FRESQUET
Courtesy El Nuevo Herald

DAVID HITCH
Courtesy Worcester Telegram and Gazette (Mass.)

HITCH
TELEGRAM
& GAZETTE
GILLETTE
SCHICK

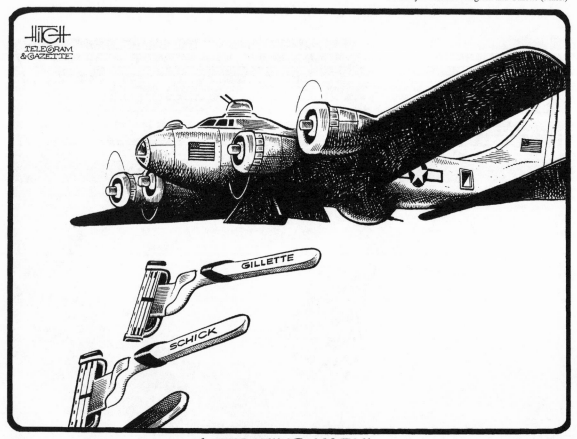

LIBERATING KABUL

CLAY BENNETT
Courtesy Christian Science Monitor

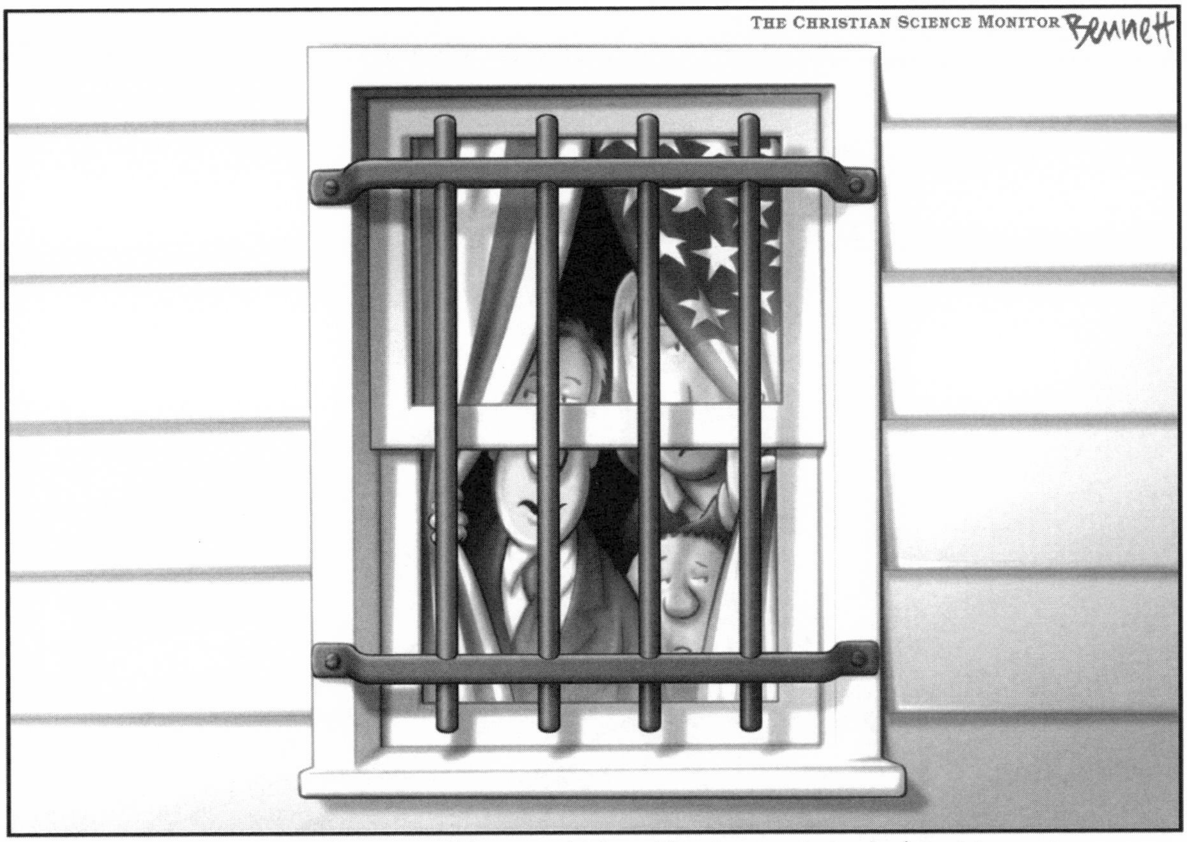
THE CHRISTIAN SCIENCE MONITOR
Bennett

'I guess it was easier than putting the terrorists behind bars.'

ALAN VITELLO
Courtesy Vitello's View

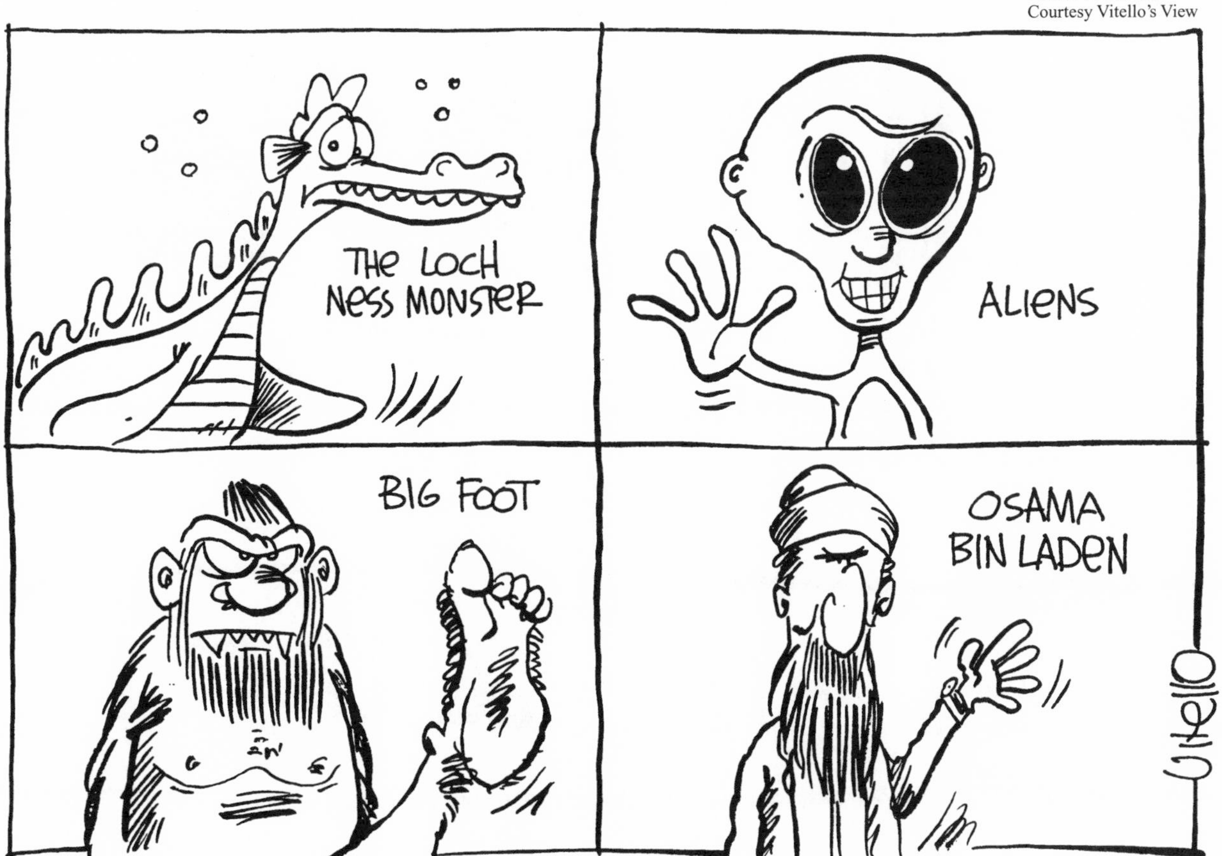
THE LOCH NESS MONSTER
ALIENS
BIG FOOT
OSAMA BIN LADEN
Vitello
DEAD? ALIVE? HERE? THERE? WHERE?....

SVEN VAN ASSCHE
Courtesy Darien Times (Conn.)

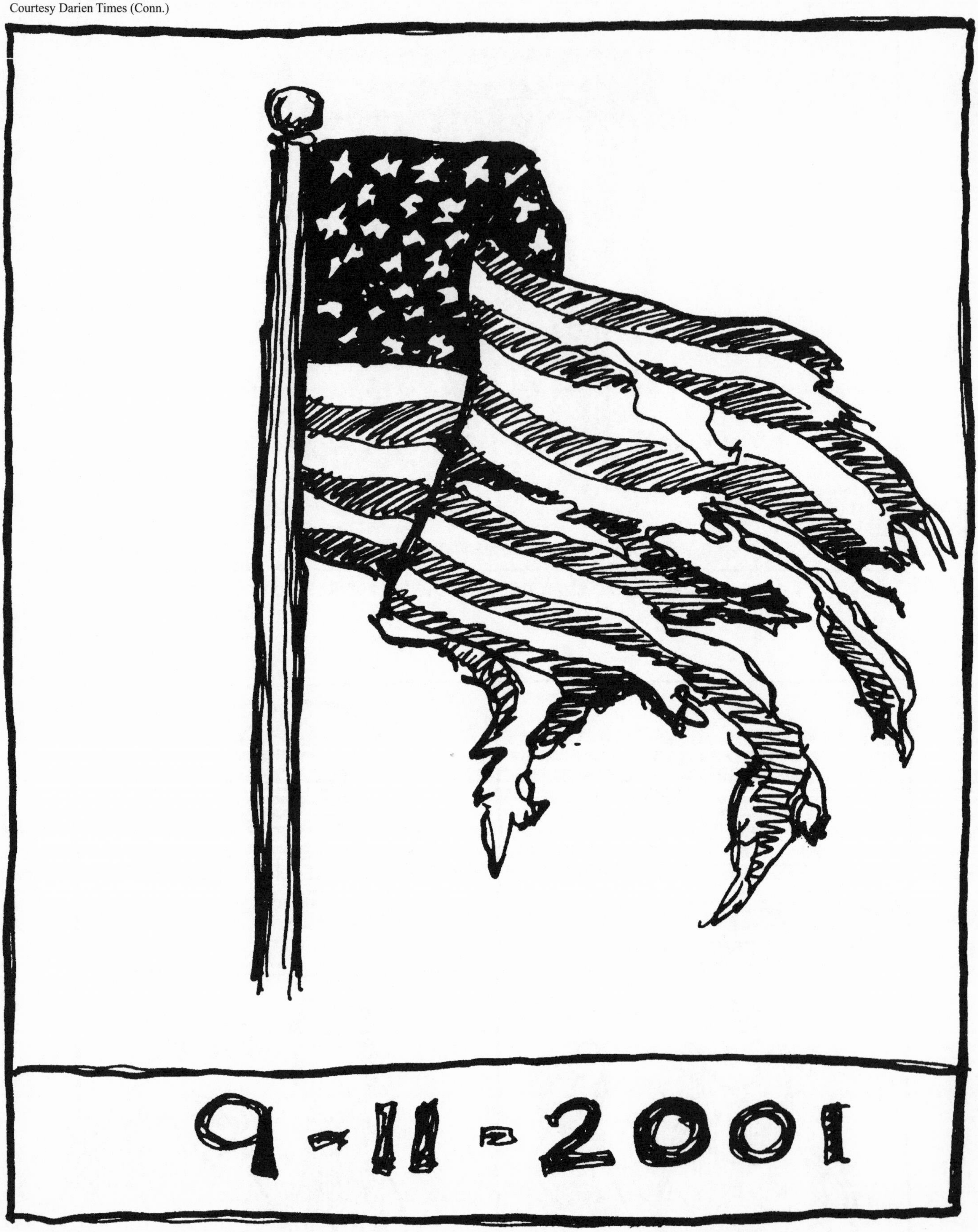
9-11-2001

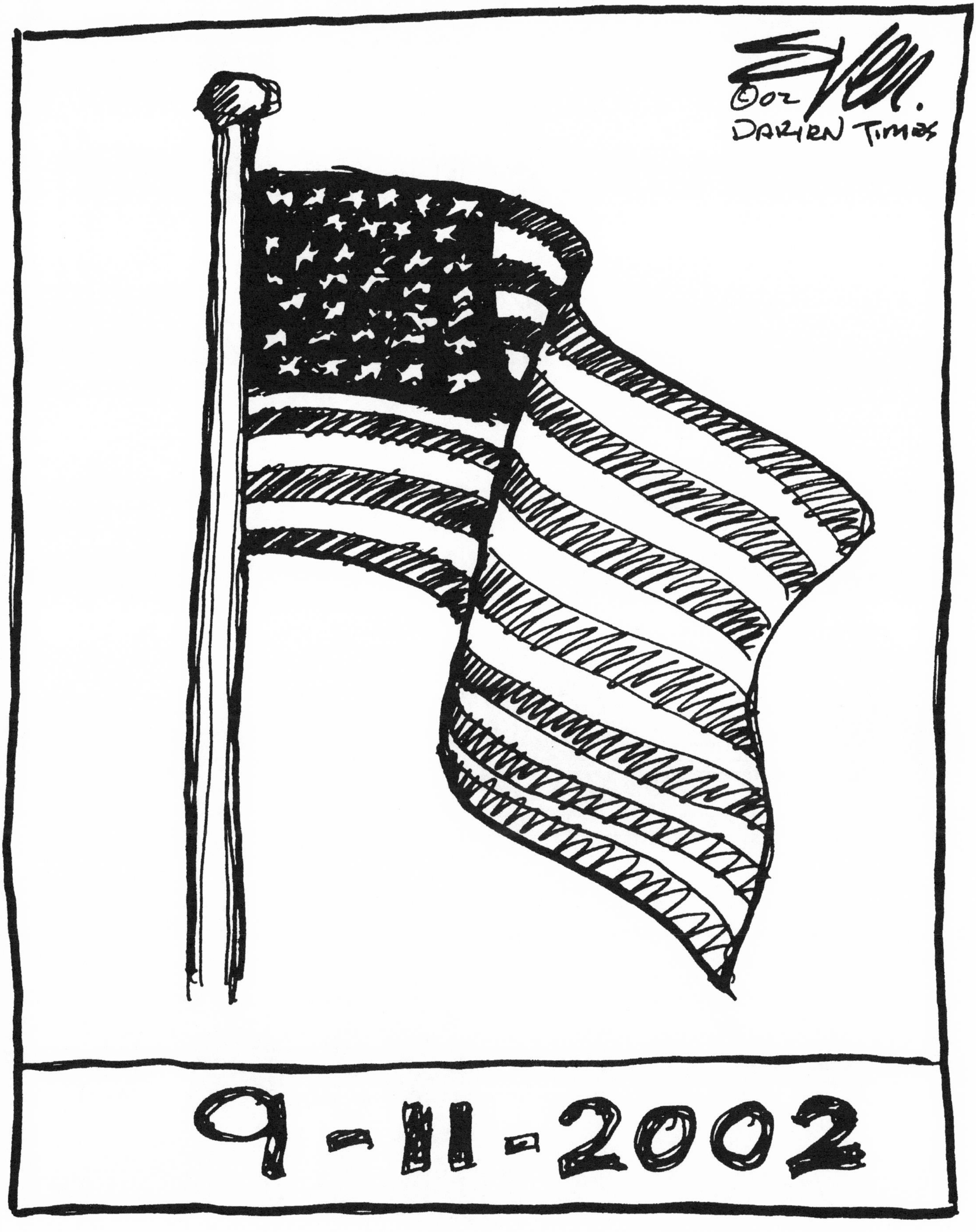
©02
DARIEN TIMES
9-11-2002

DEATH TO AMERICA!
DIRTY BOMB
HEY! I DEMAND MY CONSTITUTIONAL RIGHTS!

MIKE PETERS
Courtesy Dayton Daily News

BILL GARNER
Courtesy Washington Times

OK...HEADS YOU GET A STUDENT VISA... TAILS IT'S A VISITOR'S VISA!
VISAS

ED COLLEY
Courtesy Boston Globe South

WE DON'T CARE WHO YOU SAY YOU ARE... YOU FIT THE PROFILE.

Security concerns affect some July Fourth plans.

JAMES D. CROWE
Courtesy Mobile Register

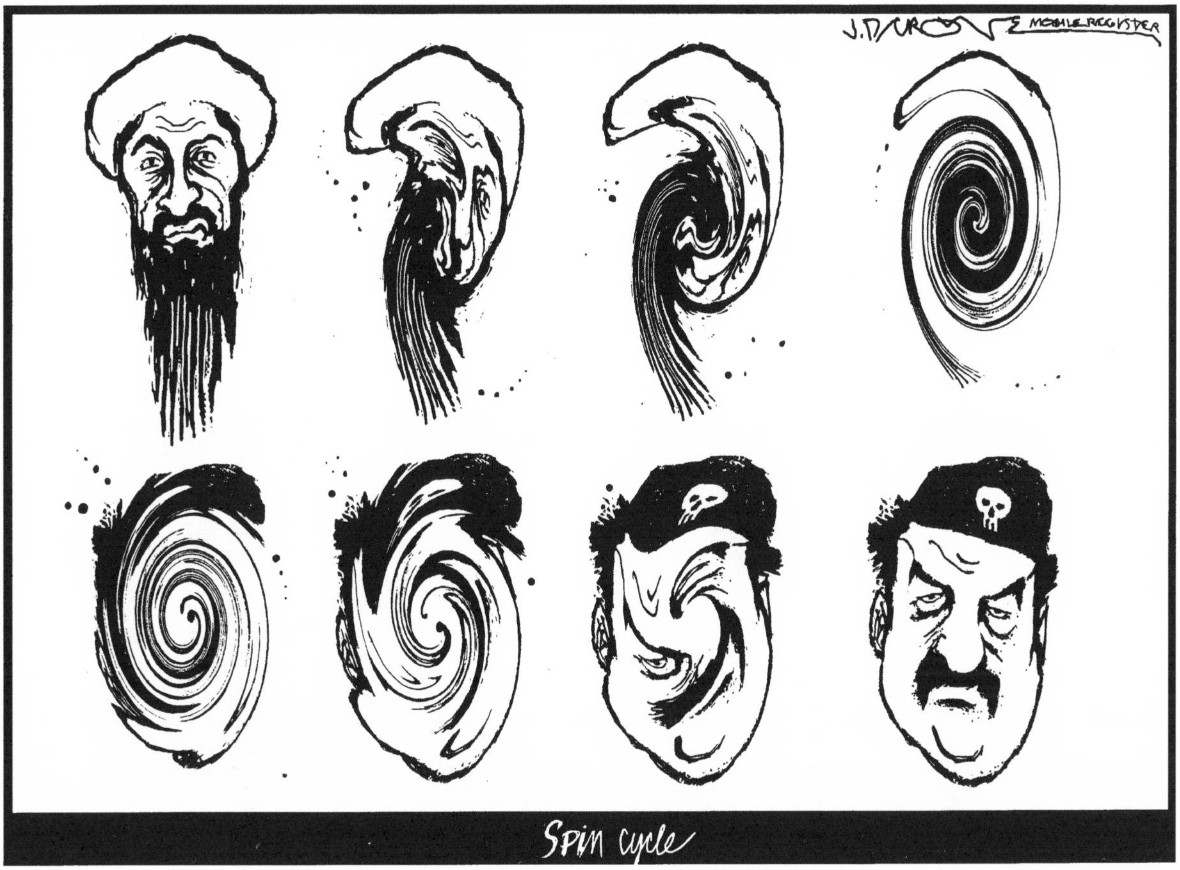
J.D. CROWE MOBILE REGISTER
Spin cycle

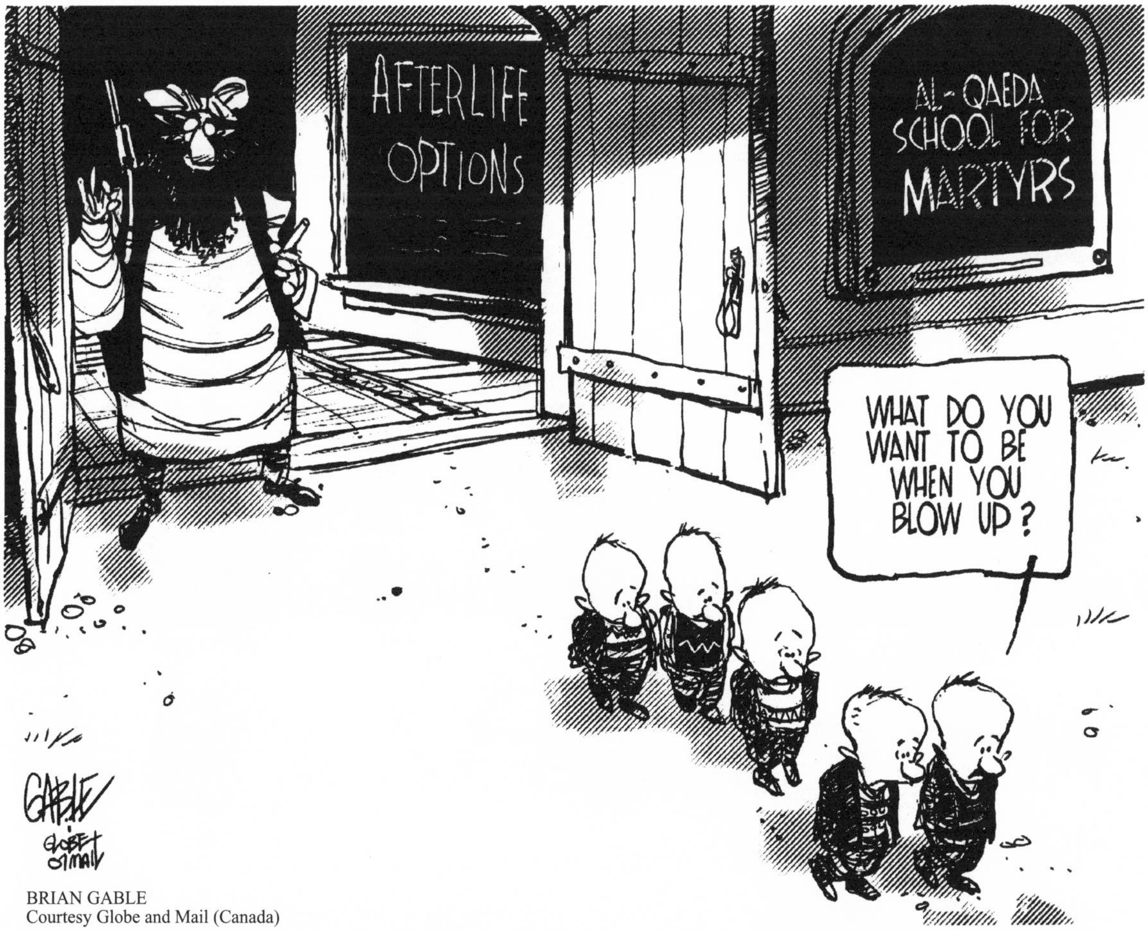
AFTERLIFE OPTIONS
AL-QAEDA SCHOOL FOR MARTYRS
WHAT DO YOU WANT TO BE WHEN YOU BLOW UP?
GABLE
GLOBE & MAIL

BRIAN GABLE
Courtesy Globe and Mail (Canada)

STEVE KELLEY
Courtesy The Times-Picayune (La.)

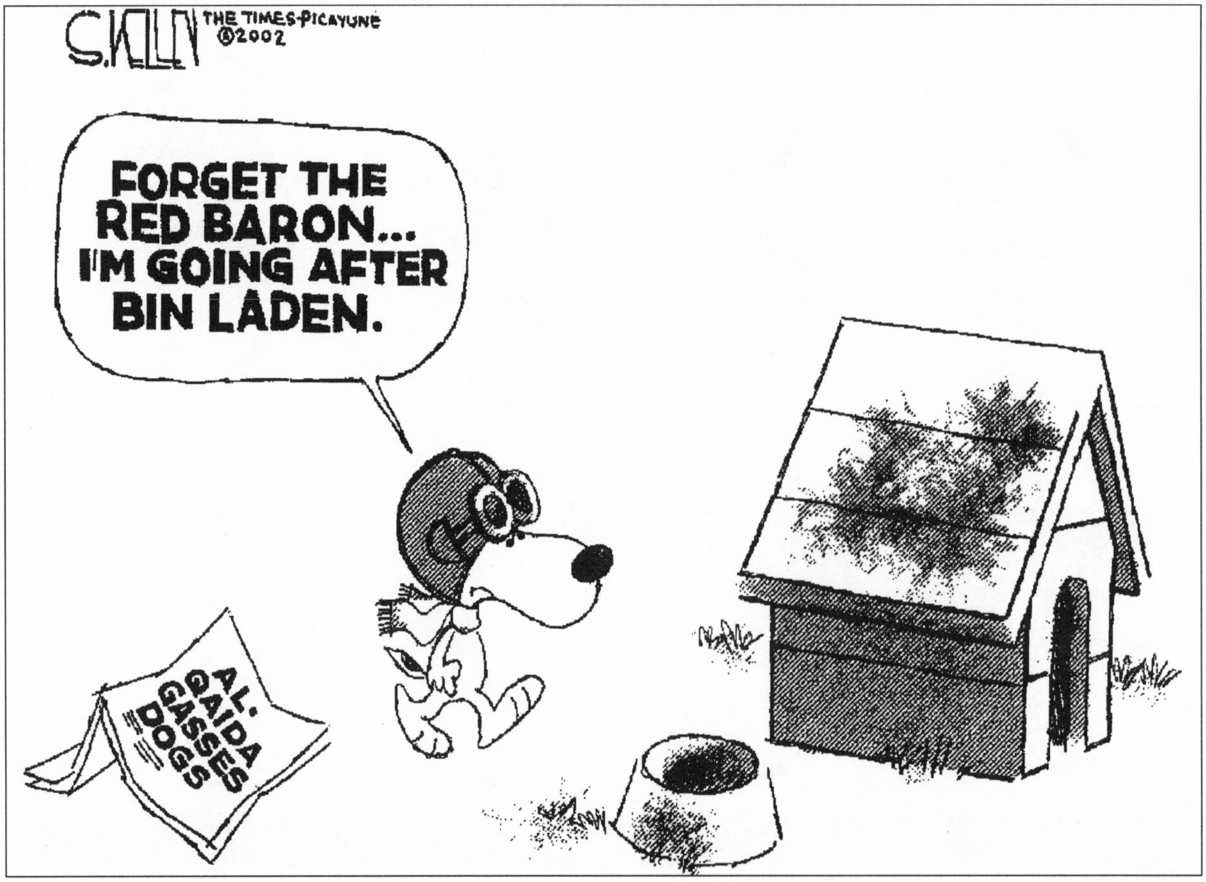
S.KELLEY
THE TIMES-PICAYUNE ©2002
FORGET THE RED BARON... I'M GOING AFTER BIN LADEN.
AL-QAIDA GASSES DOGS

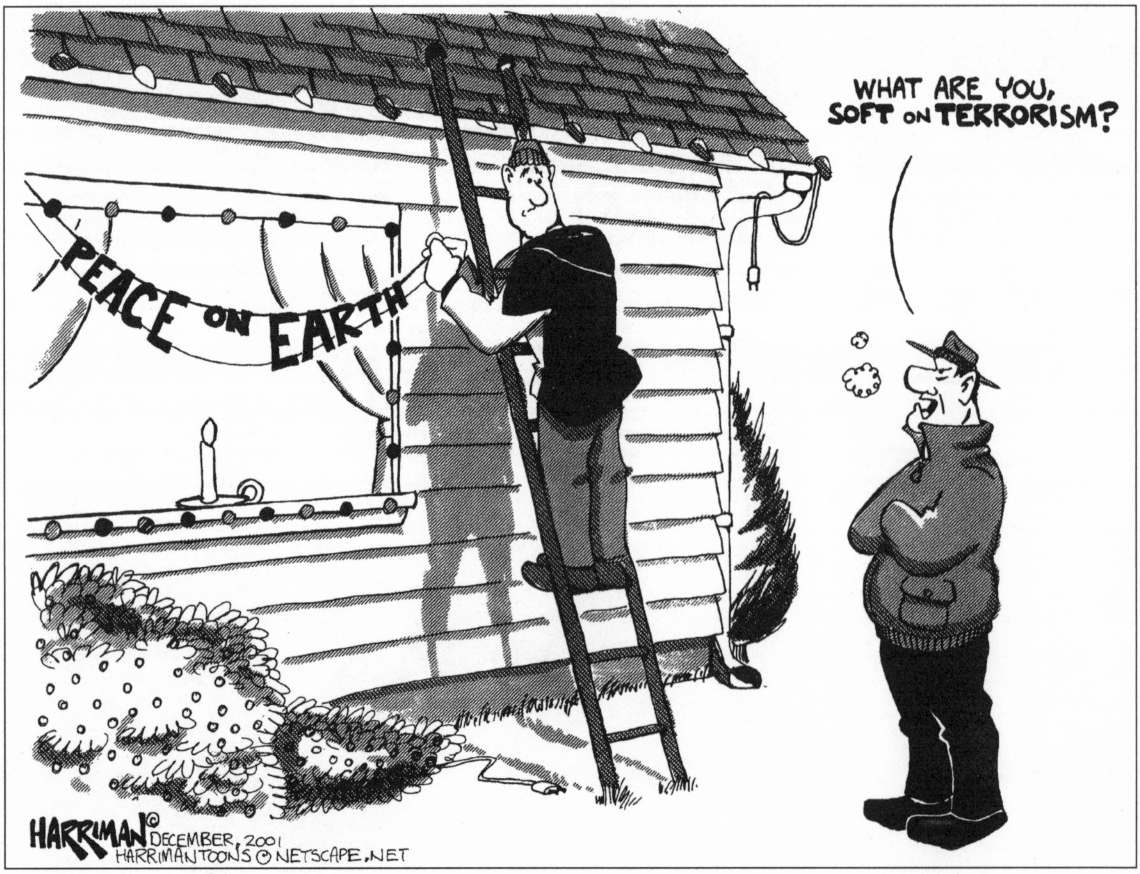
WHAT ARE YOU, SOFT ON TERRORISM?
PEACE ON EARTH
HARRIMAN© DECEMBER, 2001
HARRIMANTOONS@NETSCAPE.NET

ROB HARRIMAN
Courtesy Portland Tribune

DAVID COX
Courtesy Arkansas Democrat-Gazette

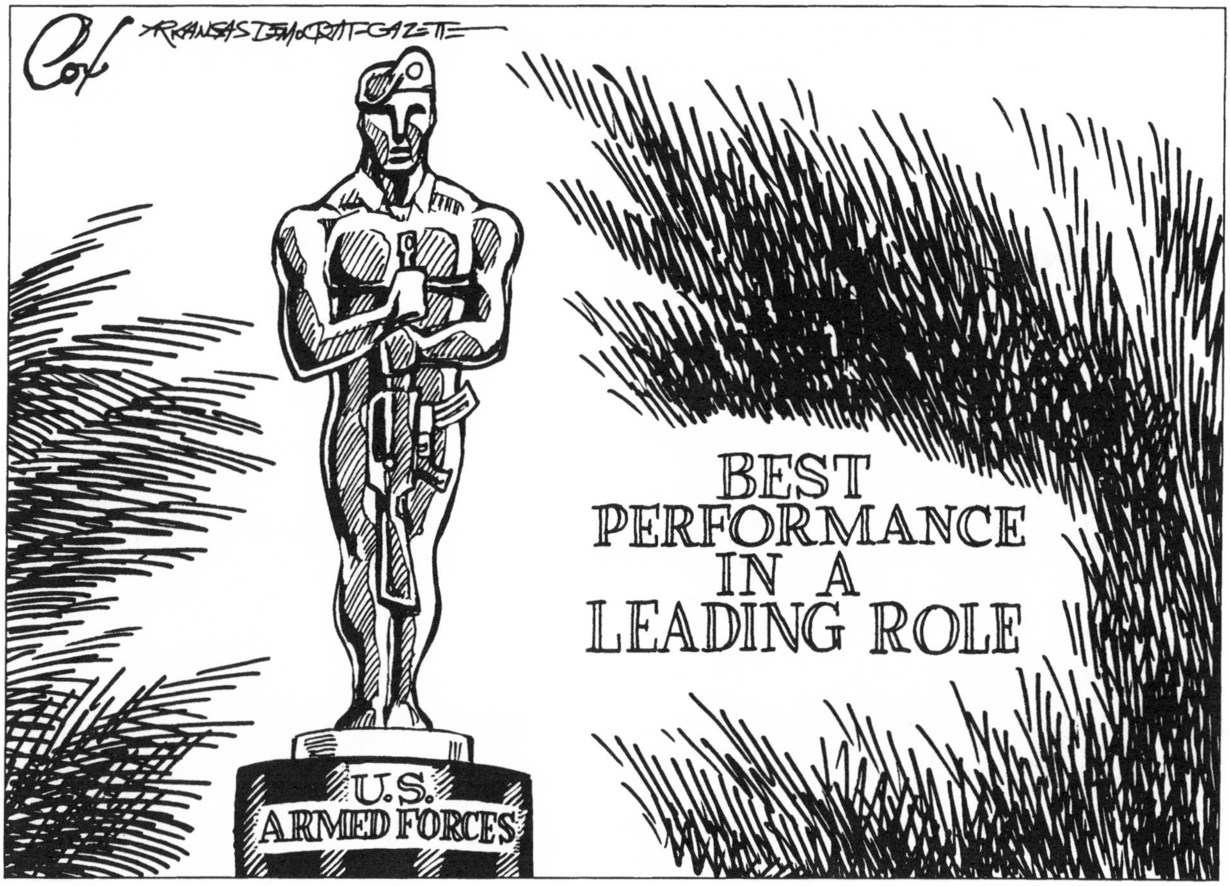
Cox ARKANSAS DEMOCRAT-GAZETTE
BEST PERFORMANCE IN A LEADING ROLE
U.S. ARMED FORCES

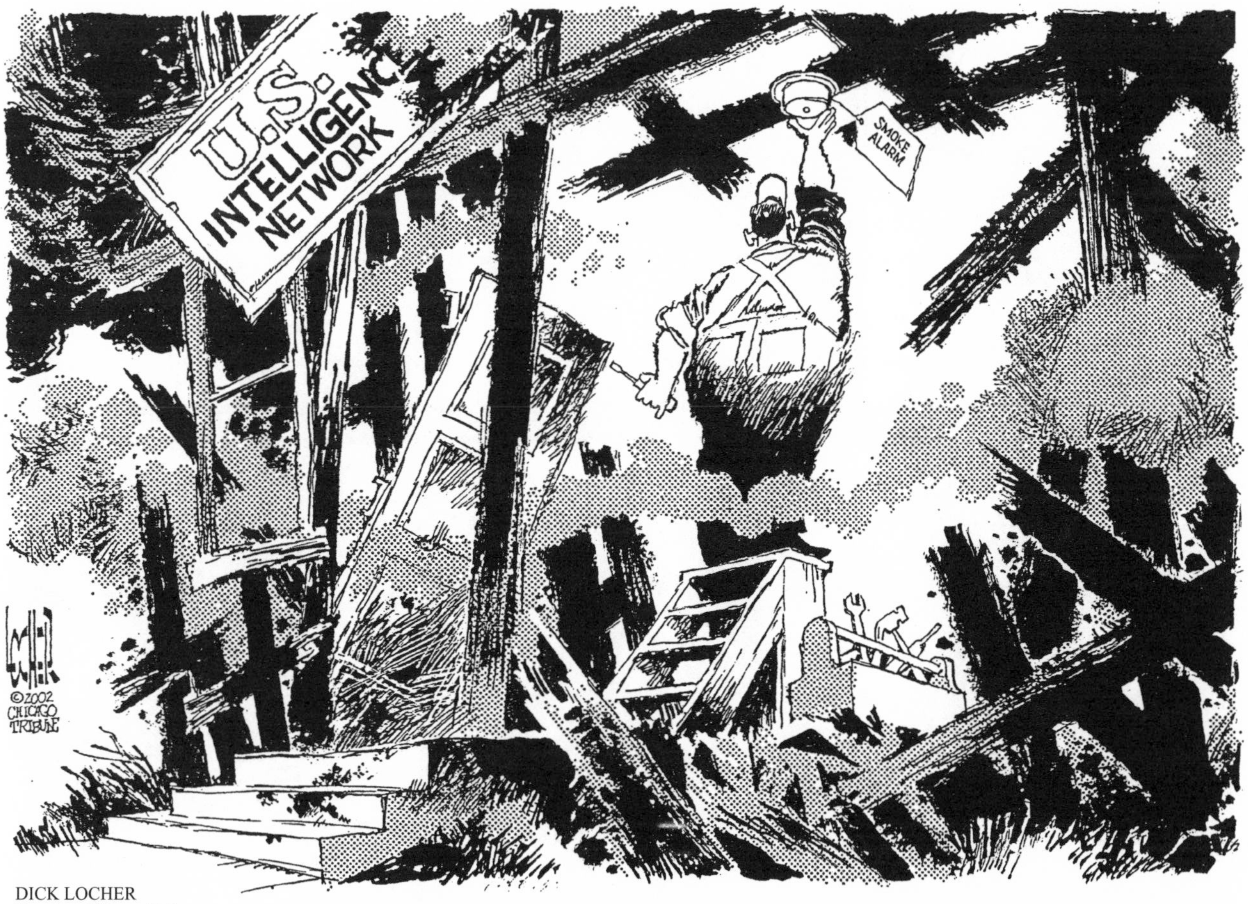
U.S. INTELLIGENCE NETWORK
SMOKE ALARM
LOCHER ©2002 CHICAGO TRIBUNE

DICK LOCHER
Courtesy Chicago Tribune

JOEL THORNHILL
Courtesy Lawrence County Record (Mo.)

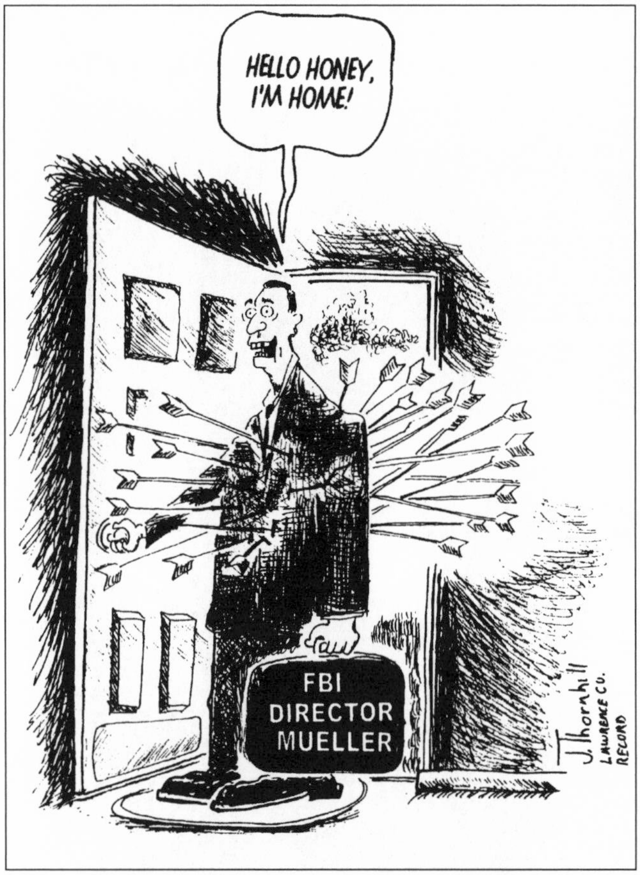
HELLO HONEY, I'M HOME!
FBI DIRECTOR MUELLER
J. Thornhill LAWRENCE CO. RECORD

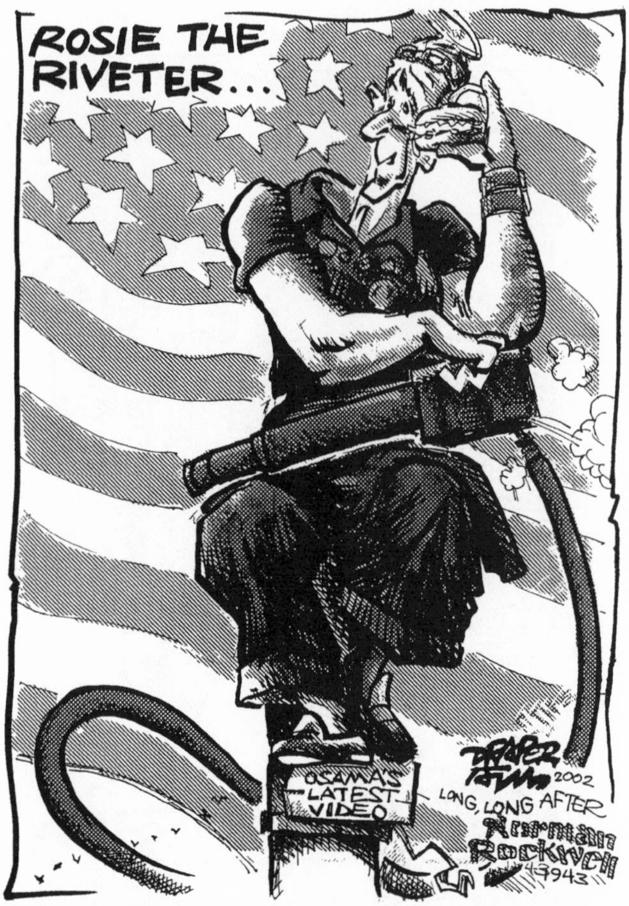
ROSIE THE RIVETER...
OSAMA'S LATEST VIDEO
DRAPER HILL 2002
LONG, LONG AFTER Norman Rockwell 1943

DRAPER HILL
Courtesy Grosse Pointe Publishing Co.

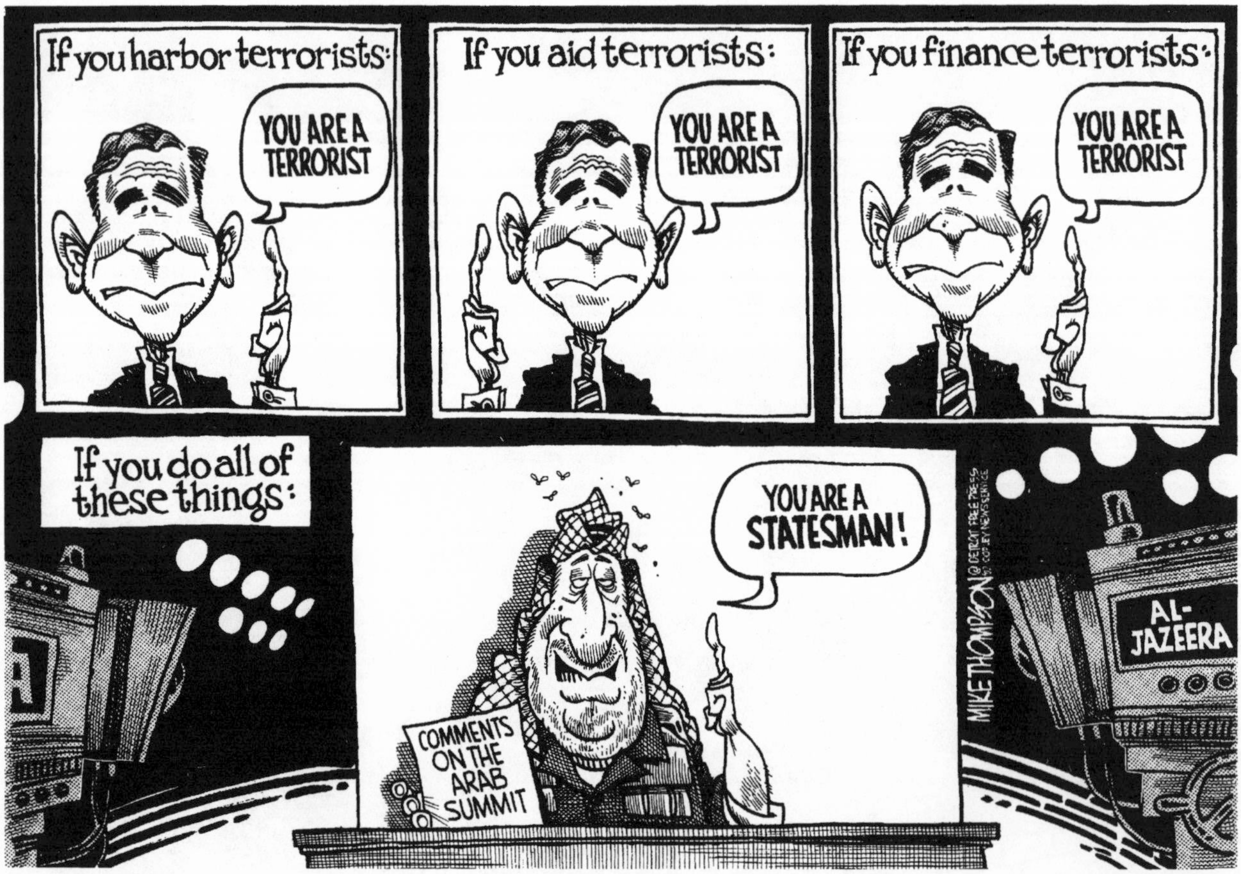
If you harbor terrorists:
YOU ARE A TERRORIST
If you aid terrorists:
YOU ARE A TERRORIST
If you finance terrorists:
YOU ARE A TERRORIST
If you do all of these things:
YOU ARE A STATESMAN!
COMMENTS ON THE ARAB SUMMIT
AL-JAZEERA
MIKE THOMPSON

MICHAEL THOMPSON
Courtesy Detroit Free Press

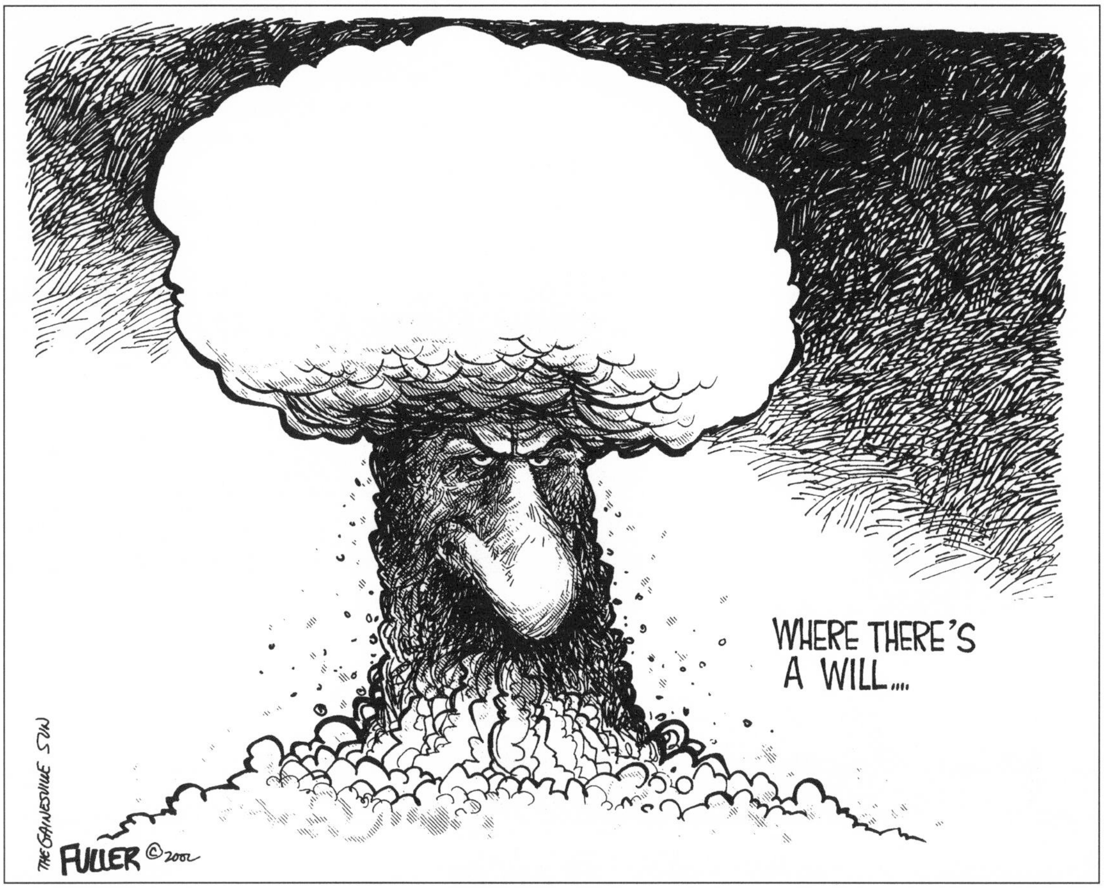
WHERE THERE'S A WILL....
THE GAINESVILLE SUN
FULLER ©2002

JAKE FULLER
Courtesy Gainesville Sun

DICK LOCHER
Courtesy Chicago Tribune

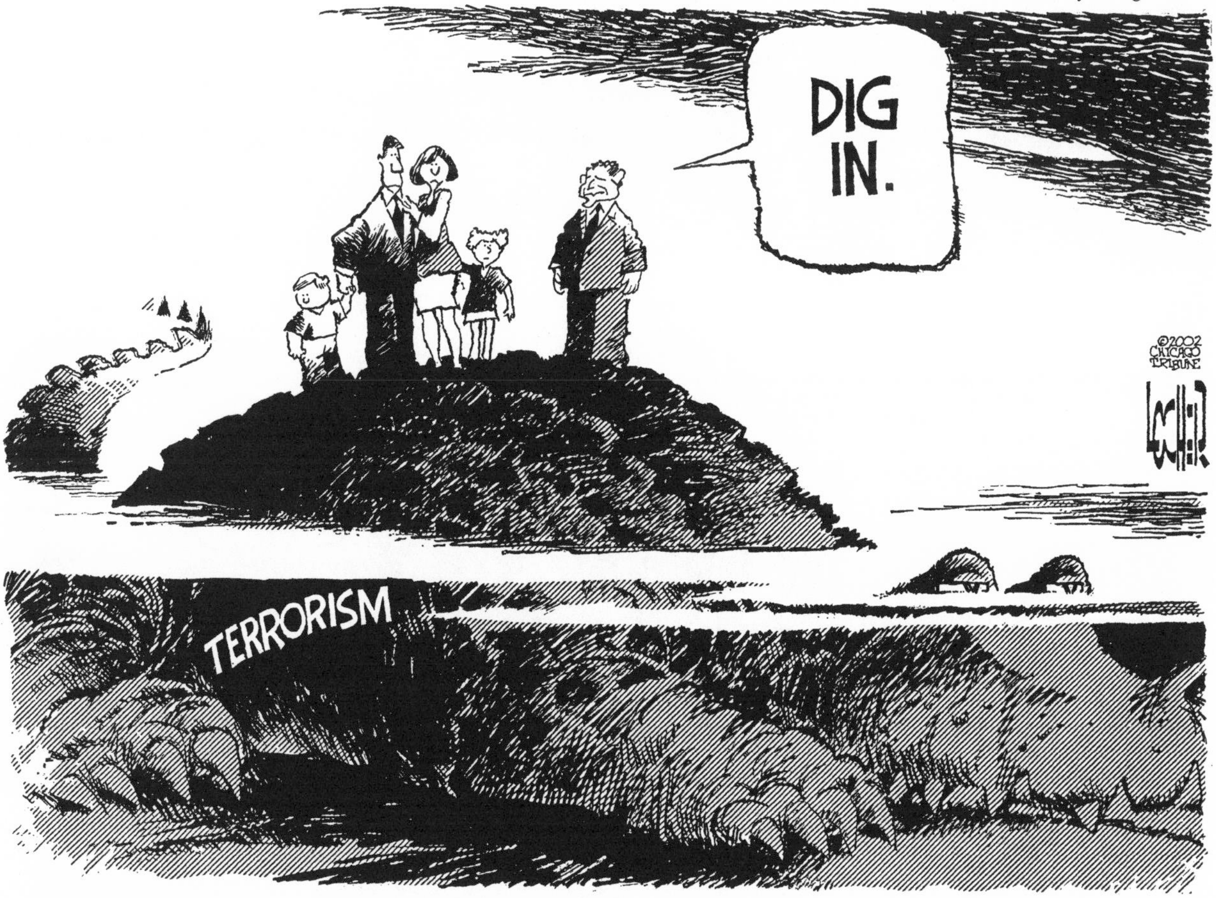
DIG IN.
TERRORISM
©2002 CHICAGO TRIBUNE
LOCHER

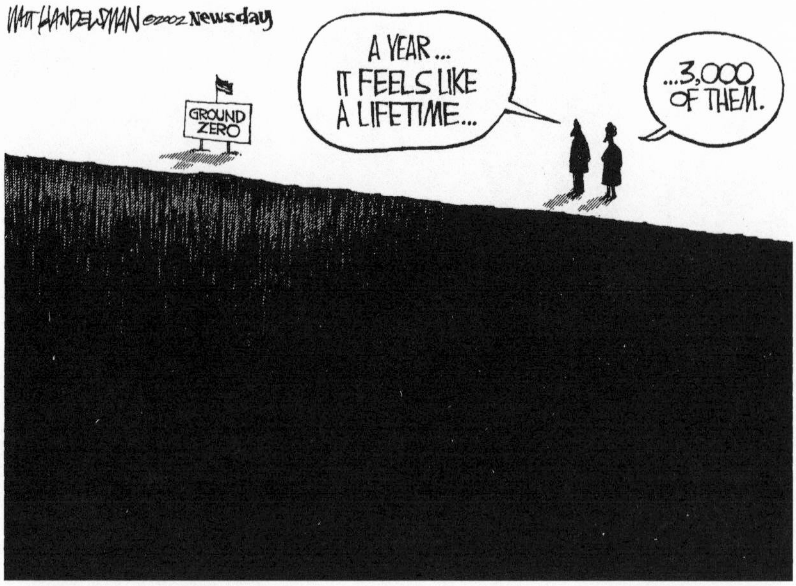
WALT HANDELSMAN ©2002 Newsday
GROUND ZERO
A YEAR... IT FEELS LIKE A LIFETIME...
...3,000 OF THEM.

WALT HANDELSMAN
Courtesy Newsday

JOHN TREVER
Courtesy Albuquerque Journal

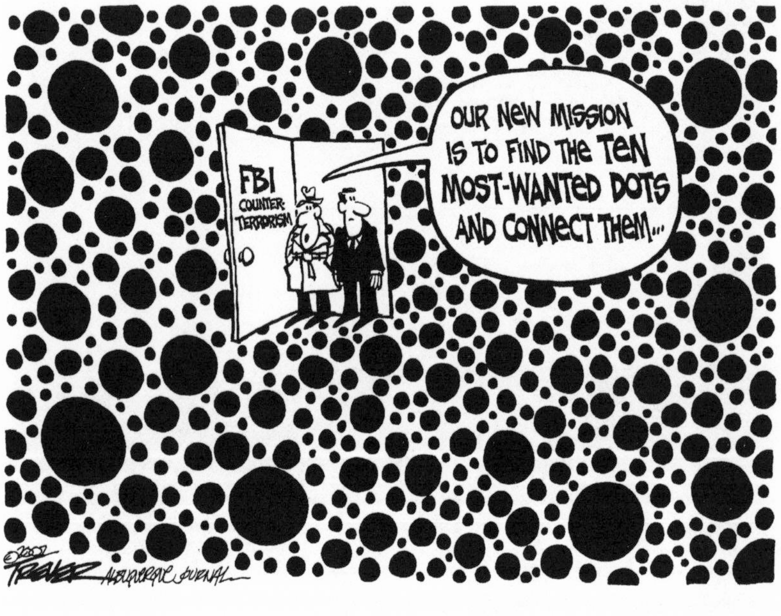
FBI COUNTER-TERRORISM
OUR NEW MISSION IS TO FIND THE TEN MOST-WANTED DOTS AND CONNECT THEM...
©2002 TREVER ALBUQUERQUE JOURNAL

NICK ANDERSON
Courtesy Louisville Courier-Journal

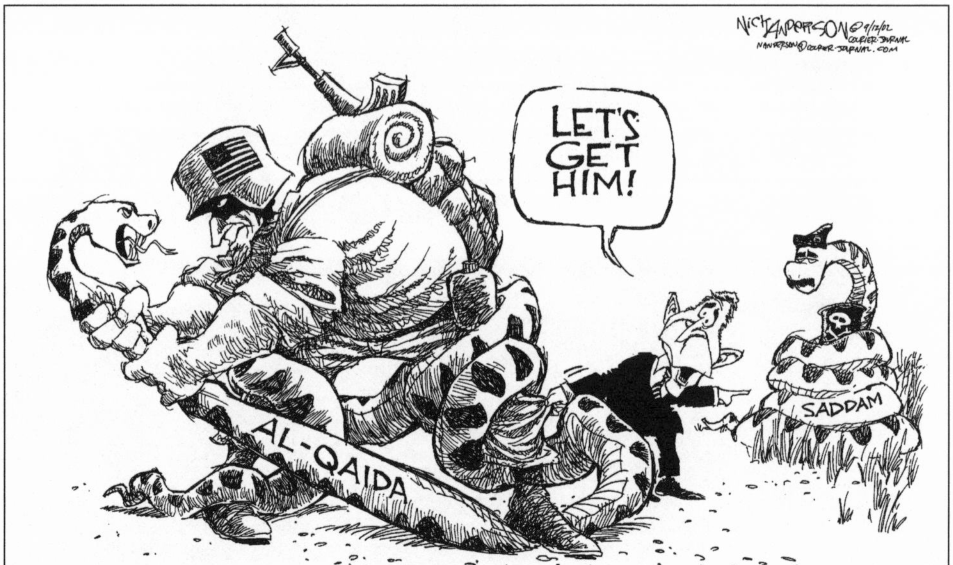
LET'S GET HIM!
AL-QAIDA
SADDAM

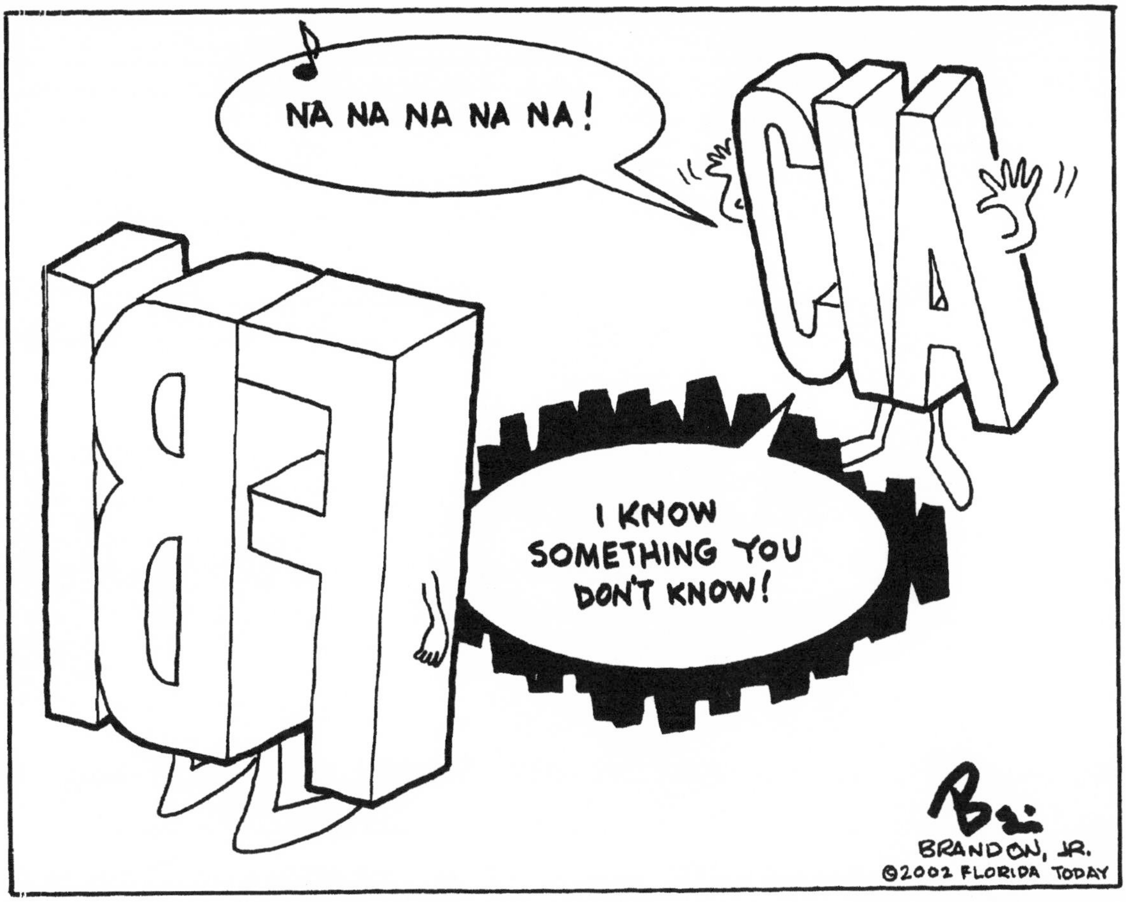
NA NA NA NA NA!
CIA
FBI
I KNOW SOMETHING YOU DON'T KNOW!
BRANDON, JR.
©2002 FLORIDA TODAY

BRUMSIC BRANDON
Courtesy Florida Today

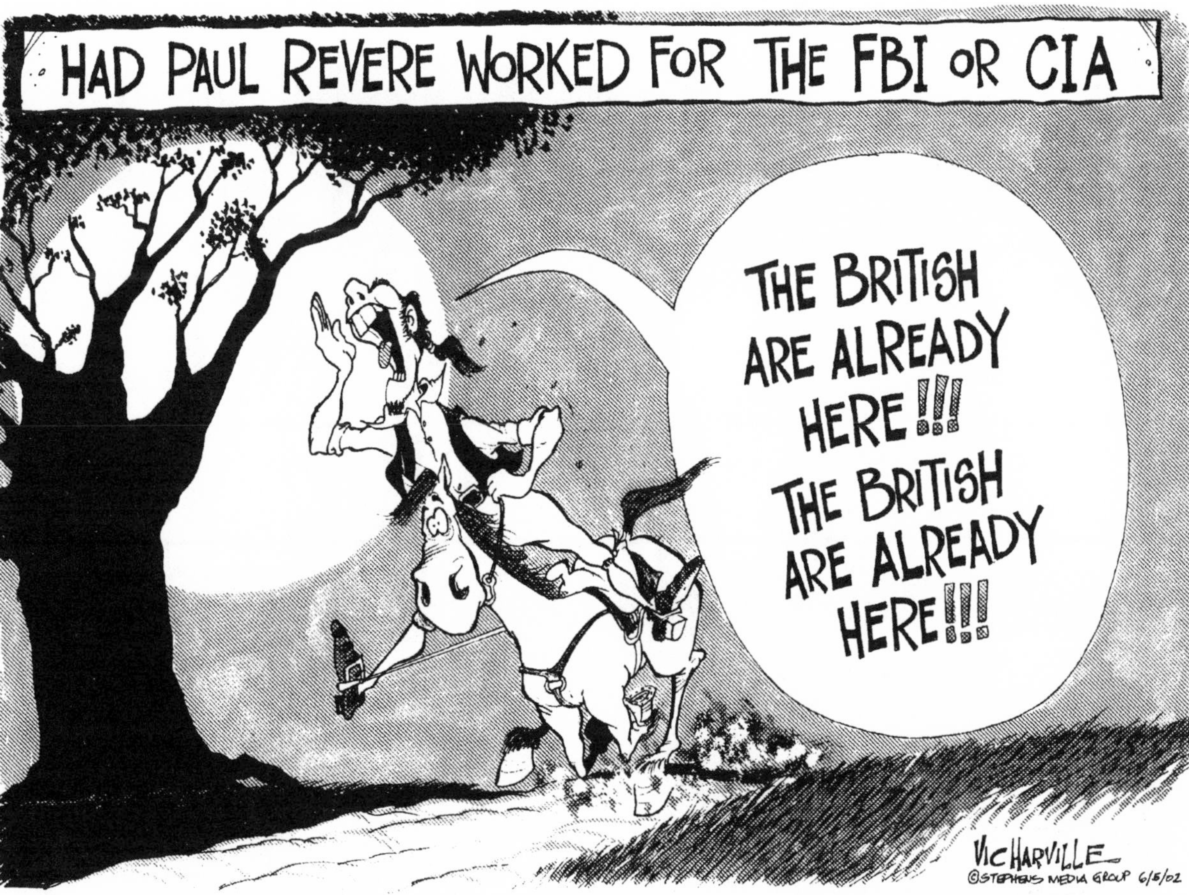
HAD PAUL REVERE WORKED FOR THE FBI OR CIA
THE BRITISH ARE ALREADY HERE!!! THE BRITISH ARE ALREADY HERE!!!
VIC HARVILLE
©STEPHENS MEDIA GROUP 6/5/02

VIC HARVILLE
Courtesy Donrey News (Ark.)

ED STEIN
Courtesy Rocky Mountain News

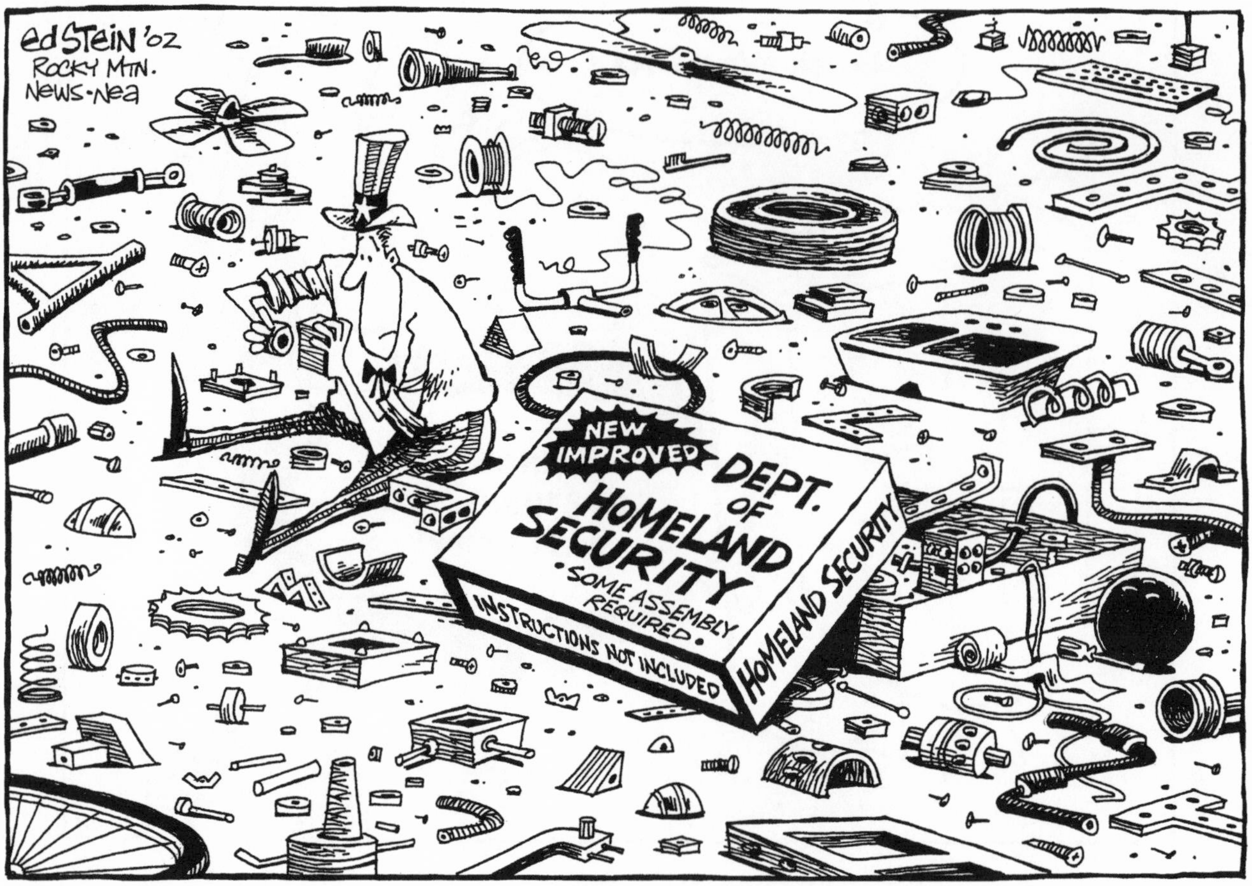

ed STeiN '02 ROCKY MTN. NEWS-NEA
NEW IMPROVED
DEPT. OF HOMELAND SECURITY
SOME ASSEMBLY REQUIRED
INSTRUCTIONS NOT INCLUDED
HOMELAND SECURITY

FRANK CAMMUSO
Courtesy Post-Standard

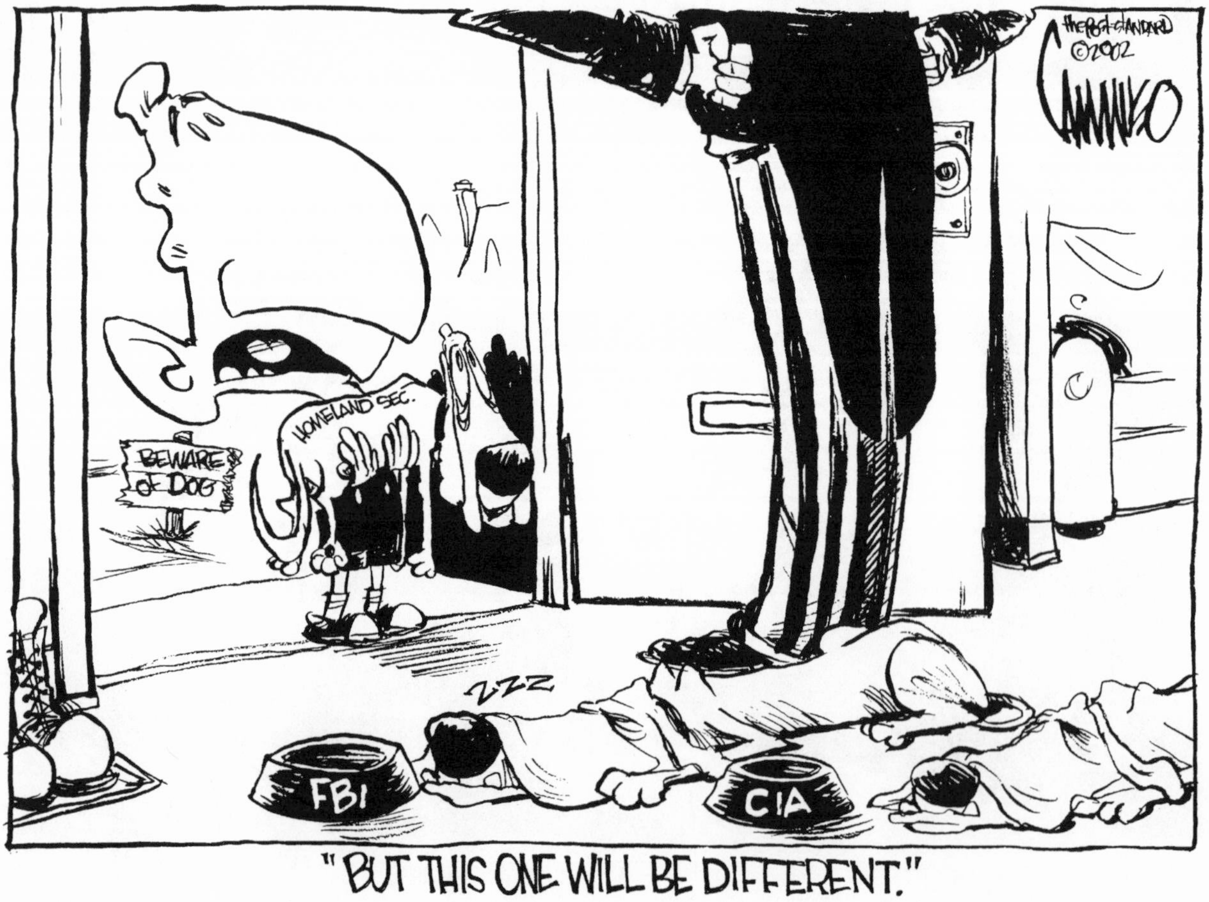

THE POST-STANDARD ©2002 CAMMUSO
HOMELAND SEC.
BEWARE OF DOG
ZZZ
FBI
CIA

"BUT THIS ONE WILL BE DIFFERENT."

Congress

Although Congress was more closely divided than it had been in almost half a century, it nevertheless could point to a number of accomplishments. The most dramatic overhaul of laws concerning campaign finance in twenty-five years was passed, along with a huge, $1.35 trillion tax cut and the biggest reorganization of government in fifty years.

A new Homeland Security Department will be headed by Tom Ridge, former governor of Pennsylvania. The new Cabinet-level super agency will combine 22 federal agencies and have 170,000 employees to protect America from terrorism. Congress also passed nationwide election standards, with billions of dollars earmarked for new voting equipment to rectify problems that have plagued voters in recent elections.

Congress also passed a whopping farm bill increasing subsidies to farmers by 80 percent. Ohio Rep. James Trafficant was expelled from Congress for taking bribes and kickbacks.

Congress did nothing about prescription drugs or health issues but did give a resounding vote of approval to President Bush's war on terrorism. A treaty called "the convention for the elimination of all forms of discrimination against women" has been ratified by 165 nations but still has seen no action in Congress.

SCOTT STANTIS
Courtesy Birmingham News

STANTIS ©2002 THE BIRMINGHAM NEWS
SO.... WHERE DO I DRAW THE LINE?....
We the People
SECURITY

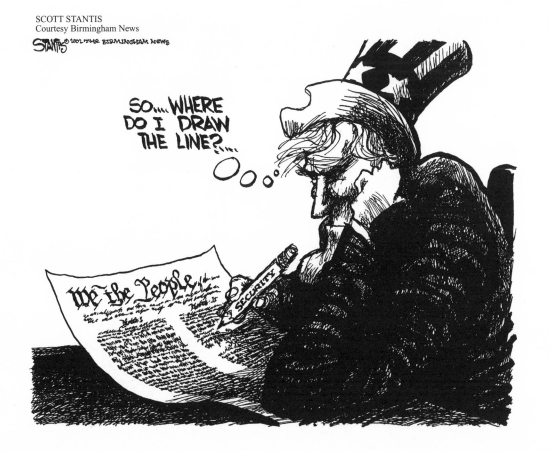

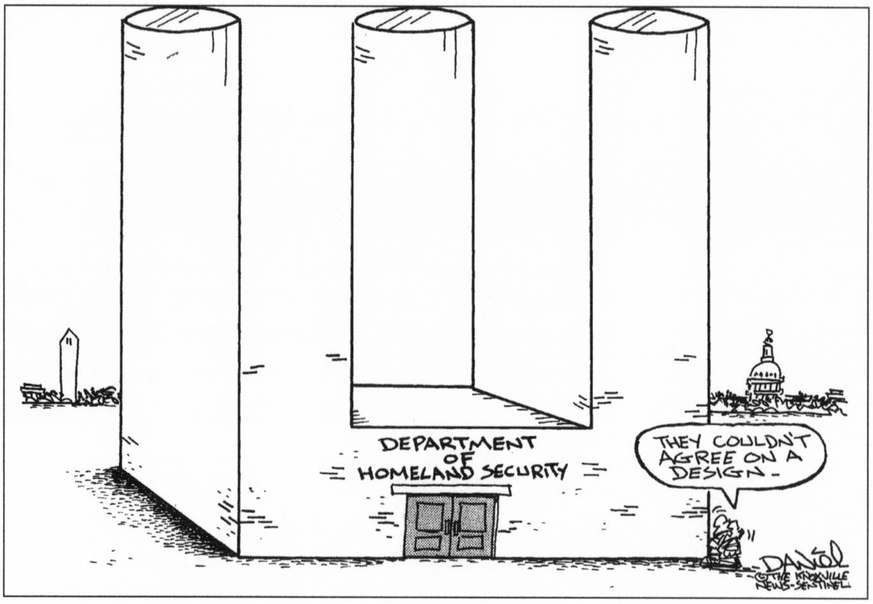
DEPARTMENT OF HOMELAND SECURITY
THEY COULDN'T AGREE ON A DESIGN-
DANIEL ©THE KNOXVILLE NEWS-SENTINEL

CHARLES DANIEL
Courtesy Knoxville News-Sentinel

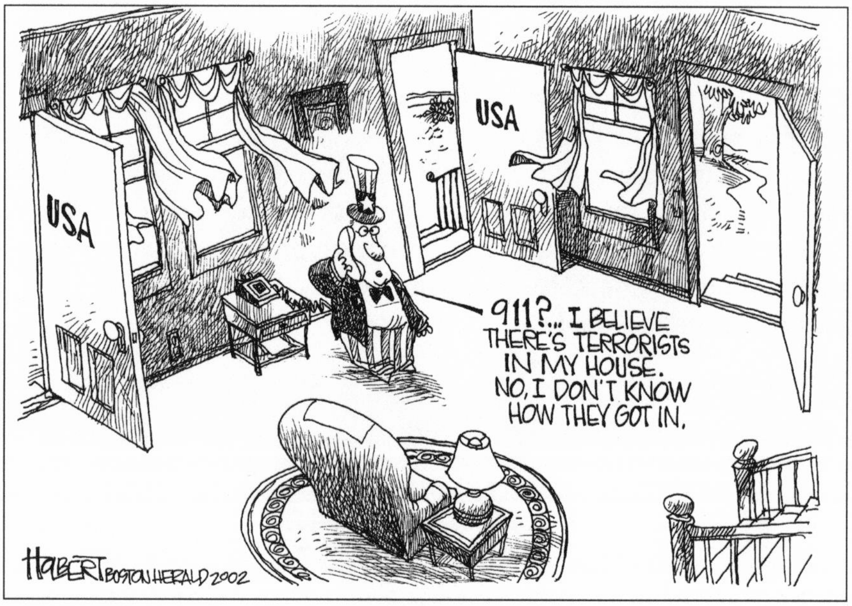
USA
USA
911?... I BELIEVE THERE'S TERRORISTS IN MY HOUSE. NO, I DON'T KNOW HOW THEY GOT IN.
HOLBERT BOSTON HERALD 2002

JERRY HOLBERT
Courtesy Boston Herald

SIGNE WILKINSON
Courtesy Philadelphia Daily News

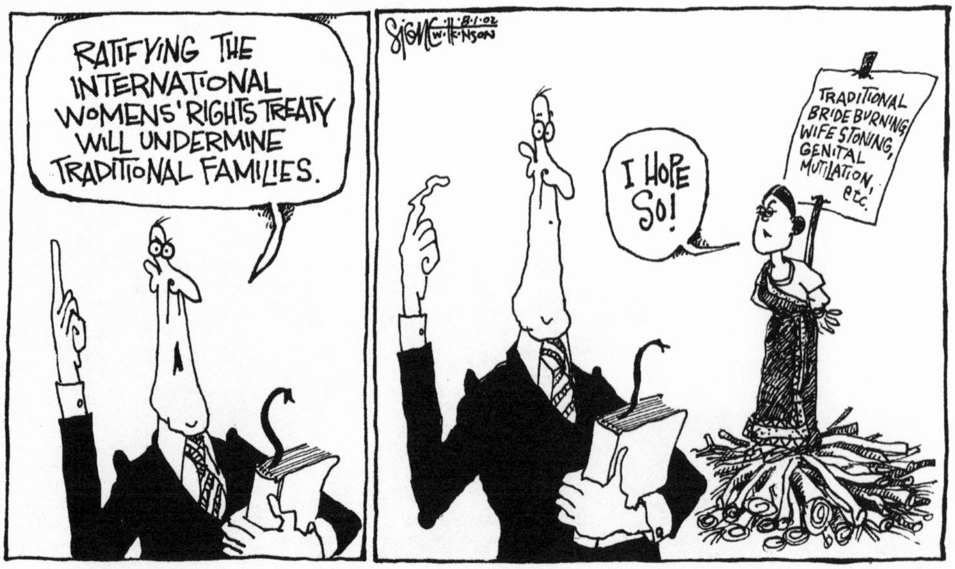
RATIFYING THE INTERNATIONAL WOMENS' RIGHTS TREATY WILL UNDERMINE TRADITIONAL FAMILIES.
SIGNE WILKINSON 8.1.02
I HOPE SO!
TRADITIONAL BRIDE BURNING, WIFE STONING, GENITAL MUTILATION, etc.

ETTA HULME
Courtesy Fort Worth Star-Telegram

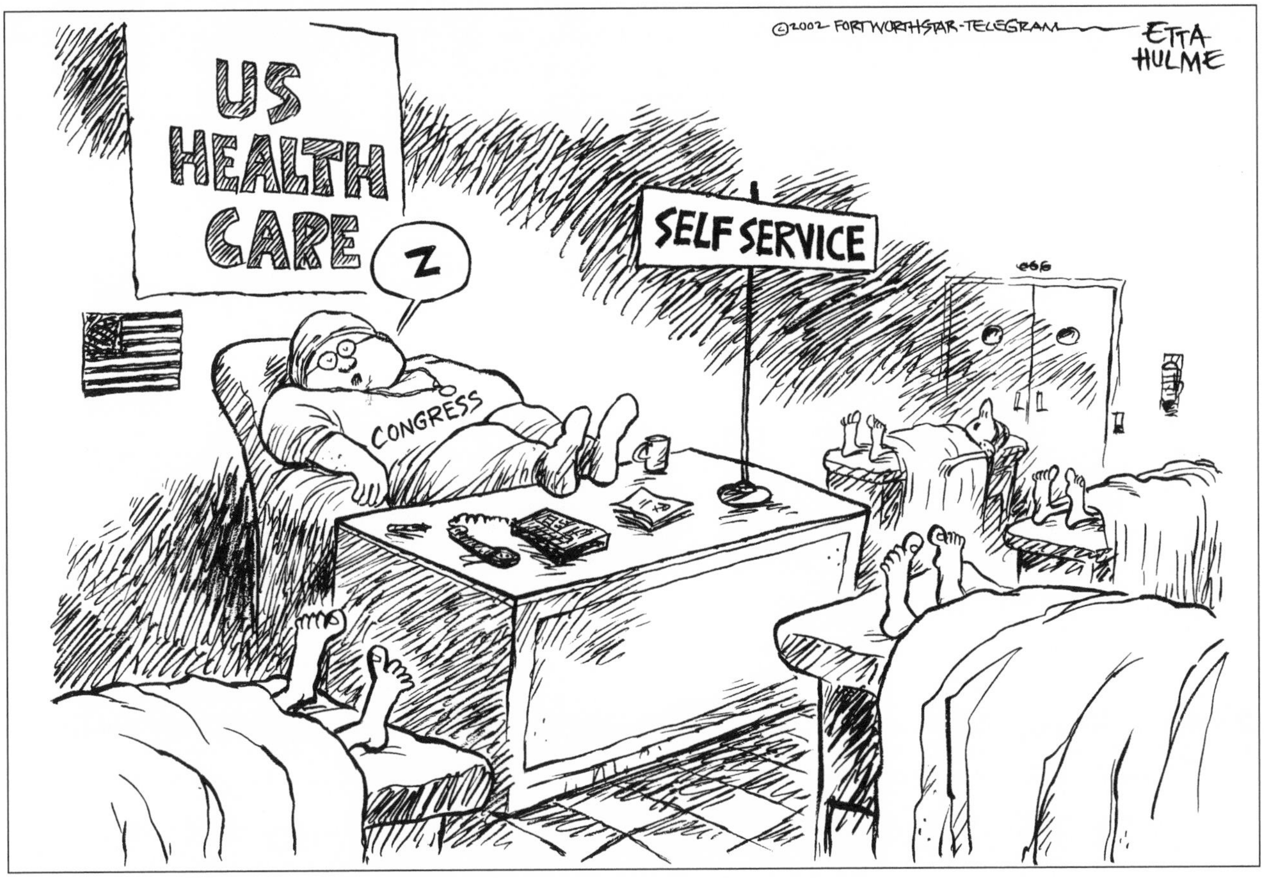

©2002 FORTWORTHSTAR-TELEGRAM
ETTA HULME
US HEALTH CARE
Z
SELF SERVICE
CONGRESS

JEFF PARKER
Courtesy Florida Today

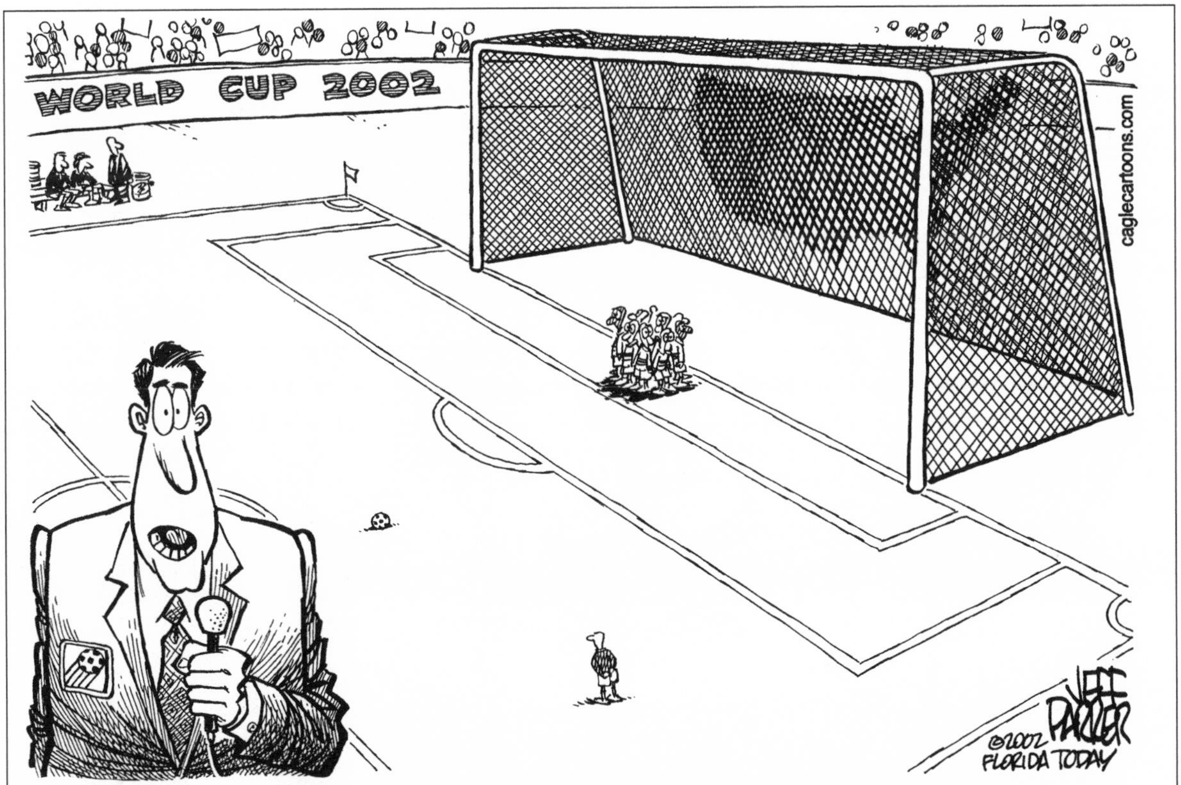

WORLD CUP 2002
caglecartoons.com
JEFF PARKER
©2002 FLORIDA TODAY
"...AND AS THE PROPOSED HOMELAND SECURITY DEPARTMENT TAKES THE FIELD, WE CAN SEE THEY SURE DO HAVE THEIR WORK CUT OUT FOR THEM WITH AN ENORMOUS GOAL TO KEEP..."

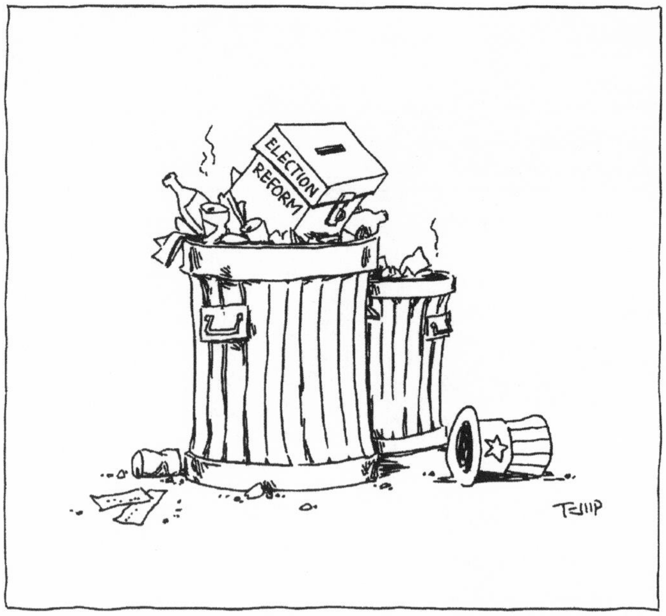
ELECTION REFORM

STEPHEN TEMPLETON
Courtesy The Observer-Times (N.C.)

MATT WUERKER
Courtesy Santa Cruz Metro

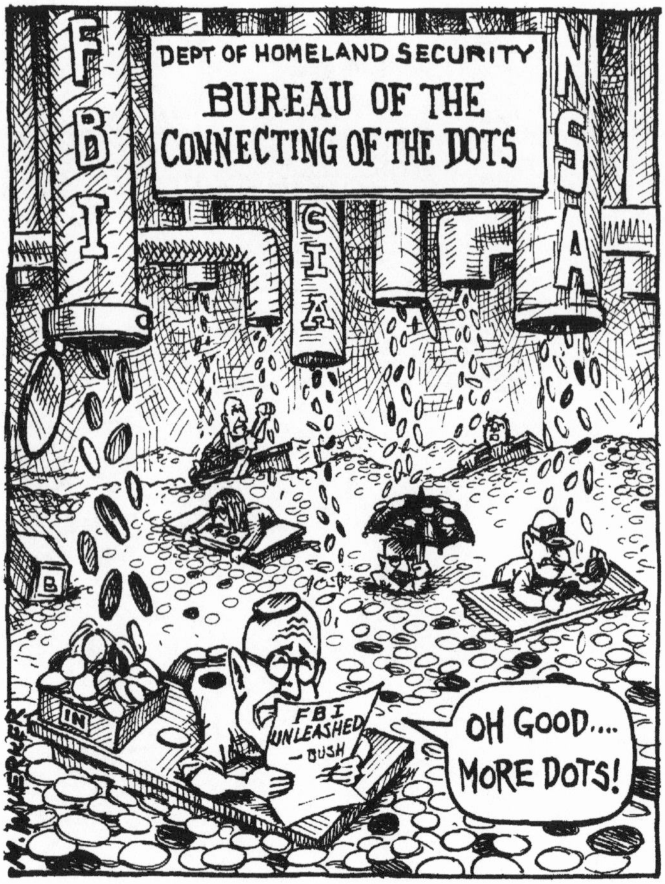
DEPT OF HOMELAND SECURITY
BUREAU OF THE CONNECTING OF THE DOTS
FBI
CIA
NSA
IN
FBI UNLEASHED — BUSH
OH GOOD.... MORE DOTS!

DREW SHENEMAN
Courtesy Newark Star-Ledger

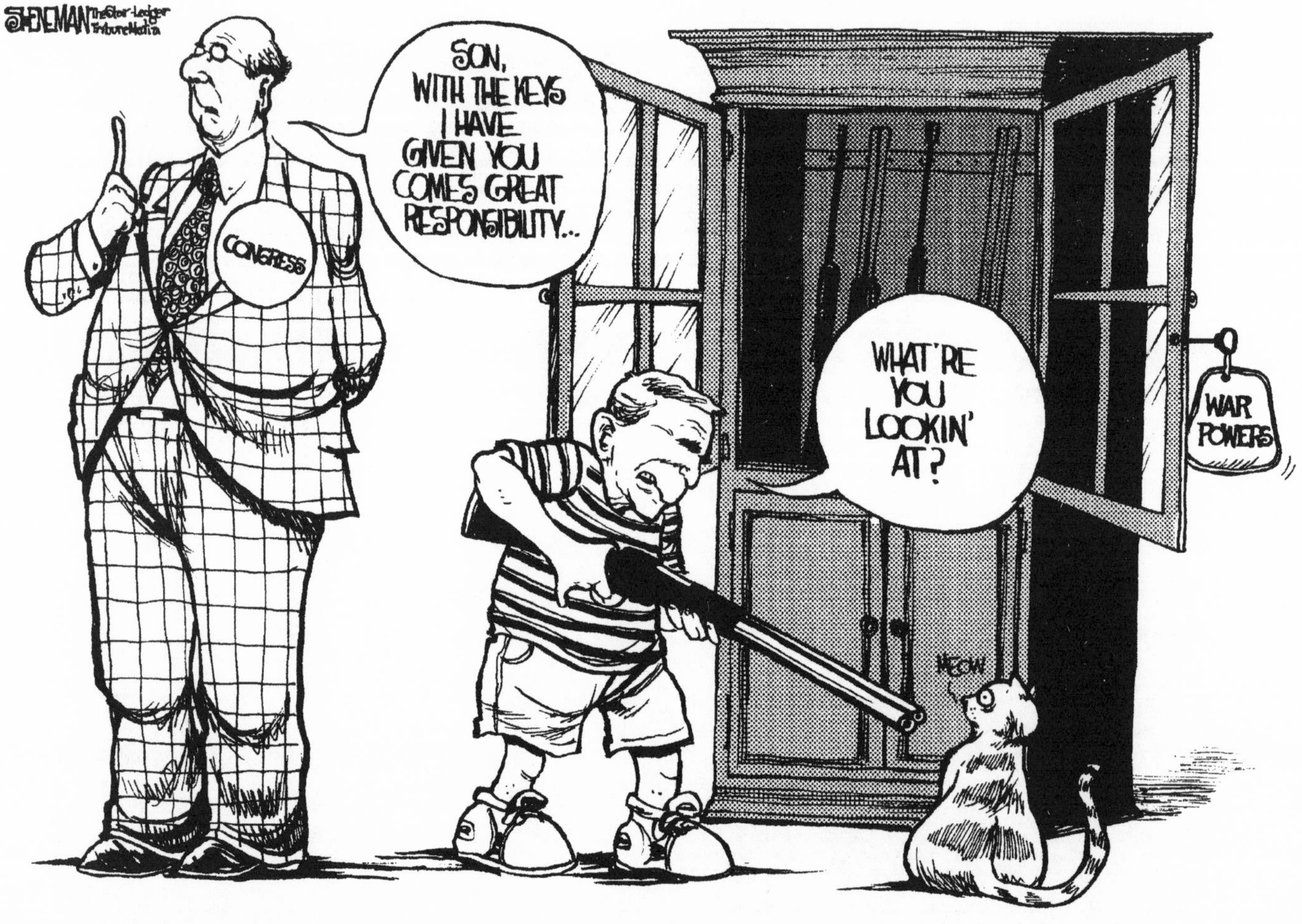
SON, WITH THE KEYS I HAVE GIVEN YOU COMES GREAT RESPONSIBILITY...
CONGRESS
WHAT'RE YOU LOOKIN' AT?
WAR POWERS
MEOW

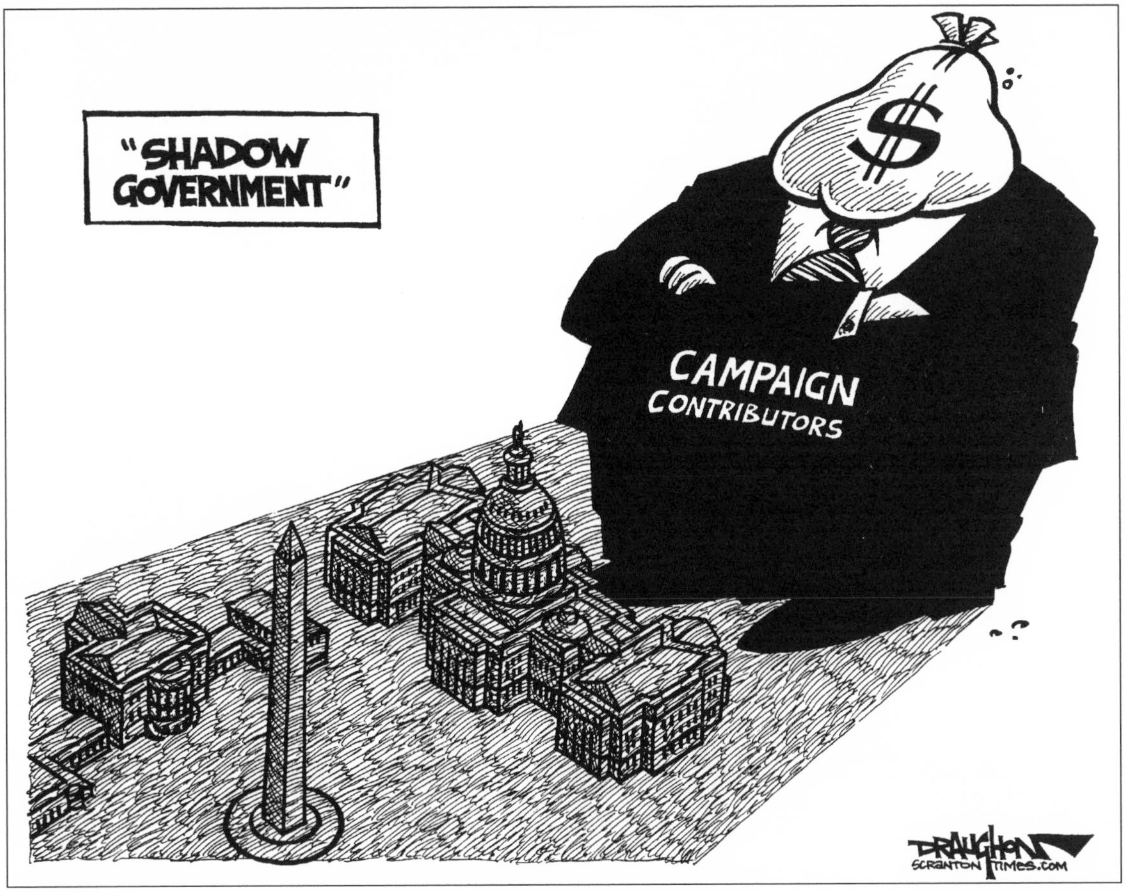
"SHADOW GOVERNMENT"
$
CAMPAIGN CONTRIBUTORS
DRAUGHON
SCRANTON TIMES.COM

DENNIS DRAUGHON
Courtesy Scranton Times

PAUL FELL
Courtesy Lincoln Journal Star

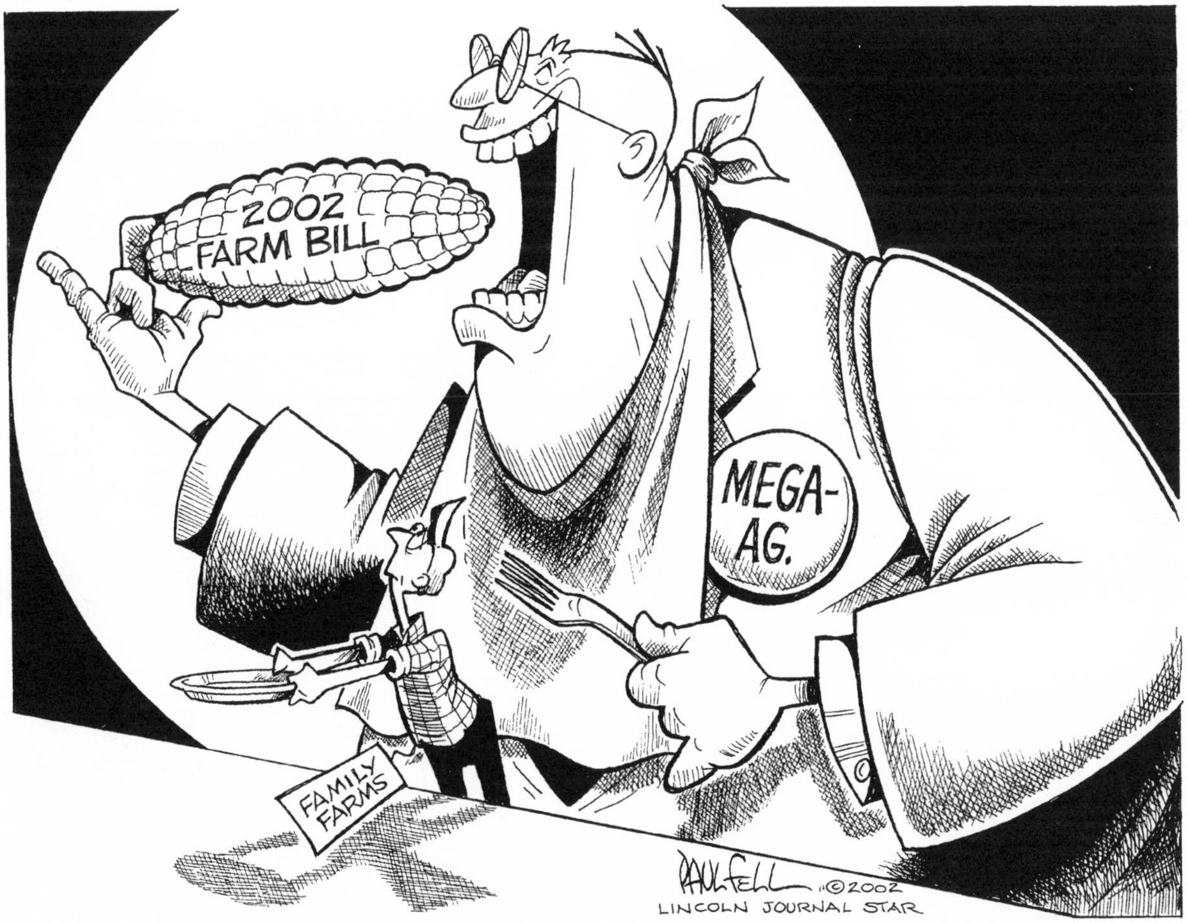
2002 FARM BILL
MEGA-AG.
FAMILY FARMS
PAUL FELL ©2002
LINCOLN JOURNAL STAR

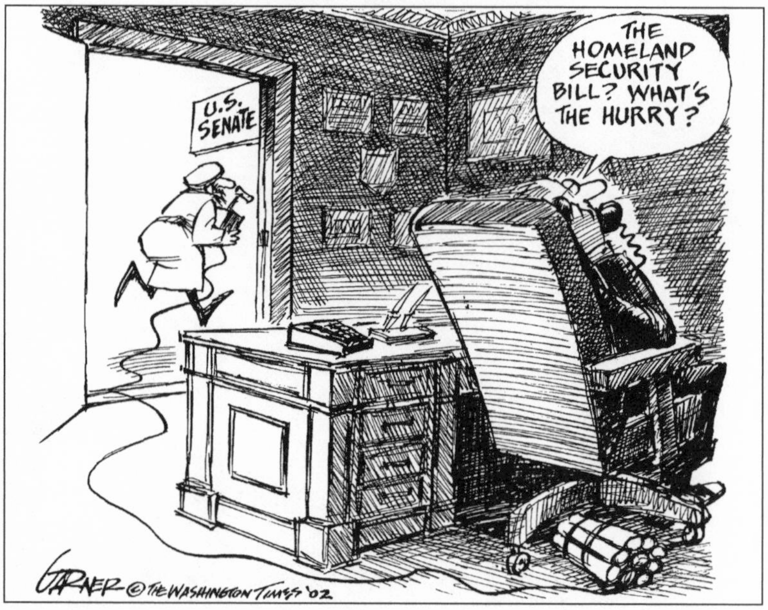
THE HOMELAND SECURITY BILL? WHAT'S THE HURRY?
U.S. SENATE
GARNER © THE WASHINGTON TIMES '02

BILL GARNER
Courtesy Washington Times

DAN O'BRIEN
Courtesy The Business Journal (Oh.)

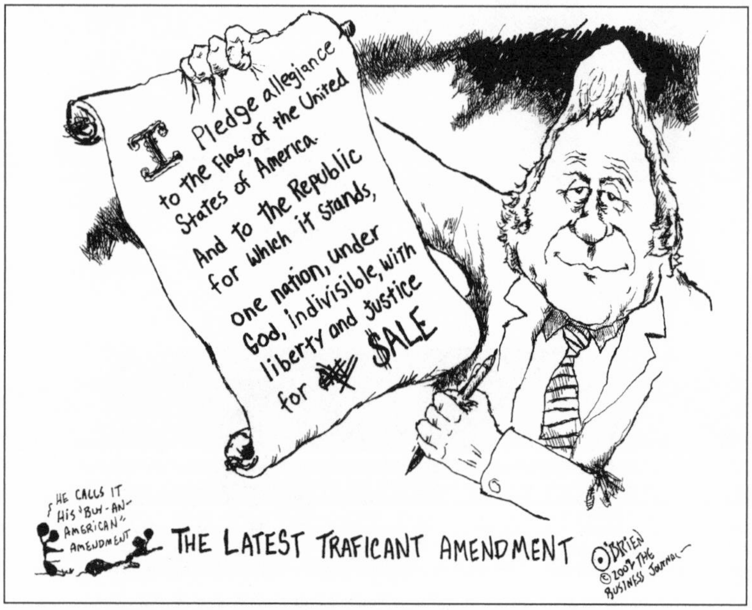
I Pledge allegiance to the Flag, of the United States of America. And to the Republic for which it stands, one nation, under God, indivisible, with liberty and justice for ALL $ALE
HE CALLS IT HIS 'BUY-AN-AMERICAN' AMENDMENT
THE LATEST TRAFICANT AMENDMENT
O'BRIEN © 2002 THE BUSINESS JOURNAL

BRIAN DUFFY
Courtesy Des Moines Register

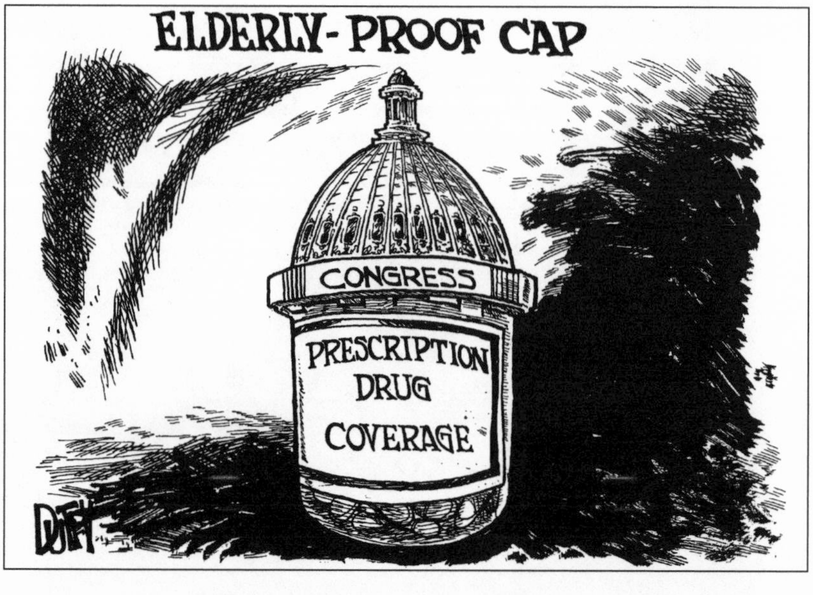
ELDERLY-PROOF CAP
CONGRESS
PRESCRIPTION DRUG COVERAGE
DUFFY

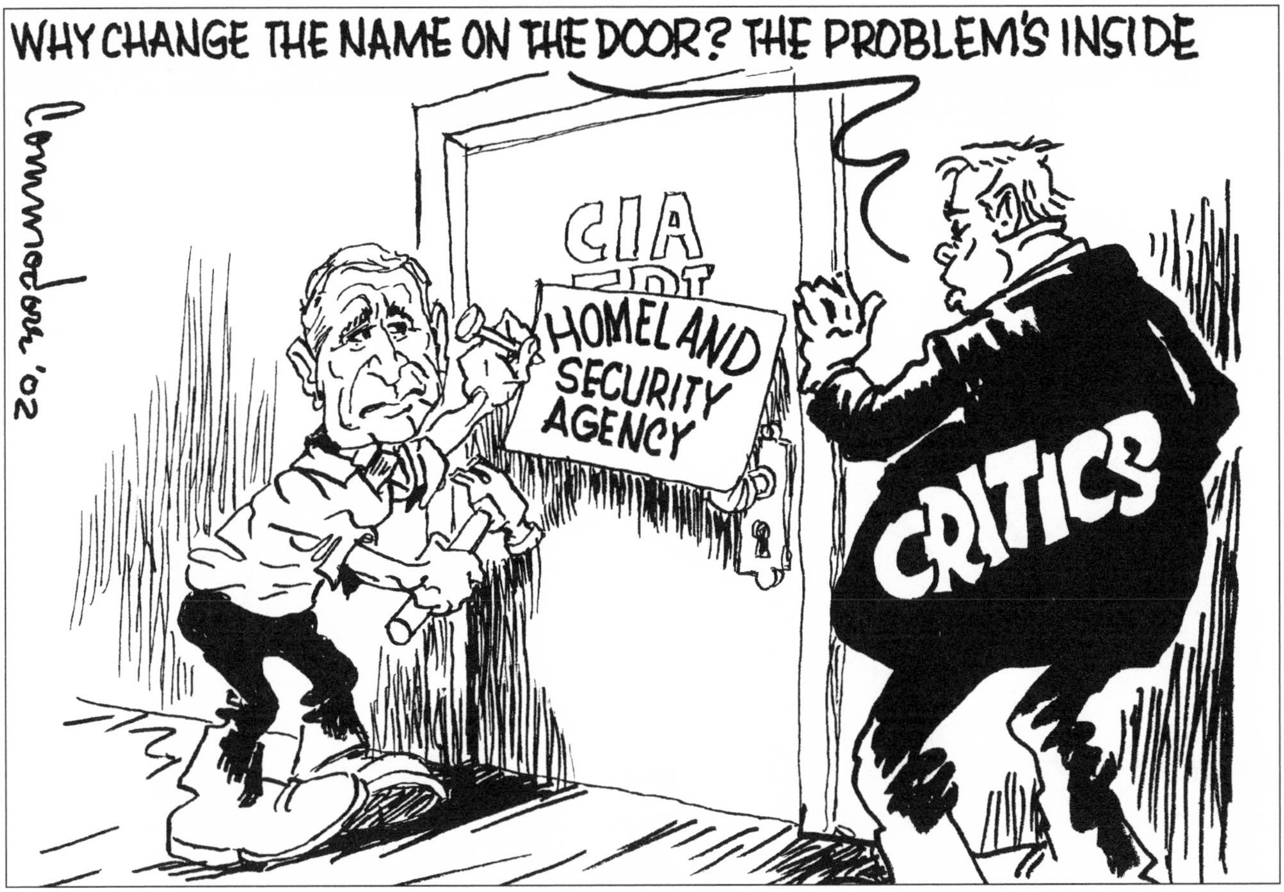
WHY CHANGE THE NAME ON THE DOOR? THE PROBLEM'S INSIDE
Commodore '02
CIA
HOMELAND SECURITY AGENCY
CRITICS

CHESTER COMMODORE
Courtesy Chicago Defender

CLAY BENNETT
Courtesy Christian Science Monitor

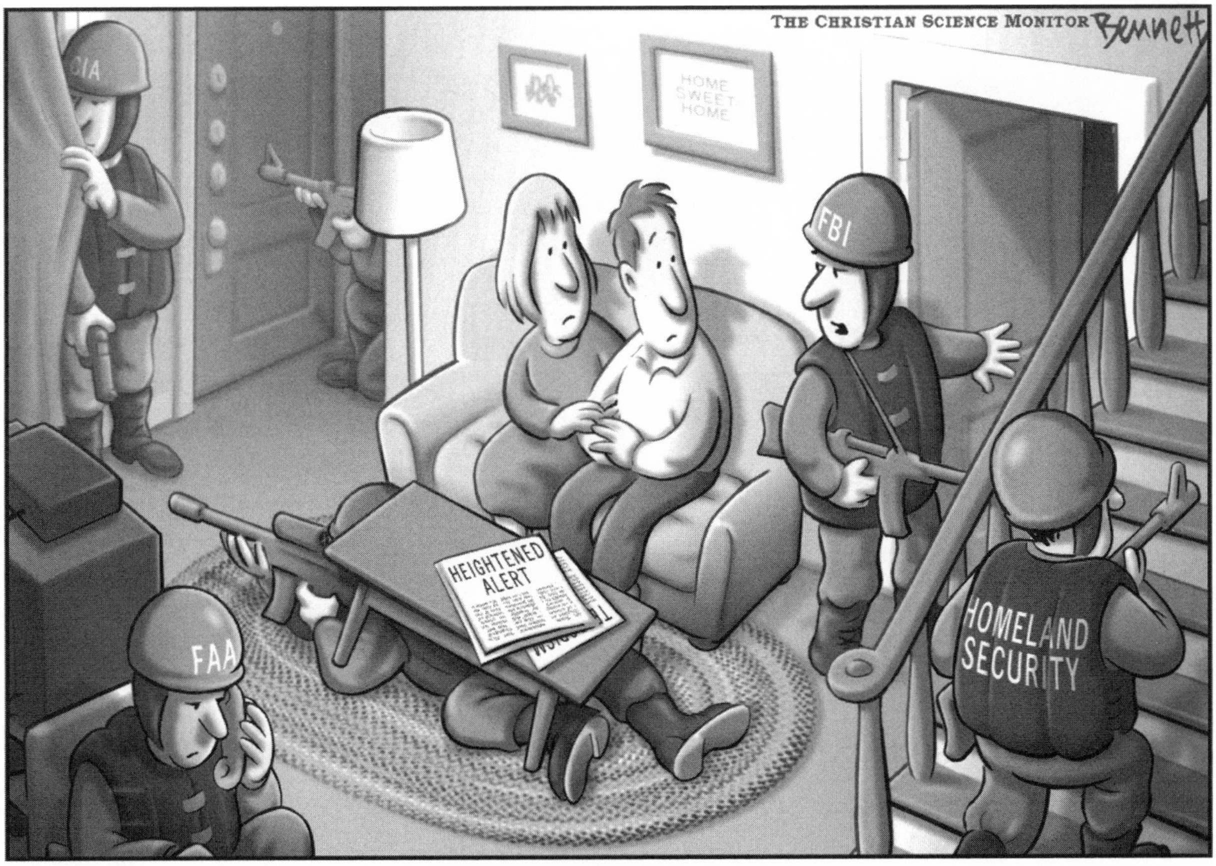
THE CHRISTIAN SCIENCE MONITOR
Bennett
HOME SWEET HOME
CIA
FBI
HEIGHTENED ALERT
FAA
HOMELAND SECURITY

'Now just act normal.'

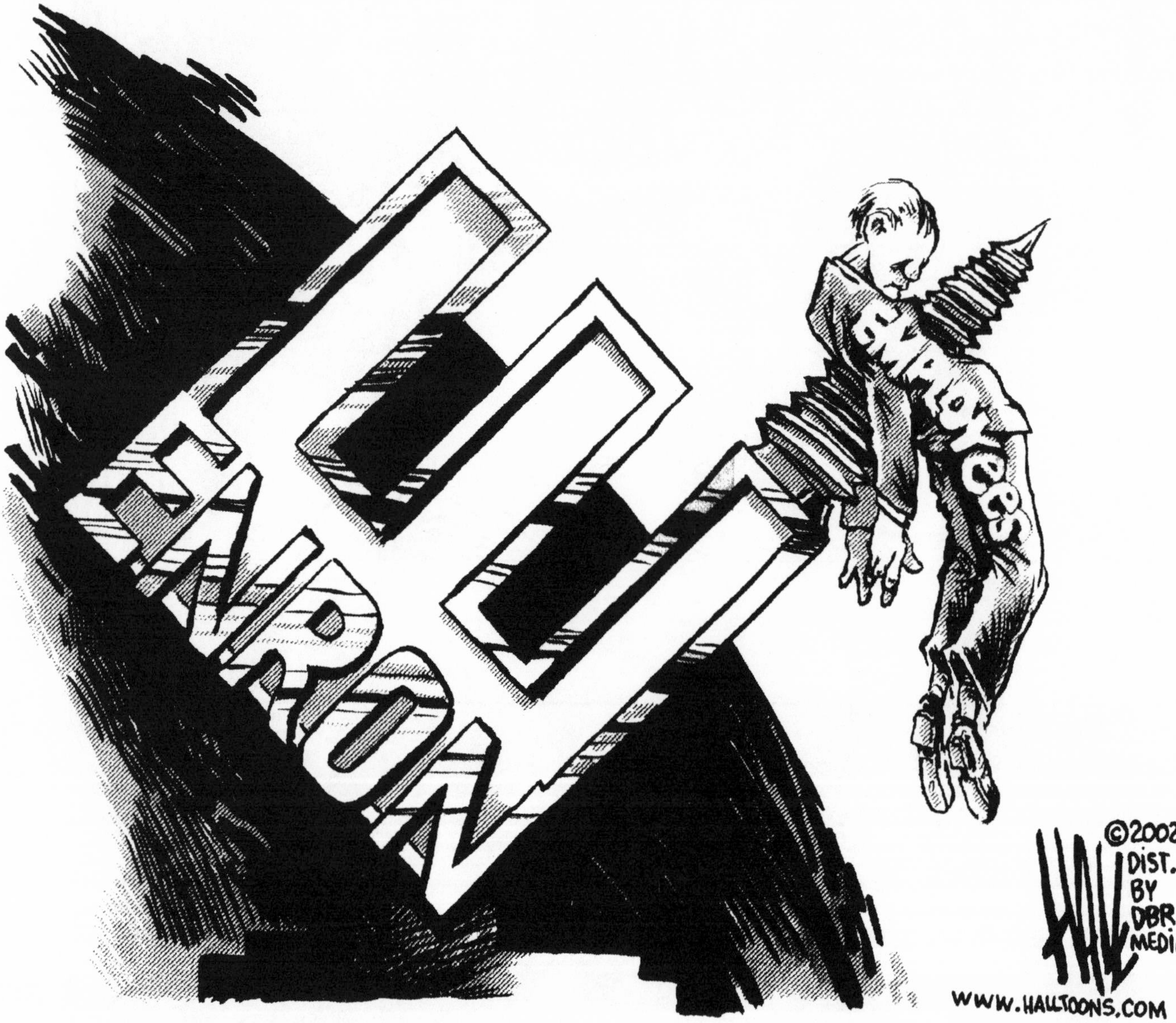
ENRON
EMPLOYEES
©2002 DIST. BY DBR MEDIA
HALL
WWW.HALLTOONS.COM

ED HALL
Courtesy Baker County Press (Fla.)

Enron / WorldCom

Fueled by Wall Street scandals, the stock market plunged in the summer to its lowest level in four years. The collapse of the energy-trading company Enron became a major story. Thousands of employees lost millions of dollars in 401(k) accounts and Enron stock, while top executives dumped their holdings before the crash. The company's auditor, Arthur Andersen, was accused of shredding documents, and top company executives faced a variety of charges, including obstruction of justice.

The story was repeated at companies such as Global Crossing and WorldCom, where executives reported a $3.8 billion accounting error, later estimated to be $5 billion. In each case, the company stock took a nosedive and thousands were laid off. Two former WorldCom executives were indicted on fraud charges.

Martha Stewart, the homemaking queen, dumped 3,928 shares of Imclone the day before the Food and Drug Administration declined to approve the firm's drug Erbitux. The company CEO, a friend of Stewart, was later charged with insider trading and perjury. Imclone stock lost 60 percent of its value after Stewart's name was linked to the scandal, and a probe of Stewart continued at year's end.

ROBERT ARIAIL
Courtesy The State (S.C.)

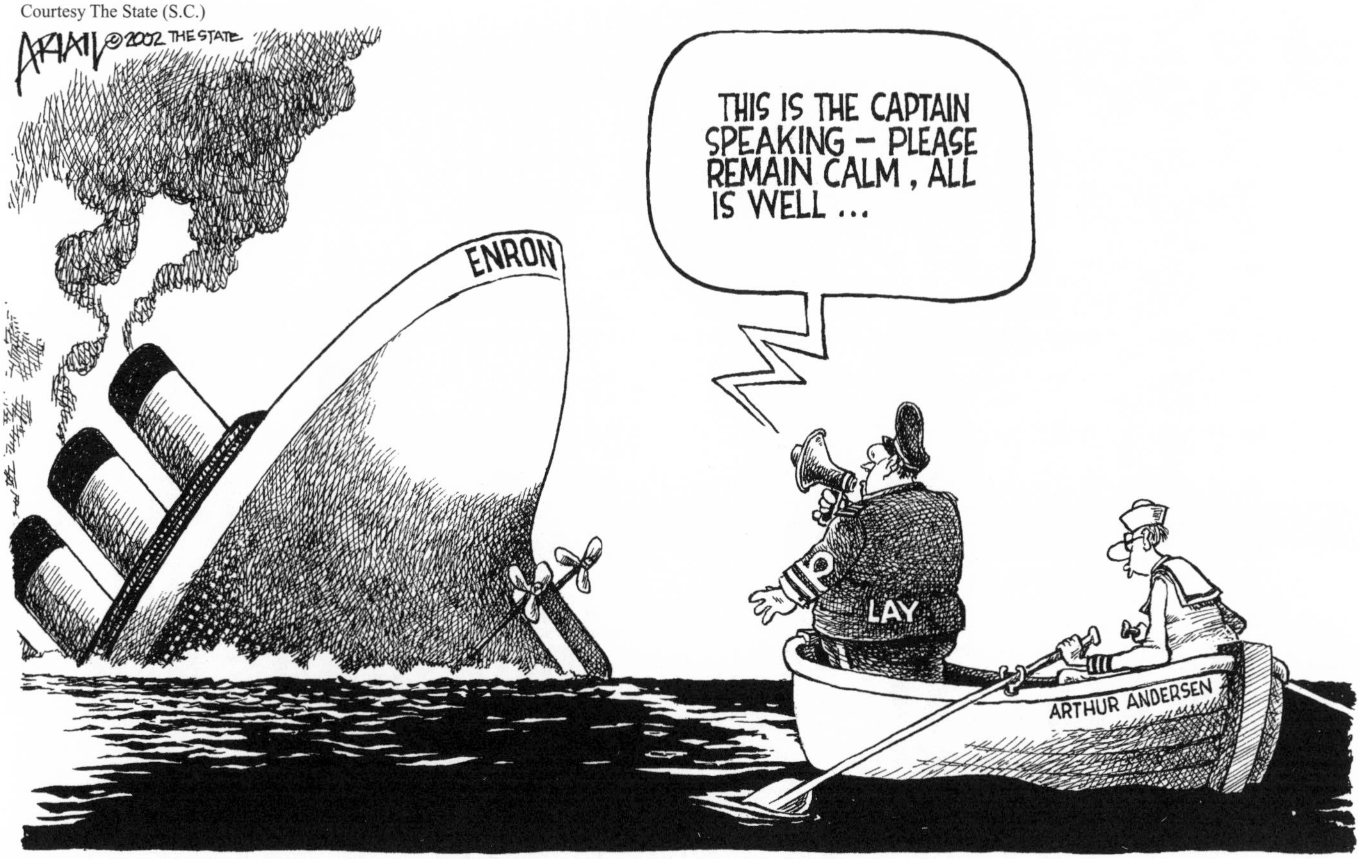
ARIAIL ©2002 THE STATE
THIS IS THE CAPTAIN SPEAKING – PLEASE REMAIN CALM, ALL IS WELL ...
ENRON
LAY
ARTHUR ANDERSEN

MALCOLM MAYES
Courtesy Edmonton Journal

MAYES Edmonton Journal
ENRON

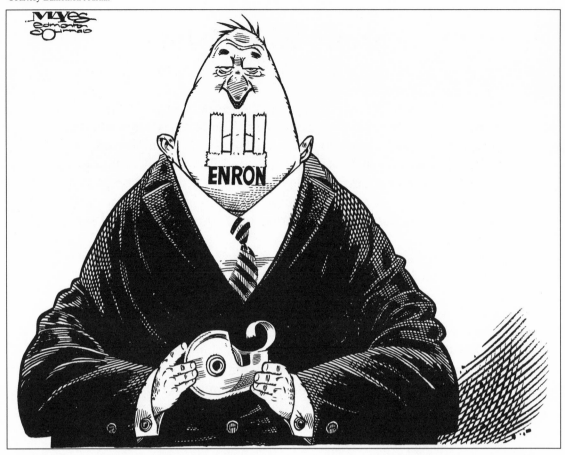

JUSTIN DeFREITAS
Courtesy Placerville Mountain Democrat (Calif.)

DeFREITAS
ADELPHIA CORP 15-20YRS.....IMCLONE 3-5YRS..... ARTHUR ANDERSEN 10-20YRS.
WORLDCOM 5-10YRS.....ENRON 6-12YRS..... TYCO 8-10YRS.....AOL TIME WARNER 5-10YRS..... ADELPHIA
THE NEW WALL STREET

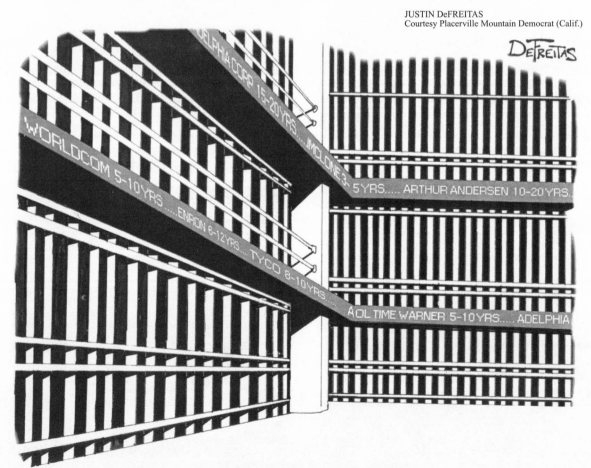

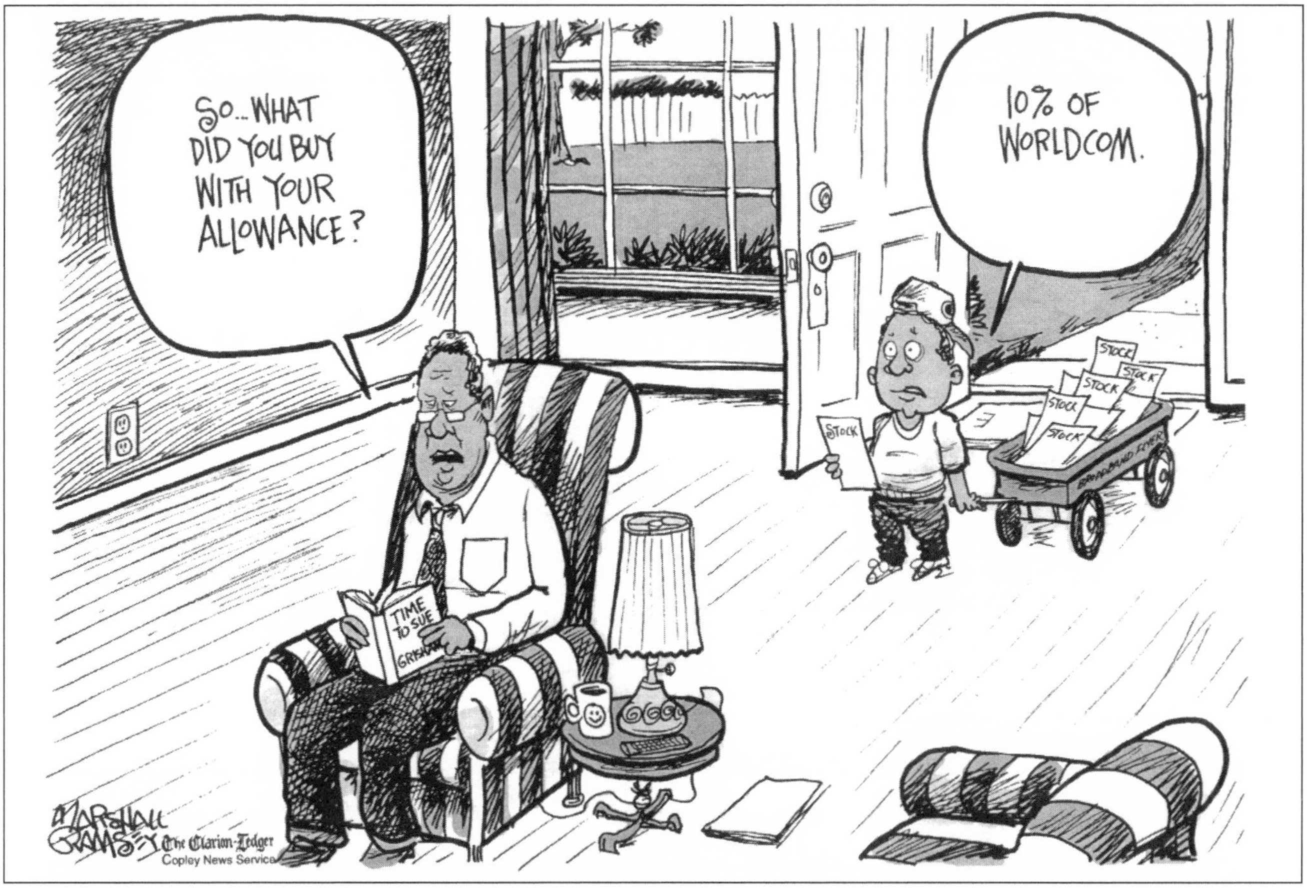
SO...WHAT DID YOU BUY WITH YOUR ALLOWANCE?
10% OF WORLDCOM.
TIME TO SUE
STOCK
MARSHALL RAMSEY The Clarion-Ledger
Copley News Service

MARSHALL RAMSEY
Courtesy The Clarion Ledger

MICHAEL THOMPSON
Courtesy Detroit Free Press

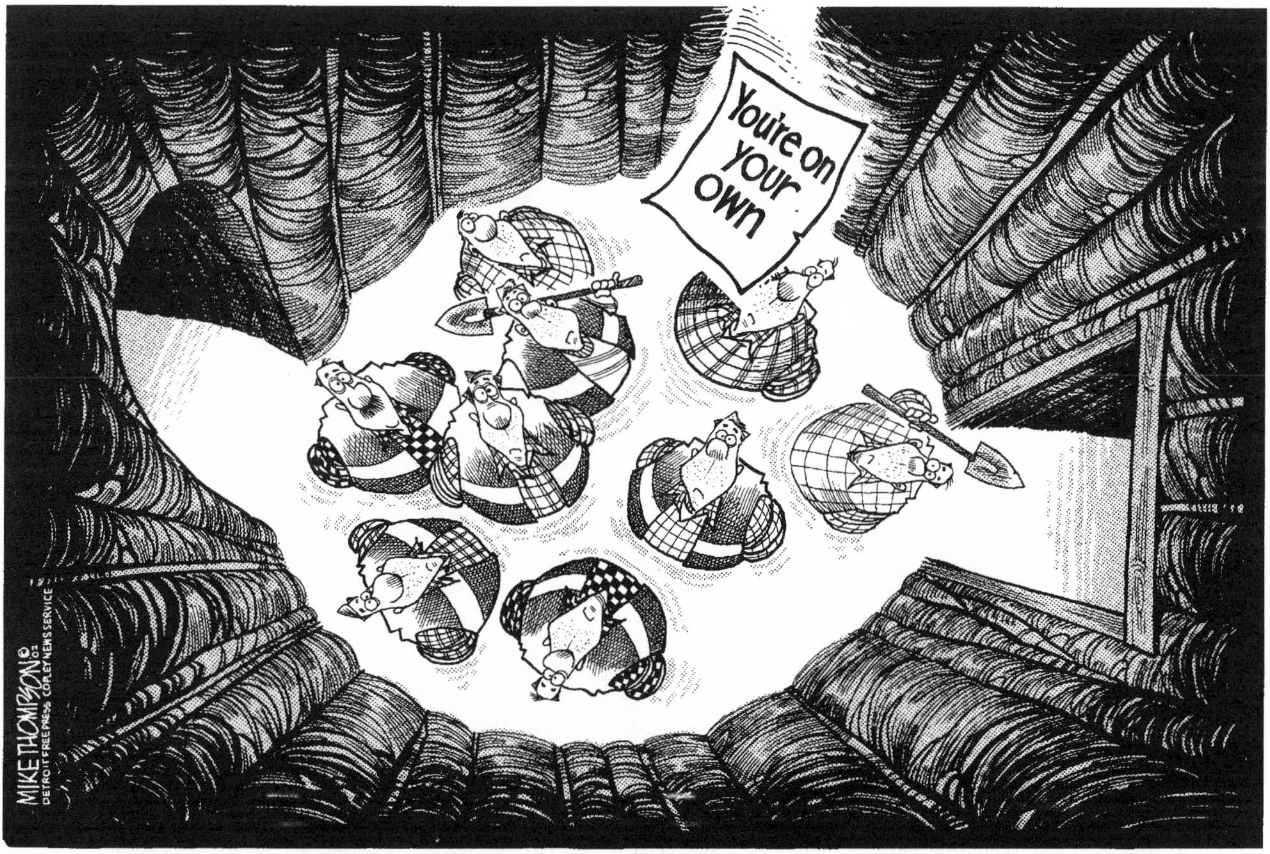
You're on your own
MIKE THOMPSON

HAD THAT MINE BEEN OWNED BY ENRON, ADELPHIA, GLOBAL CROSSING, WORLDCOM...

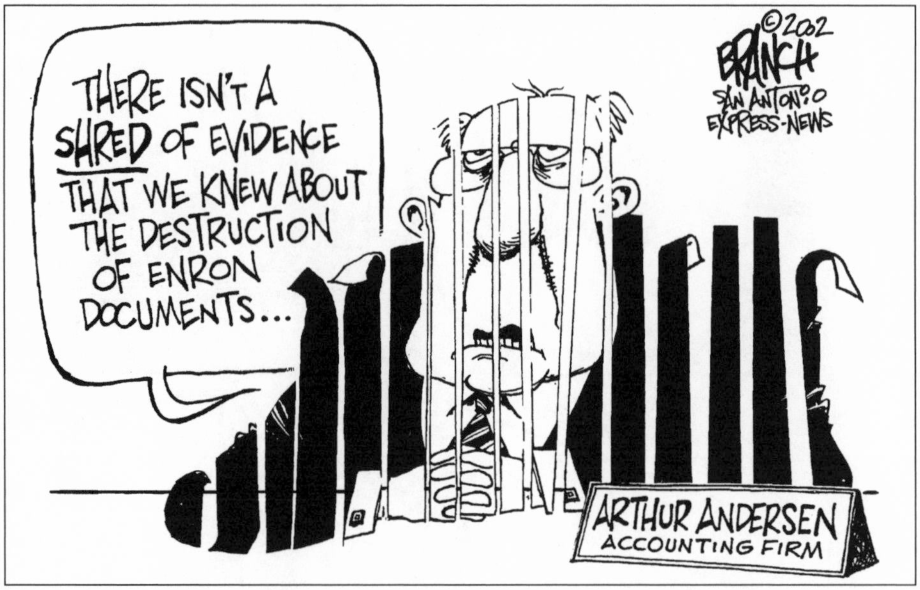
THERE ISN'T A SHRED OF EVIDENCE THAT WE KNEW ABOUT THE DESTRUCTION OF ENRON DOCUMENTS...
©2002 BRANCH SAN ANTONIO EXPRESS-NEWS
ARTHUR ANDERSEN
ACCOUNTING FIRM

JOHN BRANCH
Courtesy San Antonio Express-News

BOB RICH
Courtesy Connecticut Post

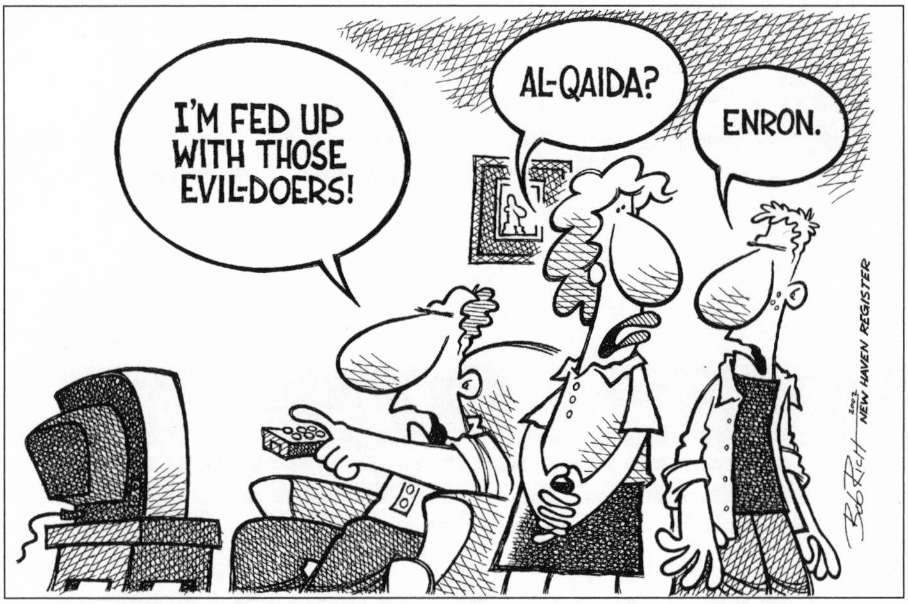
I'M FED UP WITH THOSE EVIL-DOERS!
AL-QAIDA?
ENRON.
NEW HAVEN REGISTER

SIGNE WILKINSON
Courtesy Philadelphia Daily News

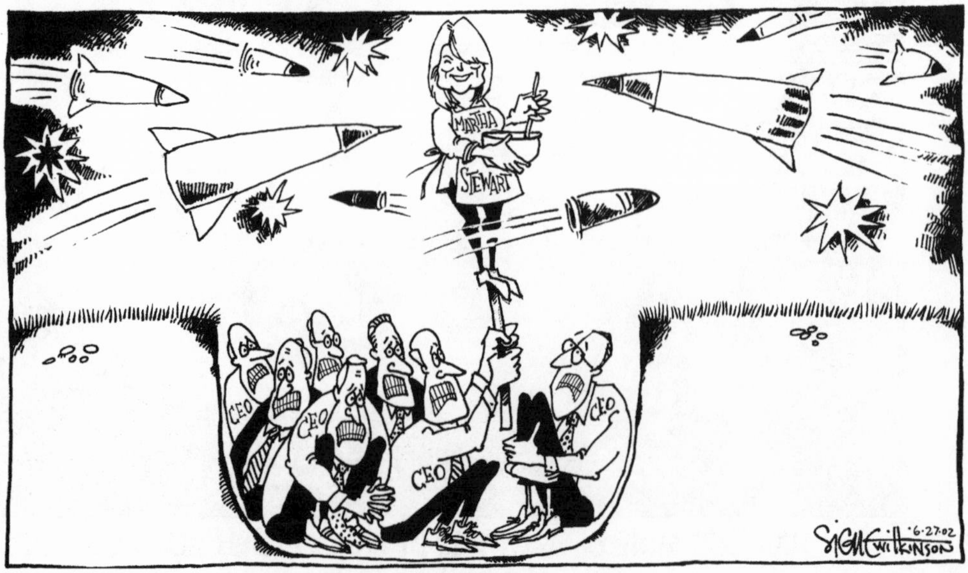
MARTHA
STEWART
CEO
CEO
CEO
CEO
6.27.02
SIGNE WILKINSON

VIC HARVILLE
Courtesy Donrey News (Ark.)

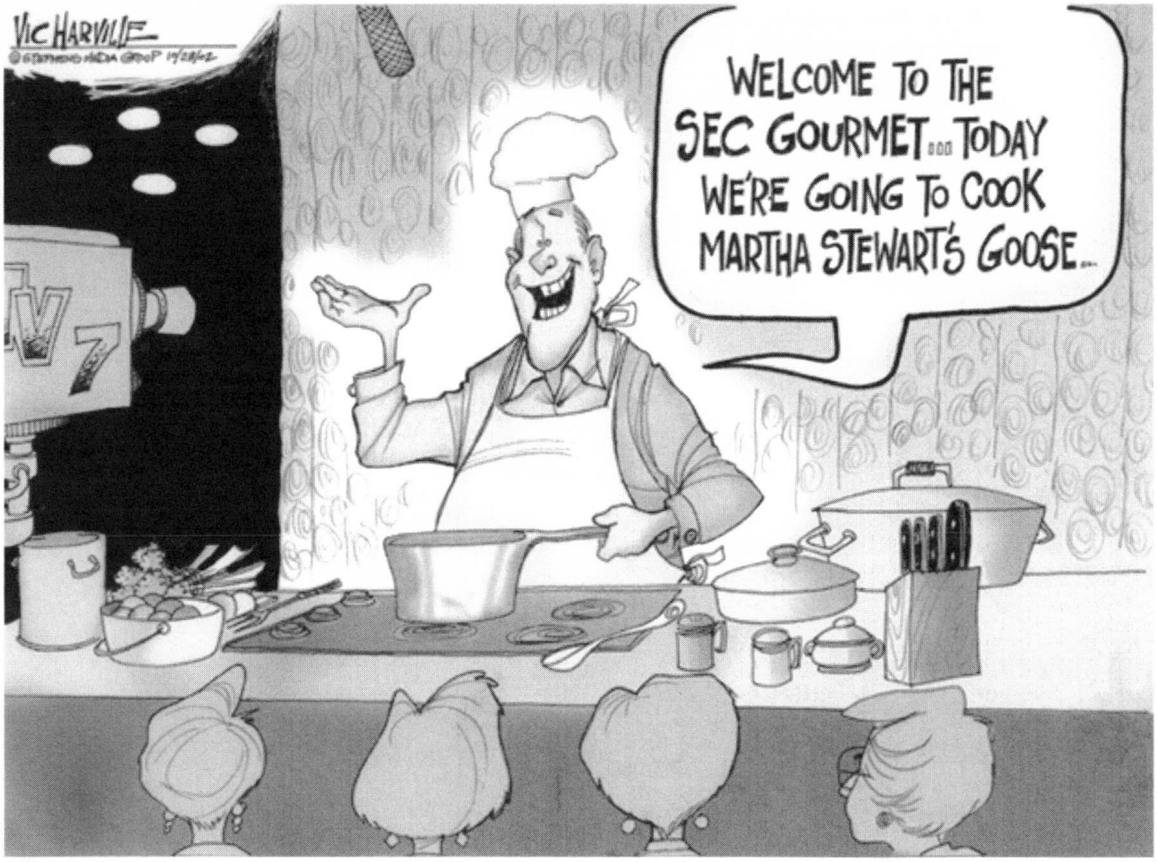

VIC HARVILLE
WELCOME TO THE SEC GOURMET... TODAY WE'RE GOING TO COOK MARTHA STEWART'S GOOSE...

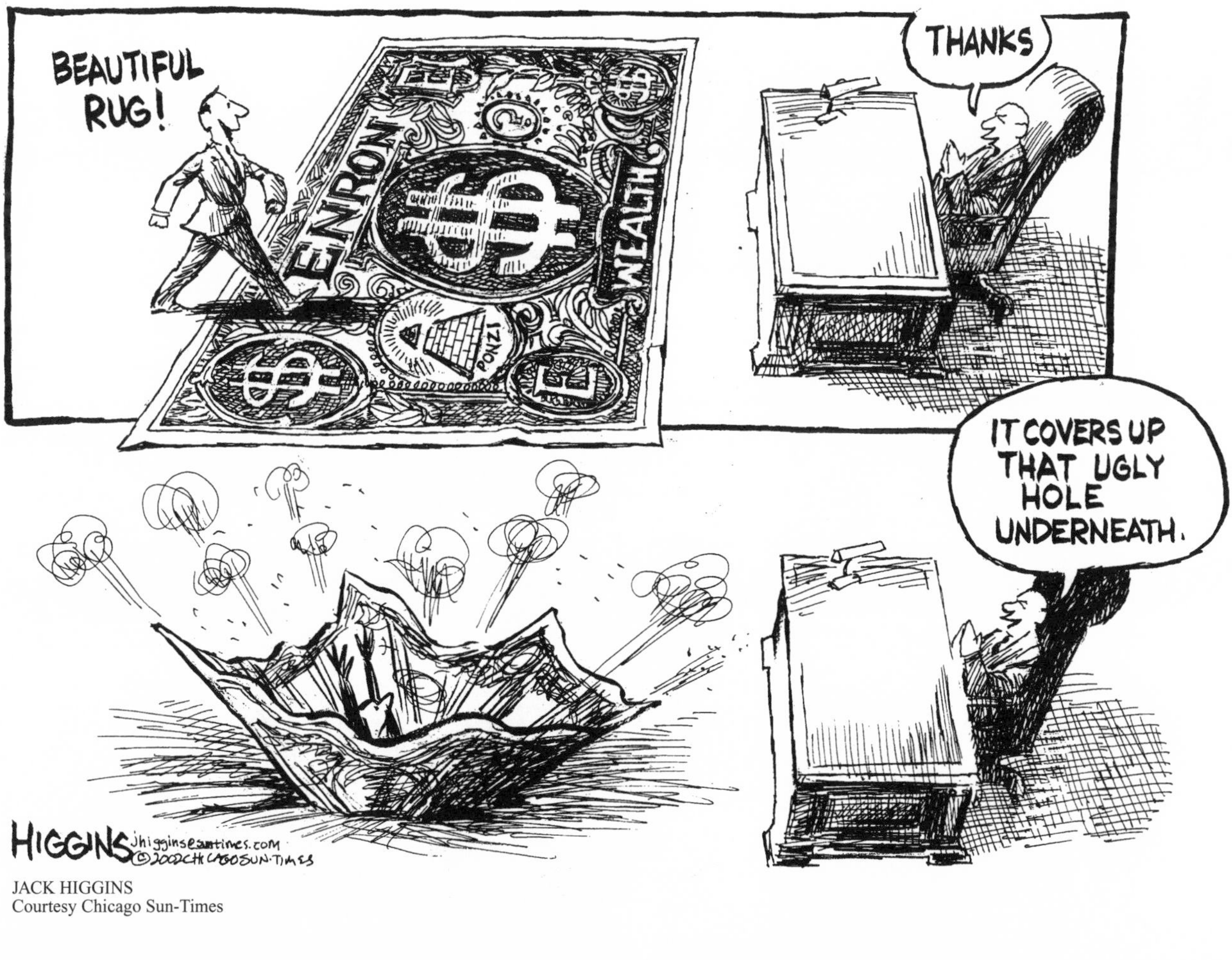

BEAUTIFUL RUG!
THANKS
ENRON
WEALTH
PONZI
IT COVERS UP THAT UGLY HOLE UNDERNEATH.
HIGGINS

JACK HIGGINS
Courtesy Chicago Sun-Times

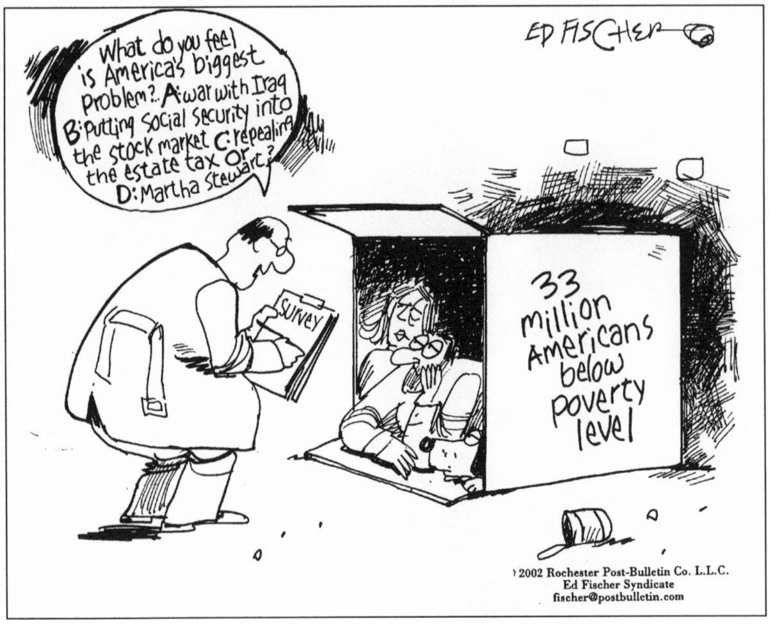
ED FISCHER
What do you feel is America's biggest Problem?. A: war with Iraq B: Putting Social Security into the stock market C: repealing the estate tax Or D: Martha Stewart?
SURVEY
33 million Americans below poverty level
© 2002 Rochester Post-Bulletin Co. L.L.C.
Ed Fischer Syndicate
fischer@postbulletin.com

ED FISCHER
Courtesy Rochester Post-Bulletin (Minn.)

JIM BORGMAN
Courtesy Cincinnati Enquirer

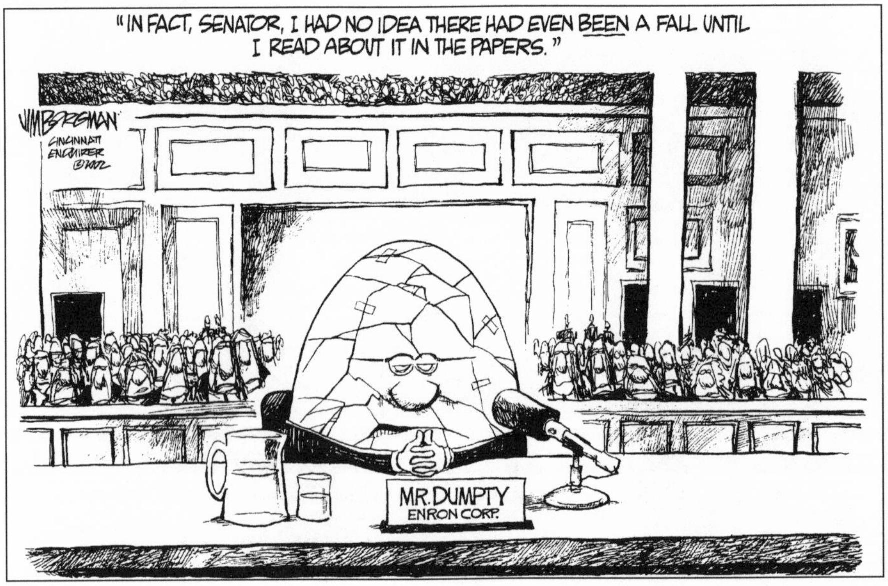
"IN FACT, SENATOR, I HAD NO IDEA THERE HAD EVEN BEEN A FALL UNTIL I READ ABOUT IT IN THE PAPERS."
JIM BORGMAN
CINCINNATI ENQUIRER ©2002
MR. DUMPTY
ENRON CORP.

JOE HELLER
Courtesy Green Bay Press-Gazette

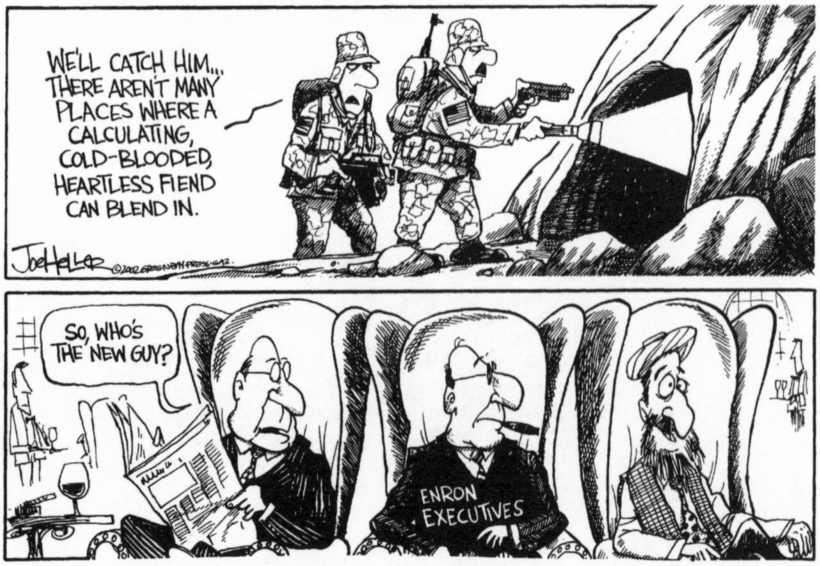
WE'LL CATCH HIM... THERE AREN'T MANY PLACES WHERE A CALCULATING, COLD-BLOODED, HEARTLESS FIEND CAN BLEND IN.
JOE HELLER
SO, WHO'S THE NEW GUY?
ENRON EXECUTIVES

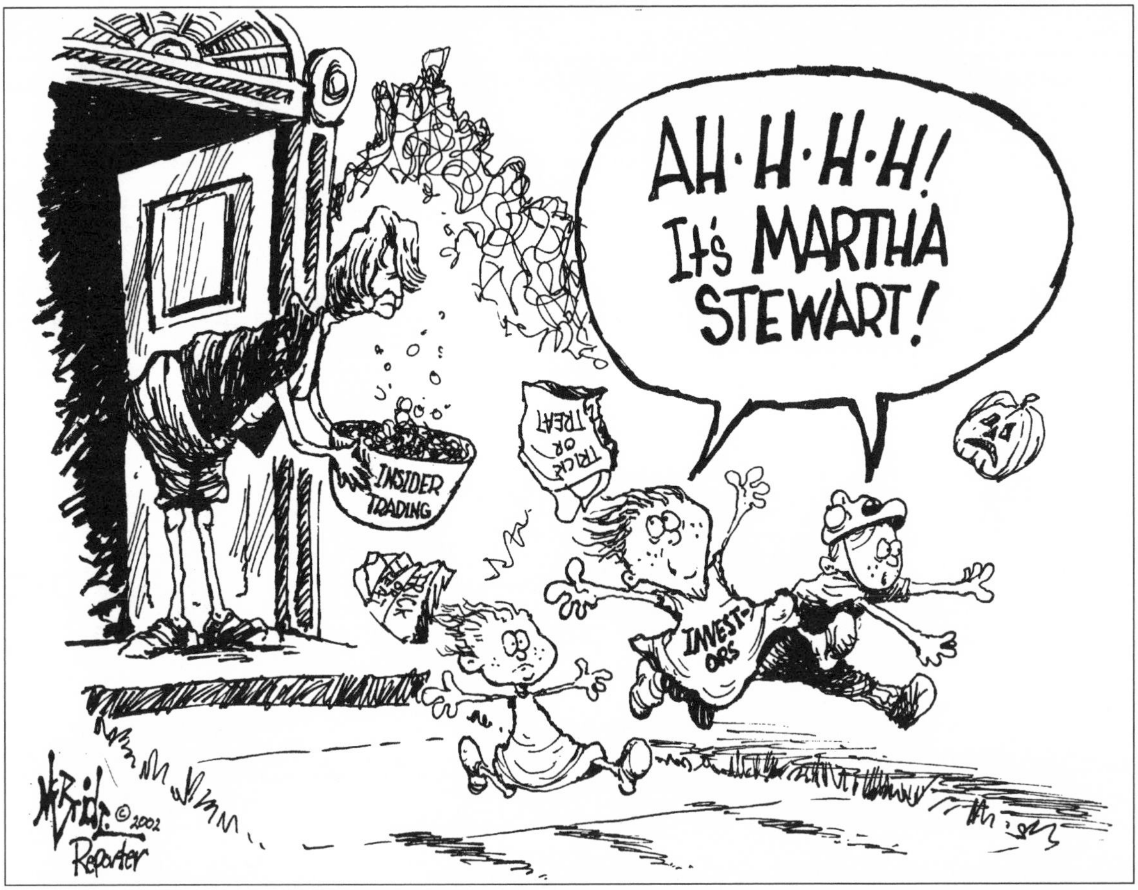
AH·H·H·H! It's MARTHA STEWART!
TRICK OR TREAT
INSIDER TRADING
INVEST-ORS
McBride ©2002 Reporter

STEVE McBRIDE
Courtesy Independence Daily Reporter (Kan.)

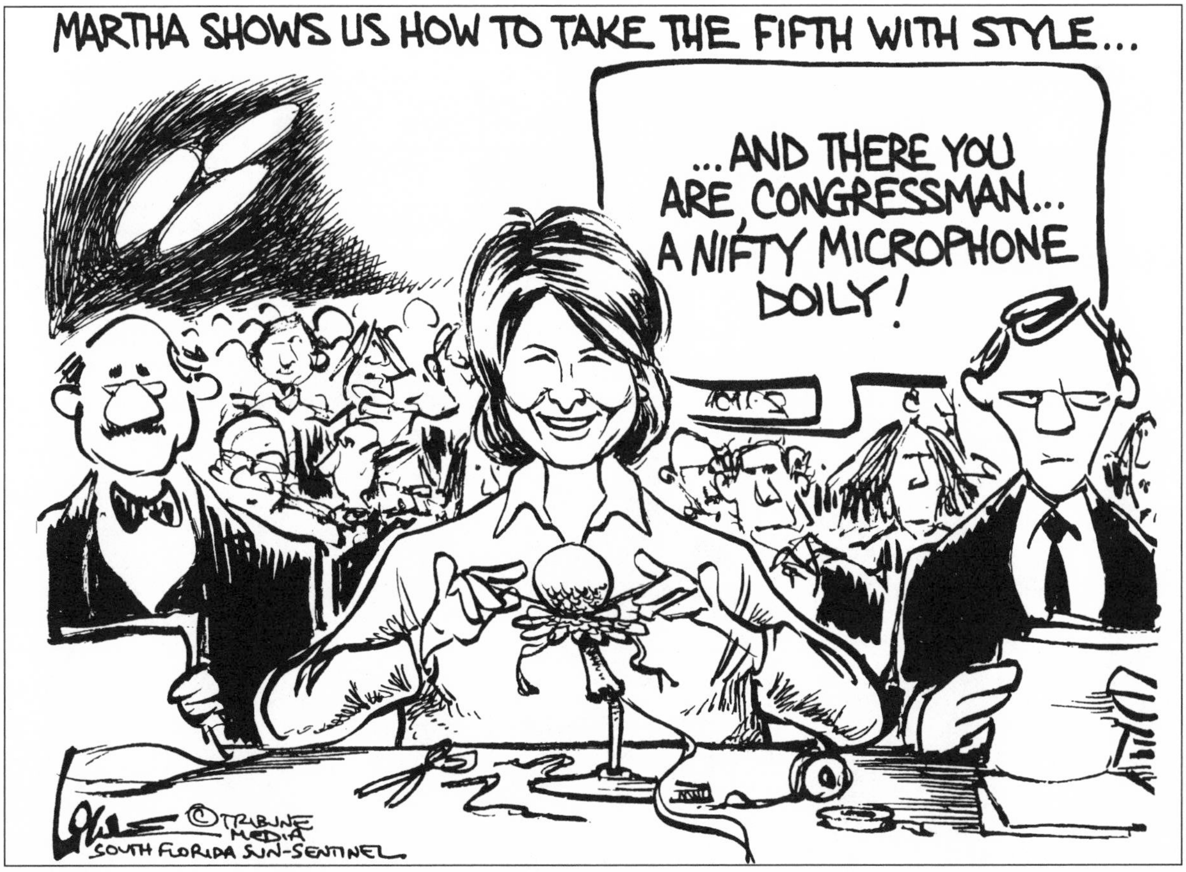
MARTHA SHOWS US HOW TO TAKE THE FIFTH WITH STYLE...
...AND THERE YOU ARE, CONGRESSMAN... A NIFTY MICROPHONE DOILY!
©TRIBUNE MEDIA
SOUTH FLORIDA SUN-SENTINEL

CHAN LOWE
Courtesy Fort Lauderdale News/Sun Sentinel

ED STEIN
Courtesy Rocky Mountain News

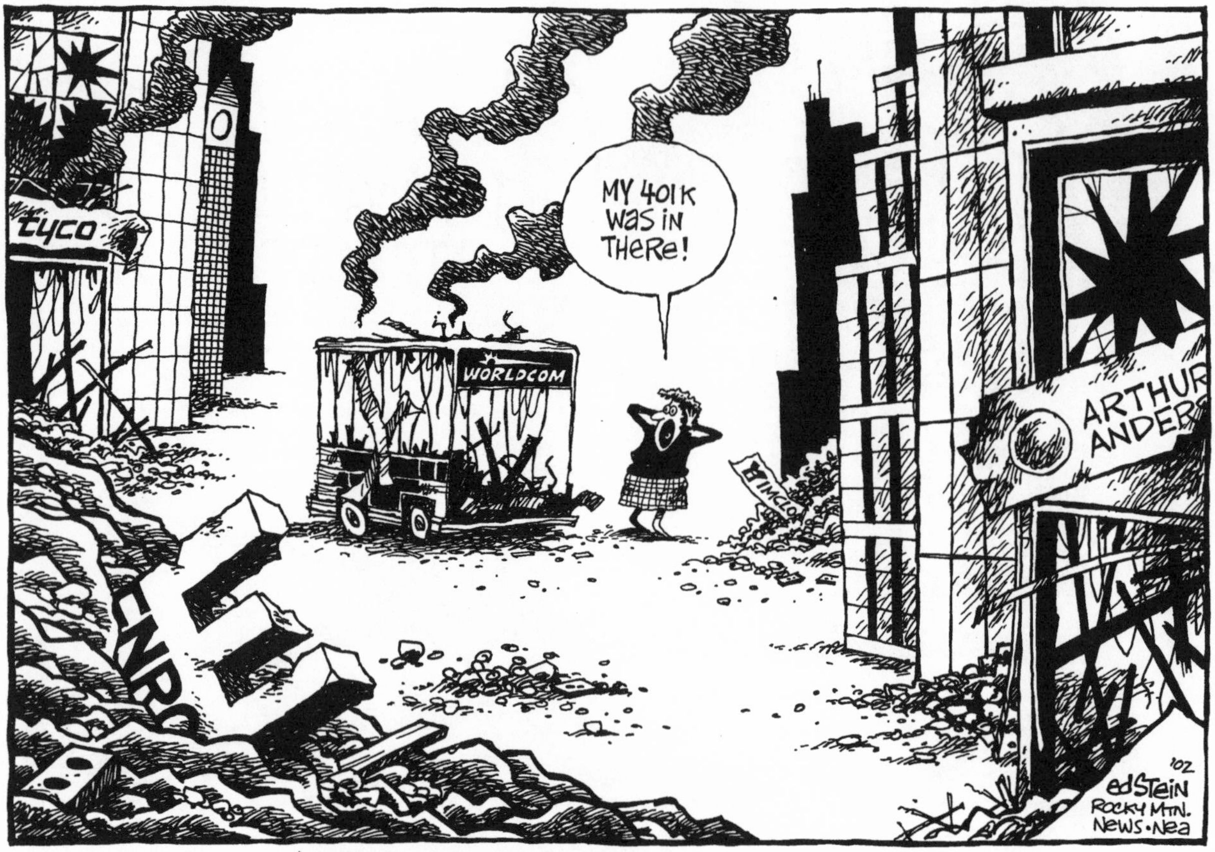
tyco
WORLDCOM
MY 401K WAS IN THERE!
ARTHUR ANDER
ENRO
'02 edStein Rocky Mtn. News•Nea

ANOTHER SUICIDE BOMBING ON WALL STREET

JACK HIGGINS
Courtesy Chicago Sun-Times

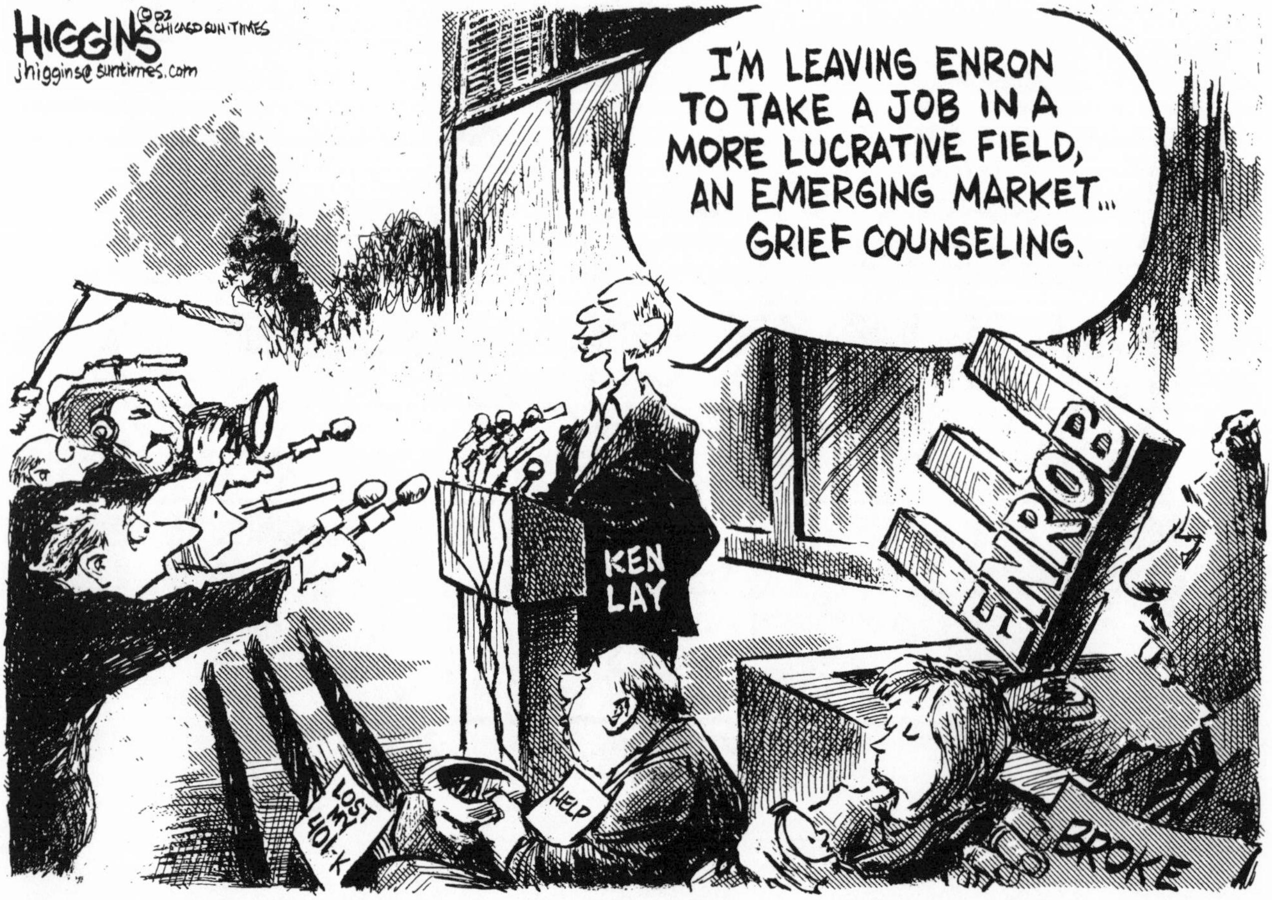
HIGGINS ©02 Chicago Sun-Times
jhiggins@suntimes.com
I'M LEAVING ENRON TO TAKE A JOB IN A MORE LUCRATIVE FIELD, AN EMERGING MARKET... GRIEF COUNSELING.
KEN LAY
LOST MY 401K
HELP
BROKE

The Economy

The U.S. economy continued to grow during the year, but at a very slow rate. As 2002 ended, unemployment stood at 5.7 percent while inflation and interest rates remained the lowest in forty years. Consumer confidence was at a nine-year low, but corporate earnings, mired in a two-year slump, were beginning to improve. Nevertheless, retail sales were up and the National Automobile Dealers Association reported a banner year. Many businesses continued to downsize, cutting payrolls and holding down spending.

President Bush invoked the Taft-Hartley Act in November to open West Coast ports after a 10-day dock workers' lockout had cost the economy $2 billion a day. The Securities and Exchange Commission began investigating business practices of hundreds of companies in the wake of the Enron scandal. The stock market resembled a roller coaster ride much of the year, but showed signs in November that the worst part of the ride might be over. The Dow Jones Industrials roared past 8,000, gaining nearly 6 percent, and the NASDAQ rose 12 percent.

The Bush Administration and Congress made it clear that oversight of the world of trade and corporate America would be strengthened and that executives responsible for business scandals would be sent to jail. Many have already been convicted.

MIKE LUCKOVICH
Courtesy Atlanta Constitution

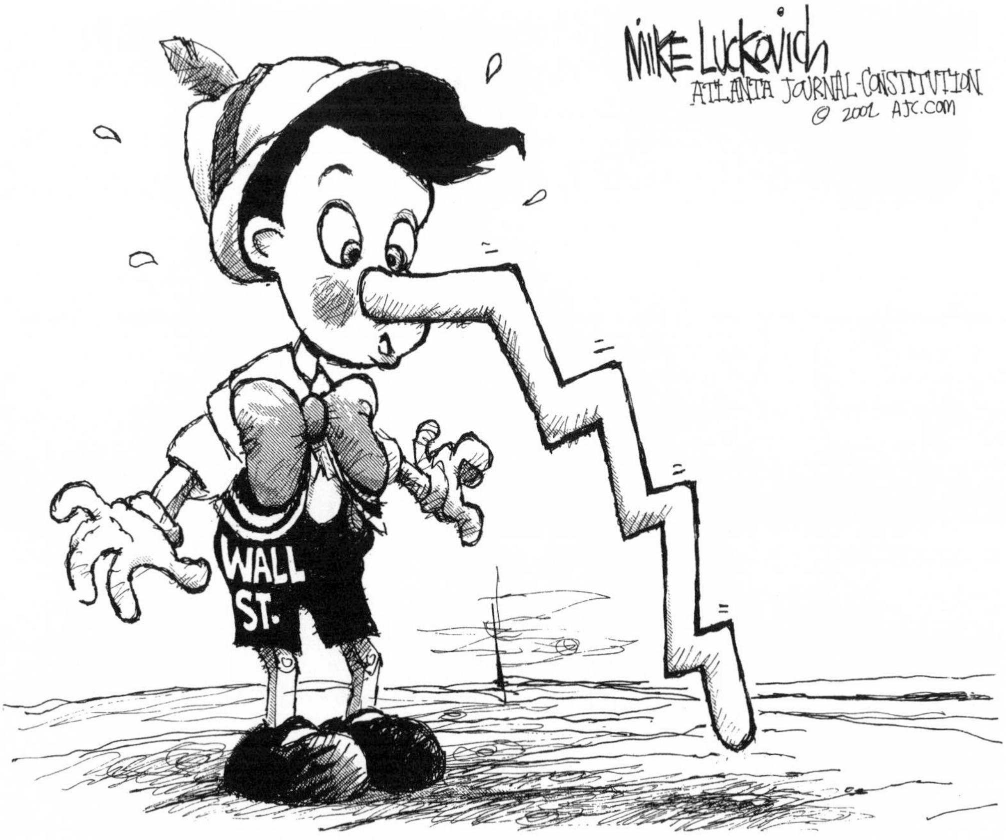
Mike Luckovich
ATLANTA JOURNAL-CONSTITUTION
© 2002 AJC.com
WALL ST.

STEVE GREENBERG
Courtesy Ventura County Star (Calif.)

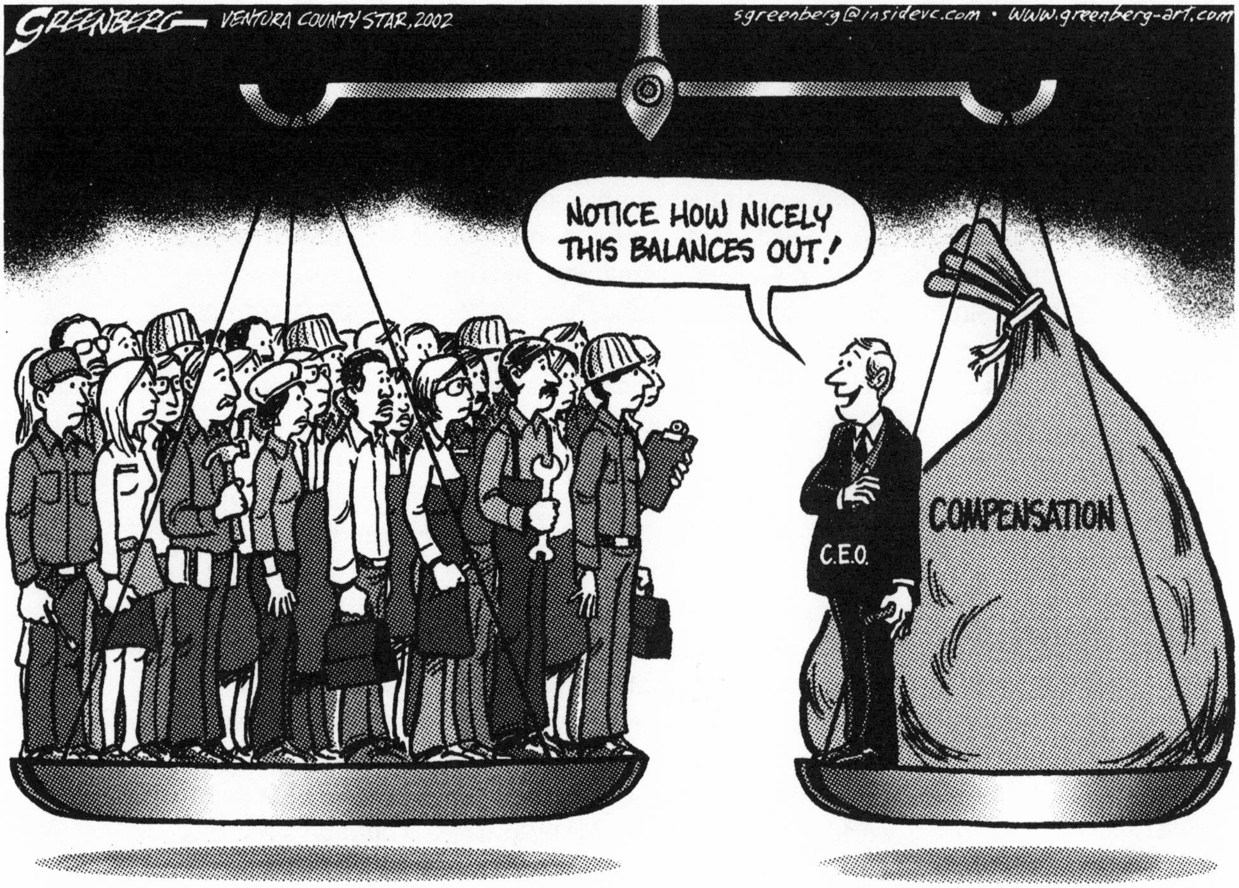
GREENBERG VENTURA COUNTY STAR, 2002
sgreenberg@insidevc.com • www.greenberg-art.com
NOTICE HOW NICELY THIS BALANCES OUT!
COMPENSATION
C.E.O.

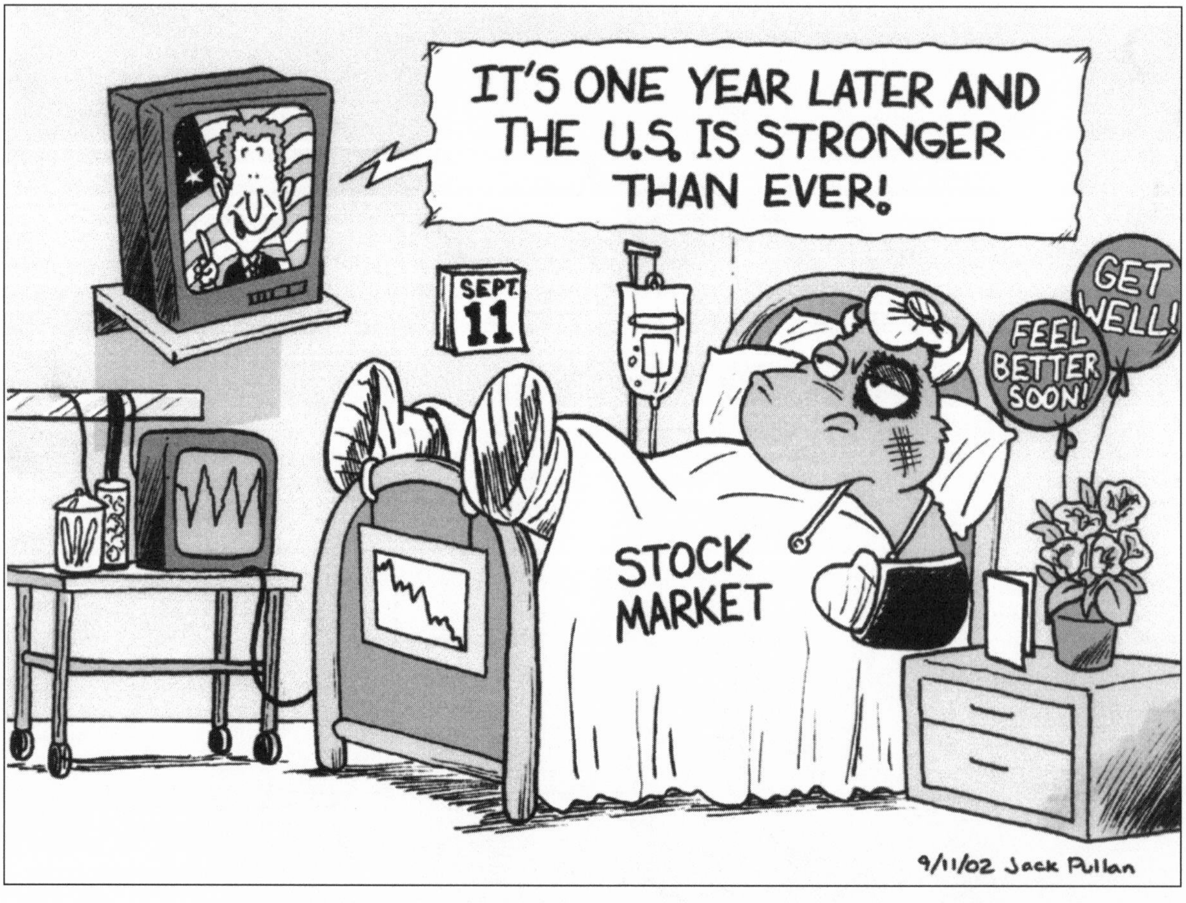
IT'S ONE YEAR LATER AND THE U.S. IS STRONGER THAN EVER!
SEPT. 11
GET WELL!
FEEL BETTER SOON!
STOCK MARKET
9/11/02 Jack Pullan

JACK PULLAN
Courtesy Sun-News Publications

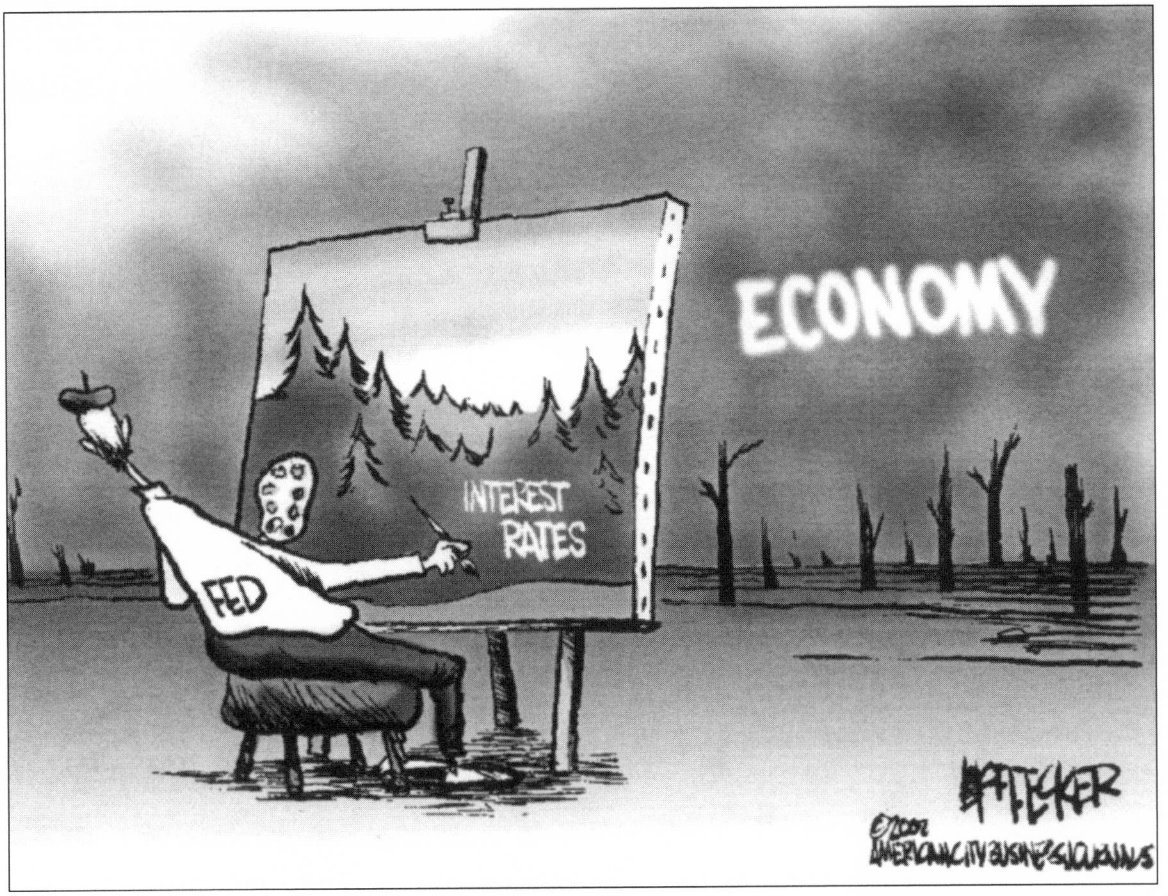
ECONOMY
INTEREST RATES
FED
HOFFECKER

JOE HOFFECKER
Courtesy Cincinnati Business Courier

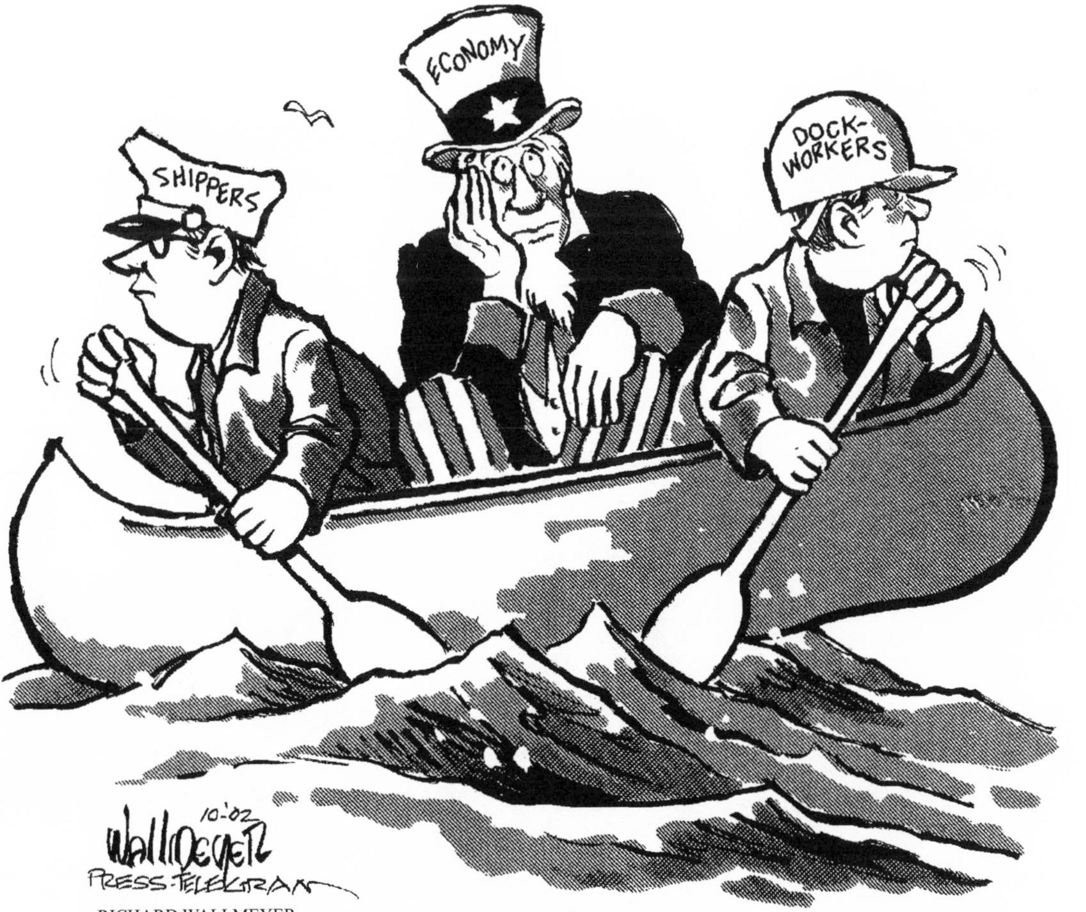
ECONOMY
SHIPPERS
DOCK-WORKERS
10-'02
WALLMEYER
PRESS-TELEGRAM

RICHARD WALLMEYER
Courtesy Long Beach Press-Telegram

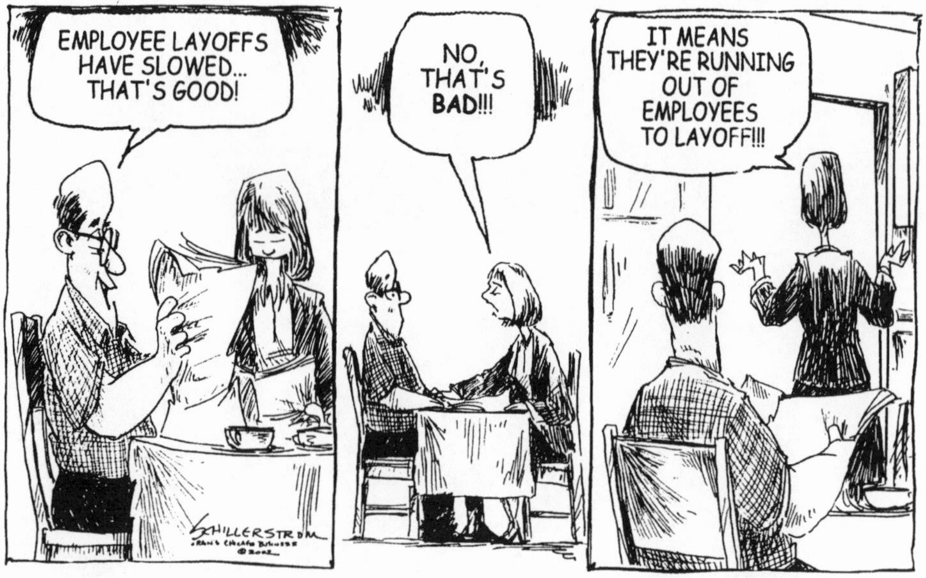
EMPLOYEE LAYOFFS HAVE SLOWED... THAT'S GOOD!
NO, THAT'S BAD!!!
IT MEANS THEY'RE RUNNING OUT OF EMPLOYEES TO LAYOFF!!!
SCHILLERSTROM

ROGER SCHILLERSTROM
Courtesy Crain Communications

CHARLES DANIEL
Courtesy Knoxville News-Sentinel

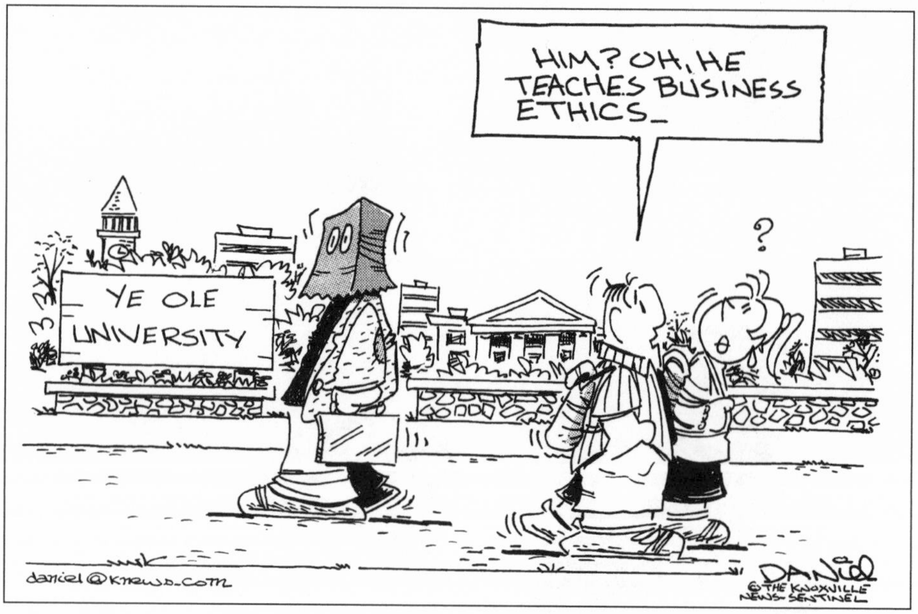
HIM? OH, HE TEACHES BUSINESS ETHICS_
YE OLE UNIVERSITY
DANIEL
© THE KNOXVILLE NEWS-SENTINEL

SVEN VAN ASSCHE
Courtesy Darien Times (Conn.)

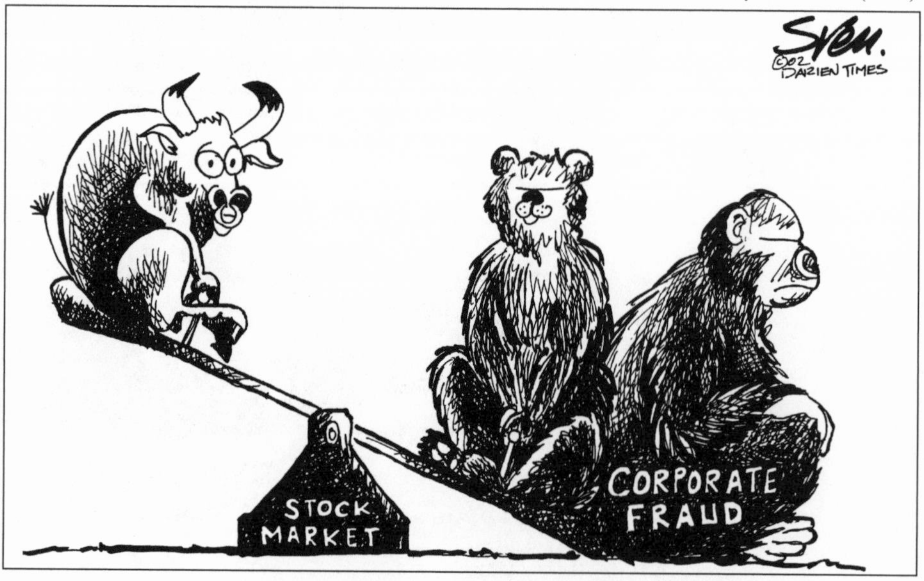
SVEN.
©02 DARIEN TIMES
STOCK MARKET
CORPORATE FRAUD

ETTA HULME
Courtesy Fort Worth Star-Telegram

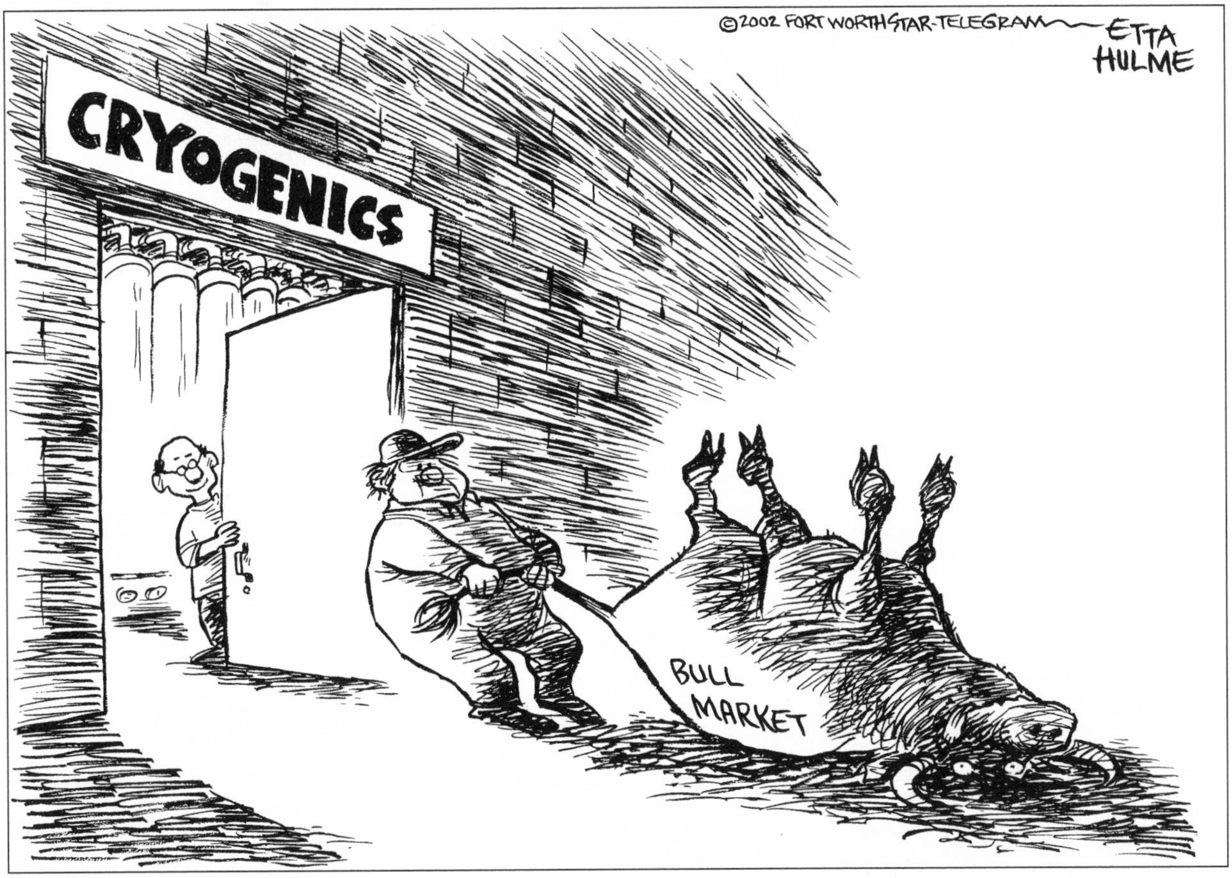
©2002 FORT WORTH STAR-TELEGRAM ETTA HULME
CRYOGENICS
BULL MARKET

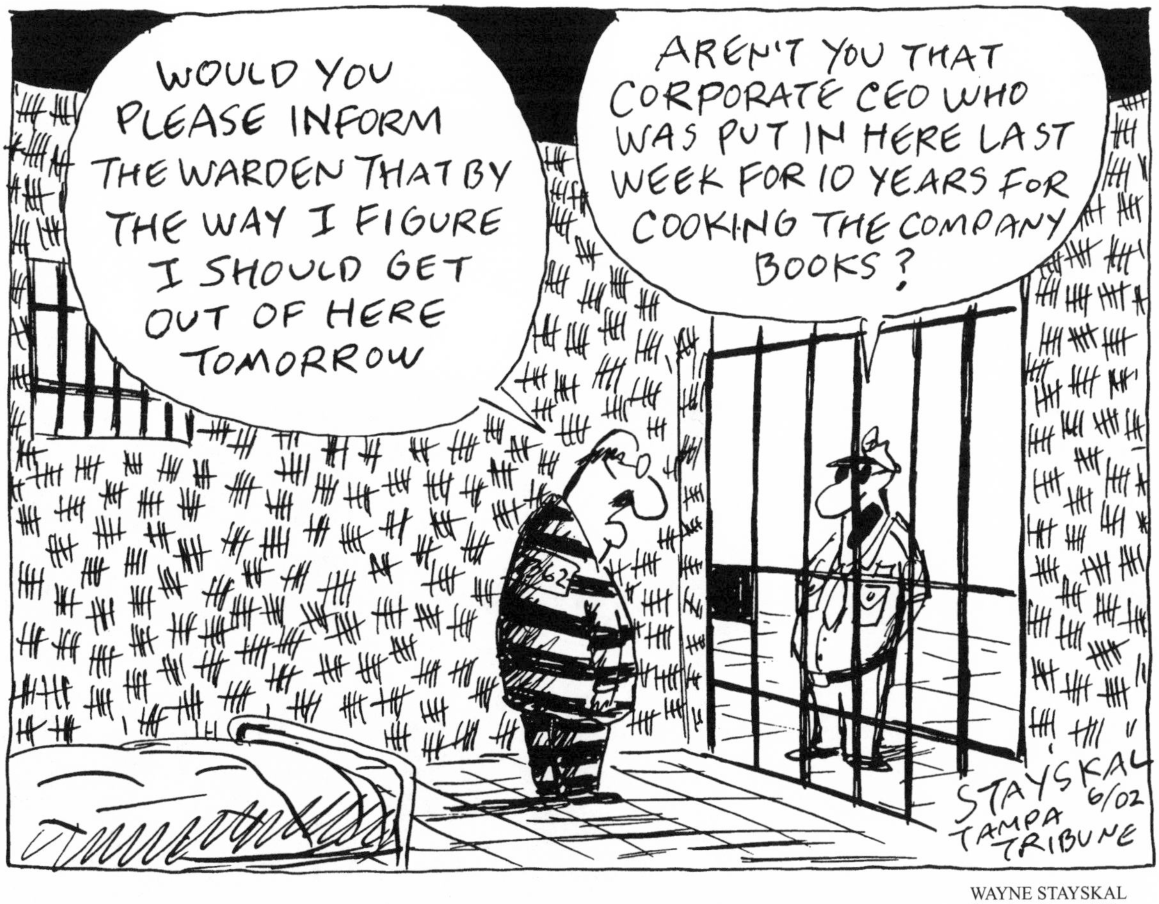
WOULD YOU PLEASE INFORM THE WARDEN THAT BY THE WAY I FIGURE I SHOULD GET OUT OF HERE TOMORROW
AREN'T YOU THAT CORPORATE CEO WHO WAS PUT IN HERE LAST WEEK FOR 10 YEARS FOR COOKING THE COMPANY BOOKS?
STAYSKAL 6/02 TAMPA TRIBUNE

WAYNE STAYSKAL
Courtesy Tampa Tribune

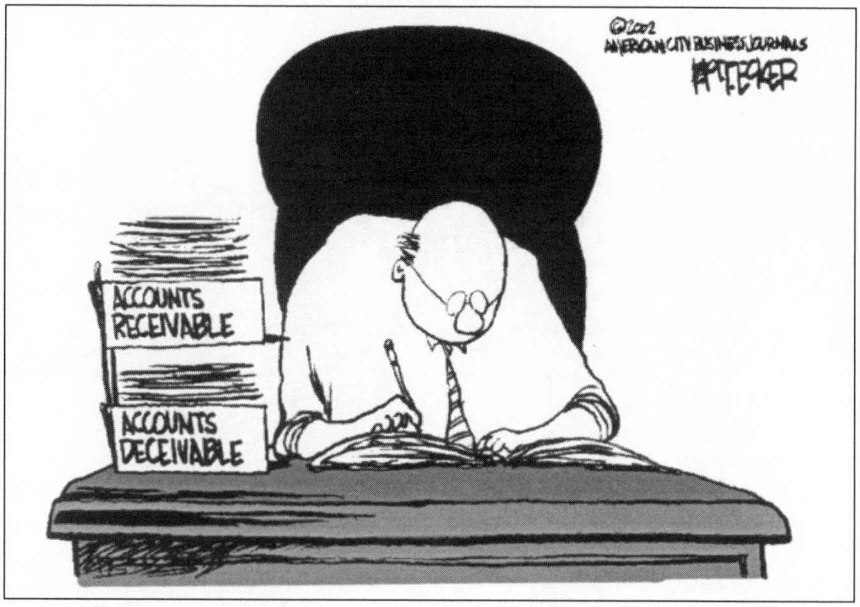
©2002
AMERICAN CITY BUSINESS JOURNALS
HOFFECKER
ACCOUNTS RECEIVABLE
ACCOUNTS DECEIVABLE

JOE HOFFECKER
Courtesy Cincinnati Business Courier

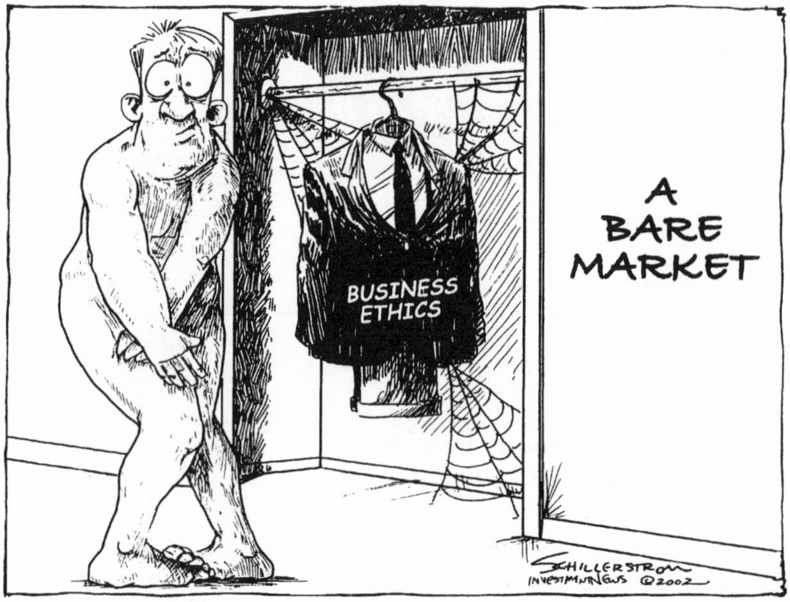
BUSINESS ETHICS
A BARE MARKET
SCHILLERSTROM
INVESTMENTNEWS ©2002

ROGER SCHILLERSTROM
Courtesy Crain Communications

JERRY BARNETT
Courtesy Indianapolis Star

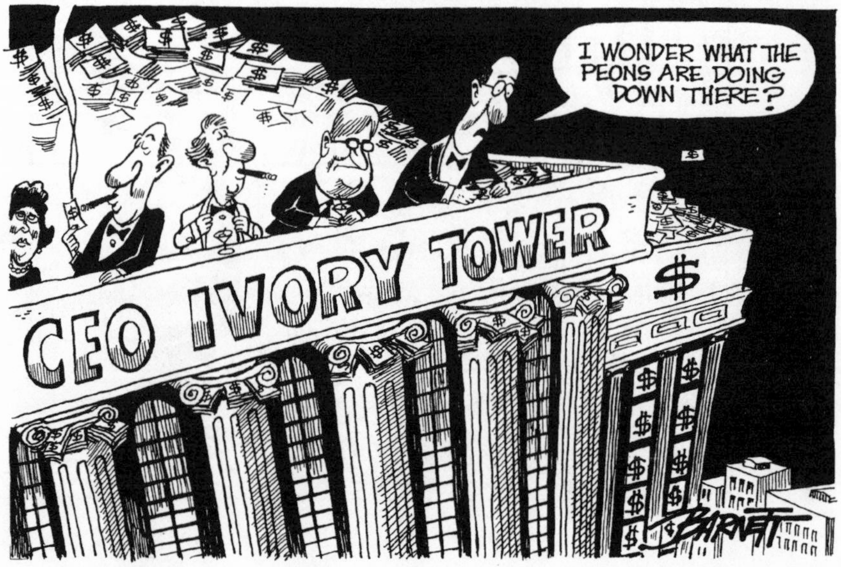
I WONDER WHAT THE PEONS ARE DOING DOWN THERE?
CEO IVORY TOWER
BARNETT

ED FISCHER
Courtesy Rochester Post-Bulletin (Minn.)

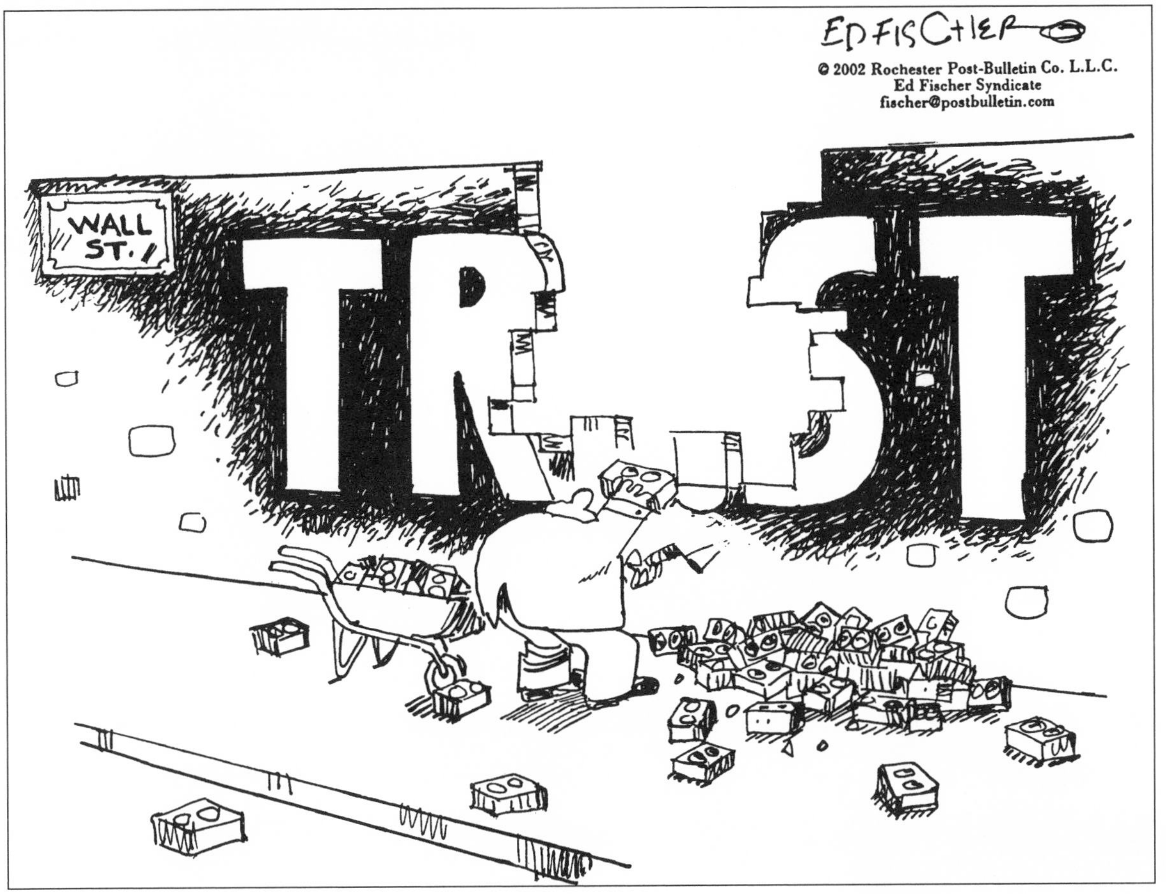
ED FISCHER
© 2002 Rochester Post-Bulletin Co. L.L.C.
Ed Fischer Syndicate
fischer@postbulletin.com
WALL ST.
TR ST

NICK ANDERSON
Courtesy Louisville Courier-Journal

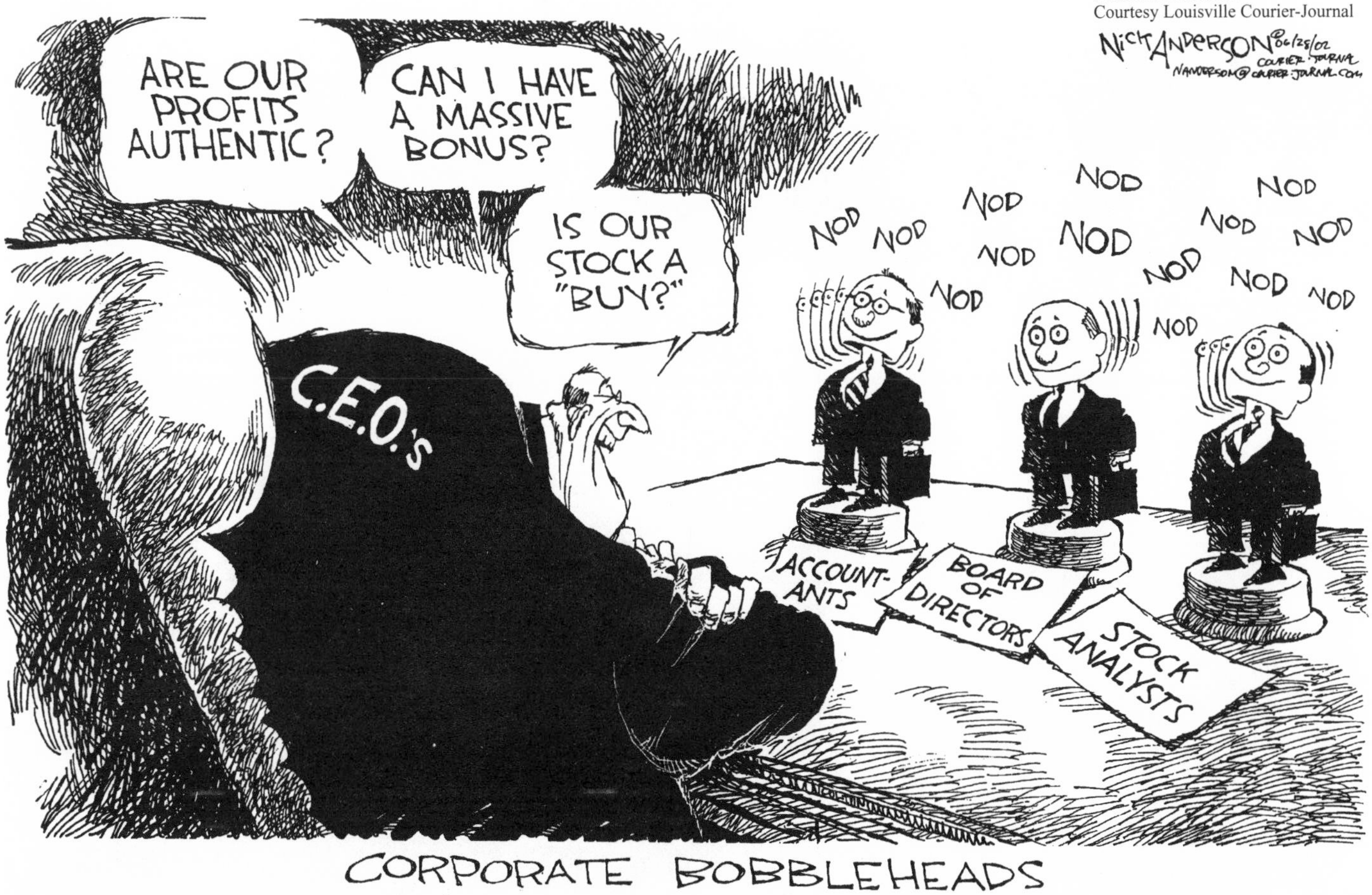
NICK ANDERSON 06/28/02
COURIER-JOURNAL
NANDERSON@COURIER-JOURNAL.COM
ARE OUR PROFITS AUTHENTIC?
CAN I HAVE A MASSIVE BONUS?
IS OUR STOCK A "BUY?"
NOD NOD NOD NOD NOD NOD NOD NOD NOD NOD NOD NOD NOD NOD
C.E.O.'s
ACCOUNT-ANTS
BOARD OF DIRECTORS
STOCK ANALYSTS

CORPORATE BOBBLEHEADS

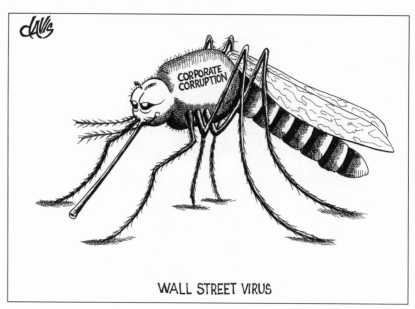

DAVIS
CORPORATE CORRUPTION
WALL STREET VIRUS

KEN DAVIS
Courtesy San Jose Business Journal

STEVE KELLEY
Courtesy The Times-Picayune (La.)

S. KELLEY THE TIMES-PICAYUNE ©2002
I DUNNO... I'M STILL A LITTLE SKEPTICAL.
STOCK MARKET
INVESTORS

RICK TUMA
Courtesy Chicago Tribune

U.S. STEEL INDUSTRY
RECOVERY PLAN
IMPORT TARIFFS
RICK TUMA
CHICAGO TRIBUNE
©2002

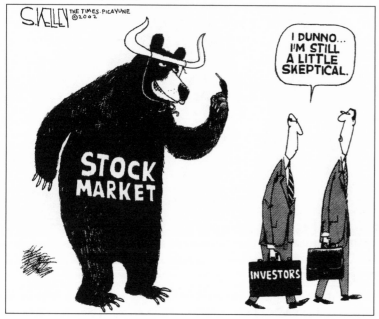

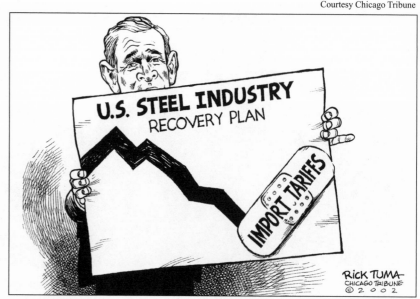

JOEL PETT
Courtesy Lexington Herald-Leader

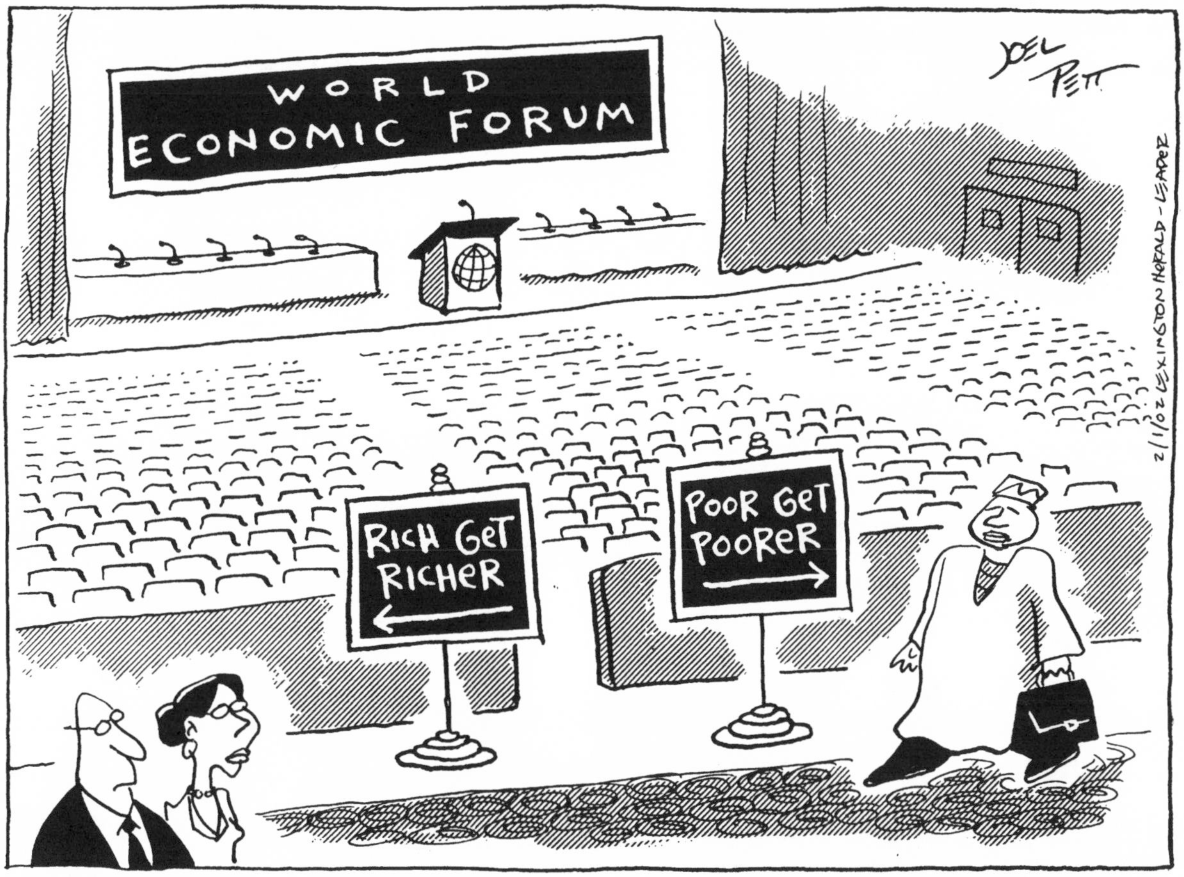
WORLD
ECONOMIC FORUM
RICH GET RICHER
POOR GET POORER
JOEL PETT
2/1/02 LEXINGTON HERALD-LEADER

CHRIS BRITT
Courtesy State Journal-Register (Ill.)

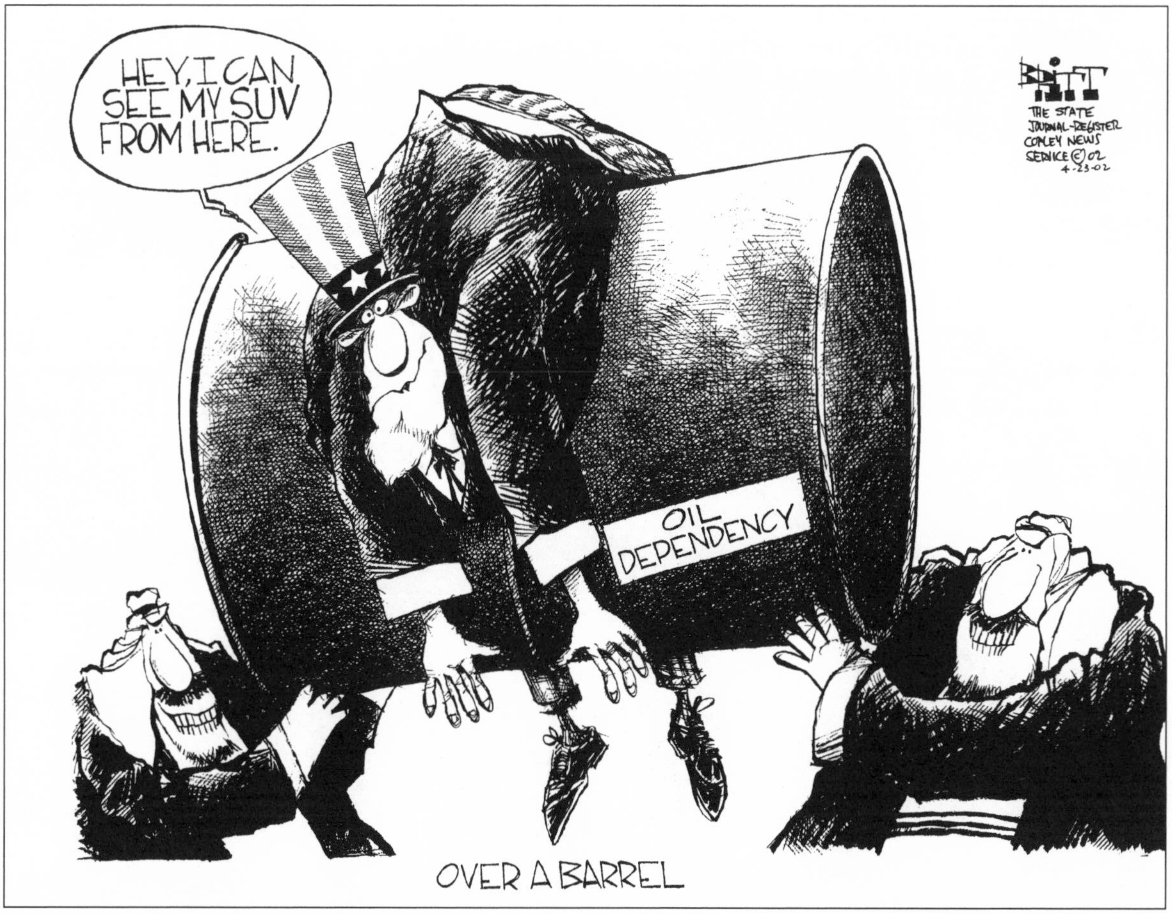
HEY, I CAN SEE MY SUV FROM HERE.
OIL DEPENDENCY
BRITT
THE STATE JOURNAL-REGISTER
COPLEY NEWS SERVICE ©02
4-23-02
OVER A BARREL

DAN O'BRIEN
Courtesy The Business Journal (Oh.)

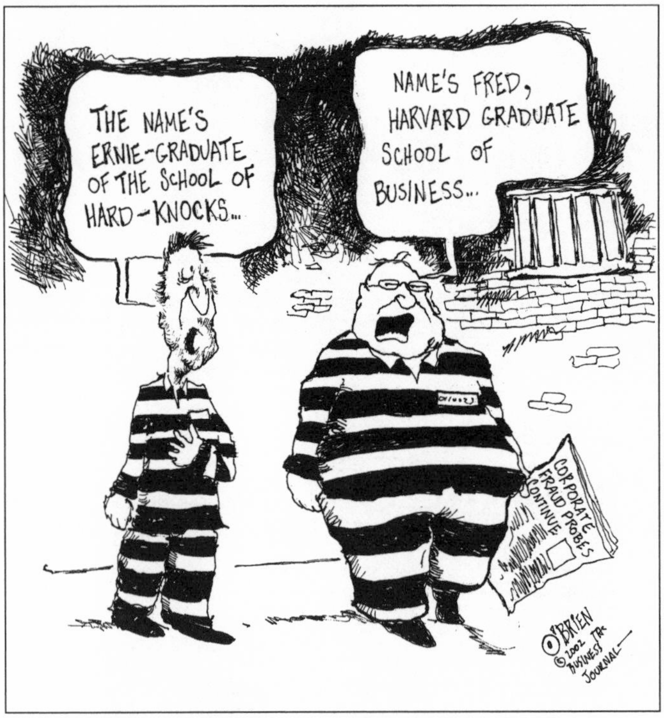
THE NAME'S ERNIE-GRADUATE OF THE SCHOOL OF HARD-KNOCKS...
NAME'S FRED, HARVARD GRADUATE SCHOOL OF BUSINESS...
CORPORATE FRAUD PROBES CONTINUE
O'BRIEN ©2002 THE BUSINESS JOURNAL

DON LANDGREN JR.
Courtesy The Landmark (Mass.)

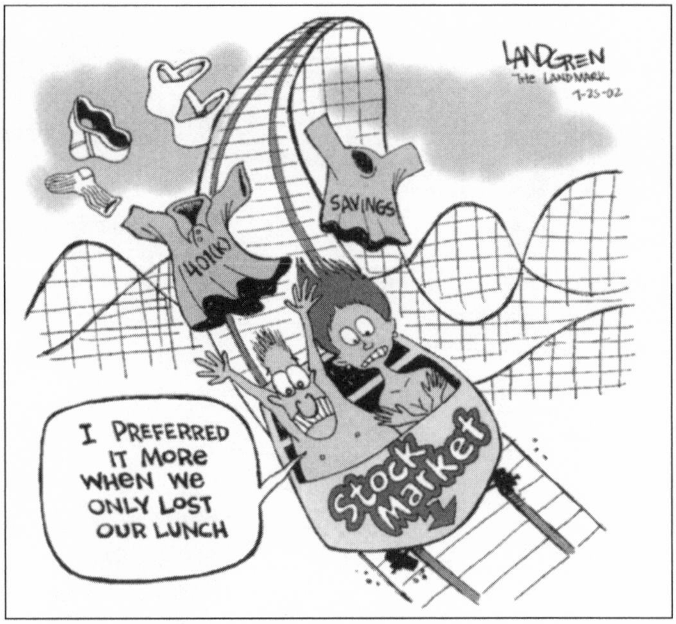
LANDGREN The LANDMARK 7-25-02
401(K)
SAVINGS
I PREFERRED IT MORE WHEN WE ONLY LOST OUR LUNCH
Stock Market

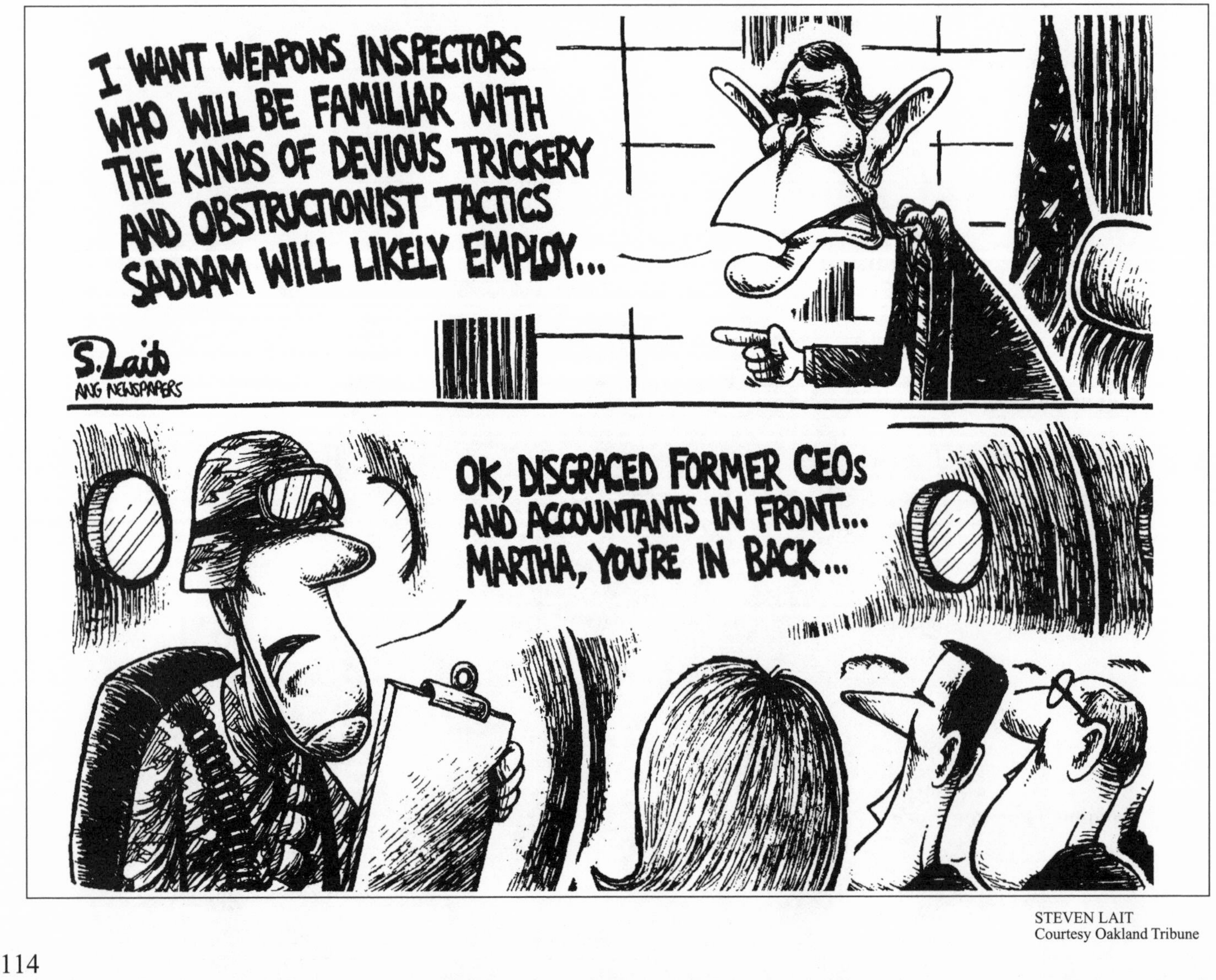
I WANT WEAPONS INSPECTORS WHO WILL BE FAMILIAR WITH THE KINDS OF DEVIOUS TRICKERY AND OBSTRUCTIONIST TACTICS SADDAM WILL LIKELY EMPLOY...
S. Lait ANG NEWSPAPERS
OK, DISGRACED FORMER CEOs AND ACCOUNTANTS IN FRONT... MARTHA, YOU'RE IN BACK...

STEVEN LAIT
Courtesy Oakland Tribune

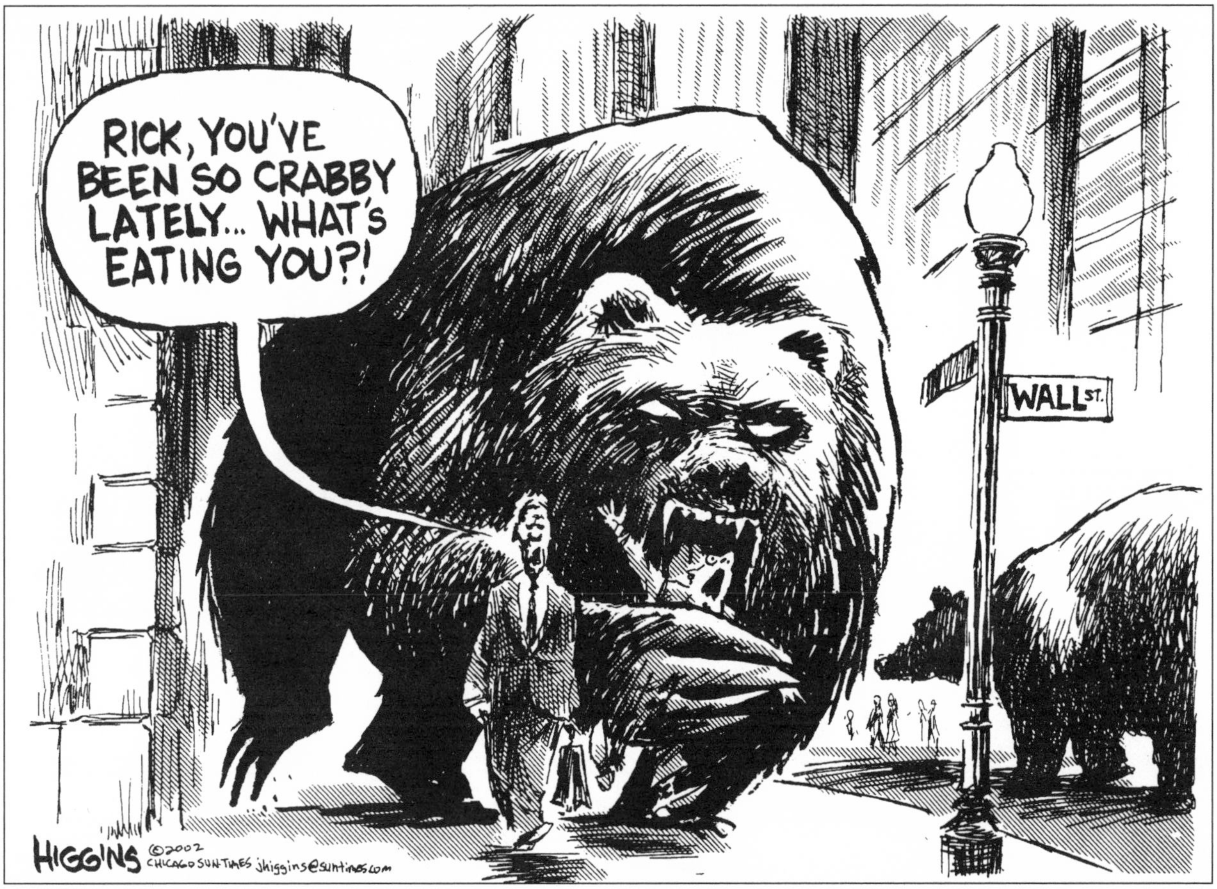
RICK, YOU'VE BEEN SO CRABBY LATELY... WHAT'S EATING YOU?!
WALL ST.
HIGGINS ©2002 CHICAGO SUN-TIMES jhiggins@suntimes.com

JACK HIGGINS
Courtesy Chicago Sun-Times

JACK CHAPMAN
Courtesy DeSoto Times Today (Miss.)

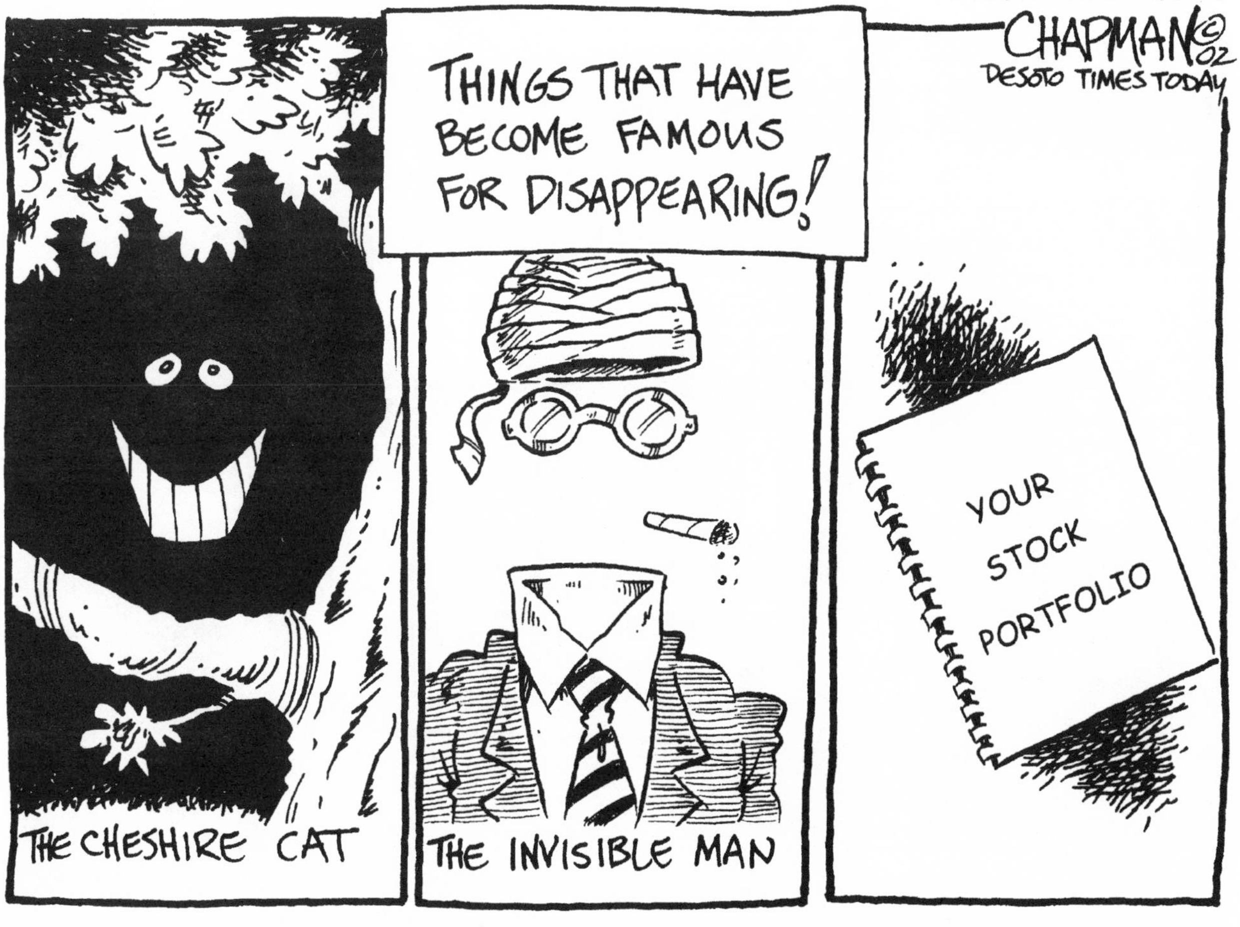
THINGS THAT HAVE BECOME FAMOUS FOR DISAPPEARING!
CHAPMAN © 02 DESOTO TIMES TODAY
THE CHESHIRE CAT
THE INVISIBLE MAN
YOUR STOCK PORTFOLIO

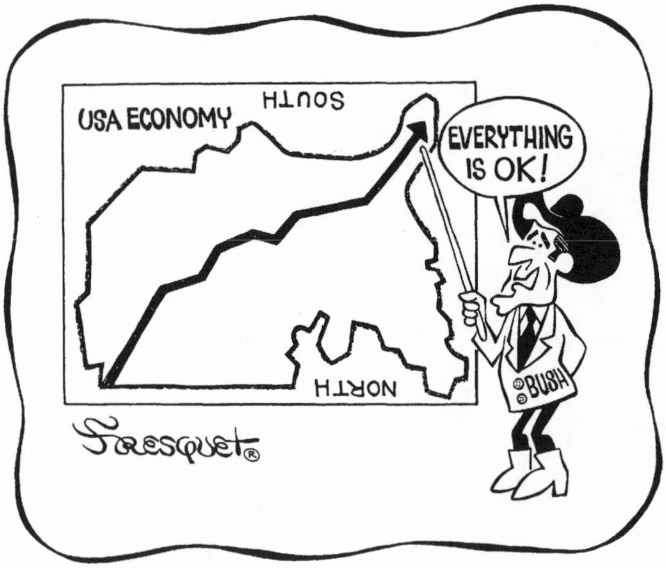
USA ECONOMY
SOUTH
NORTH
EVERYTHING IS OK!
BUSH
FRESQUET®

LAZARO FRESQUET
Courtesy El Nuevo Herald

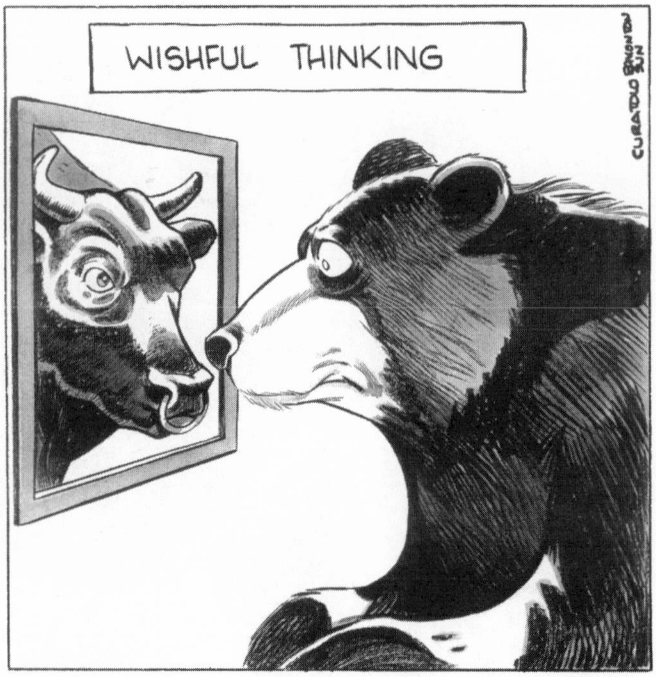
WISHFUL THINKING

FRED CURATOLO
Courtesy Edmonton Sun

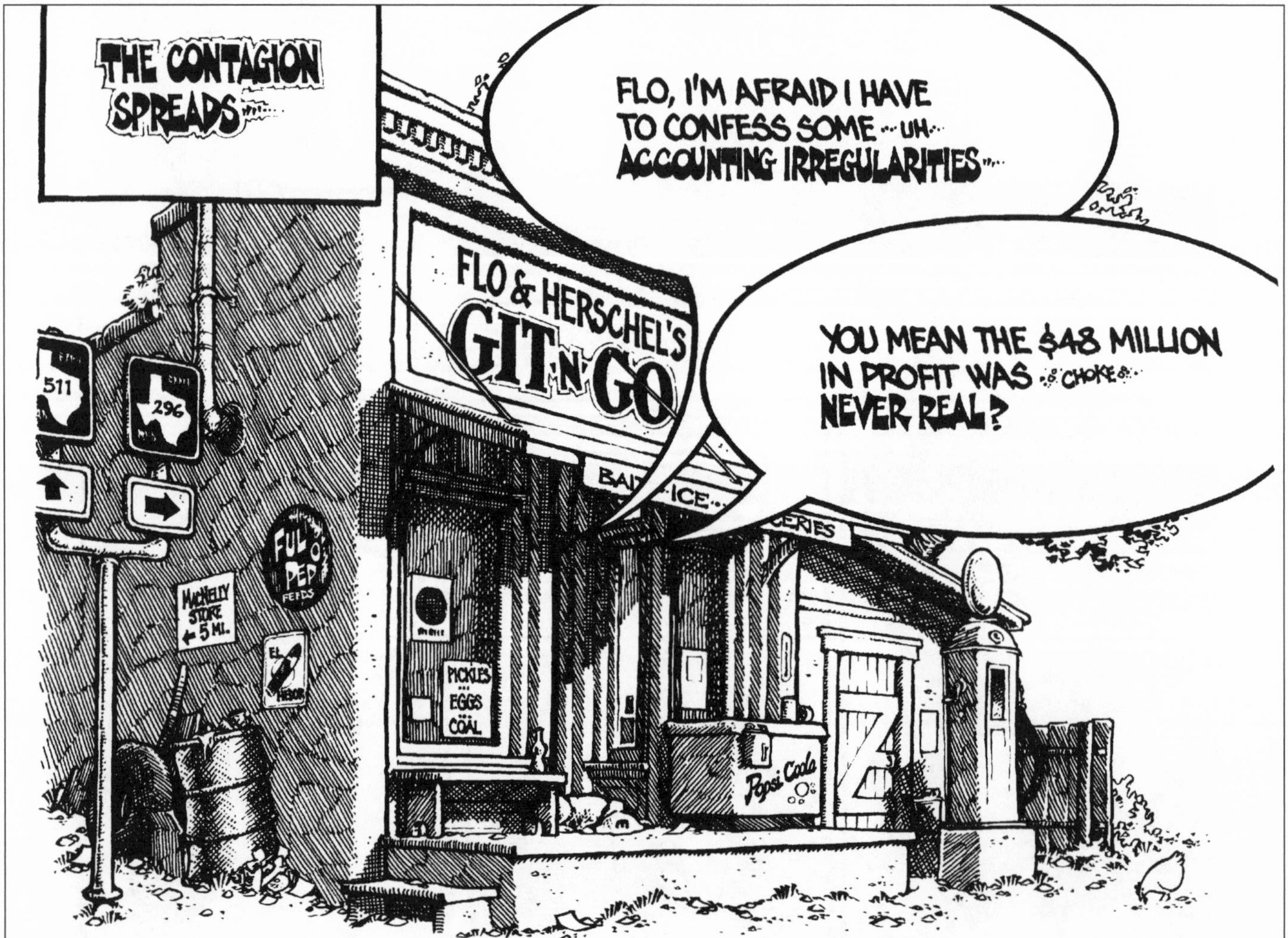
THE CONTAGION SPREADS...
FLO, I'M AFRAID I HAVE TO CONFESS SOME... UH... ACCOUNTING IRREGULARITIES...
YOU MEAN THE $48 MILLION IN PROFIT WAS ...CHOKE... NEVER REAL?
FLO & HERSCHEL'S GIT 'N' GO
511
296
FULL O' PEP FEEDS
McNELLY STORE ← 5 MI.
PICKLES EGGS COAL
Pepsi Cola

BEN SARGENT
Courtesy Austin American-Statesman

NEIL GRAHAME
Courtesy Spencer Newspapers

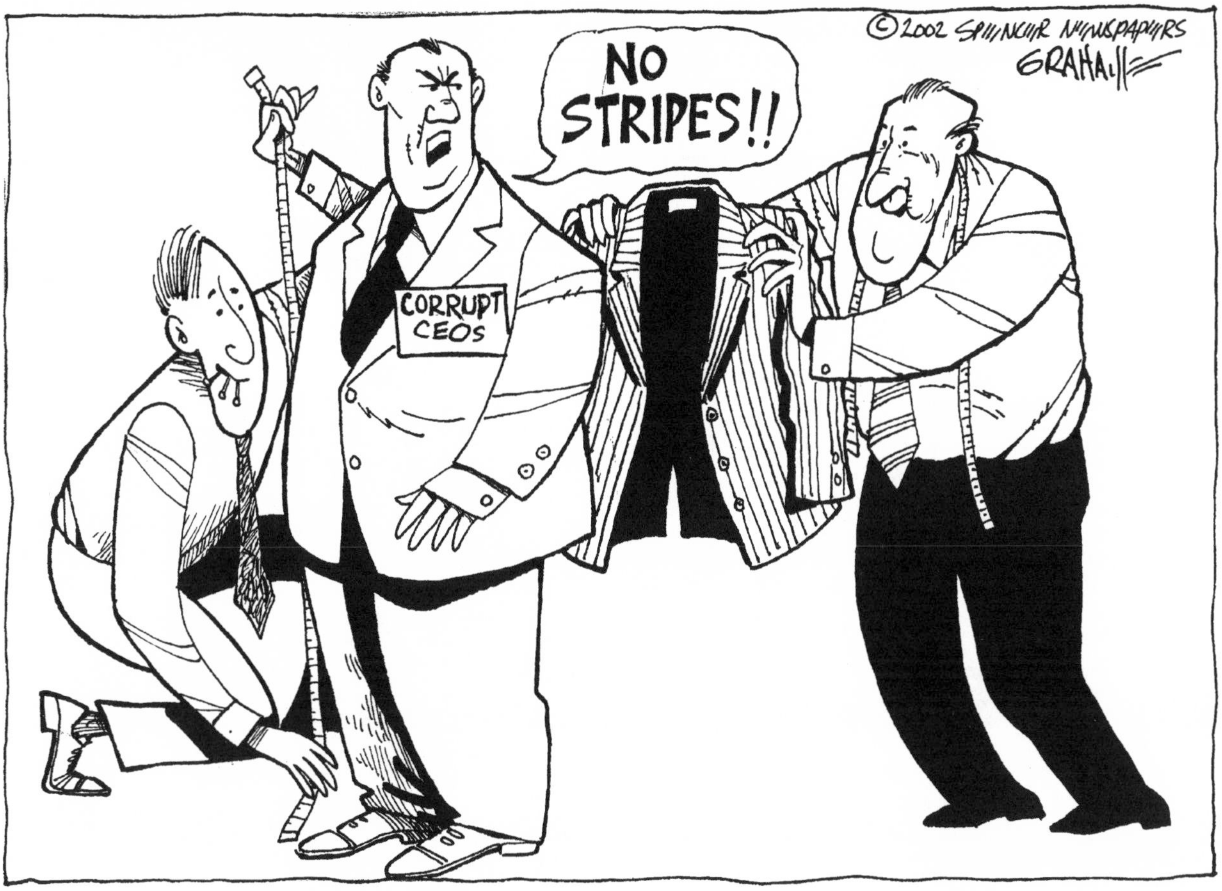
©2002 SPENCER NEWSPAPERS
GRAHAME
NO STRIPES!!
CORRUPT CEOS

DREW SHENEMAN
Courtesy Newark Star-Ledger

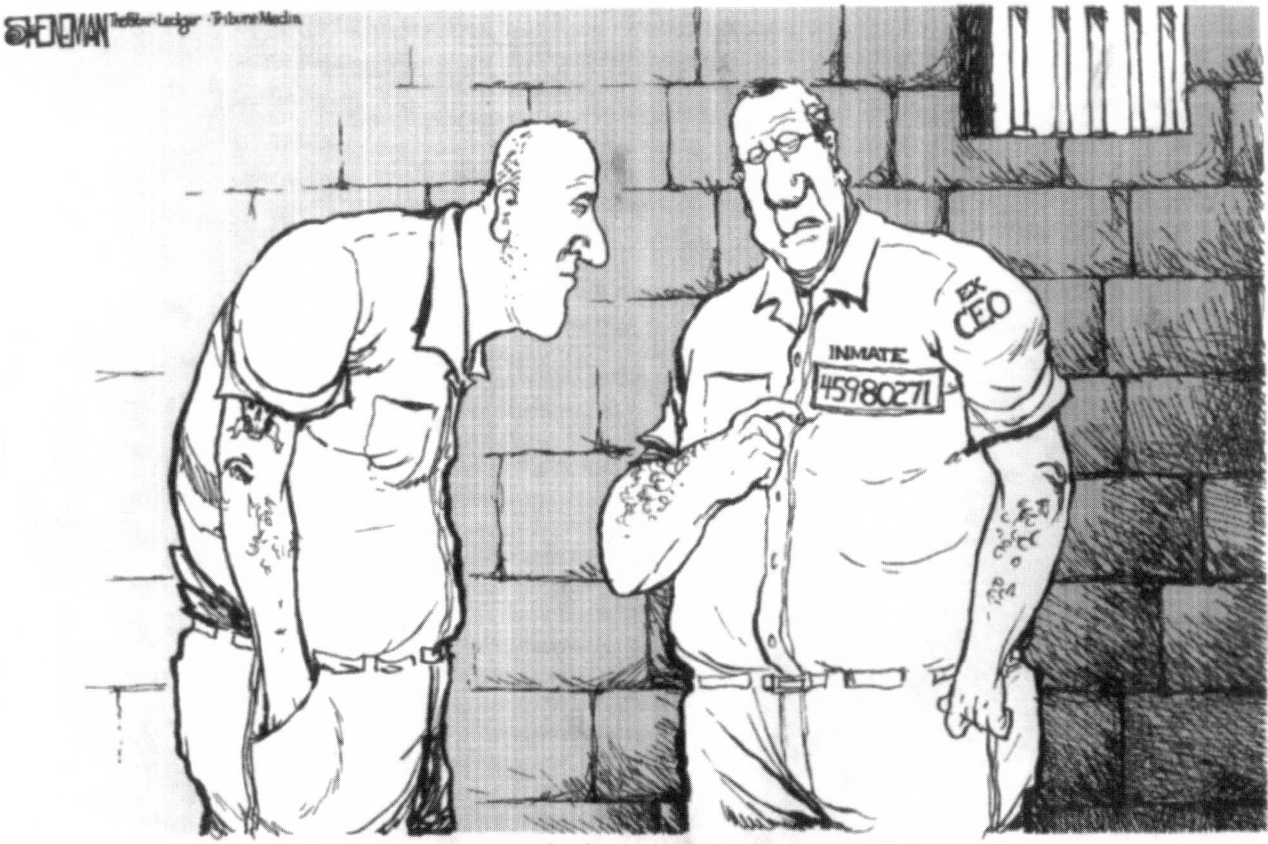
SHENEMAN
INMATE
45980271
EX CEO
"TWO MONTHS AGO, THIS WAS MY NET WORTH."

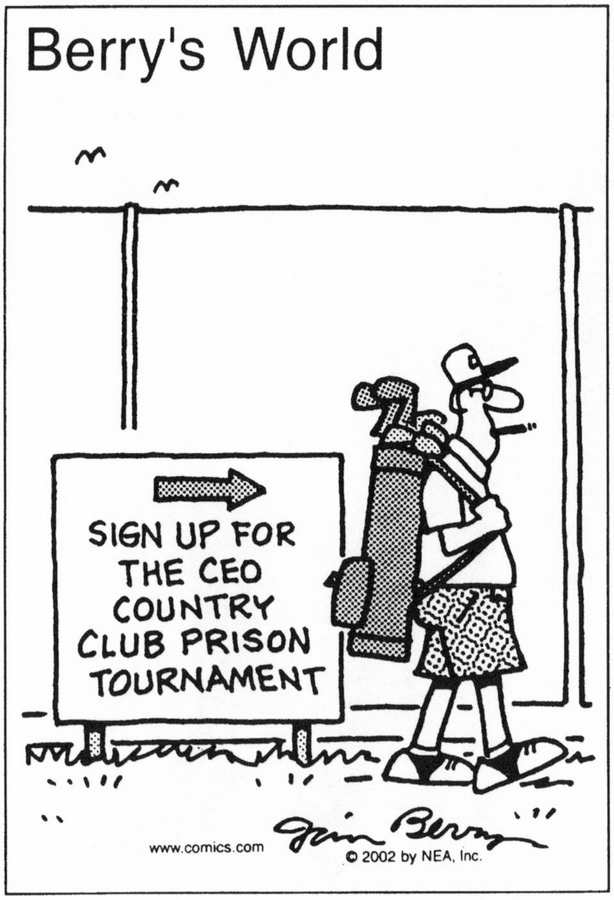
Berry's World
SIGN UP FOR THE CEO COUNTRY CLUB PRISON TOURNAMENT
www.comics.com
© 2002 by NEA, Inc.

JIM BERRY
Courtesy NEA

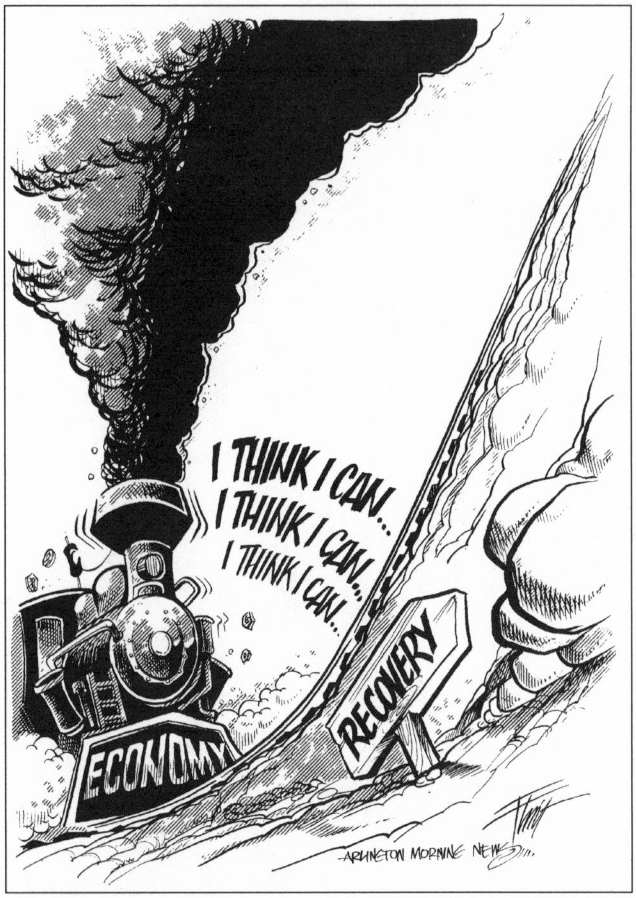
I THINK I CAN...
I THINK I CAN...
I THINK I CAN...
ECONOMY
RECOVERY
ARLINGTON MORNING NEWS

WILLIAM L. FLINT
Courtesy Arlington Morning News (Tex.)

DICK LOCHER
Courtesy Chicago Tribune

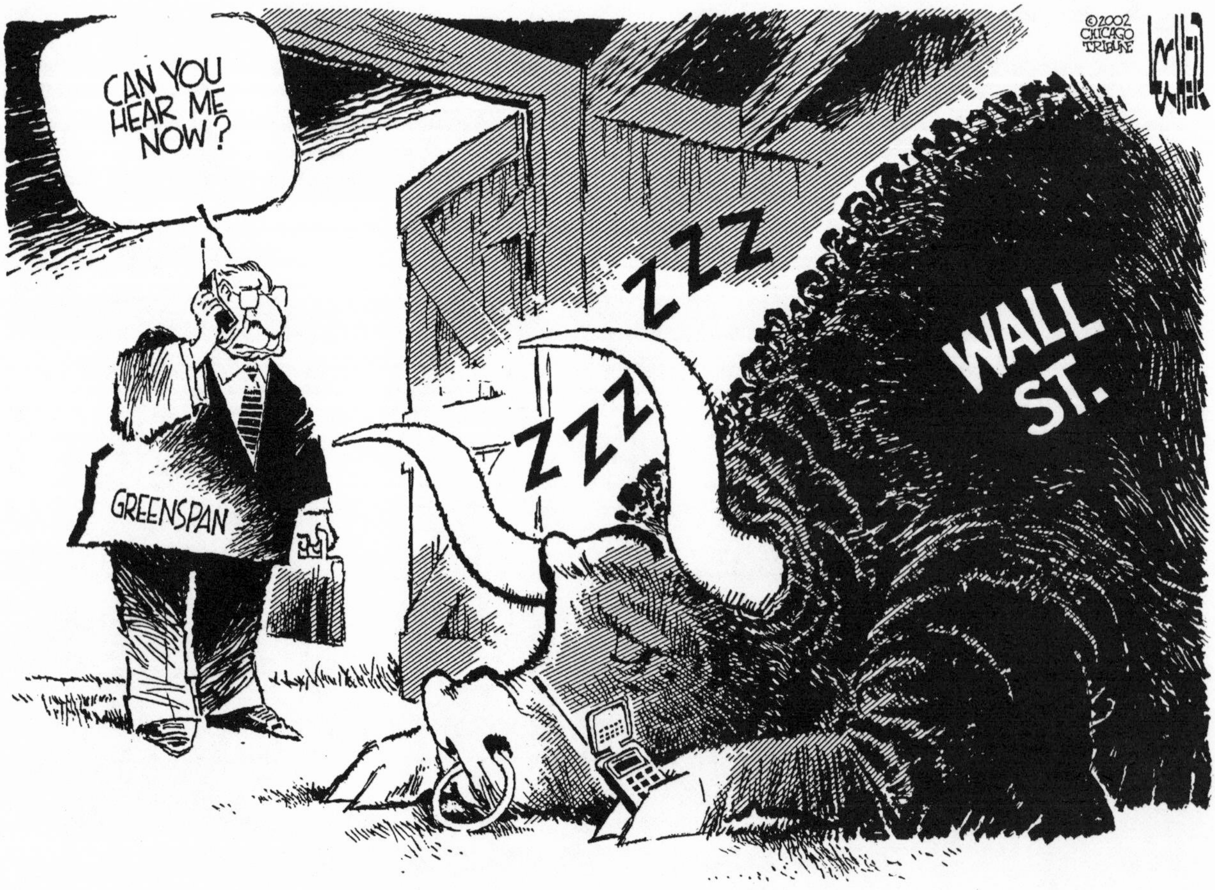
©2002 CHICAGO TRIBUNE
CAN YOU HEAR ME NOW?
ZZZ
ZZZ
WALL ST.
GREENSPAN

BEN SARGENT
Courtesy Austin American-Statesman

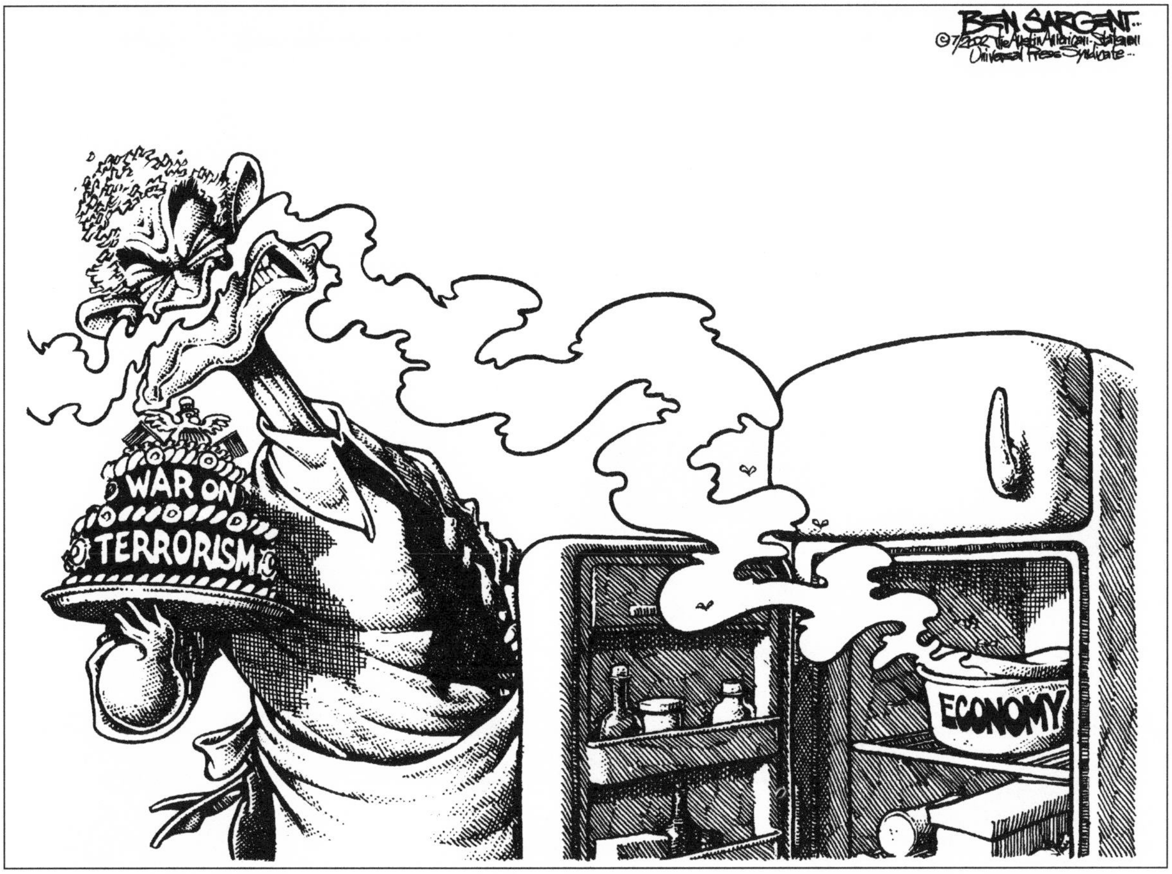
BEN SARGENT
©7/2002 The Austin American-Statesman
Universal Press Syndicate
WAR ON
TERRORISM
ECONOMY

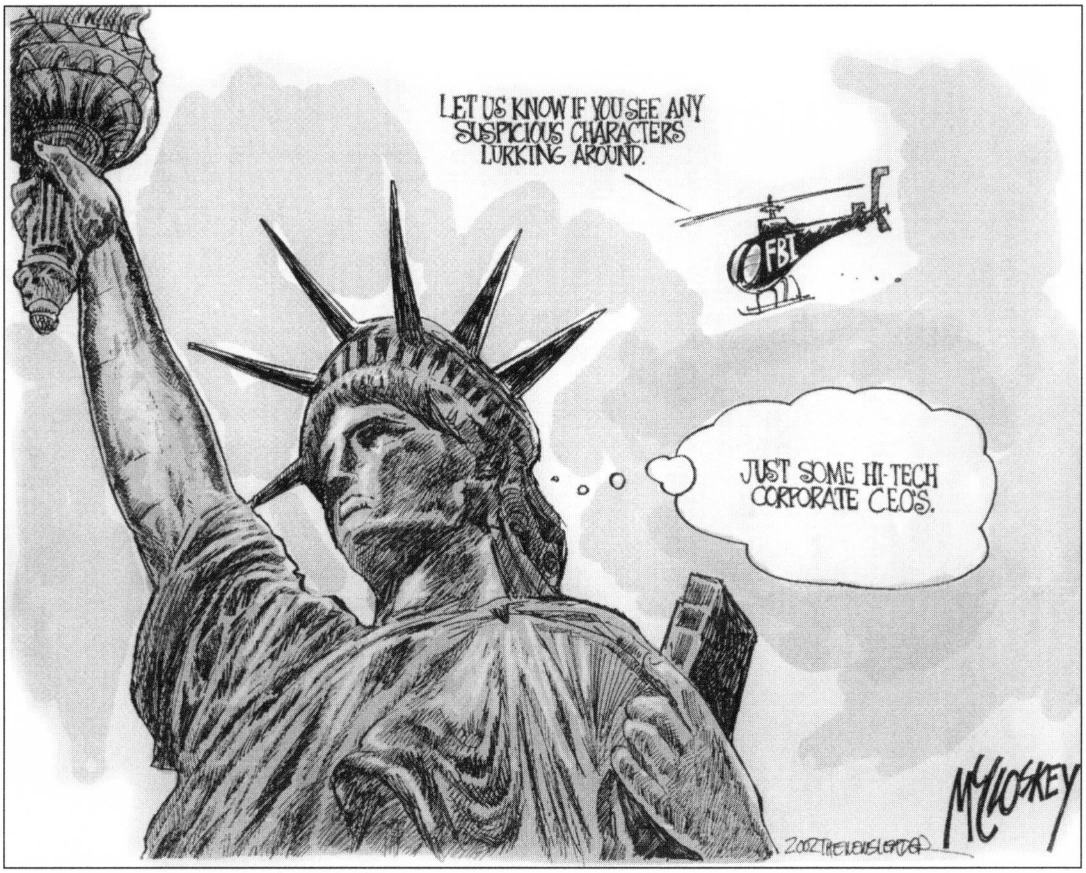
LET US KNOW IF YOU SEE ANY
SUSPICIOUS CHARACTERS
LURKING AROUND.
FBI
JUST SOME HI-TECH
CORPORATE C.E.O'S.
McCLOSKEY
2002 THE NEWS LEADER

JAMES McCLOSKEY
Courtesy Daily News Leader (Va.)

JACK OHMAN
Courtesy The Oregonian

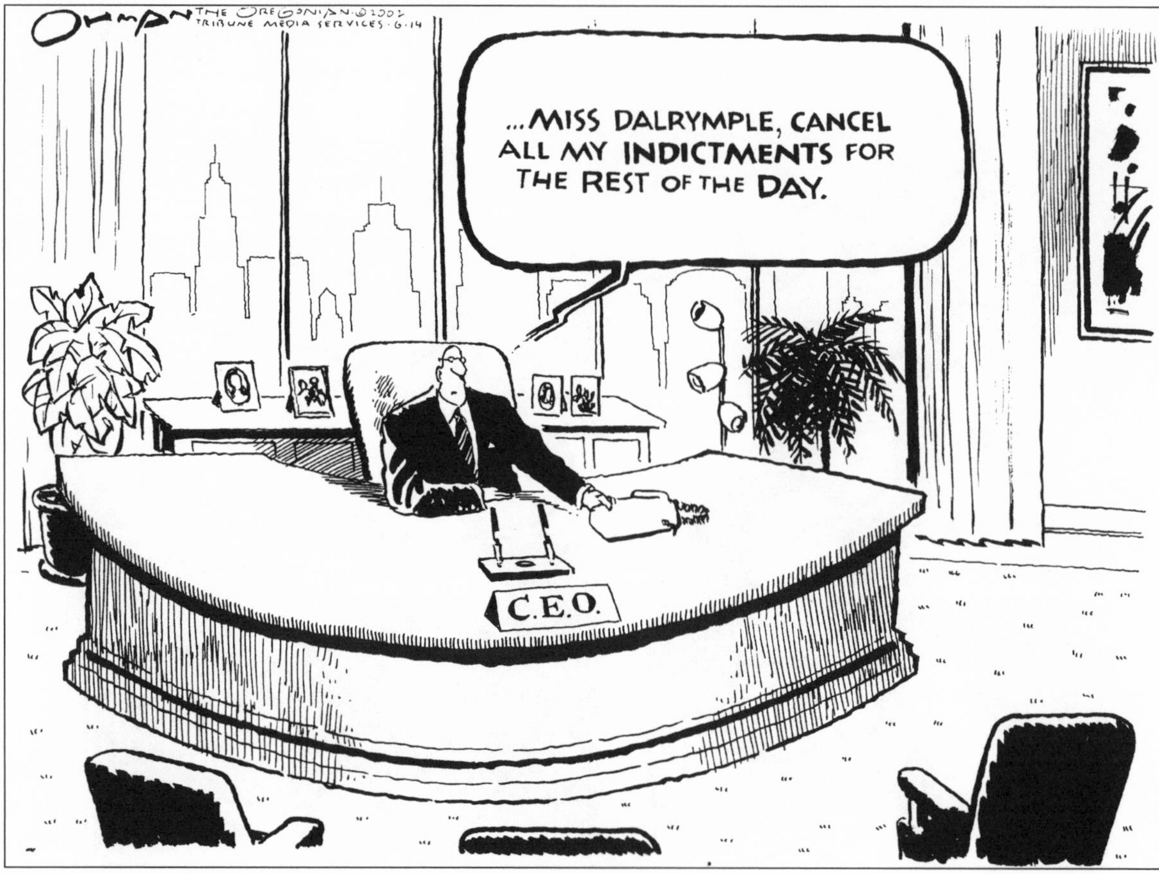
...MISS DALRYMPLE, CANCEL ALL MY INDICTMENTS FOR THE REST OF THE DAY.
C.E.O.

JAKE FULLER
Courtesy Gainesville Sun

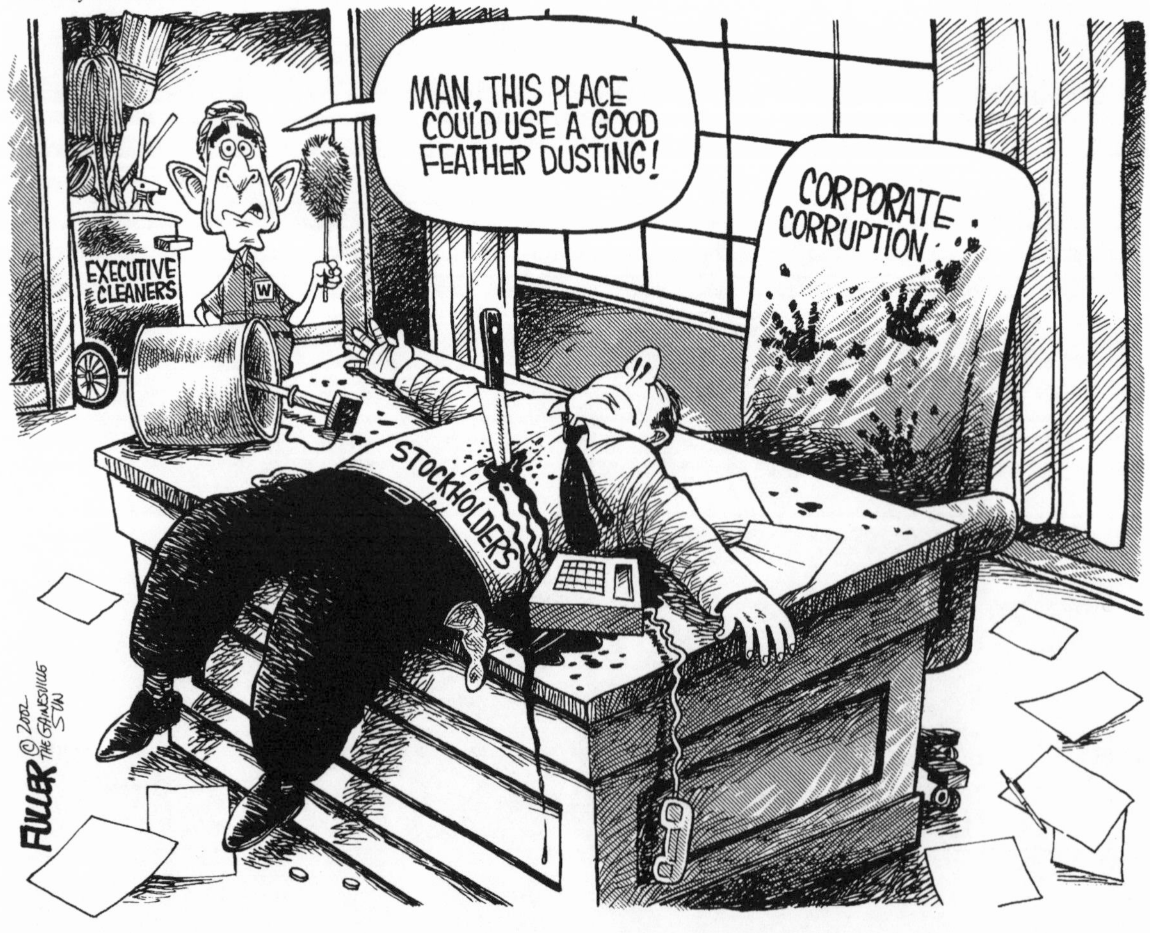
MAN, THIS PLACE COULD USE A GOOD FEATHER DUSTING!
EXECUTIVE CLEANERS
W
CORPORATE CORRUPTION
STOCKHOLDERS
FULLER

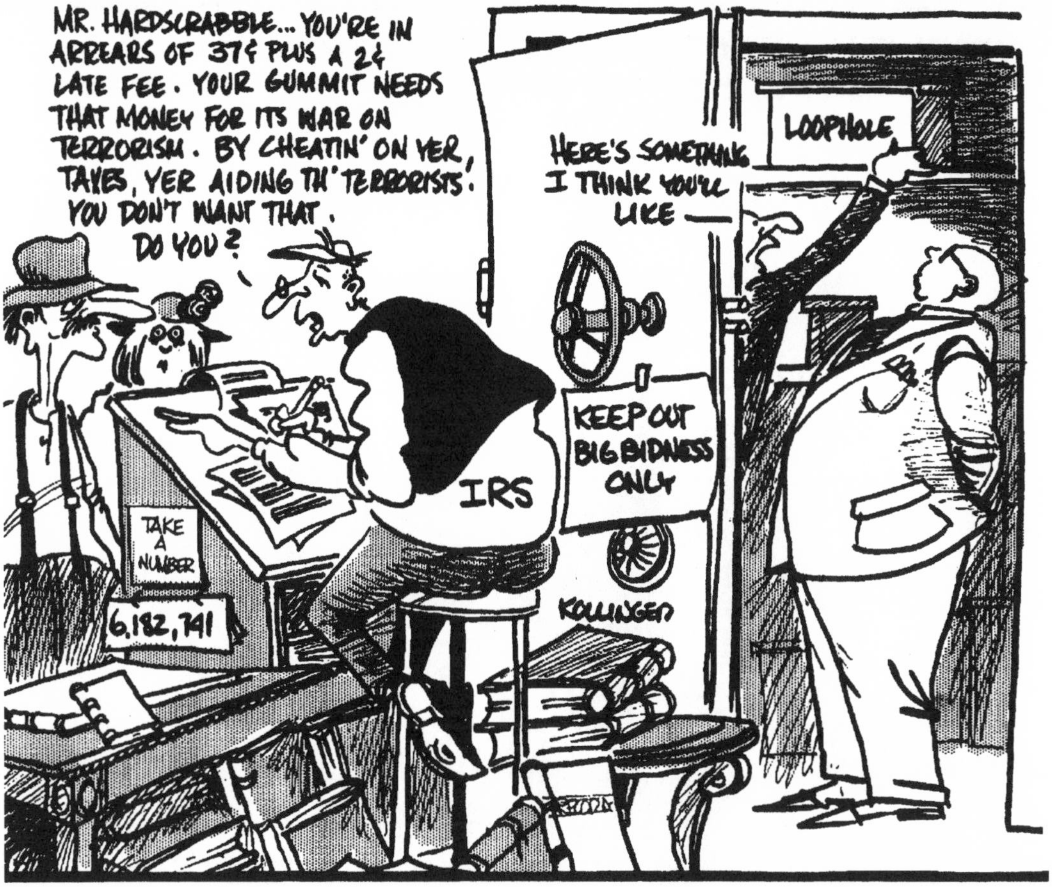
MR. HARDSCRABBLE... YOU'RE IN ARREARS OF 37¢ PLUS A 2¢ LATE FEE. YOUR GUMMIT NEEDS THAT MONEY FOR ITS WAR ON TERRORISM. BY CHEATIN' ON YER TAXES, YER AIDING TH' TERRORISTS! YOU DON'T WANT THAT. DO YOU?
HERE'S SOMETHING I THINK YOU'LL LIKE —
LOOPHOLE
KEEP OUT BIG BIDNESS ONLY
IRS
TAKE A NUMBER
6,182,741
KOLLINGER

RICK KOLLINGER
Courtesy The Star-Democrat (Md.)

FRANK CAMMUSO
Courtesy Post-Standard

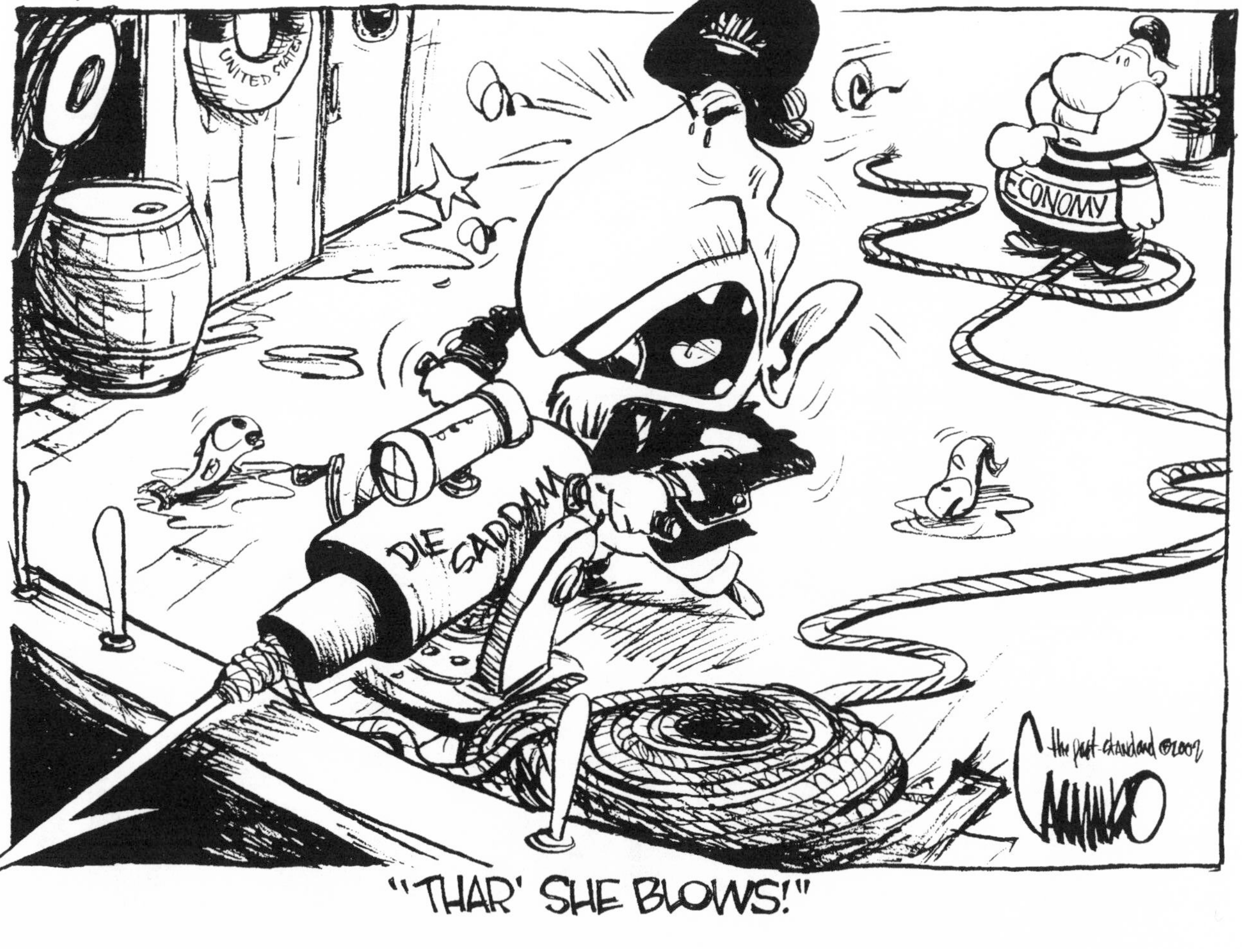
UNITED STATES
ECONOMY
DIE SADDAM
CAMMUSO

"THAR' SHE BLOWS!"

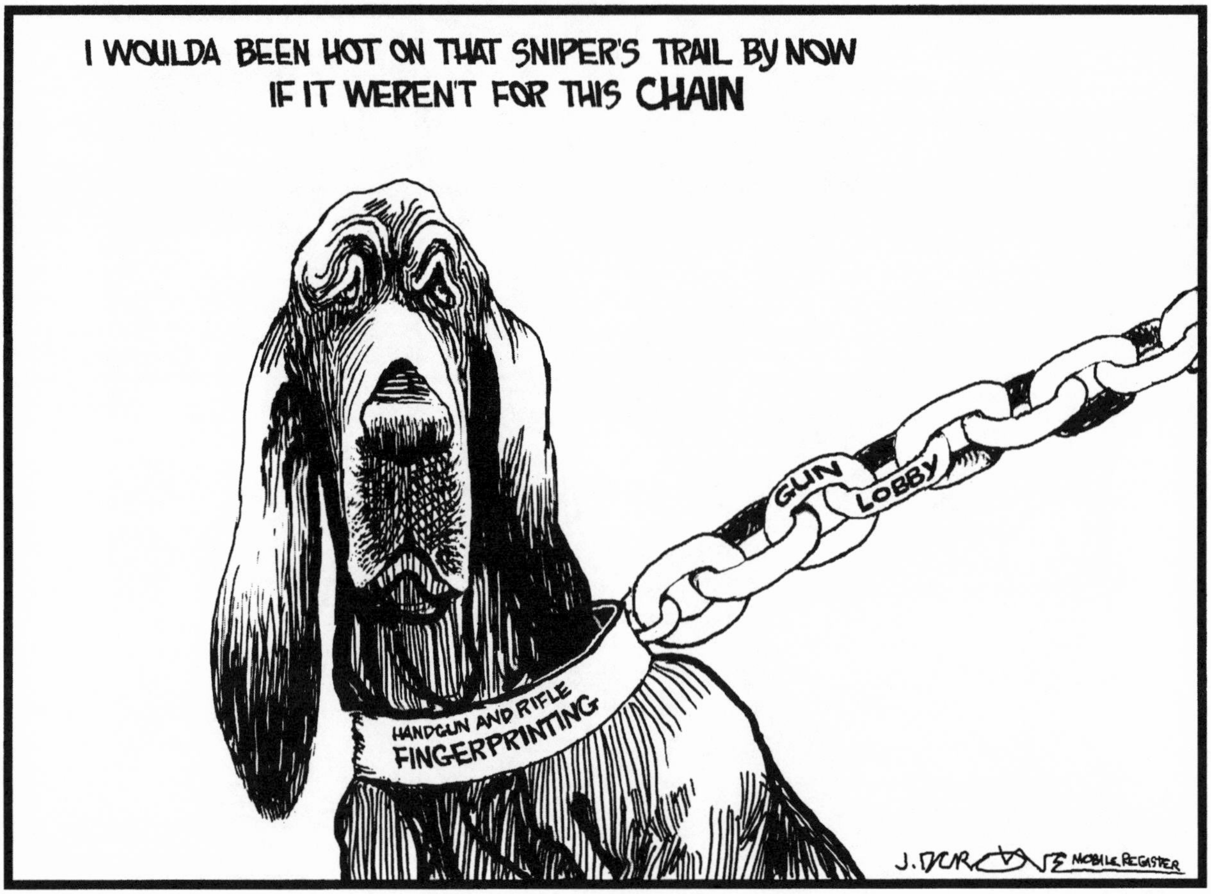
I WOULDA BEEN HOT ON THAT SNIPER'S TRAIL BY NOW
IF IT WEREN'T FOR THIS CHAIN
GUN
LOBBY
HANDGUN AND RIFLE
FINGERPRINTING
MOBILE REGISTER

JAMES D. CROWE
Courtesy Mobile Register

CLAY JONES
Courtesy The Free Lance-Star (Va.)

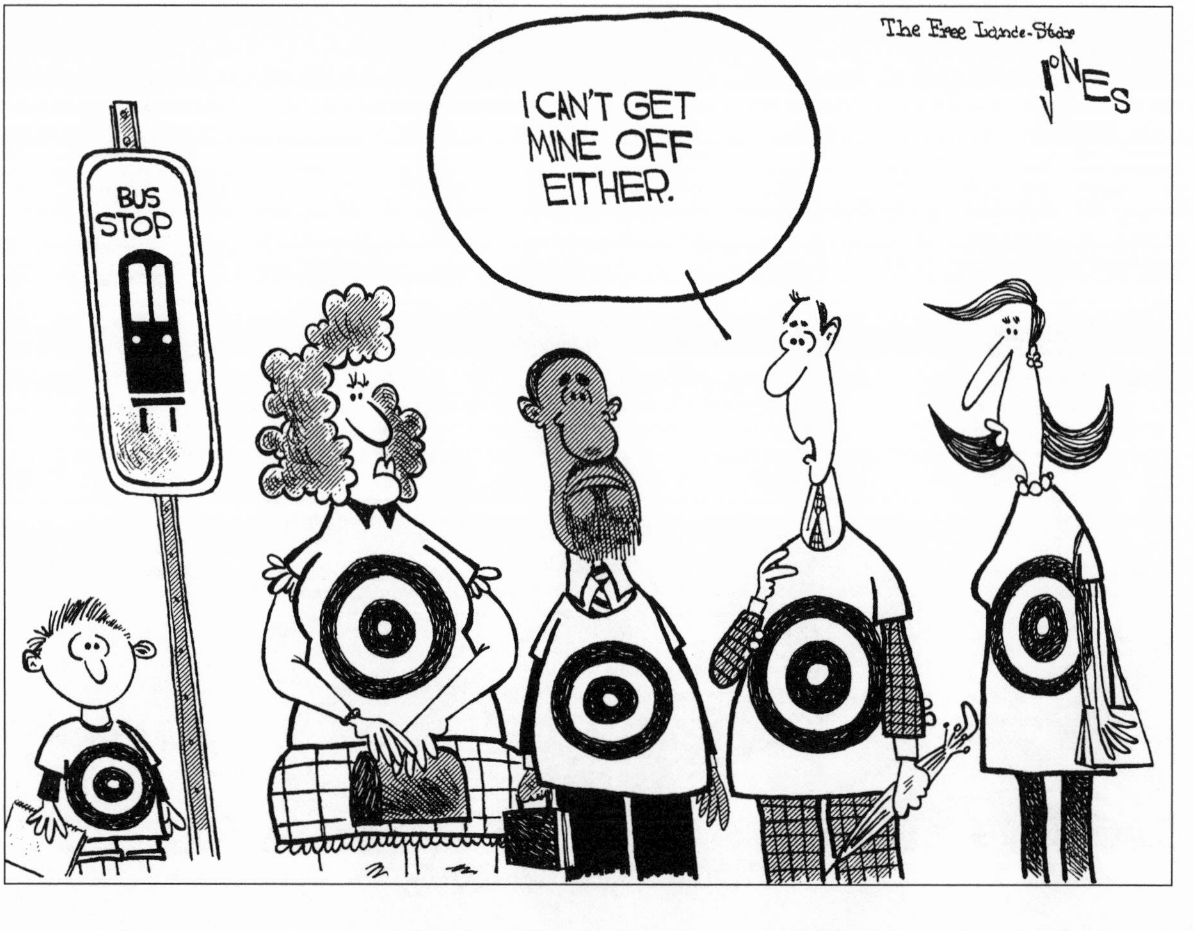
The Free Lance-Star
JONES
I CAN'T GET
MINE OFF
EITHER.
BUS
STOP

Crime

Major crimes that produced the most victims during the year occurred in the corporate world. First, Enron, the energy-trading giant, fell as a result of greed and a reckless competitive zeal to win at any cost. Other large companies soon followed. Scores of top executives were accused of using secret partnerships to hide huge debts, wildly inflating profit statements and making themselves rich in the process.

Crimes in high places in the business world have cost Americans hundreds of millions of dollars. The federal government has jailed several CEOs and continues to follow up in an effort to hold the wrongdoers accountable.

The entire country was shocked by a Washington, D.C.-area killing spree by snipers who began murdering people in public places at random. After the first few killings, many citizens grew panicky because of the deadly accuracy of the shooters. Some schools were closed and children were kept inside after authorities received communications that youngsters would be targeted. After fourteen shootings, resulting in eleven deaths, two alleged snipers were arrested at a rest stop near Frederick, Maryland.

Many children were reported missing during the year, and the trend appeared to be headed up.

SIGNE WILKINSON
Courtesy Philadelphia Daily News

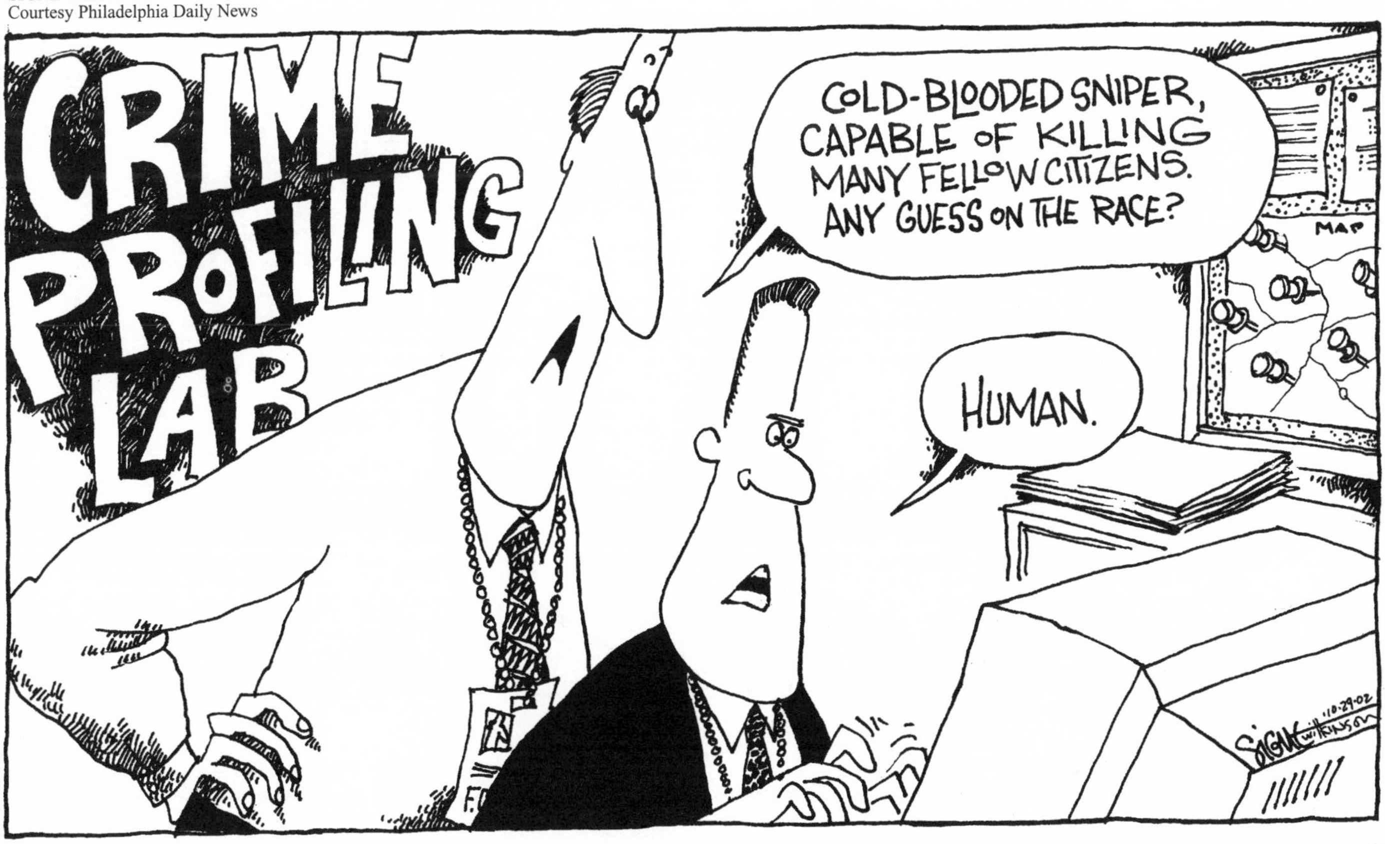
CRIME PROFILING LAB
COLD-BLOODED SNIPER, CAPABLE OF KILLING MANY FELLOW CITIZENS. ANY GUESS ON THE RACE?
HUMAN.
MAP
SIGNE WILKINSON
10.29.02

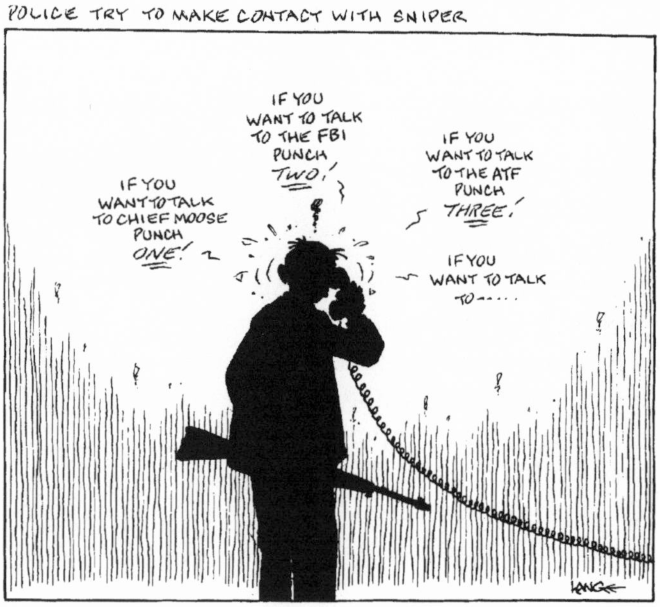
POLICE TRY TO MAKE CONTACT WITH SNIPER
IF YOU WANT TO TALK TO CHIEF MOOSE PUNCH ONE!
IF YOU WANT TO TALK TO THE FBI PUNCH TWO!
IF YOU WANT TO TALK TO THE ATF PUNCH THREE!
IF YOU WANT TO TALK TO- - - - .
LANGE

JIM LANGE
Courtesy The Daily Oklahoman

JIM BUSH
Courtesy Providence Journal (R.I.)

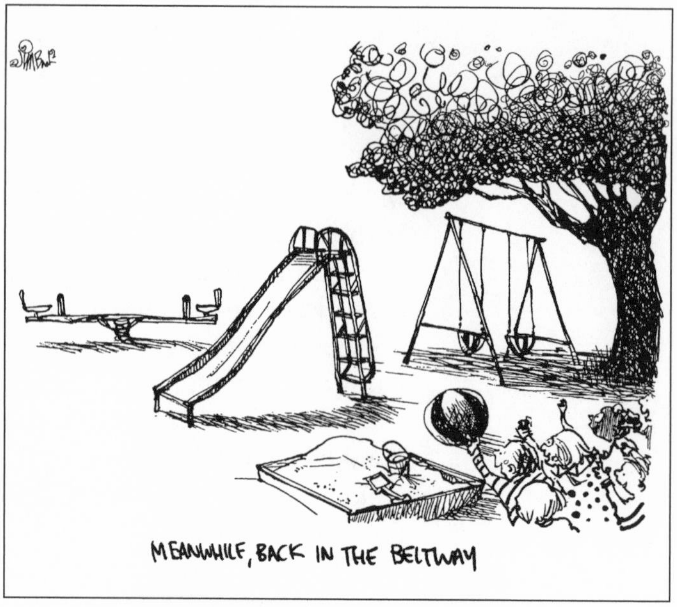
MEANWHILE, BACK IN THE BELTWAY

(drawn upon the capture of the Maryland sniper suspects)

JACK CHAPMAN
Courtesy DeSoto Times Today (Miss.)

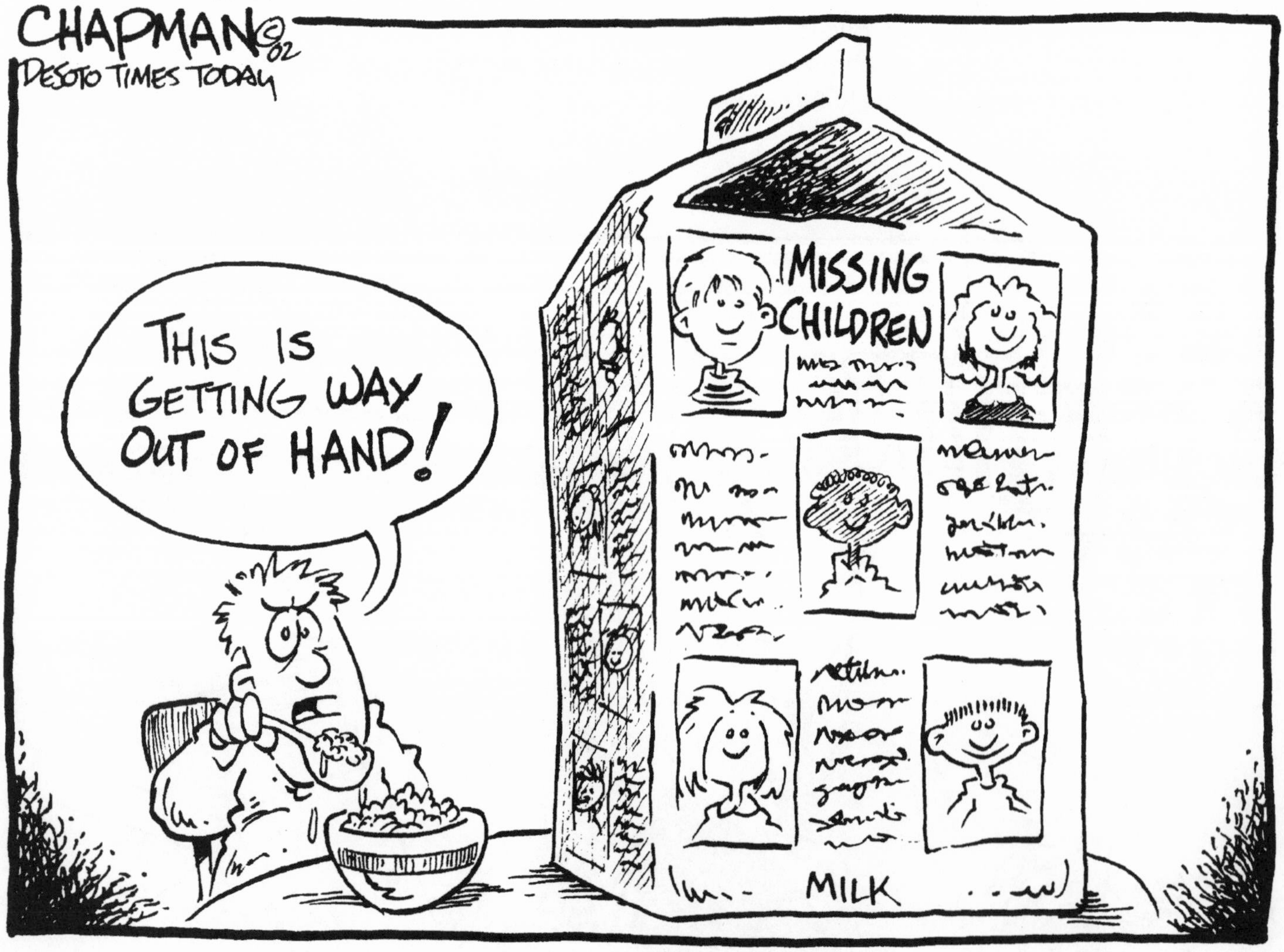
CHAPMAN © 02
DESOTO TIMES TODAY
THIS IS GETTING WAY OUT OF HAND!
MISSING CHILDREN
MILK

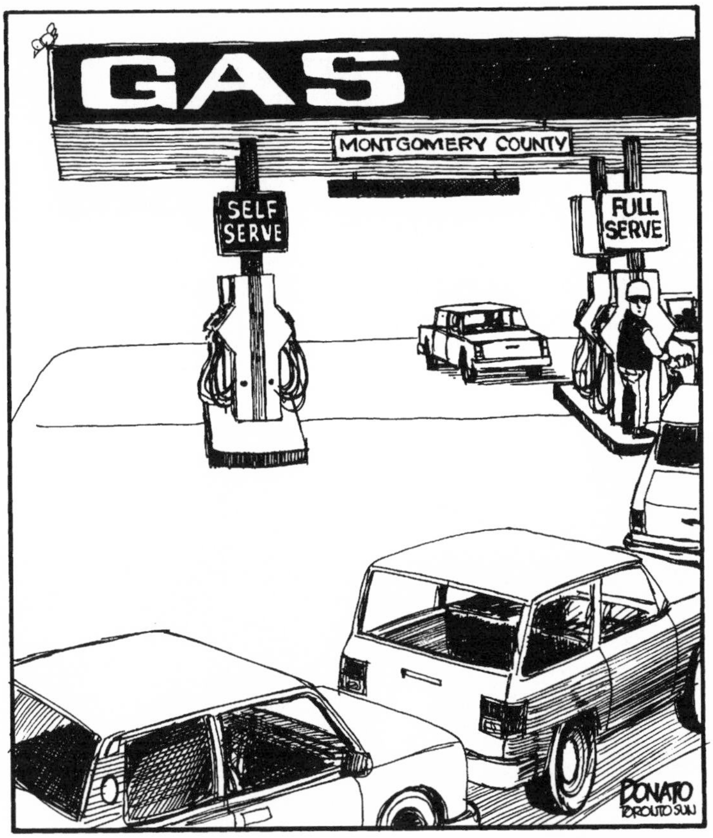
GAS
MONTGOMERY COUNTY
SELF SERVE
FULL SERVE
DONATO
TORONTO SUN

ANDY DONATO
Courtesy Toronto Sun

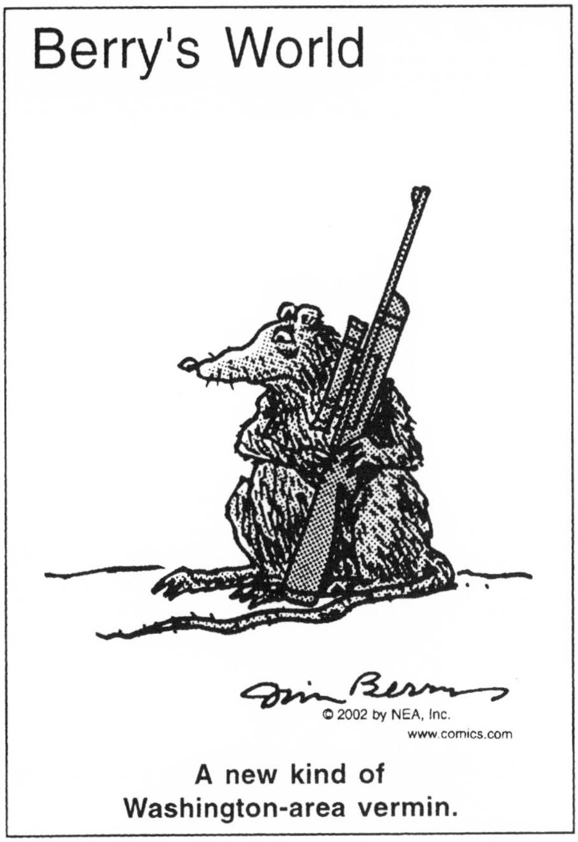
Berry's World
Jim Berry
© 2002 by NEA, Inc.
www.comics.com
A new kind of
Washington-area vermin.

JIM BERRY
Courtesy NEA

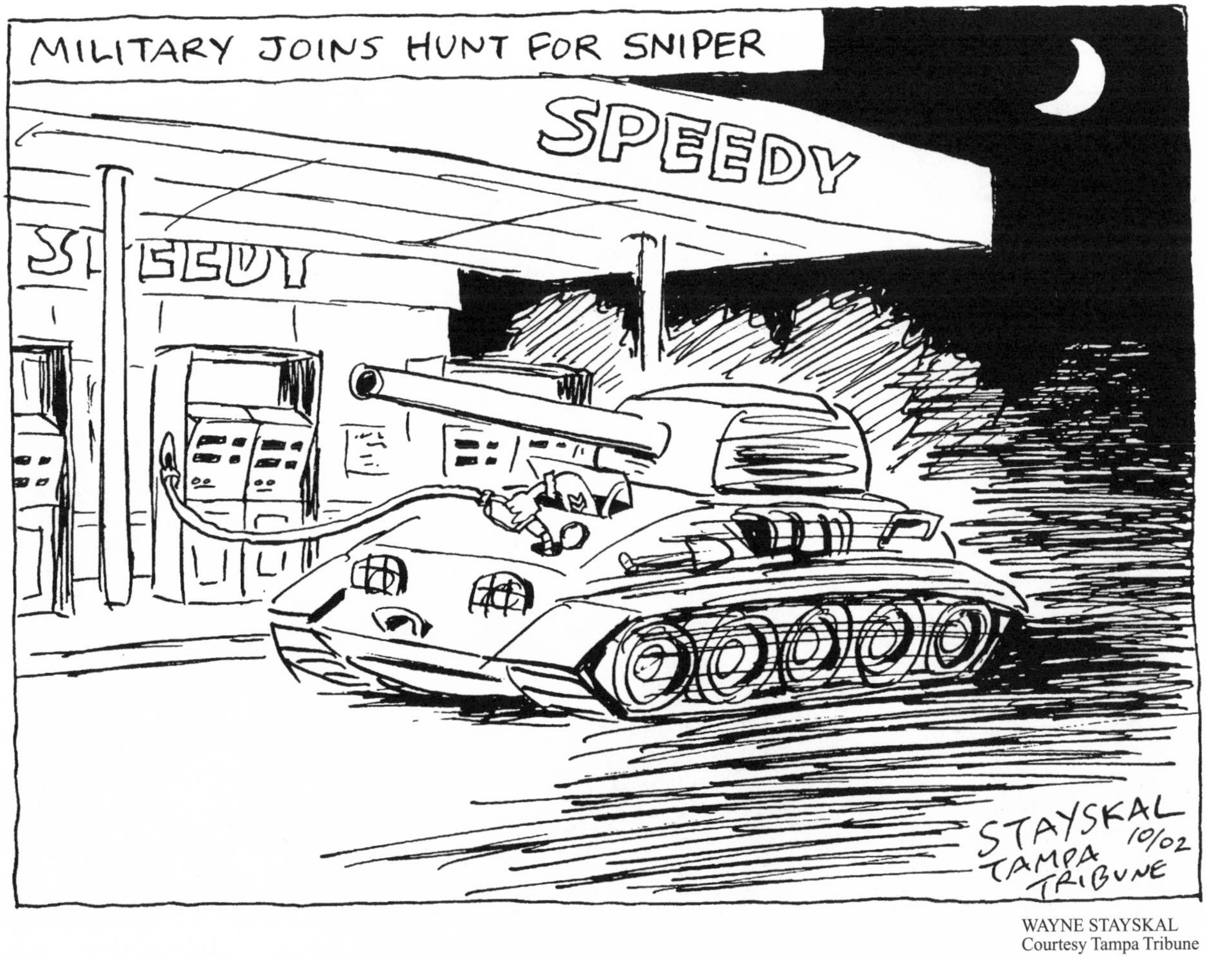
MILITARY JOINS HUNT FOR SNIPER
SPEEDY
STAYSKAL 10/02
TAMPA TRIBUNE

WAYNE STAYSKAL
Courtesy Tampa Tribune

CINDY PROCIOUS
Courtesy Huntsville Times

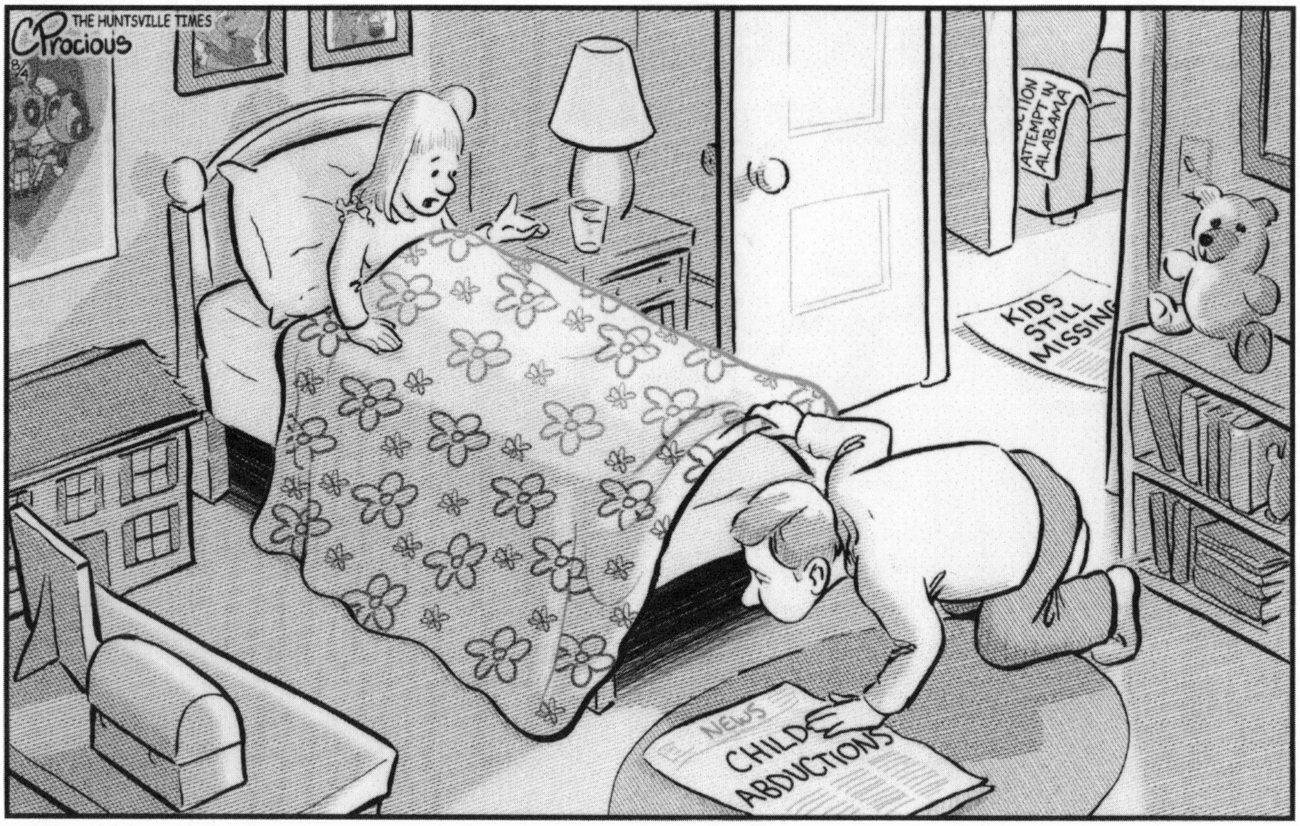

CProcious
THE HUNTSVILLE TIMES
8/4
ATTEMPT IN ALABAMA
KIDS STILL MISSING
NEWS
CHILD ABDUCTIONS

"C'MON, DAD... I'M NOT AFRAID OF MONSTERS UNDER MY BED ANYMORE."

STEVE BREEN
Courtesy San Diego Union-Tribune

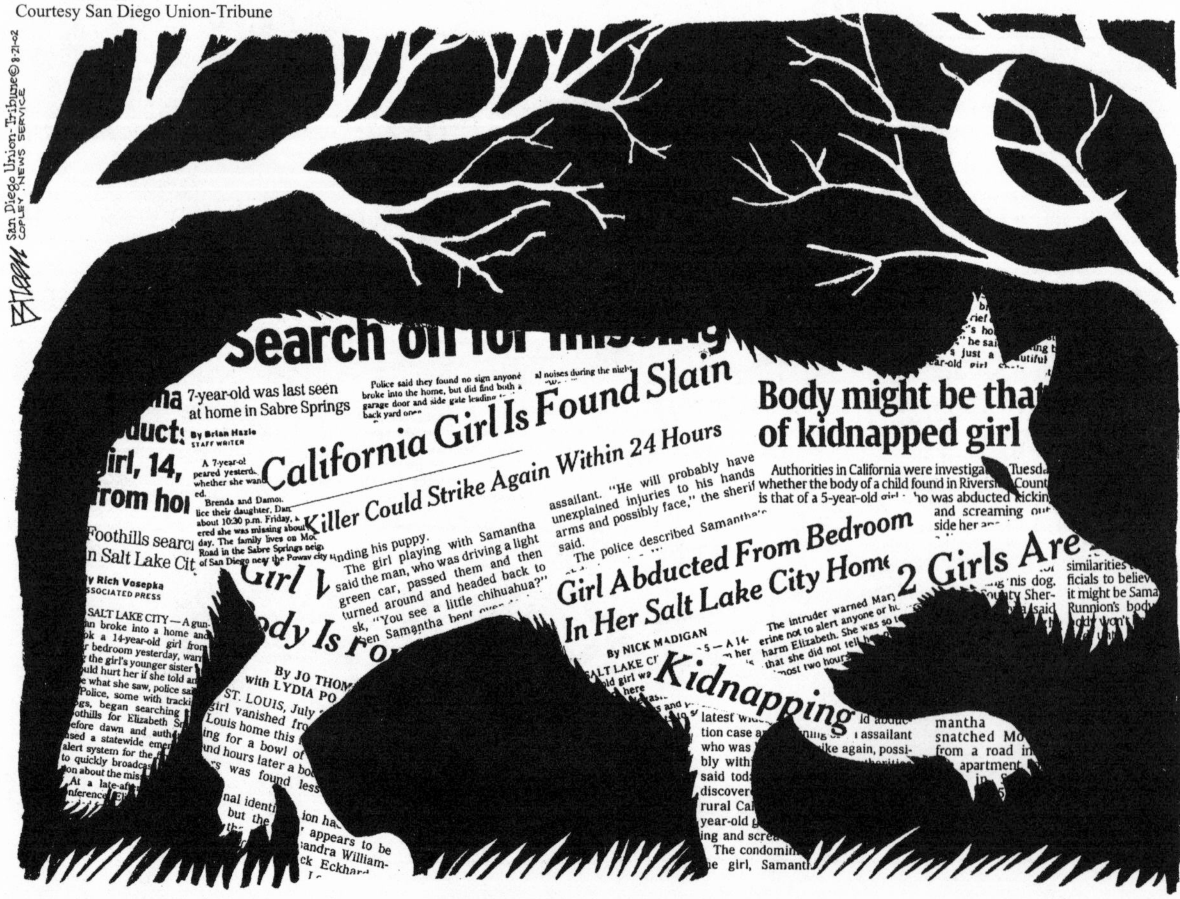

San Diego Union-Tribune ©8-21-02
COPLEY NEWS SERVICE
7-year-old was last seen at home in Sabre Springs
California Girl Is Found Slain
Killer Could Strike Again Within 24 Hours
Body might be that of kidnapped girl
Girl Abducted From Bedroom In Her Salt Lake City Hom
2 Girls Are
Kidnapping

THE BIG BAD WOLF

Society

Just as Americans remember Pearl Harbor, so do they remember the infamy of September 11, 2001. President Bush has declared that America is a nation at war—and will be for a long time to come. This fact of life was brought home to every citizen by the outpouring of love, dedication, and deep respect for the victims of 9-11 throughout the country on September 11, 2002. And with that outpouring came a clear message: WE SHALL NOT FORGET.

The Ninth Circuit Court in San Francisco ruled that the words "under God" must be removed from the Pledge of Allegiance as recited in public schools, setting off a storm of protest and outrage. Not a single U.S. senator agreed with the court, nor did an overwhelming majority of Americans.

Attorney General John Ashcroft asked Congress to approve a sweeping set of new laws that would make it easier for law enforcement agencies to track terrorists' communications over computer networks and telephones. He also sought expanded wiretap authority. Some civil libertarians oppose the idea, claiming such laws would undermine some constitutional rights. President Bush contends that such changes are essential in the modern world—in pursuing terrorist financing, for example.

SCOTT STANTIS
Courtesy Birmingham News

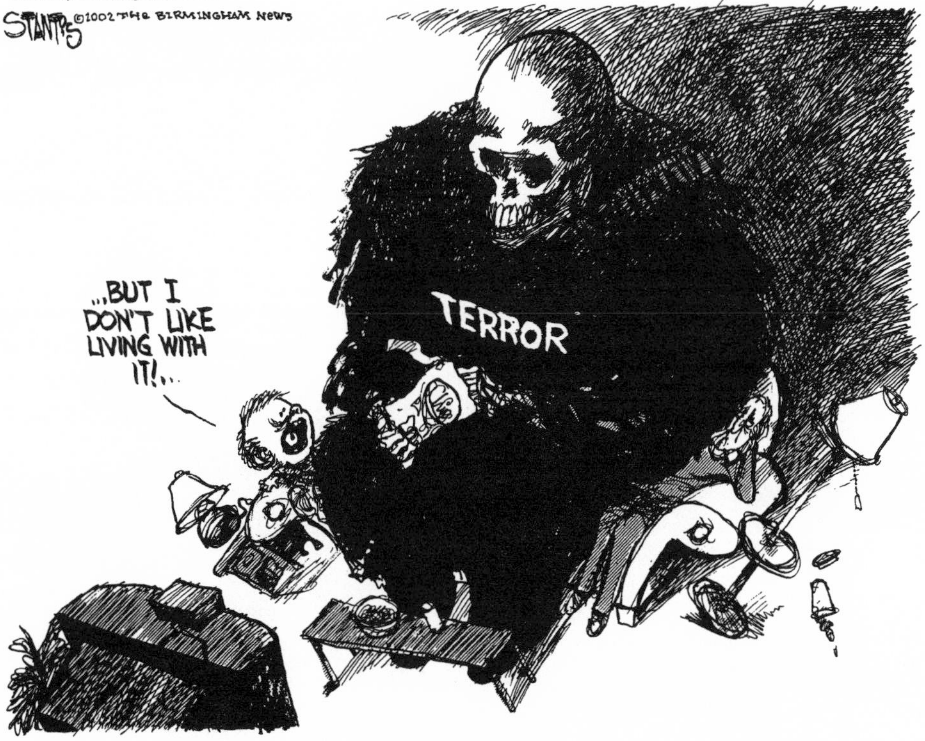
STANTIS ©2002 THE BIRMINGHAM NEWS
TERROR
...BUT I DON'T LIKE LIVING WITH IT!...

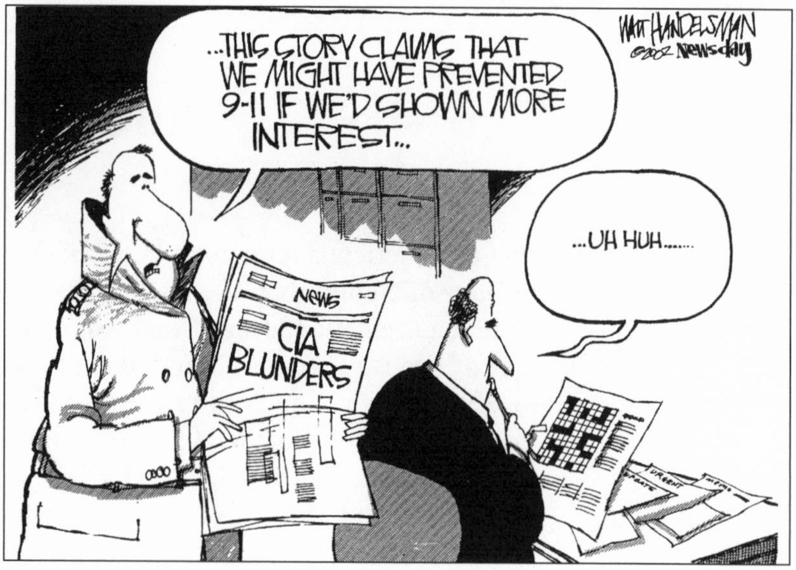
WALT HANDELSMAN ©2002 Newsday
...THIS STORY CLAIMS THAT WE MIGHT HAVE PREVENTED 9-11 IF WE'D SHOWN MORE INTEREST...
...UH HUH......
NEWS
CIA BLUNDERS

WALT HANDELSMAN
Courtesy Newsday

RANDY BISH
Courtesy Tribune-Review (Pa.)

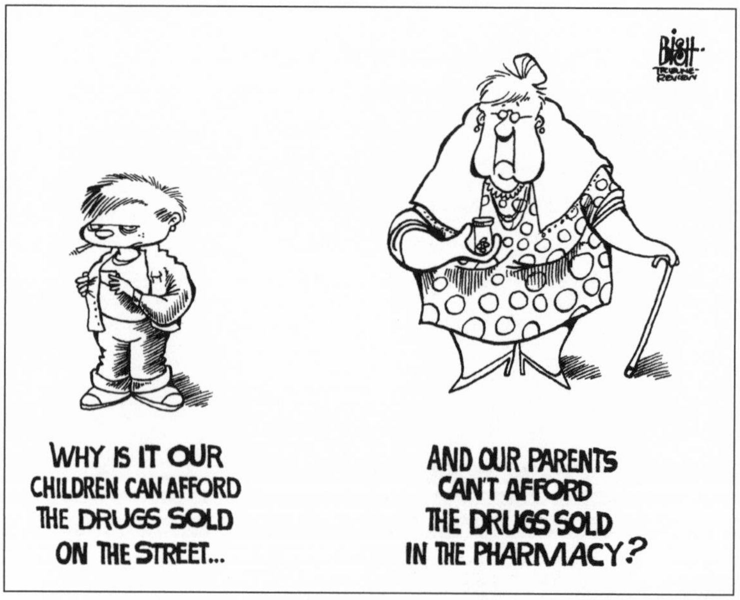
BISH TRIBUNE-REVIEW
WHY IS IT OUR CHILDREN CAN AFFORD THE DRUGS SOLD ON THE STREET...
AND OUR PARENTS CAN'T AFFORD THE DRUGS SOLD IN THE PHARMACY?

IRENE JOSLIN
Courtesy Brown County Democrat (Ind.)

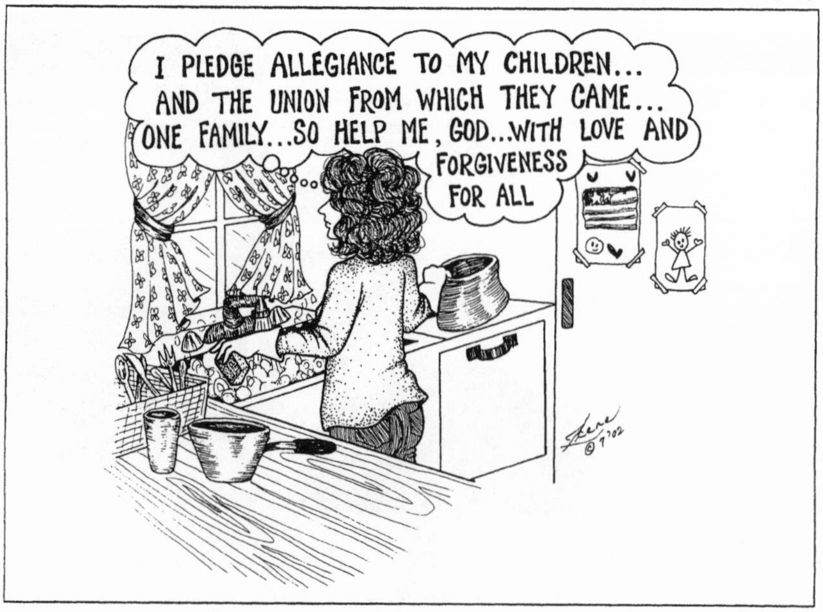
I PLEDGE ALLEGIANCE TO MY CHILDREN... AND THE UNION FROM WHICH THEY CAME... ONE FAMILY...SO HELP ME, GOD...WITH LOVE AND FORGIVENESS FOR ALL

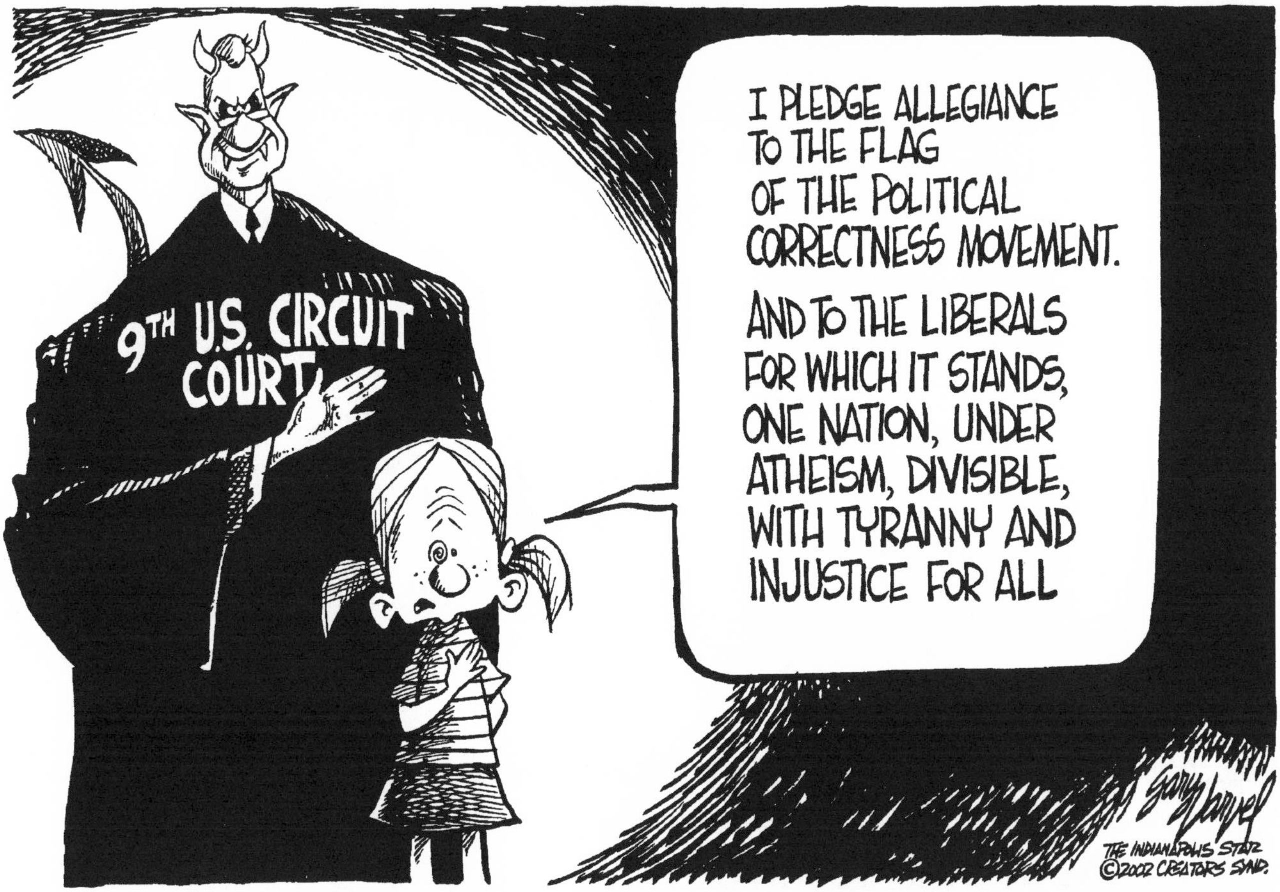
9TH U.S. CIRCUIT COURT
I PLEDGE ALLEGIANCE TO THE FLAG OF THE POLITICAL CORRECTNESS MOVEMENT.
AND TO THE LIBERALS FOR WHICH IT STANDS, ONE NATION, UNDER ATHEISM, DIVISIBLE, WITH TYRANNY AND INJUSTICE FOR ALL
THE INDIANAPOLIS STAR
©2002 CREATORS SYND.

GARY VARVEL
Courtesy Indianapolis Star

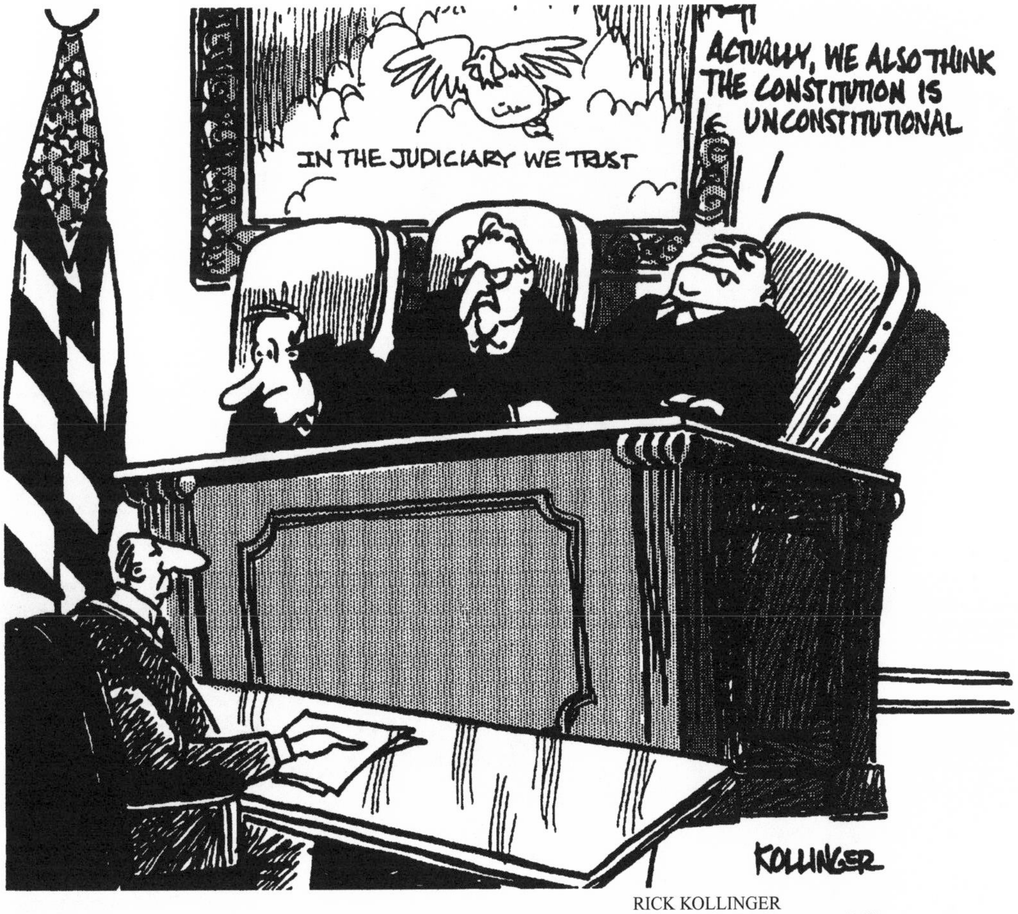
IN THE JUDICIARY WE TRUST
ACTUALLY, WE ALSO THINK THE CONSTITUTION IS UNCONSTITUTIONAL
KOLLINGER

RICK KOLLINGER
Courtesy The Star-Democrat (Md.)

MAYBE I SHOULD TELL HIM THAT THIS IS UNCONSTITUTIONAL
VALLEY FORGE, 2002

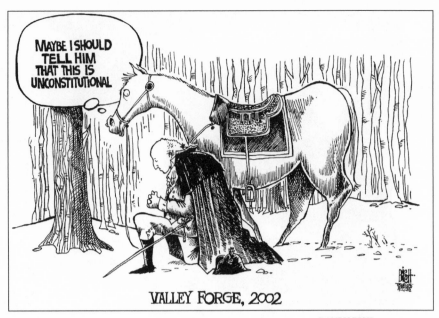

RANDY BISH
Courtesy Tribune-Review (Pa.)

"I DUNNO, TOM, THAT REFERENCE TO 'NATURE'S GOD' IS A LITTLE OUT OF ORDER, DON'T YOU THINK?"
"AND THE PART ABOUT 'ENDOWED BY THEIR CREATOR' IS REALLY OFF THE WALL..."
"PERHAPS IF YOU PRECEDED SUCH STATEMENTS BY 'ALLEGED' OR 'AS SOME BELIEVE'..."
MAJESKI TIMES LEADER AFTER TRUMBULL
IF THE DECLARATION OF INDEPENDENCE WERE WRITTEN TODAY

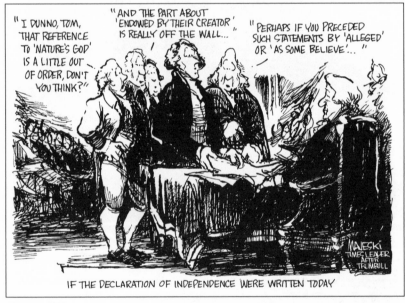

JOE MAJESKI
Courtesy The Times-Leader (Pa.)

STEVE GREENBERG
Courtesy Ventura County Star (Calif.)

ONE NATION UNDER GOD*
WITH LIBERTY AND JUSTICE FOR ALL.
* OFFER VOID IN ALASKA, ARIZONA, CALIFORNIA, HAWAII, IDAHO, MONTANA, NEVADA, OREGON and WASHINGTON
— 9th CIRCUIT COURT of APPEALS
GREENBERG — VENTURA COUNTY STAR, 2002

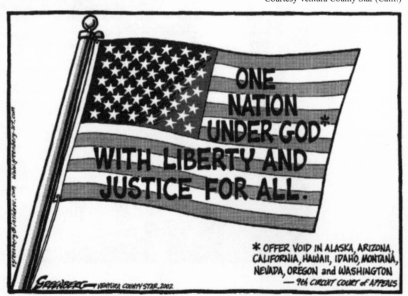

JOHN SHERFFIUS
Courtesy St. Louis Post-Dispatch

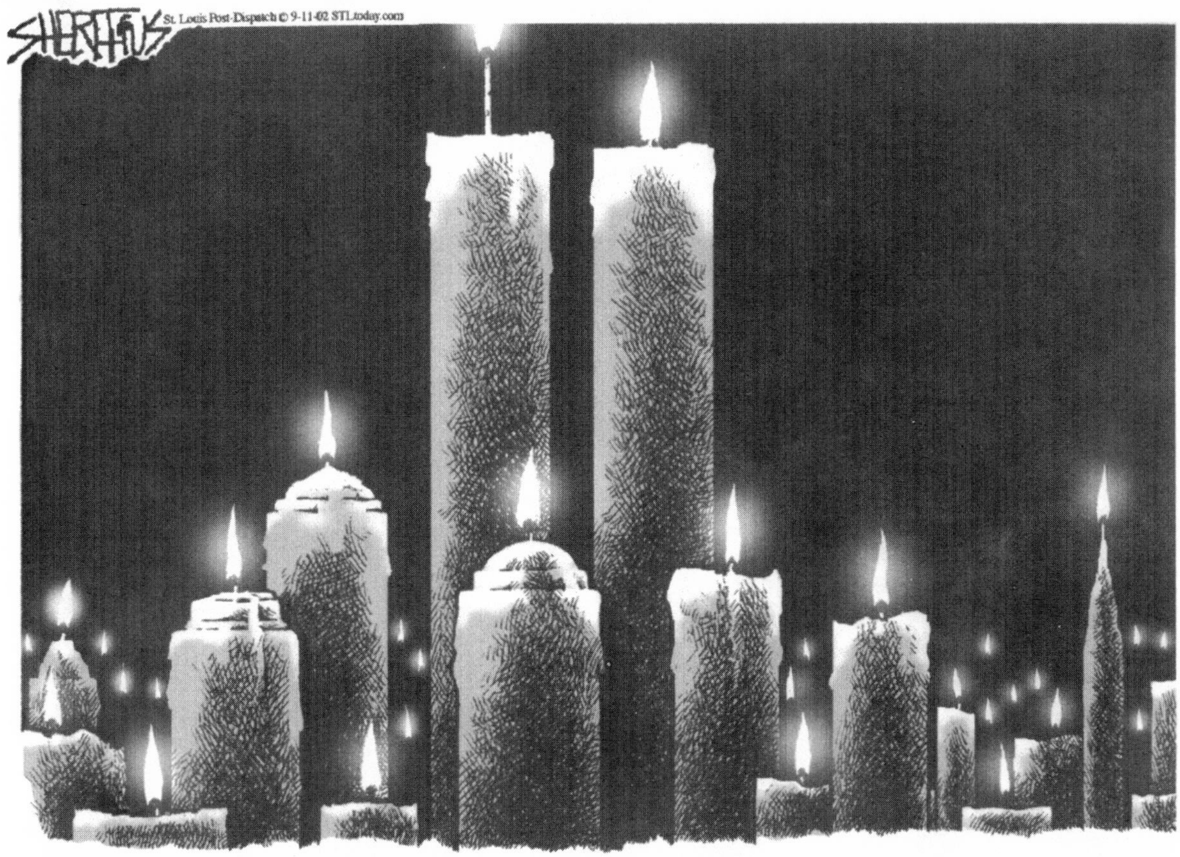
SHERFFIUS
St. Louis Post-Dispatch © 9-11-02 STLtoday.com

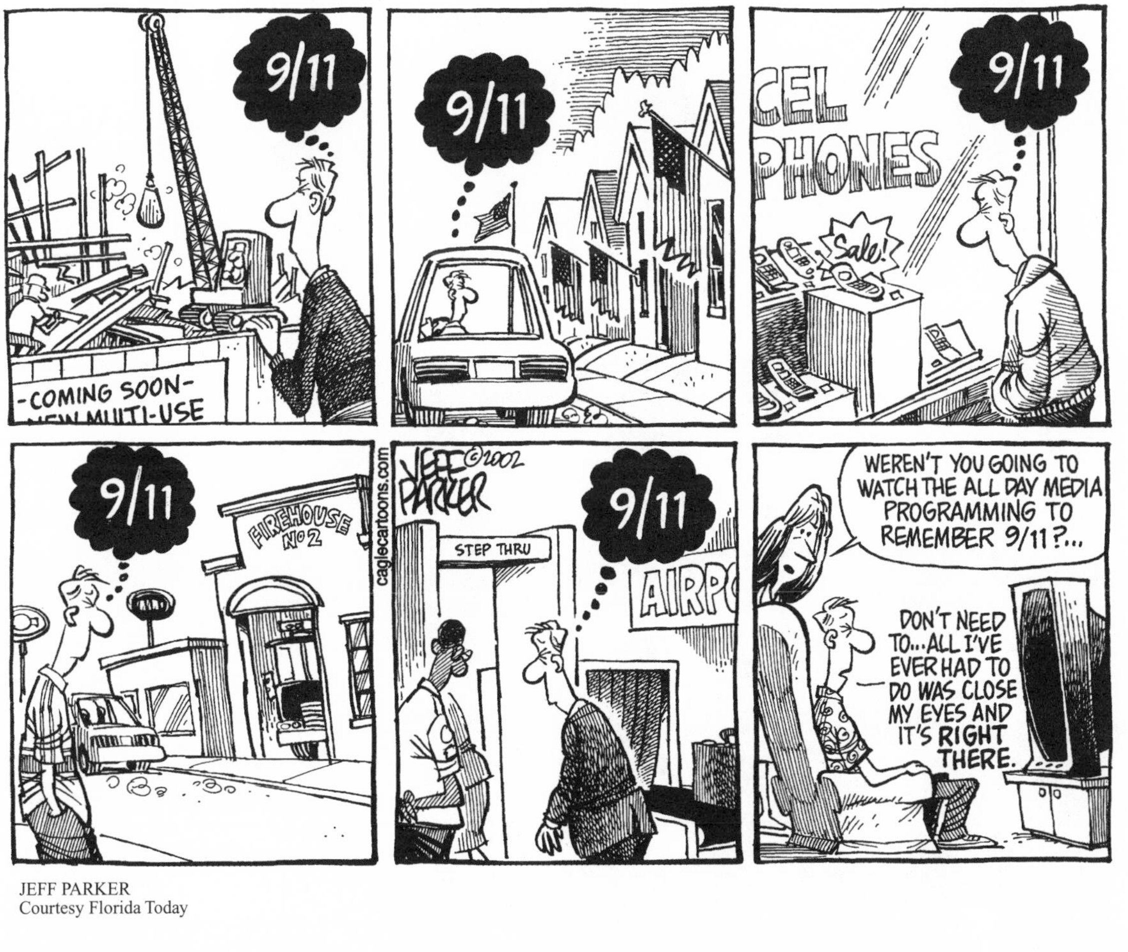
9/11
-COMING SOON-
9/11
CEL
PHONES
Sale!
9/11
9/11
FIREHOUSE
No 2
caglecartoons.com
JEFF PARKER ©2002
STEP THRU
9/11
WEREN'T YOU GOING TO WATCH THE ALL DAY MEDIA PROGRAMMING TO REMEMBER 9/11?...
DON'T NEED TO...ALL I'VE EVER HAD TO DO WAS CLOSE MY EYES AND IT'S RIGHT THERE.

JEFF PARKER
Courtesy Florida Today

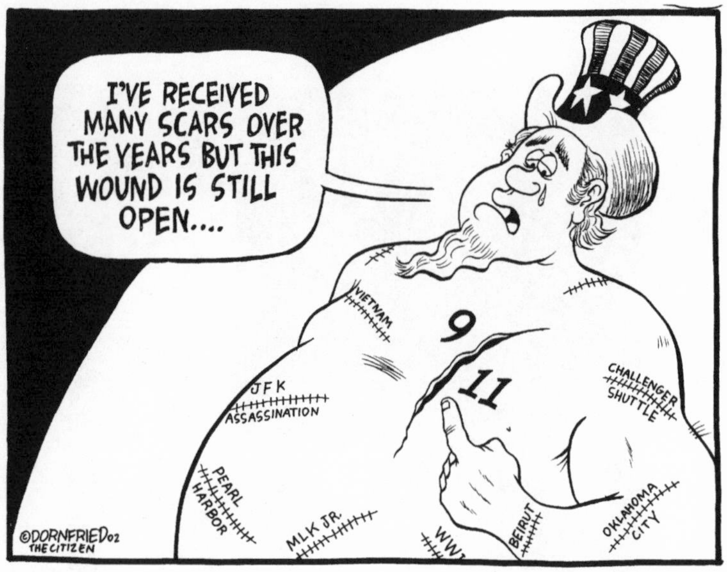

I'VE RECEIVED MANY SCARS OVER THE YEARS BUT THIS WOUND IS STILL OPEN....
VIETNAM
9
11
JFK ASSASSINATION
CHALLENGER SHUTTLE
PEARL HARBOR
MLK JR.
BEIRUT
OKLAHOMA CITY
©DORNFRIED02 THE CITIZEN

BOB DORNFRIED
Courtesy Berlin Citizen (Conn.)

BARBARA BRANDON-CROFT
Courtesy Universal Press Syndicate

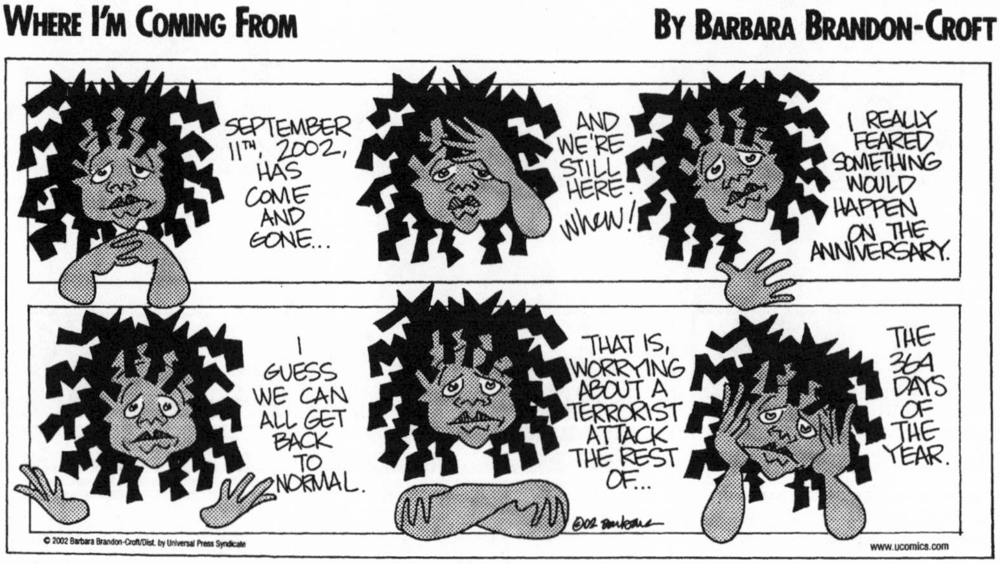

WHERE I'M COMING FROM
BY BARBARA BRANDON-CROFT
SEPTEMBER 11TH, 2002, HAS COME AND GONE...
AND WE'RE STILL HERE. WHEW!
I REALLY FEARED SOMETHING WOULD HAPPEN ON THE ANNIVERSARY.
I GUESS WE CAN ALL GET BACK TO NORMAL.
THAT IS, WORRYING ABOUT A TERRORIST ATTACK THE REST OF...
THE 364 DAYS OF THE YEAR.
© 2002 Barbara Brandon-Croft/Dist. by Universal Press Syndicate
www.ucomics.com

JERRY BARNETT
Courtesy Indianapolis Star

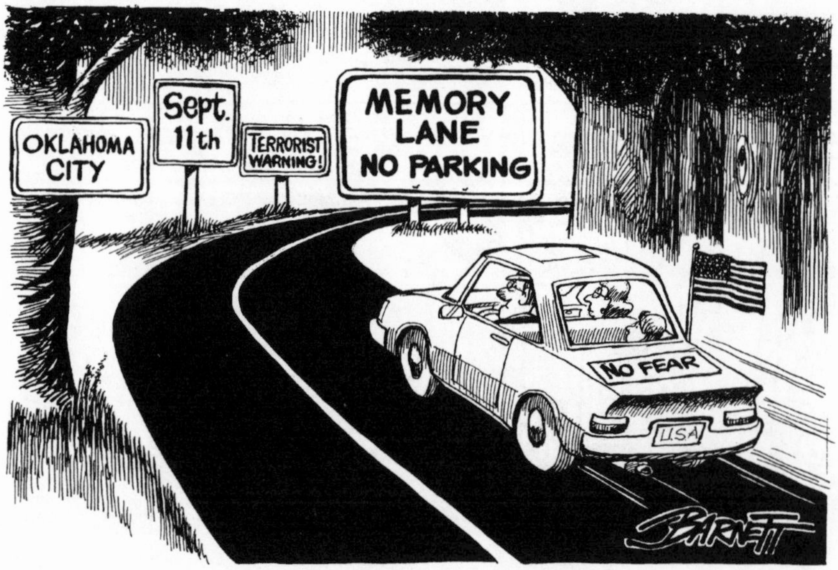

OKLAHOMA CITY
Sept. 11th
TERRORIST WARNING!
MEMORY LANE NO PARKING
NO FEAR
USA
BARNETT

MARK THORNHILL
Courtesy North County Times (Calif.)

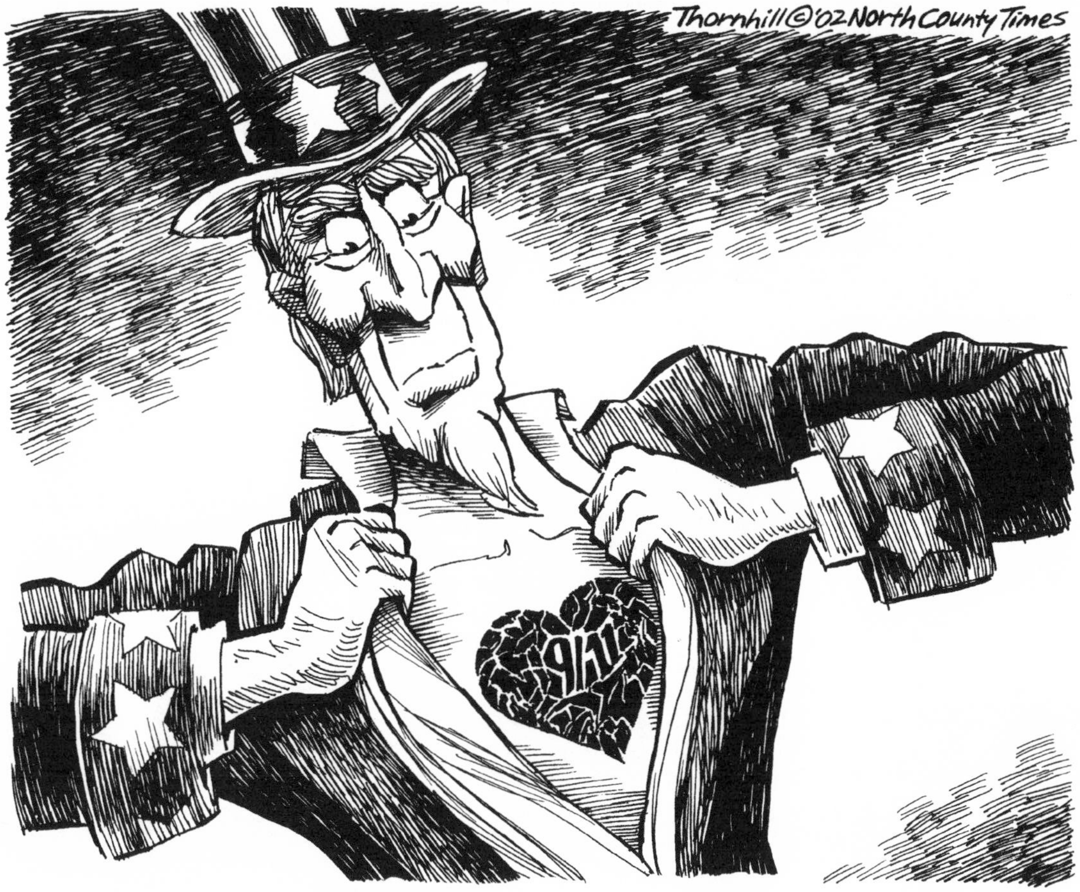
Thornhill©'02 North County Times
9/11

DOUG MacGREGOR
Courtesy Fort Myers News-Press

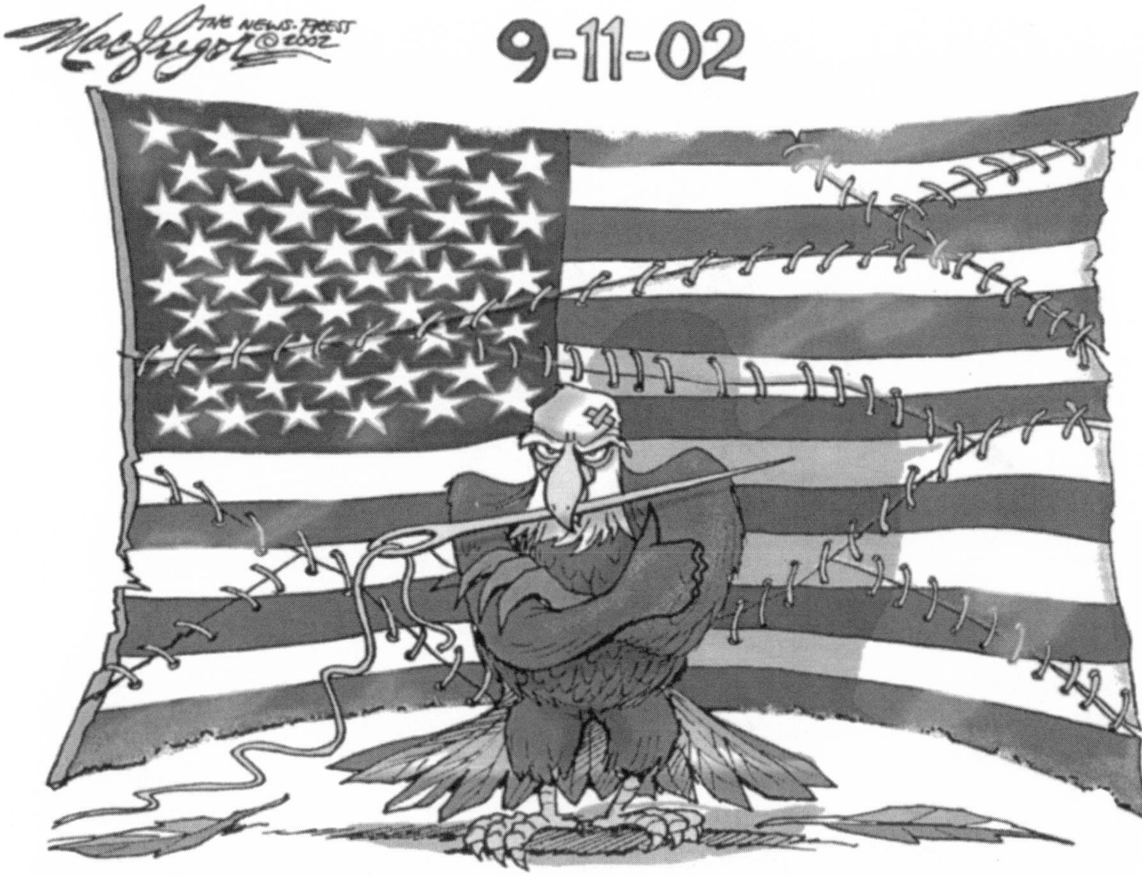
MacGregor THE NEWS-PRESS ©2002
9-11-02

GARY VARVEL
Courtesy Indianapolis Star

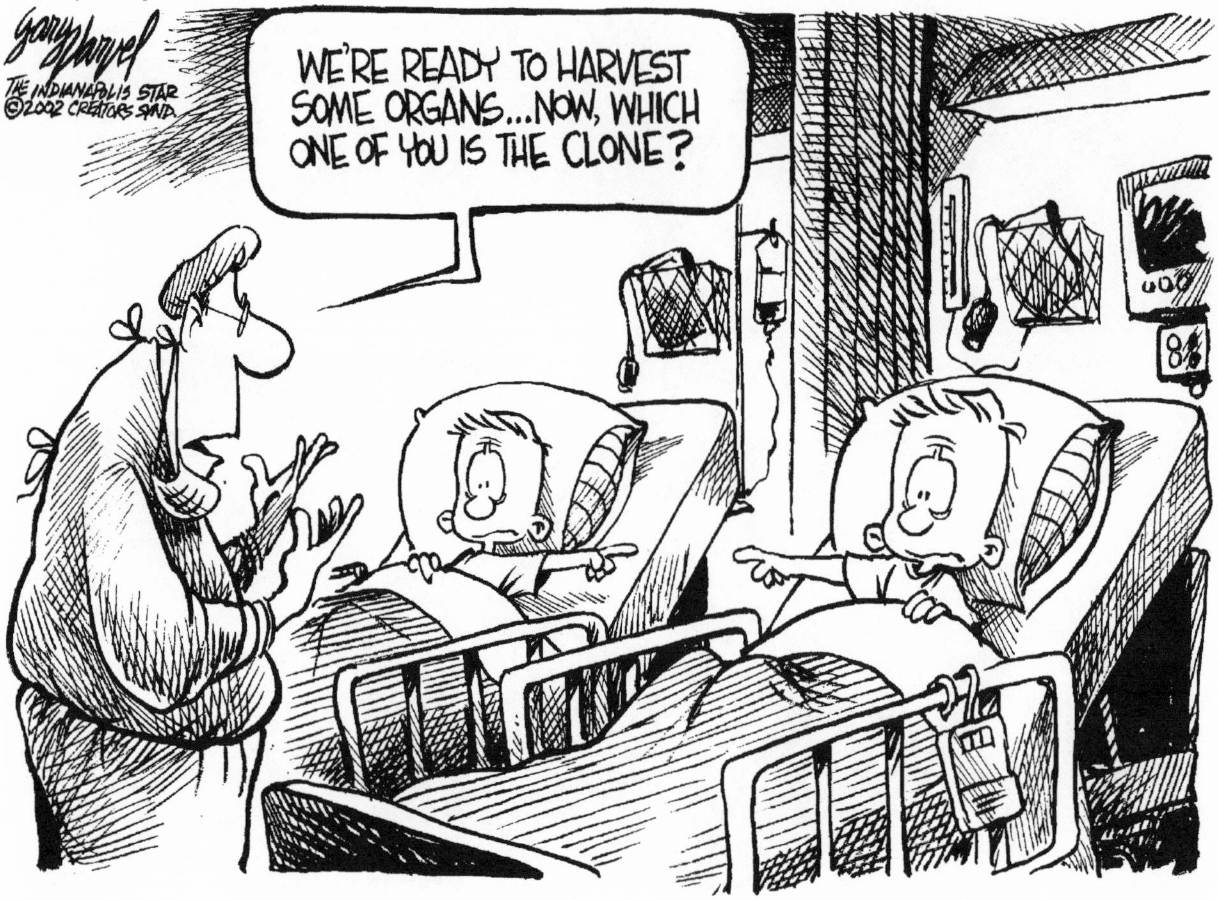
garyvarvel
THE INDIANAPOLIS STAR
©2002 CREATORS SYND.
WE'RE READY TO HARVEST SOME ORGANS...NOW, WHICH ONE OF YOU IS THE CLONE?

GILL FOX
Courtesy Fairfield Citizen News (Conn.)

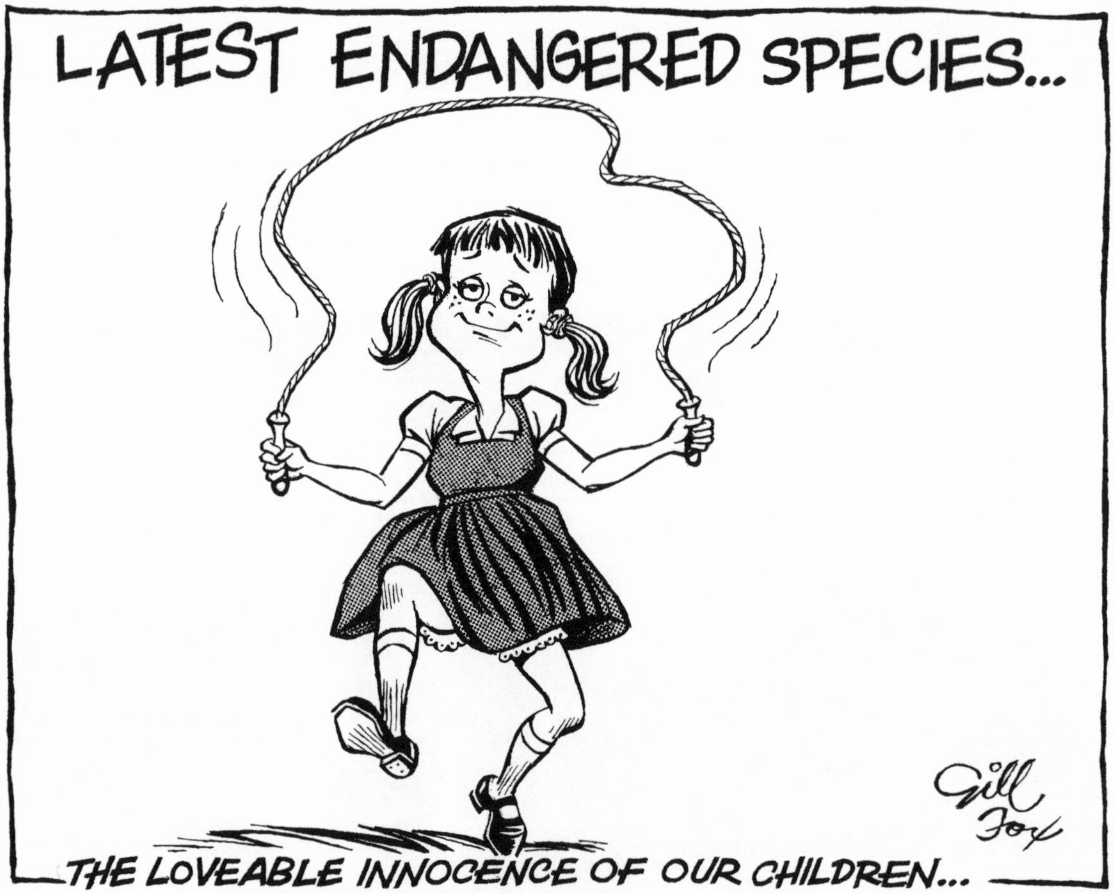
LATEST ENDANGERED SPECIES...
Gill Fox
THE LOVEABLE INNOCENCE OF OUR CHILDREN...

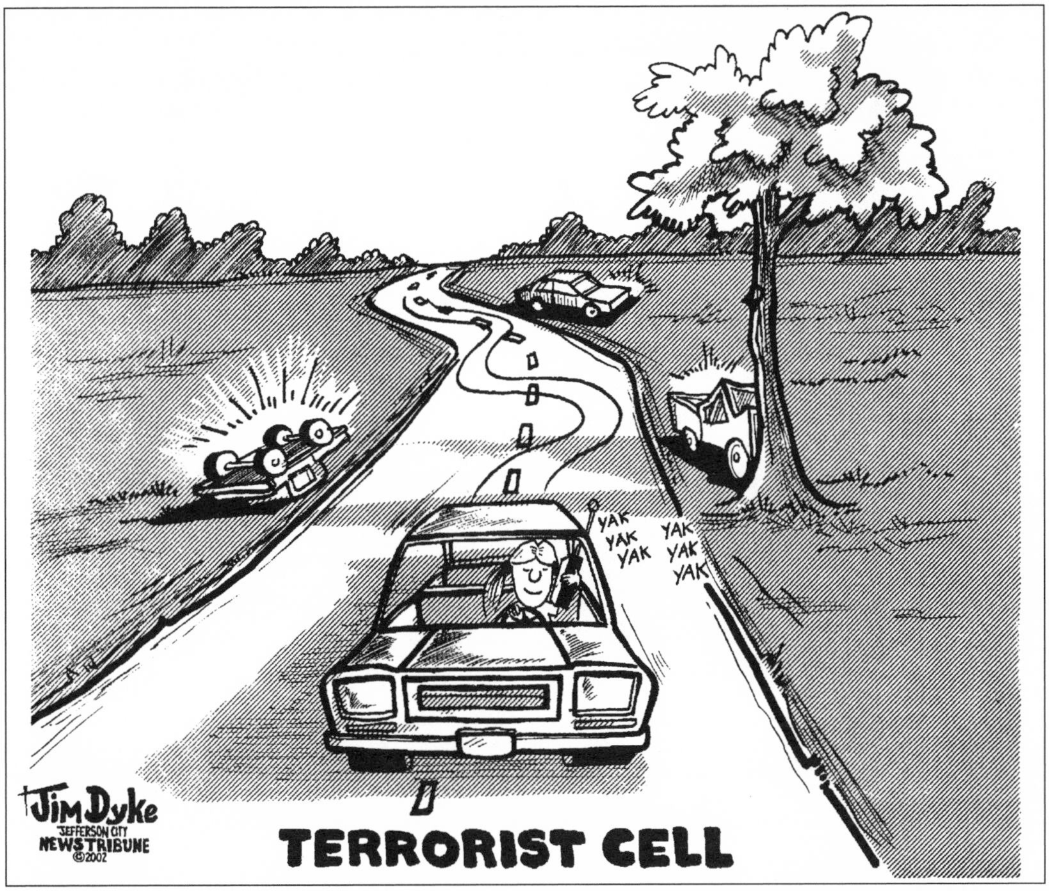
YAK YAK YAK
YAK YAK YAK
Jim Dyke
JEFFERSON CITY NEWS TRIBUNE ©2002
TERRORIST CELL

JIM DYKE
Courtesy Jefferson City News-Tribune

VIC CANTONE
Courtesy Artist Market.com Syndicate

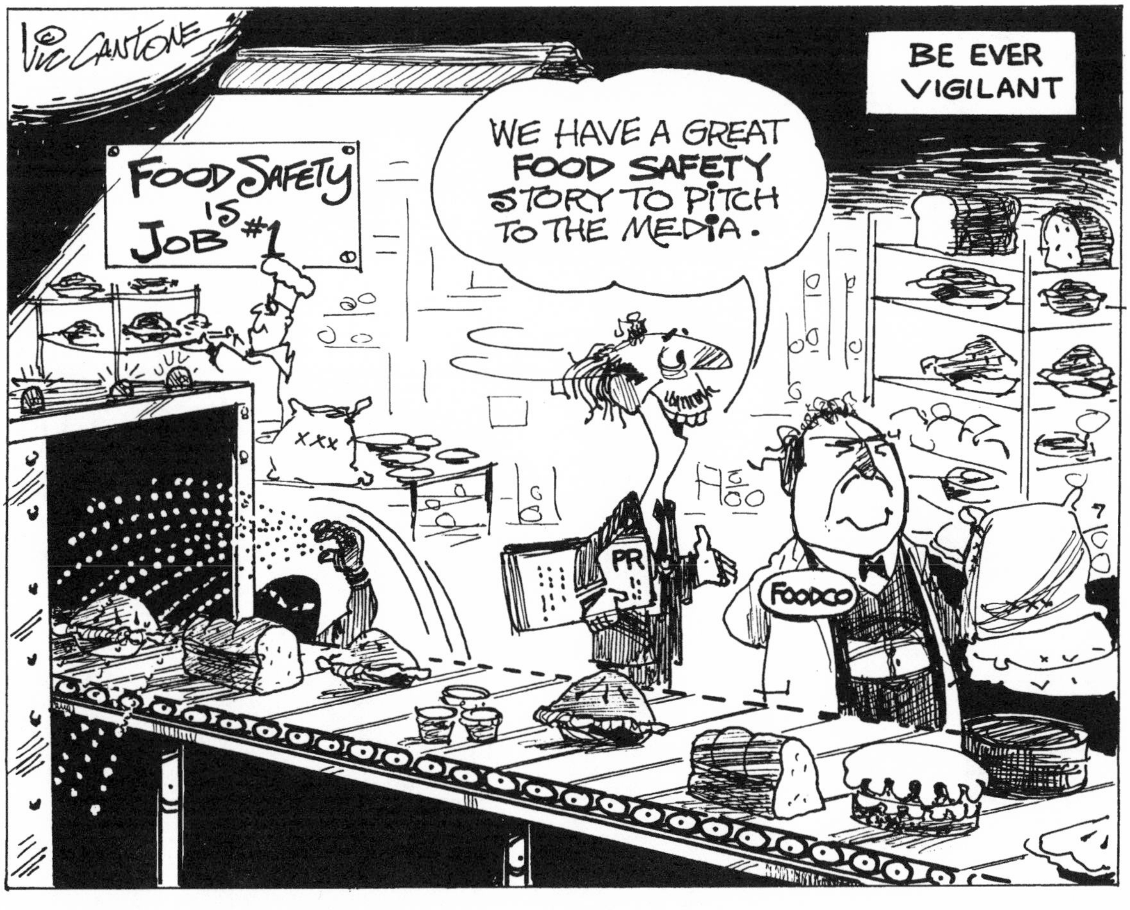
VIC CANTONE
BE EVER VIGILANT
FOOD SAFETY IS JOB #1
WE HAVE A GREAT FOOD SAFETY STORY TO PITCH TO THE MEDIA.
PR
FOODCO

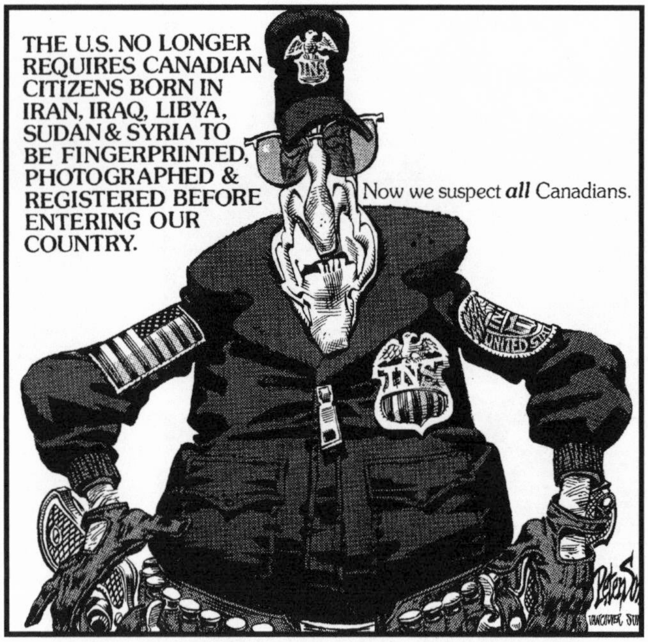
THE U.S. NO LONGER REQUIRES CANADIAN CITIZENS BORN IN IRAN, IRAQ, LIBYA, SUDAN & SYRIA TO BE FINGERPRINTED, PHOTOGRAPHED & REGISTERED BEFORE ENTERING OUR COUNTRY.
Now we suspect *all* Canadians.
INS
INS

ROY PETERSON
Courtesy Vancouver Sun

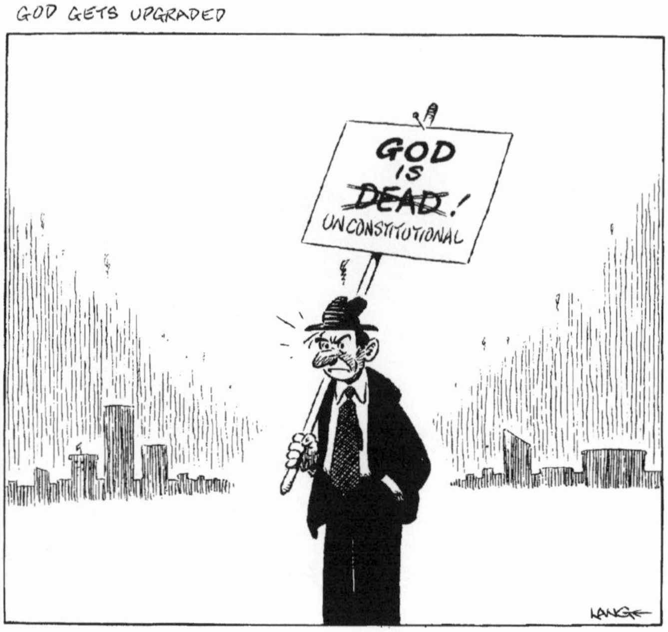
GOD GETS UPGRADED
GOD IS ~~DEAD~~! UNCONSTITUTIONAL
LANGE

JIM LANGE
Courtesy The Daily Oklahoman

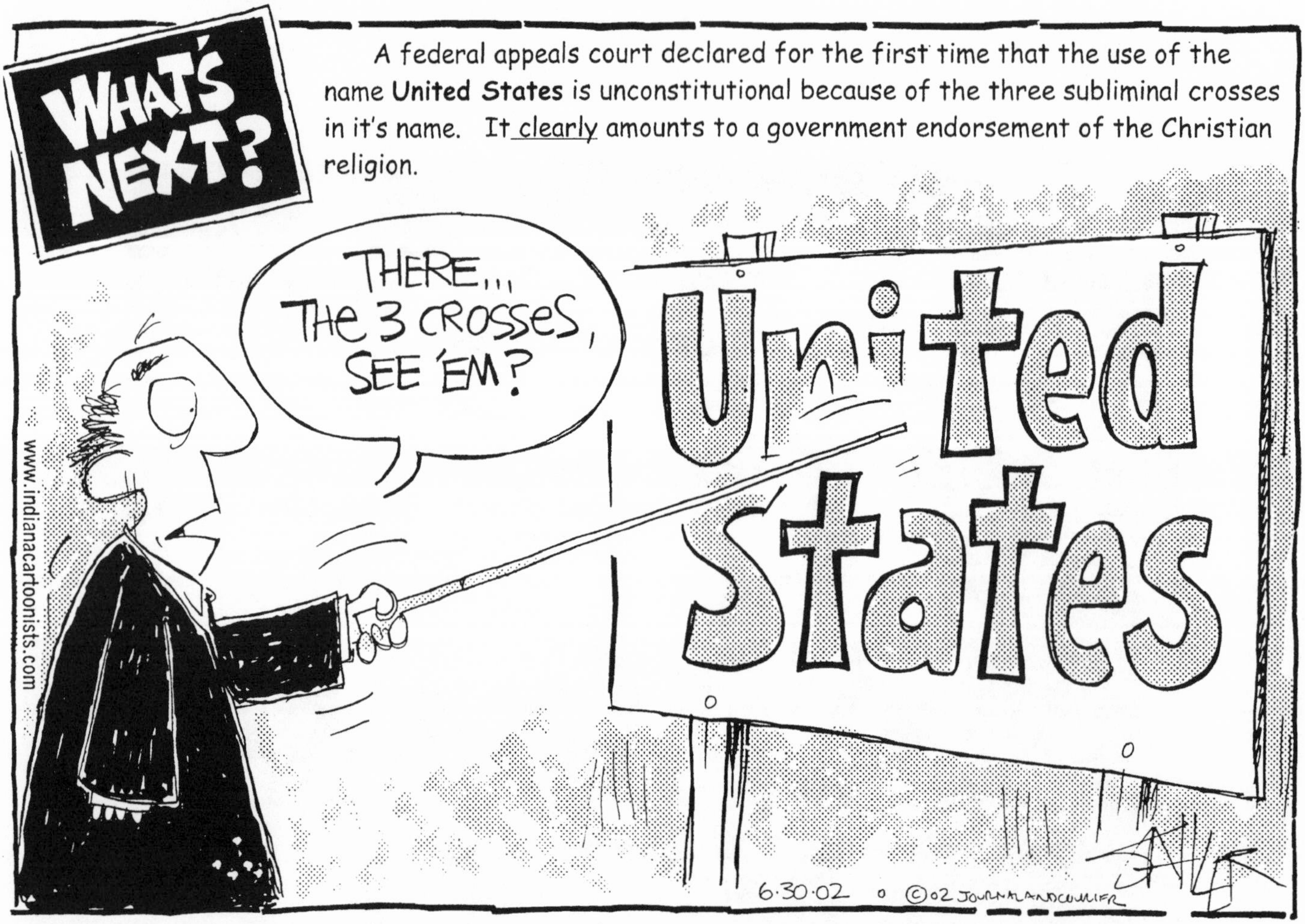
WHAT'S NEXT?
A federal appeals court declared for the first time that the use of the name **United States** is unconstitutional because of the three subliminal crosses in it's name. It clearly amounts to a government endorsement of the Christian religion.
THERE,,, THE 3 CROSSES, SEE 'EM?
United States
www.indianacartoonists.com
6·30·02

DAVE SATTLER
Courtesy Lafayette Journal-Courier (Ind.)

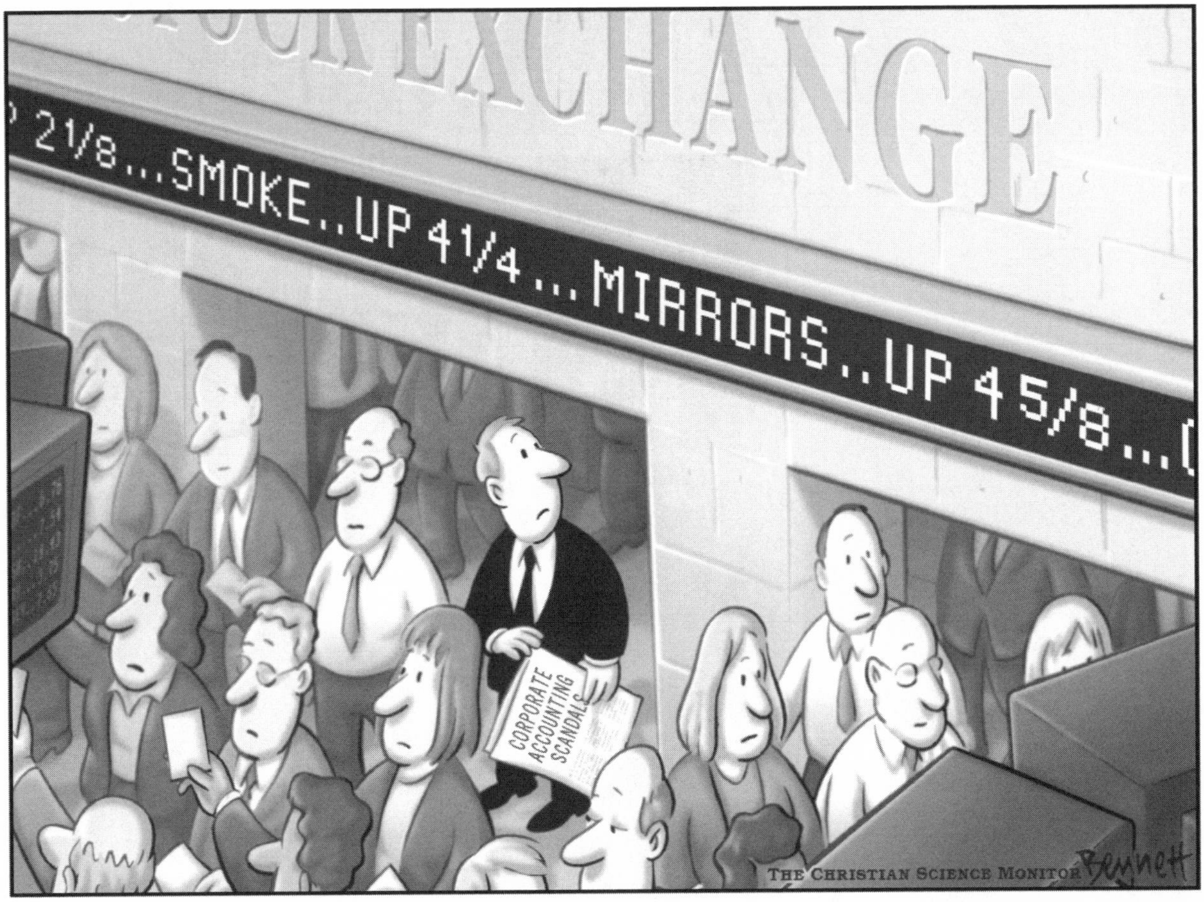
EXCHANGE
21/8...SMOKE..UP 41/4...MIRRORS..UP 45/8...
CORPORATE ACCOUNTING SCANDALS
THE CHRISTIAN SCIENCE MONITOR
BENNETT

CLAY BENNETT
Courtesy Christian Science Monitor

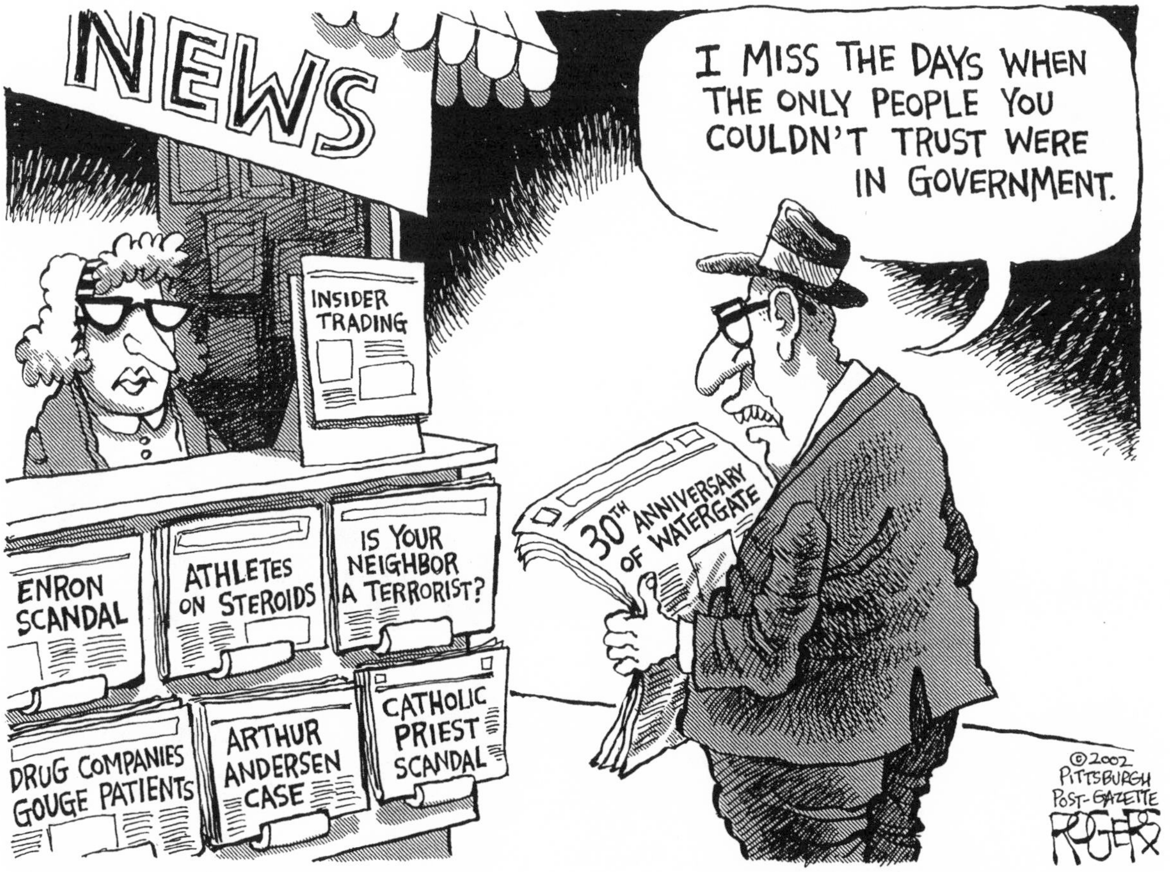
NEWS
I MISS THE DAYS WHEN THE ONLY PEOPLE YOU COULDN'T TRUST WERE IN GOVERNMENT.
INSIDER TRADING
30TH ANNIVERSARY OF WATERGATE
ENRON SCANDAL
ATHLETES ON STEROIDS
IS YOUR NEIGHBOR A TERRORIST?
DRUG COMPANIES GOUGE PATIENTS
ARTHUR ANDERSEN CASE
CATHOLIC PRIEST SCANDAL
©2002 PITTSBURGH POST-GAZETTE
ROGERS

ROB ROGERS
Courtesy Pittsburgh Post-Gazette

AMERICA 2002
MARTHA STEWART
MOM
Steroids
BASEBALL
USA OVERWEIGHT
APPLE PIE
(WHAT'S NEXT, THE PLEDGE OF ALLEGIANCE?)
LALO ALCARAZ ©2002

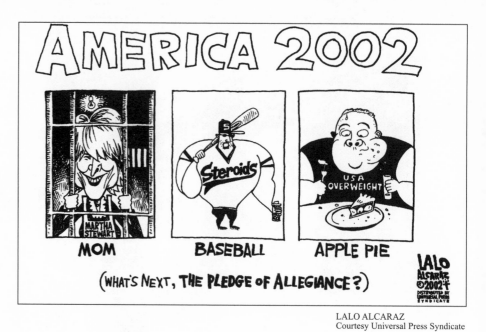

LALO ALCARAZ
Courtesy Universal Press Syndicate

DANI AGUILA
Courtesy Filipino Reporter

"SEEDLING OF FAITH, CANDLES OF HOPE AND LOVE..."
In Memoriam
©2002 el dani IN MANILA FILIPINO REPORTER, New York City

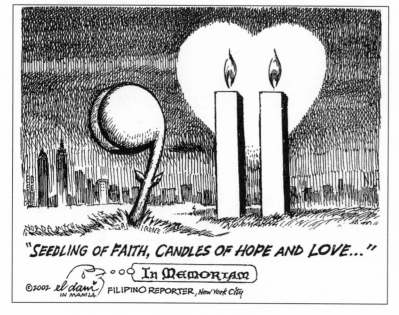

BARBARA BRANDON-CROFT
Courtesy Universal Press Syndicate

WHERE I'M COMING FROM
BY BARBARA BRANDON-CROFT
HOW MUCH SURVEILLANCE IS TOO MUCH? WHAT ABOUT OUR CIVIL LIBERTIES?
CAN WE LIVE WITH THE EXTRA SCRUTINY IN OUR PORTS OF TRAVEL?
SHOULD WE HAVE TO ENDURE ADDED EYES ON US...
WHEN WE VISIT NATIONAL MONUMENTS, SHOPPING MALLS, RESTAURANTS, MOVIE THEATERS?
WHO'D A THOUGHT WE'D EVER SEE A LEVEL PLAYING FIELD?
FINALLY, EVERYONE GETS A TASTE OF WHAT IT IS TO BE BLACK IN AMERICA.
www.ucomics.com
©02 Barbara
© 2002 Barbara Brandon-Croft/Dist. by Universal Press Syndicate

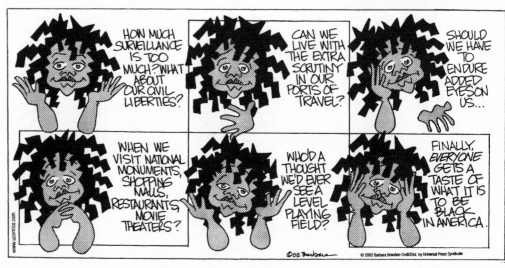

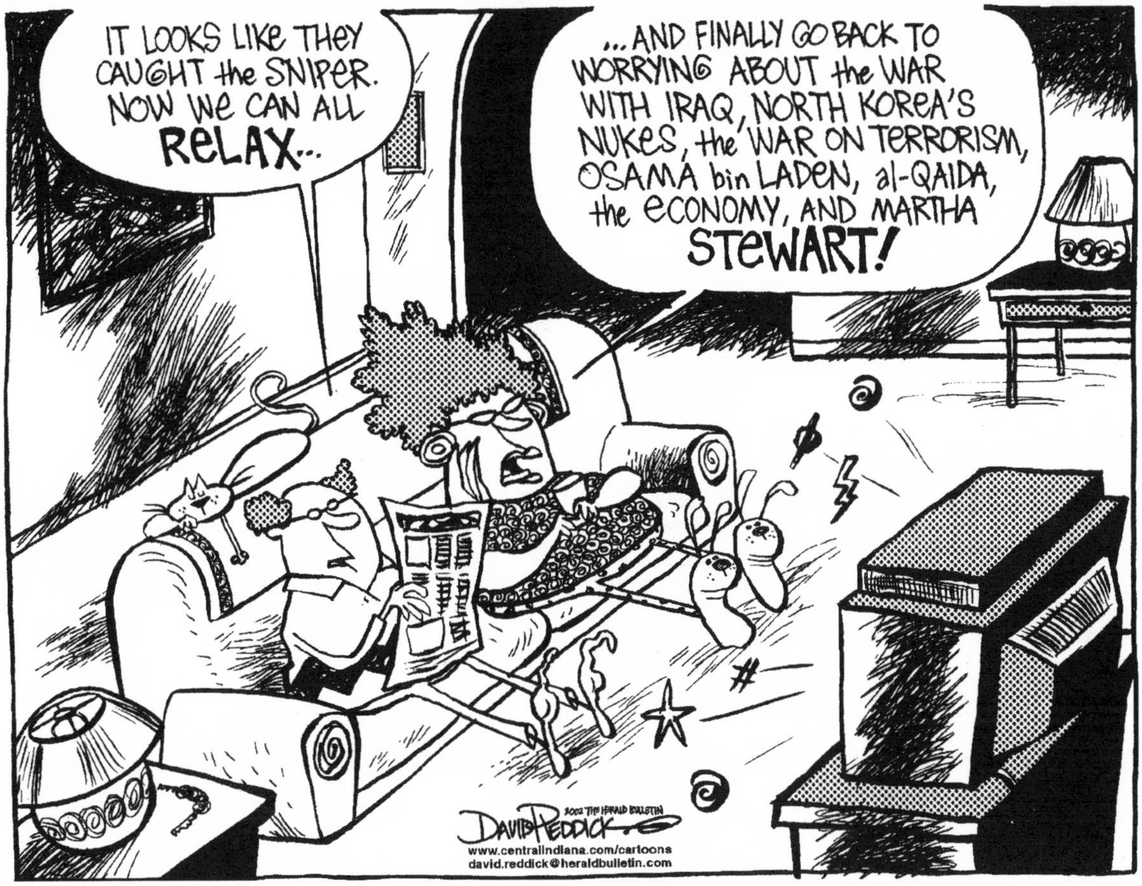
IT LOOKS LIKE THEY CAUGHT THE SNIPER. NOW WE CAN ALL RELAX...
...AND FINALLY GO BACK TO WORRYING ABOUT THE WAR WITH IRAQ, NORTH KOREA'S NUKES, THE WAR ON TERRORISM, OSAMA BIN LADEN, AL-QAIDA, THE ECONOMY, AND MARTHA STEWART!
DAVID REDDICK ©2002 THE HERALD BULLETIN
www.centralindiana.com/cartoons
david.reddick@heraldbulletin.com

DAVID REDDICK
Courtesy The Herald Bulletin (Ind.)

ETTA HULME
Courtesy Fort Worth Star-Telegram

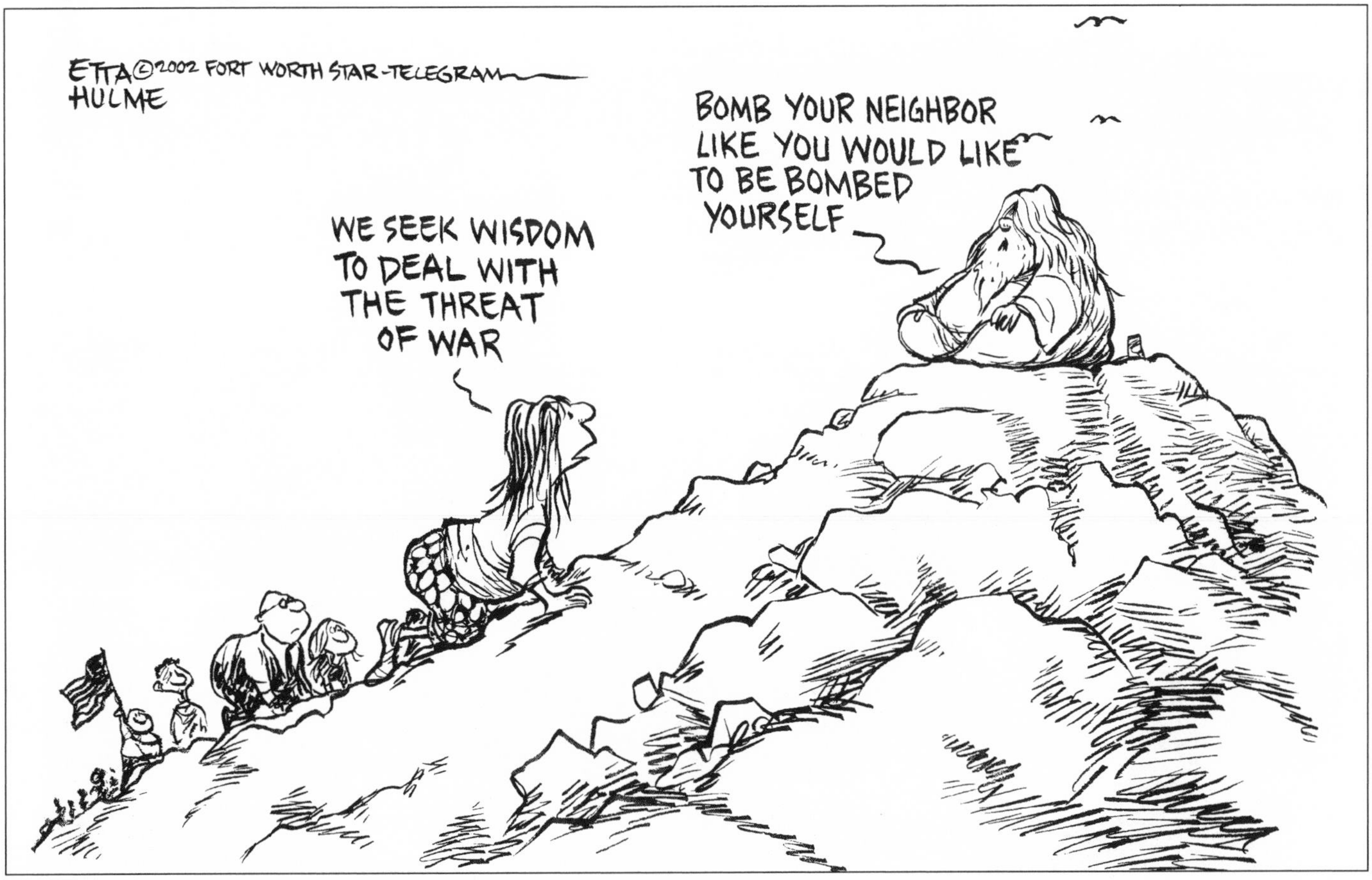
ETTA HULME ©2002 FORT WORTH STAR-TELEGRAM
WE SEEK WISDOM TO DEAL WITH THE THREAT OF WAR
BOMB YOUR NEIGHBOR LIKE YOU WOULD LIKE TO BE BOMBED YOURSELF

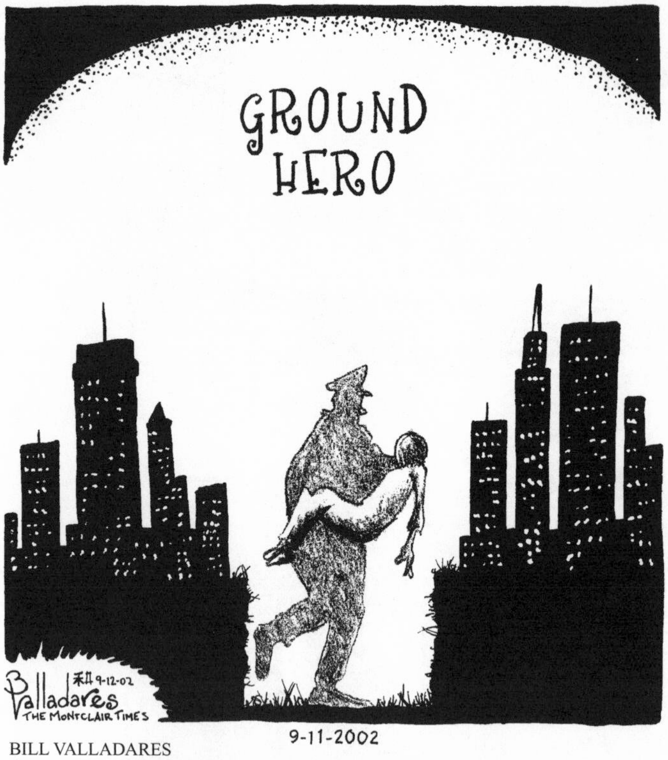
GROUND
HERO
Valladares 9-12-02
THE MONTCLAIR TIMES
9-11-2002

BILL VALLADARES
Courtesy Montclair Times (N.J.)

CLIFF LEVERETTE
Courtesy Magnolia Gazette (Miss.)

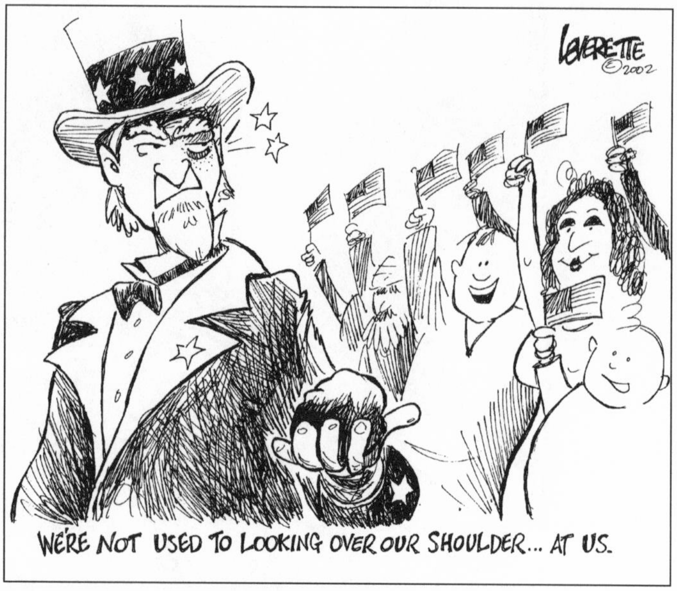
LEVERETTE ©2002
WE'RE NOT USED TO LOOKING OVER OUR SHOULDER... AT US.

BOB LANG
Courtesy Editorial Services

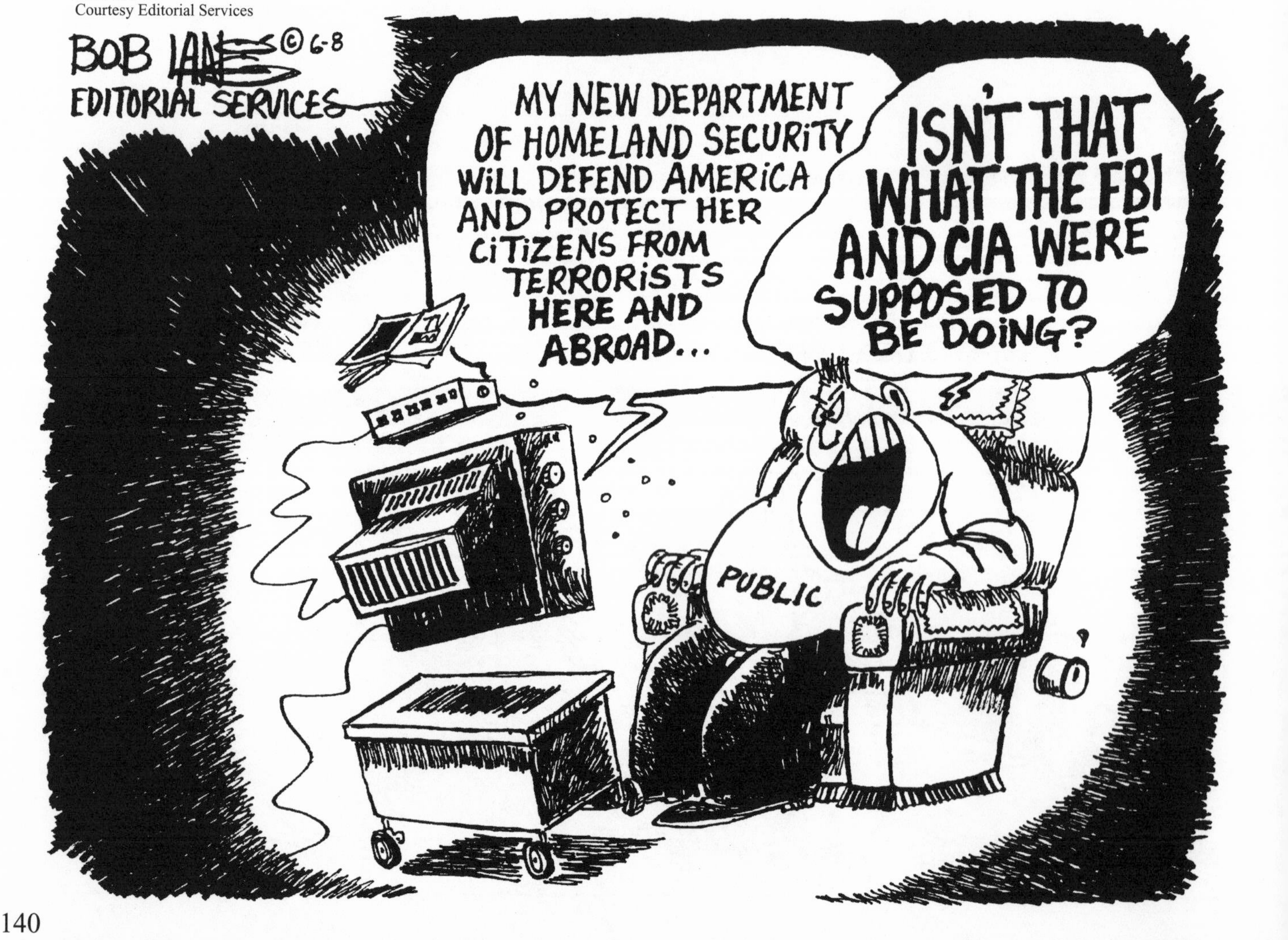
BOB LANG ©6-8
EDITORIAL SERVICES
MY NEW DEPARTMENT OF HOMELAND SECURITY WILL DEFEND AMERICA AND PROTECT HER CITIZENS FROM TERRORISTS HERE AND ABROAD...
ISN'T THAT WHAT THE FBI AND CIA WERE SUPPOSED TO BE DOING?
PUBLIC

JOSEPH F. O'MAHONEY
Courtesy The Patriot Ledger (Mass.)

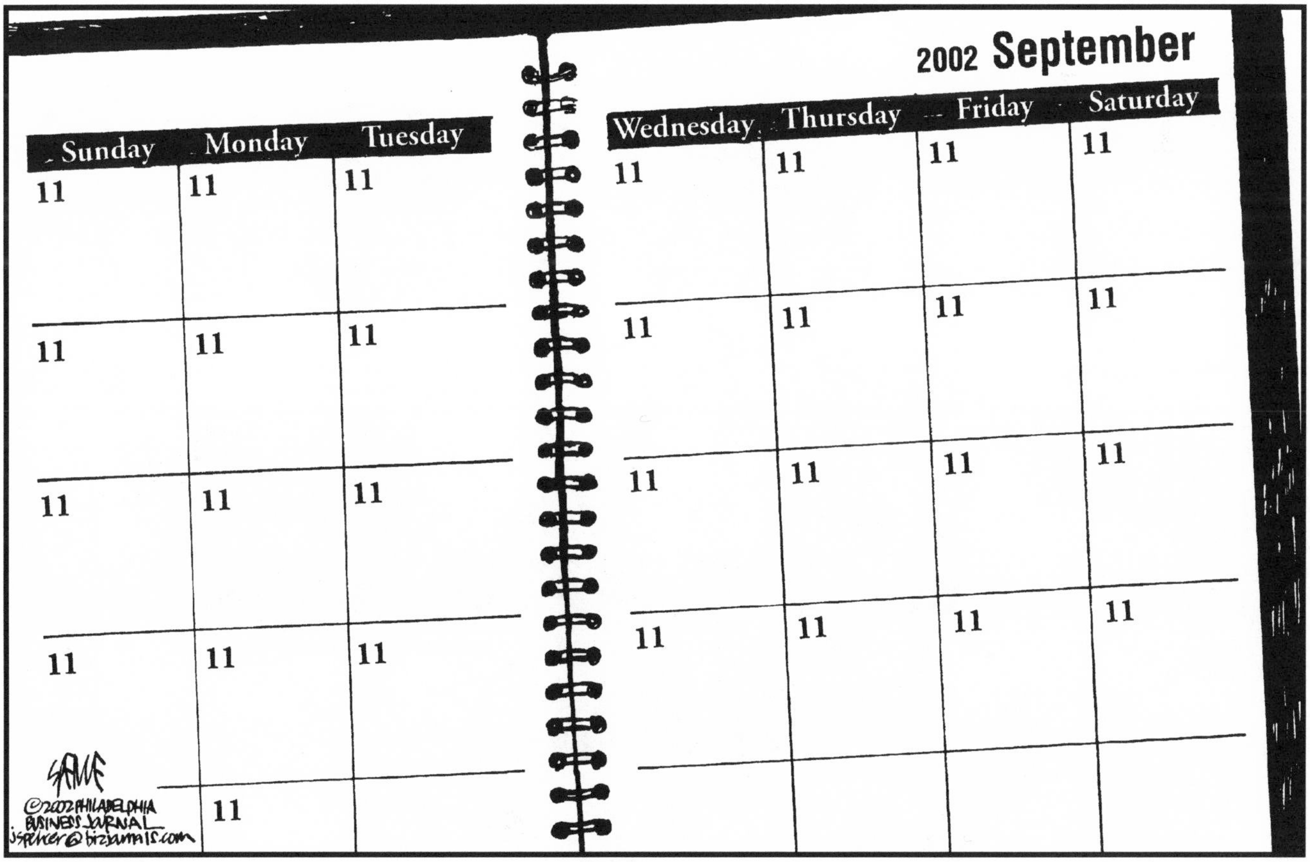

Sunday	Monday	Tuesday		Wednesday	Thursday	Friday	Saturday
							2002 **September**
11	11	11		11	11	11	11
11	11	11		11	11	11	11
11	11	11		11	11	11	11
11	11	11		11	11	11	11
	11						

JOHN SPENCER
Courtesy Philadelphia Business Journal

JOHN SHERFFIUS
Courtesy St. Louis Post-Dispatch

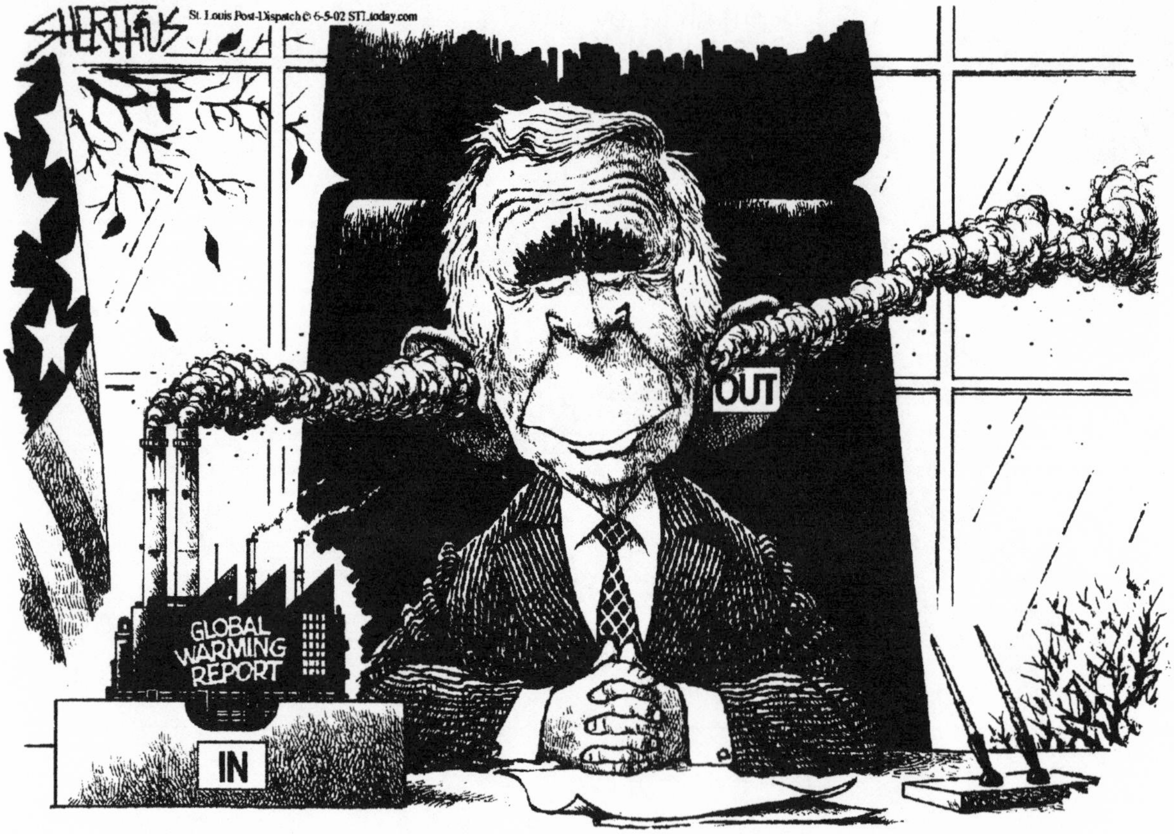
SHERFFIUS
St. Louis Post-Dispatch © 6-5-02 STLtoday.com
GLOBAL WARMING REPORT
OUT
IN

DREW SHENEMAN
Courtesy Newark Star-Ledger

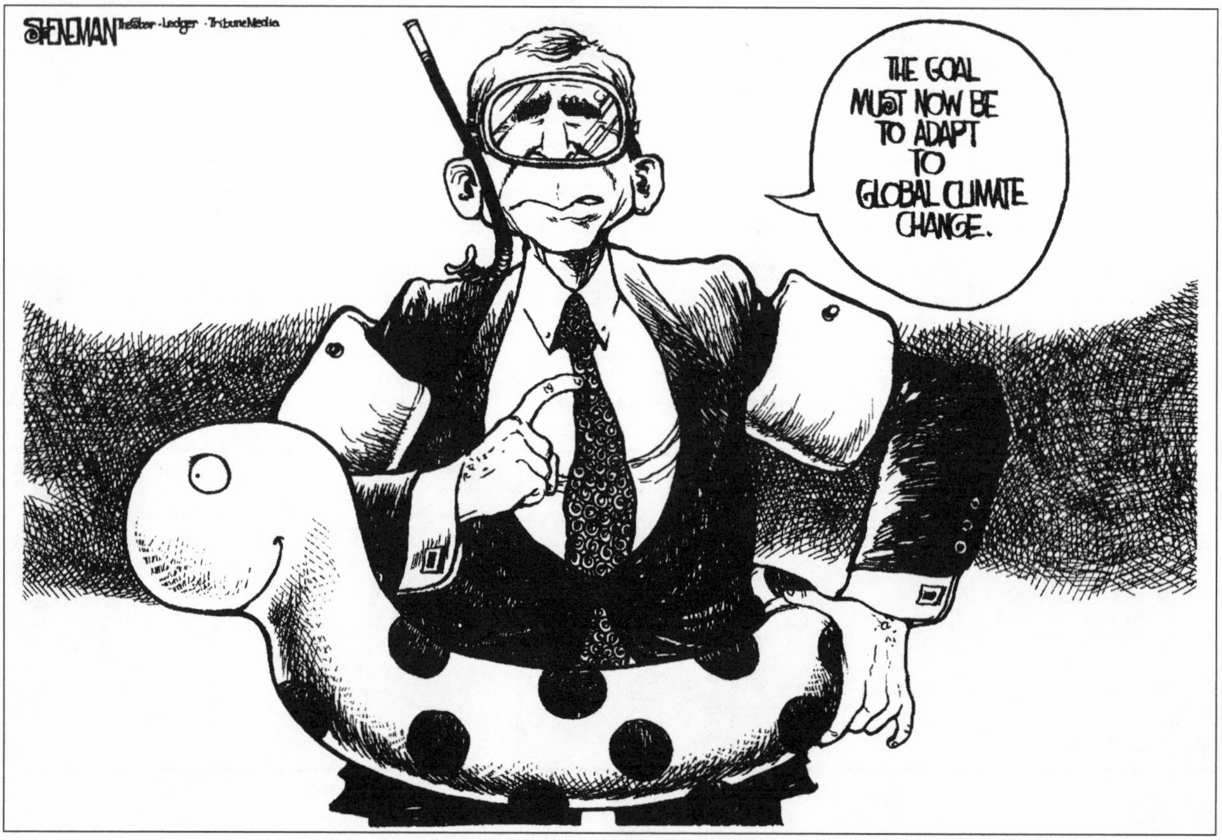
SHENEMAN
THE GOAL MUST NOW BE TO ADAPT TO GLOBAL CLIMATE CHANGE.

Health / Environment

It was reported late in the year that women now make up half of all the world's AIDS victims. Africa remains the hardest hit by this epidemic, with women accounting for 58 percent of infected adults in the sub-Sahara. An estimated 42 million people are now living with HIV/AIDS, an increase of 5 million in 2002. Starvation threatens 14.4 million in Africa, not only because of famine but also because of the impact of AIDS on the economy.

Congress failed to resolve the growing problem of costly prescription drugs for seniors, but the issue is on its agenda in 2003. The western states were hit with the worst wild land fires in more than ninety years, and in Pike National Forest more than 5,400 people were forced to evacuate. Eight states fought the raging fires before they were controlled. The most severe drought in a century took a heavy toll on western wildlife.

The worst outbreak of West Nile virus, a mosquito-borne disease, left several dead in Louisiana, then spread to other states. A widely distributed report claimed that 60 percent of all Americans, including children, are obese. Fast food restaurants were cited as a primary cause.

ROB ROGERS
Courtesy Pittsburgh Post-Gazette

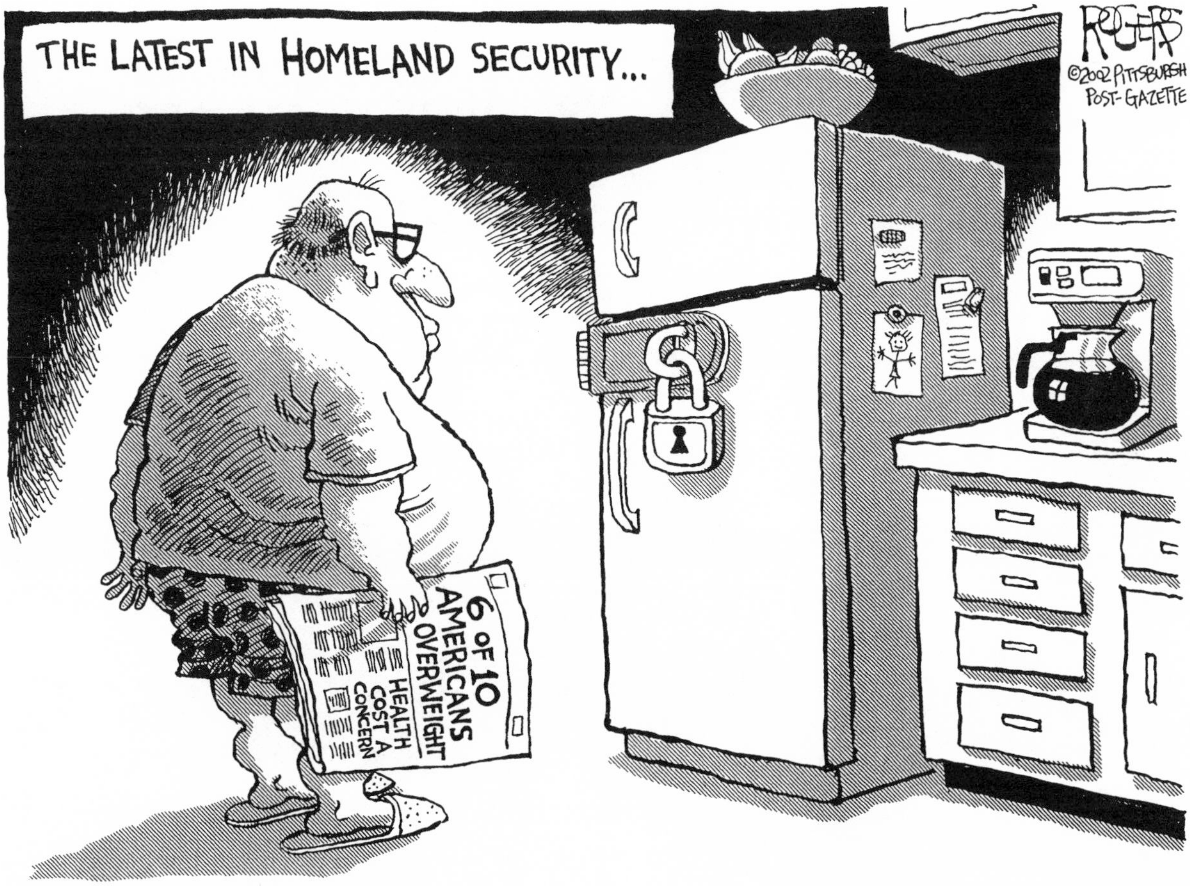
THE LATEST IN HOMELAND SECURITY...
ROGERS
©2002 PITTSBURGH POST-GAZETTE
6 OF 10 AMERICANS OVERWEIGHT
HEALTH COST A CONCERN

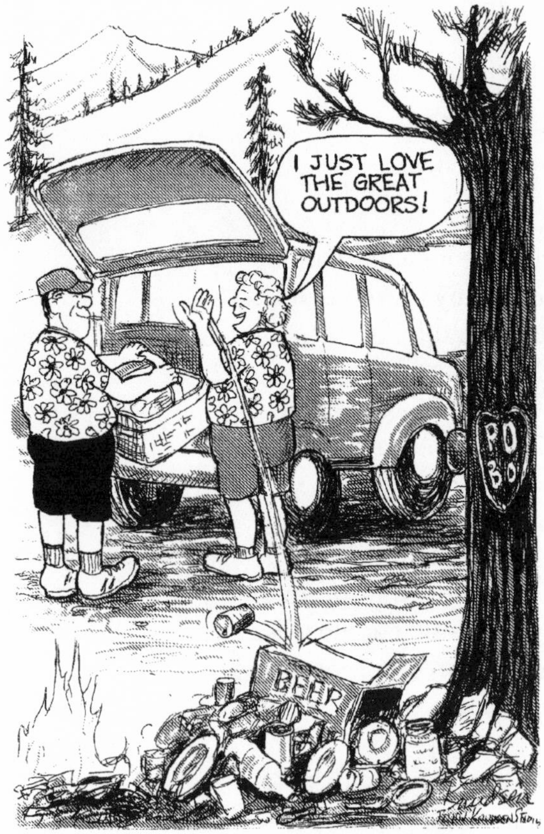
I JUST LOVE THE GREAT OUTDOORS!
BEER

JOHN KNUDSEN
Courtesy St. Louis Review

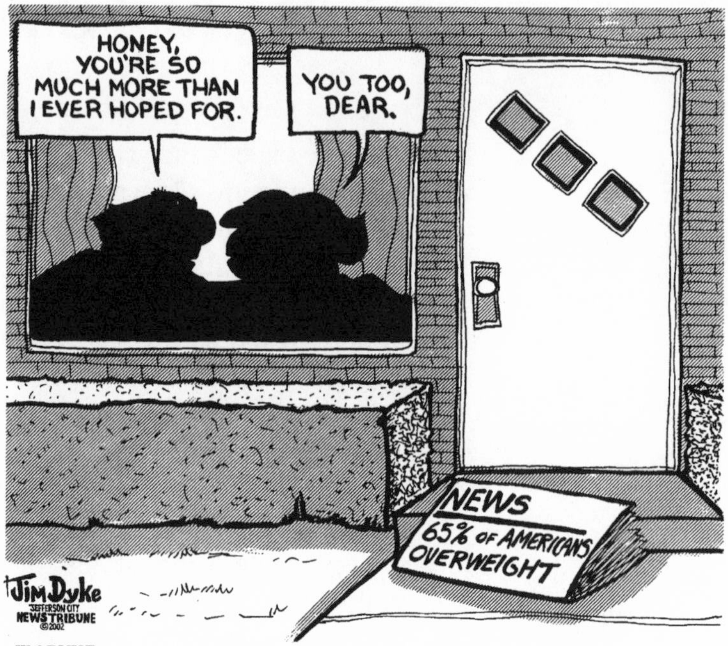
HONEY, YOU'RE SO MUCH MORE THAN I EVER HOPED FOR.
YOU TOO, DEAR.
NEWS
65% OF AMERICANS OVERWEIGHT
Jim Dyke JEFFERSON CITY NEWS TRIBUNE ©2002

JIM DYKE
Courtesy Jefferson City News-Tribune

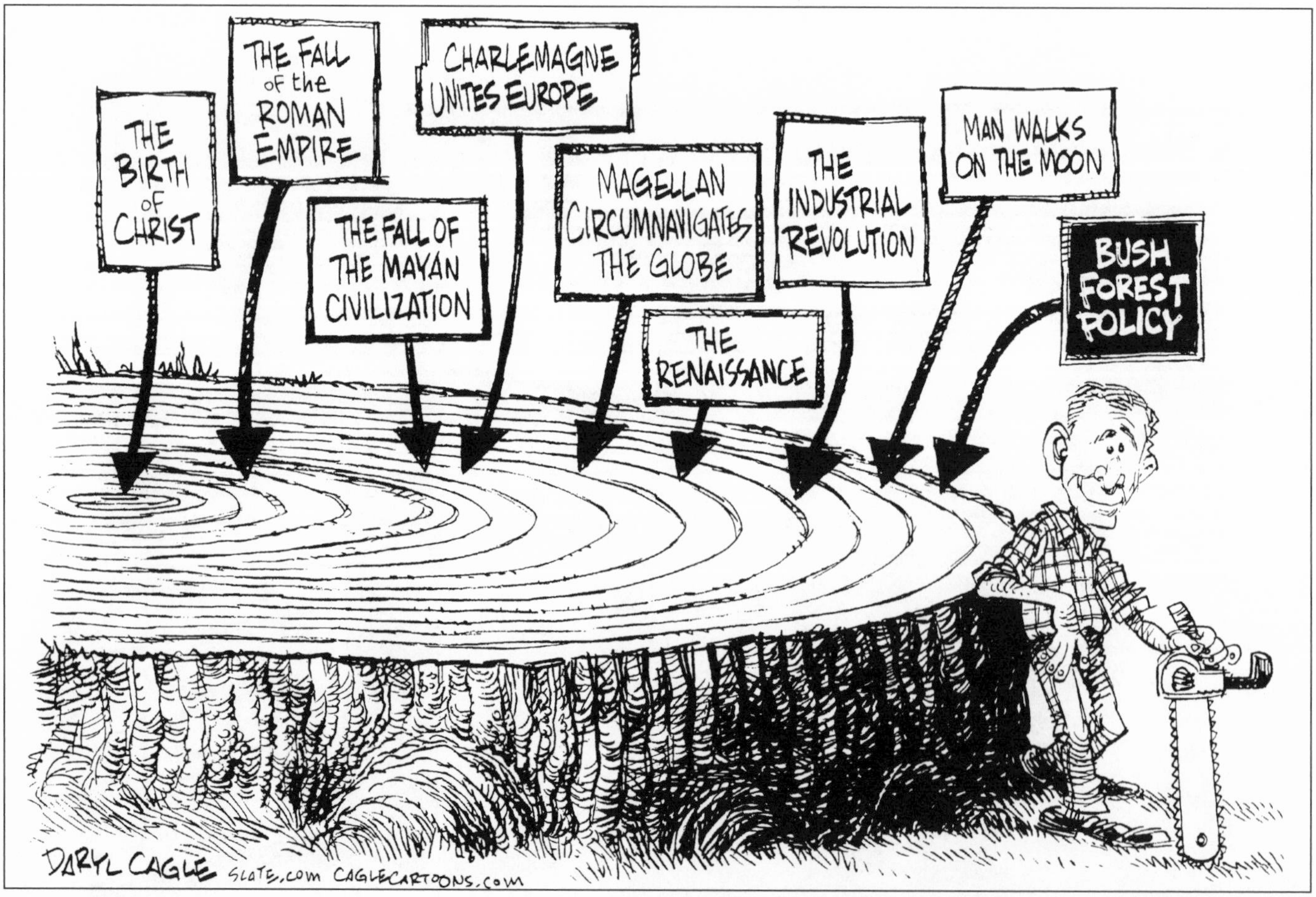
THE BIRTH of CHRIST
THE FALL of the ROMAN EMPIRE
THE FALL OF THE MAYAN CIVILIZATION
CHARLEMAGNE UNITES EUROPE
MAGELLAN CIRCUMNAVIGATES THE GLOBE
THE RENAISSANCE
THE INDUSTRIAL REVOLUTION
MAN WALKS ON THE MOON
BUSH FOREST POLICY
DARYL CAGLE SLATE.com CAGLECARTOONS.com

DARYL CAGLE
Courtesy caglecartoons.com

DENNIS DRAUGHON
Courtesy Scranton Times

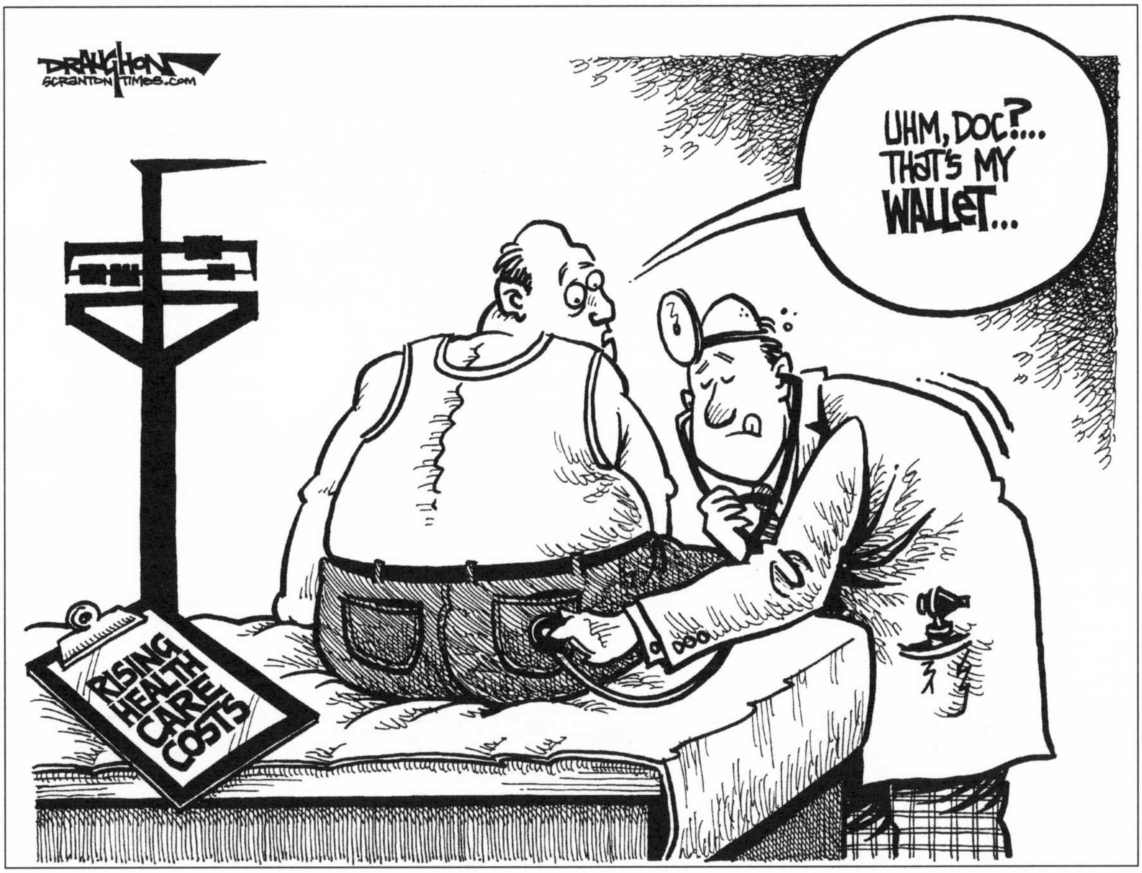
DRAUGHON SCRANTONTIMES.COM
UHM, DOC?... THAT'S MY WALLET...
RISING HEALTH CARE COSTS

TOM STIGLICH
Courtesy Northeast Times (Pa.)

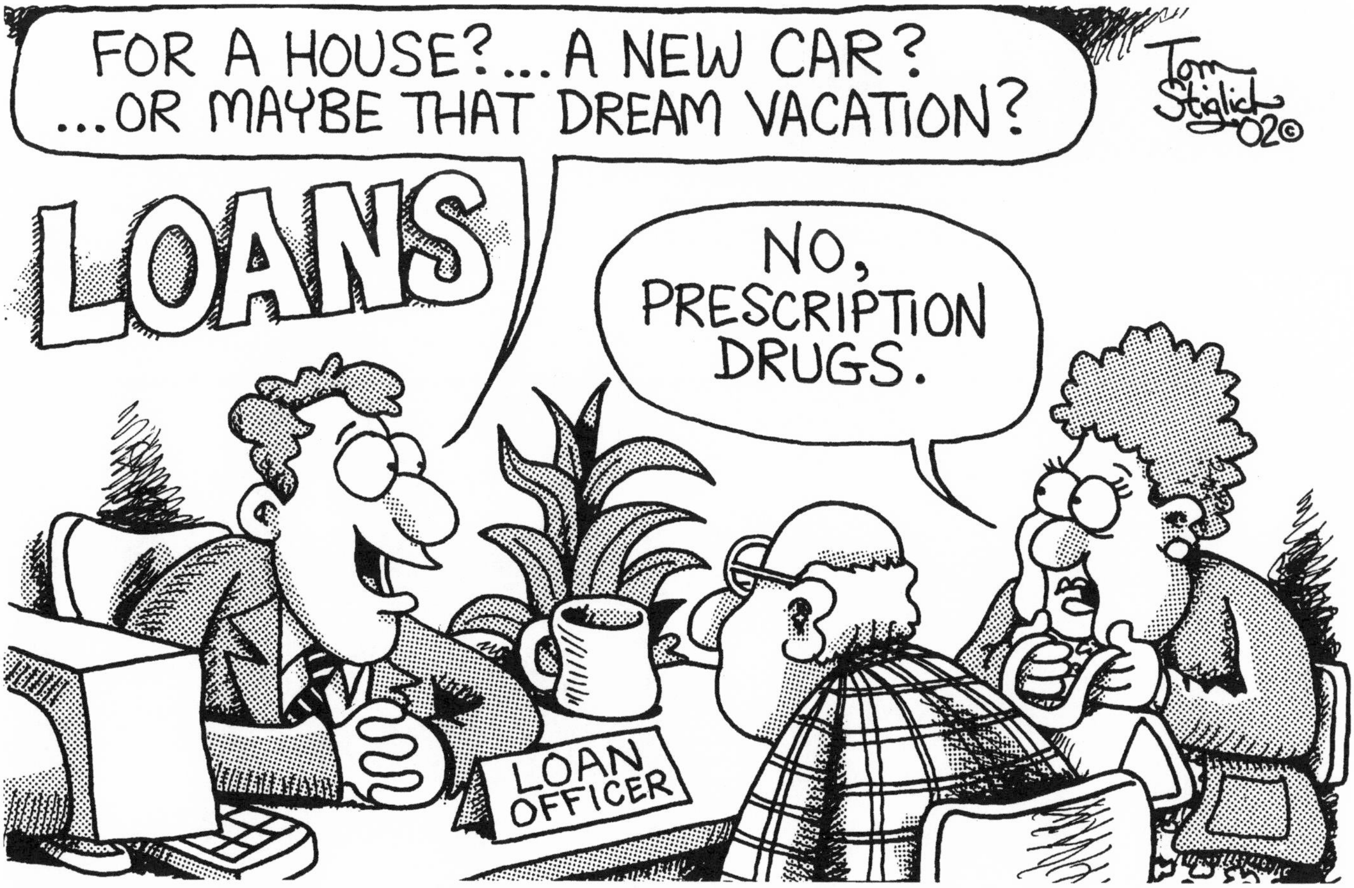
FOR A HOUSE?... A NEW CAR? ...OR MAYBE THAT DREAM VACATION?
Tom Stiglich 02©
LOANS
NO, PRESCRIPTION DRUGS.
LOAN OFFICER

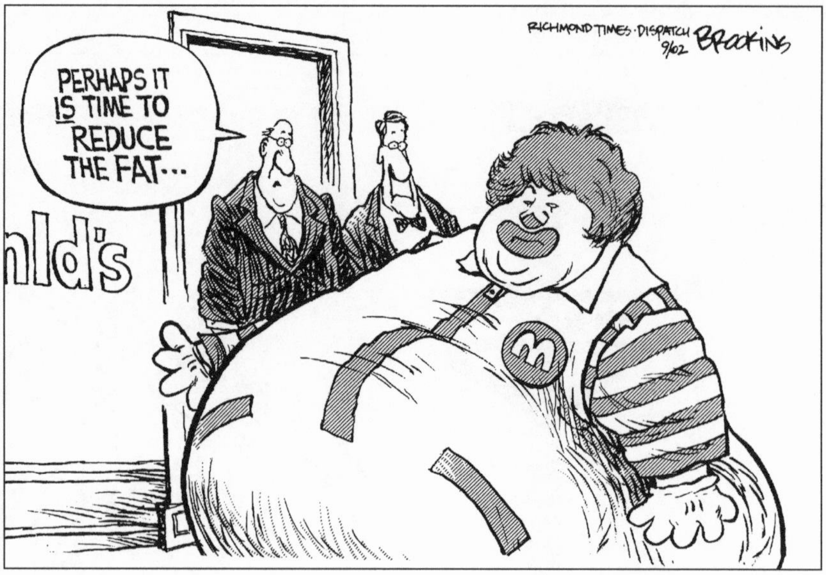
RICHMOND TIMES-DISPATCH 9/02 BROOKINS
PERHAPS IT IS TIME TO REDUCE THE FAT...
nld's

GARY BROOKINS
Courtesy Richmond Times-Dispatch

KEN DAVIS
Courtesy San Jose Business Journal

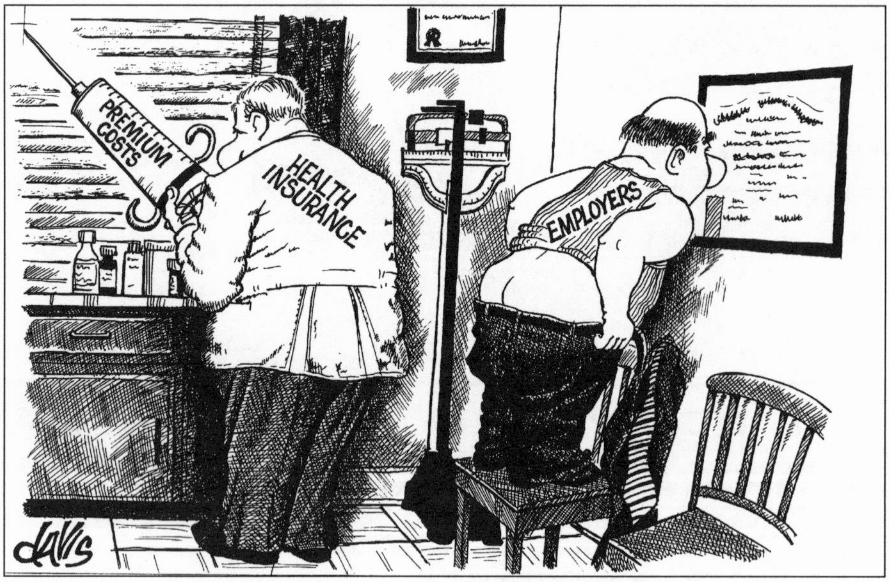
PREMIUM COSTS
HEALTH INSURANCE
EMPLOYERS
DAVIS

DON LANDGREN JR.
Courtesy The Landmark (Mass.)

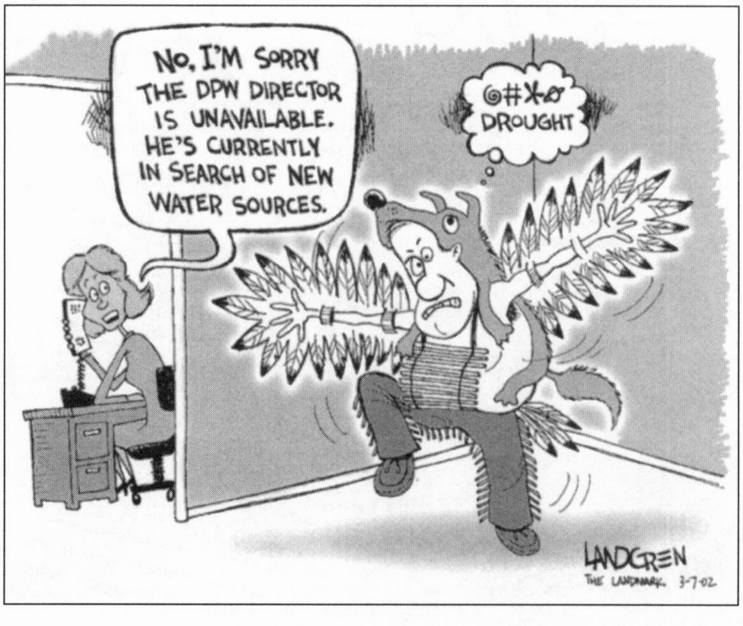
NO, I'M SORRY THE DPW DIRECTOR IS UNAVAILABLE. HE'S CURRENTLY IN SEARCH OF NEW WATER SOURCES.
DROUGHT
LANDGREN
THE LANDMARK 3-7-02

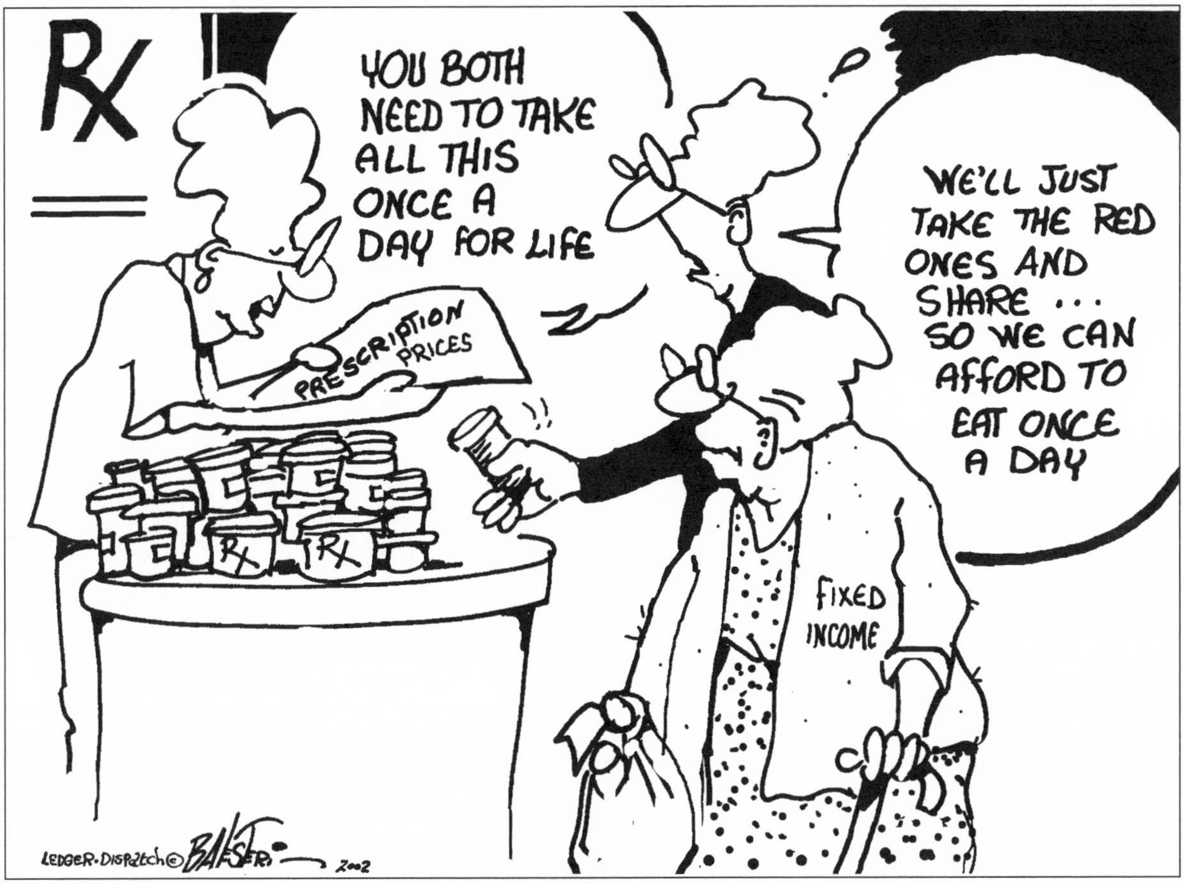
RX
YOU BOTH NEED TO TAKE ALL THIS ONCE A DAY FOR LIFE
PRESCRIPTION PRICES
WE'LL JUST TAKE THE RED ONES AND SHARE . . . SO WE CAN AFFORD TO EAT ONCE A DAY
FIXED INCOME
LEDGER-DISPATCH© BALESTERI 2002

ANNETTE BALESTERI
Courtesy Ledger-Dispatch (Calif.)

MICHAEL RAMIREZ
Courtesy Los Angeles Times

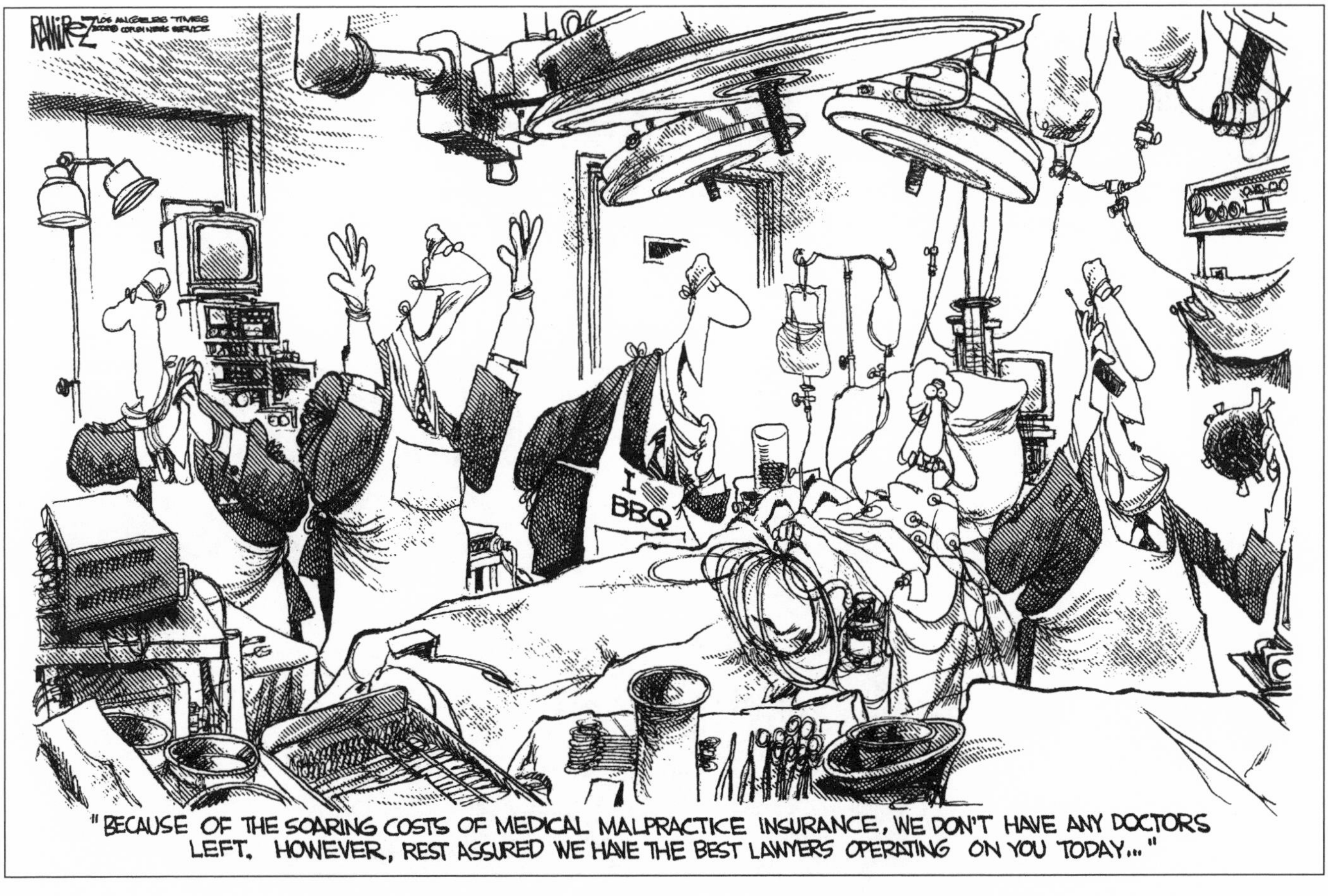
RAMIREZ
I BBQ
"BECAUSE OF THE SOARING COSTS OF MEDICAL MALPRACTICE INSURANCE, WE DON'T HAVE ANY DOCTORS LEFT. HOWEVER, REST ASSURED WE HAVE THE BEST LAWYERS OPERATING ON YOU TODAY..."

WE COULD TRY TO RUIN THE AMERICANS' NATIONAL PARKS, O'GREAT AL-CREEPO?
THEY'LL DO THAT TO THEMSELVES.
TERRORIST
THE CHATTANOOGA TIMES
PLANTE

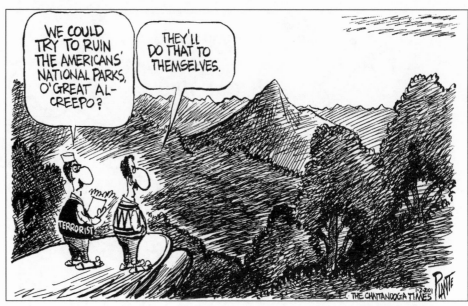

BRUCE PLANTE
Courtesy Chattanooga Times

NICK ANDERSON
Courtesy Louisville Courier-Journal

NEWS ITEM: BUSH PROPOSES THAT WE "ADAPT" TO GLOBAL WARMING...
AIR CONDITIONING

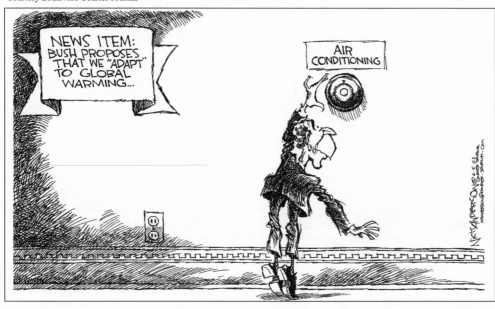

WILLIAM WALLACE
Courtesy Casper Star Tribune (Wy.)

WALLACE '02
© casper star-tribune
'02
WEST NILE
VIRUS
DRACULA
!!
REALITY'S SCARIER!
SNIPER KILLS

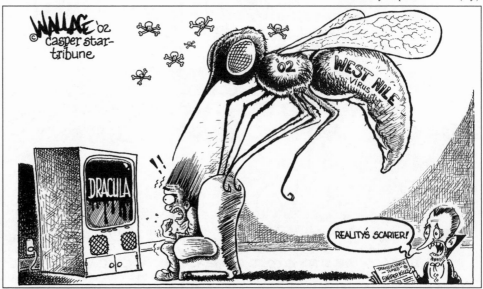

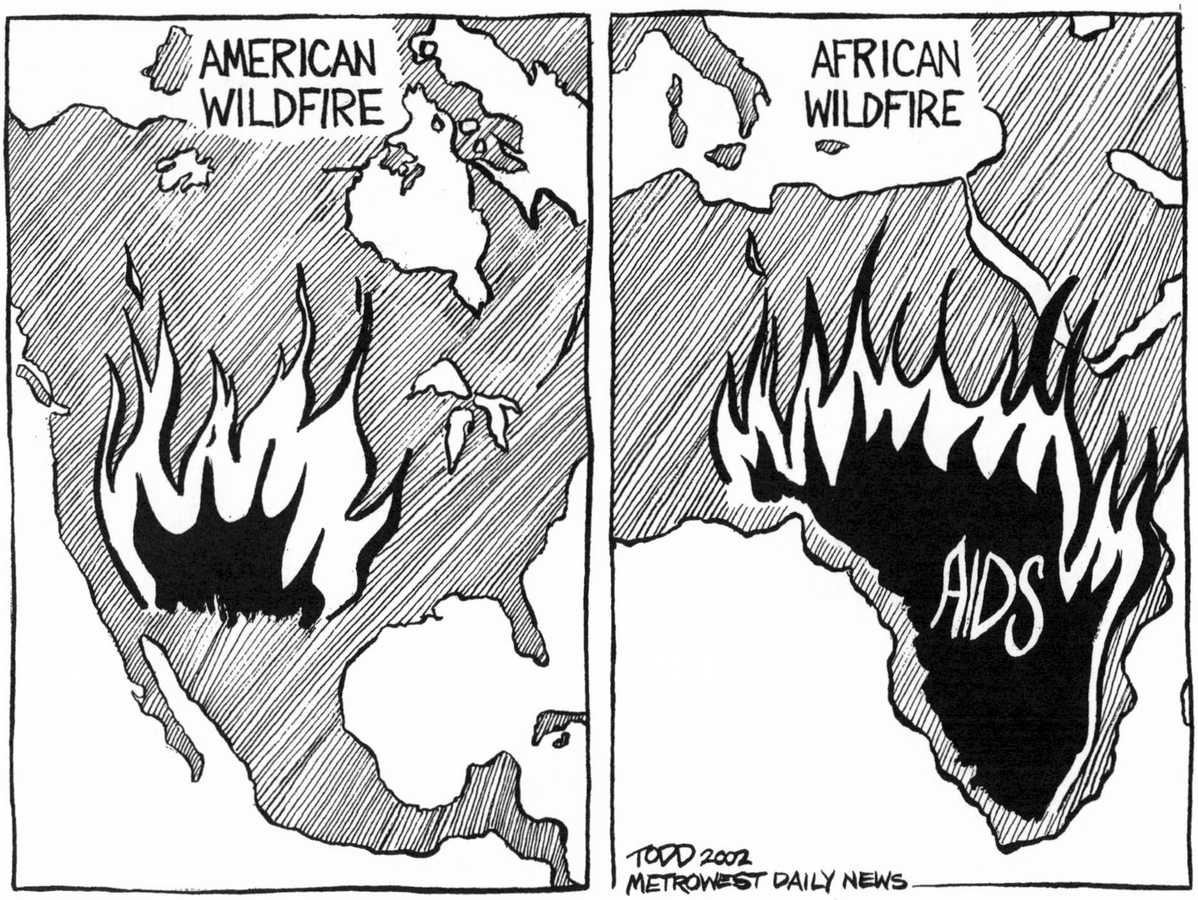
AMERICAN WILDFIRE
AFRICAN WILDFIRE
AIDS
TODD 2002
METROWEST DAILY NEWS

JONATHAN TODD
Courtesy Metrowest Daily News (Mass.)

JAMES CASCIARI
Courtesy Vero Beach Press-Journal

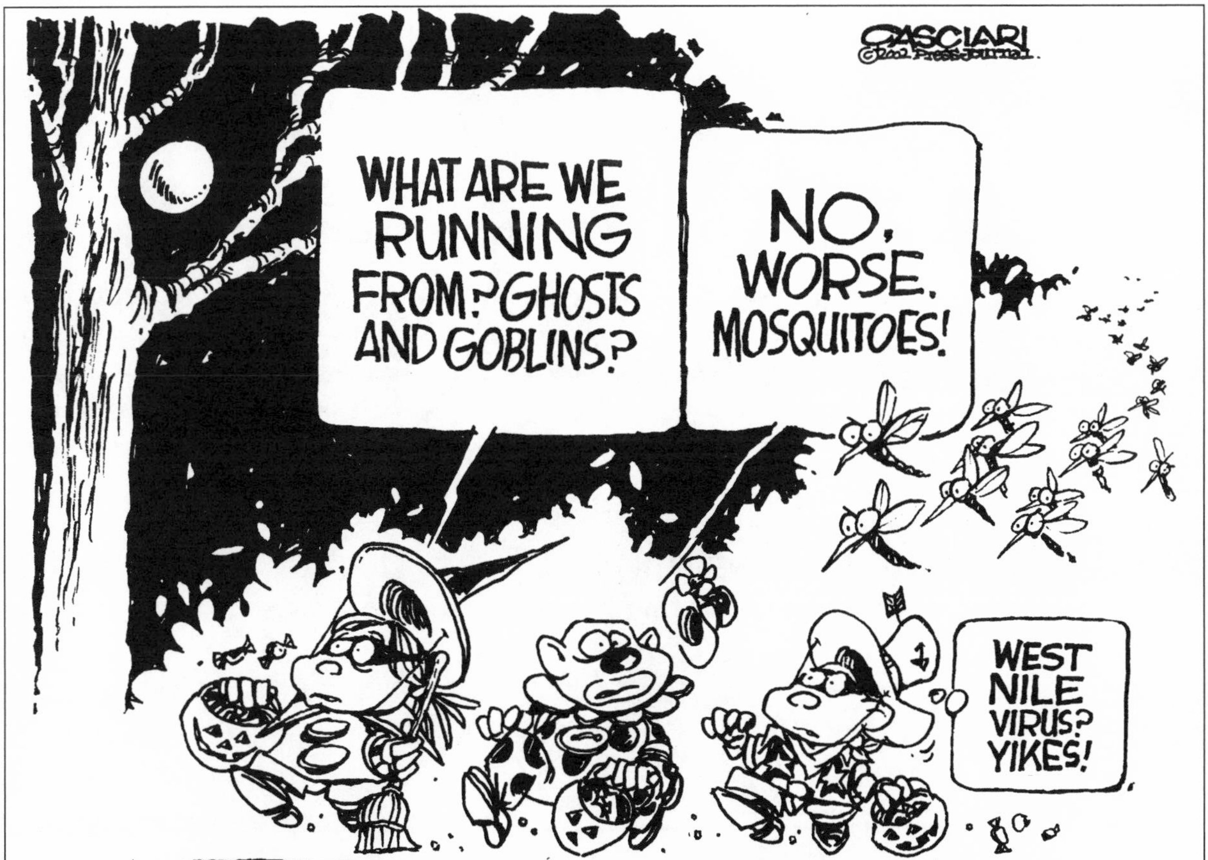
CASCIARI
WHAT ARE WE RUNNING FROM? GHOSTS AND GOBLINS?
NO, WORSE. MOSQUITOES!
WEST NILE VIRUS? YIKES!

RICK McKEE
Courtesy Augusta Chronicle

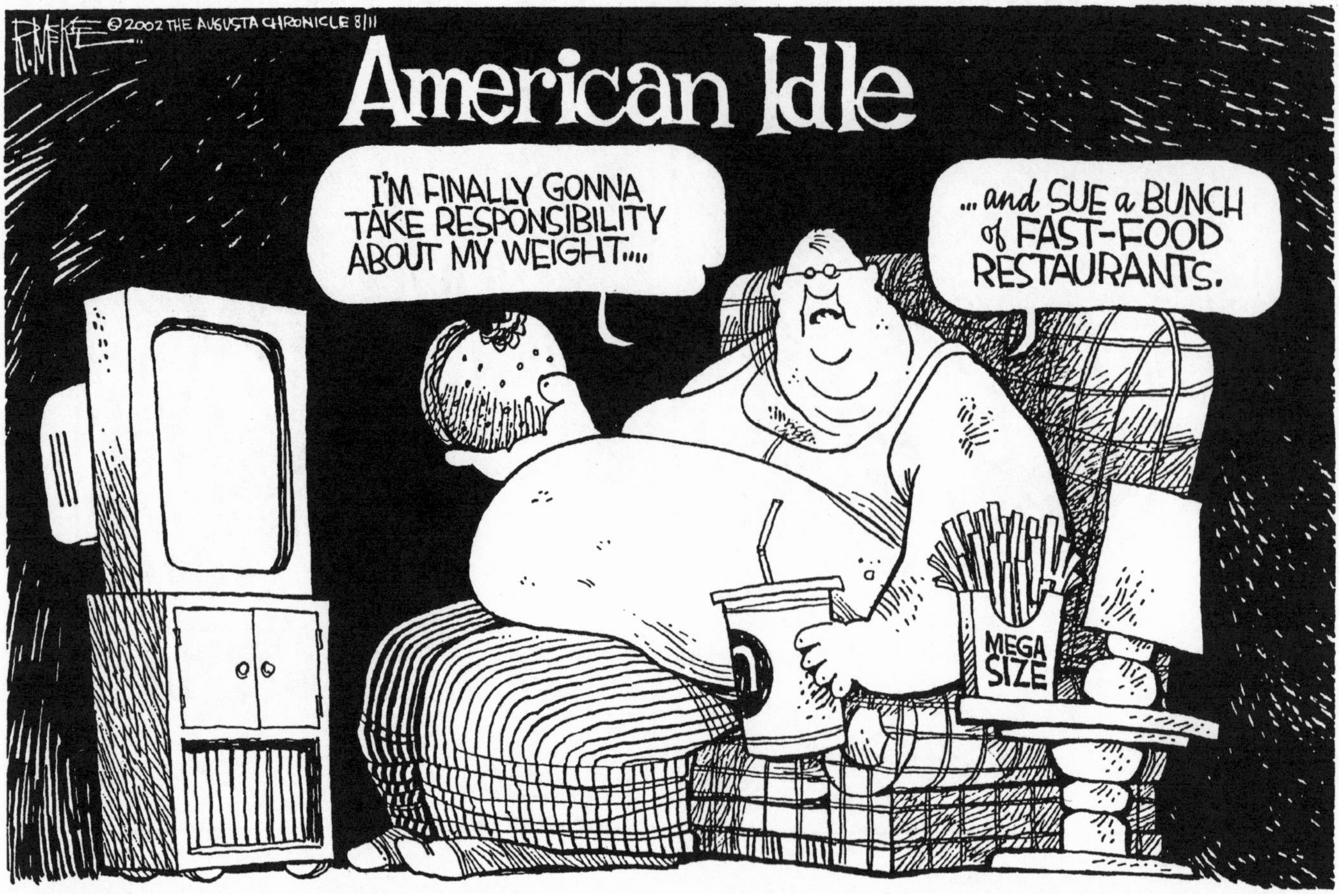

R. McKEE © 2002 THE AUGUSTA CHRONICLE 8/11
American Idle
I'M FINALLY GONNA TAKE RESPONSIBILITY ABOUT MY WEIGHT....
...and SUE a BUNCH of FAST-FOOD RESTAURANTS.
MEGA SIZE

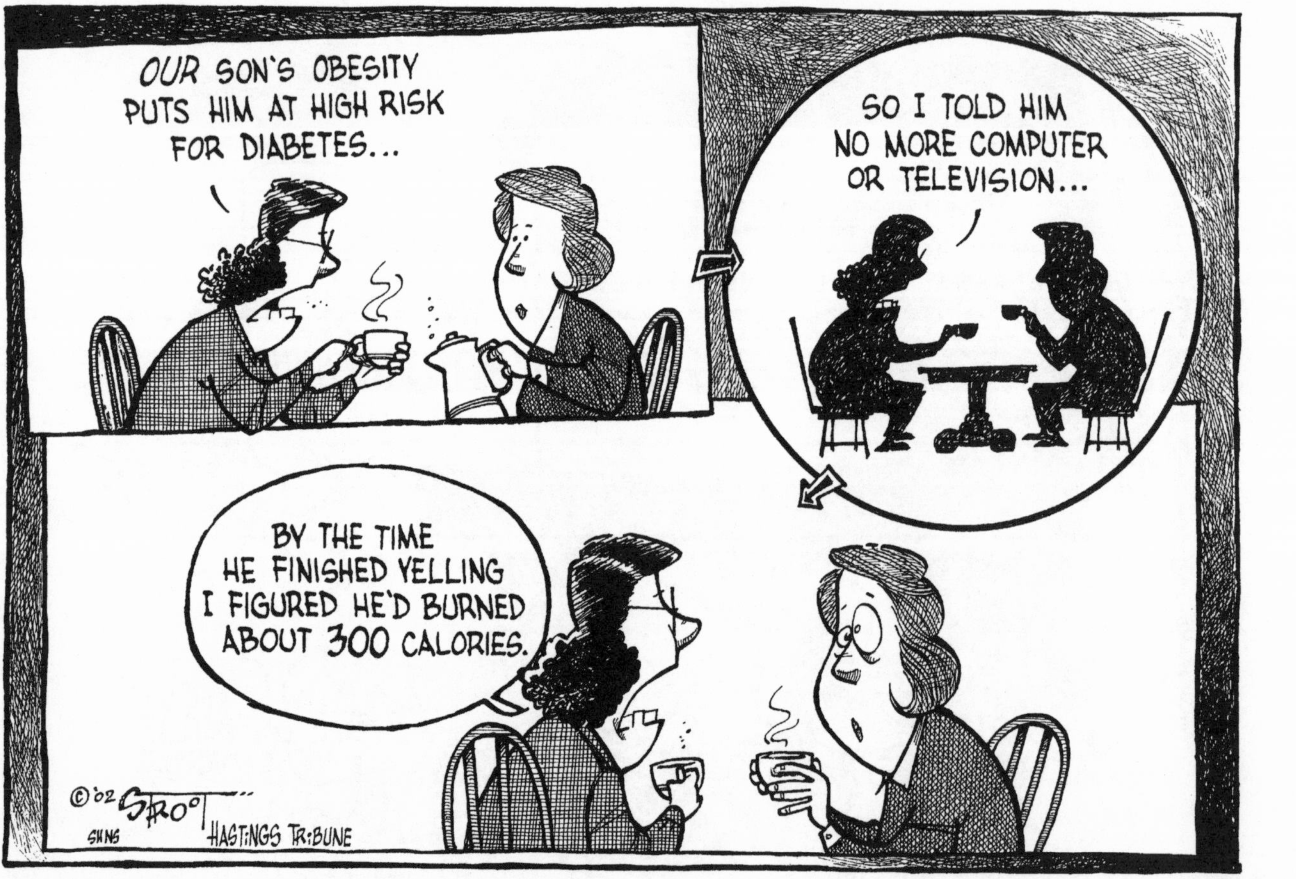

OUR SON'S OBESITY PUTS HIM AT HIGH RISK FOR DIABETES...
SO I TOLD HIM NO MORE COMPUTER OR TELEVISION...
BY THE TIME HE FINISHED YELLING I FIGURED HE'D BURNED ABOUT 300 CALORIES.
©'02 STROOT SHNS HASTINGS TRIBUNE

WAYNE STROOT
Courtesy Hastings Tribune

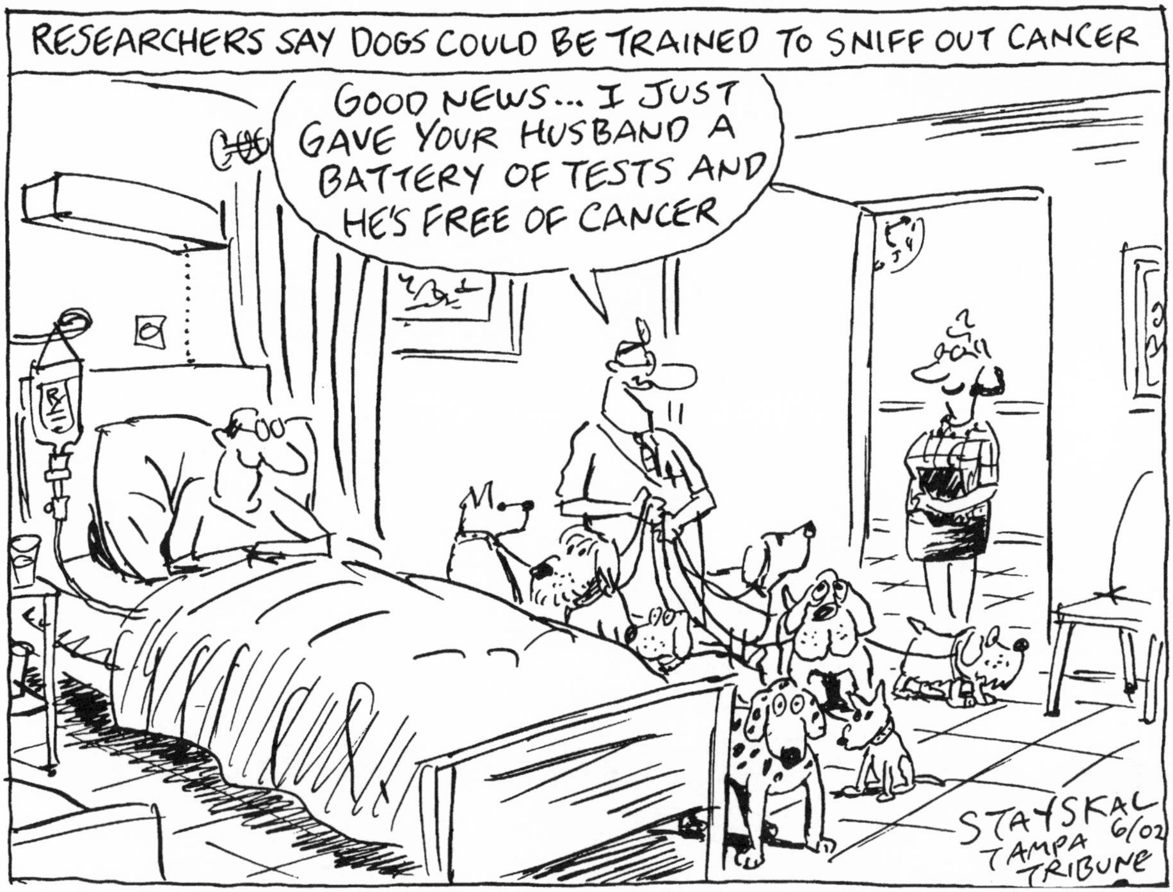
RESEARCHERS SAY DOGS COULD BE TRAINED TO SNIFF OUT CANCER
GOOD NEWS... I JUST GAVE YOUR HUSBAND A BATTERY OF TESTS AND HE'S FREE OF CANCER
STAYSKAL 6/02 TAMPA TRIBUNE

WAYNE STAYSKAL
Courtesy Tampa Tribune

ED STEIN
Courtesy Rocky Mountain News

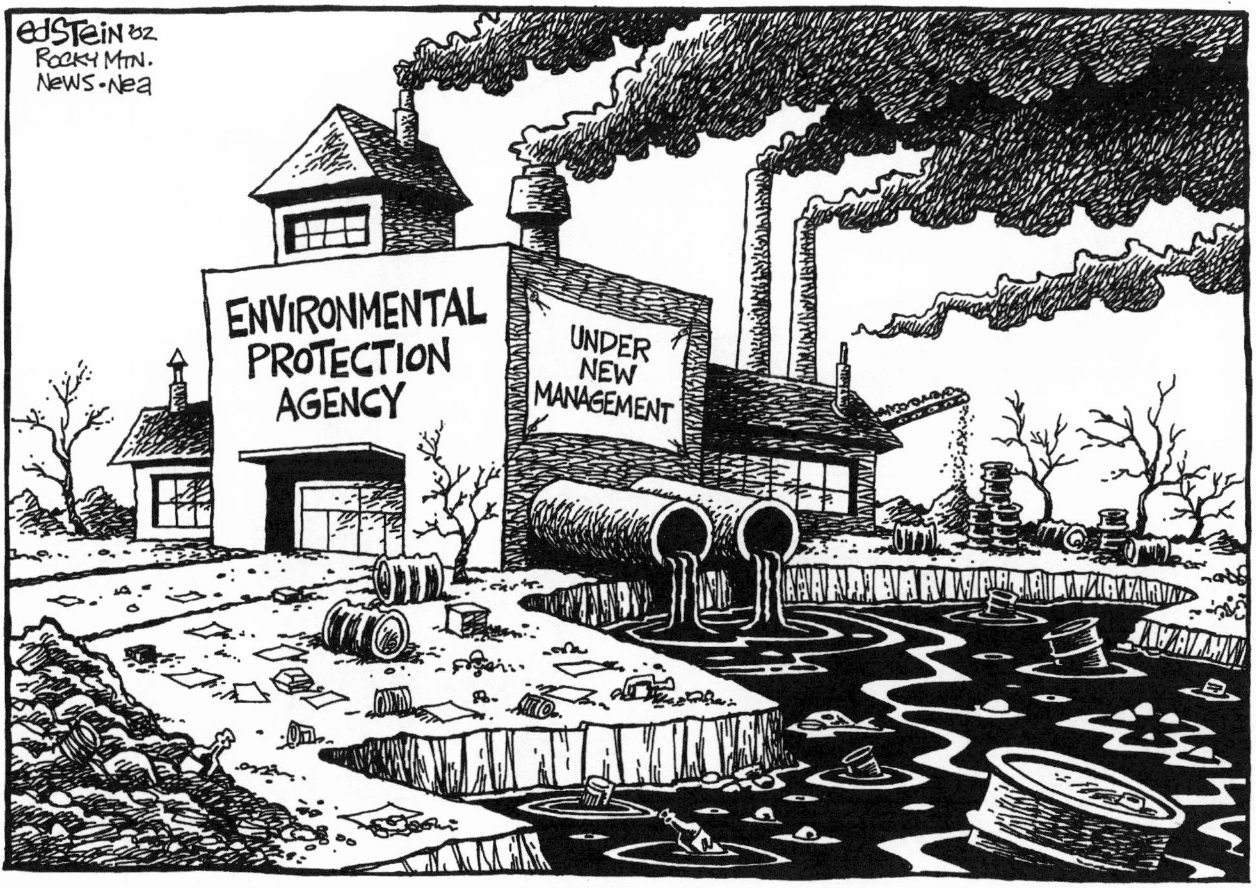
edSTein '02 ROCKY MTN. NEWS•NEA
ENVIRONMENTAL PROTECTION AGENCY
UNDER NEW MANAGEMENT

JOHN SHERFFIUS
Courtesy St. Louis Post-Dispatch

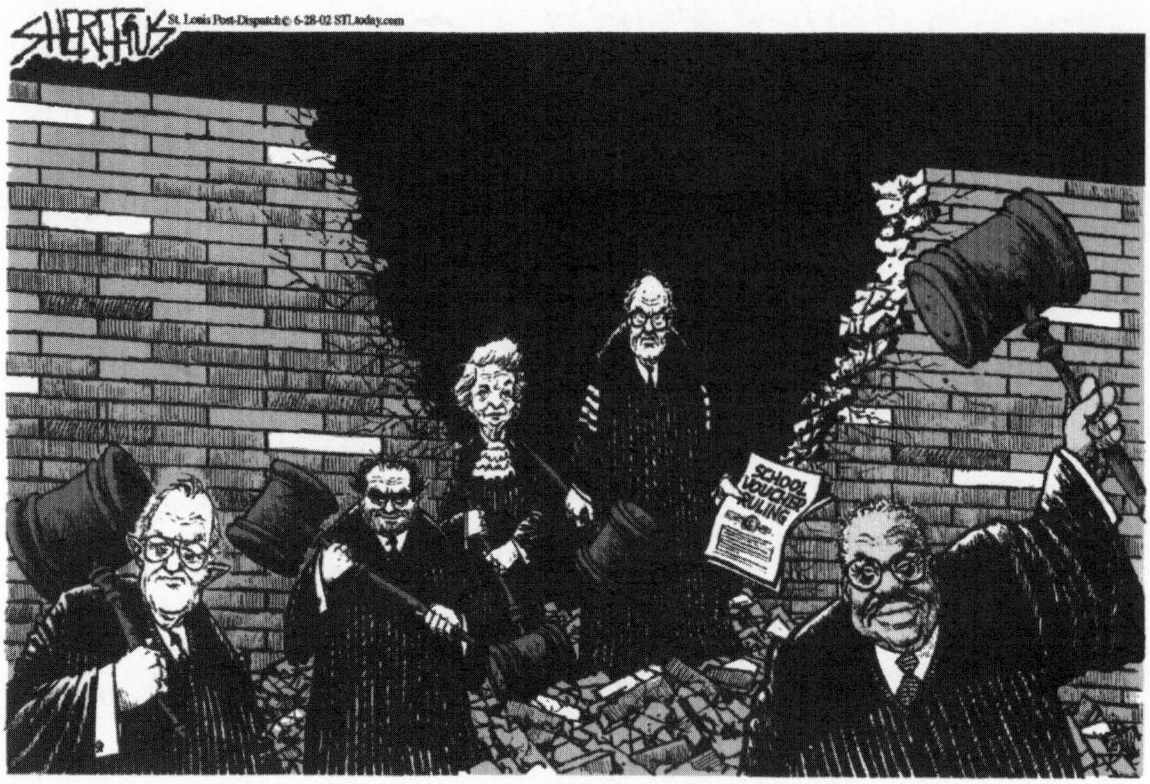
SHERFFIUS
St. Louis Post-Dispatch © 6-28-02 STLtoday.com
SCHOOL VOUCHER RULING

...one nation funding God...

DREW SHENEMAN
Courtesy Newark Star-Ledger

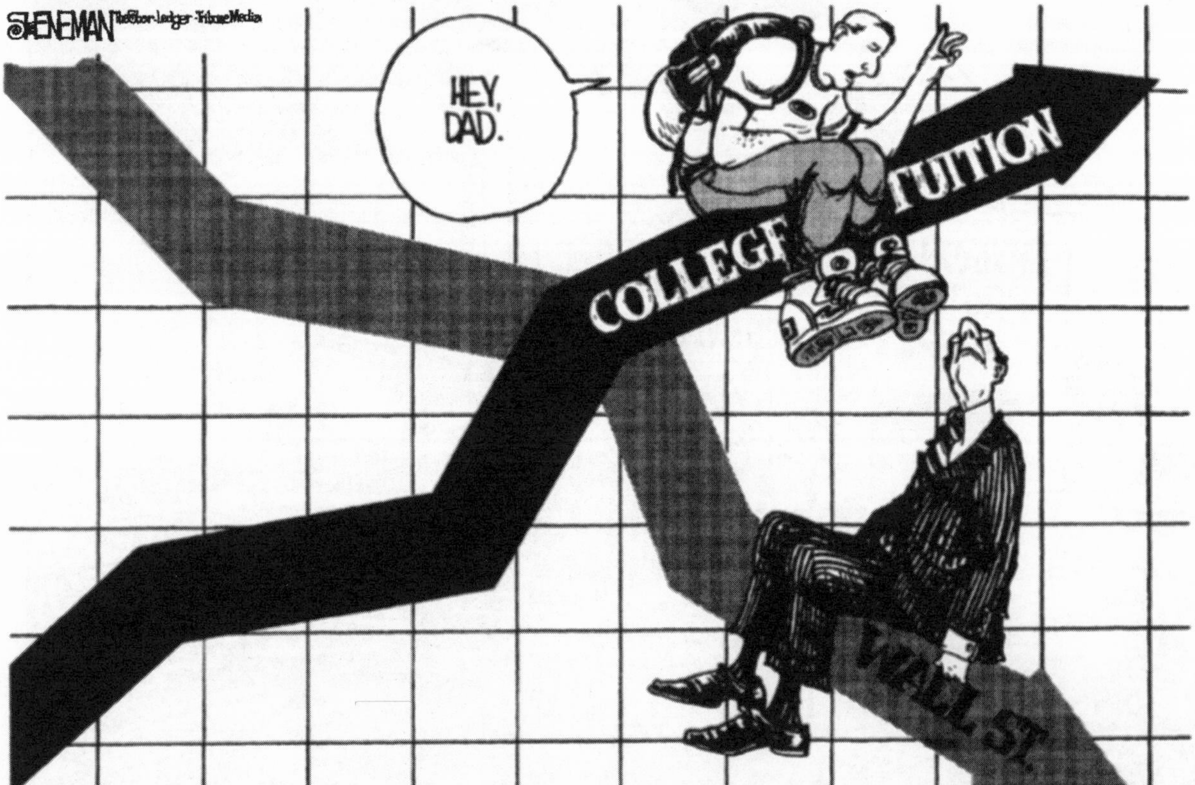
SHENEMAN
HEY, DAD.
COLLEGE TUITION
WALL ST.

Education

San Francisco's Ninth Circuit Court ruled that reciting the Pledge of Allegiance in public schools was an "unconstitutional endorsement" of religion because of the words "under God," which were added by Congress in 1954. The edict immediately hit the airwaves and newspapers across the country with a loud bang. President Bush called the ruling "ridiculous," and few rushed to strike the offending words.

Cell phones have not only been causing wrecks and road rage on the streets and highways, but they are disrupting classrooms as well. As a result, many schools have established rules forbidding them.

While the cost of a college education continues to shoot up, there is no shortage of students seeking admission. Many states have failed to increase funding for education sufficiently, and many universities are being forced to turn away well-qualified applicants.

There is also a real shortage of public school teachers because of chronic low pay and other continuing issues. The matter of school vouchers remained highly controversial but some school districts were beginning to accept the idea.

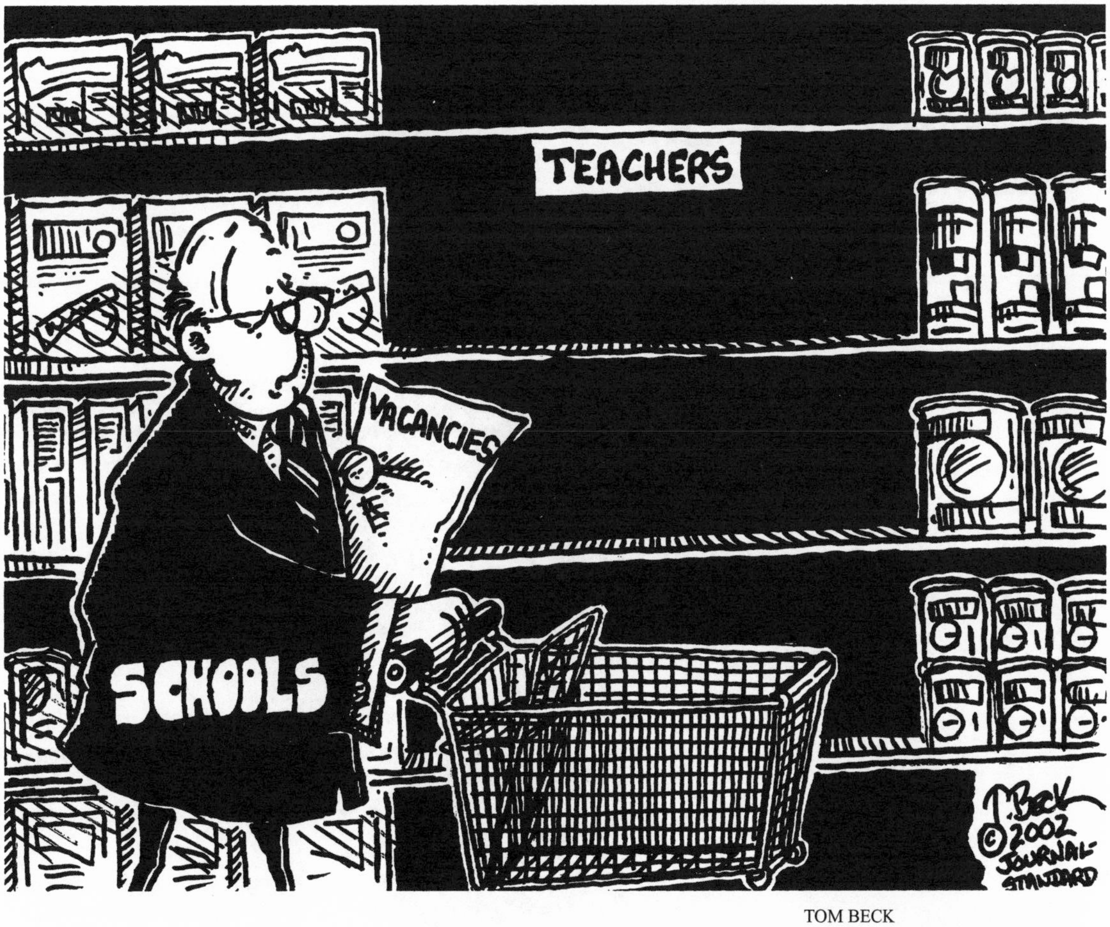
TEACHERS
VACANCIES
SCHOOLS
T. BECK
©2002
JOURNAL-STANDARD

TOM BECK
Courtesy Freeport Journal-Standard (Ill.)

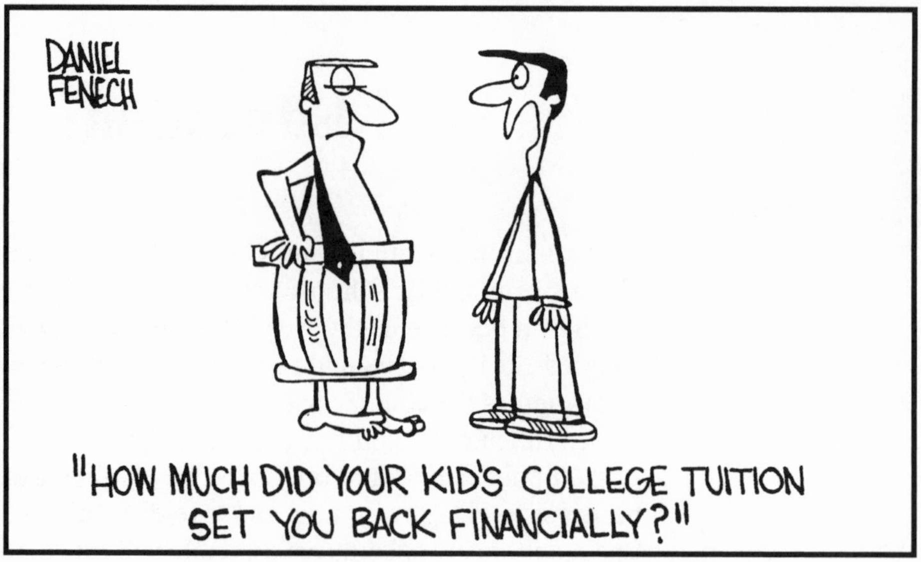
DANIEL FENECH
"HOW MUCH DID YOUR KID'S COLLEGE TUITION SET YOU BACK FINANCIALLY?"

DANIEL FENECH
Courtesy Saline Reporter (Mich.)

GLENN K. FODEN
Courtesy Patuxent Publishing

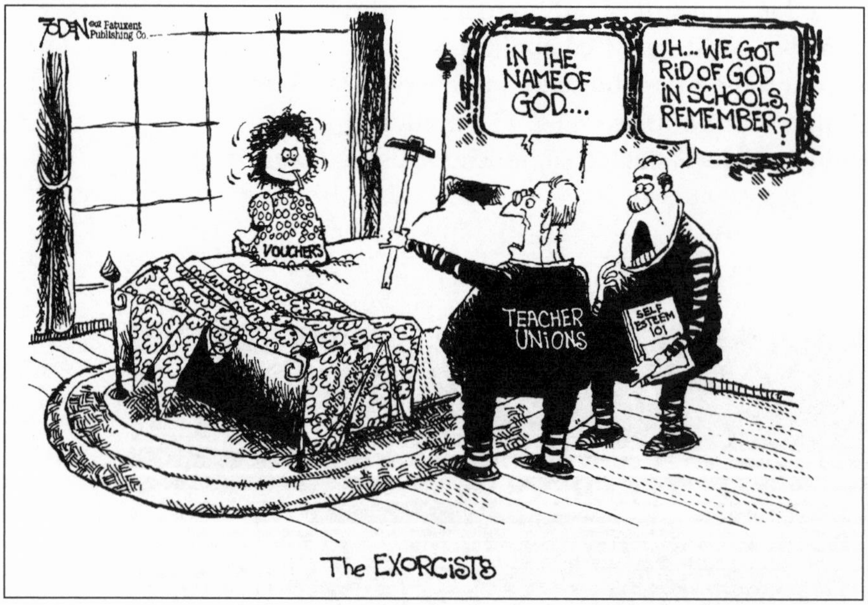
FODEN ©02 Patuxent Publishing Co.
IN THE NAME OF GOD...
UH... WE GOT RID OF GOD IN SCHOOLS, REMEMBER?
VOUCHERS
TEACHER UNIONS
SELF ESTEEM 101
The EXORCISTS

MARK THORNHILL
Courtesy North County Times (Calif.)

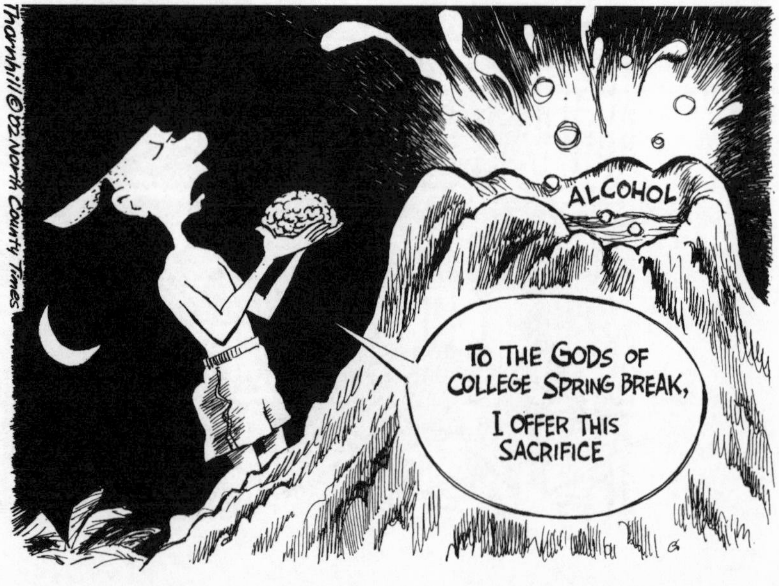
Thornhill ©02 North County Times
ALCOHOL
TO THE GODS OF COLLEGE SPRING BREAK,
I OFFER THIS SACRIFICE

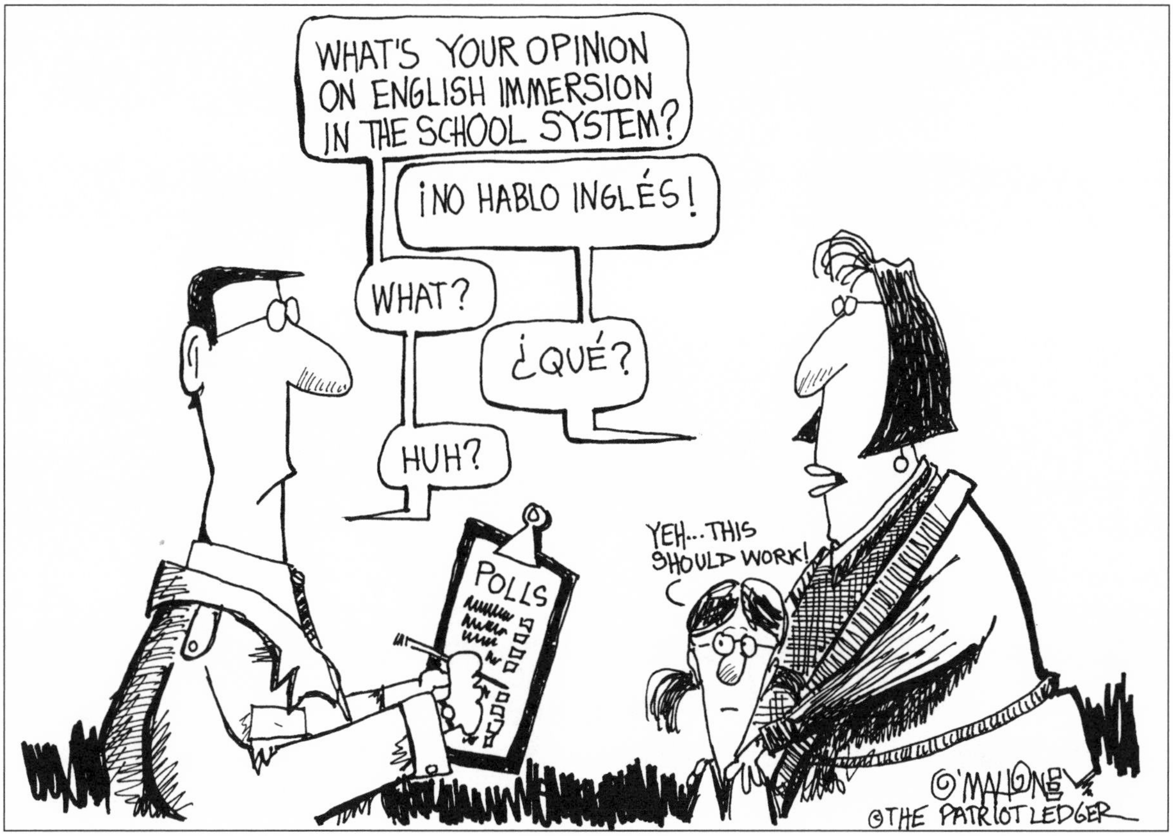
WHAT'S YOUR OPINION ON ENGLISH IMMERSION IN THE SCHOOL SYSTEM?
¡NO HABLO INGLÉS!
WHAT?
¿QUÉ?
HUH?
POLLS
YEH... THIS SHOULD WORK!
©O'MAHONEY
©THE PATRIOT LEDGER

JOSEPH F. O'MAHONEY
Courtesy The Patriot Ledger (Mass.)

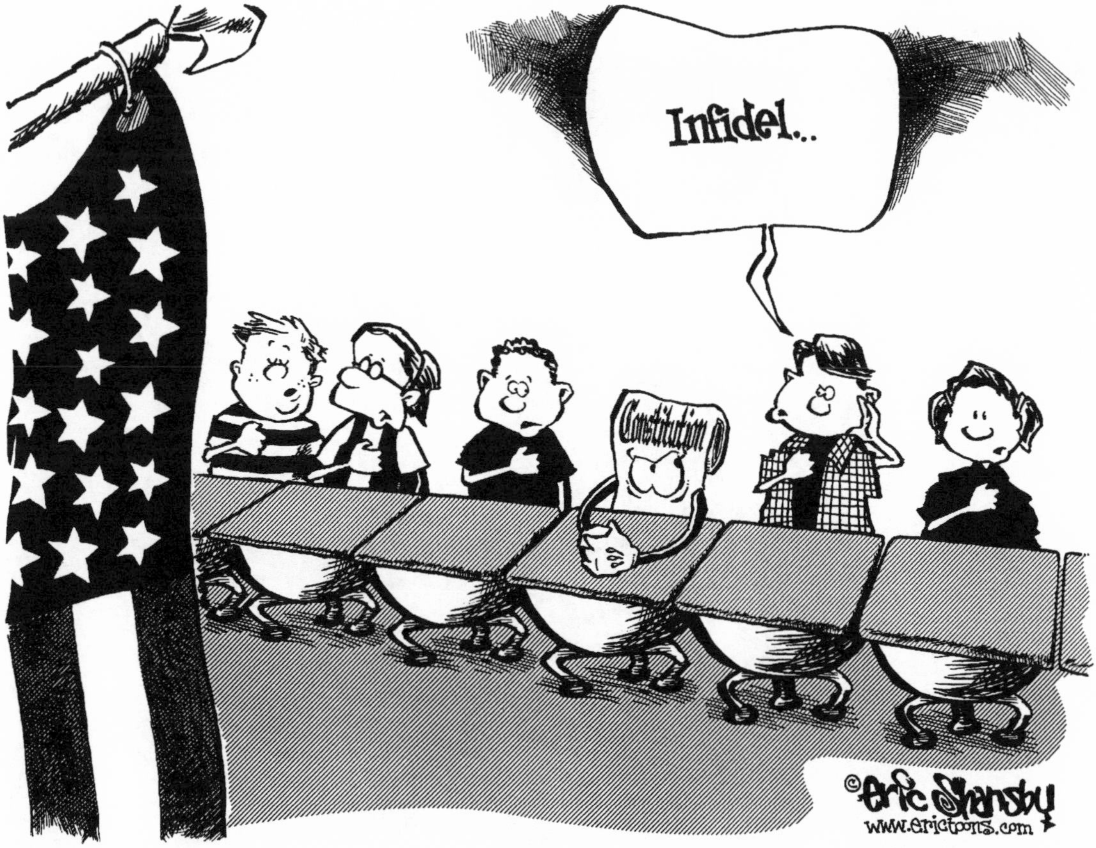
Infidel...
Constitution
©eric shansby
www.erictoons.com

ERIC SHANSBY
Courtesy The Sentinel (Md.)

WILLIAM L. FLINT
Courtesy Arlington Morning News (Tex.)

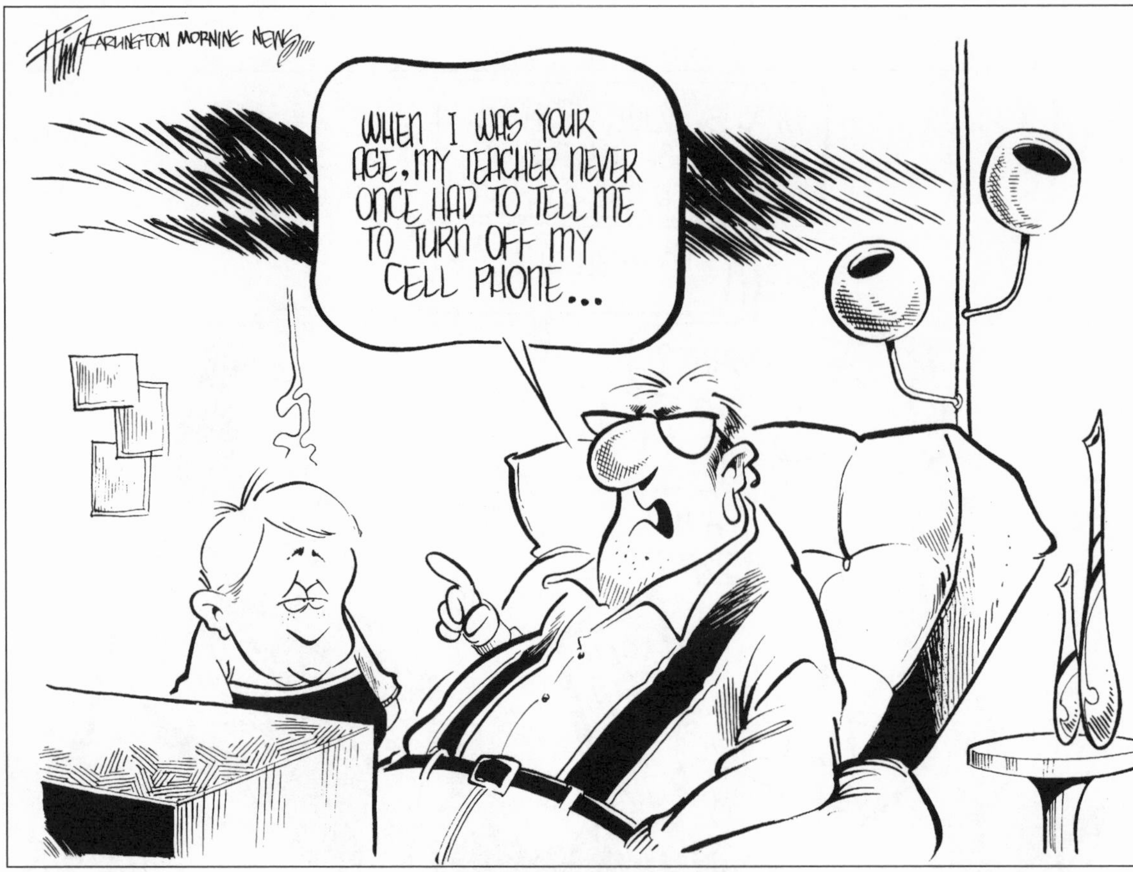
FLINT ARLINGTON MORNING NEWS
WHEN I WAS YOUR AGE, MY TEACHER NEVER ONCE HAD TO TELL ME TO TURN OFF MY CELL PHONE...

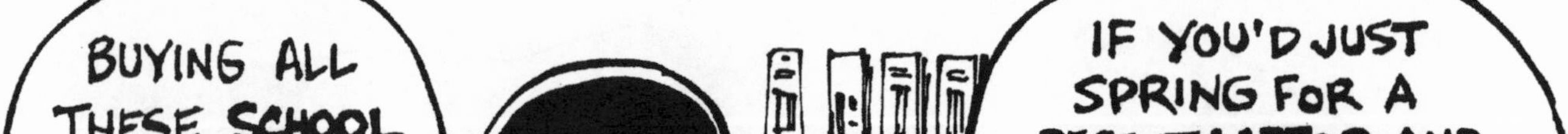
BUYING ALL THESE SCHOOL SUPPLIES IS GETTING PRETTY EXPENSIVE
IF YOU'D JUST SPRING FOR A DECENT LAPTOP AND A PALM PILOT, WE WOULDN'T NEED HALF THIS STUFF!
QUAST © 2002 ROCKFORD REGISTER STAR

BRUCE QUAST
Courtesy Rockford Register-Star

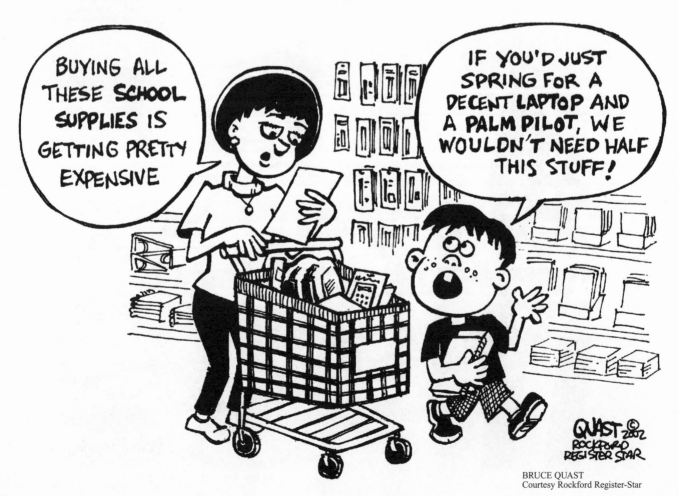

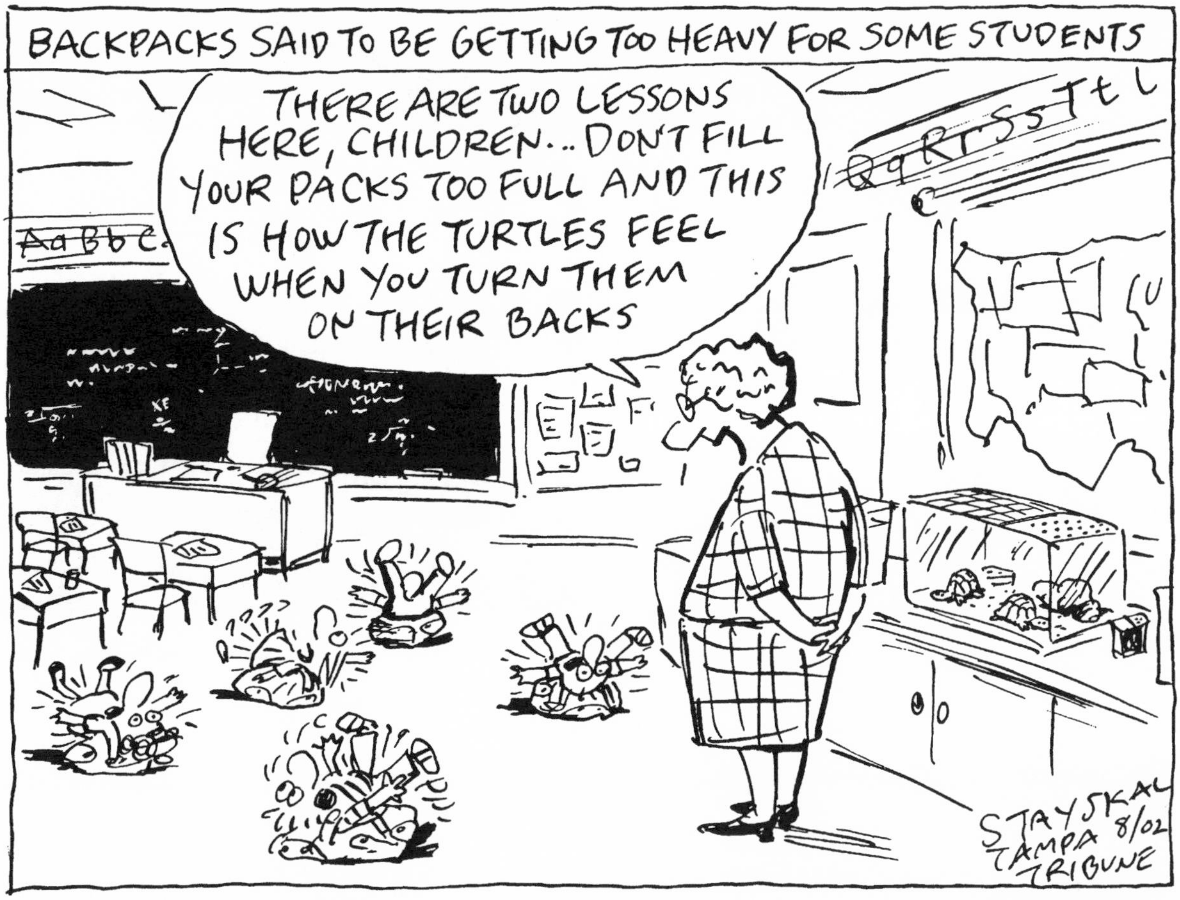
BACKPACKS SAID TO BE GETTING TOO HEAVY FOR SOME STUDENTS
THERE ARE TWO LESSONS HERE, CHILDREN...DON'T FILL YOUR PACKS TOO FULL AND THIS IS HOW THE TURTLES FEEL WHEN YOU TURN THEM ON THEIR BACKS
STAYSKAL 8/02 TAMPA TRIBUNE

WAYNE STAYSKAL
Courtesy Tampa Tribune

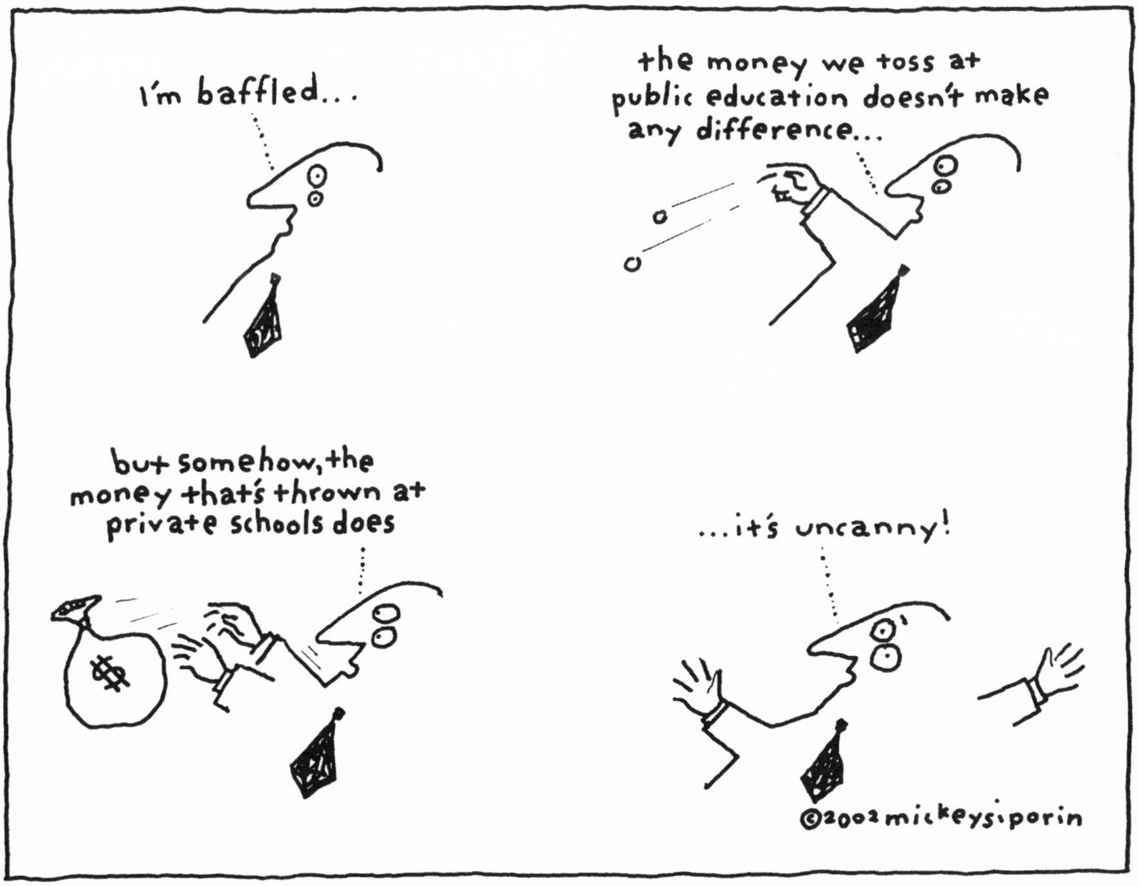
I'm baffled...
the money we toss at public education doesn't make any difference...
but somehow, the money that's thrown at private schools does
...it's uncanny!
©2002 mickeysiporin

MICKEY SIPORIN
Courtesy Newark Star-Ledger

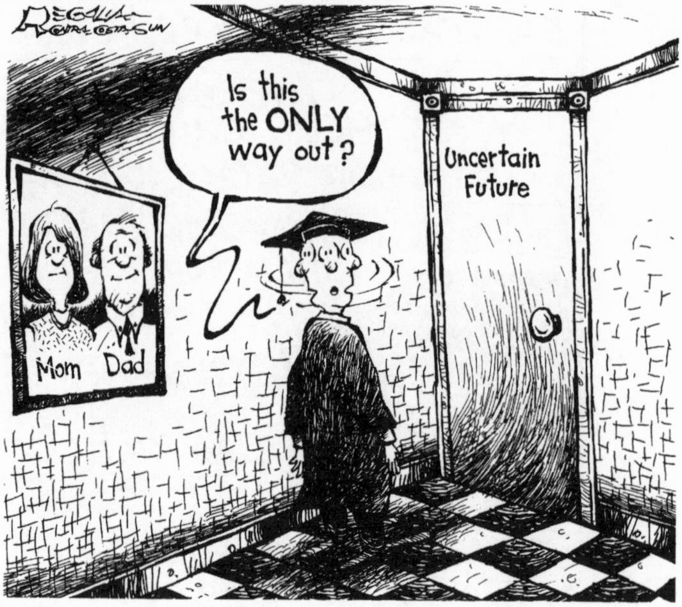
REGALIA CONTRA COSTA SUN
Is this the ONLY way out?
Uncertain Future
Mom
Dad

DOUGLAS REGALIA
Courtesy Contra Costa Times (Calif.)

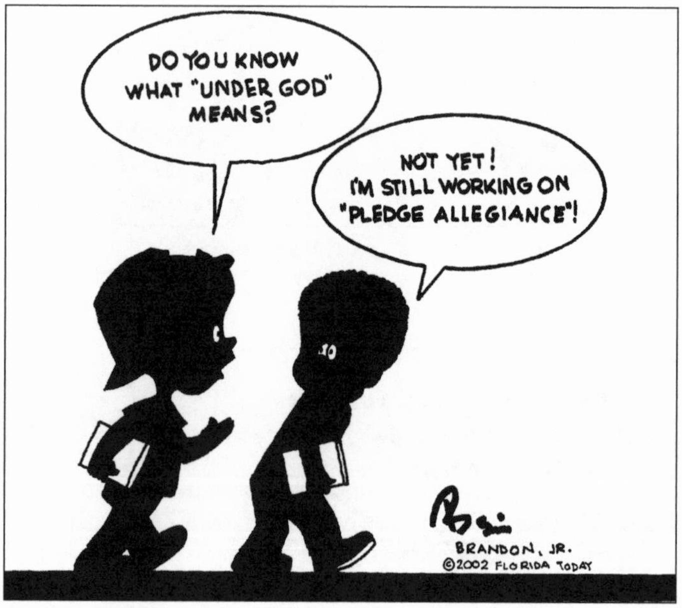
DO YOU KNOW WHAT "UNDER GOD" MEANS?
NOT YET! I'M STILL WORKING ON "PLEDGE ALLEGIANCE"!
BRANDON, JR.
©2002 FLORIDA TODAY

BRUMSIC BRANDON
Courtesy Florida Today

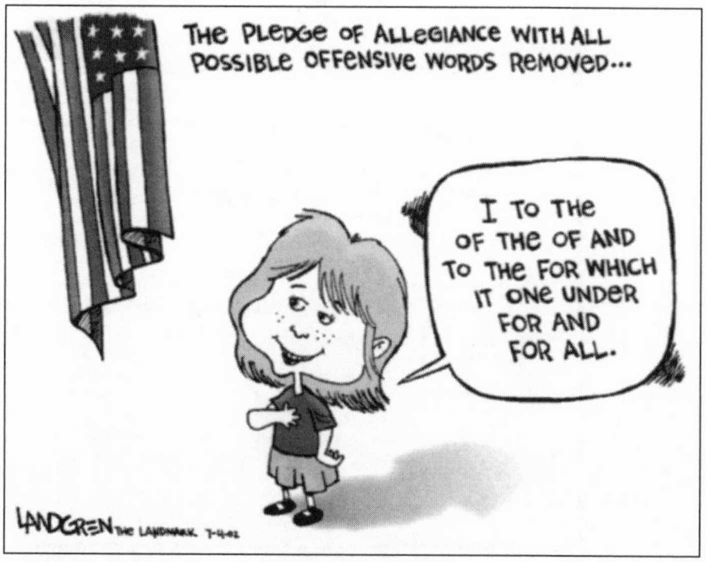
THE PLEDGE OF ALLEGIANCE WITH ALL POSSIBLE OFFENSIVE WORDS REMOVED...
I TO THE OF THE OF AND TO THE FOR WHICH IT ONE UNDER FOR AND FOR ALL.
LANDGREN THE LANDMARK 7-4-02

DON LANDGREN JR.
Courtesy The Landmark (Mass.)

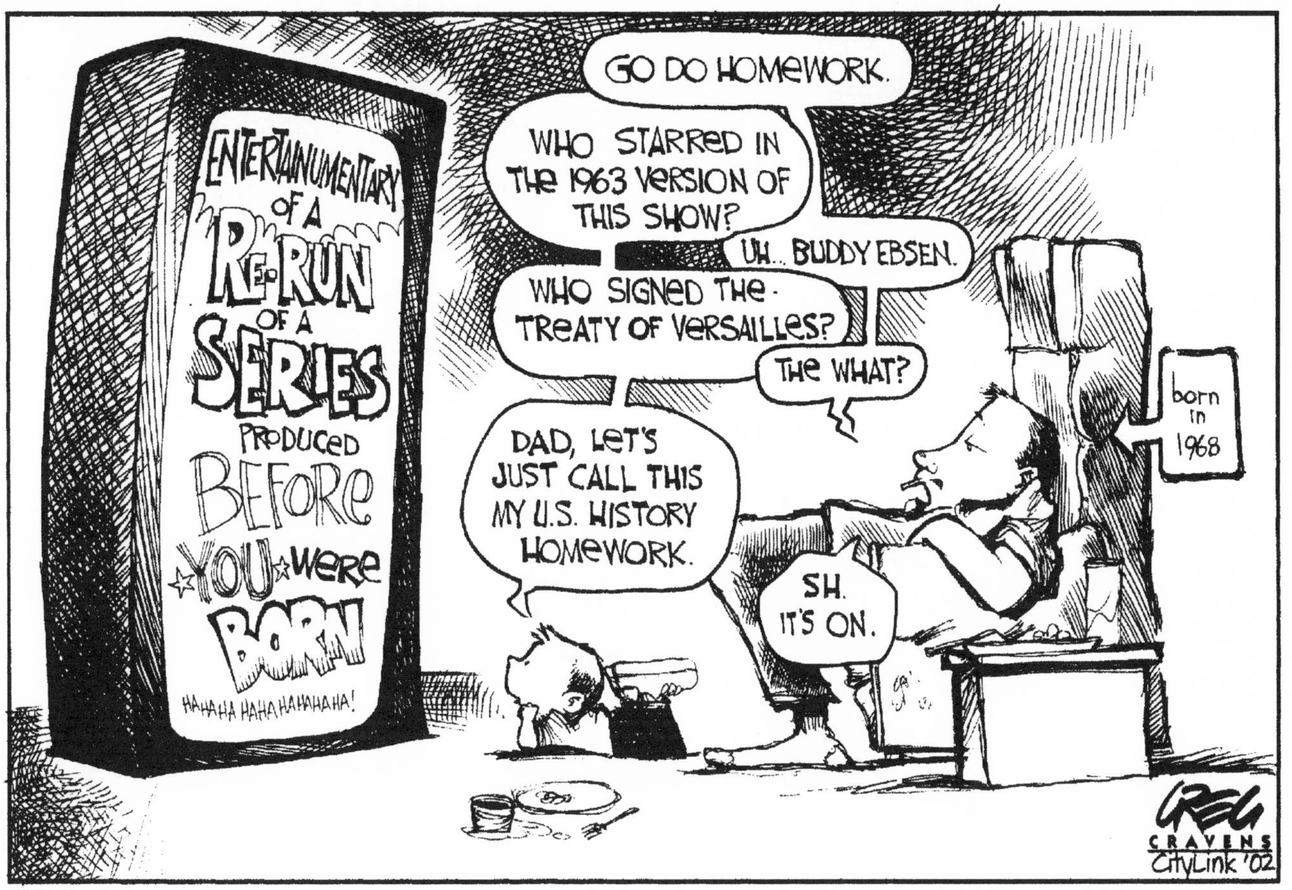
ENTERTAINUMENTARY OF A RE-RUN OF A SERIES PRODUCED BEFORE YOU WERE BORN
HAHAHA HAHA HAHAHAHA!
GO DO HOMEWORK.
WHO STARRED IN THE 1963 VERSION OF THIS SHOW?
UH... BUDDY EBSEN.
WHO SIGNED THE TREATY OF VERSAILLES?
THE WHAT?
born in 1968
DAD, LET'S JUST CALL THIS MY U.S. HISTORY HOMEWORK.
SH. IT'S ON.
GREG CRAVENS
CityLink '02

GREG CRAVENS
Courtesy ANG Newspapers

GARY MARKSTEIN
Courtesy Milwaukee Journal Sentinel

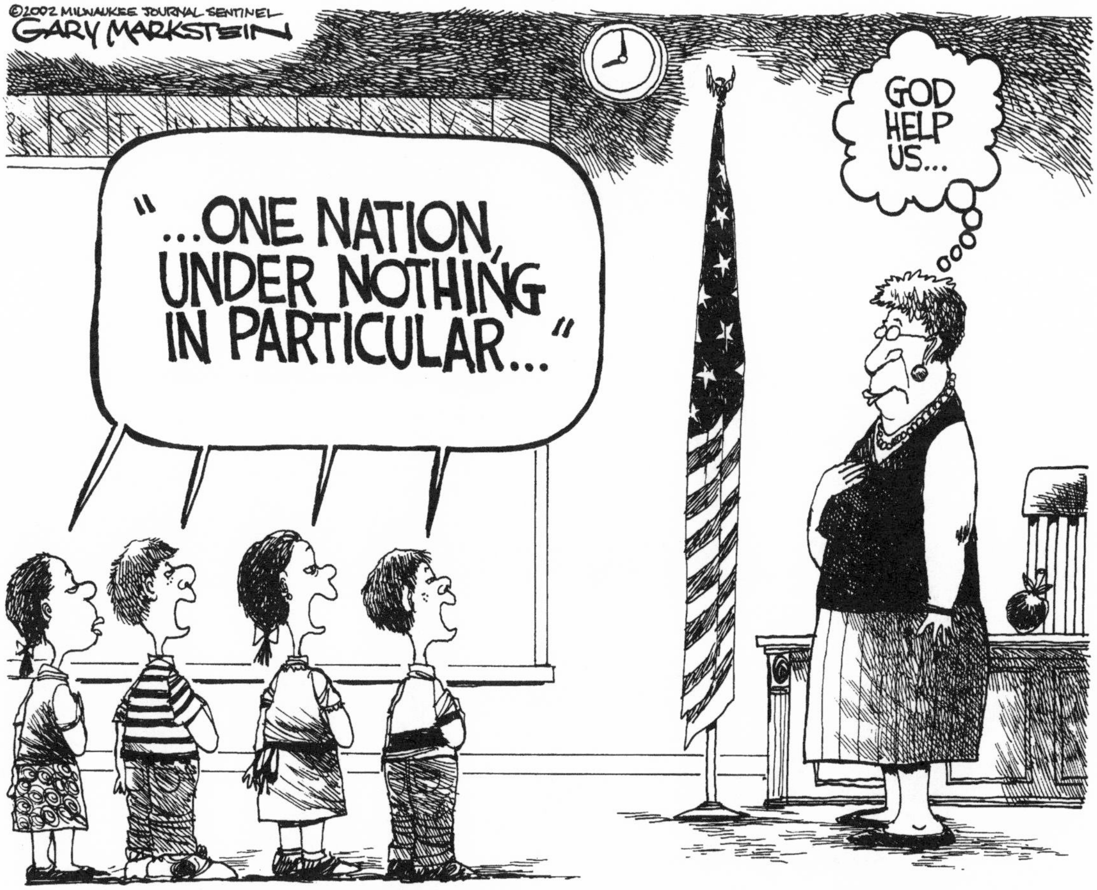
©2002 MILWAUKEE JOURNAL SENTINEL
GARY MARKSTEIN
"...ONE NATION, UNDER NOTHING IN PARTICULAR..."
GOD HELP US...

MICHAEL CAVNA
Courtesy San Diego Union-Tribune

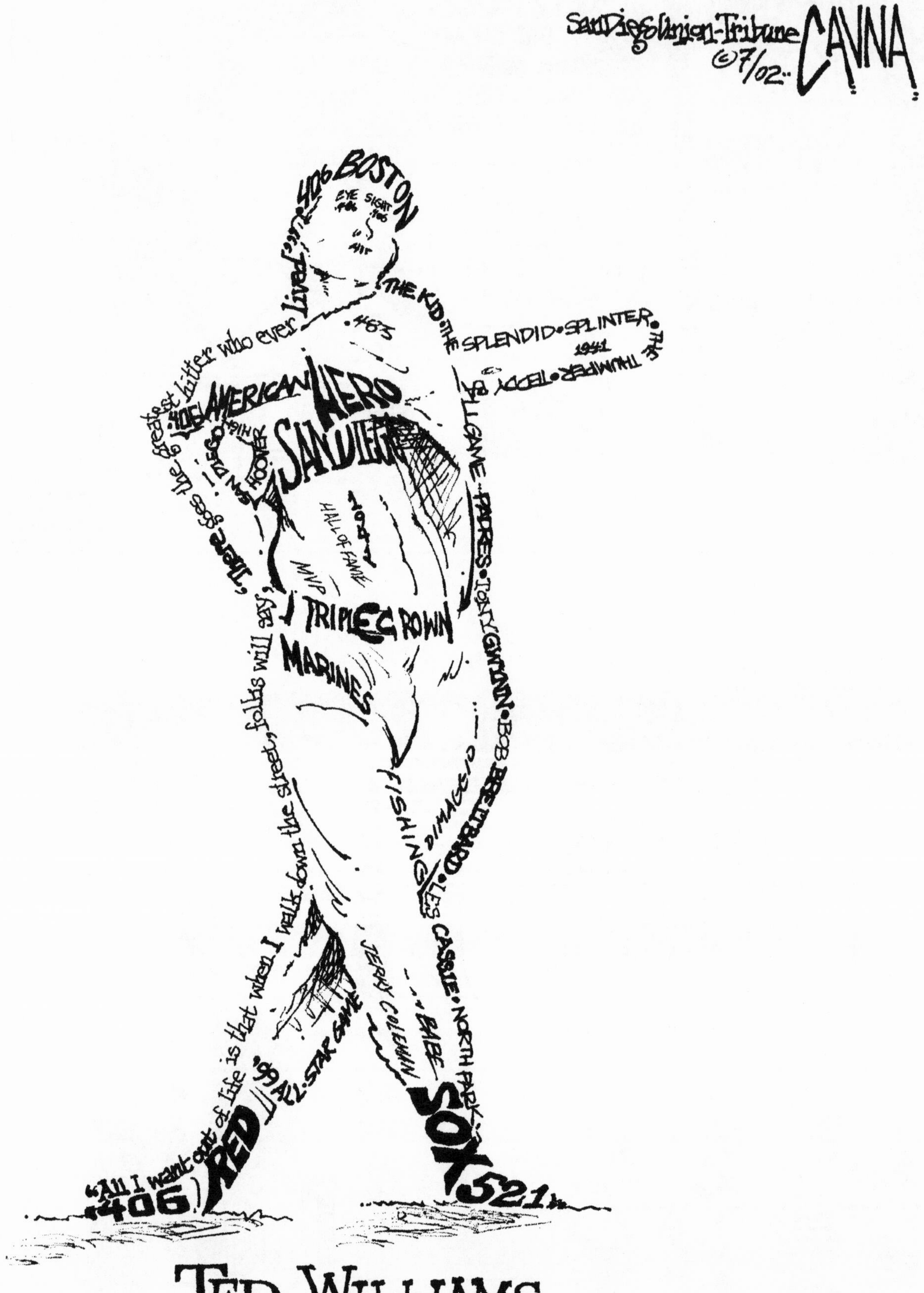
SanDiegoUnion-Tribune ©7/02 CAVNA
.406 BOSTON
EYE SIGHT
"All I want out of life is that when I walk down the street, folks will say, 'There goes the greatest hitter who ever lived.'"
THE KID
THE SPLENDID SPLINTER
THE THUMPER
TEDDY BALLGAME
.483
AMERICAN HERO
SAN DIEGO
HALL OF FAME
MVP
TRIPLE CROWN
MARINES
PADRES
TONY GWYNN
BOBBY DOERR
DIMAGGIO
FISHING
LES CASSIE
NORTH PARK
JERRY COLEMAN
BABE
'99 ALL-STAR GAME
RED SOX
.406
521
TED WILLIAMS
1918 • 2002

Sports

Before the 2002 Winter Olympics opened in Salt Lake City there was growing concern over the cost of this historic event. It is getting more and more difficult for Olympic boosters to persuade corporations to spend millions of dollars to help foot the bills. And over the years there has been a steady decline in television viewers, which means shrinking revenue from that source.

Then came Skategate—the scandal over the gold-medal winner in pairs skating—in which a French judge allegedly was pressured to vote for the Russian team in exchange for a Russian vote in a later competition. The incident forced a thorough housecleaning and is expected to bring about overdue changes in selecting judges and awarding medals in future Olympics.

Major League Baseball fended off a threatened strike, and an all-California World Series saw the Anaheim Angels beat the San Francisco Giants in seven games. Steroid use seemed to have become widespread in sports, and baseball's greatest hitter, Ted Williams, died at the age of 83. There was a family squabble over whether to freeze Williams' body and put it in cryogenic suspension.

GARY MARKSTEIN
Courtesy Milwaukee Journal Sentinel

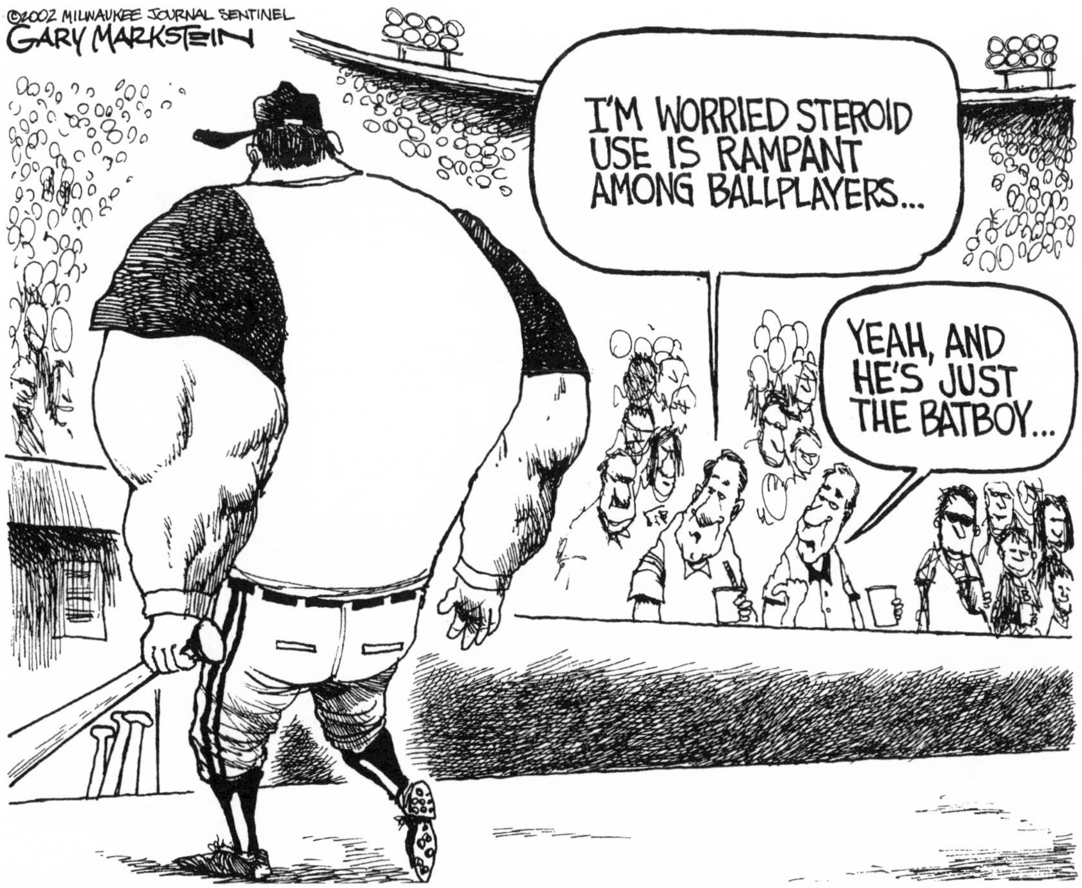
©2002 MILWAUKEE JOURNAL SENTINEL
GARY MARKSTEIN
I'M WORRIED STEROID USE IS RAMPANT AMONG BALLPLAYERS...
YEAH, AND HE'S JUST THE BATBOY...

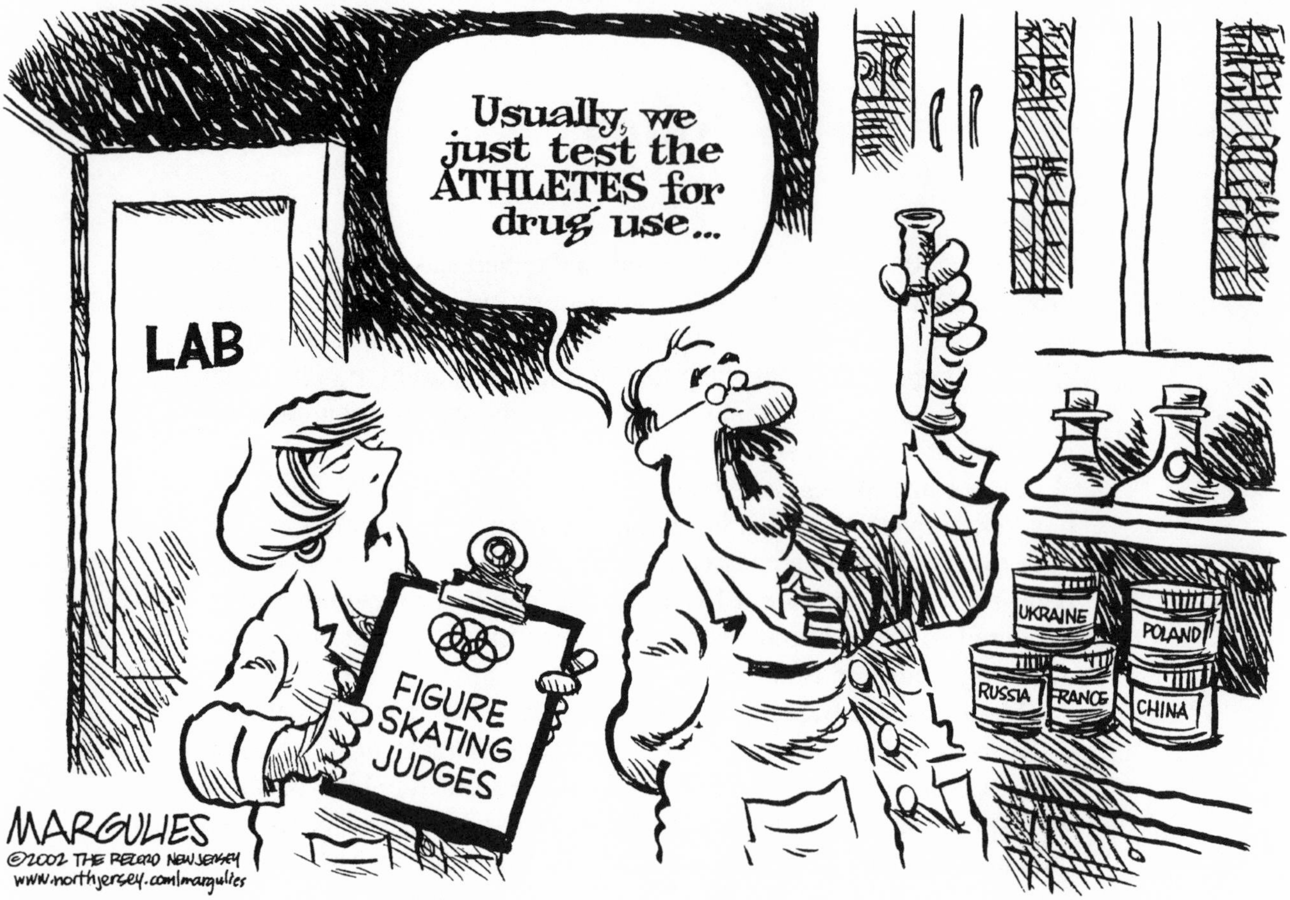
Usually, we just test the ATHLETES for drug use...
LAB
FIGURE SKATING JUDGES
UKRAINE
POLAND
RUSSIA
FRANCE
CHINA
MARGULIES
©2002 THE RECORD NEW JERSEY
www.northjersey.com/margulies

JIMMY MARGULIES
Courtesy The Record (N.J.)

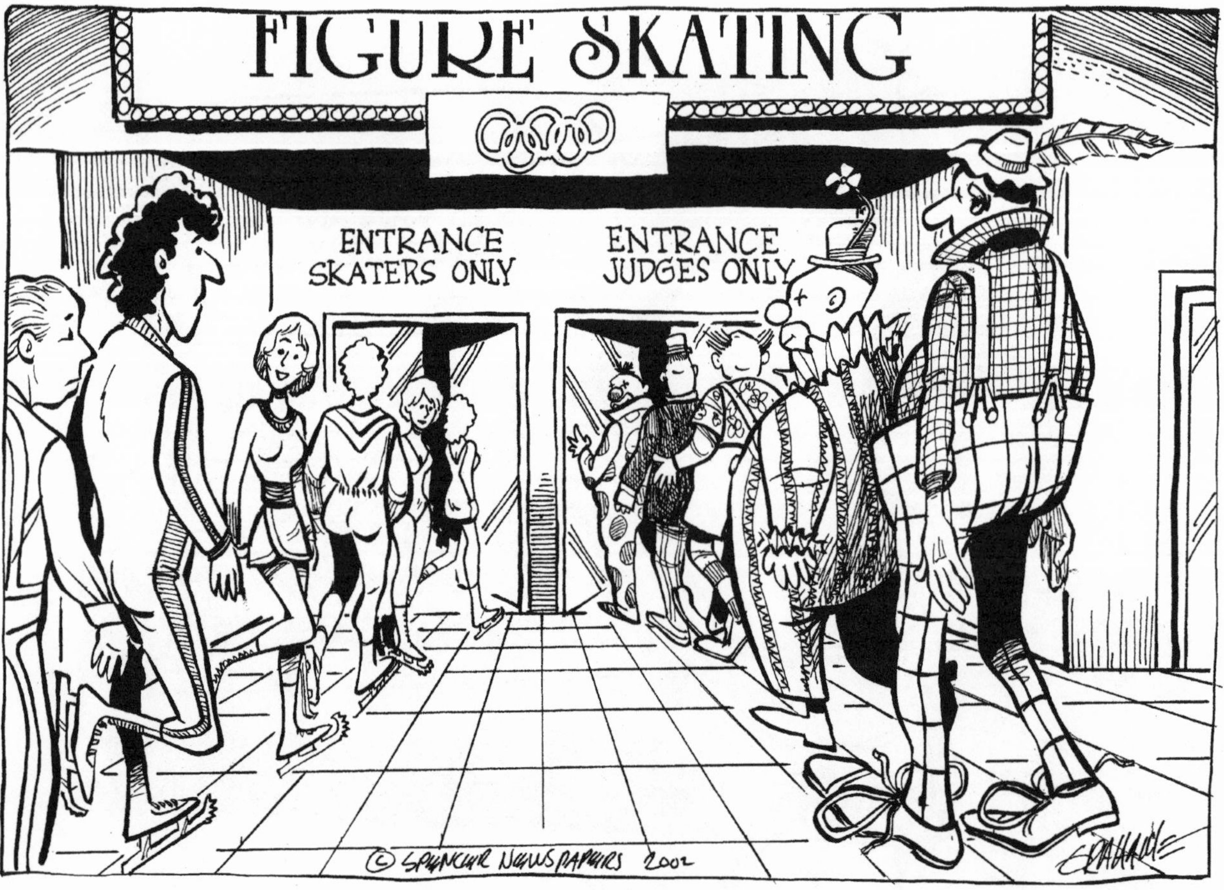
FIGURE SKATING
ENTRANCE SKATERS ONLY
ENTRANCE JUDGES ONLY
© SPENCER NEWSPAPERS 2002
GRAHAME

NEIL GRAHAME
Courtesy Spencer Newspapers

STACY CURTIS
Courtesy The Times (Ind.)

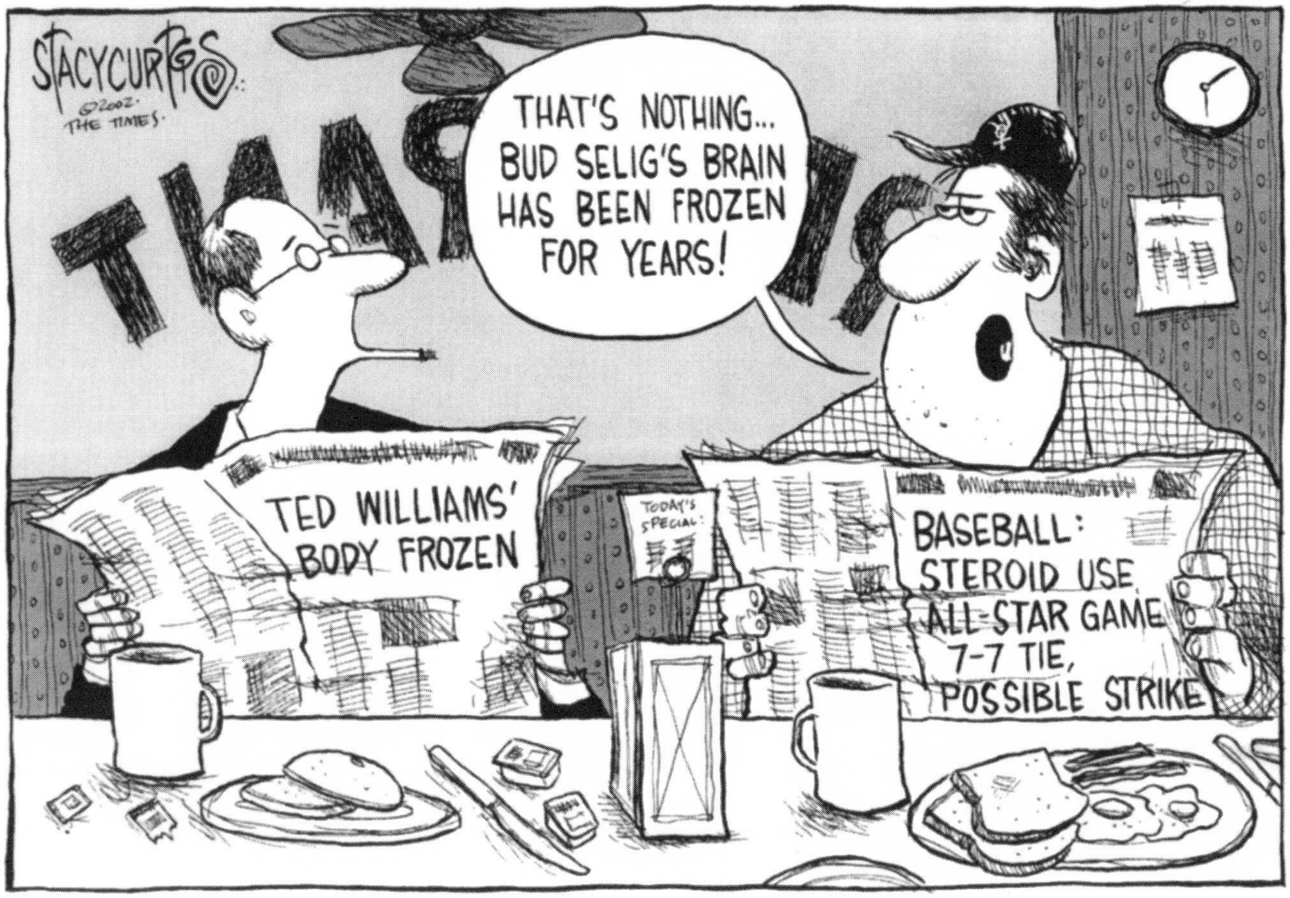
STACYCURTIS ©2002 THE TIMES
THAT'S NOTHING... BUD SELIG'S BRAIN HAS BEEN FROZEN FOR YEARS!
TED WILLIAMS' BODY FROZEN
TODAY'S SPECIAL:
BASEBALL: STEROID USE ALL-STAR GAME 7-7 TIE, POSSIBLE STRIKE

RICK McKEE
Courtesy Augusta Chronicle

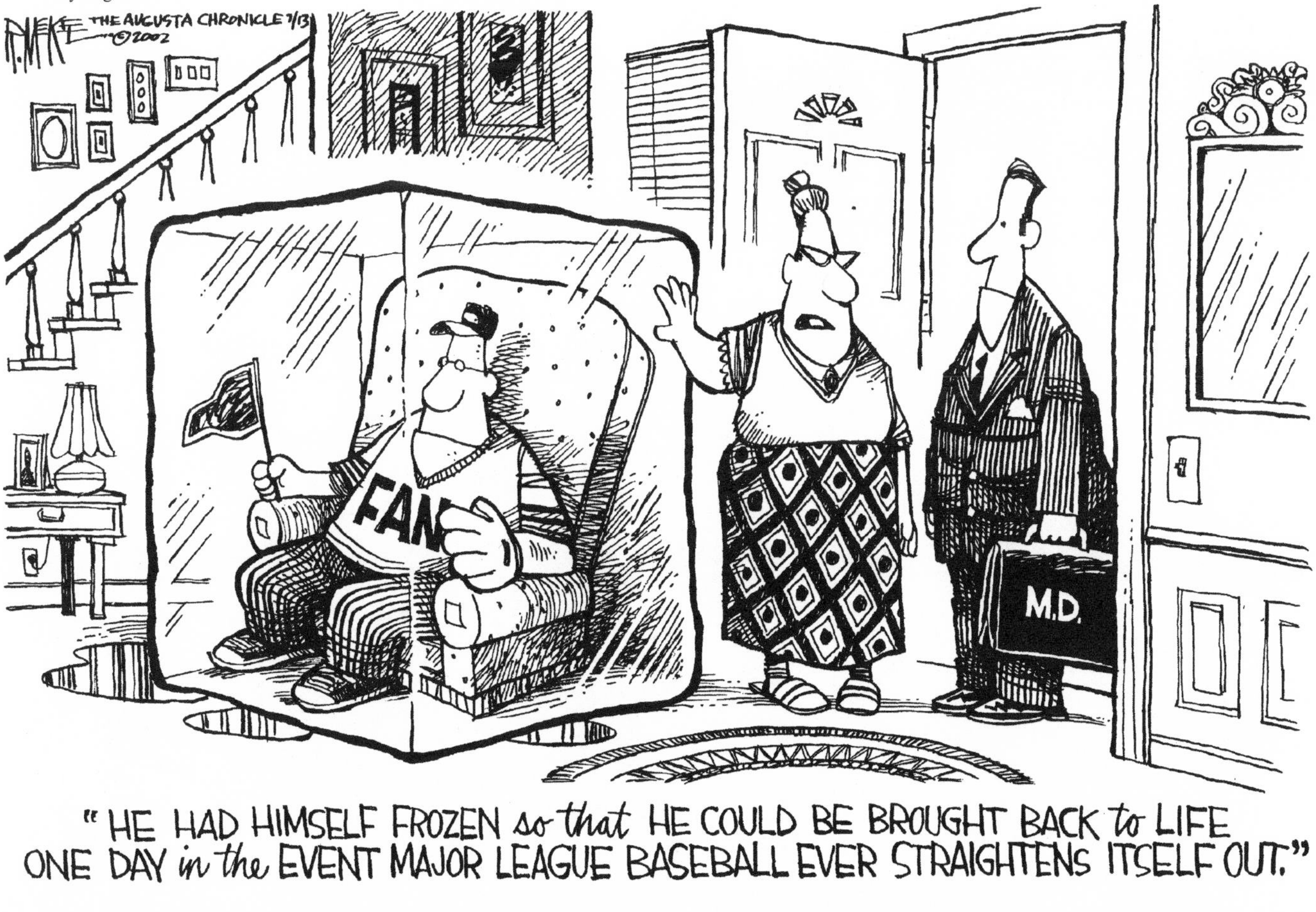
THE AUGUSTA CHRONICLE ©2002
FAN
M.D.
"HE HAD HIMSELF FROZEN so that HE COULD BE BROUGHT BACK to LIFE ONE DAY in the EVENT MAJOR LEAGUE BASEBALL EVER STRAIGHTENS ITSELF OUT."

MAJOR LEAGUE $TRIKE TALK
PLAYER$
OWNER$
COULD BE THE FINAL DUEL!
JACK JURDEN
WILMINGTON NEWS JOURNAL

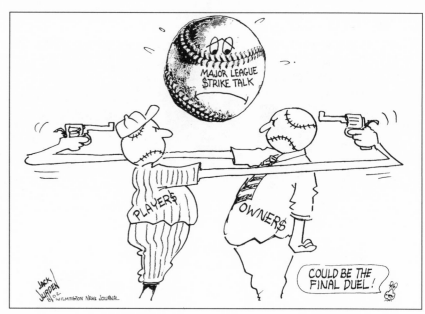

JACK JURDEN
Courtesy Wilmington News Journal

...FANTASIC!! SO MR SELIG WANTS ME TO SHRED EVERY TEAM'S BOOKS AND CLAIM MAJOR LEAGUE BASEBALL IS A NON-PROFIT ORGANIZATION!!!
HR DOCK
SINCE 2002

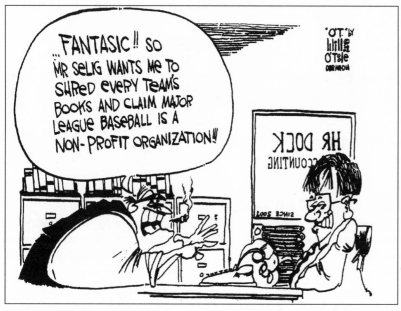

WILL O'TOOLE
Courtesy Home News & Tribune (N.J.)

DARYL CAGLE
Courtesy caglecartoons.com

GLUTTONS
Greedies
BIG Heads
JERKS
I SWITCHED TO SOCCER
DARYL CAGLE SLATE.com

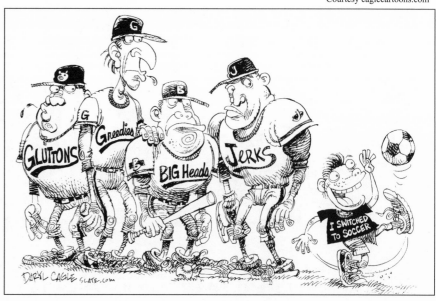

PLAYERS' UNION
FANS
STRIKE
TIM HARTMAN ©2002

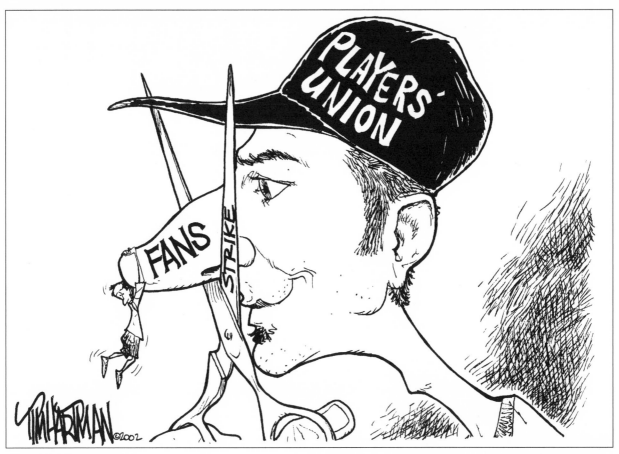

TIM HARTMAN
Courtesy Beaver County Times (Pa.)

CHAN LOWE
Courtesy Fort Lauderdale News/Sun Sentinel

LOWE
SOUTH FLORIDA SUN-SENTINEL ©TRIBUNE MEDIA

"EVEN THOUGH THEY AVERTED A STRIKE, I GET THIS NAGGING FEELING THAT THE BASIC NATURE OF THE GAME WILL NEVER BE THE SAME."

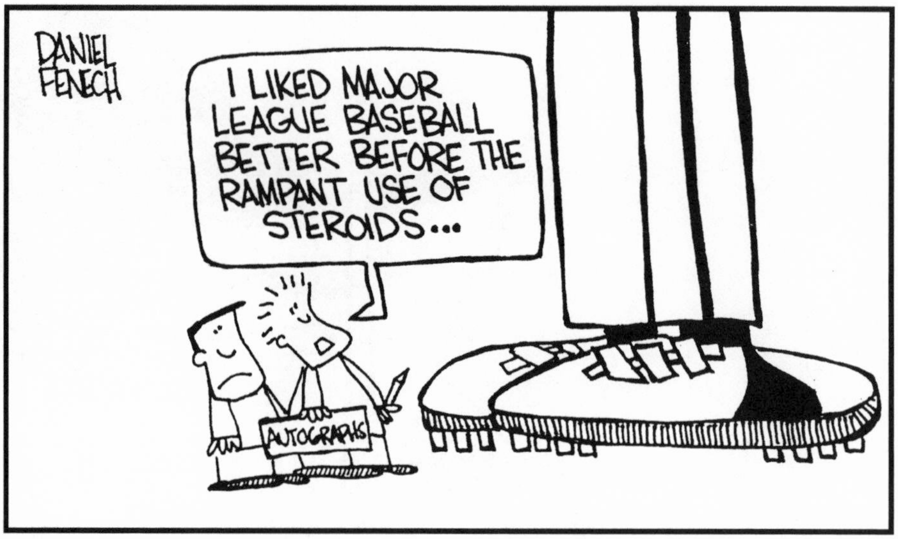
DANIEL FENECH
I LIKED MAJOR LEAGUE BASEBALL BETTER BEFORE THE RAMPANT USE OF STEROIDS...
AUTOGRAPHS

DANIEL FENECH
Courtesy Saline Reporter (Mich.)

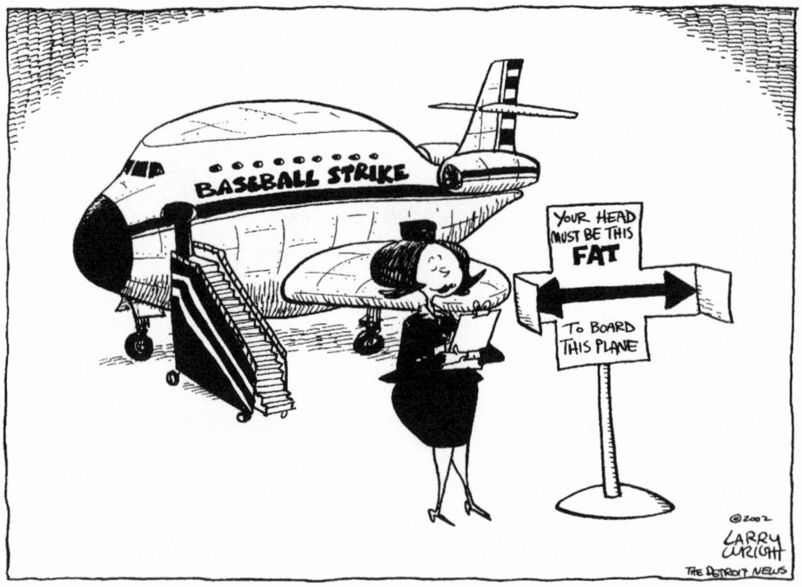
BASEBALL STRIKE
YOUR HEAD MUST BE THIS FAT
TO BOARD THIS PLANE
©2002 LARRY WRIGHT
THE DETROIT NEWS

LARRY WRIGHT
Courtesy Detroit News

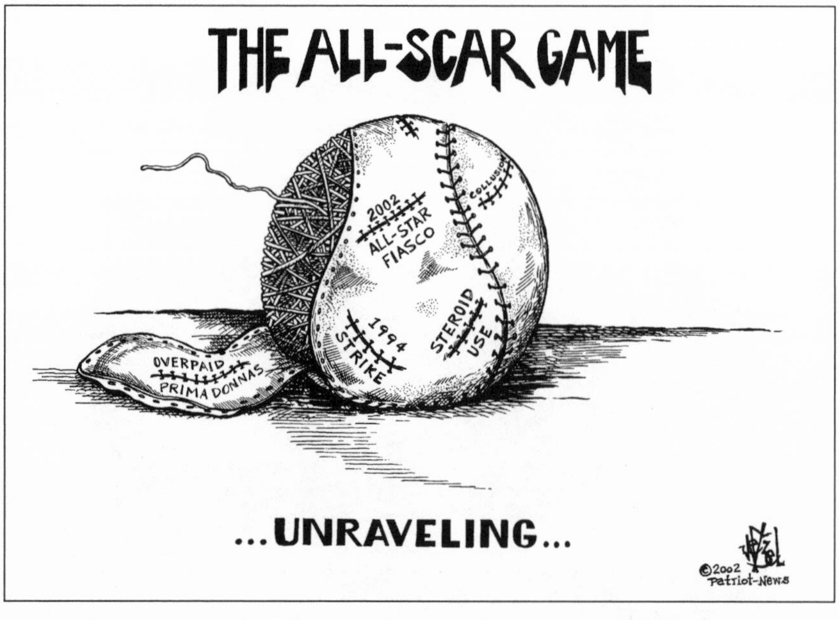
THE ALL-SCAR GAME
2002 ALL-STAR FIASCO
COLLUSION
STEROID USE
1994 STRIKE
OVERPAID PRIMA DONNAS
...UNRAVELING...
©2002 Patriot-News

STEVE WETZEL
Courtesy The Patriot-News (Pa.)

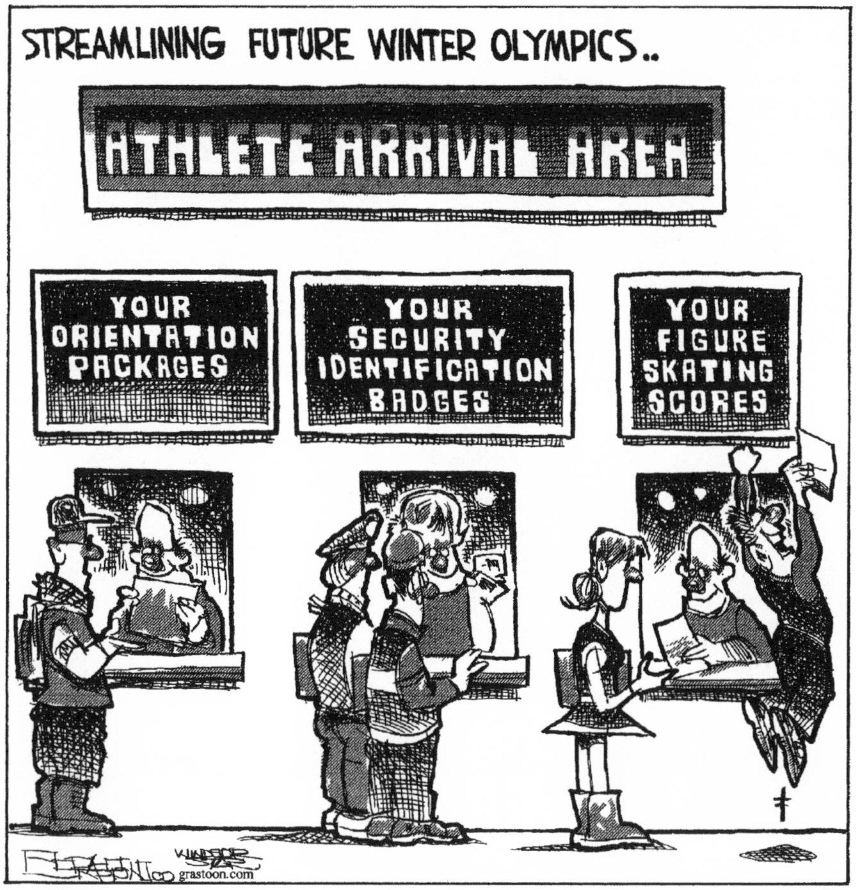
STREAMLINING FUTURE WINTER OLYMPICS..
ATHLETE ARRIVAL AREA
YOUR ORIENTATION PACKAGES
YOUR SECURITY IDENTIFICATION BADGES
YOUR FIGURE SKATING SCORES
grastoon.com

MIKE GRASTON
Courtesy Windsor Star

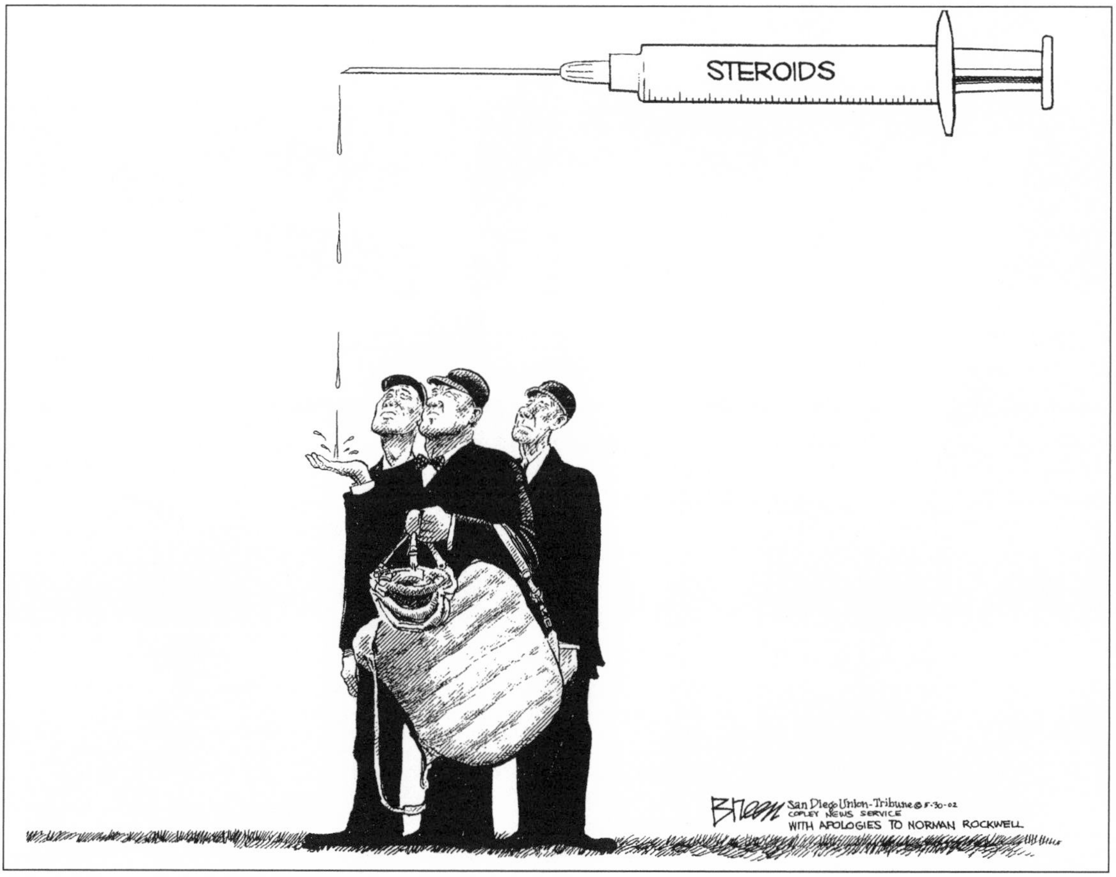
STEROIDS
San Diego Union-Tribune © 5-30-02
COPLEY NEWS SERVICE
WITH APOLOGIES TO NORMAN ROCKWELL

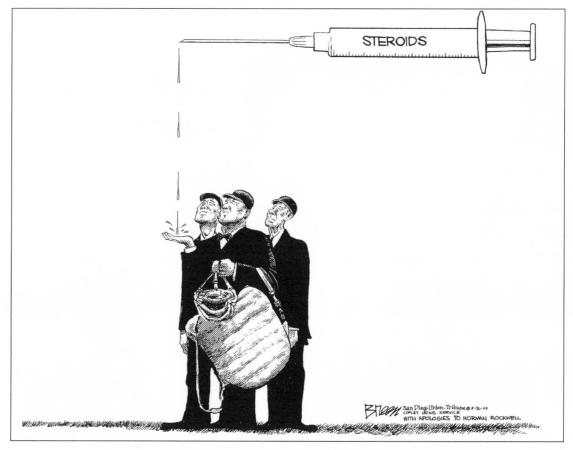

STEVE BREEN
Courtesy San Diego Union-Tribune

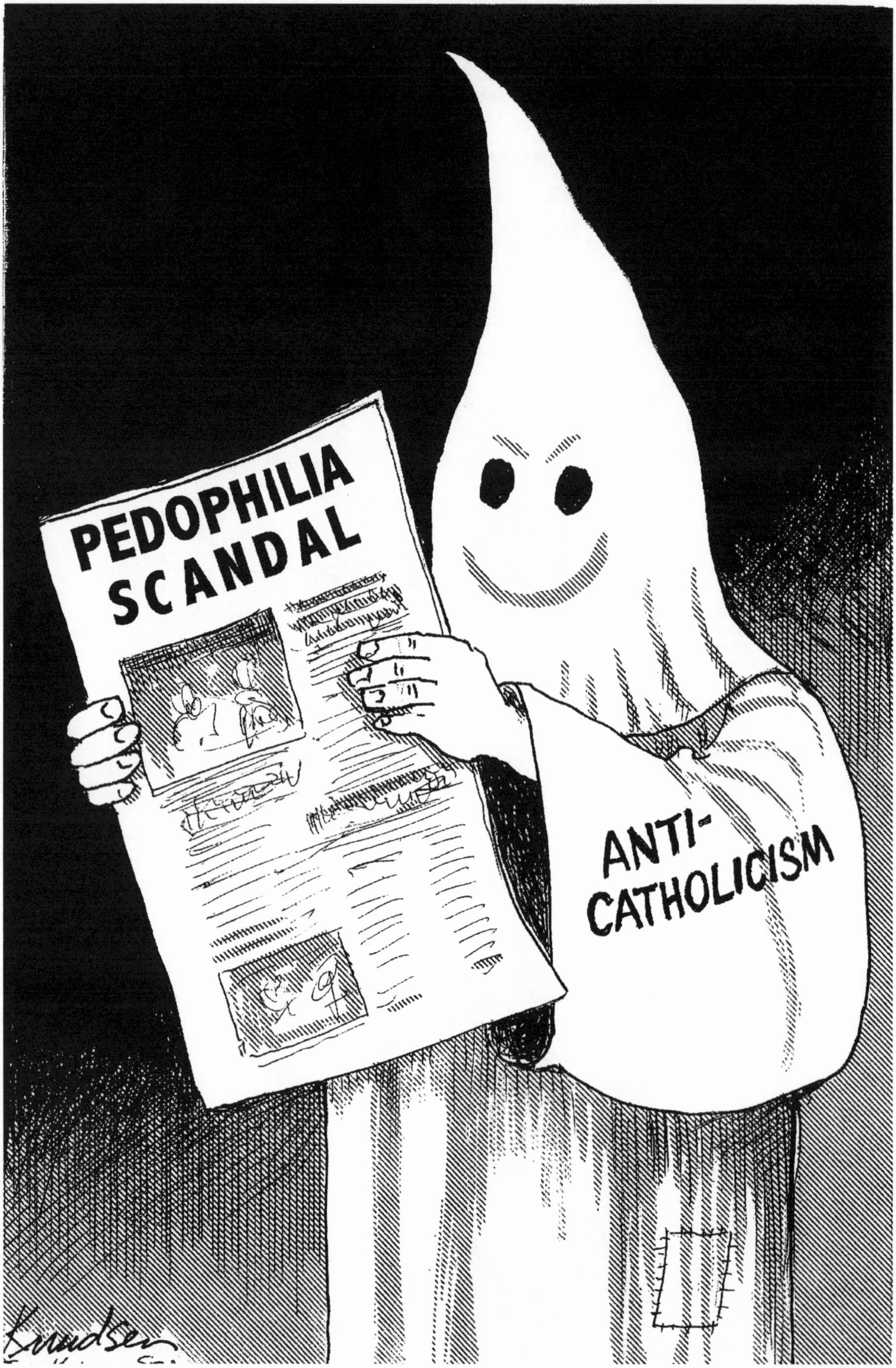
PEDOPHILIA SCANDAL
ANTI-CATHOLICISM
Knudsen

JOHN KNUDSEN
Courtesy St. Louis Review

Church in Crisis

Charges of widespread pedophilia and sexual misconduct by priests continued to rock the Catholic Church throughout 2002. In 1984 criminal and civil charges were leveled against a Louisiana priest, who pleaded guilty to molesting eleven boys. For the next eighteen years, sexual allegations were filed against some 1,200 priests in the U.S. The pattern of widespread abuse apparently was ignored and covered up by some church leaders for years.

An FBI sting operation uncovered a pedophile ring operating on the internet, and some forty arrests were made, including several priests. Pope John Paul II issued a statement expressing his personal grief over the scandal and summoned cardinals to the Vatican to discuss the matter. The Church has already paid families millions of dollars to settle abuse cases.

This is not merely an American affliction. The Church faces thousands of sex-abuse-related lawsuits in Canada, while parishes in Mexico, Poland, and France are having to deal with similar cases. The church in Ireland agreed to contribute $110 million to a $400 million settlement for children abused in church-run schools over the past thirty years.

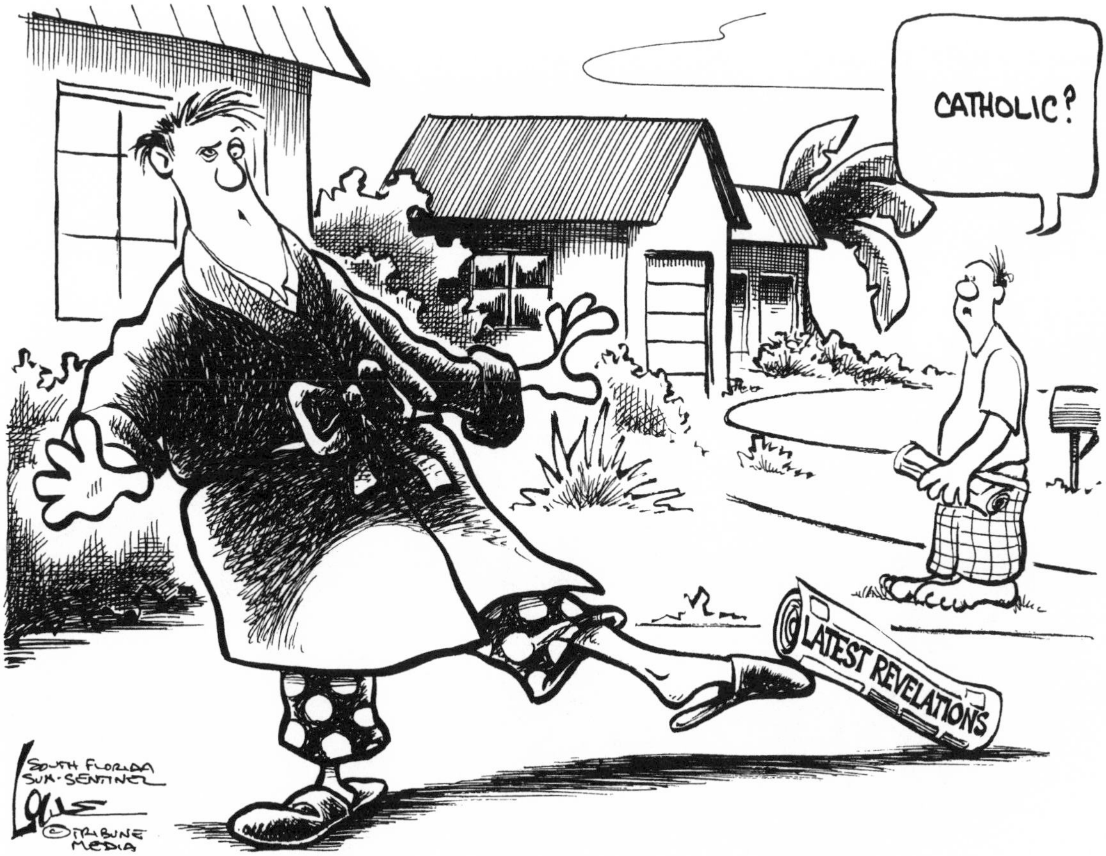
CATHOLIC?
LATEST REVELATIONS
SOUTH FLORIDA SUN-SENTINEL
©TRIBUNE MEDIA

CHAN LOWE
Courtesy Fort Lauderdale News/Sun Sentinel

PAUL CONRAD
Courtesy Los Angeles Times

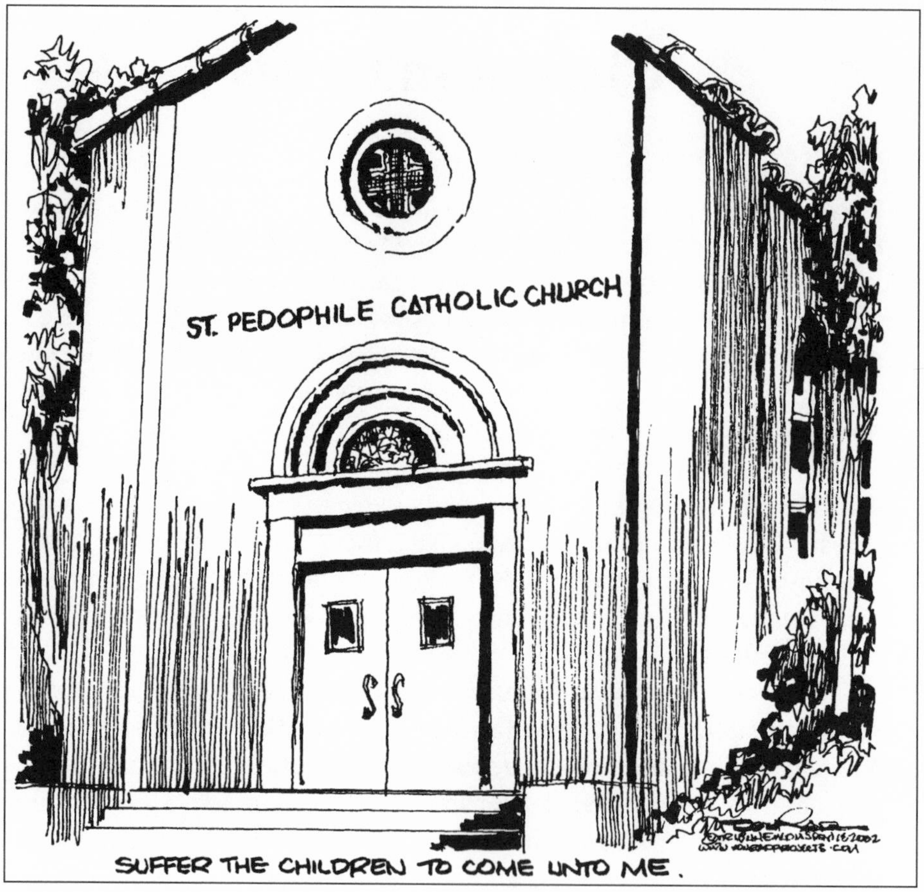
ST. PEDOPHILE CATHOLIC CHURCH
SUFFER THE CHILDREN TO COME UNTO ME.

ROBERT ARIAIL
Courtesy The State (S.C.)

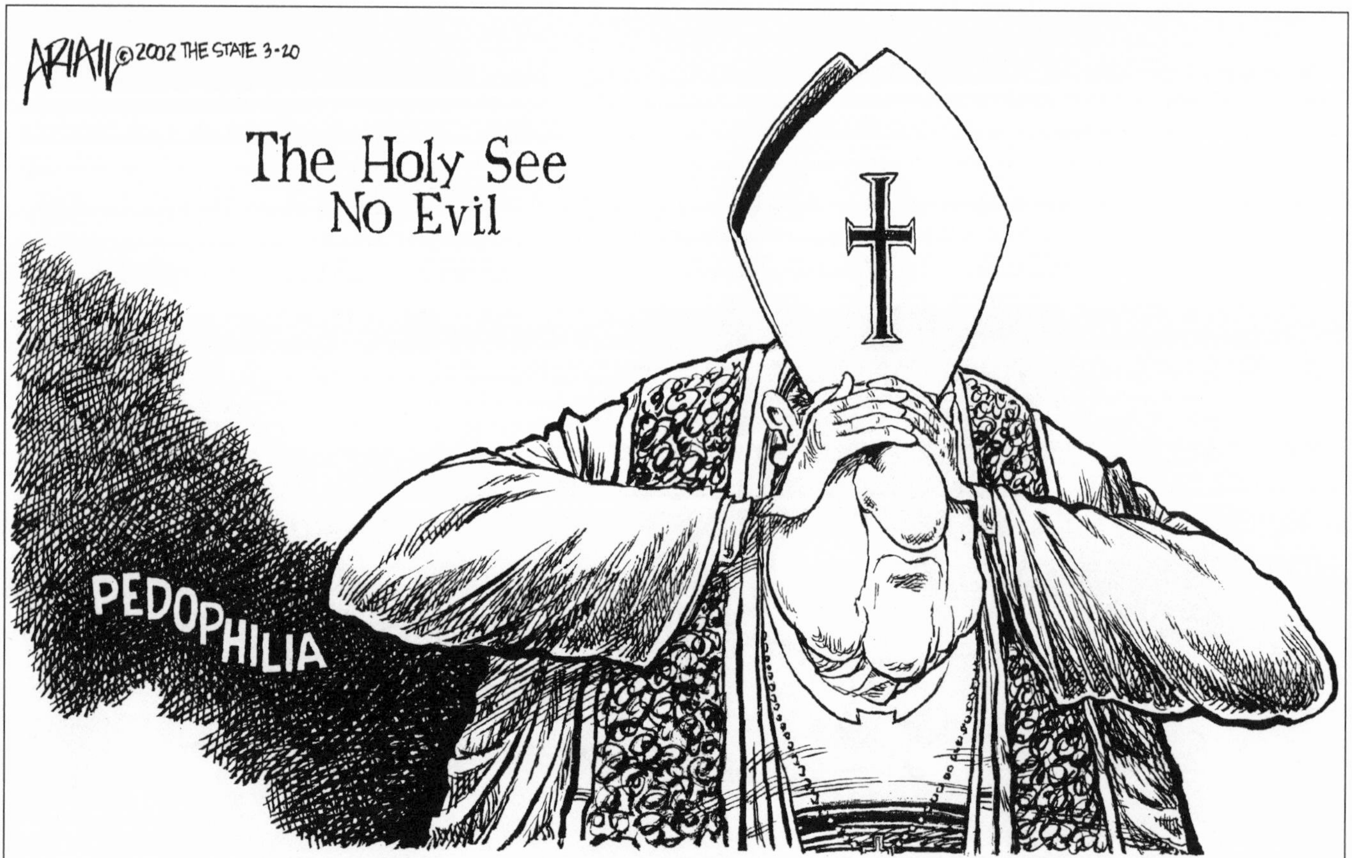
ARIAIL ©2002 THE STATE 3-20
The Holy See
No Evil
PEDOPHILIA

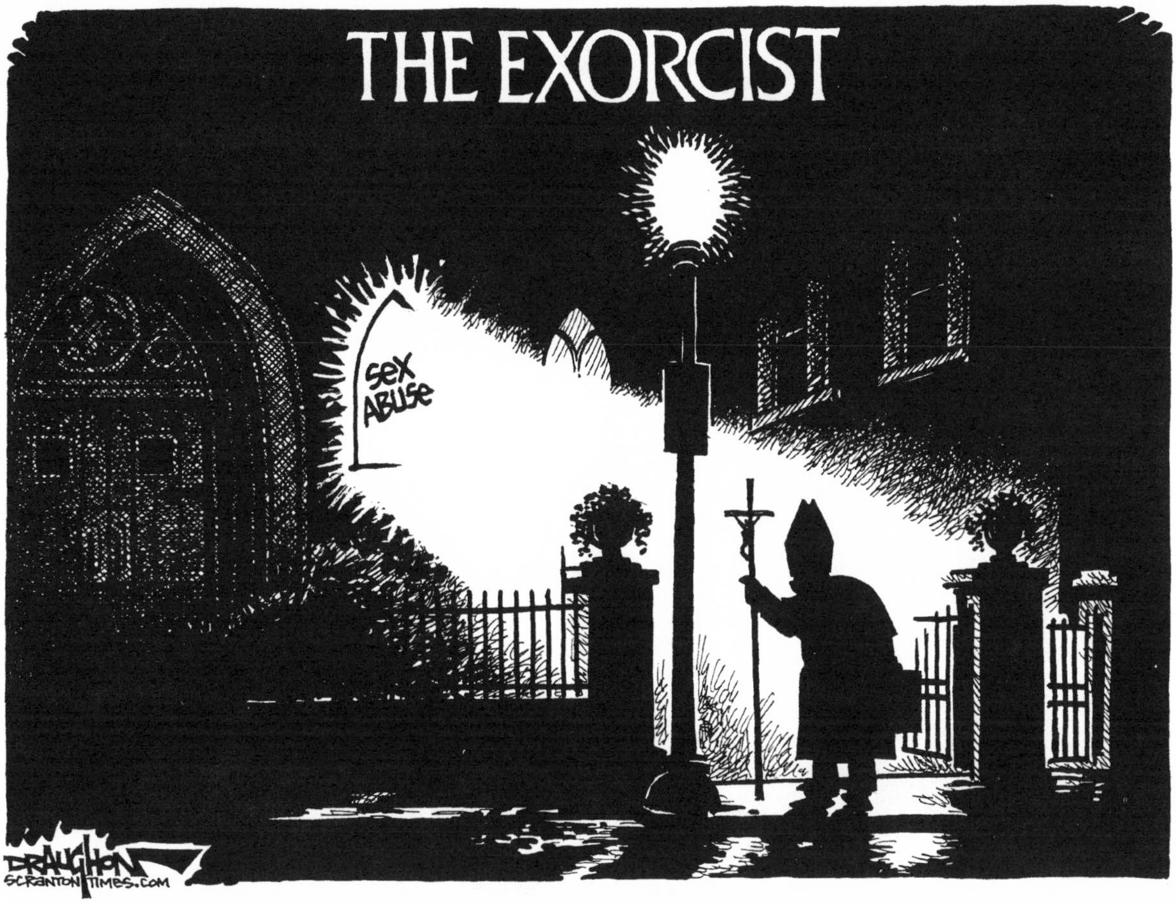
THE EXORCIST
SEX ABUSE
DRAUGHON
SCRANTONTIMES.COM

DENNIS DRAUGHON
Courtesy Scranton Times

MICHAEL RAMIREZ
Courtesy Los Angeles Times

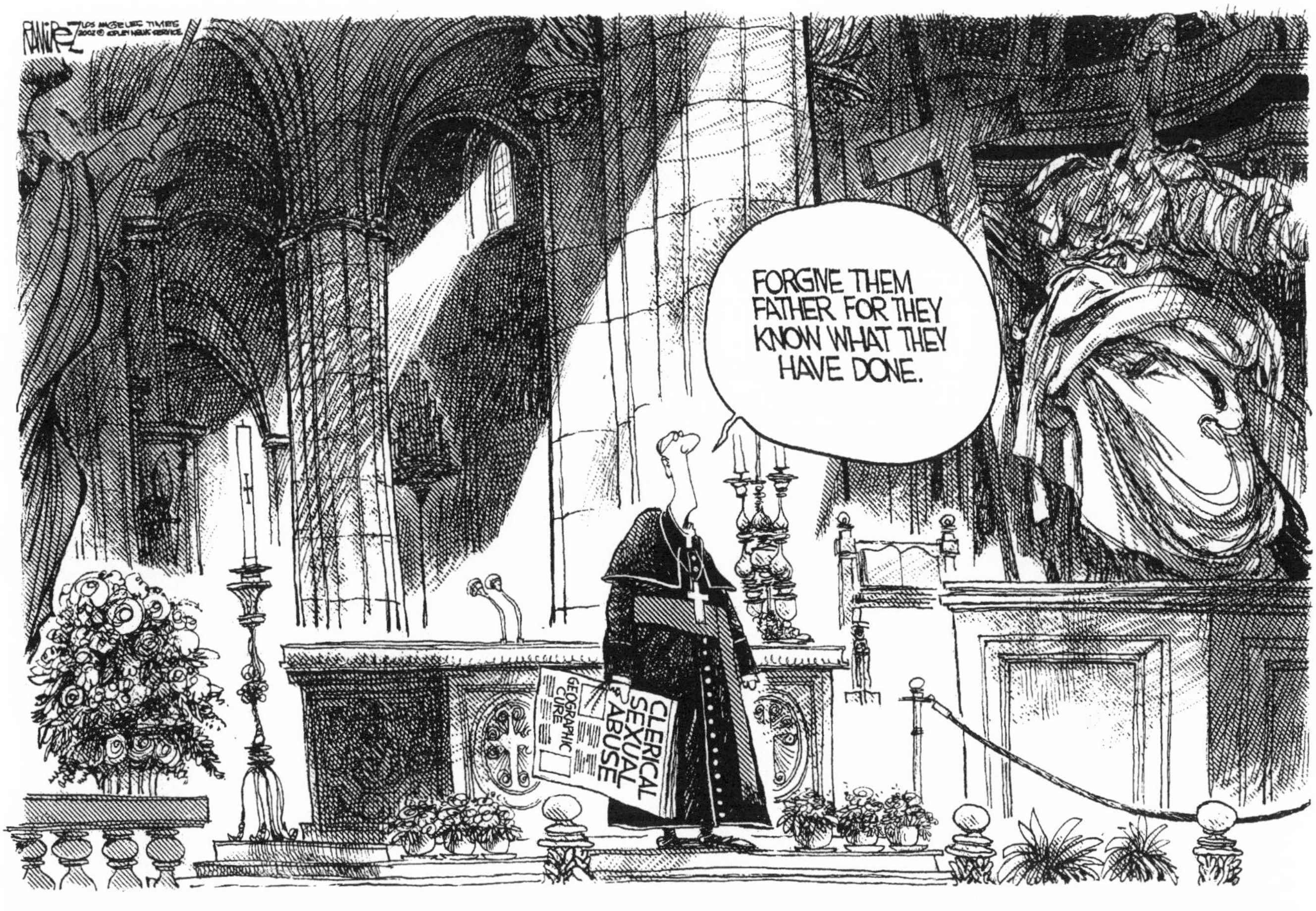
FORGIVE THEM FATHER FOR THEY KNOW WHAT THEY HAVE DONE.
CLERICAL SEXUAL ABUSE

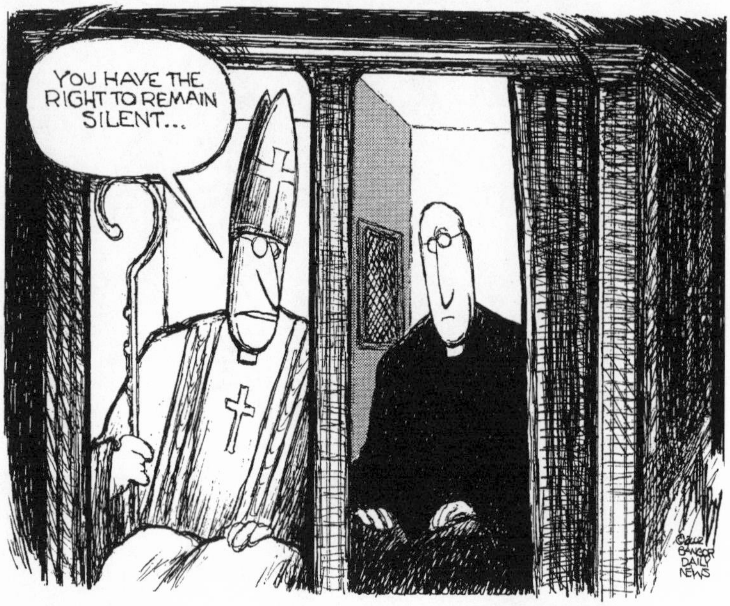
YOU HAVE THE RIGHT TO REMAIN SILENT...

GEORGE DANBY
Courtesy Bangor Daily News

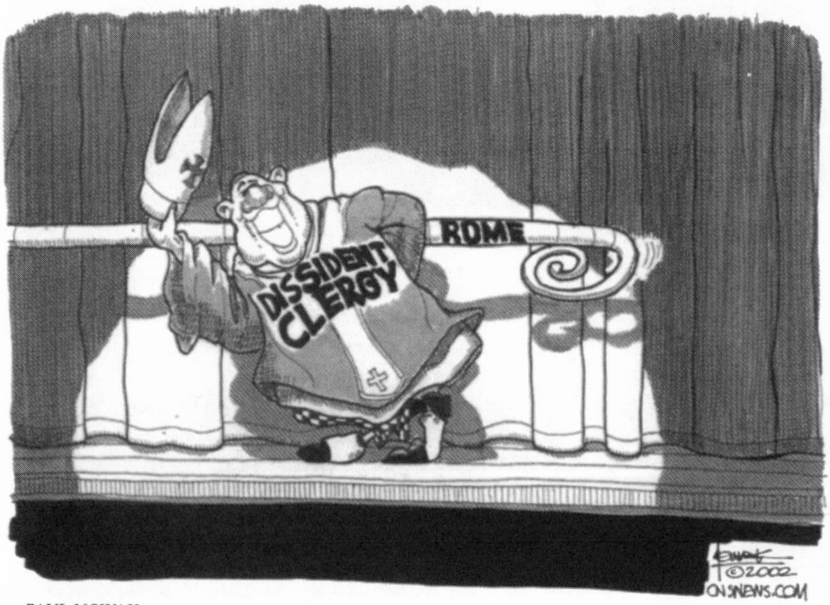
ROME
DISSIDENT CLERGY
©2002
CNSNEWS.COM

PAUL NOWAK
Courtesy Scripps-Howard News Service

J. R. ROSE
Courtesy Byrd Newspapers

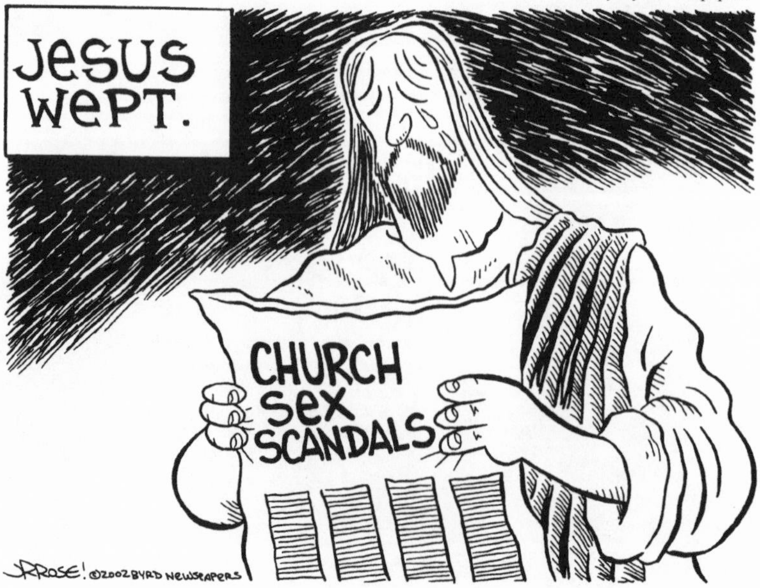
JESUS WEPT.
CHURCH SEX SCANDALS
©2002 BYRD NEWSPAPERS

ED COLLEY
Courtesy Boston Globe South

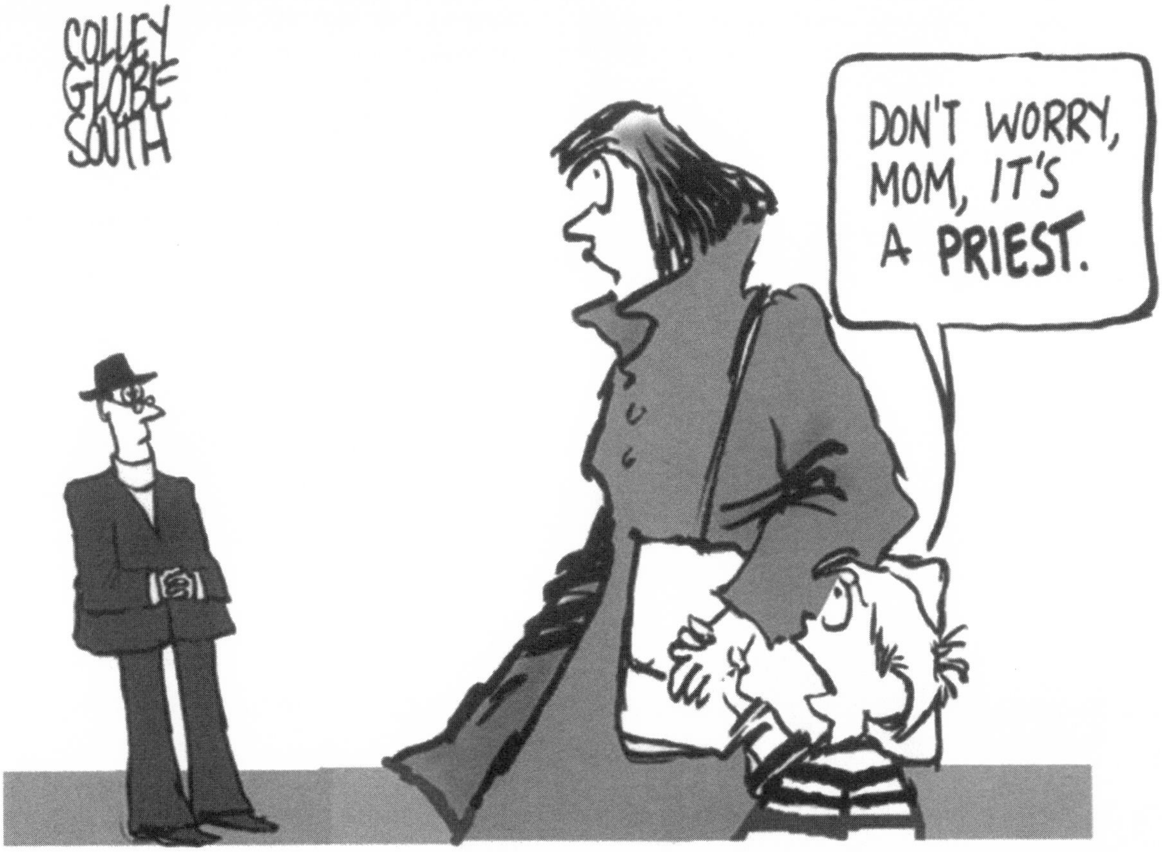
COLLEY GLOBE SOUTH
DON'T WORRY, MOM, IT'S A PRIEST.

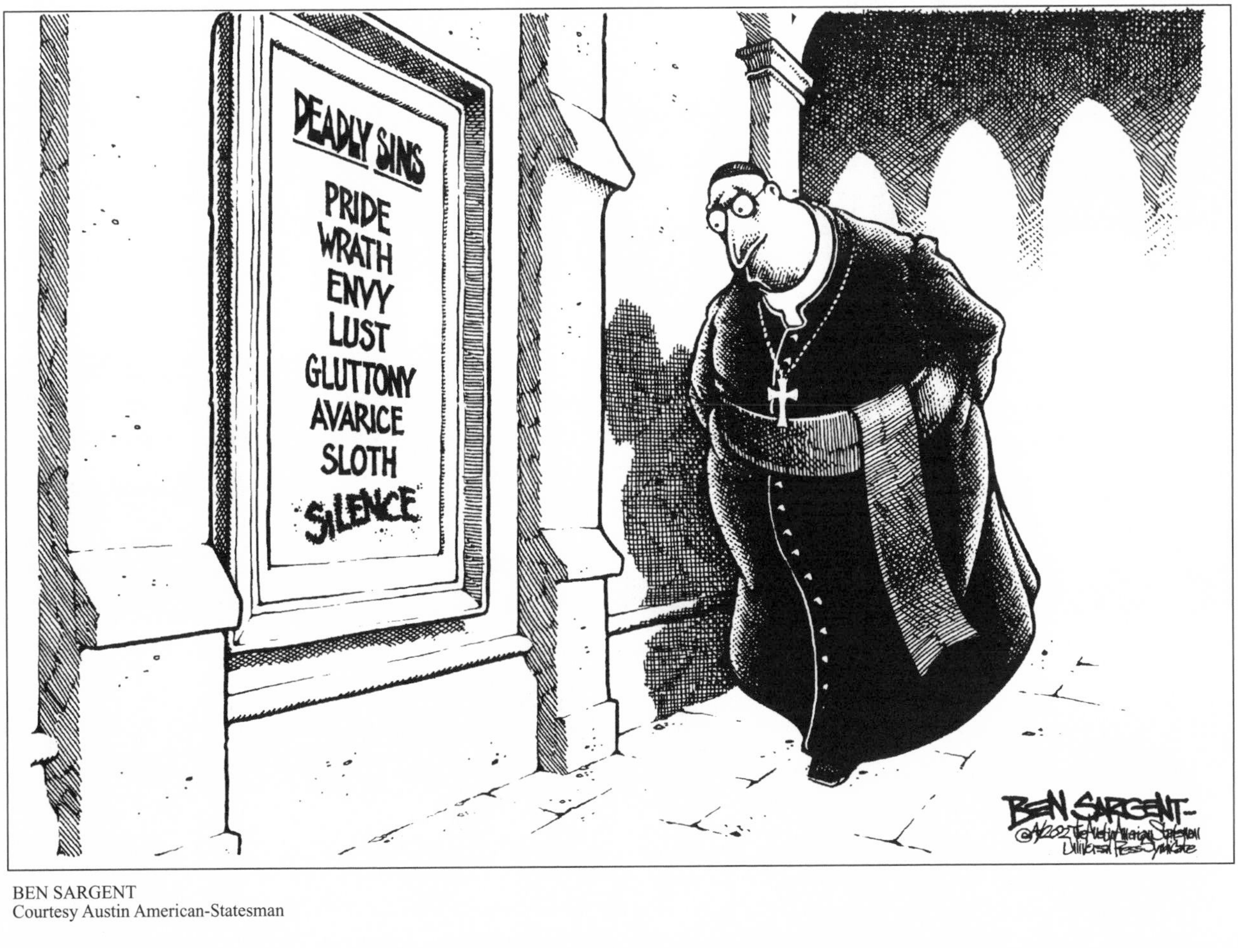
DEADLY SINS
PRIDE
WRATH
ENVY
LUST
GLUTTONY
AVARICE
SLOTH
SILENCE
BEN SARGENT

BEN SARGENT
Courtesy Austin American-Statesman

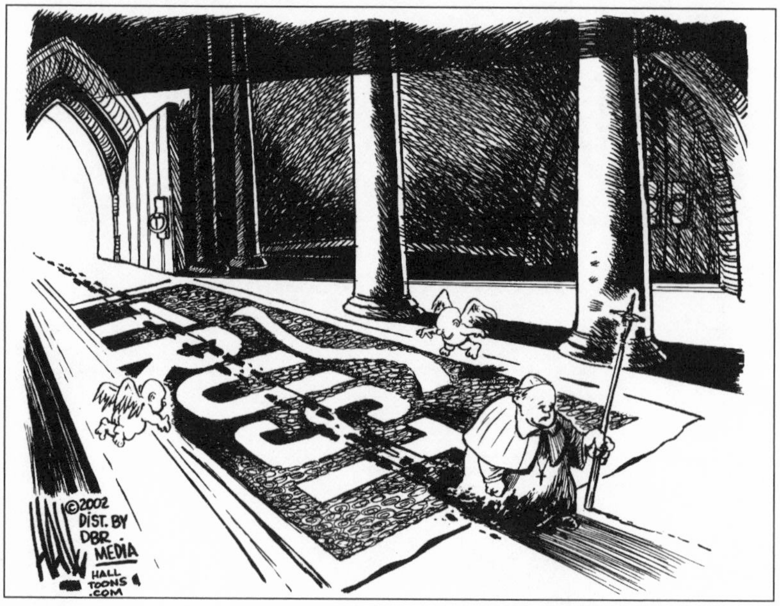
TRUST
HALL
©2002 DIST. BY DBR MEDIA
HALL TOONS .COM

ED HALL
Courtesy Baker County Press (Fla.)

JIM BORGMAN
Courtesy Cincinnati Enquirer

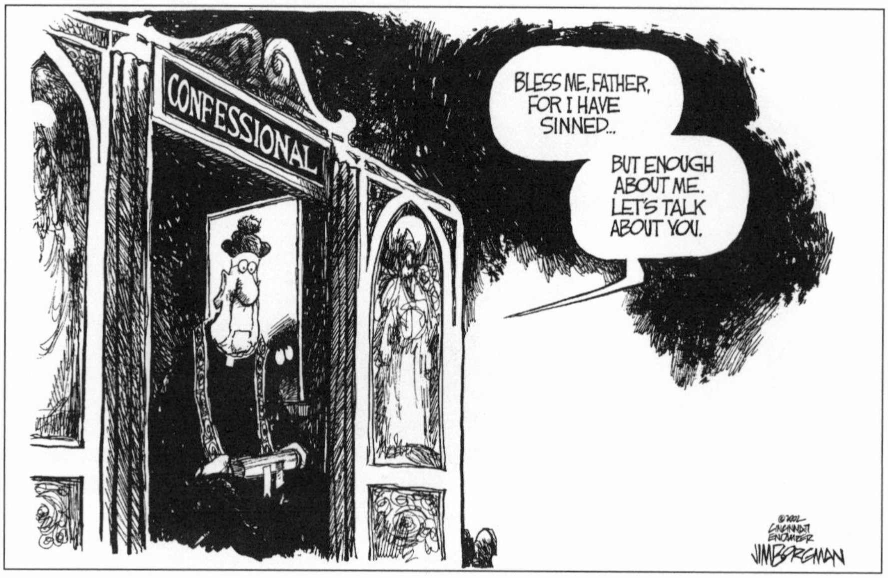
CONFESSIONAL
BLESS ME, FATHER, FOR I HAVE SINNED...
BUT ENOUGH ABOUT ME. LET'S TALK ABOUT YOU.
JIMBORGMAN

WALT HANDELSMAN
Courtesy Newsday

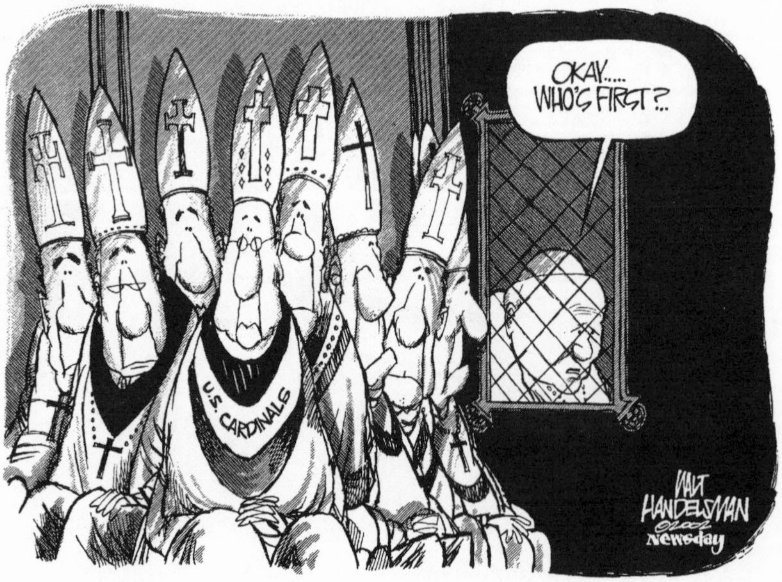
OKAY..... WHO'S FIRST?..
U.S. CARDINALS
WALT HANDELSMAN ©2002 Newsday

BOB GORRELL
Courtesy America Online News

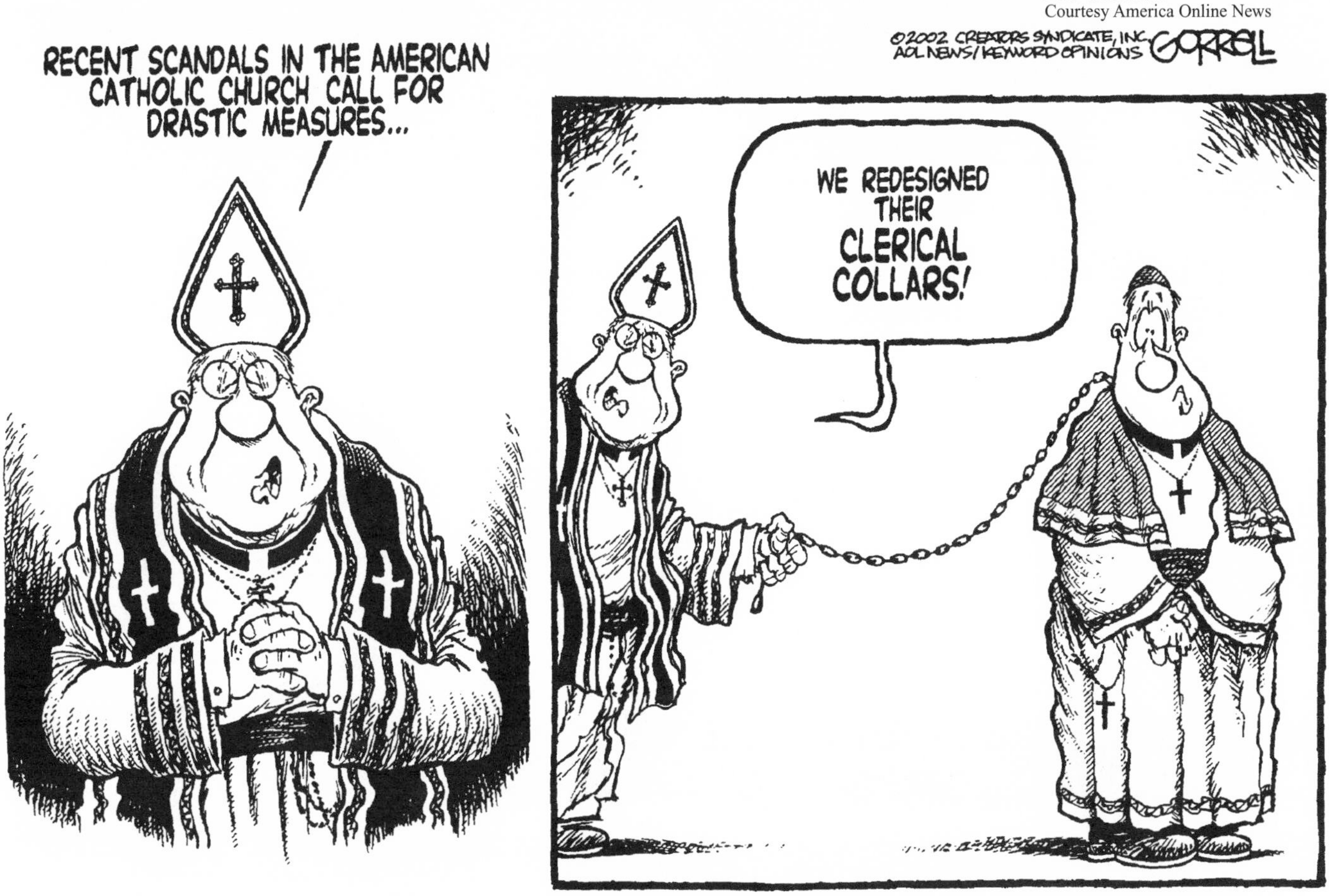
©2002 CREATORS SYNDICATE, INC.
AOL NEWS/KEYWORD OPINIONS
GORRELL
RECENT SCANDALS IN THE AMERICAN CATHOLIC CHURCH CALL FOR DRASTIC MEASURES...
WE REDESIGNED THEIR CLERICAL COLLARS!

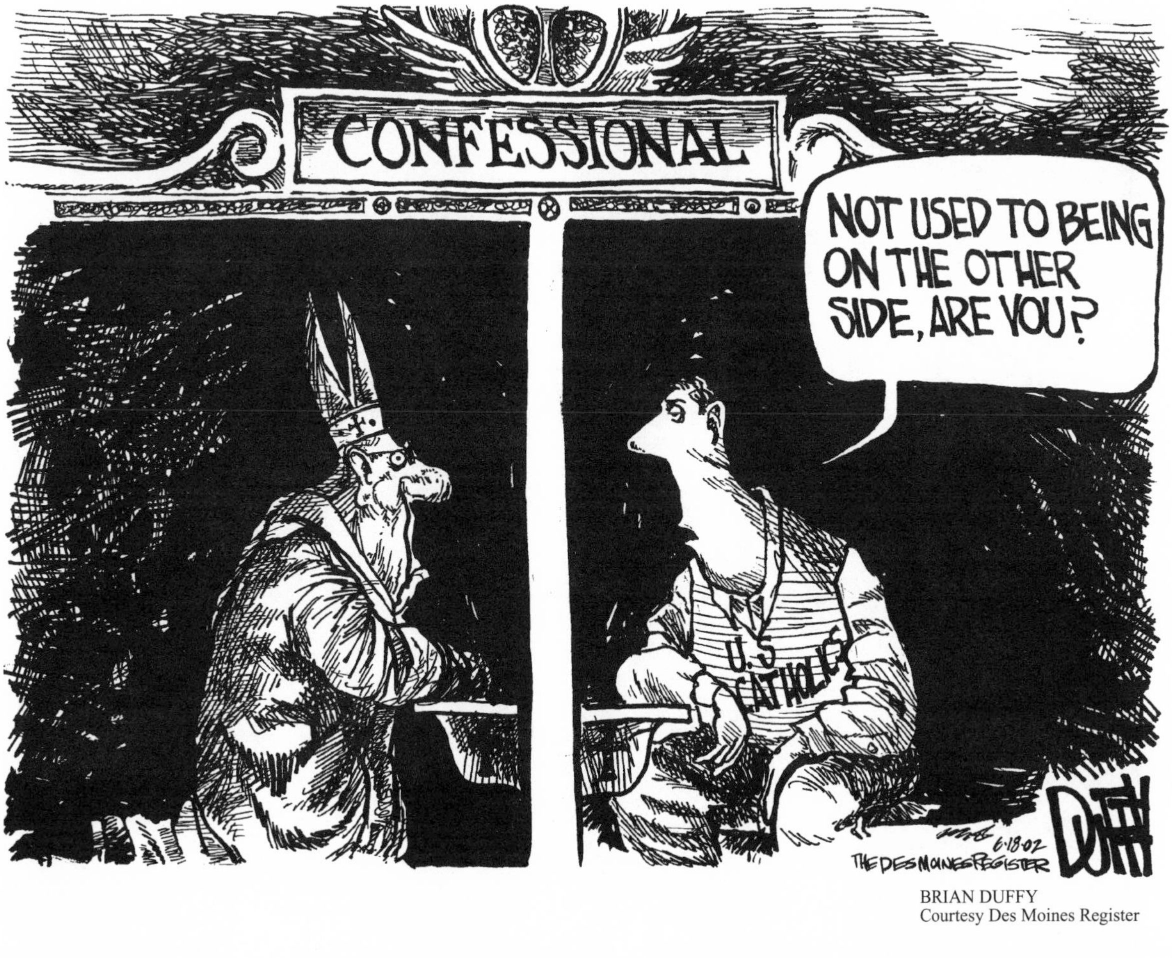
CONFESSIONAL
NOT USED TO BEING ON THE OTHER SIDE, ARE YOU?
U.S. CATHOLIC
6-18-02
THE DES MOINES REGISTER
DUFFY

BRIAN DUFFY
Courtesy Des Moines Register

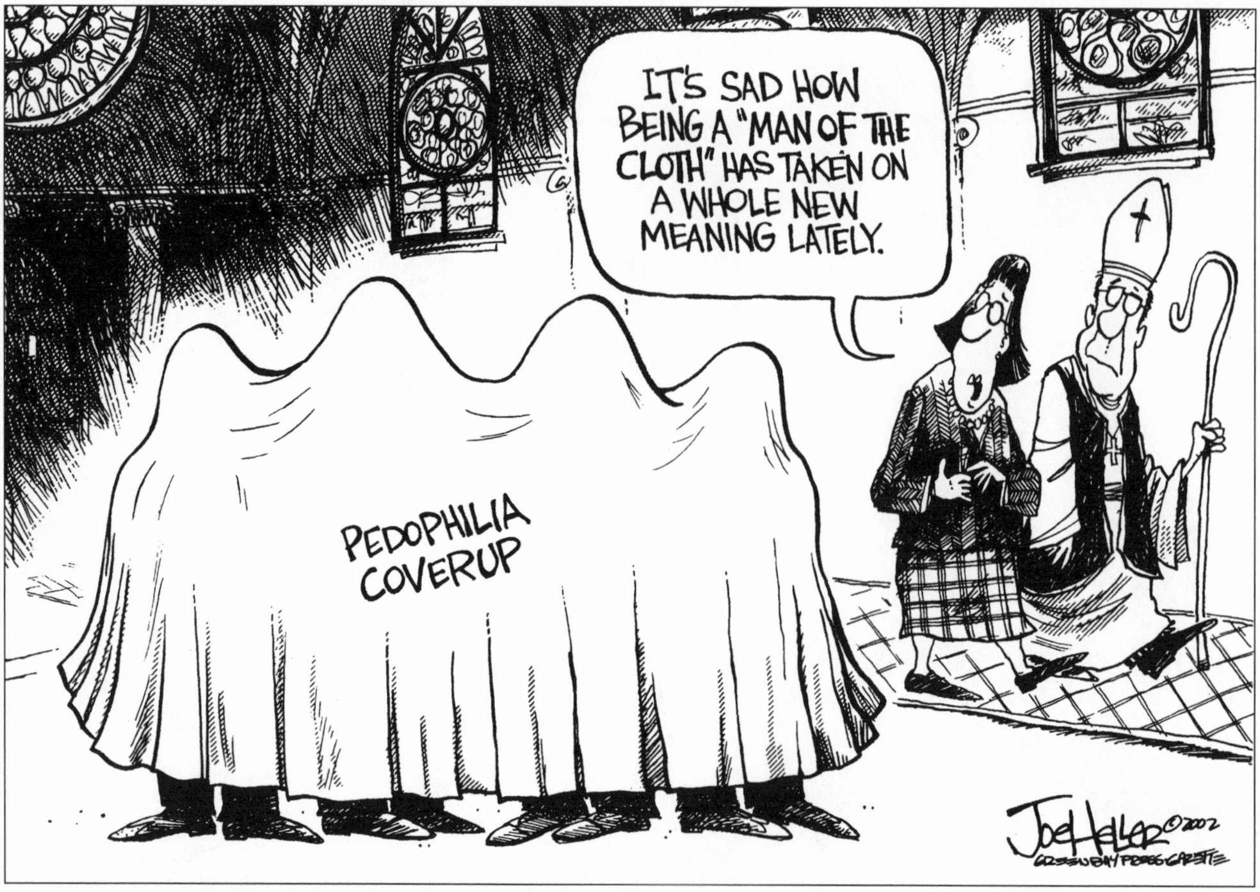
IT'S SAD HOW BEING A "MAN OF THE CLOTH" HAS TAKEN ON A WHOLE NEW MEANING LATELY.
PEDOPHILIA COVERUP
JOE HELLER ©2002 GREEN BAY PRESS-GAZETTE

JOE HELLER
Courtesy Green Bay Press-Gazette

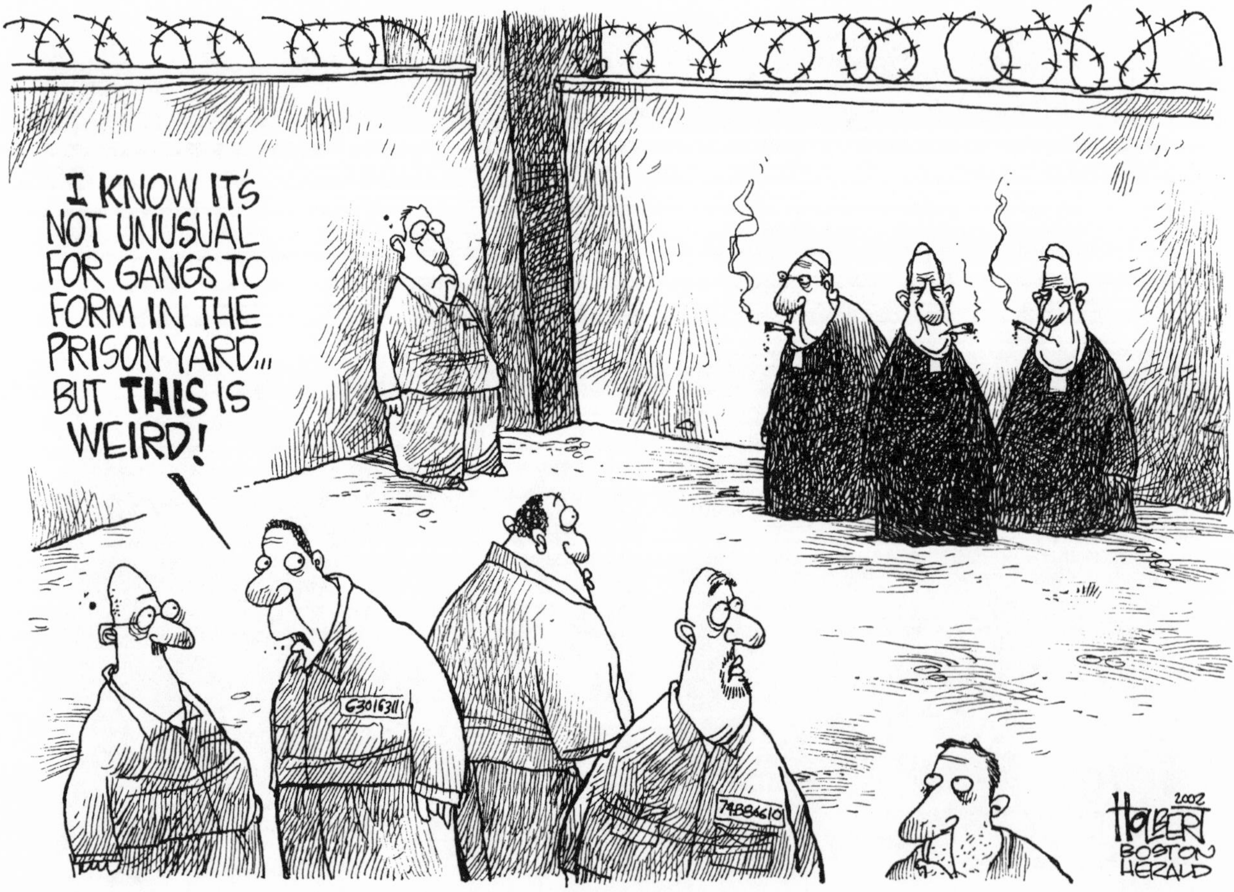
I KNOW IT'S NOT UNUSUAL FOR GANGS TO FORM IN THE PRISON YARD... BUT **THIS** IS WEIRD!
63016311
79886610
2002 HOLBERT BOSTON HERALD

JERRY HOLBERT
Courtesy Boston Herald

Media / Entertainment

Islamic militants kidnapped and murdered *Wall Street Journal* reporter Danny Pearl in Pakistan in March. A group of conspirators carefully set a death trap for Pearl and then lured him into it with deceit and lies. Then he was brutally killed. The 38-year-old Pearl disappeared in January while covering a story in Pakistan.

Hollywood's two top acting awards during the year went to black performers. Denzel Washington won the best actor Oscar for his work in *Training Day.* Halle Berry captured best actress honors for *Monster's Ball.* Berry was the first black female to be named best actress in the Oscars' 74-year history.

The general public concluded that the media was guilty of excessive coverage of the Washington, D.C.-area sniper case. Television and newspapers advised people to stay off the streets and to guard their children enroute to school—or even to keep them home altogether. It was a genuine feeding frenzy until arrests were made. Polls show that Americans believe the media seeks out the negative—not the positive—in society. Decency in broadcasting received another black eye when one program staged a sexual act in St. Patrick's Cathedral while a reporter broadcast the event live on radio.

SELECTIVE JOURNALISM
HALL
©2002 BAKER COUNTY PRESS
HALLTOONS.COM

ED HALL
Courtesy Baker County Press (Fla.)

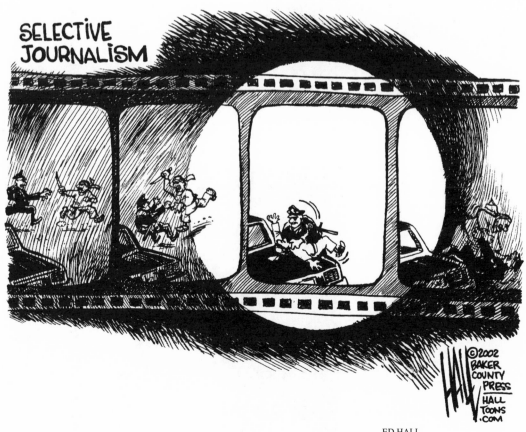

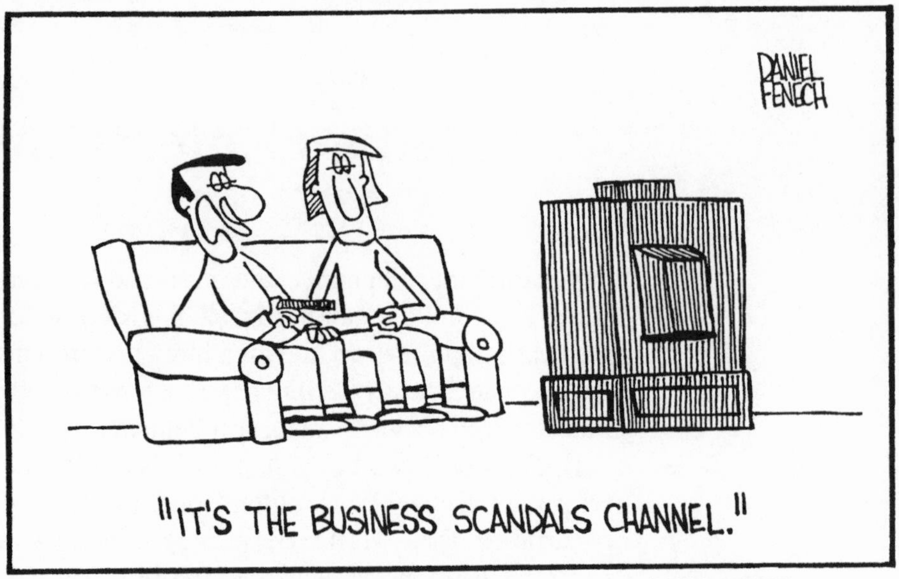
DANIEL FENECH
"IT'S THE BUSINESS SCANDALS CHANNEL."

DANIEL FENECH
Courtesy Saline Reporter (Mich.)

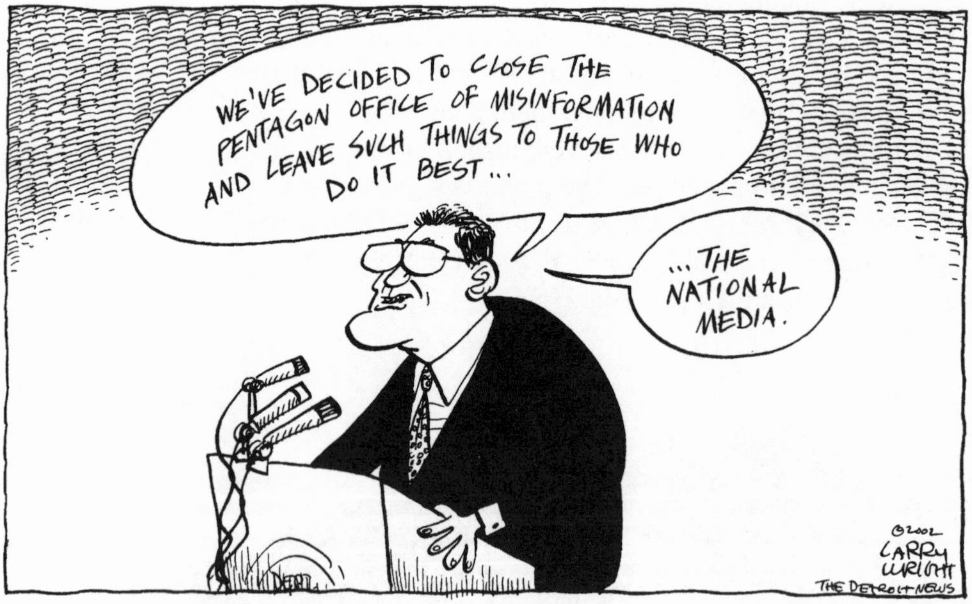
WE'VE DECIDED TO CLOSE THE PENTAGON OFFICE OF MISINFORMATION AND LEAVE SUCH THINGS TO THOSE WHO DO IT BEST...
...THE NATIONAL MEDIA.
©2002 LARRY WRIGHT THE DETROIT NEWS

LARRY WRIGHT
Courtesy Detroit News

JIMMY MARGULIES
Courtesy The Record (N.J.)

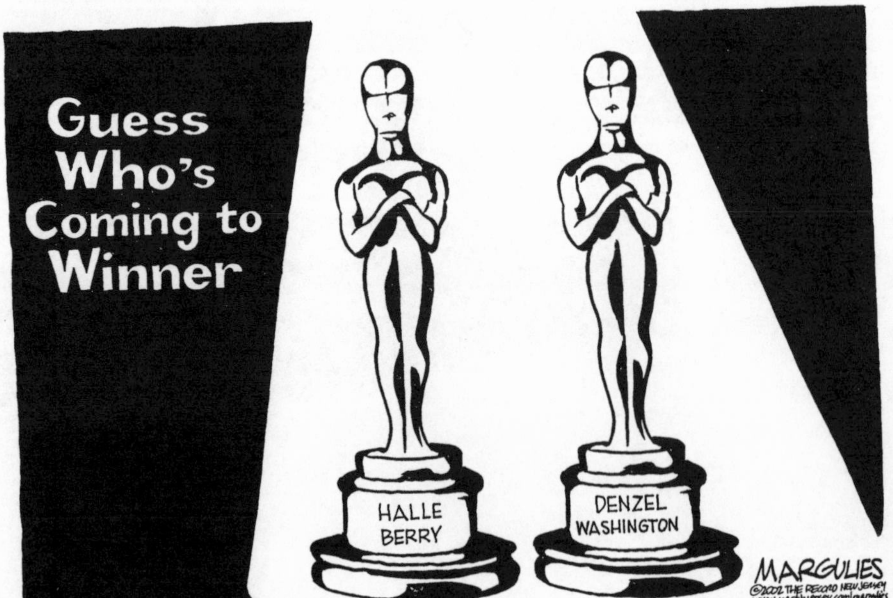
Guess Who's Coming to Winner
HALLE BERRY
DENZEL WASHINGTON
MARGULIES

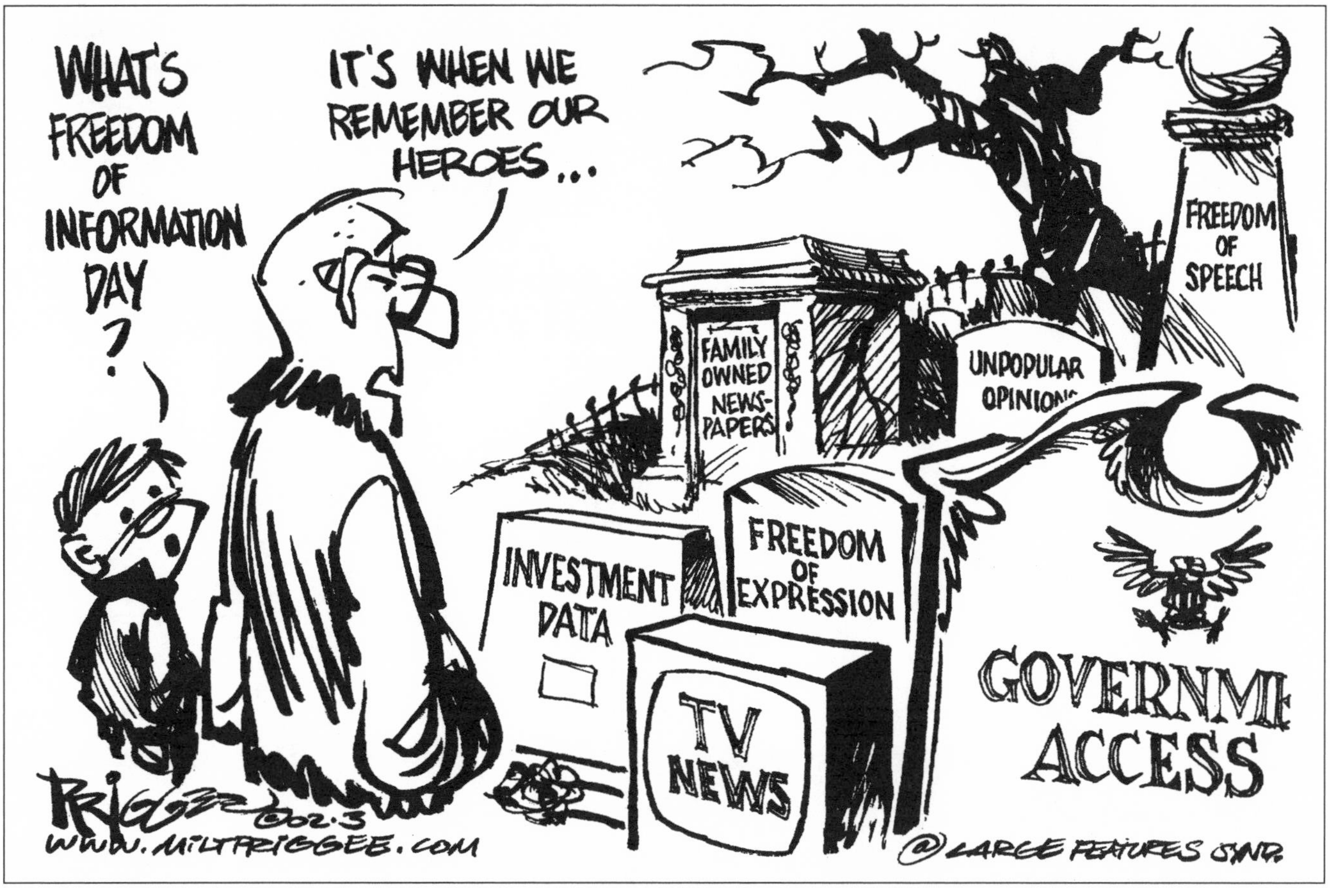
WHAT'S FREEDOM OF INFORMATION DAY ?
IT'S WHEN WE REMEMBER OUR HEROES...
FAMILY OWNED NEWS-PAPERS
UNPOPULAR OPINIONS
FREEDOM OF SPEECH
INVESTMENT DATA
FREEDOM OF EXPRESSION
TV NEWS
GOVERNME ACCESS
PRIGGEE ©02.3
WWW.MILTPRIGGEE.COM
@ LARGE FEATURES SYND.

MILT PRIGGEE
Courtesy miltpriggee.com

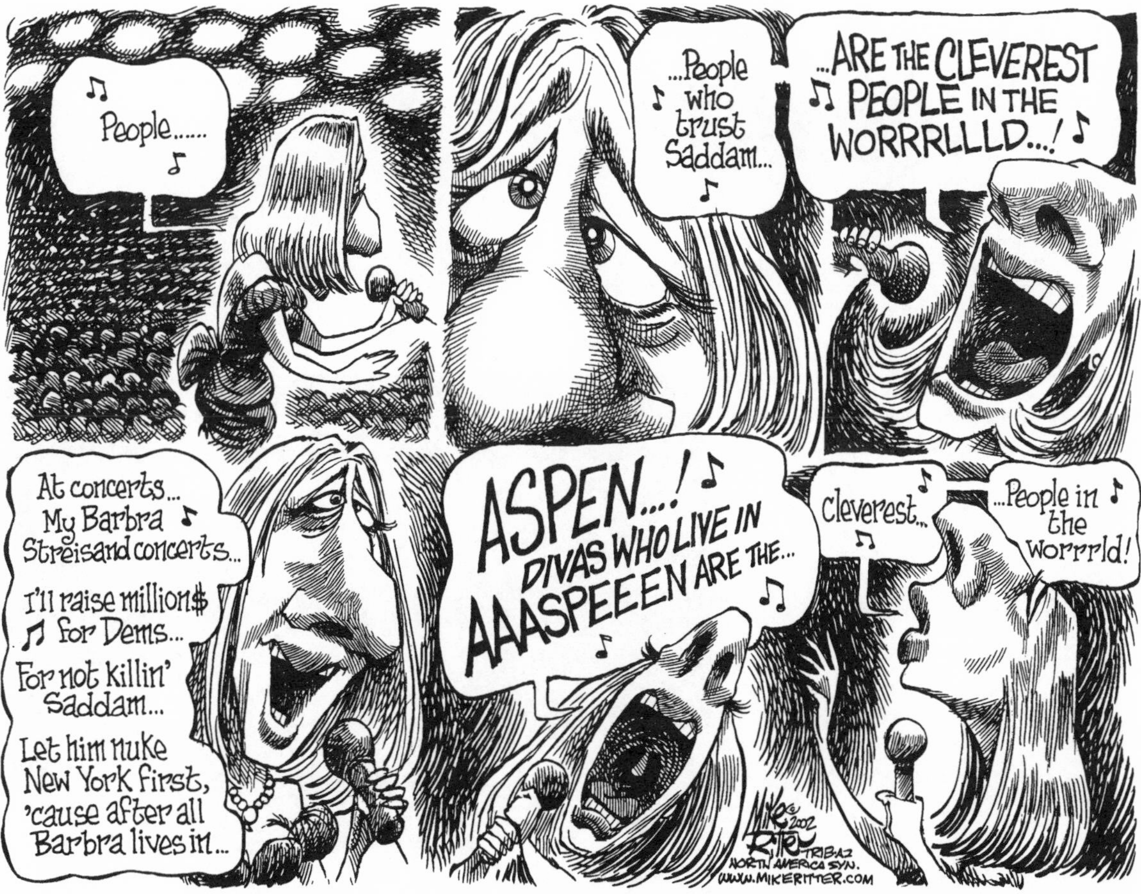
People......
...People who trust Saddam...
...ARE THE CLEVEREST PEOPLE IN THE WORRRLLLD...!
At concerts... My Barbra Streisand concerts...
I'll raise million$ for Dems...
For not killin' Saddam...
Let him nuke New York first, 'cause after all Barbra lives in...
ASPEN...!
DIVAS WHO LIVE IN AAASPEEEN ARE THE...
Cleverest...
...People in the worrrld!
MIKE RITTER ©2002 TRIB-AZ NORTH AMERICA SYN.
WWW.MIKERITTER.COM

MIKE RITTER
Courtesy Tribune Newspapers

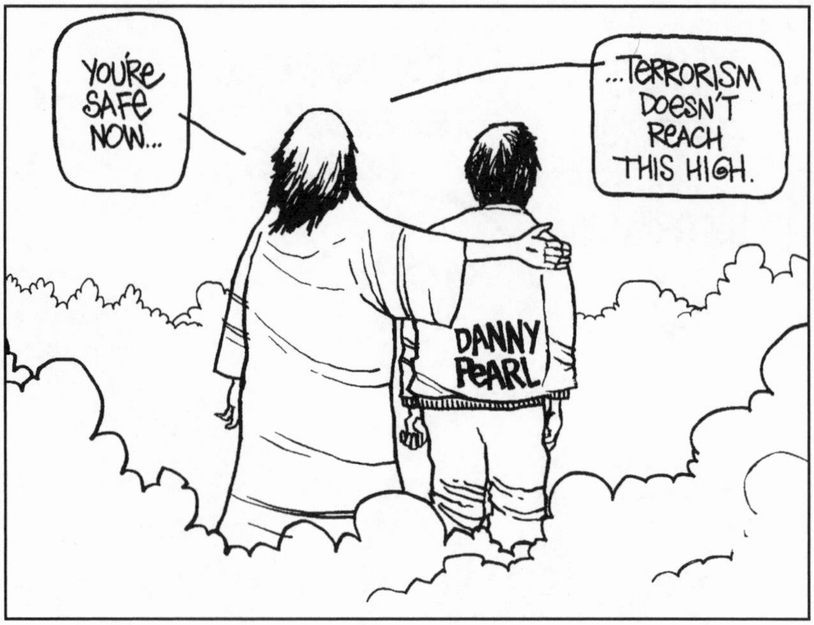

YOU'RE SAFE NOW...
...TERRORISM DOESN'T REACH THIS HIGH.
DANNY PEARL

DAVID REDDICK
Courtesy The Herald Bulletin (Ind.)

BILL MANGOLD
Courtesy Heritage Newspapers

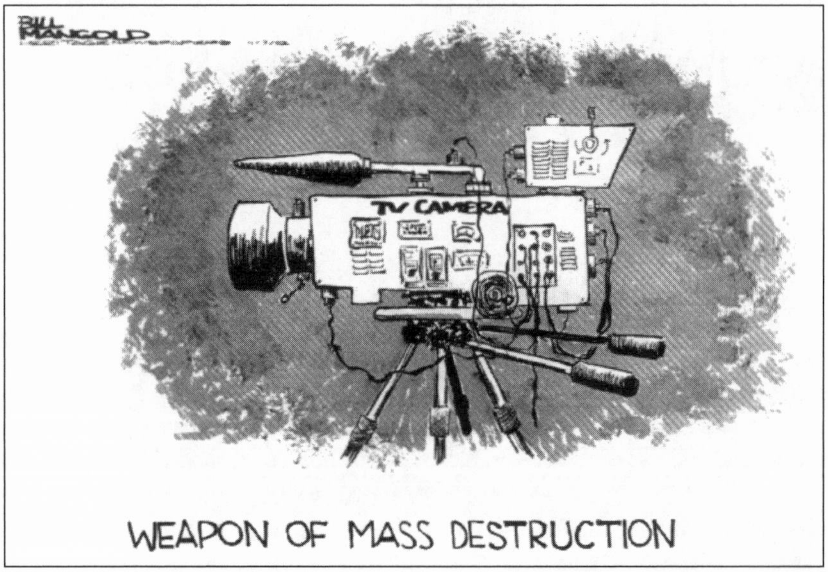

BILL MANGOLD
TV CAMERA
WEAPON OF MASS DESTRUCTION

BRUCE PLANTE
Courtesy Chattanooga Times

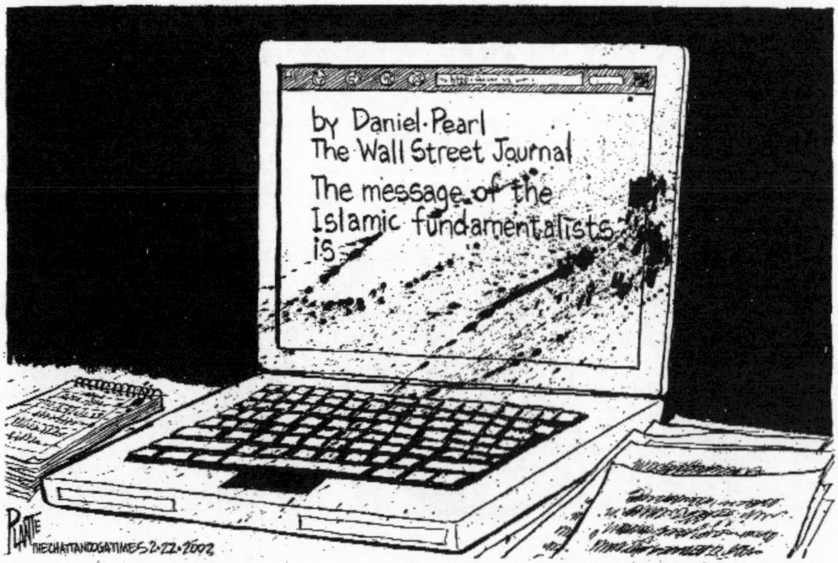

by Daniel·Pearl
The Wall Street Journal
The message of the
Islamic fundamentalists
is
PLANTE
THECHATTANOOGATIMES 2·22·2002

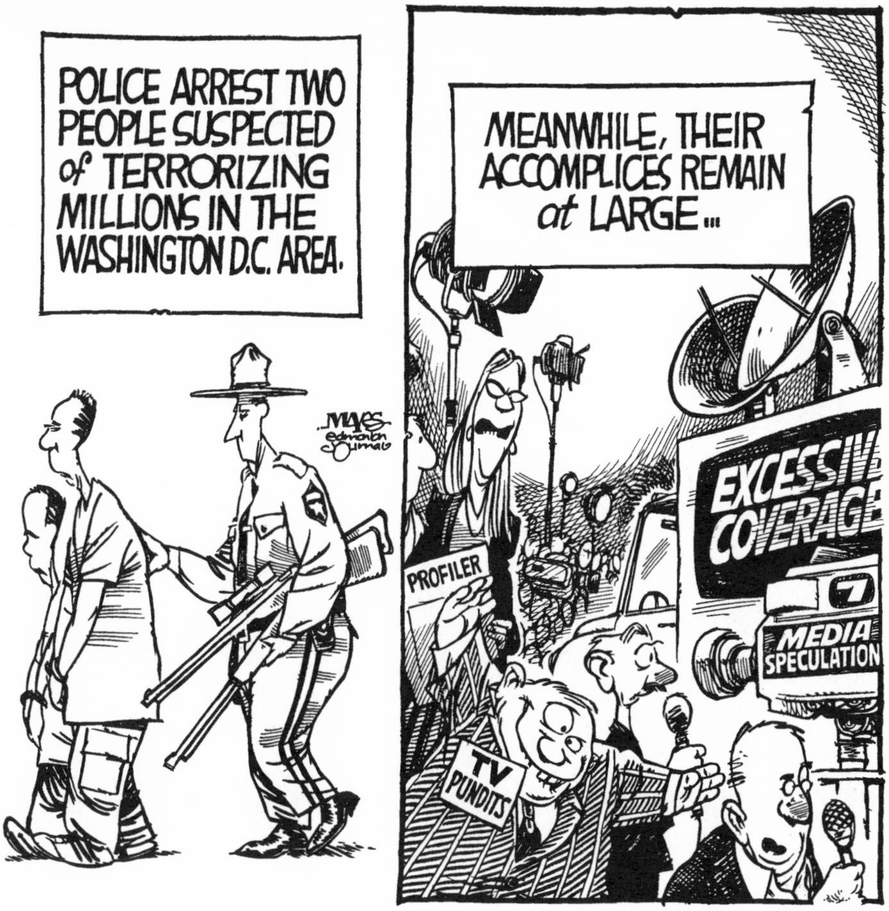
POLICE ARREST TWO PEOPLE SUSPECTED of TERRORIZING MILLIONS IN THE WASHINGTON D.C. AREA.
MEANWHILE, THEIR ACCOMPLICES REMAIN at LARGE...
MAYES
PROFILER
TV PUNDITS
EXCESSIV
COVERAGE
7
MEDIA SPECULATION

MALCOLM MAYES
Courtesy Edmonton Journal

MICHAEL OSBUN
Courtesy Citrus City Chronicle (Fla.)

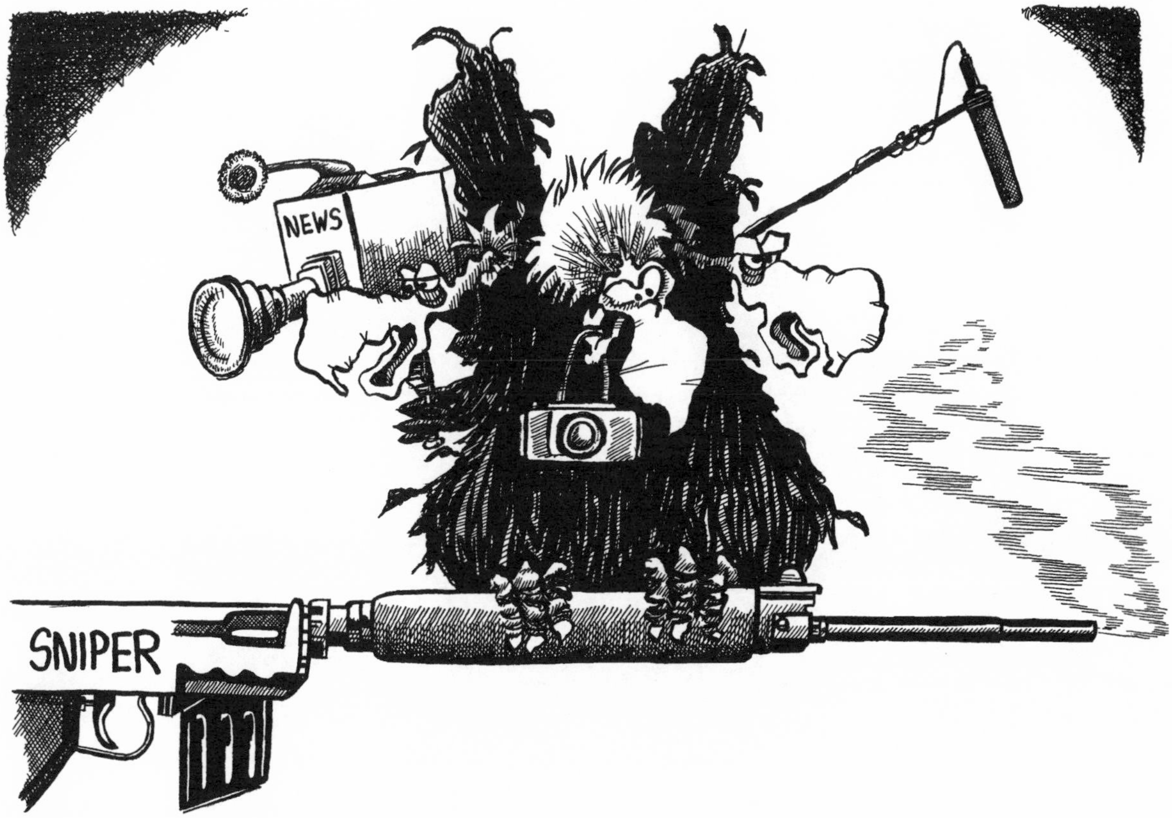
NEWS
SNIPER

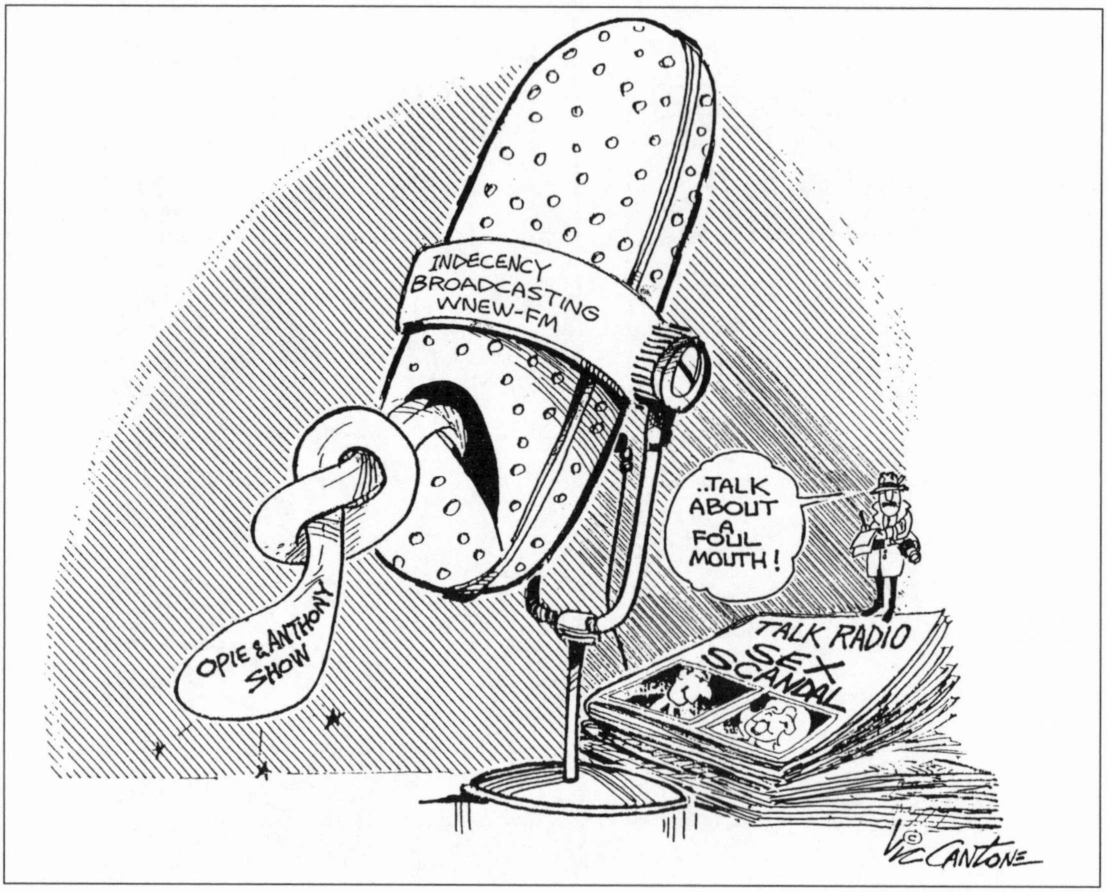
INDECENCY
BROADCASTING
WNEW-FM
OPIE & ANTHONY
SHOW
..TALK
ABOUT
A
FOUL
MOUTH!
TALK RADIO
SEX
SCANDAL
VIC CANTONE

VIC CANTONE
Courtesy Artist Market.com Syndicate

ADENLE ADEWALE
Courtesy This Day Newspapers (Nigeria)

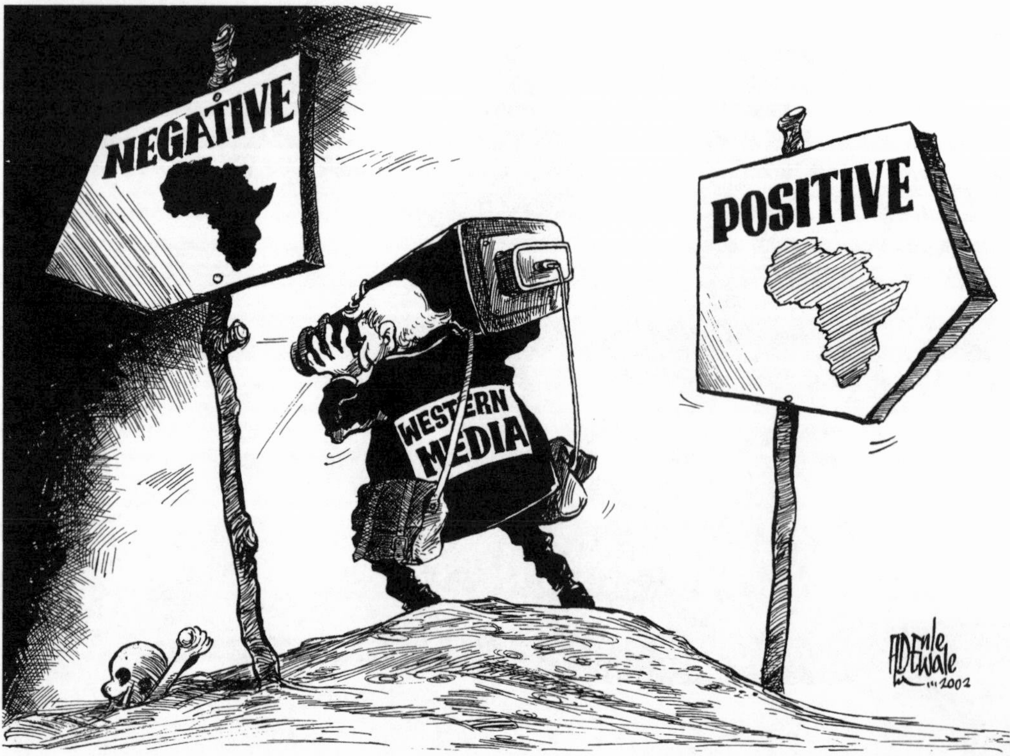
NEGATIVE
POSITIVE
WESTERN
MEDIA
ADEWALE
2002

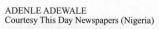

Canada

Canadian Prime Minister Jean Chrétien announced in August that he would step down in 2004 instead of seeking a fourth consecutive term. Paul Martin, his longtime finance minister, is the top contender to succeed him. Chrétien met with the ailing 82-year-old Pope John Paul II on the latter's visit to Canada and also called upon George Bush in Washington. The U.S. had placed tariffs on steel, lumber, and textiles that Canadians felt were too high. Debate renewed over a possible unified currency with the U.S.

The Canadian government faces two major problems: low funding for the military and weak national security, the latter bringing increased complaints from the U.S.

Canada added 326,000 jobs in the first seven months of 2002 as many U.S. businesses took advantage of the weak Canadian dollar to add workers at their plants north of the border. Politicians were demanding new rules on ethics in government as the prime minister stood accused by some of being in the pockets of corporate donors. Canada's hockey team won the gold medal at the Olympics at Salt Lake City, and the nation mourned the death of the Queen Mother of England.

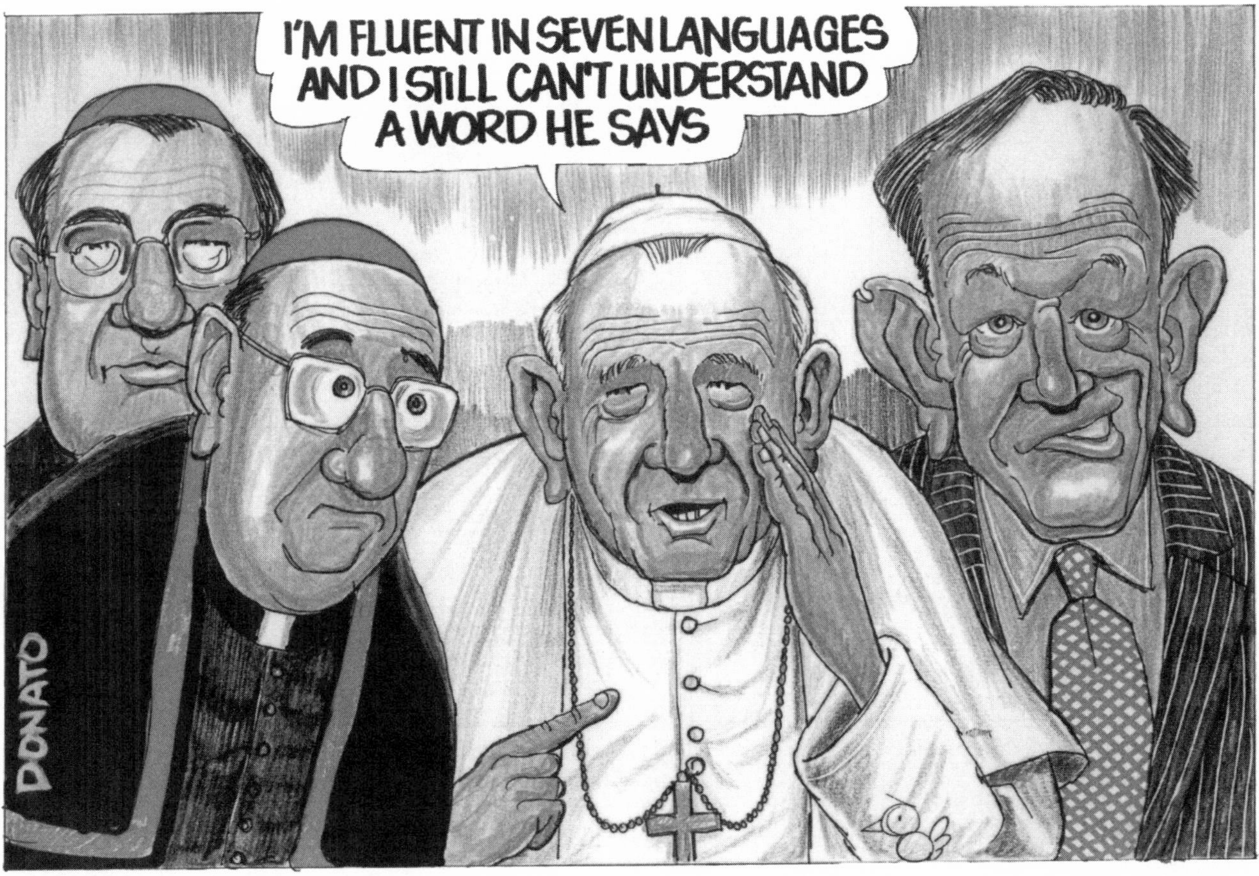
I'M FLUENT IN SEVEN LANGUAGES AND I STILL CAN'T UNDERSTAND A WORD HE SAYS
DONATO

ANDY DONATO
Courtesy Toronto Sun

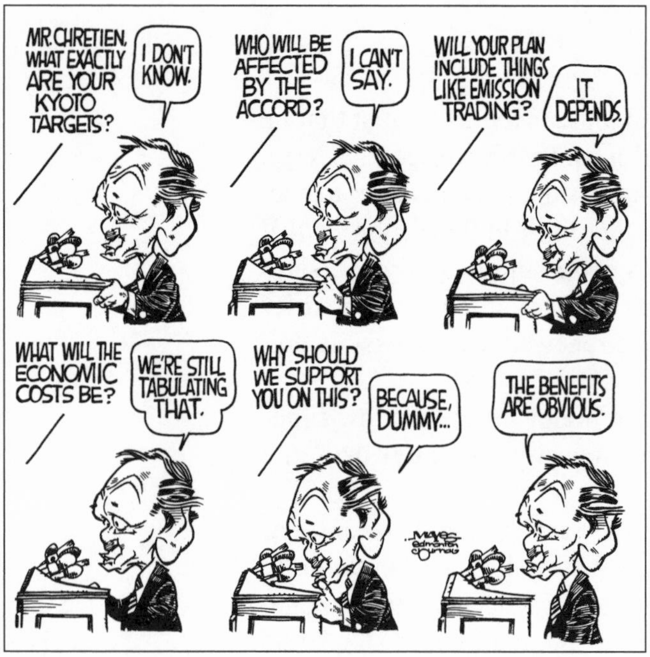
MR. CHRETIEN, WHAT EXACTLY ARE YOUR KYOTO TARGETS?
I DON'T KNOW.
WHO WILL BE AFFECTED BY THE ACCORD?
I CAN'T SAY.
WILL YOUR PLAN INCLUDE THINGS LIKE EMISSION TRADING?
IT DEPENDS.
WHAT WILL THE ECONOMIC COSTS BE?
WE'RE STILL TABULATING THAT.
WHY SHOULD WE SUPPORT YOU ON THIS?
BECAUSE, DUMMY...
THE BENEFITS ARE OBVIOUS.

MALCOLM MAYES
Courtesy Edmonton Journal

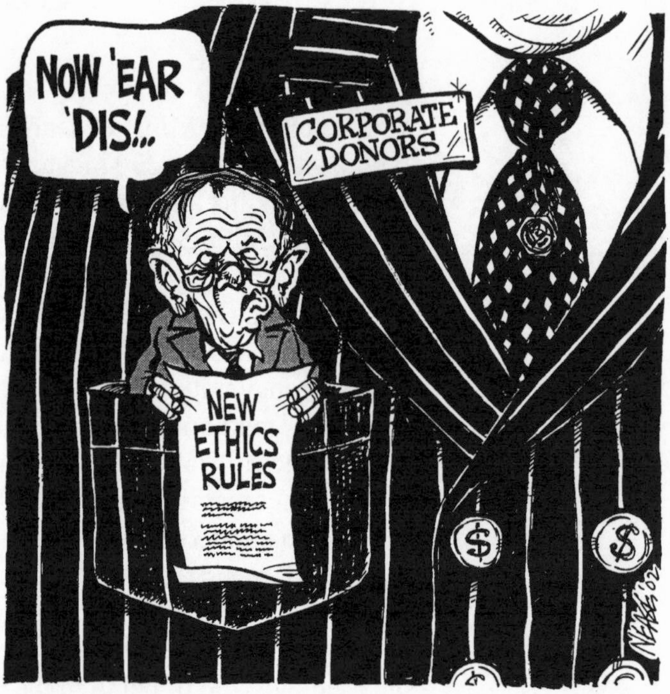
NOW 'EAR 'DIS!..
CORPORATE DONORS
NEW ETHICS RULES

STEVE NEASE
Courtesy Toronto Sun

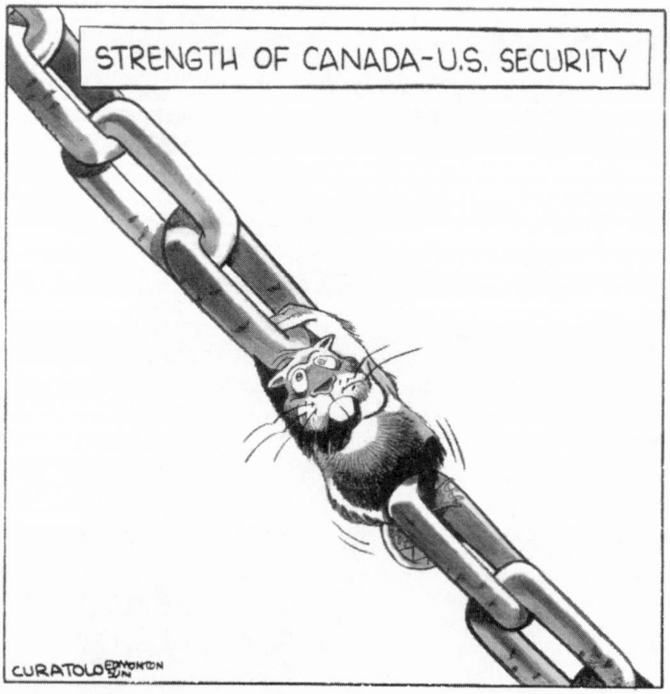
STRENGTH OF CANADA-U.S. SECURITY
CURATOLO

FRED CURATOLO
Courtesy Edmonton Sun

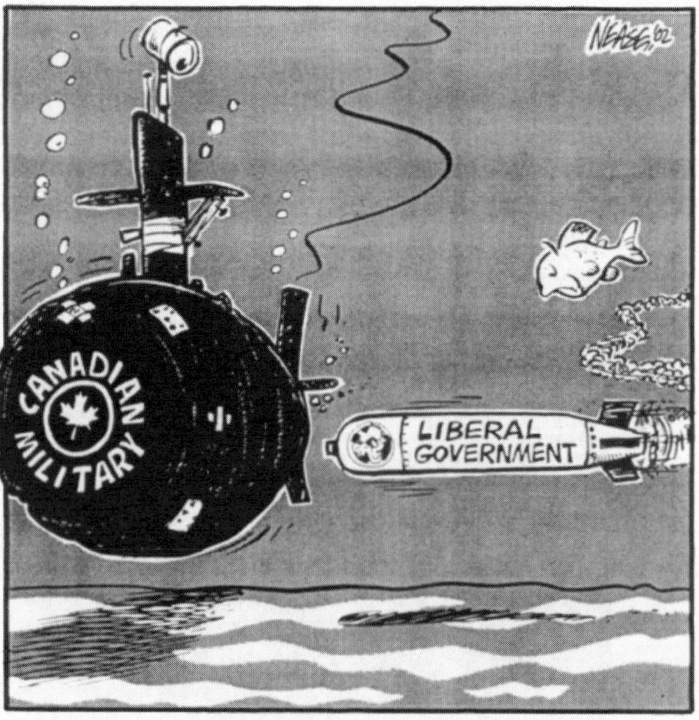
CANADIAN MILITARY
LIBERAL GOVERNMENT

STEVE NEASE
Courtesy St. John's Telegraph Journal

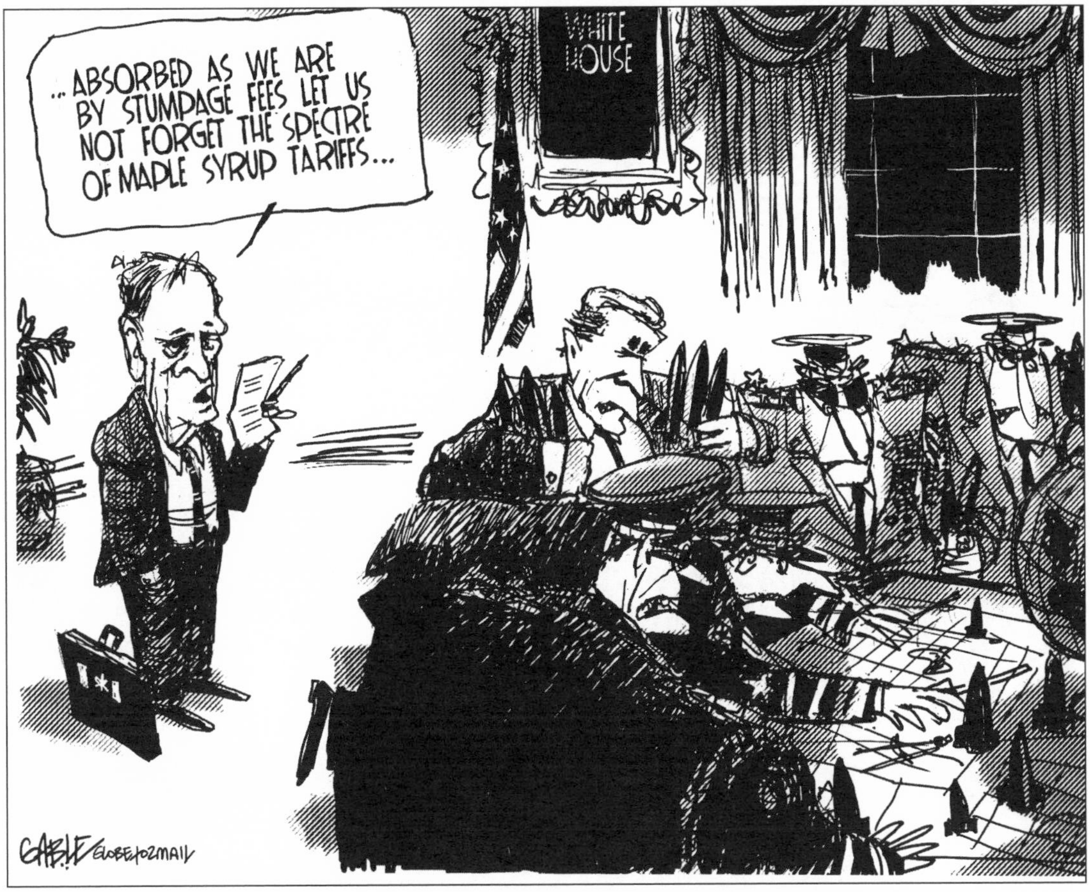
... ABSORBED AS WE ARE BY STUMPAGE FEES LET US NOT FORGET THE SPECTRE OF MAPLE SYRUP TARIFFS...
WHITE HOUSE
GABLE GLOBE&MAIL

BRIAN GABLE
Courtesy Globe and Mail (Canada)

GAREME MACKAY
Courtesy Hamilton Spectator

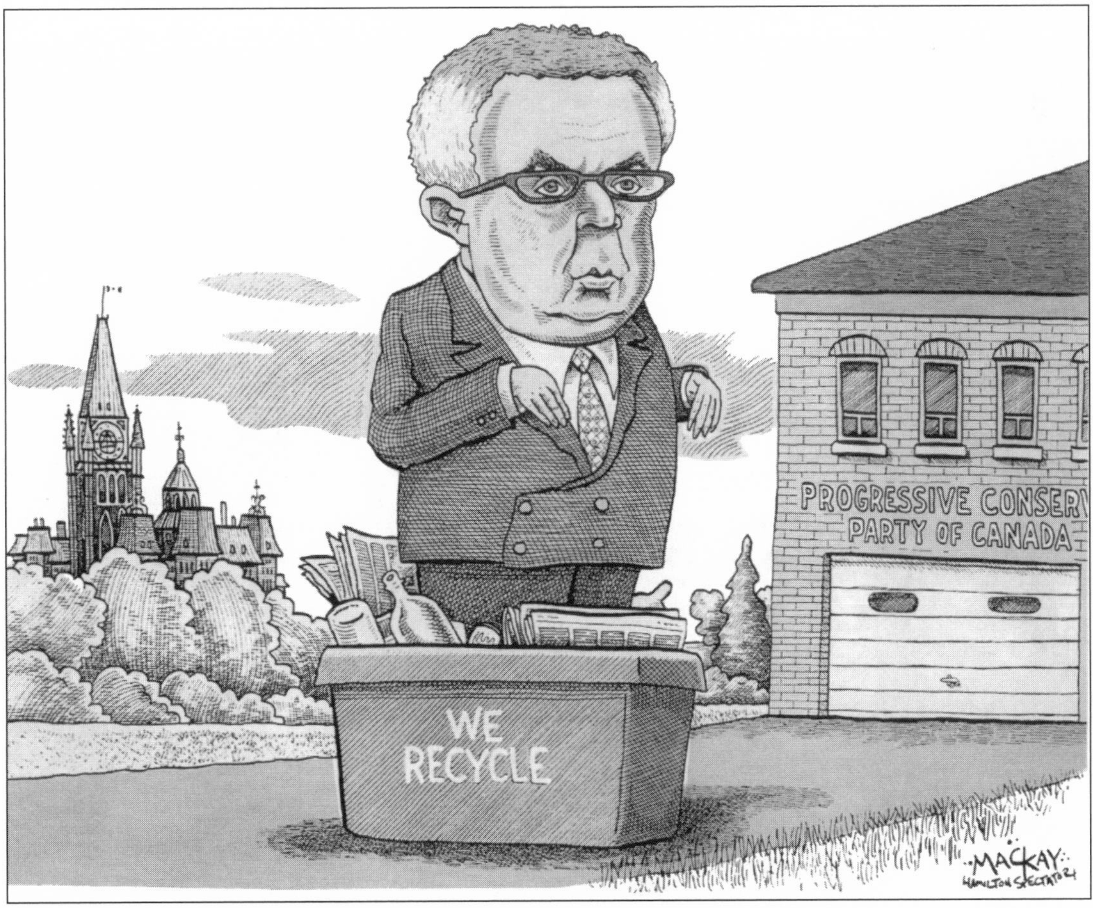
PROGRESSIVE CONSERV
PARTY OF CANADA
WE RECYCLE
MACKAY HAMILTON SPECTATOR

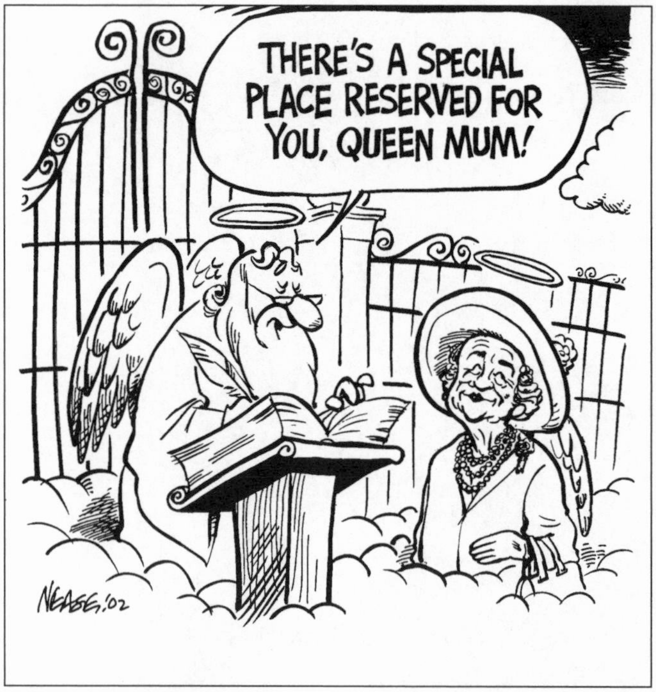
THERE'S A SPECIAL PLACE RESERVED FOR YOU, QUEEN MUM!
NEASE '02

STEVE NEASE
Courtesy Kingston Whig-Standard

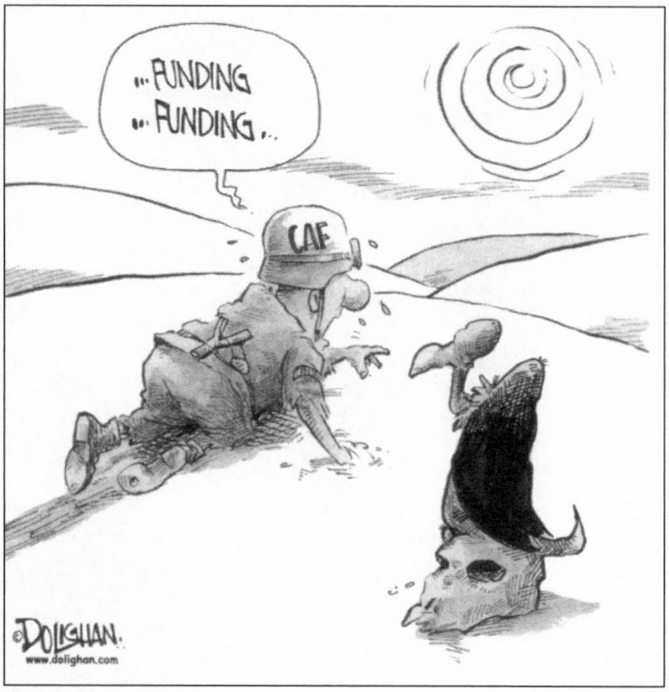
...FUNDING ...FUNDING...
CAF
DOLIGHAN
www.dolighan.com

TIM DOLIGHAN
Courtesy Toronto Sun

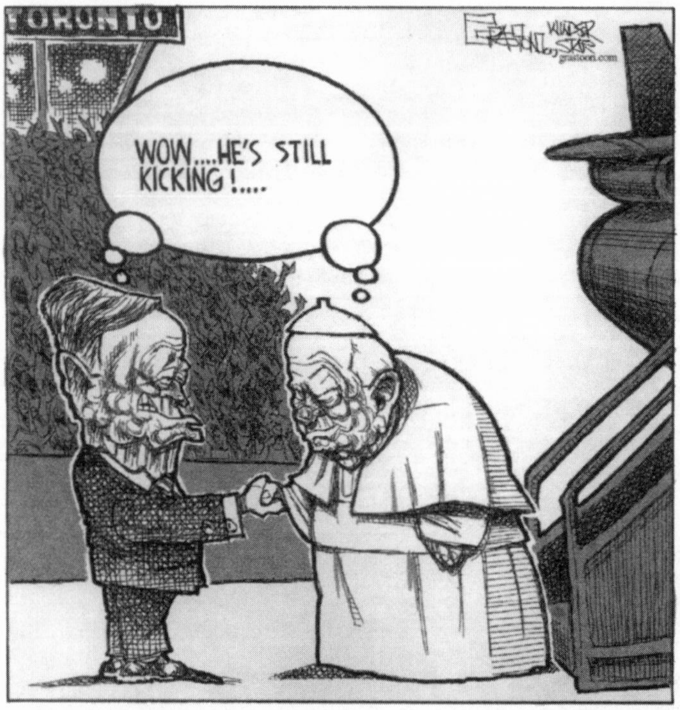
TORONTO
WOW....HE'S STILL KICKING!....
WINDSOR STAR

MIKE GRASTON
Courtesy Windsor Star

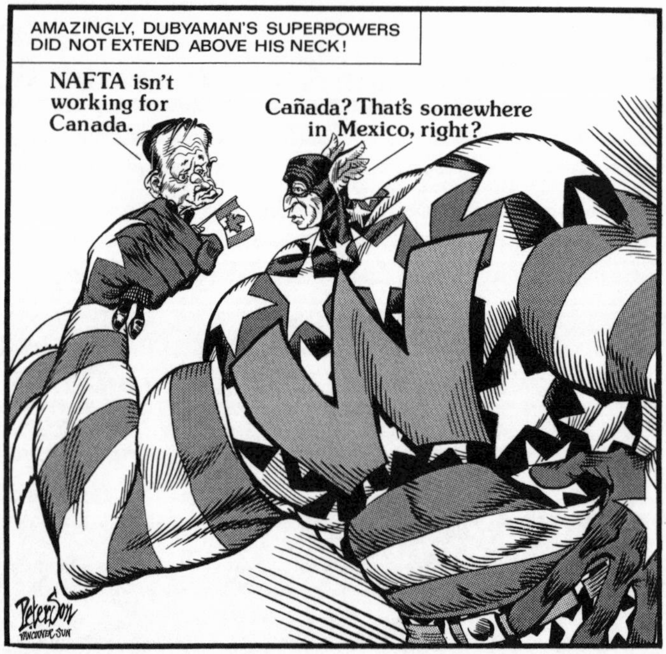
AMAZINGLY, DUBYAMAN'S SUPERPOWERS DID NOT EXTEND ABOVE HIS NECK!
NAFTA isn't working for Canada.
Cañada? That's somewhere in Mexico, right?
Peterson
VANCOUVER SUN

ROY PETERSON
Courtesy Vancouver Sun

MIKE GRASTON
Courtesy Windsor Star

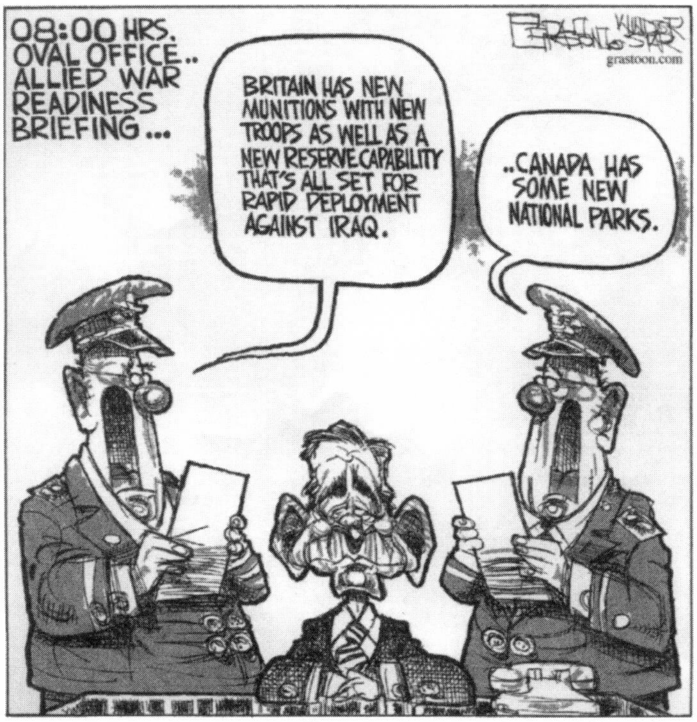

08:00 HRS. OVAL OFFICE.. ALLIED WAR READINESS BRIEFING...
BRITAIN HAS NEW MUNITIONS WITH NEW TROOPS AS WELL AS A NEW RESERVE CAPABILITY THAT'S ALL SET FOR RAPID DEPLOYMENT AGAINST IRAQ.
..CANADA HAS SOME NEW NATIONAL PARKS.
grastoon.com

ROY PETERSON
Courtesy Vancouver Sun

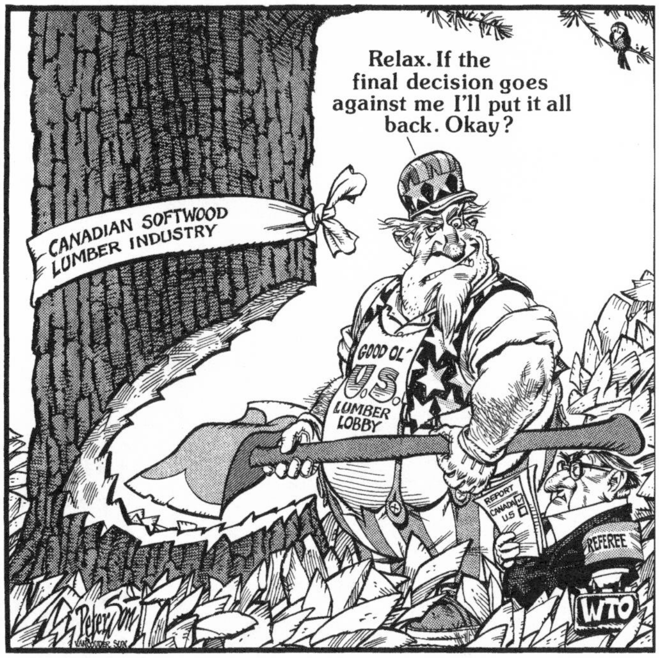

Relax. If the final decision goes against me I'll put it all back. Okay?
CANADIAN SOFTWOOD LUMBER INDUSTRY
GOOD OL' U.S. LUMBER LOBBY
REPORT
CANADA
US
REFEREE
WTO

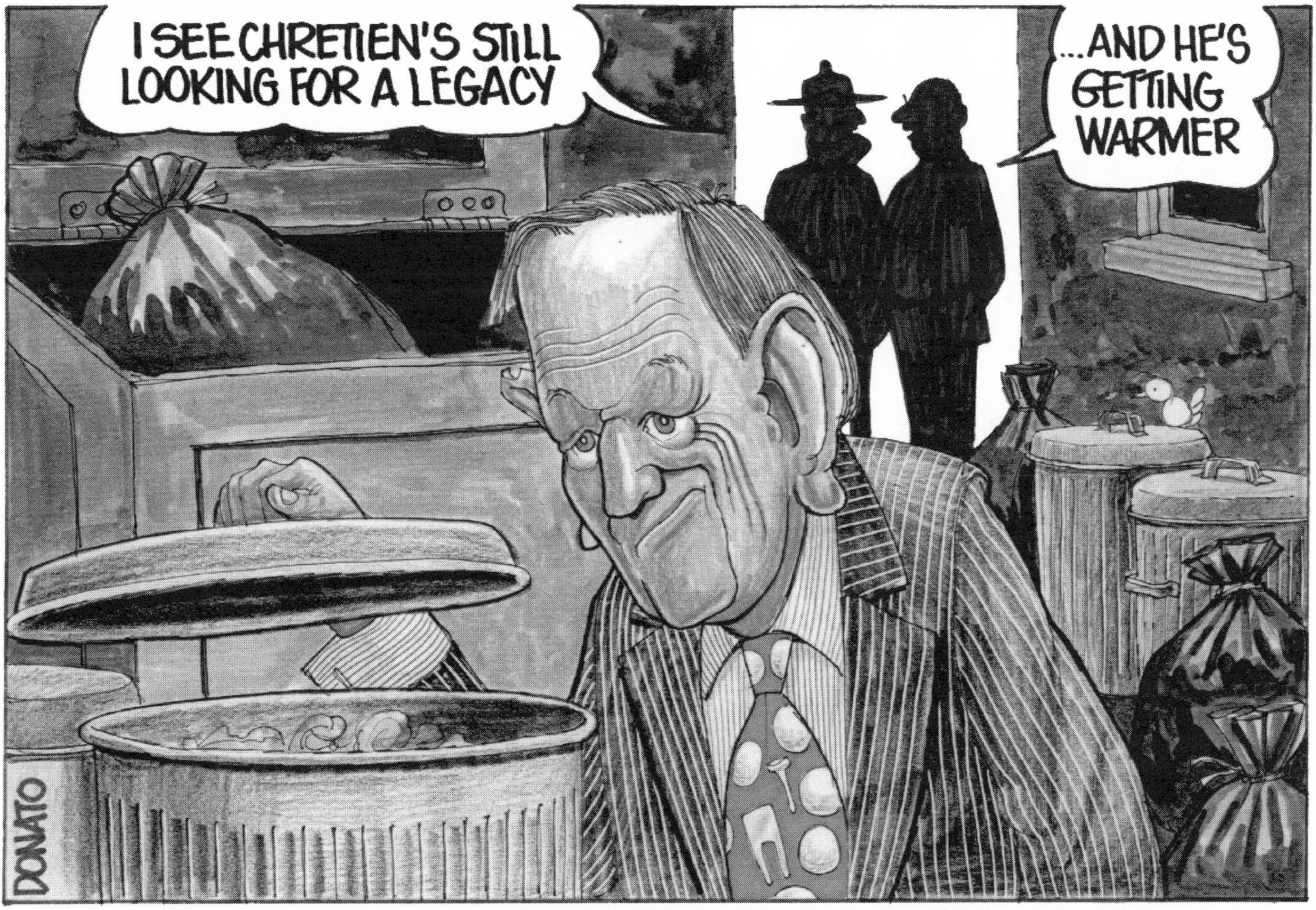

I SEE CHRETIEN'S STILL LOOKING FOR A LEGACY
...AND HE'S GETTING WARMER
DONATO

ANDY DONATO
Courtesy Toronto Sun

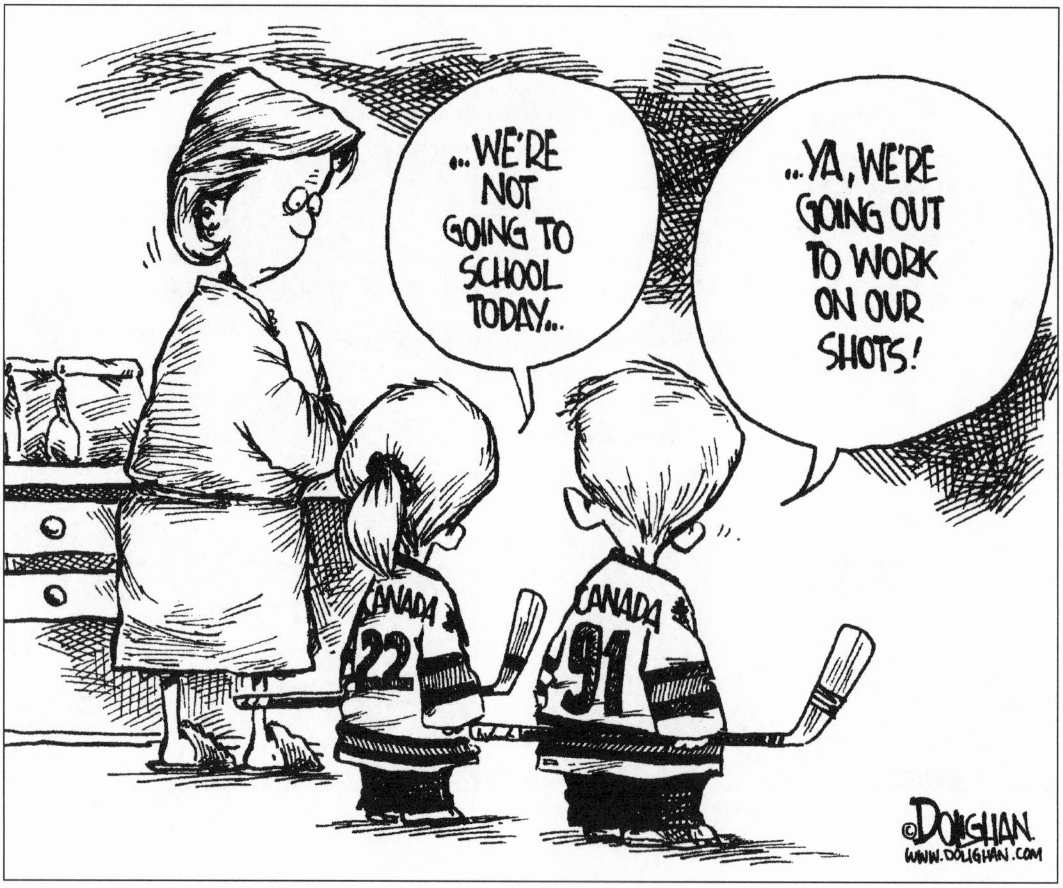
...WE'RE NOT GOING TO SCHOOL TODAY...
...YA, WE'RE GOING OUT TO WORK ON OUR SHOTS!
CANADA 22
CANADA 91
©DOLIGHAN
WWW.DOLIGHAN.COM

TIM DOLIGHAN
Courtesy Toronto Sun

GAREME MACKAY
Courtesy Hamilton Spectator

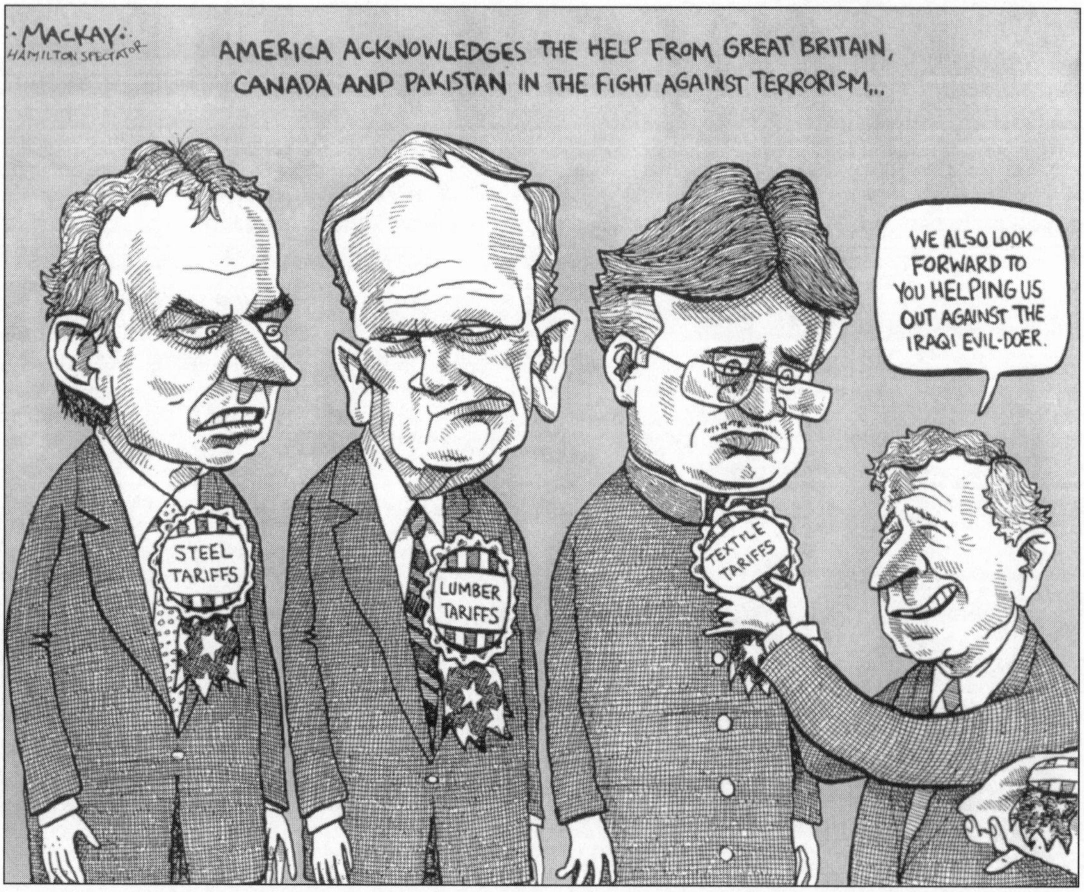
MACKAY HAMILTON SPECTATOR
AMERICA ACKNOWLEDGES THE HELP FROM GREAT BRITAIN, CANADA AND PAKISTAN IN THE FIGHT AGAINST TERRORISM...
WE ALSO LOOK FORWARD TO YOU HELPING US OUT AGAINST THE IRAQI EVIL-DOER.
STEEL TARIFFS
LUMBER TARIFFS
TEXTILE TARIFFS

. . . and Other Issues

Jimmy Carter in October was awarded the Nobel Peace Prize, the third U.S. president, after Theodore Roosevelt in 1906 and Woodrow Wilson in 1919, to be so honored. The Nobel selection committee said that the award was intended to recognize Carter's approach to peace as a positive contrast to President Bush's threats of war against Iraq. The committee also admitted that the choice of Carter also was meant to be a "kick in the leg" to all that follow the same line as the United States. Carter also paid a visit to Fidel Castro and urged a change in U.S.-Cuban relations.

Polls showed that 75 percent of all Americans, including 90 percent of whites, are opposed to the payment of reparations to blacks because their ancestors were enslaved. Some, however, continued to press for Congress to act on this issue. Some liberal media accused the U.S. of mistreating al-Qaida and Taliban suspects being held at Guantanamo Bay in Cuba. The FBI and the CIA drew criticism after 9-11 because America was caught off guard, and the Senate began looking into the matter.

Well-known figures who died during the year included Ted Williams, Milton Berle, Sam Snead, Johnny Unitas, Rod Steiger, Dave Thomas, historian Stephen Ambrose, and the Queen Mother of England.

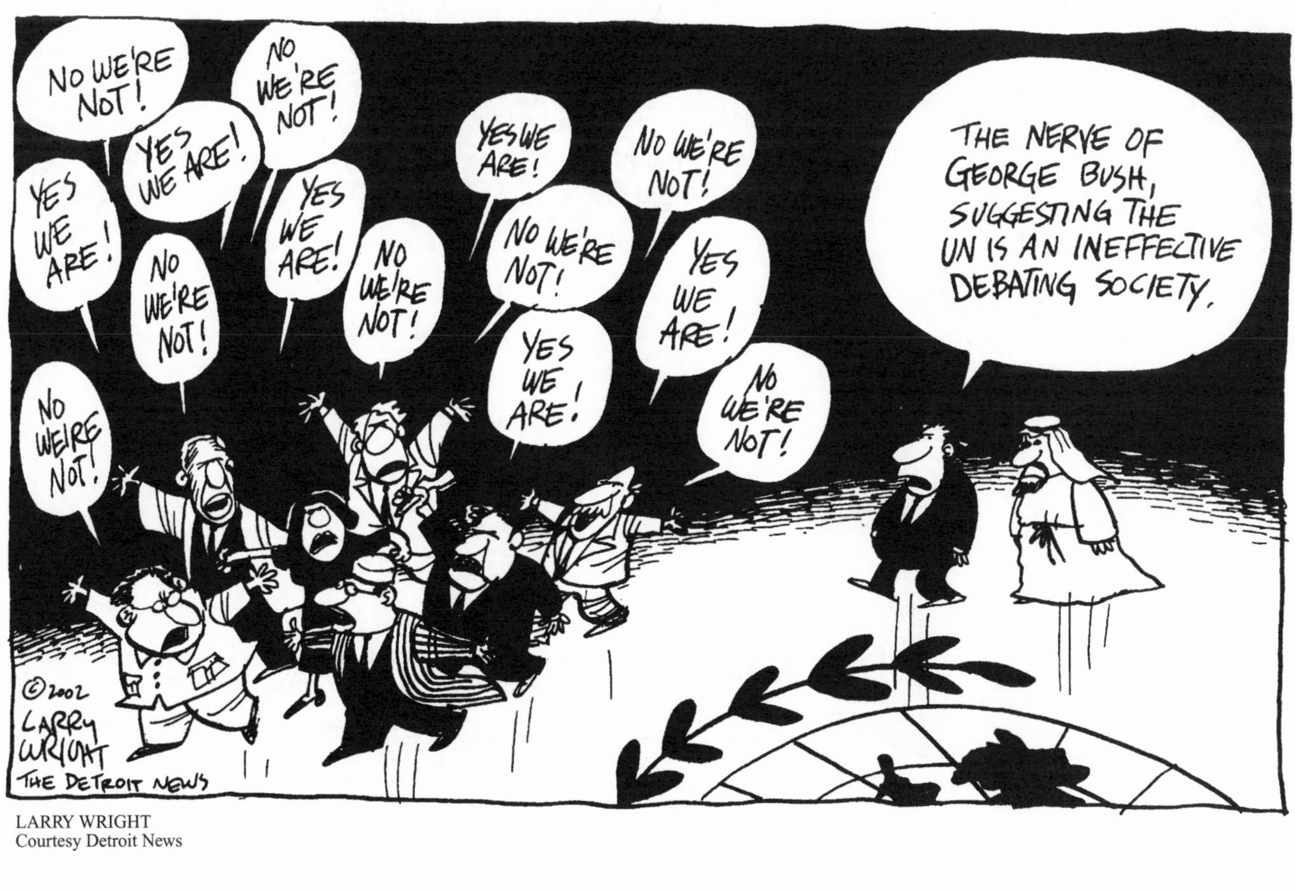
NO WE'RE NOT!
NO WE'RE NOT!
YES WE ARE!
YES WE ARE!
YES WE ARE!
NO WE'RE NOT!
NO WE'RE NOT!
YES WE ARE!
NO WE'RE NOT!
NO WE'RE NOT!
YES WE ARE!
YES WE ARE!
NO WE'RE NOT!
NO WE'RE NOT!
THE NERVE OF GEORGE BUSH, SUGGESTING THE UN IS AN INEFFECTIVE DEBATING SOCIETY.
©2002 LARRY WRIGHT THE DETROIT NEWS

LARRY WRIGHT
Courtesy Detroit News

JAMES D. CROWE
Courtesy Mobile Register

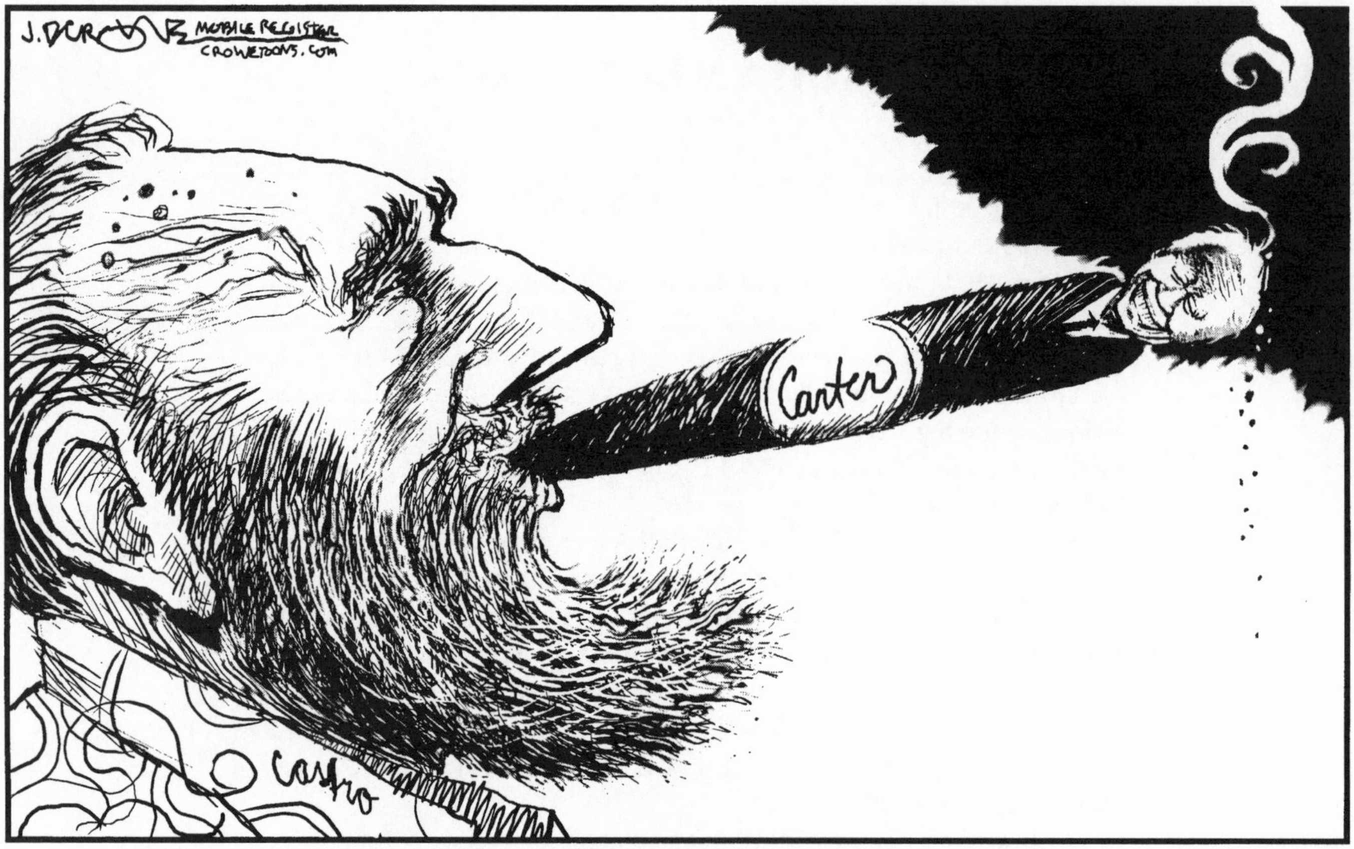
J. D. CROWE MOBILE REGISTER CROWETOONS.COM
Carter
Castro

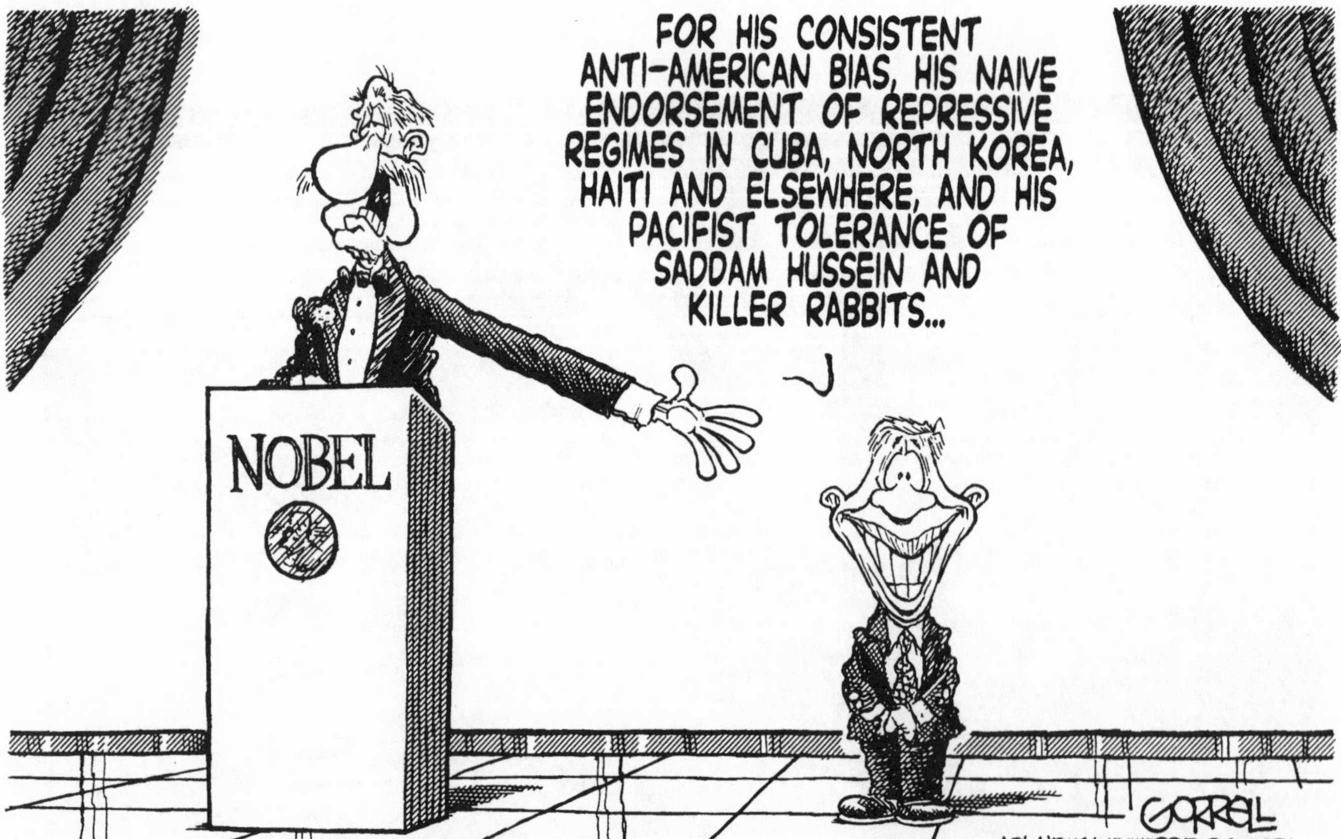
FOR HIS CONSISTENT ANTI-AMERICAN BIAS, HIS NAIVE ENDORSEMENT OF REPRESSIVE REGIMES IN CUBA, NORTH KOREA, HAITI AND ELSEWHERE, AND HIS PACIFIST TOLERANCE OF SADDAM HUSSEIN AND KILLER RABBITS...
NOBEL
GORRELL
AOL NEWS/KEYWORD BOB GORRELL
©2002 CREATORS SYNDICATE, INC.

BOB GORRELL
Courtesy America Online News

JAMES McCLOSKEY
Courtesy Daily News Leader (Va.)

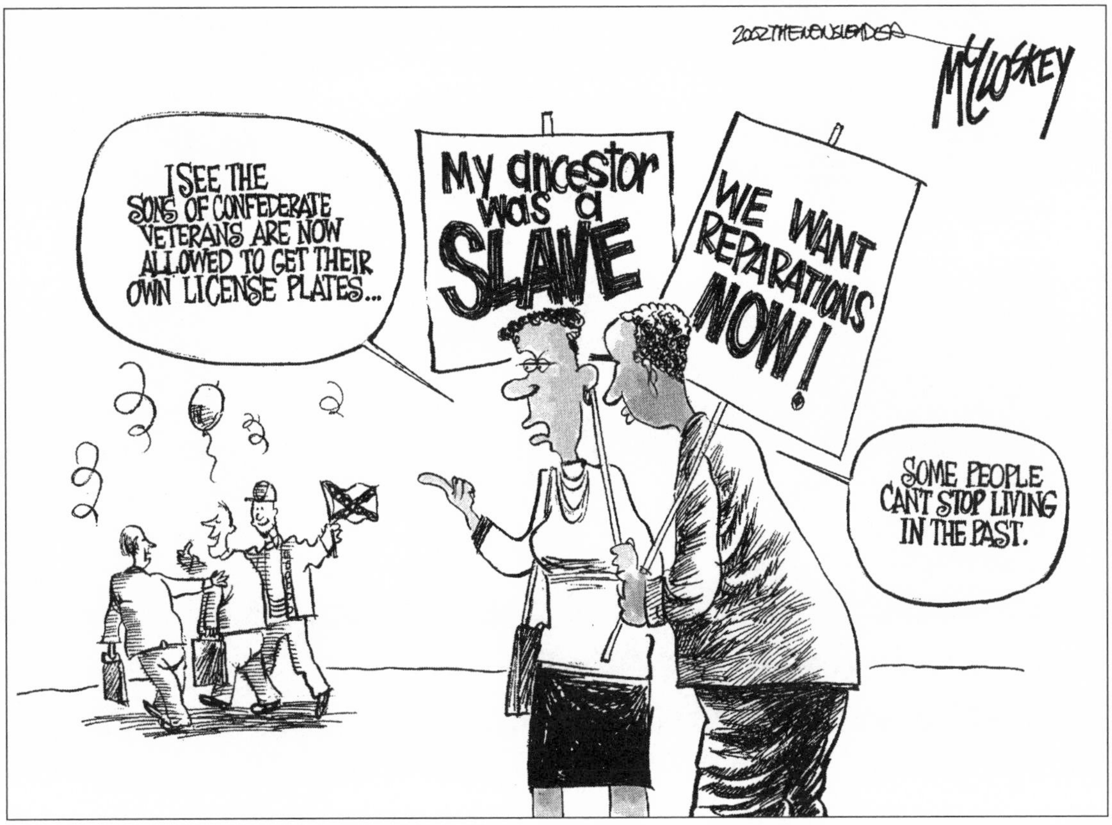

I SEE THE SONS OF CONFEDERATE VETERANS ARE NOW ALLOWED TO GET THEIR OWN LICENSE PLATES...
My ancestor was a SLAVE
WE WANT REPARATIONS NOW!
SOME PEOPLE CAN'T STOP LIVING IN THE PAST.
McCLOSKEY

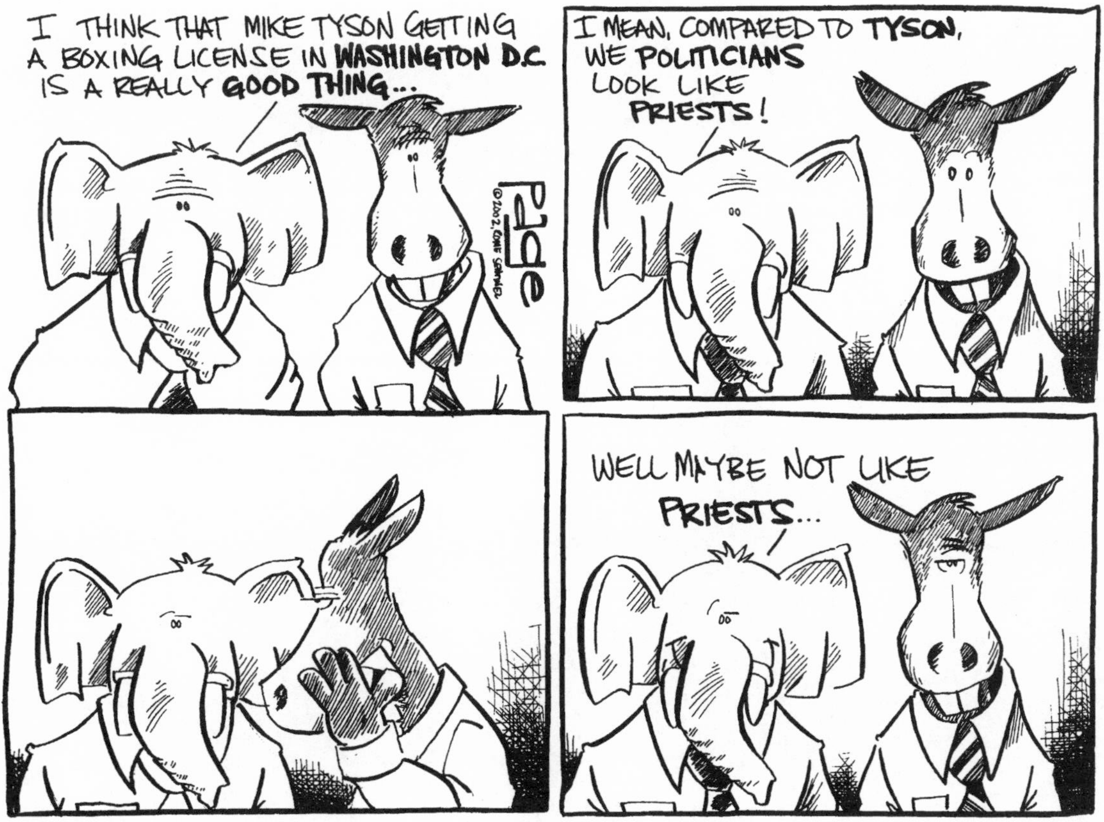

I THINK THAT MIKE TYSON GETTING A BOXING LICENSE IN WASHINGTON D.C. IS A REALLY GOOD THING...
PAGE
I MEAN, COMPARED TO TYSON, WE POLITICIANS LOOK LIKE PRIESTS!
WELL MAYBE NOT LIKE PRIESTS...

FRANK PAGE
Courtesy Rome Daily Sentinel (N.Y.)

SCOTT STANTIS
Courtesy Birmingham News

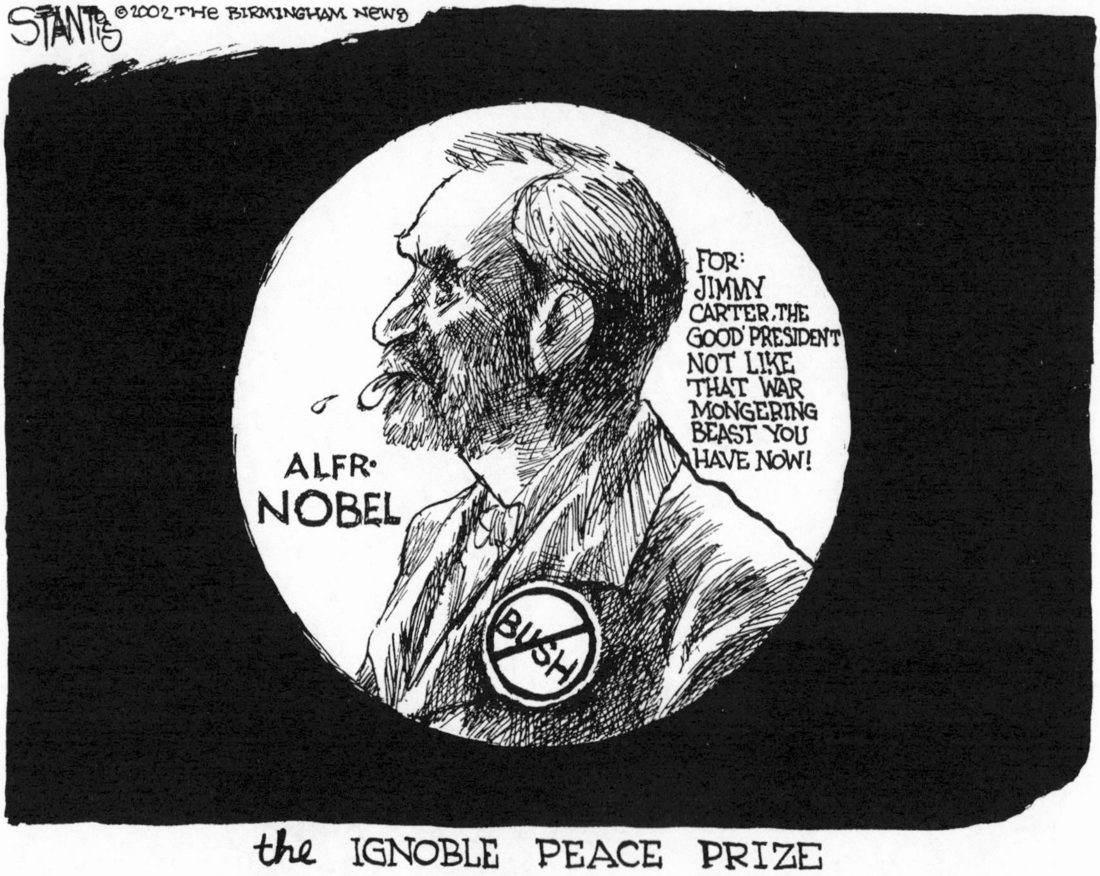
STANTIS ©2002 THE BIRMINGHAM NEWS
FOR: JIMMY CARTER, THE GOOD PRESIDENT NOT LIKE THAT WAR MONGERING BEAST YOU HAVE NOW!
ALFR. NOBEL
BUSH
the IGNOBLE PEACE PRIZE

MICHAEL RAMIREZ
Courtesy Los Angeles Times

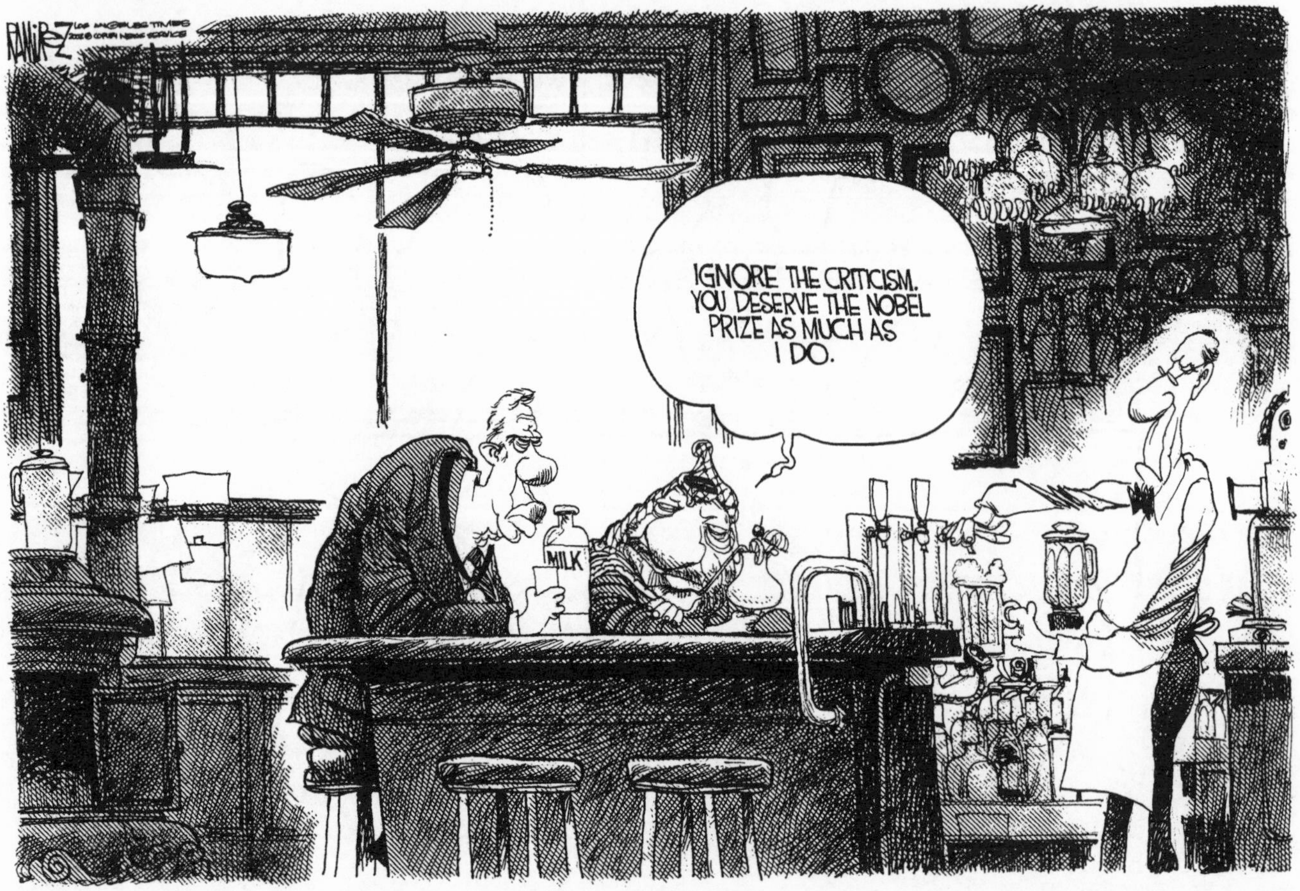
RAMIREZ
IGNORE THE CRITICISM. YOU DESERVE THE NOBEL PRIZE AS MUCH AS I DO.
MILK

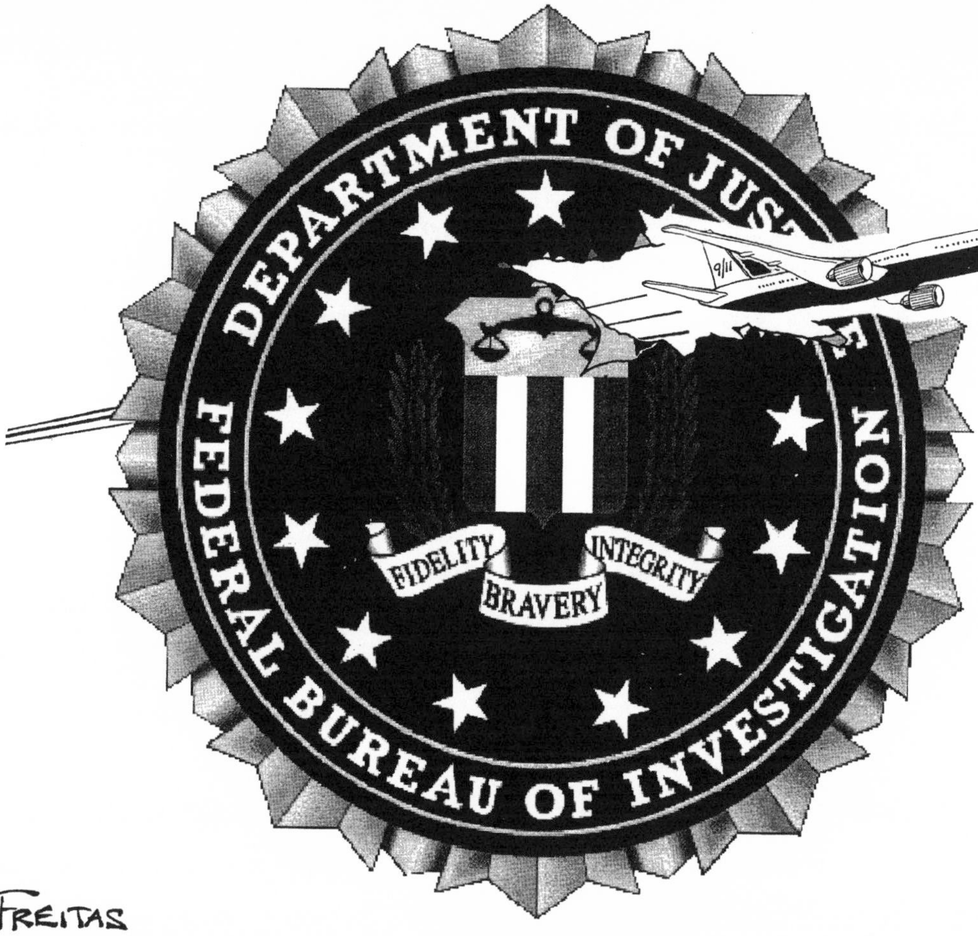
DEPARTMENT OF JUSTICE
FEDERAL BUREAU OF INVESTIGATION
FIDELITY
BRAVERY
INTEGRITY
9/11
DEFREITAS

JUSTIN DeFREITAS
Courtesy Placerville Mountain Democrat (Calif.)

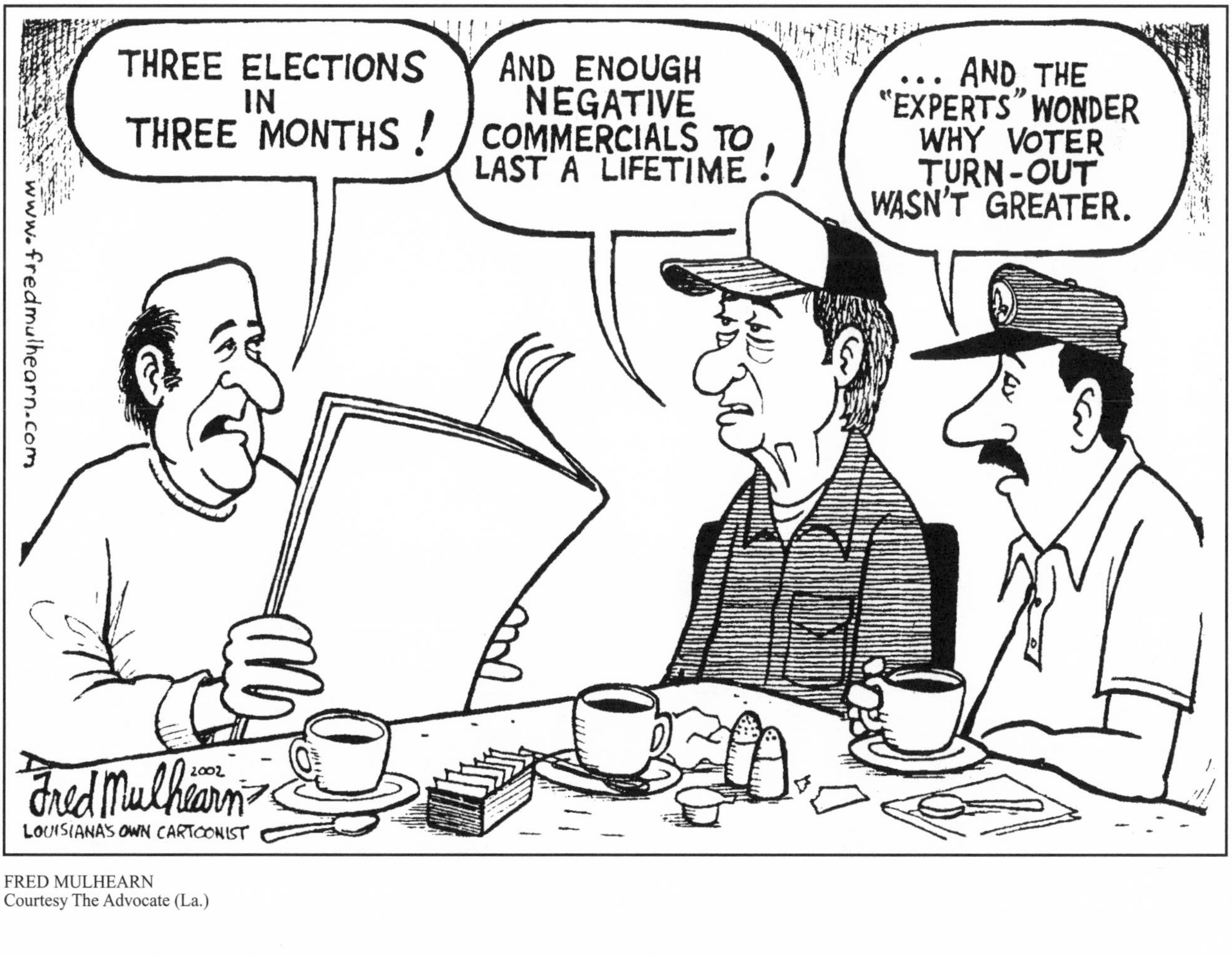
THREE ELECTIONS IN THREE MONTHS!
AND ENOUGH NEGATIVE COMMERCIALS TO LAST A LIFETIME!
... AND THE "EXPERTS" WONDER WHY VOTER TURN-OUT WASN'T GREATER.
www.fredmulhearn.com
Fred Mulhearn 2002
LOUISIANA'S OWN CARTOONIST

FRED MULHEARN
Courtesy The Advocate (La.)

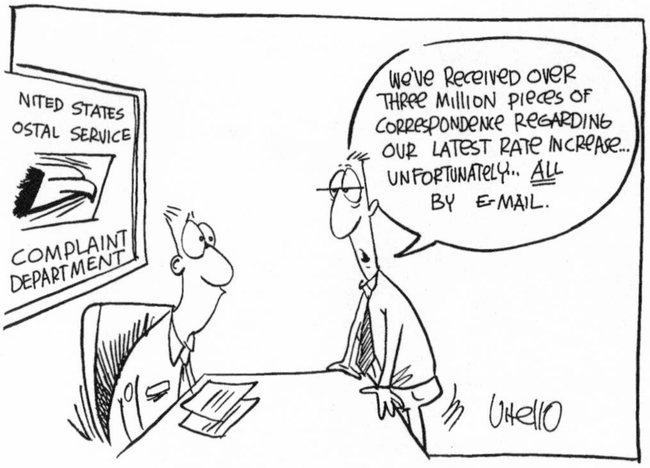
NITED STATES
OSTAL SERVICE
COMPLAINT DEPARTMENT
We've Received over three million pieces of correspondence regarding our latest rate increase... unfortunately.. ALL by E-MAIL.
Vitello

ALAN VITELLO
Courtesy Vitello's View

CLIFF LEVERETTE
Courtesy Magnolia Gazette (Miss.)

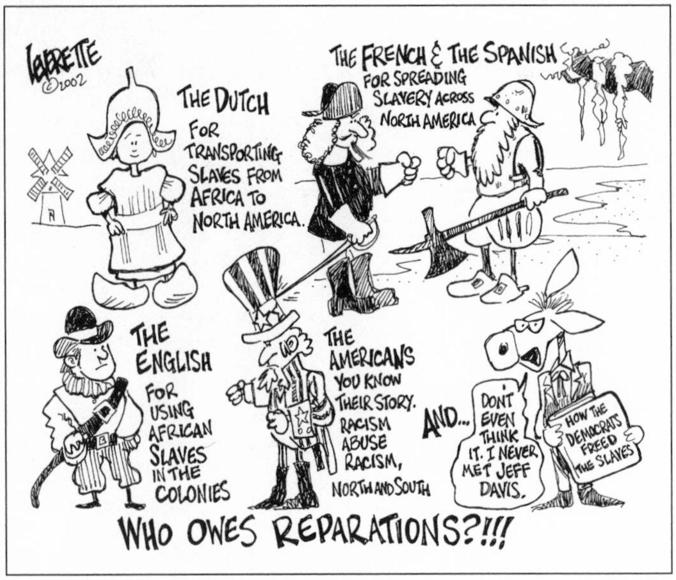
LEVERETTE ©2002
THE DUTCH FOR TRANSPORTING SLAVES FROM AFRICA TO NORTH AMERICA.
THE FRENCH & THE SPANISH FOR SPREADING SLAVERY ACROSS NORTH AMERICA
THE ENGLISH FOR USING AFRICAN SLAVES IN THE COLONIES
THE AMERICANS YOU KNOW THEIR STORY. RACISM ABUSE RACISM, NORTH AND SOUTH
AND...
DON'T EVEN THINK IT. I NEVER MET JEFF DAVIS.
HOW THE DEMOCRATS FREED THE SLAVES
WHO OWES REPARATIONS?!!!

DOUG MacGREGOR
Courtesy Fort Myers News-Press

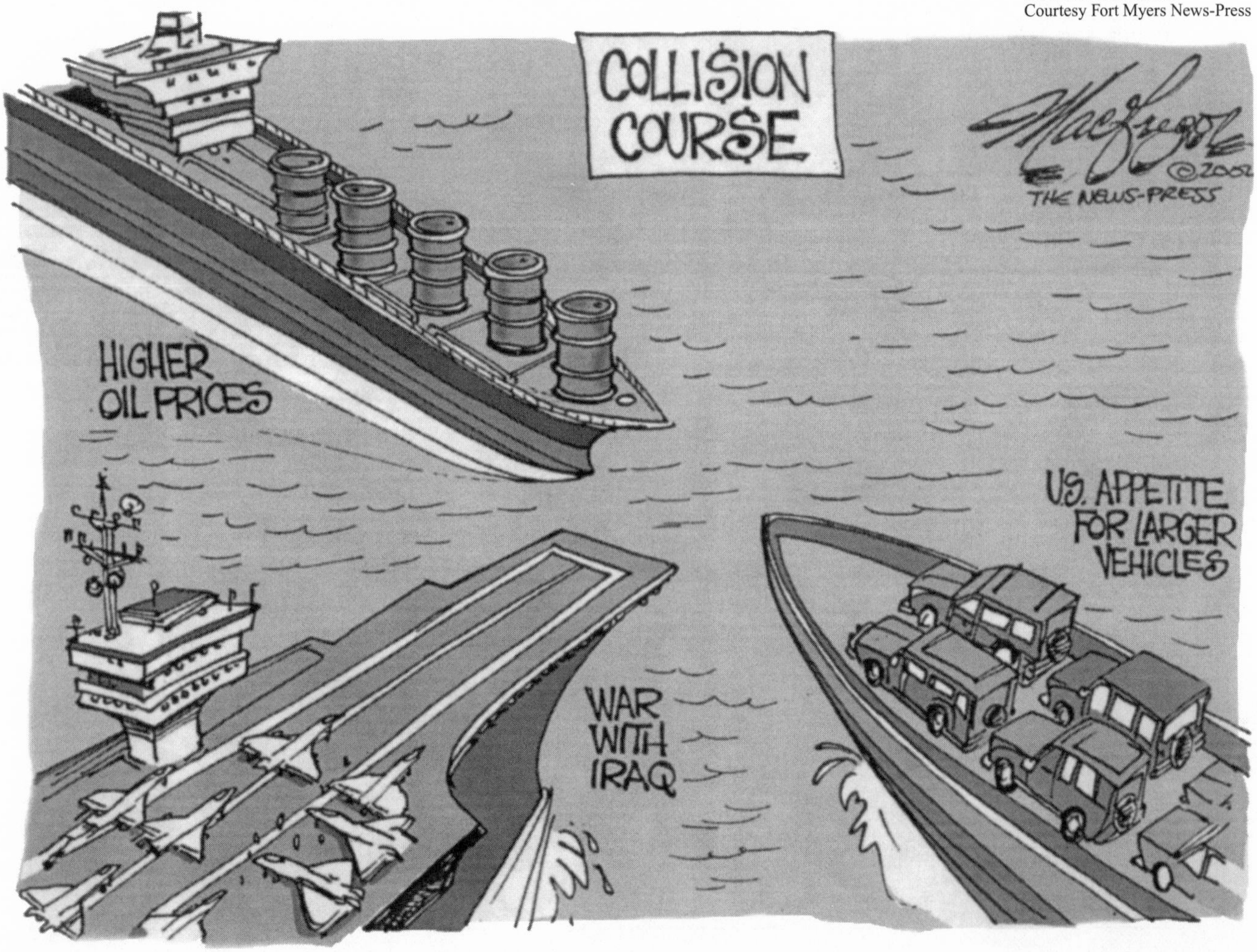
COLLI$ION COUR$E
MacGregor ©2002 THE NEWS-PRESS
HIGHER OIL PRICES
U.S. APPETITE FOR LARGER VEHICLES
WAR WITH IRAQ

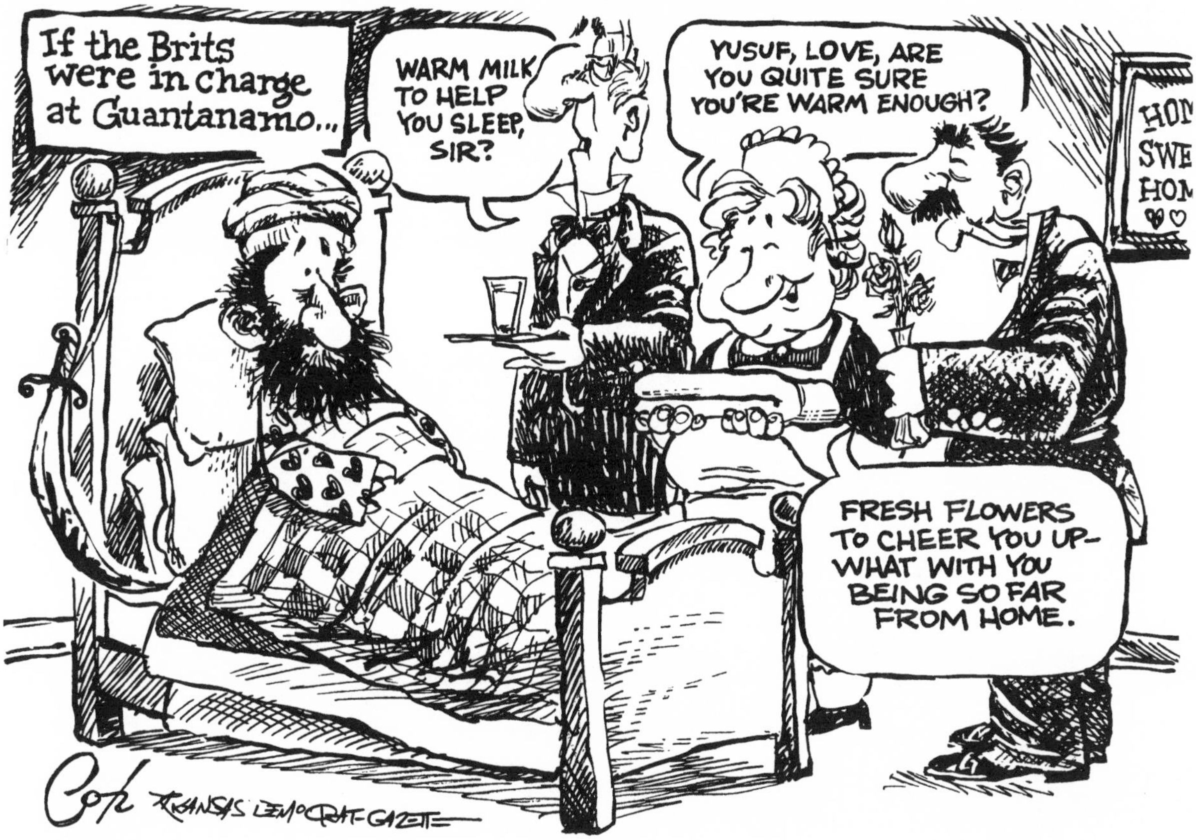
If the Brits were in charge at Guantanamo...
WARM MILK TO HELP YOU SLEEP, SIR?
YUSUF, LOVE, ARE YOU QUITE SURE YOU'RE WARM ENOUGH?
FRESH FLOWERS TO CHEER YOU UP- WHAT WITH YOU BEING SO FAR FROM HOME.
Cox ARKANSAS DEMOCRAT-GAZETTE

DAVID COX
Courtesy Arkansas Democrat-Gazette

MIKE KEEFE
Courtesy Denver Post

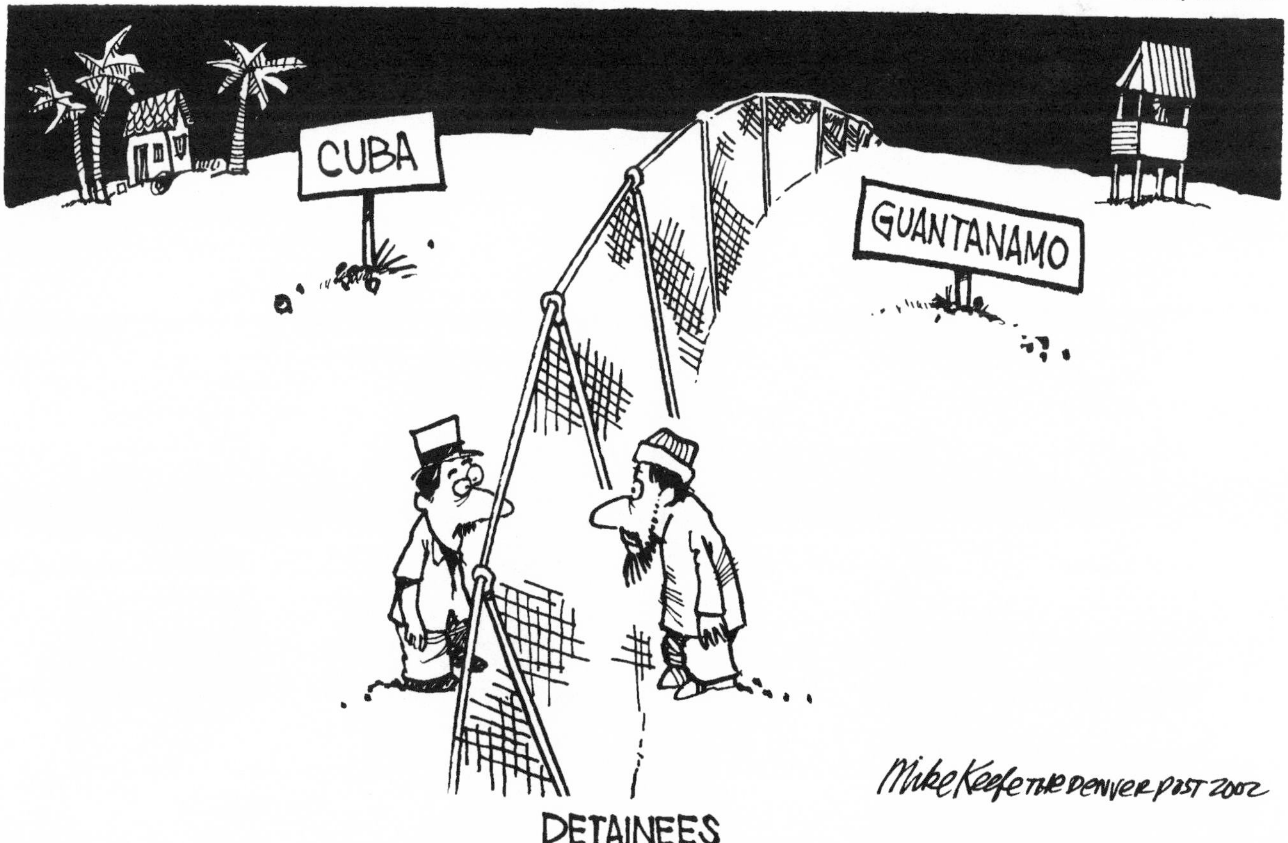
CUBA
GUANTANAMO
Mike Keefe THE DENVER POST 2002
DETAINEES

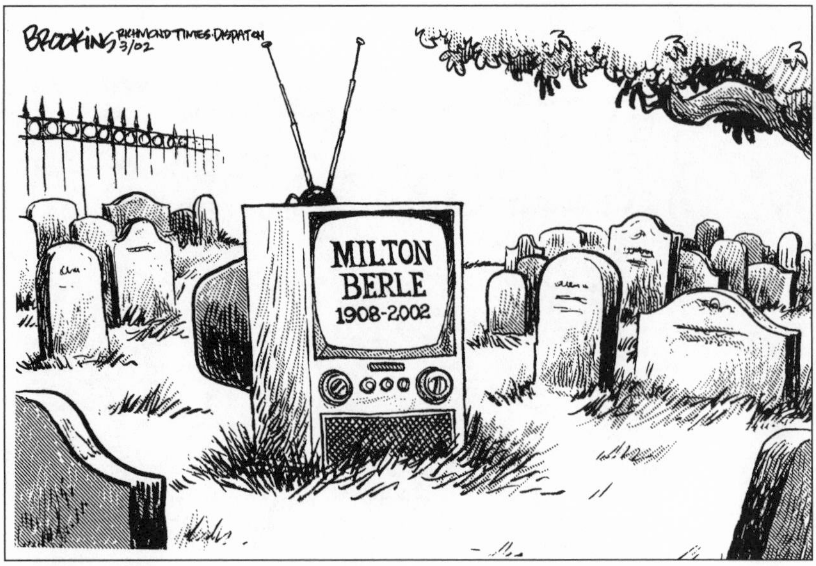
BROOKINS RICHMOND TIMES-DISPATCH 3/02
MILTON BERLE
1908-2002

GARY BROOKINS
Courtesy Richmond Times-Dispatch

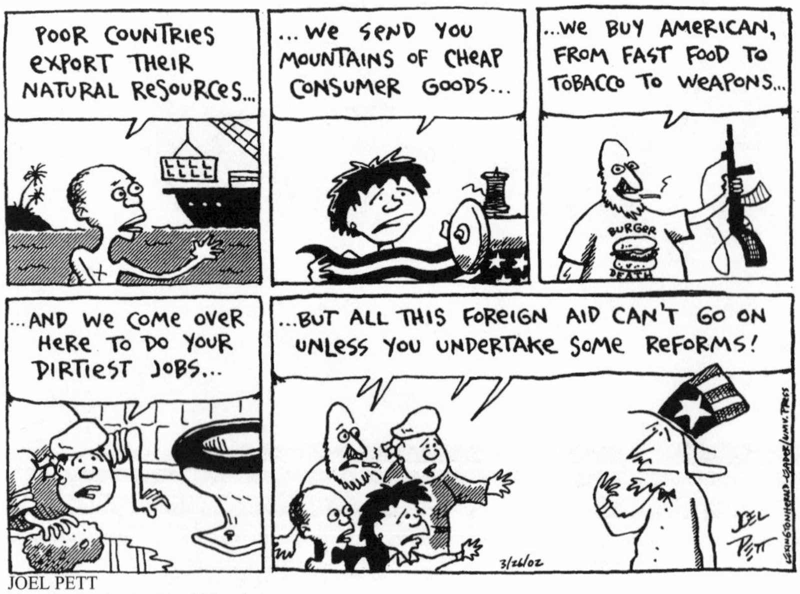
POOR COUNTRIES EXPORT THEIR NATURAL RESOURCES...
...WE SEND YOU MOUNTAINS OF CHEAP CONSUMER GOODS...
...WE BUY AMERICAN, FROM FAST FOOD TO TOBACCO TO WEAPONS...
BURGER
DEATH
...AND WE COME OVER HERE TO DO YOUR DIRTIEST JOBS...
...BUT ALL THIS FOREIGN AID CAN'T GO ON UNLESS YOU UNDERTAKE SOME REFORMS!
3/26/02
JOEL PETT

JOEL PETT
Courtesy Lexington Herald-Leader

BILL MANGOLD
Courtesy Heritage Newspapers

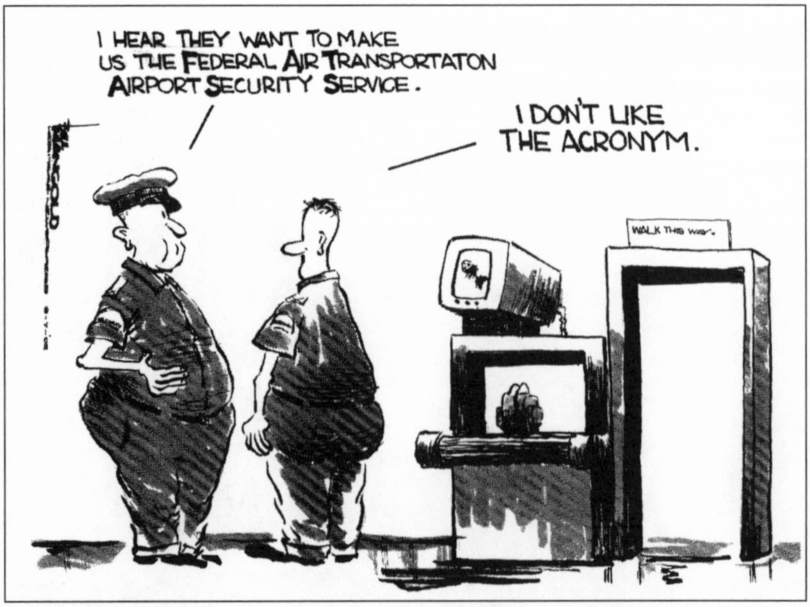
I HEAR THEY WANT TO MAKE US THE FEDERAL AIR TRANSPORTATON AIRPORT SECURITY SERVICE.
I DON'T LIKE THE ACRONYM.
WALK THIS WAY.
MANGOLD

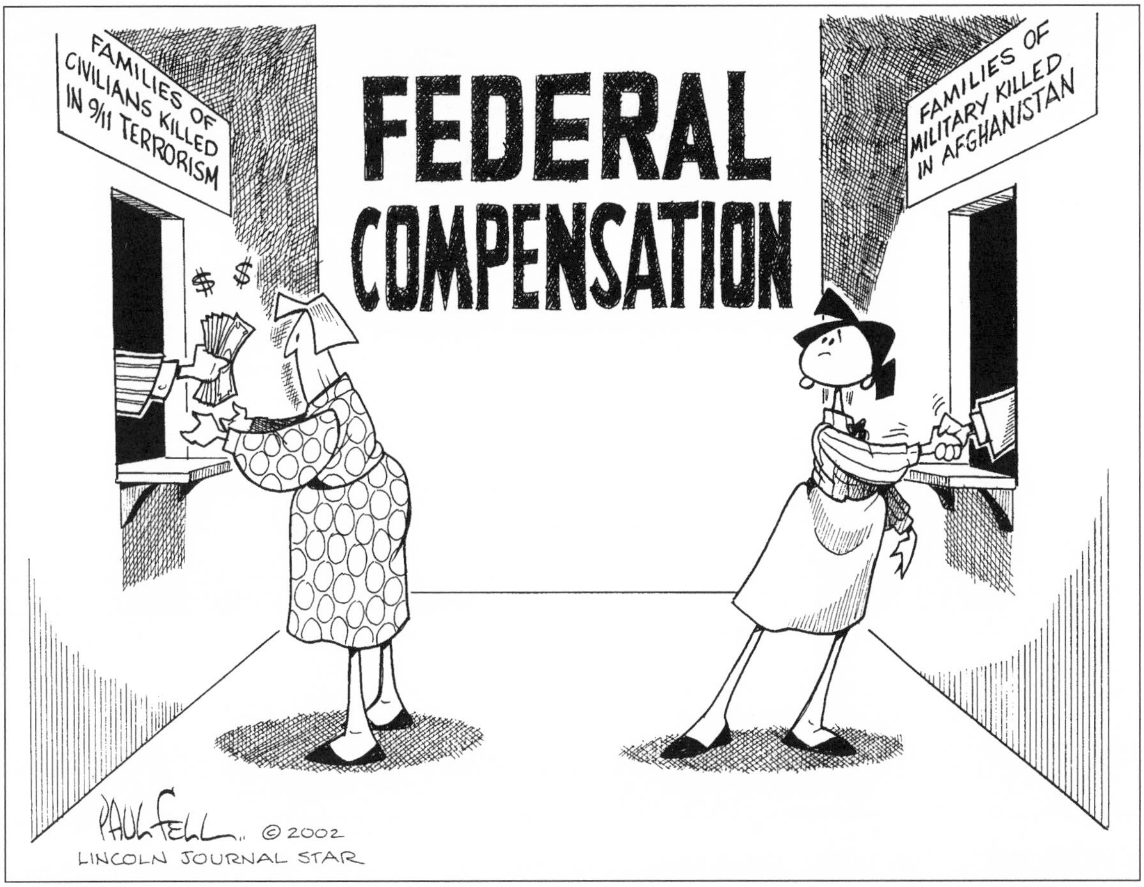
FEDERAL COMPENSATION
FAMILIES OF CIVILIANS KILLED IN 9/11 TERRORISM
FAMILIES OF MILITARY KILLED IN AFGHANISTAN
$ $
PAUL FELL © 2002
LINCOLN JOURNAL STAR

PAUL FELL
Courtesy Lincoln Journal Star

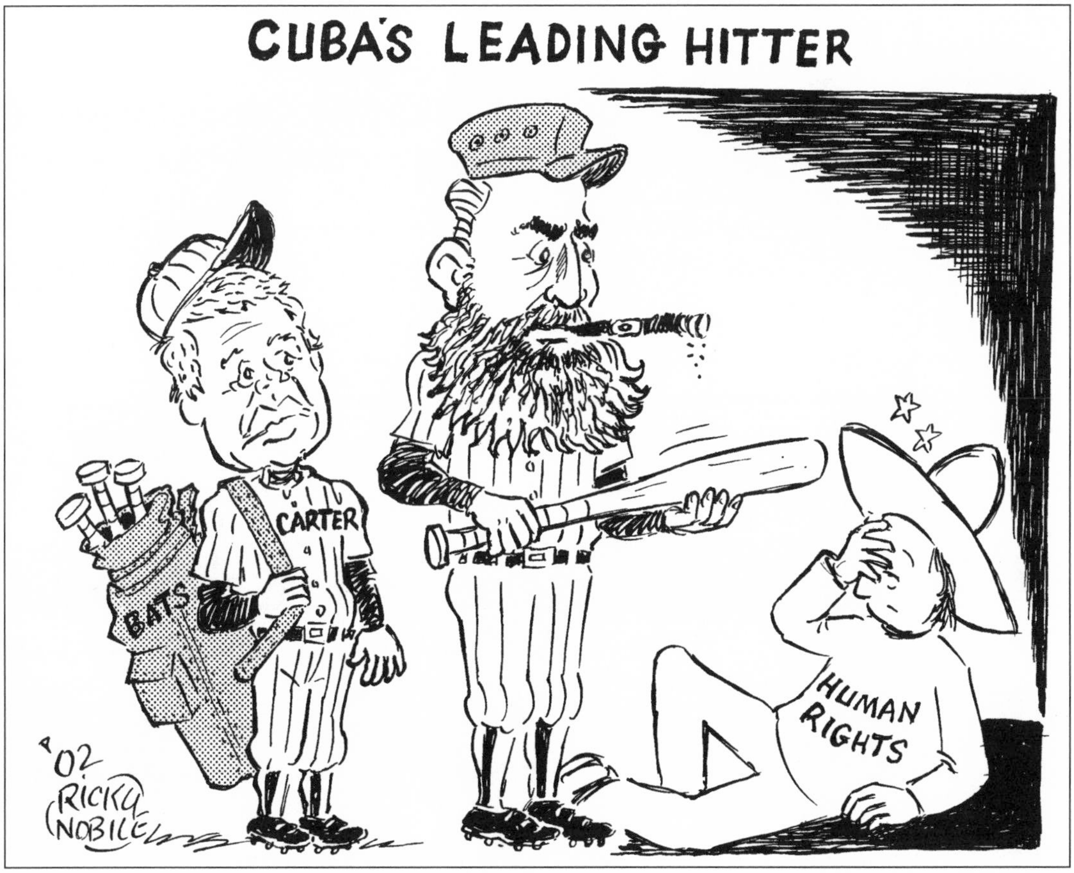
CUBA'S LEADING HITTER
CARTER
BATS
HUMAN RIGHTS
'02 RICKY NOBILE

RICKY NOBILE
Courtesy Hattiesburg American

GRANDPA? IT'S ME, TIM.... NO, NOTHING'S WRONG, I JUST WANTED TO TELL YOU THAT I LOVE YOU.
PHONE
©BAKER 2001

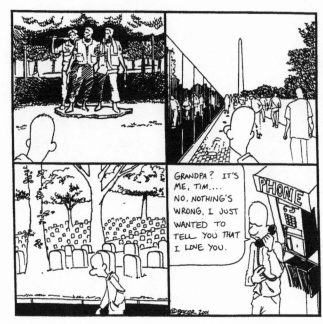

MARK BAKER
Courtesy Army Times

GENE AUTRY
ANGELS
WORLD SERIES
CLOUD NINE
10-02
Wallmeyer
PRESS-TELEGRAM

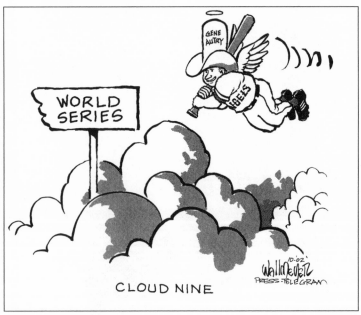

RICHARD WALLMEYER
Courtesy Long Beach Press-Telegram

JIM BORGMAN
Courtesy Cincinnati Enquirer

JIMBORGMAN
CINCINNATI ENQUIRER ©2002
WHAT'S YOUR POINT?
Nobel
Peace
Prize
IRAQ OR BUST!
USA! USA! USA! USA! USA! USA!
JIMMY CARTER

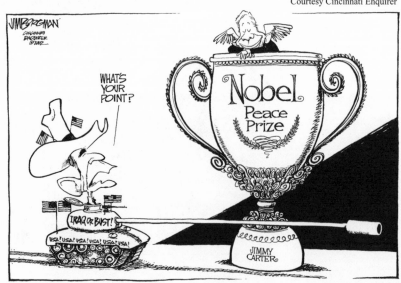

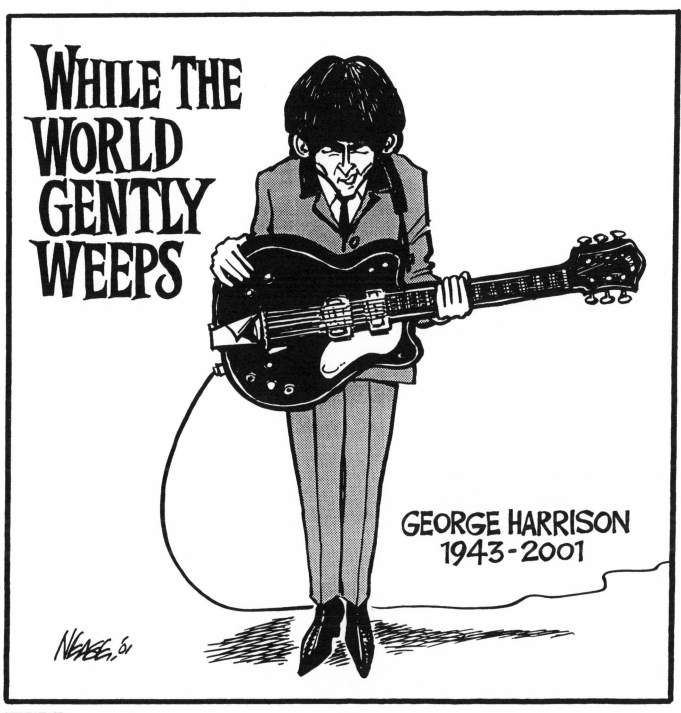

WHILE THE WORLD GENTLY WEEPS

GEORGE HARRISON
1943-2001

STEVE NEASE
Courtesy St. John's Telegraph Journal

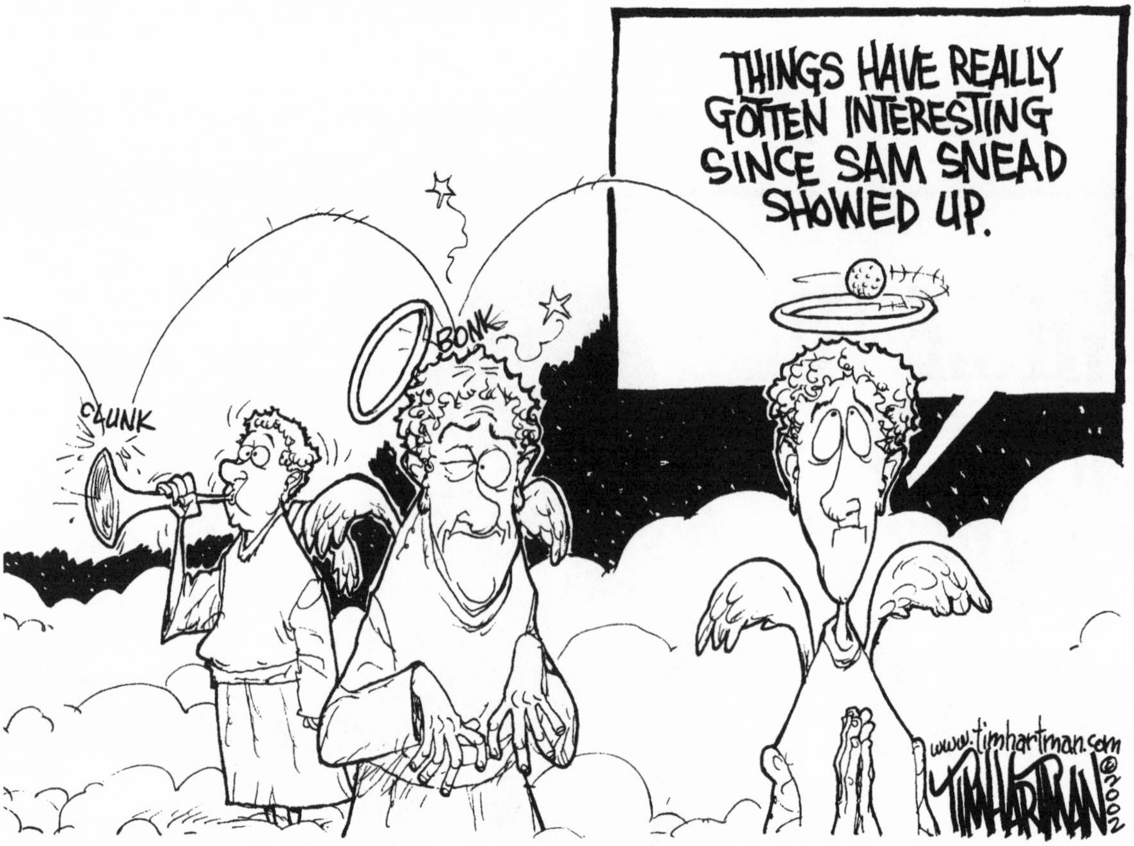
THINGS HAVE REALLY GOTTEN INTERESTING SINCE SAM SNEAD SHOWED UP.
CLUNK
BONK
www.timhartman.com
TIMHARTMAN
©2002

TIM HARTMAN
Courtesy Beaver County Times (Pa.)

DOUG MacGREGOR
Courtesy Fort Myers News-Press

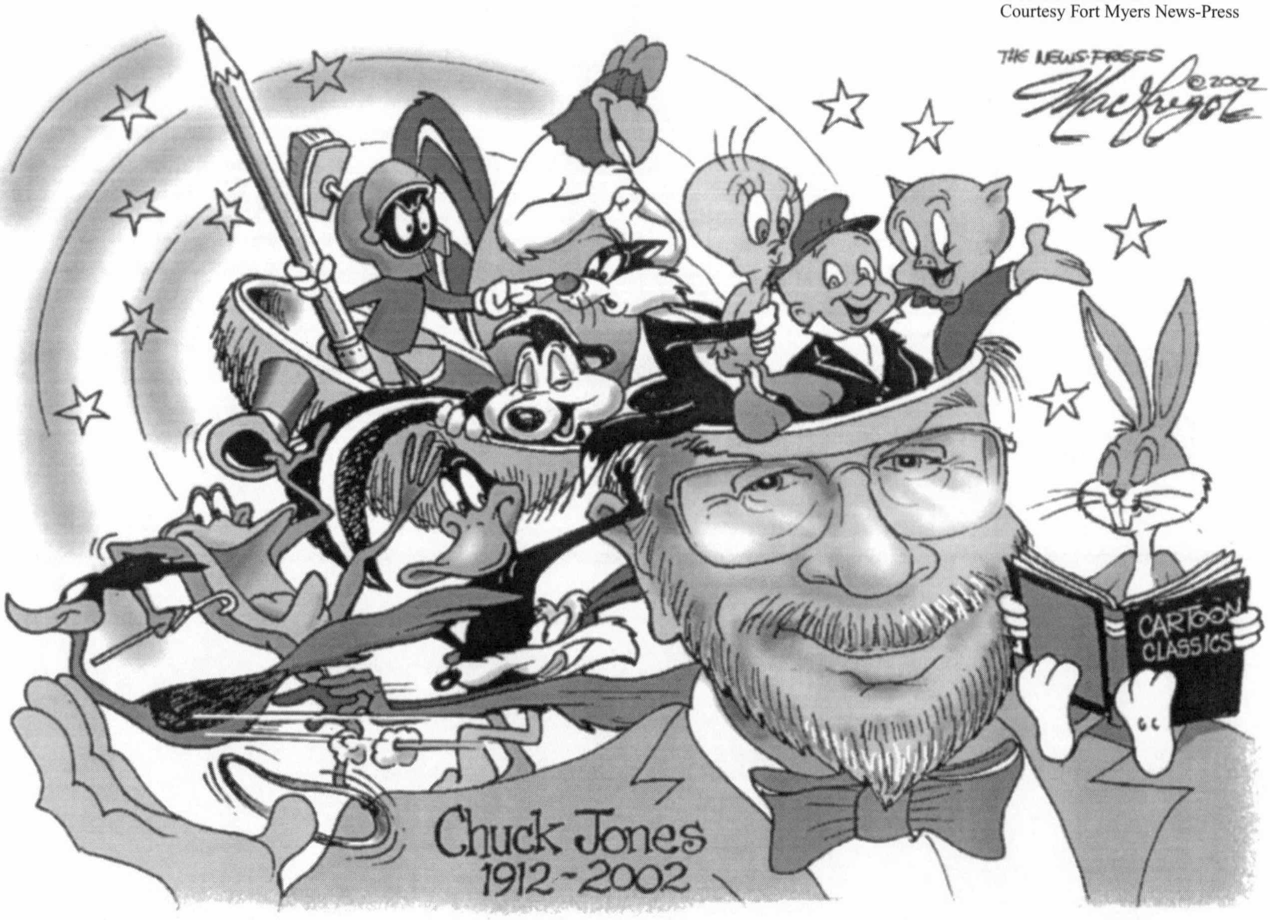
THE NEWS-PRESS
©2002
MacGregor
CARTOON CLASSICS
Chuck Jones
1912-2002

JEFF STAHLER
Courtesy Cincinnati Post

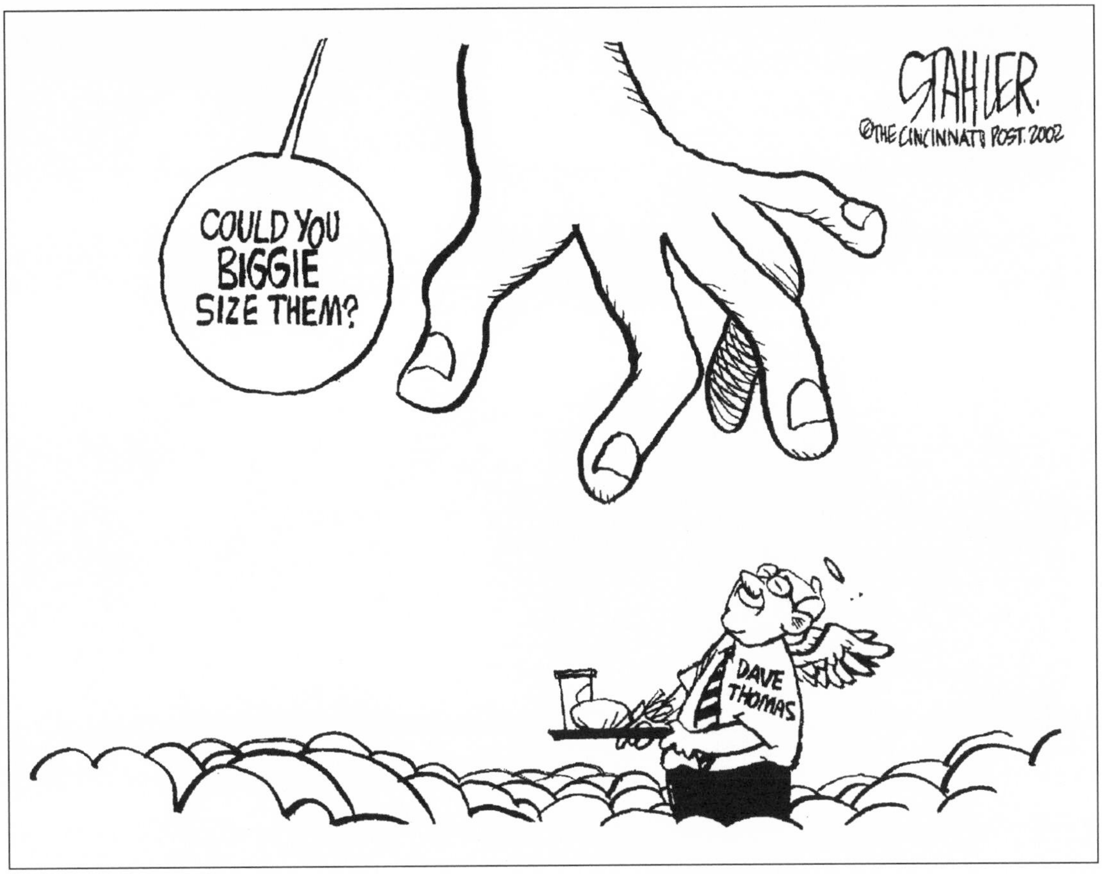
STAHLER
©THE CINCINNATI POST. 2002
COULD YOU BIGGIE SIZE THEM?
DAVE THOMAS

MICHAEL CAVNA
Courtesy San Diego Union-Tribune

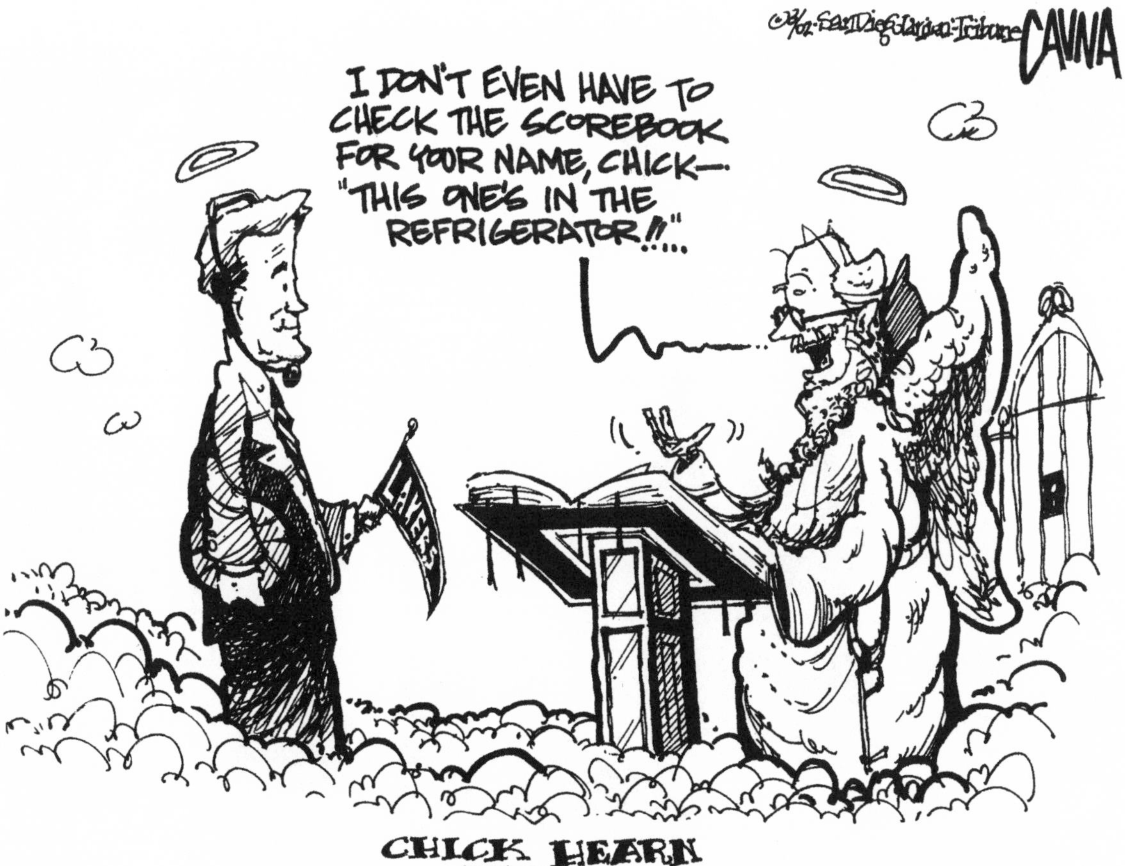
CAVNA
I DON'T EVEN HAVE TO CHECK THE SCOREBOOK FOR YOUR NAME, CHICK— "THIS ONE'S IN THE REFRIGERATOR!!"...
CHICK HEARN
1916–2002

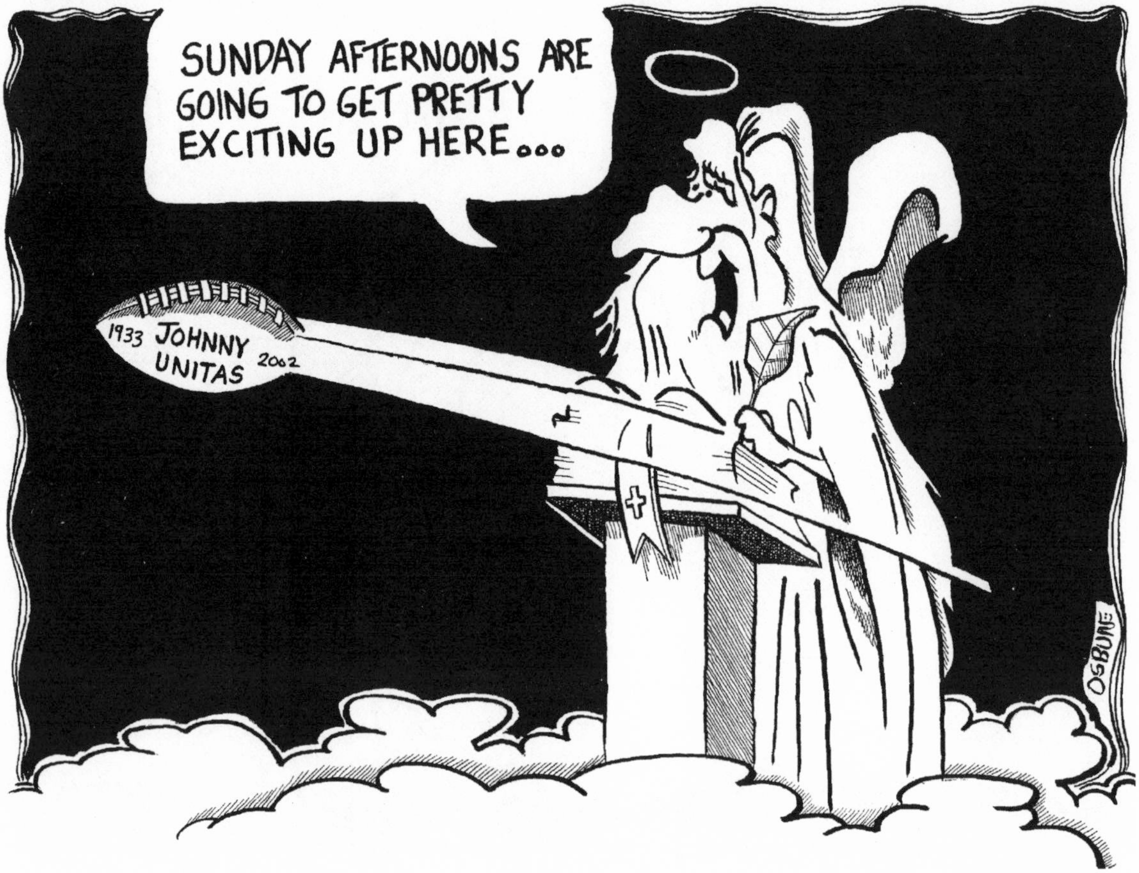
SUNDAY AFTERNOONS ARE GOING TO GET PRETTY EXCITING UP HERE...
1933 JOHNNY UNITAS 2002
OSBURE

MICHAEL OSBUN
Courtesy Citrus City Chronicle (Fla.)

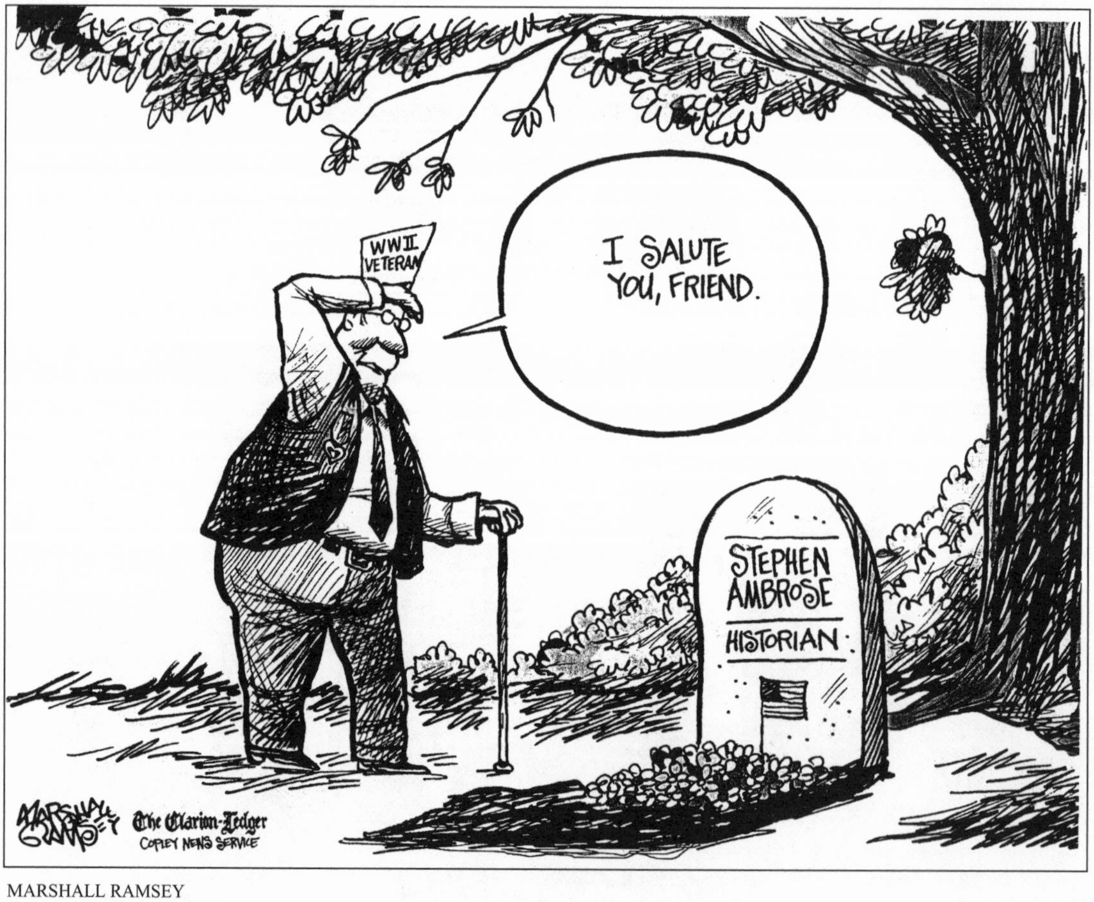
WWII VETERAN
I SALUTE YOU, FRIEND.
STEPHEN AMBROSE
HISTORIAN
The Clarion-Ledger
COPLEY NEWS SERVICE

MARSHALL RAMSEY
Courtesy The Clarion Ledger

Past Award Winners

PULITZER PRIZE

1922—Rollin Kirby, New York World
1923—No award given
1924—J.N. Darling, New York Herald-Tribune
1925—Rollin Kirby, New York World
1926—D.R. Fitzpatrick, St. Louis Post-Dispatch
1927—Nelson Harding, Brooklyn Eagle
1928—Nelson Harding, Brooklyn Eagle
1929—Rollin Kirby, New York World
1930—Charles Macauley, Brooklyn Eagle
1931—Edmund Duffy, Baltimore Sun
1932—John T. McCutcheon, Chicago Tribune
1933—H.M. Talburt, Washington Daily News
1934—Edmund Duffy, Baltimore Sun
1935—Ross A. Lewis, Milwaukee Journal
1936—No award given
1937—C.D. Batchelor, New York Daily News
1938—Vaughn Shoemaker, Chicago Daily News
1939—Charles G. Werner, Daily Oklahoman
1940—Edmund Duffy, Baltimore Sun
1941—Jacob Burck, Chicago Times
1942—Herbert L. Block, NEA
1943—Jay N. Darling, New York Herald-Tribune
1944—Clifford K. Berryman, Washington Star
1945—Bill Mauldin, United Features Syndicate
1946—Bruce Russell, Los Angeles Times
1947—Vaughn Shoemaker, Chicago Daily News
1948—Reuben L. ("Rube") Goldberg, New York Sun
1949—Lute Pease, Newark Evening News
1950—James T. Berryman, Washington Star
1951—Reginald W. Manning, Arizona Republic
1952—Fred L. Packer, New York Mirror
1953—Edward D. Kuekes, Cleveland Plain Dealer
1954—Herbert L. Block, Washington Post
1955—Daniel R. Fitzpatrick, St. Louis Post-Dispatch
1956—Robert York, Louisville Times
1957—Tom Little, Nashville Tennessean
1958—Bruce M. Shanks, Buffalo Evening News
1959—Bill Mauldin, St. Louis Post-Dispatch
1960—No award given
1961—Carey Orr, Chicago Tribune
1962—Edmund S. Valtman, Hartford Times
1963—Frank Miller, Des Moines Register
1964—Paul Conrad, Denver Post
1965—No award given
1966—Don Wright, Miami News
1967—Patrick B. Oliphant, Denver Post
1968—Eugene Gray Payne, Charlotte Observer
1969—John Fischetti, Chicago Daily News
1970—Thomas F. Darcy, Newsday
1971—Paul Conrad, Los Angeles Times
1972—Jeffrey K. MacNelly, Richmond News Leader
1973—No award given
1974—Paul Szep, Boston Globe
1975—Garry Trudeau, Universal Press Syndicate
1976—Tony Auth, Philadelphia Enquirer
1977—Paul Szep, Boston Globe

1978—Jeff MacNelly, Richmond News Leader
1979—Herbert Block, Washington Post
1980—Don Wright, Miami News
1981—Mike Peters, Dayton Daily News
1982—Ben Sargent, Austin American-Statesman
1983—Dick Locher, Chicago Tribune
1984—Paul Conrad, Los Angeles Times
1985—Jeff MacNelly, Chicago Tribune
1986—Jules Feiffer, Universal Press Syndicate
1987—Berke Breathed, Washington Post Writers Group
1988—Doug Marlette, Atlanta Constitution
1989—Jack Higgins, Chicago Sun-Times
1990—Tom Toles, Buffalo News
1991—Jim Borgman, Cincinnati Enquirer
1992—Signe Wilkinson, Philadelphia Daily News
1993—Steve Benson, Arizona Republic
1994—Michael Ramirez, Memphis Commercial Appeal
1995—Mike Luckovich, Atlanta Constitution
1996—Jim Morin, Miami Herald
1997—Walt Handelsman, New Orleans Times-Picayune
1998—Steve Breen, Asbury Park Press
1999—David Horsey, Seattle Post-Intelligencer
2000—Joel Pett, Lexington Herald-Leader
2001—Ann Telnaes, Tribune Media Services
2002—Clay Bennett, Christian Science Monitor

NATIONAL SOCIETY OF PROFESSIONAL JOURNALISTS AWARD (SIGMA DELTA CHI AWARD)

1942—Jacob Burck, Chicago Times
1943—Charles Werner, Chicago Sun
1944—Henry Barrow, Associated Press
1945—Reuben L. Goldberg, New York Sun
1946—Dorman H. Smith, NEA
1947—Bruce Russell, Los Angeles Times
1948—Herbert Block, Washington Post
1949—Herbert Block, Washington Post
1950—Bruce Russell, Los Angeles Times
1951—Herbert Block, Washington Post and
　　　Bruce Russell, Los Angeles Times
1952—Cecil Jensen, Chicago Daily News
1953—John Fischetti, NEA
1954—Calvin Alley, Memphis Commercial Appeal
1955—John Fischetti, NEA
1956—Herbert Block, Washington Post
1957—Scott Long, Minneapolis Tribune
1958—Clifford H. Baldowski, Atlanta Constitution
1959—Charles G. Brooks, Birmingham News
1960—Dan Dowling, New York Herald-Tribune
1961—Frank Interlandi, Des Moines Register
1962—Paul Conrad, Denver Post
1963—William Mauldin, Chicago Sun-Times
1964—Charles Bissell, Nashville Tennessean
1965—Roy Justus, Minneapolis Star
1966—Patrick Oliphant, Denver Post

1967—Eugene Payne, Charlotte Observer
1968—Paul Conrad, Los Angeles Times
1969—William Mauldin, Chicago Sun-Times
1970—Paul Conrad, Los Angeles Times
1971—Hugh Haynie, Louisville Courier-Journal
1972—William Mauldin, Chicago Sun-Times
1973—Paul Szep, Boston Globe
1974—Mike Peters, Dayton Daily News
1975—Tony Auth, Philadelphia Enquirer
1976—Paul Szep, Boston Globe
1977—Don Wright, Miami News
1978—Jim Borgman, Cincinnati Enquirer
1979—John P. Trever, Albuquerque Journal
1980—Paul Conrad, Los Angeles Times
1981—Paul Conrad, Los Angeles Times
1982—Dick Locher, Chicago Tribune
1983—Rob Lawlor, Philadelphia Daily News
1984—Mike Lane, Baltimore Evening Sun
1985—Doug Marlette, Charlotte Observer
1986—Mike Keefe, Denver Post
1987—Paul Conrad, Los Angeles Times
1988—Jack Higgins, Chicago Sun-Times
1989—Don Wright, Palm Beach Post
1990—Jeff MacNelly, Chicago Tribune
1991—Walt Handelsman, New Orleans Times-Picayune
1992—Robert Ariail, Columbia State
1993—Herbert Block, Washington Post
1994—Jim Borgman, Cincinnati Enquirer
1995—Michael Ramirez, Memphis Commercial Appeal
1996—Paul Conrad, Los Angeles Times
1997—Michael Ramirez, Los Angeles Times
1998—Jack Higgins, Chicago Sun-Times
1999—Mike Thompson, Detroit Free Press
2000—Nick Anderson, Louisville Courier-Journal
2001—Clay Bennett, Christian Science Monitor

NATIONAL NEWSPAPER AWARD/CANADA

1949—Jack Boothe, Toronto Globe and Mail
1950—James G. Reidford, Montreal Star
1951—Len Norris, Vancouver Sun
1952—Robert La Palme, Le Devoir, Montreal
1953—Robert W. Chambers, Halifax Chronicle-Herald
1954—John Collins, Montreal Gazette
1955—Merle R. Tingley, London Free Press

1956—James G. Reidford, Toronto Globe and Mail
1957—James G. Reidford, Toronto Globe and Mail
1958—Raoul Hunter, Le Soleil, Quebec
1959—Duncan Macpherson, Toronto Star
1960—Duncan Macpherson, Toronto Star
1961—Ed McNally, Montreal Star
1962—Duncan Macpherson, Toronto Star
1963—Jan Kamienski, Winnipeg Tribune
1964—Ed McNally, Montreal Star
1965—Duncan Macpherson, Toronto Star
1966—Robert W. Chambers, Halifax Chronicle-Herald
1967—Raoul Hunter, Le Soleil, Quebec
1968—Roy Peterson, Vancouver Sun
1969—Edward Uluschak, Edmonton Journal
1970—Duncan Macpherson, Toronto Daily Star
1971—Yardley Jones, Toronto Daily Star
1972—Duncan Macpherson, Toronto Star
1973—John Collins, Montreal Gazette
1974—Blaine, Hamilton Spectator
1975—Roy Peterson, Vancouver Sun
1976—Andy Donato, Toronto Sun
1977—Terry Mosher, Montreal Gazette
1978—Terry Mosher, Montreal Gazette
1979—Edd Uluschak, Edmonton Journal
1980—Vic Roschkov, Toronto Star
1981—Tom Innes, Calgary Herald
1982—Blaine, Hamilton Spectator
1983—Dale Cummings, Winnipeg Free Press
1984—Roy Peterson, Vancouver Sun
1985—Ed Franklin, Toronto Globe and Mail
1986—Brian Gable, Regina Leader-Post
1987—Raffi Anderian, Ottawa Citizen
1988—Vance Rodewalt, Calgary Herald
1989—Cameron Cardow, Regina Leader-Post
1990—Roy Peterson, Vancouver Sun
1991—Guy Badeaux, Le Droit, Ottawa
1992—Bruce Mackinnon, Halifax Herald
1993—Bruce Mackinnon, Halifax Herald
1994—Roy Peterson, Vancouver Sun
1995—Brian Gable, Toronto Globe and Mail
1996—Roy Peterson, Vancouver Sun
1997—Serge Chapleau, La Presse
1998—Roy Peterson, Vancouver Sun
1999—Serge Chapleau, La Presse
2000—Serge Chapleau, La Presse
2001—Brian Gable, Toronto Globe and Mail

Index of Cartoonists

INDEX OF CARTOONISTS

Complete Your CARTOON COLLECTION

Previous editions of this timeless classic are available for those wishing to update their collection of the most provocative moments of the past three decades. In the early days the topics were the oil crisis, Richard Nixon's presidency, Watergate, and the Vietnam War. Those subjects have given way to the Clinton impeachment trial, the historic 2000 presidential election, and the terrorist attack on America. Most important, in the end, the wit and wisdom of the editorial cartoonists prevail on the pages of these op-ed editorials, where one can find memories and much, much more in the work of the nation's finest cartoonists.

Select from the following supply of past editions

_____ 1972 Edition $18.95 pb (F)	_____ 1984 Edition $18.95 pb (F)	_____ 1995 Edition $14.95 pb
_____ 1974 Edition $18.95 pb (F)	_____ 1985 Edition $18.95 pb (F)	_____ 1996 Edition $14.95 pb
_____ 1975 Edition $18.95 pb (F)	_____ 1986 Edition $18.95 pb (F)	_____ 1997 Edition $14.95 pb
_____ 1976 Edition $18.95 pb (F)	_____ 1987 Edition $14.95 pb	_____ 1998 Edition $14.95 pb
_____ 1977 Edition $18.95 pb (F)	_____ 1988 Edition $14.95 pb	_____ 1999 Edition $14.95 pb
_____ 1978 Edition $18.95 pb (F)	_____ 1989 Edition $18.95 pb (F)	_____ 2000 Edition $14.95 pb
_____ 1979 Edition $18.95 pb (F)	_____ 1990 Edition $14.95 pb	_____ 2001 Edition $14.95 pb
_____ 1980 Edition $18.95 pb (F)	_____ 1991 Edition $14.95 pb	_____ 2002 Edition $14.95 pb
_____ 1981 Edition $18.95 pb (F)	_____ 1992 Edition $14.95 pb	_____ 2003 Edition $14.95 pb
_____ 1982 Edition $18.95 pb (F)	_____ 1993 Edition $14.95 pb	_____ Add me to the list of standing
_____ 1983 Edition $18.95 pb (F)	_____ 1994 Edition $14.95 pb	orders

Please include $2.75 for 4th Class Postage and handling or $5.35 for UPS Ground Shipment plus $.75 for each additional copy ordered.

Total enclosed: _____

NAME _____

ADDRESS _____

CITY_____STATE_____ ZIP_____

Make checks payable to:

PELICAN PUBLISHING COMPANY
P.O. Box 3110, Dept. 6BEC
Gretna, Louisiana 70054-3110

CREDIT CARD ORDERS CALL 1-800-843-1724 or 1-888-5-PELICAN or go to e-pelican.com
Jefferson Parish residents add 8¾% tax. All other Louisiana residents add 4% tax.
Please visit our Web site at www.pelicanpub.com or e-mail us at sales@pelicanpub.com